The prevailing idea of Lord Palmerston is that he occupied the British premiership for almost ten years by basing his policies on 'crude belligerence abroad and class fear at home'. This book, founded on extensive new archival research, shows that the received view of Palmerston is an inversion of the truth. In common with nearly all Victorian politicians, and more ably than most of them, it is argued that Palmerston worked for the co-operation of social classes, and for the avoidance of war on a scale that might disrupt the economy and exacerbate social tensions. As Prime Minister, he managed the transition to democracy in advance of the Second Reform Act by taking politics to the people in platform oratory that Gladstone, among others, first denounced and then emulated; and by inviting the self-styled representatives of the middle class into the 'citadel of power', the Cabinet, which had hitherto been almost exclusively an aristocratic preserve.

The success of Palmerston's methods invited Tory and radical misrepresentation, inasmuch as a genius for adaptation could easily be taken for legerdemain. In this study policies and political relationships are examined in depth and in considerable detail in order to discover the real substance of Palmerston's achievements. His ability to laugh publicly at himself and others was a measure of the authority he enjoyed in his time.

Palmerston and Liberalism, 1855–1865

Palmerston and Liberalism, 1855–1865

E. D. STEELE

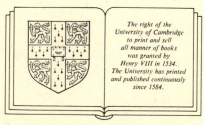

The right of the
University of Cambridge
to print and sell
all manner of books
was granted by
Henry VIII in 1534.
The University has printed
and published continuously
since 1584.

CAMBRIDGE UNIVERSITY PRESS

Cambridge

New York   Port Chester

Melbourne   Sydney

Published by the Press Syndicate of the University of Cambridge
The Pitt Building, Trumpington Street, Cambridge CB2 1RP
40 West 20th Street, New York, NY 10011, USA
10 Stamford Road, Oakleigh, Melbourne 3166, Australia

© Cambridge University Press 1991

First published 1991

Printed in Great Britain at the University Press, Cambridge

British Library cataloguing in publication data
Steele, E. D.
Palmerston and Liberalism, 1855–1865
1. Great Britain. Palmerston, Henry John Temple, Viscount,
1784–1865
I. Title
941.081092

Library of Congress cataloguing in publication data
Steele, E. D.
Palmerston and Liberalism, 1855–1865/E. D. Steele.
p. cm.
Includes bibliographical references and index.
1. Palmerston, Henry John Temple, Viscount, 1784–1865.   2. Great
Britain – Politics and government – 1837–1901.   3. Liberalism – Great
Britain – History – 19th century.   I. Title.
DA536.P2S74   1991   90–40491   941.081′092–dc20   CIP

ISBN 0 521 40045 7 hardback

'...he devoted more time and ability to the work of understanding the people than any democratic politician of his age.'

(*The Daily News*, 25 October 1865, on the death of Lord Palmerston)

Contents

Maps

Preface

I have to acknowledge the permission of the Trustees of the Broadlands Archive Trust to quote from the papers of the third Viscount Palmerston and the seventh Earl of Shaftesbury, which I saw when they were in the care of the National Register of Archives. I am deeply grateful to the Trustees, to the owners and custodians of the other manuscript sources listed in the bibliography, and to Dr Mark Curthoys who provided me with transcripts from two collections. The staffs of the National Register of Archives, the Department of Manuscripts in the British Library, the National Library of Wales, the Bodleian Library, and other institutions were most helpful.

My principal debts of gratitude incurred in the making of this book and its submission to a publisher are to those whom I now thank. Professor W. R. Ward and Professor W. A. Speck found time to read the whole manuscript; their advice and encouragement were invaluable. Professor Derek Beales, Dr Colin Matthew and Dr Richard Whiting commented on parts of the manuscript, and I discussed aspects of it with Dr Roy Bridge, Dr Christopher Challis, and Dr Keith Wilson: I am particularly indebted to Keith Wilson, in whose *British Foreign Secretaries and Foreign Policy* the substance of chapters 3, 10, and 11 first appeared. I should also like to thank Mr William Davies of the Cambridge University Press and Mr Michael Sissons of Peters, Fraser and Dunlop. My wife's affection and support made the book possible: I cannot hope to repay all that I owe to her.

27 May 1990   E. D. Steele

1 Serpents Island
2 Mouths of the Danube (to Moldavia 1856; to direct Ottoman rule 1857)
Vienna
R. Danube
Budapest
AUSTRIAN EMPIRE
R. Dneister
R. Prut
RUSSIA
Jassy
Moldavia
Bolgrad
R. Prut
S. Bessarabia
Transylvania
1
Wallachia
R. Danube
2
Bucharest
Bosnia
Belgrade
Serbia
R. Danube
Herzegovina
OTTOMAN EMPIRE
BLACK SEA
Bulgaria
Montenegro
ADRIATIC SEA
Constantinople
Salonica
Thessaly
Epirus
AEGEAN SEA
GREECE
Athens
0 150 miles
0 150 km
Frontiers of independent states
Frontiers of autonomous principalities
Crete

1 Turkey in Europe after the Crimean War

2 Italy in 1859

SWITZERLAND

SAVOY

AUSTRIAN EMPIRE

LOMBARDY

VENETIA

R. Po

Milan

Venice

Turin

R. Po

FRANCE

PIEDMONT

PARMA

MODENA

1

NICE

(KINGDOM OF SARDINIA)

Florence

R. Arno

TUSCANY

2

CORSICA
(French)

3

SARDINIA

4

R. Tiber Rome

NAPLES

Naples

0   50   100   150 miles

Papal States
1 Romagna (or Legations)
2 Marches
3 Umbria
4 Patrimony of St Peter

Palermo

SICILY

xv

Part I
Realities

1

Introduction

Purpose

Liberalism is historically a collection of ideas and attitudes, not a coherent theory. It cannot profitably be studied in any other way than through its meaning in practice. Its best minds tend, revealingly, to be also classifiable as conservatives, Burke for example or radicals, like J. S. Mill. Or else they were, like Guizot in France, politicians first. In the middle of the last century, the United States stood for democracy, while Britain represented a liberalism which belonged to that age. With all their similarities the contemporary British and American constitutions differed fundamentally in defining the political nation. The 1832 Reform Act perpetuated the exclusion of a large majority of adult men from the electorate. The second Reform Act of 1867 brought in a franchise sufficiently wide to be termed democratic: but it was not until 1918 that Britain arrived at manhood suffrage, seventy years behind France and fifty behind Germany. The character of British parliamentary government as late as 1867, after household suffrage had been extended to the whole of the United Kingdom, was publicly described by Gladstone in these words: 'The natural condition of a healthy society is that governing functions should be discharged in the main by the leisured class...whatever control a good system may impose by popular suffrage.'[1] By 'the leisured class' he meant primarily the aristocracy and gentry who comprised an absolute majority in the House of Commons before 1885, and in the cabinet before 1905. The landed class had earlier acquired considerable wealth from sources other than agriculture, and the process of assimilating their supposed rivals, the businessmen raised up by a continuing industrial revolution, was far advanced. The anachronistic primacy of land endured for good reasons. The leading radical thinker of the mid-nineteenth century, J. S. Mill, paid tribute to the virtues of a class which he often criticized severely: he did not believe that 'any rulers in history have been actuated by a more sincere

3

desire to do their duty towards the poorer portion of their countrymen'.[2]
He wrote that in 1861, when Palmerston was prime minister for the second
time.

   This liberalism was common to both the historic parties; by Continental
standards, the Tories were unquestionably liberals. In his *Constitutional
History of England*, a classic published in the same year as Mill's *Considerations
on Representative Government*, Erskine May explained the paradox of landed
rule in an ever more industrial and urban society by the willingness of
aristocratic politicians to adopt 'progressive' policies – the adjective is
May's.[3] The Liberals, as the Whigs generally preferred to be known
halfway through the century, were not always better than the Tories at
being 'progressive': Palmerston had been a colleague and follower of the
Tory George Canning, the first British statesman to acknowledge, ten years
before the Great Reform Act, the supremacy of public opinion over the
constitutional trinity of Crown, Lords and Commons. In Canning's view,
the strength of public opinion in an increasingly populous and thriving
nation was quite effectively expressed through the medium of a fast
growing, and, as regards middle-class papers then, free press: so much so
that he considered it unwise to diminish the independence of government
and legislature. Gladstone, a youthful disciple, ascribed his opposition to
the 1832 Act to Canning's influence as well as Burke's. By contrast, and in
spite of Canning's politics, Palmerston took the evolutionary approach to
change that balanced the fear of revolution in Burke.[4] The Canningite
strain in the Liberals from 1830, when Palmerston, Melbourne and others
entered Lord Grey's cabinet, helped to broaden the outlook of their very
aristocratic leadership.

   The extraordinary success of Victorian liberalism, with a small 'l', is
undeniable. Britain combined progress with stability; the social tensions of
the previous sixty years declined rapidly from the end of the 1840s. The
adaptability of her traditional institutions was envied on the Continent,
while civil war in America discredited the working model of democracy.
Palmerston's contribution to the British achievement, appreciated at the
time, has suffered at the hands of historians. Often critical of him as a
foreign secretary, they have been harsher in their judgements of his
performance as prime minister. To Mr A. J. P. Taylor, writing after the last
war, his place in domestic political history is 'an empty one'.[5] In Professor
Vincent's influential study of the Liberal party at this period, its reshaping
owes little to a leader who was not an authentic Liberal.[6] More recently,
there has been a disposition to concede Palmerston's 'genuine and
dominant Liberalism' when he was prime minister. Yet for two years his
first ministry depended on the votes of doubtful Liberals or reluctant
opponents; his second came in with a majority of thirteen in June 1859,
which by-elections eroded. In the circumstances, he has sometimes seemed

to be an expert in survival, with small interest in domestic policy, relying on a generation's more or less successful conduct of British international relations to impress the House and the electorate.[7] It is asked how far he controlled his cabinet and party outside Foreign Office matters.

The purpose of this book is to show how Palmerston accustomed the country to the idea of democracy, in a peculiarly British version, before it began to operate through household suffrage after 1867. In doing so, he pursued policies that were liberal and his own. It is said that in so far as they were his they 'involved crude belligerence abroad and class fear at home'.[8] The reality is quite different. Palmerston seldom made the mistake of underrating the intelligence of the national audience which he reached through a press that was expanding rapidly after the abolition of news-paper stamp duty in 1855: Victorian politicians were far less likely than today's to talk down. His main themes were the co-operation of classes and national security. An element of 'class fear' may have been present in the minds of the propertied, including men of small property: but only in the sense that their calculations favoured a Palmerston ministry for its assurance of prosperity and stability. When Palmerston fell in 1858, and whenever his governments were threatened, the price of Consols on the London Stock Exchange declined in sympathy, revealing how the investing public felt, irrespective of party. As for 'crude belligerence abroad' the readiness to use force in Palmerston's policy towards China, Japan and Brazil was not evident in his handling of relations with France and America. He and his foreign secretaries were charged with applying a double standard: Palmerston contended that it was inherent in in-ternational statecraft, and the voters upheld him in 1857. The behaviour of other powers – and particularly of France and America – was indis-tinguishable; their warships, and French troops, joined Britain's in her Far Eastern operations. In Europe, Palmerston's appeasement or conciliation, according to taste, of France in the crisis of January and February 1858 was so unpopular that his opponents in all parts of the House were emboldened to overthrow him. The realization that he had been right strongly affected opinion next year, when his vindication by events undermined the Derby ministry.

The case for regarding Palmerston's influence as constructive does not rest upon his legislative record; although his governments were responsible for more legislation than is sometimes supposed. Gladstone's administra-tions, on the other hand, were identified with their additions to the statute book. Yet Gladstonian Liberalism did not differ essentially from Liberalism as Palmerston left it. It is important to realize the extent to which both men and their contemporaries thought and spoke in terms of class. The actual and potential conflicts of interest under capitalism were well understood. Liberal policy and rhetoric were directed, above all, to securing harmony between classes, as the domestic prerequisite of the confidence on which depended the pace of economic expansion with its social benefits. Between 1855 and 1865 the Liberals embraced class collaboration without the reservations of the old Whig leadership. While the shift was a collective one, Palmerston's political will was felt – notably by Gladstone – to have been instrumental in the process. Landed primacy was safe for the foreseeable future; Cobden put its extended life at the best part of a century.[9] Palmerston was not the old cynic, now reactionary, now populist, of hostile portraits, but an intelligent, courageous politician who had overcome his doubts of a few years back about the prospects for the Liberal party. The analysis of party and factional strengths received less attention from him than it has from historians: the institutional structures of a modern party had yet to develop, the habits of eighteenth-century connexions had ceased to be respectable, and the mid-century electorate and public displayed a permanent Liberal bias.[10] The Liberals consolidated their position by showing that they were more 'progressive' than their Tory rivals. In building up that advantage, Palmerston compensated for the narrow majorities, or no majority at all, which the uneven distribution of the voters was liable to produce. 'The strength of the government', he had occasion to remind his chief whip, 'consists not simply in the balance of votes…in the…Commons but mainly in favourable public opinion'.[11]

Exaggerating, typically, the significance of their own kind, Cobden told Bright that a Palmerston ministry had 'no other basis but the trading and manufacturing constituencies'.[12] The economic health of these communities was decisive for the success of Palmerstonian Liberalism. Their self-styled representatives, Cobden, Bright and a likeminded handful, were disappointed, if not really surprised, at confirmation that substantial businessmen in the industrial towns shared the outlook of their metropolitan counterparts, who had long been associated with the landed interest in Parliament and government. The élites of Birmingham, Manchester, Leeds and the rest were satisfied with very little besides good management of the economy, which Palmerston and his chancellors of the exchequer provided: they wanted to know that they too were fit to participate, on the modest scale commensurate with their lack of experience, in the running of the country. The promotion of M. T. Baines in December 1855 introduced a representative of the provincial middle class into the cabinet for the first time; his brother Edward edited the *Leeds Mercury*, the family newspaper which was a force in regional politics. Then on the formation of his second administration in 1859, Palmerston invited Cobden and his friend Milner Gibson to join. 'Why don't you come into the citadel of power?' Palmerston asked Cobden when they met. Cobden resisted the offer, painfully conscious of all that he had said against the prime minister over the years, but pledged himself to support the cabinet so long as Milner

Gibson, who had not refused, was a member. 'Almost without exception', Cobden's old associates from the Anti-Corn Law League urged him to go in: their pressure, not Palmerston's impelled him to give that unsolicited pledge.[13] A middle-class and radical presence at the heart of government was what he and they had always desired. Palmerston's offer had the approval of Lord John Russell and Gladstone, though other colleagues were uneasy. The Cobdenite radicals, so few in Parliament, were a potential threat to the continued acceptance of landed rule in a changing Britain; it made excellent sense to disarm them with office. Henceforth the radically inclined middle-classes, never a large minority, were firmly attached to Liberalism, however critical they might be of its policies.

Old deference, new prosperity and intelligent political management elicited a similar response from working-class voters and the voteless mass. Palmerston's speeches outside Parliament were seen as novel in going over the heads of MPs not merely to commend his policies but to imply a direct relationship between premier and people: it seemed that he was bypassing Parliament; opponents and rivals were disapproving, even outraged. No realistic politician ignored the unenfranchised altogether: Palmerston was accused of courting them. His oratory in the big towns encouraged a community of interest and sentiment through a shared responsibility from which no one was excluded. When his cabinet was more broadly based in the sixties, he singled out the upper working-class and treated them as if they already possessed the franchise in the numbers admitted by the 1867 Reform Act. A 'viable class society'[14] needed a rhetoric that asserted a parity of esteem among classes whose inequality was fundamental to the economic and political order. Palmerston met the need with authority and insight. He did not expect to be heard quite solemnly when he compared himself to a working man in front of working men.[15] Nor was he: but they appreciated the significance of what he said in recognition of their political worth. They were men with skills and good wages, the natural leaders of their class, steadily more bourgeois in character and more numerous with the industrial trend. Without their participation no movement from below could be really dangerous. Their enthusiasm for Chartism had been limited. No sharp divide separated them from the lower reaches of the middle-class. British social structure with its absence of rigid divisions lent itself to the language of unity.

Palmerston talked of his government's commitment to what he called 'progressive improvement'. To posterity, it is most obvious in the form of lighter taxation made possible by economic growth. The ability of aristocratic politicians to govern cheaply was a strong recommendation; another was the libertarianism which they shared with other classes. '... rapid and pen-stroke improvements may suit despotic countries, where the nation is compelled to obey impulses which proceed from above', said

Palmerston at Leeds in 1860, '... [but] in a country like this where public
opinion is as powerful as ... edicts of the governing authority, time and
delay are essentially necessary'.[16] This general explanation of his caution in
legislating carries conviction: there was no groundswell of opinion in favour
of major reforms. The new political style which Palmerston embodied as
prime minister took the urgency out of Parliamentary reform. His
conciliation of Dissent went far to isolate those militant Nonconformists
whose contribution to radical politics was disproportionate. One of the
deepest divisions in society was apparently that between the Establishment
and Dissent: but for many people there was not the gulf visible to zealots
on either side. Palmerston shaped his policy accordingly, with the result
that relations between Churchmen and Dissenters were better at the time
of his death than they had ever been, or were to be again for the rest of the
century and beyond. Though his own views were of the broadest, he used
his ecclesiastical patronage to elevate sympathizers with the strongest
religious current of the age, the neo-puritanism common to the Low
Church and most of Dissent. What he looked for in a bishop, he declared
from the platform, was concern to make denominational boundaries 'as
little perceptible as possible'. These appointments were undoubtedly
popular; he claimed credit on the hustings for choosing 'earnest and pious
men ... above the narrow prejudices which sometimes separate sect from
sect'.[17] In the perspective of a unifying Protestantism, secular differences
were diminished. E. B. Pusey, clearer-sighted and more generous than some
High Churchmen, was prepared to tell his followers that Palmerston
deserved the Church's gratitude and advised them to vote Liberal at the
election of 1865.[18]

   The public and business demanded security from invasion and protection
for the spread of global interests. They also wanted their country to have
a say in the affairs of Europe, as befitted a great power, and to advocate the
export of constitutionalism. All this they expected to enjoy without a war
against another European power or the United States that might jeopardize
prosperity and revive the social perils of the struggle with the French
Revolution and the first Napoleon. Britain's military limitations had been
exposed in the Crimea. Palmerston's diplomacy afterwards satisfied the
conflicting requirements of his countrymen; they forgave his mistakes.
Moreover, he invited them to make a virtue of necessity and see British
weakness as another aspect of political superiority to the Continent, thus
annexing a favourite radical argument: 'it is not by keeping up menacing
establishments that real, substantial and useful influence is to be acquired',
he said when the war was over. The British were encouraged in their notion
that they were Europe's tutors: 'most of the improvements which have
been made elsewhere', he asserted, were 'owing to the proof that England
had given of the prosperity and happiness which constitutional monarchy

extends'. He linked foreign with domestic policy to foster a collective self-respect in which class antagonism would be reconciled. 'The character of a nation', he said in the industrial North, 'both in its own esteem, and in the consideration it receives from other nations, is built up by the aggregate good behaviour of all ... classes'.[19] However exaggerated those claims were, they reinforced the idea of his country's reputation as bound up with the emulation that her freedom, wealth and order excited, and with the avoidance of anything like aggression towards other great states. Little of this features in a conventional picture of Palmerston. Teaching Britain to accept her place in a dangerous world needed some courage in a politician so clearly identified with the recent war.

Napoleon III let it be known in 1855 and again in 1859 that he wished Palmerston to be prime minister; with little diplomatic reserve on the second occasion. Palmerston neither liked nor trusted the Emperor and France; in private, he quoted approvingly the judgement of the Orleanist statesman Guizot on the Second Empire and its creator: 'I hate the man, I detest the system, but it is the only thing for the present.'[20] The relationship with the Emperor was indispensable to Palmerston's foreign policy, and therefore to his policy as a whole. This Napoleon was an anglophil, and believed himself to be a liberal; he also had a healthy respect for British seapower and financial resources, remembering how they had helped his uncle's enemies. On Britain's side, co-operation with France gave her more weight in the councils of Europe than she would otherwise have carried after her showing in the Crimea.

Palmerston's handling of France, whose ambitions inspired such apprehension across the Channel, increased his ascendancy in the Commons. By the early sixties his command of the House amounted to a species of dictatorship: exercised 'by common consent', wrote a supporter on the back benches; 'by making all parties laugh at one another', complained the High Church Bishop Wilberforce without a trace of humour.[21] As with Salisbury in the next generation, the liberty to indulge a strong sense of the ridiculous was a measure of his authority. The narrowness of its electoral base and social composition made the House more, not less, sensitive than some later Parliaments to the ascertainable, or the surmised, wishes of the country. The secret of Palmerston's hold over the Commons lay in their acknowledgement of him as the supreme interpreter of public opinion; especially after his resurrection from political death in 1858–59, the opposition and dissident Liberals were extremely reluctant to risk defeating him again. They had learnt not to underestimate his talent for anticipating the views that the public would disclose: in the words of the supporter just quoted, he had 'the ... gift of saying tonight what no one expects but a great majority will agree to tomorrow'.[22] This was a period of transition, skilfully managed, with Palmerston at the centre. From

the vantage point of the cabinet his intellectual colleague, Sir George
Cornewall Lewis, described the British political system in the prime
minister's last years as 'an aristocratico-democratic representative constitution'.[23]

This book is not the detailed history of Palmerston's ten years at the head
of the Liberal party, but an interpretation: the summary of ten years in the
next section may be useful. Each chapter after the first addresses one or
more of the questions involved in an estimate of his statesmanship. Chapter
2 of Part I explores the political relationship with Gladstone which is
central to an assessment of both men. The subject of chapter 3 is
Palmerston's establishment of himself in the premiership during the war
that brought him to the highest office, and the consolidation of his position
in the year of peace leading up to his electoral triumph of 1857. The
ambiguity in his Canningite origins was finally resolved; he emerged as an
authentic Liberal at home and abroad.

Chapters 4–6 of Part II are devoted to parties and connections from the
angle of Palmerston's pre-eminence over the ten years: 4 to the main body
of Whigs and Liberals as far as 1861; 5 to the Peelites, few but influential,
whom Liberalism absorbed, and the radicals more closely integrated with
the party after 1859; 6 to the Tory opposition. Chapter 7 examines one of
Palmerston's undoubted strengths, his religious policy, and 8 the economic
management of his governments with the wider implications for national
stability. Chapter 9 deals with his political ascendancy in its consolidating
phase of 1862–5 when it was seriously challenged only once, on Schleswig-
Holstein; a long section goes into the social foundations of politics at the
time of his death.

In Part III, chapters 10 and 11 cover foreign policy after the Crimean
war; both Palmerston's foreign secretaries were clearly subordinate
ministers.[24] The dominant theme is his need to reconcile the assertion of
continuing great power status, and the furtherance of old interests and new,
with the preservation of confidence vital to the economy and best served by
peace. An imperfect solution to this problem was supplied by the Anglo-
French relationship, which turned on the understanding between the
British prime minister and the French emperor. Chapter 12 treats Ireland
as a foreign country: Palmerston saw it as such, alien in race and religion
outside the North-East corner. Chapter 13 divides the empire of the day into
its three main components: India, the colonies of settlement, and the
'informal empire' of comparatively recent historiography. The emphasis is
on the mixture of realism and humanity that characterized the imperial
policies of Palmerston's governments.

A summary of ten years

Palmerston became prime minister for the first time in February 1855, nearly a year after Britain and France had gone to war with Russia.[25] Lord Aberdeen's coalition of Liberals and Peelites, in which Palmerston took the Home Office, had resigned at the end of January following its defeat on the radical J. A. Roebuck's motion for an inquiry into the direction of the war – 'the Sebastopol Committee'. Palmerston's reputation from his long service as foreign secretary and his enthusiasm for the war, made him the obvious choice in the eyes of his party, the opposition and the public; at the Home Office he bore little responsibility for the government's failures. The Peelite group held the balance of power in that Parliament. Without them and without Palmerston, whose refusal was decisive, Lord Derby gave up the attempt to form a Tory-led coalition. The Liberal leader, Russell, had alienated his colleagues by resigning before Roebuck's motion was put to the vote. Palmerston's ministry was another cabinet of Liberals and Peelites: but three of the five Peelites in the cabinet left it before the close of February; ostensibly as a protest against the Commons' perseverance with their inquiry into the war. They were replaced with Liberals, including Russell, and a lone Tory peer. Palmerston prosecuted the war with a new vigour; sending Russell, at the same time, to represent Britain at peace negotiations in Vienna. In the spring and summer, the government survived the attacks of the Tories, dissident Liberals and seceding Peelites, as well as Russell's enforced resignation in July over his conduct and defence of the abortive negotiations at Vienna. The fall of Sebastopol in September vindicated the optimism which Palmerston shared with the public, but not with a majority of his ministers, or of the Commons. The expansion of a limited conflict was prevented by France's desire for peace on terms not very different from those available before the outbreak of hostilities. The Treaty of Paris signed in 1856 secured the Ottoman empire against Russian encroachment for some time to come.

Peace did not end the government's preoccupation with foreign problems. The implementation of the treaty where Russia and Turkey met in the Balkans required determined diplomacy and a show of naval strength in the Black Sea. These methods were less successful elsewhere in the same year. They failed to impress the Bourbon Kingdom of Naples, which called the Anglo-French bluff. The concern of business for its American trade inhibited ministers from endeavouring to treat the United States like Russia after Paris. The Americans got the better of Britain in the disputes which came to a head in the middle of 1856. An expedition sent against Persia in the autumn – an Indian rather than a British affair – coincided with the start of operations in China that continued intermittently for four years. The circumstances in which the China war, or wars, began gave the opposition at Westminster and its allies a narrow victory in March 1857 on Cobden's motion censuring the morality of British actions. Palmerston countered with a dissolution: and won a remarkable personal triumph. The Liberals were returned with the biggest majority since 1835.

When the new parliament met, the government turned to promised domestic legislation, and particularly the consideration of a reform bill. Its plans were overshadowed by the spread of the Indian Mutiny from May, and a severe financial crisis in October and November. Ministers went to the rescue of an overlent banking system and authorized the Bank of England to ignore the statutory restriction on its note issue. In spite of these distractions, a cabinet committee that included Palmerston made real progress with a scheme of parliamentary reform. At that point, the government was suddenly faced with an alarming conflict of French and British imperatives. The attempted assassination of Napoleon III in January 1858 by conspirators based in Britain naturally produced strongly worded French demands, official and unofficial, for preventive measures. The freedom enjoyed by political exiles, revolutionaries and reactionaries alike, was not something that could be set aside at foreign dictation. All the cabinet felt able to propose was a modification of the criminal law making conspiracy to commit murder abroad a felony instead of a misdemeanour. Even this gesture was resented in the Commons and outside; when the bill embodying it came before the House in February, the radical Milner Gibson carried by nineteen votes an amendment criticizing ministerial deference to France. The prevailing atmosphere left Palmerston and his colleagues no option but to resign.

It was widely assumed that this reverse would end the career of a statesman in his seventies. Palmerston confounded expectations by taking as readily to the leadership of opposition as he had to the premiership. The minority administration of Lord Derby relied on the tolerance of Liberals who were unwilling to restore Palmerston. Tory mistakes assisted the latter's recapture of his party. The cabinet was obliged to substitute, in effect, his reorganization of Indian government for theirs. The other piece of legislation that embarrassed them in the session of 1858 was the provision for admitting Jews to Parliament. It had Derby's support, consistently with his declaration on taking office that the government did not intend to be 'stationary' in its policies. Five members of the cabinet declined to follow the prime minister in voting for the Jew Bill, which their party had steadily opposed for years. The episode did nothing to dispel the impression of obscurantism which the Tories gave on religious questions. The government pinned its hopes on the larger issue of parliamentary reform: but its bill introduced in March 1859 did not touch the £10 household franchise, and the changes that were proposed could not make up for the omission. Defeated on the point, Derby dissolved. The gain of twenty-six seats compared with 1857 left the Tories in a minority still, and vulnerable once the Liberals agreed among themselves.

The slow recovery in Palmerston's position had quickened from January 1859 with the approach of war on the Continent. While both parties advocated neutrality in the Italian conflict between France and Austria that began in April, the Tory bias was Austrian, and the Liberal, French. The public's strongest feeling was apprehension of France. The Tories' anxiety to conciliate Napoleon, having evicted Palmerston for doing so, did not allay the Emperor's suspicions of a party that was historically anti-French. The Royal Navy's command of the sea was briefly in question as ironclads and iron ships replaced the old fleets of Britain and France. The suppression of the Indian Mutiny, not yet complete, strained the resources of a small regular army. Palmerston had those uncomfortable facts in mind when he was overthrown. The Tories were thought to have lost sight of them: the resulting alarm on the Stock Exchange at the end of April inflicted heavy losses on dealers and investors. Rumours of a Franco-Russian alliance were taken to presage a great European war into which Britain would be inexorably drawn on the side of Austria and her expected German allies, that is, on the weaker side. Palmerston had maintained his links with Napoleon III in opposition, meeting him in Paris in August 1858 and again at Compiègne – a well-publicized visit – in November. The ex-premier's sympathy with the Italian national aspirations championed by France and her ally Sardinia was less important than the belief that he could preserve Britain's neutrality and improve her relations with France. This is the setting of his return to power.

The Liberal majority on the vote of 10/11 June that removed Derby was only thirteen. Palmerston needed to win over beforehand nearly all those Liberals who had helped to turn him out, together with the remaining handful of unabsorbed Peelites. Russell, who had gone against him in March 1857 as well as February 1858, still wanted to be prime minister, but eventually consented to serve under his rival. A meeting of Liberal MPs on 6 June confirmed the understandings reached between these and other leading figures: the basis of unity was continued neutrality in the war raging in Italy, and a broader representation of all sections of the party in the personnel and policies of a new government. The cabinet that Palmerston subsequently formed was composed of eight Whigs or Liberals, two radicals and no fewer than six Peelites. The Peelite share excited some unfriendly comment: it represented the abilities of individuals, and not a collective identity which had never been clear-cut and was fading. Gladstone's to the Treasury was a surprising appointment; he had voted with the Tories in the division that brought them down. The most significant choice was that of Milner Gibson, representing the radicalism of the Manchester School. At the time, the pressure of these disparate elements in the same cabinet, and the smallness of the Liberal majority, did not suggest that the government would last long. It was helped to survive by the Tories' preference for opposition after their setbacks in office. The breadth of Liberalism made it hard to attack successfully; this also applied to attacks from within.

At the prime minister's insistence, Gladstonian budgets carrying through the fiscal enterprise begun in 1853 provided for a high level of defence expenditure to secure Britain from invasion and maintain her international standing. The hints and threats of resignation that came from Gladstone were never taken further: the certainty of political isolation deterred him. Without the modernization of the navy, the government could not have asserted itself abroad to the extent that it did. As Palmerston had always pointed out, the Anglo-French relationship central to his foreign policy was beneficial only so long as France did not dominate, her superiority on land balanced by Britain's at sea. The spectacular rise of the Volunteer movement from 1859 bore witness to public anxiety. Relief exaggerated the significance of British support for France and Sardinia in the unification of Italy between 1859 and 1861. There was extravagant rejoicing when Washington gave way to Britain and France over the seizure of Confederate envoys from the British steamer *Trent* in November 1861. Britain's inability to do anything for the Poles when they rebelled against Russia in 1863, or to save Schleswig and Holstein for Denmark the year after, attracted more criticism in Parliament than it did outside. The national response to the possibility of intervention, however limited, in the American Civil War was similar: Gladstone's pressure on his colleagues to recognize the Confederacy in 1862 was not popular, despite the widespread partiality for the South.

Here Britain disappointed France, as she disappointed Britain over the Danish duchies. In the East the two countries co-ordinated their diplomacy and use of force; jointly occupying Canton in 1857–58, and Peking in 1860 to end the China wars. A little later, the French navy assisted in bombarding the Japanese into submission to Western requirements. When the French expedition to the Lebanon in 1860–61 made Palmerston fear for the integrity of the Ottoman empire, Napoleon and his advisers were at pains to reassure him that they only meant to safeguard the Christians of the region from present and future oppression. For all the dislike and suspicion evident in their dealings with one another, Britain and France were drawn together by their liberal sympathies in Europe and their interests in the wider world. The inspiration of the symbolic Anglo-French commercial treaty in 1860 was as much political as economic.

The Liberal advance at the election of 1865, three months before Palmerston died in office, was not merely confirmation of a personal ascendancy unknown since the Younger Pitt's day. The party, and politics with it, had changed. The proposal to introduce life peerages in 1856 is an indication of Palmerston's modernity. His reservations about Parliamentary reform after the mid-fifties are often misrepresented. The bill of 1860 brought in by his government sought to reduce the £10 household franchise to £6; in respect of that central provision it went further than the Russell–Gladstone bill of 1866. Neither Parliament nor the public was ready for life peerages or a second instalment of reform. One of his successes was the Divorce Act of 1857. He reminded electors in 1859 of his responsibility for that measure: few bills have been so bitterly contested on their way through the Commons, or can more properly be designated progressive. His endorsement of the abolition of church rates and qualifying oaths for Dissenters did not get either into law; the Lords and the Tories persisted in their obstruction. But he won over the moderate majority of Dissent by his well-advertised choice of a number of prelates whom they found congenial.

Cobden's complaint in the sixties that he had become a 'demagogue' is revealing of the nature of Palmerston's influence. Lord Salisbury observed in 1881 that power had moved from Parliament to the platform: Palmerston saw that the shift was inevitable.[26] His appearances in major industrial centres were a development of the tendency, strongly marked in his case before the premiership, to address a larger audience through the newspapers. Gladstone denounced, and then imitated, him. Derby and Disraeli perceived the importance of the change without adapting to it. Their comparative neglect of urban Toryism contrasted with Palmerston's cultivation of Liberalism in the big towns. The sparing distribution of political office and titles added to the satisfaction of local notables with his policies. The solid support for him in the industrial areas was demonstrated in 1860 when his known objection to Gladstone's timing of paper duty repeal for that year encouraged the Lords to throw the bill out. There was little enthusiasm even in supposedly radical towns for Gladstone's protests at the Lords' action. From then on, Palmerston spoke of the virtues of the working class, specifically, in an obvious anticipation of a democratic franchise before very long. It is a mistake to judge him by the paucity of major legislation under his governments.

Palmerston before the premiership

Palmerston does not lack for biographies: the latest by Professor Kenneth Bourne promises to be definitive when the second volume, taking on from 1841, is published. The son of the second Viscount, an Anglo-Irish landowner, by his second wife, from a wealthy City family, Henry Temple succeeded his father at the age of seventeen in 1802. From Harrow he proceeded to the universities of Edinburgh and Cambridge, at both of which he was a serious student. Palmerston's tastes and his manner have tended to obscure the fact that he was a very clever man: the superficial impression was of a genial, shrewd philistine; the antithesis, apparently, of highminded, reflective contemporaries like Peel or Russell. A considerable womanizer, he eventually married the widowed Lady Cowper in 1839, who had been his mistress for many years; at least one of the children of her first marriage was believed to be Palmerston's. At Cambridge he took to politics on the Pittite side; his rank, wealth and discernible talent secured a pocket borough in 1807, later exchanged for the prestigious representation of the university (1811–31). Office as a lord of the Admiralty preceded his election, and in 1809 he became secretary at war, holding the post for nearly twenty years. The War Office trained him in administration during the greatest of Britain's wars before 1914; a hard worker, he ran a much-criticized bureaucratic machine competently without making a name for himself. He remained outside the cabinet until 1827 when he entered it as an adherent of Canning after Wellington and Peel had refused to serve under a prime minister who supported Catholic emancipation. It was a turning point in Palmerston's career. Canning and Catholic emancipation set him on the road to the premiership. After Canning's death he sat in the cabinets of Goderich and Wellington, resigning with the other Canningites in 1828 over the Duke's unwillingness to make even a small gesture of parliamentary reform.[27]

Within a couple of months he was writing of 'the leaden weight of Tory narrow-mindedness'. Then, as later, he was impatient of conservative fears that threatened his country's ability to 'keep... up to her station among the improving nations of civilized Europe'. In this short spell out of office he attacked the foreign policy of the government he had left to such effect that he was given the Foreign Office in Lord Grey's Whig-led coalition of 1830.[28] His approach was, and remained, Canning's: a liberal bias abroad should not be too pronounced; it was essential to maintain 'an influence both with the free, and the despot'. He was similarly careful on the reform bills of 1831 and 1832; Whig colleagues were particularly critical of his reluctance to support, as he finally did, the threat of a large creation of peers that induced the Lords to give way. The Tories continued to look on him as someone who might be persuaded to return. After more than twenty years with the Liberals, he seriously considered rejoining his old party in response to Derby's overtures in 1852. As a member of the three Liberal cabinets since 1830, he had endorsed all their notable reforms, but questioned Russell's abandonment of the doctrine that the 1832 Act was final. Palmerston saw no reason yet to strengthen the 'democratic element' in the Commons. On the other hand, the ties of two decades were reinforced by dislike of the Tories' slowness to drop agricultural protection, and of the unashamed reactionaries on their backbenches.[29]

The coolness between Palmerston and the Liberals at this time owed more to differences with Russell which centred on the conduct of foreign policy than to anything else. Russell was clearly jealous of a reputation that overshadowed his own, and had become increasingly concerned about Palmerston's independence during his third term (1846–51) at the Foreign Office. His colleague's authority had grown with success over the first two terms (1830–34, 1835–41). He built upon Canning's policy to establish a Greek Kingdom guaranteed by absolutist Russia and liberal France as well as Britain (1832). Britain and the bourgeois monarchy of Louis Philippe also conferred statehood on the insurgent Belgians, and got the Dutch out of the country by force (1830–33). In the Iberian peninsula co-operation with France enabled Palmerston to promote the constitutional cause boldly. Britain was instrumental in the expulsion of Don Miguel from Portugal (1834), and played an important part in the defeat of the first Carlist rising in Spain (1833–39). Diplomacy was backed up by the deployment of British seapower and volunteers. Palmerston allowed himself to picture the Quadruple Alliance of 1834 between Britain, France and the two peninsular monarchies as 'a Western confederacy of free states...a political and moral power in Europe'.[30] Spain under the regency of Queen Cristina and the Portugal of Maria II did not fulfil his hopes. At the other end of the Mediterranean Britain obtained the agreement of the conservative powers – Russia, Austria, and Prussia – to defend Turkey against France's Egyptian protégé, Mehemet Ali. His forces retreated before the amphibious operations of British and Austrian squadrons combined with the revolt they raised in occupied territory. Admiral Napier's blockade of, and threat to bombard, Alexandria completed the pasha's rout; he renounced the conquests of many years. Palmerston crowned his achievement in the Near East with the convention of 1841, to which Turkey and the five great powers were parties, closing the Straits to foreign warships in peacetime. Russia's security from the unwelcome presence of Western navies in the Black Sea was balanced by the five powers' commitment to the defence of Turkey. The negotiation of the Straits Convention was evidence of the British foreign secretary's European status.

Some of his colleagues had objected both to siding with the conservative powers and to being told too little when policy was in the making. He countered by intimating his readiness to resign. 'You know how advantageous and necessary I think Palmerston's holding the Seals to your ministry', wrote one of these opponents to the prime minister, Melbourne.[31] The foreign secretary's reputation was further enhanced by the forcible widening of commercial access to China (1839–42). He exploited an unpromising position in the Far East with great success so far as domestic politics were concerned. The Tories sought to censure the government for being drawn into hostilities by merchants engaged in the opium trade, legal under the British flag but illegal in China. The debate featured the celebrated oration of his colleague Macaulay, who professed to despise chauvinism, on 'that victorious flag' in the Orient.[32] The opposition had miscalculated, as they acknowledged when they came into office by gratefully accepting the outcome of the war. The Treaty of Nanking (1842) embodied Palmerston's objectives: extraterritorial rights in the specified ports open to commerce, a reasonable tariff, and the cession of Hong Kong. He was understandably gratified by the Tory conversion, attributable to the prevailing depression: 'These Asiatic triumphs...will relieve the Government from embarrassments of all kinds', he commented. 'Our manufacturers will get employment, our merchants will find a market, and Goulburn [chancellor of the exchequer] will find money.'[33] His expectations of China were much too high, but the public and business shared them. He went out admired by both sides, and beyond Westminster.

The Court, the new prime minister, Russell, and others were apprehensive of Palmerston's return to the Foreign Office in 1846; he was offered, and declined, the Colonies. 'I am well aware', he observed in a letter written for royal eyes, 'that some...at home and abroad have imbibed the notion that I am more indifferent than I ought to be as to running the risk of war.' He argued persuasively that he had averted or contained conflict.[34] There is no mention, in this letter, of the feeling against him in France, where the memory of his diplomatic victory over her in 1840 had been kept green by his attacks on the Tories for being too conciliatory in their efforts to improve relations. He had also used strong language in criticizing the surrender of disputed territory to the United States in the Ashburton Treaty (1842). Such outspokenness reflected impatience to take foreign affairs out of the hands of those whom he unfairly designated 'a set of geese'.[35] Restored to office, he was not lacking in prudence when powerful states were involved. He put peace with them before the encouragement of Continental liberalism. Britain's moral support did not save Sardinia from defeat by Austria when she tried to establish the constitutional Kingdom of Northern Italy which Palmerston had made an aim of British policy. The Mediterranean fleet was not used to prevent the Neapolitan Bourbon reconquest of Sicily, where the revolutions of 1848 began; although Britain and France insisted on a delay for negotiation with the rebels. By the end of 1849 reaction was triumphant everywhere in Italy outside Sardinia, as it was in the German lands and Hungary. Mediating in the quarrel between Germans and Danes over Schleswig and Holstein Palmerston concurred in setting aside the right of self-determination. The security of the Danish monarchy, lying on the Baltic approaches, was considered a British interest.[36]

The contrast between such realism and his vocal championship of European liberals called for an explanation. The latter, Palmerston told the

Commons in July 1849, gave Britain a claim to the gratitude of a liberal Europe in the near future while his practical diplomacy ensured the safety of their own country and promoted Continental peace. His defence emphasized a pragmatic response to the Second Republic, democracy overturning a liberal regime. Its advent naturally revived old fears, which the election of Louis Napoleon Bonaparte as president in December 1848 intensified. It was his duty, Palmerston contended, to remain close to the power that geography, military manpower, and rivalry at sea made potentially more dangerous, and more helpful, to Britain than any other. 'What business is it of ours', he asked, 'whether the French nation thinks proper to be governed by a King, an emperor, a president or a consul?'[37] His opponents were routed in the House: he was more vulnerable in cabinet. Russell removed him from the Foreign Office in December 1851 for approving, in conversation with the French ambassador, of the coup that established a Bonapartist dictatorship. Palmerston had found Louis Napoleon easier to work with than Louis Philippe and his ministers, and felt, moreover, that he offered the best hope of averting renewed civil war. Russell believed that the contradictions of the foreign secretary's policy could no longer be tolerated.[38] A few weeks earlier, Palmerston had once again advertised his dislike of authoritarian regimes offensively to a friendly monarch. Stopped by the cabinet from meeting the Hungarian patriot Kossuth, he met a deputation of London radicals instead, who thanked him for his sympathetic attitude to the exile. Palmerston did not admonish them for the violently hostile references in the address to the Austrian and Russian emperors whose armies had put down the Hungarian revolt. Britain's role in Europe, he said, required 'a good deal of judicious bottle holding'; the picture a sporting metaphor conjured up was immortalized in a *Punch* cartoon.[39] Russell chose to ignore the force of this recent remark, and treated the prompt approval of Louis Napoleon's coup as incompatible with Palmerston's politics as well as the collective responsibility of cabinet.

The foreign secretary's removal had been discussed at intervals for several years. His popularity on the Tory backbenches and the radical wing of the Liberal party held Russell back: 'both would be ready to receive him as their leader', the prime minister told the Queen.[40] She and her husband objected to Palmerston's contention that a revolution ought to be judged on its merits; their liberalism was timid and restricted. Ties with other royal houses especially through the spreading Coburg connection, influenced them against him. It took the cumulative unease in cabinet to make Russell act decisively on the complaints at Court. Palmerston's language in encouraging Continental liberals and reproving governments for slowness to change threatened practical co-operation with the conservative powers. The formidable Austrian chancellor, Prince Schwarzenberg, exasperated by the British minister's 'eternal insinuations', invited him to make war on the Hapsburg empire.[41] Like other foreigners, he pointed to the methods that Britain was compelled to employ in Ireland to hold that country down; they were not easy to reconcile with accepted ideas of liberty. Palmerston's cabinet colleagues, though not the Court, agreed that a liberal state should be broadly identified with liberal causes. It was the presentation of that side of his policy which exercised them. His behaviour, needlessly provocative towards great states, was overbearing when small ones offended. His treatment of Greece, condemned by the Lords in June 1850, was upheld in the Commons on a congratulatory motion tabled, significantly, by a radical. The public were better pleased than the House with Palmerston's justification of his actions: but those who opposed him were nevertheless impressed by his performance. Gladstone admitted to himself that the speech was 'extraordinary and masterly'; the Tory Edward Stanley, in his diary, called it 'equally eloquent, popular and indiscreet'.[42]

A good debater from long practice, Palmerston rose on this occasion to Parliamentary heights no one had thought him capable of scaling. Speaking for four and a half hours, with scarcely a note, he successfully resisted the indictment in opposing speeches. It seemed hard to justify the use of the Mediterranean fleet to collect relatively modest compensation due from the Greek government to, among others, a Gibraltarian Jew of dubious reputation answering to the name of Don Pacifico. It was harder to explain the delay in informing the envoy to Greece of the agreement, reached at the cabinet's insistence, with the Greek and French representatives in London, which would have lifted the British blockade. Palmerston's colleagues backed him to preserve the life of a weak administration; he was replying to them as much as to the Tories and Peelites. He did not plead, he asserted, the right and duty of Britain to see that her subjects abroad enjoyed the security of Roman citizens in the ancient world.[43] This claim could have no basis in international law, and was obviously unenforceable against powerful countries. It was a declaration of equality with nations strong enough to behave in the same way towards inferiors, and as such it went down very well. France, a co-guarantor of the Greek state, had recalled her ambassador from London in protest at the coercion of Athens; but he was soon back at his post. Before this famous victory of Palmerston's, which was greater than the majority of forty-six on Roebuck's motion indicated, Russell told the Queen that he would not remain in office without a change of foreign secretary. Afterwards, Palmerston declined to consider further the apparently tempting offer of the leadership in the Commons in place of Russell, who proposed to continue as prime minister with a peerage.

It appeared impossible to move Palmerston against his will. He had hinted in his speech at the attempts of ministers and the Court to get him out of the Foreign Office. When it came in December 1851, his dismissal had the predicted effect of upsetting the government. He took an early opportunity to put his old colleagues in a minority on the militia bill introduced to allay public anxiety about the condition of national defences in the face of a Bonapartist France. Palmerston complained that the bill was inadequate. The display of patriotic vigilance was not needed for his popularity, which had grown steadily. He believed that if Liberal MPs were invited to vote, 'by ballot', on the leadership of the party, he would displace Russell. However, he did not venture to suggest the experiment: '...there he is...he cannot be put down, nor put away', wrote Palmerston, explaining why he consented to serve beside him in Aberdeen's coalition.[44]

After Russell had turned it down, Aberdeen entrusted the Foreign Office to Lord Clarendon, who had been one of Palmerston's critics in Liberal cabinets. The Whig elder statesman, Lord Lansdowne, persuaded Palmerston to join as Home Secretary. While Aberdeen and Russell excluded him from any of the key posts, the administration could not stand without the man whose influence they wanted to confine. The political liking for him stretched across the House from Tories to those radicals who were to support the war against Russia. In the eyes of the latter, his record abroad more than made up for his doubts for Parliamentary reform. He took resistance to the coalition's reform bill to the extent of announcing a resignation which he withdrew. The approach of war eclipsed a domestic question that had failed to excite the public; the bill was dropped after its introduction. But Palmerston did not again oppose reform openly. His position on the war was a strong one, and grew stronger. He held that the conflict could have been prevented by resolute diplomacy and a better understanding with France. The Russians invaded the Ottoman empire in October 1853 because they were unconvinced of the Anglo-French will to stop them; hostilities with Britain and France commenced in March 1854 after two months' notice to quite the Sultan's territory had been ignored. Palmerston saw the struggle as a means of liberating Europe from the straitjacket of the Vienna settlement forty years earlier. At the same time, he did not envisage war on the scale of that period: the impending clash, he commented 'must as far as we are concerned have a very limited range'.[45] He was never reckless in the sphere of policy which he had made his own.

The public gave Palmerston the credit for a collective decision to stand up to Russia. The clamour for firmness in defence of the British interests seen as bound up with the integrity of the Ottoman empire[46] was followed by indignation at the plight of the expeditionary force in the Crimea. The losses inflicted by enemy action were much smaller than the mortality for which the incompetence or worse of the military, officialdom, and responsible ministers were blamed. The dissatisfaction assumed such proportions that there was alarm for aristocratic government itself. Russell, like Palmerston, was not one of the ministers pilloried for the Crimean failures. He responded to the national outcry by questioning Aberdeen's fitness to head the administration, and by proposing Palmerston for the War Office. Colleagues thought Russell was influenced by personal ambition rather than concern for the country. At the cabinet in December, Palmerston spoke contemptuously of such opportunism and earned the gratitude of those present. Appreciation of this solidarity with them eased his inevitable succession to the leadership in the Commons when Russell resigned in January 1855, unable to withstand Roebuck's motion due for debate at the end of the month. Palmerston defended the government in the debate: that he was unsuccessful hardly mattered; it was accepted that Aberdeen and his fellow Peelite Newcastle at the War Office were on trial, and not the entire cabinet.

A majority of 157 for the motion swept Aberdeen out of office. The Queen was warned to avoid any display of unwillingness to send for a man whom she and the Prince viewed with apprehension. She summoned Palmerston after both the party chiefs, Derby and then Russell, found they could not induce him to enter a government led by either. Derby disparaged Palmerston to her while indicating that he was indispensable: 'Lord Palmerston was totally unfit... very deaf... very blind... seventy-one years old... his day had gone by'.[47] It is one of the classic misjudgements of British political history. Power, as every student of politics knows, is the great rejuvenator. Believing in himself as prime minister, Palmerston was ready to adapt to changes which it seemed the current excitement might accelerate in an unwelcome fashion. In retrospect, there was no real middle-class alternative to the primacy of landed politicians: in February 1855 it did look as if that primacy would be foreshortened. He came to the premiership understanding the need to demonstrate that he was – to use Erskine May's term – more 'progressive' than his Liberal and Tory rivals, and unafraid of the radicals.

2

Palmerston and Gladstone

As a comparatively young man still, a Canningite minister not yet enlisted among the Whigs, Palmerston let fall the inveterate prejudice that usually guided him within the political and social framework he wished to pursue. The Tories he described as being, within that common framework, 'the il-liberals'.[1] His origins were never forgotten when he changed sides; in 1858 a far from uncritical friend and confidant, Sir George Cornewall Lewis, noted in his diary that 'the rank and file of the party...think Lord Palmerston is more tory than liberal in his tendencies'.[2] If Lewis was right, the arche-typal Whig, Lord John Russell, understood Palmerston better than the Liberal backbenchers of the mid-1850s. Although estranged from Palmer-ston at the time, Russell was scrupulously fair to him in this respect, at any rate in the intimacy of extremely frank and interesting letters to his kinsman by marriage, Dean Elliot. 'It has pleased some...in want of a leader', he wrote, 'to set me up in opposition to Palmerston. Yet...on many...ques-tions...I do not differ from him, and upon some...I have shown myself less favourable to popular measures.' The situation of parties compelled Palmer-ston not to alienate support from Tories like G. W. P. Bentinck's following, who preferred him to Disraeli; but Russell was emphatic: '*However, he is always liberal.*'[3] The comparison with Gladstone is instructive. Herbert Gladstone once excused his father's vindication of aristocracy as against plutocracy by saying that it emanated from 'inborn, natural conservatism'.[4] Much more revealing is Gladstone's own rather puzzled self-analysis in the second Palmerston ministry: 'It is true', he told his wife, 'that I seem to be both at the Conservative and at the Radical ends of the Cabinet. I do not know how it has come about, but it was not my desire.'[5] He proclaimed his debt to Peel. What he owed to Palmerston does not appear to have been similarly acknowledged. This phase of his political education began with secession from the new Palmerston government in 1855. Palmerston's deference to public opinion, in the shape of vociferous backing for the Sebastopol Committee, decided Gladstone and two other Peelites to leave.[6]

23

A man such as Gladstone was, steeped in Thomas à Kempis and Pascal,[7] could not but find Palmerston's unashamed worldliness hard to bear, aggravating as it did their natural incompatibility. To the end of their lengthy association in the cabinet of 1859–65, he felt sorely tried by the necessity of encountering the prime minister in prolonged argument. After a cabinet of January 1863, Palmerston had been 'bumptious...in his tone', he complained; next year he expressed his relief that 'the nightmare of the Palmerston correspondence has at least for the present passed away'.[8] The antagonism was really personal rather than political. Gladstone's vehement denunciations of Palmerston and his policies in which he indulged during the second half of the 1850s[9] must be set beside his candid explanation of the differences between them as having arisen 'more on account of his temper and views of public conduct than of any political opinions'.[10] It was Palmerston's style that he could not stomach, blinding himself to the implications of an approach to politics which Palmerston was then still developing. Long seen for, and himself modestly aware of being, a formidable parliamentarian and a brilliant administrator, he considered Palmerston's growing populism at the head of government abhorrent and perilous.[11] He was loath to accept the need for cultivating public opinion more directly than had hitherto been thought either seemly or prudent; and equally loath to concede the wisdom of deferring to it, not exceptionally, but as a matter of course, once it became clear. He followed where Palmerston led. In its obituary of Palmerston, *The Times* held up his comprehension of 'a great fact' and establishment of 'a great doctrine'. While Peel 'on two great occasions...sacrificed to public opinion...Lord Palmerston bowed to this deity, recognized its power, and used it as he could'. As *The Times* noticed, Palmerston had often been accused of merely keeping himself in office by compliance with public moods.[12] His critics, with Gladstone prominent among them, went further and charged him with exciting feeling in order to maintain his position by ostentatiously gratifying it.

Palmerston's courtship of public opinion had a more serious purpose than the enjoyment of office. It was integral to his ordered conception of the state, to the fullest exposition of which the House of Commons listened in 1859. A constitutional monarchy assumed the existence of a landed class, whose essential function was 'the maintenance of a balance between the different powers which comprised the fabric of our representative constitution'. The successful discharge of that function and the toleration of 'aristocratical institutions' in a progressively more industrialized and urbanized country depended on leadership and example, which demanded favourable publicity.[13] Palmerston did not think the press could do his work for him, believing that it reflected rather than made opinion, and that its judgements were ultimately commercial ones, for the most part.[14] His relationship with Delane of *The Times*, while close, was unsentimental, on both sides.[15] There was irony in Palmerston's public assertion that 'contributors to the press are the favourites and the ornaments of the social circles into which they enter'.[16] He shared Cobden's view that 'the true test of the tendency of parties is in the utterances of their leaders'.[17] The value of the press to him, as to Cobden, lay in the extensive coverage it was able to give, after production costs came down in 1855, to the speeches of politicians in whom its readership had an avid interest, whether sympathetic or not. '...what an immense advantage you have in the full reports of your arguments', wrote Cobden to Bright during the latter's agitation for Parliamentary reform in 1858: 'We would have given our ears for three columns of the *Times* in 1841.'[18] Those speeches of Bright's like others in a similar strain elsewhere, were not made to a predominantly landed House of Commons. When he had beaten off the wartime attacks of assorted enemies on his premiership, Palmerston sought to consolidate the victory by seeking out audiences, in Salford, Manchester and Liverpool, of the kind that Cobden and Bright hoped to turn against aristocratic primacy in government and society.

Palmerston's themes in his Northern speeches of 1856 were national freedom, strength, and prosperity; Britain's superiority over other countries in these respects; the internal and external policies to safeguard and enhance her interests and prospects; and the readiness of her traditional rulers to continue doing everything expected of them to secure the stable conditions for further advances at home and abroad. In making this last point, he contrived that it should harmonize with the responsibilities, which he tactfully stressed, of the substantial citizens whom he was addressing.[19] It is not easy to see why the speeches should have aroused such indignation in Gladstone, except that they were very well received. He fastened on the prime minister's references to foreign affairs. 'I wish I could believe myself under the influence of opium', he lamented to Lord Aberdeen, 'so shocked do I feel at the...shameful part which we seem to be playing before the world...The evil is greatly aggravated by the demonstration at Manchester and the far more absurd one at Liverpool. I do not think they add a jot to his real strength.'[20] He repeated these comments in a letter to his brother Robertson Gladstone, a leading provincial radical and civic politician in Liverpool. The speeches and their reception had done 'serious mischief', and would 'powerfully encourage' Palmerston.[21] The prime minister's supporters naturally thought otherwise. A particularly significant reaction was that of the British minister to Russia, Lord Wodehouse, telling how Palmerston's treatment in the big Northern towns had noticeably strengthened the government's hand in diplomacy. The strictly controlled Russian press paid a great deal of attention to British politics. 'The amount of trouble they bestow on us', wrote Wodehouse of that press, 'is a very fair measure of our influence.'[22] To many in all parties besides Gladstone, Palmerston appeared overbearing and provocative. In his speeches the prime minister was concerned to counter the parliamentarians by bringing public opinion to bear. He took the criticism of himself, and offered a reasoned reply.

It was familiar and slanted towards his audience. His policy and methods were those which 'all enlightened statesmen will adopt, and ... all intelligent people will justify and approve'. To the old charge that he selected weak states for his displays of strength, he answered, not altogether convincingly, that they abused their feebleness: 'Larger powers are above these things.' He presented foreign policy as an extension of British liberties, by 'moral authority' in the case of European states with large forces. 'A nation exercises a potent influence when it is seen to exhibit a bright example of internal order and morality', he said, '... then it is that even those who may feel that our institutions are not in exact accordance with their own theoretic notions of government are yet consciously impelled to imitate our progress...' By affirming that British constitutionalism was for export, like free trade and with it, he delighted his hearers, who had the additional satisfaction of being complimented upon the contrast between their municipal independence and administrative centralization in Europe. Linking Britain's power and prestige abroad and what he termed 'progressive improvement' at home, was fundamental to Palmerston's outlook. While he certainly drew on his popularity to resist ill-considered demands, as they seemed to him, for Parliamentary reform,[23] he did not go in search of foreign adventures in order to circumvent domestic reforms in general. By 'progressive improvement' he meant exactly what he said, and did: '... why should we not endeavour to be perpetually ameliorating ... laws and institutions, which, being human, cannot be perfect, but which, according to the progress of society and the change of circumstances must be continually in need of emendation and extension?[24] It was a Burkean idea of reform: and also Gladstone's. It should be clear why Palmerstonian politics were hard to attack effectively from any political quarter, radical, Peelite, Tory or disaffected Liberal.

In the fifties, Gladstone inclined to see himself and his political associates as marked out by fidelity to Peel's statecraft. None other than Sir James Graham, among those associates, warned him against entertaining an illusion. 'The policy of Peel', advised Graham, 'is still the policy to which I adhere. But this confession of faith is no valid security for practical conduct. Most of Palmerston's administration would make this same profession...'[25] Gladstone would never admit that Palmerston was personally committed to Peelism in this sense: but the policies of his first government bore Graham out. Unquestionably the ablest and most dangerous opponent of that government, because he could by sheer eloquence gather votes from all over the House, Gladstone assailed its departures from the safe course, whatever it might be. The preoccupation with safety, and his share of responsibility for the conflict with Russia, inhibited his wartime opposition. For instance, he disliked the financial arrangements of his successor at the Treasury, Lewis, and especially the resort to borrowing. He had to tell his disappointed radical brother, that he could not well have exploited 'minor points' in an attempt to defeat the scheme when, for good short-term reasons, he would himself have been obliged to propose a loan in preference to still higher taxation.[26] After the peace in 1856, he felt free to attack the government vigorously for not making reductions in the army and navy estimates that would take Britain back towards pre-war levels of expenditure, and help to ensure a more pacific foreign policy.[27] However, he took a long stride in the direction of political reality when he interpreted the 1857 general election's decisive result as sanctioning a departure from the objectives he had tried to reaffirm before the polls. 'My sentiments in regard to...finance and foreign policy', he stated, 'are precisely what they have been. The difference...is that the ministry...now...have title to plead...the presumable approval of a very great part of the country.'[28]

The election had been occasioned by the hollowest of Parliamentary victories over Palmerston during ten years at the head of his party, the defeat on Cobden's motion condemning the handling of recent events in China. Palmerston occupied a strong position politically, if not morally. As he argued in the House beforehand, the events shortly to be censured had arisen out of 'a predetermined system...But...who were the authors of that system?...Why...the Government of Sir Robert Peel'.[29] If the electorate did not care very much for the rights and wrongs of what had happened at Canton, it was partly because they, too, appreciated this; and partly because Palmerston had provided, as nearly as possible, through the Crimean War and since, the 'fair government' for which Gladstone appealed at the election.[30] The electors' verdict drove Gladstone to reflect where he stood. His opinions were unchanged, but to him and those who sympathized with him, it was 'a matter of the utmost delicacy to consider the tone and manner in which they shall seek to give effect to their views'. On reflection, he found this limiting: 'I ought rather to have said it will be governed by the same motives than to have used words which might seem to imply that it would of necessity be identical in form.'[31] The shift in his thinking, which was encouraged by his friend, the High Church leader Bishop Wilberforce, whose detestation of Palmerston was contained by a truly ecclesiastical awareness of the need to co-exist with the unrighteous. The Bishop strenuously opposed the government's Divorce Bill in the summer of 1857, and well knew how unpopular determined resistance to it in the Commons must be. He was anxious that Gladstone, in whom he saw his religious and political ideal of a future prime minister,[32] should not damage his prospects by putting up 'a very great fight' against the bill.[33] Wilberforce's advice, reinforced by that of the Duke of Newcastle,[34] went unheeded. Gladstone proceeded to that 'direct collision with Palmerston' which the Bishop had pleaded with him to avoid. Gladstone quite mistakenly replied that 'Politically the question carries no venom in it.'[35] Palmerston attached considerable importance to the bill; it was his resolution that overcame Gladstone's delaying tactics in the Commons. As predicted, the struggle did him no good. The House wondered at his judgement in drawing to their notice the disproportionate upper-class propensity to sexual immorality.[36]

Gladstone, Russell, Bright, and the Tories brought Palmerston low only by exploiting popular nationalism against him. The Tory leadership's part in defeating the government on the radical Milner Gibson's amendment to the Conspiracy to Murder Bill was scarcely consistent. They had recognized the bill as the least that could be done to appease the understandable anger in France at the activities of political exiles here, culminating in the preparations for the attempt on Napoleon III's life in January 1858.[37] Gladstone had a clearer perception than either Russell or Bright of the risk to Britain's security involved in compounding the offence to France by throwing out even so modest and inadequate a proposal, all the government felt able to introduce. He was acting, he assured his wife, to protect 'the very foundations of national liberty' from 'the Colonels' Bill'[38] – the name it had been given from the attitude of the French military in the crisis. His speech on Milner Gibson's amendment, one of his Parliamentary triumphs, contained a fulsome tribute to Napoleon as a friend of Britain and a cooler acquiescence in the desirability of perpetuating the French alliance. He blamed the government both for straining Anglo-French relations by being in the wrong over Rumania and other international problems, and for truckling to France over the bill. He skilfully turned to account the pride in British constitutionalism which Palmerston had stimulated : 'These times are grave for liberty. We talk of progress...more than ever does responsibility centre upon the institutions of England...I say that a measure passed by this House...the chief hope of freedom – which attempts to establish a moral complicity between us and those who seek safety in repressive measures will be a blow...to that sacred cause in every country...'[39] Untypically, Gladstone exulted in Palmerston's downfall : '...he was hooted...by the crowd in the Park!'.[40]

In a long letter almost immediately afterwards to his old colleague, Lord Canning, governor-general of India, he discussed the likely settlement of politics following the upheaval. The day before he had written to his brother Robertson, 'the Liberal party...is released from a most discreditable position as the supporters of the worst government of our time'.[41]

To Canning he put the crucial question about Palmerston, 'Will he come back?', and set himself to answer it. He saw no hope for the Tories, whom he had just declined to rejoin as a member of Derby's cabinet. 'What seems clearest is that the new ministry cannot last long. They are in a sad minority within Parliament and in a decided minority without. Miracles of policy such as convert...opponents are rare and not to be thought of.' Of his own Peelite grouping, he said merely: '...our power...which lies among the independent liberals, is not great'. Concentrating upon the Liberals, he related how Palmerston was bent on getting into office again and retained the loyalty of many; but wound up: 'I hold...that Lord John Russell will gain the upper hand. I doubt Palmerston's capacity to vie with him. He has no legislative spirit or power, and very little knowledge of public business and...his popularity is gone.'[42] Personal antagonism surely inspired much of this extraordinary misjudgment; less than three months later, Gladstone was minimizing his political differences with Palmerston. The letter to Canning strongly suggests that he never seriously believed he would be justified in re-entering a Tory cabinet. The impression that he did so believe was derived from Derby's renewed offer of a cabinet place in May, from the qualified support which Gladstone, like Russell and Bright, extended to the government while the Liberals were trying to sort themselves out, and from his acceptance of a government mission to the Ionian Islands.[43]

Derby's approaches to Gladstone aroused mixed feelings in his party. When the first was made on Palmerston's resignation, and *The Times* announced his inclusion in the new cabinet, his Tory brother, Captain John Gladstone, MP, sent him a word of congratulation and warning: 'You will have no easy task before you, but I hope that the House will at any rate for some time show forbearance.'[44] The Tories' dislike of Peelites remained strong, although they had largely swallowed Peelism; and Gladstone would be bound to lose much of the sympathy for him on the other side. Such general hostility might be expected to break forth when the opportunity presented itself, and disable him politically. This consideration must have weighed with him if he was tempted by Derby's offers. *The Times*'s announcement prompted the radical brother to write: 'we cannot, for the life of us, understand how...you are ever to get on with Lord Derby and his administration...'[45] As for the support that Gladstone gave Derby, he was soon disappointed in the Tory government; but contributed to keeping it in office so long as it was the only alternative to a Palmerston restoration.[46] The decision to undertake the Ionian mission was accompanied by careful avoidance of any political strings that might be attached to an imperial duty: 'My circumspection...has...been enormous', he reassured Lord Aberdeen, who had no faith in a Tory revival either.[47]

In Gladstone's absence, Palmerston was rewarded for having devoted his

energies to the routine of leadership in opposition, holding regular meetings
with ex-cabinet ministers; and for having taken pains to conciliate Russell
through the tactful medium of Lewis.[48] The menace of a great international
conflict found him relatively well placed to take advantage of rising public
alarm at the open threat of war between Austria and France, with the
whole European balance in consequent jeopardy. Moreover, the government's intention of strengthening its authority and the electoral base of
Toryism by meeting a persistent demand for revision of the 1832 Reform
Act, was working in favour of its Whig and moderate Whig rivals. For this
the latter had Bright to thank. He had seized the chance of pressurizing a
weak ministry and a disunited Liberal party by launching an agitation for
a radical reform bill.[49] Those vastly experienced statesmen, Palmerston and
Russell, could plausibly claim that they were best fitted to devise legislation
that would prove as broadly satisfactory as the 1832 Act.[50] Gladstone
described Parliamentary reform before setting out for Greece as an
'unattractive subject'.[51] He wrote to the Duke of Newcastle at the end of
January 1859, saying that he did not see his way to 'being right and being
also practicable'[52] with regard to the question. Within days he had
confirmation from Bulwer Lytton, the Tory colonial secretary, that anxiety
about developments in Europe was pushing all else aside in men's minds at
home: 'Affairs as to war…may suddenly lift up Palmerston into a power
no one dreamed he could have again.'[53] There was really no other choice
as prime minister if the threat of war intensified and the choice were to be
made.

The Tories played into Palmerston's hands by dissolving upon their
reform bill in April. War between France, her Sardinian ally, and Austria
broke out during the election. Almost simultaneously, a tremendous panic
took possession of the City and the investing public on the circumstantial
report carried by newspapers of a Franco-Russian treaty providing for an
offensive and defensive alliance, which was naturally suspected of being
aimed at Britain.[54] Earlier in the month the French ambassador had called
on the foreign secretary, Napoleon's old acquaintance, Lord Malmesbury
and 'talked wildly about alliance with France to conquer all Europe by
means of steam fleets which would land anywhere'.[55] It made sense in this
atmosphere to suppose that the French had looked elsewhere for their ally
in the conquest of Europe. The London Stock Exchange's worst collapse for
many years was not irrational in the circumstances. Consols fell by up to $7\frac{1}{8}$
in the last days of April; while reputable foreign securities were unsaleable;
British railway shares, a favourite investment, dropped sharply in line with
the funds. Fifty-one members failed on the Stock Exchange.[56] For these
disasters *The Times* City column roundly blamed 'the wilful blindness of the
Derby Cabinet to the dangers…threatening this country'.[57]

Speaking in his constituency on 30 April Pakington, the First Lord of the

Admiralty, referred with dismay to the scale of the losses: '...there has been a state of things in the City...for the last few days hardly to be remembered...panic...ruin falling on a number of persons, failure to an extent I am...afraid to mention...depreciation of property which is most serious'. He attributed the crash mainly to the credulity of the press and restated the government's policy of neutrality; but added ominously that it might be difficult to persevere in that policy during a general war on the Continent.[58] Next week Disraeli, denying the existence of the rumoured Franco-Russian treaty, said 'these erroneous statements...have, I believe, ruined many virtuous families in this country'; yet, while he asserted that the government wanted peace, he envisaged stationing 'our armies on the German frontier...our fleets...in the Mediterranean or the Adriatic, to watch events', awaiting the moment when the war might be ended and the affairs of Europe settled. Palmerston was the beneficiary of this striking lack of confidence in the Tories' ability to manage foreign policy.[59]

Palmerston declared that his introduction of the Conspiracy to Murder Bill to preserve better relations with France than now existed had been vindicated. There was no part of his political life to which he looked back with more satisfaction: 'if great care had not been taken to mislead the public mind...the universal feeling of honest Englishmen would have been that we were right'. But he had learnt his lesson in 1858, and repeated it: 'Public opinion ran wild...when a nation takes up an opinion you might as well think of stopping a wild horse...'[60] Sympathetic to Sardinia but afraid of France, British opinion was quite unconvinced that the country's interests required her to incur the risk of war.[61] It was enough for Palmerston to have come out strongly on the stronger side, and at the same time to have intimated that a new government stood better with France. Gladstone was 'not prepared to dismiss the government on grounds of political morality';[62] he voted in their lobby on the motion of no confidence that removed them early in June. But his action in then joining Palmerston's cabinet inevitably called his political morals in question. He defended himself by emphasizing his agreement with Palmerston and Russell over Italy, mentioning, however, his unwillingness 'to be the one remaining Ishmael of the House of Commons'.[63] Some eighteen months had elapsed since he confided in Robertson, 'It was much against my will that I retired from office, and I should hail the opportunity of returning to it honourably.'[64] Whether or not his return conformed to his fine sense of honour evidently troubled him. The compromises inherent in political life always bore hard upon his conscience.

In one of his two important speeches during the election Palmerston had made much of the Divorce Act, which he rightly deemed a major social reform; and of his controversial episcopal appointments to lessen the gap between Church and Dissent. He presented his selections as 'men above the narrow prejudices which sometimes separate sect from sect', and 'a great advantage to the religious interests of the country'.[65] Gladstone, who had furiously resented the selection of 'thorough No-Churchmen',[66] professed to have elicited assurances about Palmerston's intentions in a matter vital to him.[67] Religious and economic policy were two fertile areas of potential disagreement with Palmerston besides Parliamentary reform, which definitely ranked third, though it had assumed greater significance in his eyes. Gladstone had so little in common with Palmerston that the prime minister did not originally intend him for the Treasury, but for a lesser cabinet post. Gladstone meant to take nothing else, it is true.[68] However, his position was not so strong, particularly after his vote of confidence in Derby's administration, that he could dictate to Palmerston. Wishing to ensure the best use of Gladstone's talents in a government with a small and uncertain majority, Lewis, a singularly disinterested politician, advised Palmerston that he would waive his claim to the Treasury, for which his name had been put down.[69] Once appointed, Gladstone hoped to use the leverage of finance to affect policy widely; but he fully realized that his influence in a Palmerston cabinet must depend substantially on the response of public opinion.

He advertised this political truth in a speech of October 1859, choosing a dinner at which, he remarked in his diary, 'no small part of England was represented'[70] – businessmen and politicians gathered for a banquet given to the directors of the company owning the SS *Great Eastern*. He sketched the limits of policy he would observe. These were determined, he recognized, firstly by 'the sentiments which animate the mass of the people'; if the masses desired 'thrift and economy', then it was his 'duty and…pleasure' to oblige. It might be that unprecedented prosperity ruled out a reversion to the principles of ministries headed by Wellington, Grey, Melbourne, and Peel – a reminder that both parties had long appreciated the political and social arguments for keeping general expenditure down. If these tried principles were rejected by the people, it would be vain to expect the Chancellor of the Exchequer to prevail. To move the public in the right direction, he asked for the help of 'those intelligent and really governing classes of which we have here an important portion'. They had it in their power 'to do something at least towards…some lightening of the burdens…on the noble-minded artisans and…peasantry of England'.[71] It was in accordance with these general considerations that Gladstone conducted his budgetary battles in the six years ahead. Palmerston's restored popularity overshadowed his own throughout the period, and his standing with 'the really governing classes' never rivalled the prime minister's. When Palmerston proved obdurate, Gladstone gave way rather than go into lasting political isolation. That would be his fate, if he resigned again; so Palmerston forcibly reminded him in their interview of 6 June 1860 when Gladstone was on the verge of going.[72]

Palmerston prepared for Gladstone's resignation that summer by arranging for Lewis to replace him when it arrived, as the prime minister thought was 'not unlikely'.[73] Lewis lacked Gladstone's virtuosity as a financier, but he had been a sound chancellor in war and commercial crisis. His character and abilities made him an influential figure in cabinet and Parliament.[74] Without him to fall back on, Palmerston would have had more difficulty in handling Gladstone during the government's formative years. The critical dispute in 1860 over money for the fortification of naval bases ended in a way that underlined Palmerston's command of the ministry. Lewis commented a week after Palmerston had spoken to him about succeeding their colleague: 'The Gladstone drama has pretty well reached its *dénouement*...having left the high ground of "insuperable objection", and having begun to parley, he is not likely to hold out much longer. *Château qui parle et femme qui écoute, l'un et l'autre va se rendre.*'[75] Thereafter, when the annual confrontation over defence estimates came round, Gladstone fought hard; but a remark to his wife about army expenditure in 1861 sums up his tactics: 'Up to a certain point, I must certainly make a stand.'[76] He told the Commons in the budget debates later in the year that the country would not let him change the structure of taxation as he wished, getting rid of the income tax, his stated aim when chancellor before the Crimean War. He rejected out of hand the suggestion that he was bound to adhere to his old finance.[77] All he could do and did, was to secure, by insistent questioning, the stabilization of peacetime expenditure at a level well above that of his previous term at the Treasury, and to profit by the growing national wealth to cut the incidence of taxation appreciably. He consented to borrow, but nevertheless effected a reduction of debt and interest.[78] To such economy, Palmerston was not averse; without it the Liberal party would have been vulnerable at the next election.[79]

The fiscal success attended by such friction between the two men was a joint achievement even in respect of the Anglo-French commercial treaty and the repeal of the paper duties. Palmerston agreed to the first with some doubts; he was saved by the victory in the Commons from the consequences of his resolve to disavow the second and the budget of 1861, if the House went the other way.[80] It was patent that, as Palmerston told him, many of the votes furnishing the slender margin of survival were cast reluctantly to deliver the government from grave embarrassment and possible collapse.[81] Gladstone took note of the prime minister's warning that he was being hurt by suspicion of his links with Bright. Speaking on the budget, he repudiated the idea that he and Bright held similar views; and sought to dispel such fears by clarifying his philosophy of taxation. He did not covertly intend 'shifting the burden from commodities to property and effecting thereby a considerable alteration in the relative position of classes'.[82] This put in perspective his past references to alleviating indirect taxes, which he had conceived as part of a general process of reduction.[83] His subsequent allusions to this subject were uncompromising in their social conservatism. Of graduated taxation, he said in 1862 'there is nothing more plausible': but it would lead to 'that source of all evils, discord between class and class'.[84] It would injure the 'labouring class', he observed in 1863: the undiscouraged accumulation of capital created the climate of confidence indispensable to the security and welfare of rich and poor, and drove down interest rates, which were the most important factor in determining employment and wages.[85] He upheld differential taxation, however, where it benefited landowners, in the levying of succession duty compared with its equivalent on personal property; the illiquidity of landed inheritances might otherwise result in forced sales and the infliction of 'suffering and almost... torture'.[86] The importance of these conventional arguments lay in the emphasis with which he deployed them.

Gladstone proposed that the government should retire when it withdrew the reform bill to which it was pledged. The incident occurred three days after his momentous interview with Palmerston. Russell, who had done most to commit the government to the bill, promptly denied that ministers were under any obligation to resign. 'I said I would not resign', noted Palmerston in his diary. 'Gladstone's motive evidently was to cover under a general resignation his own failure... and to escape from being a party to fortification loan.'[87] The prime minister believed Gladstone tried that summer to impose his will on the cabinet by brandishing the threat of resignation.[88] Whatever the truth of that may have been, Gladstone's greater tractability made for a real political partnership with Palmerston, which their mutual dislike must not be permitted to obscure. Even over religion, they seem to have succeeded in avoiding serious clashes, except once. The exception was Gladstone's attempt to press Wilberforce's candidacy for the archbishopric of York.[89] Palmerston looked on Wilberforce's labours as subversive of the religious goodwill which he had effectively promoted.[90] '... there was a greater storm... in the cabinet than I ever heard before', Gladstone informed his wife.[91] That this should have caused a more heated discussion than any excited by the issues of financial and defence policy, shows how politically charged religious questions were. The episode no doubt helped Gladstone's developing realism about the Establishment in a society which High Churchmen could not hope to dominate.[92] He began to make direct contact with prominent Dissenting ministers, whose access to Palmerston was through Lord Shaftesbury. He joked mildly about the experience to his wife when he had tea with some of them: 'What odd predicaments and situations life abounds with.'[93] Roman Catholicism united Palmerston and Gladstone in hostility to it. 'I am as sincere a Protestant as any... and also... as much an anti-Catholic', said the prime minister, speaking in the Commons. Like Gladstone, he was sure that the temporal power of the Popes would not endure.[94] He was more certain than Gladstone, perhaps, of the Papacy's decline as a spiritual power. Gladstone wanted not merely to do away with the temporal power but to tie down the Papacy in the exercise of its spiritual functions, suggesting to the Italians that they should stipulate for the accountability to Victor Emanuel II's government of the Pope's every 'counsellor...and every agent.'[95]

Starting in the autumn of 1860, Palmerston and Gladstone between them visited Leeds, Edinburgh, Manchester, Sheffield, Newcastle, and the surrounding industrial district, York, Southampton, Glasgow, Bradford, Bolton, and Liverpool, listing only those cities and towns where their advent was staged as a major event. They spoke, too, in smaller places with which they had some connection, where speeches might often provide continuity with those delivered in the big centres of population, as did the usual variety of addresses in London. By their presence and oratory, they reached communities and classes. The theme uppermost in their speeches was class collaboration, throughout the social structure and under the freely accepted leadership of aristocracy. Of the two, Gladstone referred more explicitly and frequently to aristocratic fulfilment of duty. He had a higher conception of aristocracy than Palmerston who, in keeping with his outlook, treated it as a fact rather than an ideal. Gladstone's references to his class have to be seen in the context of worry in its ranks that it was neither sufficiently numerous nor dedicated to fill its traditional rôle, while the upper middle class added so rapidly to its numbers and wealth as to make its continued acquiescence in aristocratic primacy problematical.[96] Gladstone was replying to the uncomfortably loud assertions made familiar by Cobden and Bright that the landowners had had their day. There could not have been more powerful spokesmen for a supposedly obsolete class. For Gladstone saw no inconsistency between eloquently championing its undiminished relevance, and a legitimate pride in his own plebeian origins. Proud though he was of his father's humble beginnings in Scotland, an emotion voiced on his Edinburgh visit of January 1862, he said then: 'I am very sensible of the great advantages of birth...strongly and deeply rooted...the privileges of...aristocracy depend...above all, on the strong conviction of the people that its existence is beneficial to the country at large.'[97] Up and down Britain, he dwelt on popular esteem for the class his father had entered and in which the son had firmly settled himself by marriage and landownership. He would not admit to being afraid of middle-class competition: the conditions prevailing since the Great Reform Act, he said at Oxford in November 1861, had already obliged 'the higher class' to compete with the middle class: 'I confidently state...the result has been to stimulate...that higher class...to confirm and strengthen their position...'[98] He did not hesitate to compare the middle class unfavourably with their social superiors in the understanding of property as a God-given trust for society. What an outcry there would be, he pointed out at Newcastle in November 1862, if a landowner abused his rights in a way morally resembling the behaviour of some mill-owners in the stricken cotton industry. These businessmen were 'using the rights of property in a manner which, if extensively followed, would bring all property to destruction'.[99]

Gladstone lectured, and Palmerston flattered, the middle class. The flattery was, however, directed to fostering a consciousness of social solidarity. At Sheffield the prime minister warmly commended the 'energy, intelligence...integrity' of the town's large employers, and spoke of the openness of their class to workers ambitious of rising.[100] A carefully selected working-class audience in Glasgow heard him say how wrong it was of industrial capital and labour to view each other, as in the recent past, with distrust and worse: 'The capitalist, instead of grudging the wages...due to merit and exertion, is glad to find the wages and advantages of labour may go on increasing, and the labourer...ought to see...with...satisfaction the accumulation of fortunes...'[101] He ascribed improving class relations to the flexibility and resilience of a political and economic framework with which he and Gladstone contrasted the current breakdown of 'what may be called American democracy'. They hailed 'the closer union' of classes. It was the outstanding feature of his time in politics, according to Gladstone.[102] To him, at a Volunteer dinner in 1864, the middle class was 'in a very great degree the cement between the upper and the lower classes'.[103] Their contribution to social control through enlightened factory discipline gained his warm approval: 'It is impossible to overstate the importance of this fact.'[104] Both he and Palmerston did not think it possible for government and society to better significantly the lot of those in the lower reaches of the working class, the unskilled and intermittently employed, and they said so; the prime minister even stated at Leeds that in a free economy 'the greater the development of industry...the greater the accumulation of population, the more will this class exist'.[105] If he was correct, the more important it became to be sure of the skilled men and steady wage-earners, whose example counted for so much with the less fortunate members of their class.[106] This element was indispensable, Palmerston and Gladstone made it clear, to the social hierarchy. The prime minister designated it 'the strength and stamina of the country'.[107] Yet to landed politicians, a question mark remained over the true disposition of urban workers. Gladstone enthused about a model of class relations, 'the happy social condition' of the countryside, which compensated the agricultural labourers, he contended, for their below average wages.[108] Palmerston simply put the rural classes, taken together, above the other components of 'the national fabric'.[109]

Palmerston and Gladstone associated free trade with empire in their speeches. The prime minister took pride in the development of 'informal empire'. Foreign states owed their conquest to armed force: 'we', observed Palmerston quite frankly, 'have achieved triumphs, we have made aggressions, but we make them of a very different kind. The capital and skill of Englishmen are spread over the whole surface of the globe.'[110] Gladstone denied he was an anti-imperialist. He retained an old preoccupation with the colonies of settlement, growing very satisfactorily under free trade and therefore capable of lightening Britain's responsibility of imperial protection, of which, he was careful to say, she did not desire to be entirely relieved. The scale of Britain's profitable involvement abroad perturbed him: 'What nation…has had its factories, …interests, …ships in every part of the habitable world.' He pleaded for a recognition of 'over-extended responsibilities', by which he only meant territorial commitments. The British flag must cover her immense international trade: maritime and overseas commercial activity, by the domestic prosperity to which it gave rise, 'had done much…to bind together the…classes…'.[111] There was, then, a close likeness between his idea of empire and Palmerston's though talk of successful aggression, by whatever means, could not but be repugnant to him. Over Europe, whence Britain feared attack, he and Palmerston differed, in public and in private, as to its probability. Addressing the Volunteers at Chester in October 1860, he did not find the imminence of invasion credible, but went on: 'I rejoice that at a time when the elements of danger are rife in Europe and the greatest questions stand for solution…England should both morally and physically be strong.'[112] This speech was interpreted for what it was: an announcement that he had no insuperable differences with the prime minister over foreign policy and defence.[113] Bright, for one, was surprised and shocked that Gladstone should 'glorify the Volunteers',[114] an offence which he repeated more than once; though his highest praise for them was as part of the country's 'pacific apparatus', unifying the classes.[115] For the rest, Gladstone and Palmerston, when speaking around Britain on foreign affairs, sounded themes that were in the latter's speeches of 1856 in the North: the spread of British constitutionalism, now more evident, the moral authority this conferred, and the right and duty of a vigorous diplomacy short of war. It must be said that Gladstone practically left Palmerston to make his own excuses outside Parliament for the failure of such diplomacy in the Dano-German conflict of 1863–64. Palmerston relied, even more than in Parliament, upon a literally winning candour: 'Ships sailing on the sea cannot stop armies on land.'[116]

The management of public opinion had become inseparable from the business of government instead of being an awkward complication of Parliamentary politics. Palmerston offset his narrow victory in the

Realities

Commons debate on his policy towards Denmark by a series of speeches outside. Their reception was eagerly watched. Russell, who had moved nearer to him during the government's term, congratulated the prime minister: 'It is clear your popularity is a plant of hardy growth and deep roots, as the real embarrassments of the Danish question have not shaken it.'[117] Not that Palmerston put any great faith in his popularity. The ephemeral character of such collective emotion evoked a wryly cynical reaction in him; he had earlier cautioned Russell, an almost naively vain man, against the excitement of industrial towns where a celebrity 'would be followed by cheering and acclaiming crowds...like any of us or...the Pasha of Egypt or...any other lion'.[118]His attitude to the ablest among the middle class which admired him was one of dislike and distrust; he once described Cobden as 'being like all middle-class men who have raised themselves by money making or by talent, very vain under the semblance of not being so'.[119] He was keenly alive to the inherent limitations on love of country in the capitalists who constantly solicited the action of their government. The expansion of Russia in Central Asia after, as before, the Crimean war would go on in the nature of things, he rightly predicted in a minute at the end of his career; and he inserted the mordant comment: 'she will be at no loss to find plenty of *patriotic* Englishmen who will vie with each other in alacrity to make for her those lines of railway essential to enable her to become in Asia a formidable enemy of England'.[120]

Palmerston was in several ways less of a conservative than Gladstone. He favoured reinforcement of the House of Lords by peerages for life, recruited more widely than from the lawyers whose admission was the immediate question.[121] 'It is like the beginning of the end', mourned Gladstone's Peelite friend and fellow-member for Oxford University, Sir William Heathcote.[122] Gladstone himself reacted little less violently: '...it is impossible', he said in the Commons, 'that there could arise in this country a graver question than that involved in the creation of peers for life'.[123] Palmerston had recommended a life barony for Lord Wensleydale without consulting his colleagues, but Lewis's diary lists half a dozen cabinets which discussed the constitutionality of the step and its 'very questionable wisdom'.[124] Palmerston's proposal and its fate seemed to Gladstone compelling evidence of 'the present political disorganization'.[125] The prime minister was also thwarted in his wish to confer hereditary peerages on two industrialists; something that Gladstone did not venture to do until the mid-1880s.[126] Palmerston was somewhat ahead of his colleagues in other respects. He championed 'progressive improvement' that was bold according to the ideas of the day, in its restriction of property-rights; and used forthright language, as on the Crowded Dwellings Bill in 1857: the opponents of the measure, he remarked caustically, 'said that an Englishman's home was his castle. In this case, every builder's house was his dungeon, and into this unhealthy dungeon ... for the sake of private gain, they crowded a number of persons who could not live together with safety to either body or mind ... '[127] He refused to apologize for these comments: it was the government, rather, which had been wrongly accused of 'tyrannous interference ... '.[128] Gladstone had a 'mind ... full of misgivings' on the extension of factory legislation that took place under the second Palmerston government.[129] Too much should not be made of this divergence between men, both of whom were sincerely paternalist in their outlook, with Palmerston more appreciative of the value of state intervention in setting a minimum standard.

They did continue to differ over the future and purpose of income tax after Gladstone had submitted, for the time being, to a level of expenditure much higher than he would have liked. Gladstone still looked forward to abolition of the tax as too productive of revenue for the good of governments tempted to be uneconomical. His intentions were not, on an abstract plane, less liberal than Palmerston's. It may be that the prime minister had the better of the purely fiscal and the human argument. On the first, he observed to Russell, who had suddenly sided with the chancellor: 'All taxes ... are practically income taxes'; but the Treasury received the whole of income tax, while the price of articles subject to indirect taxation reflected the cost of borrowing by importers or producers to pay duty.[130] As to the relative personal impact of income tax and indirect taxation, Palmerston argued that the former, unlike the latter, was levied upon tax-payers all of whom could comfortably afford to pay.[131] Who was the working man's friend here? On the revived question of Parliamentary reform, as on finance, Gladstone undoubtedly secured the advantage in publicity with most radicals.[132] Well-known passages in his speeches did have an encouraging sound to them, without seriously alarming the public.[133] Yet there were balancing passages. Enough has been quoted to show how little of a radical he was. Any lingering doubt should be removed by the exculpatory letter he wrote in answer to Palmerston's strictures on the wording of his remarks in the debate of May 1864 on Baines's Borough Franchise Bill.[134] It does appear that Gladstone owed his progressive reputation in the 1860s largely to Cobden's and Bright's preference for him among landed politicians. His principal attraction, at least for Bright, may have been his animus against Palmerston.[135] 'Gladstone whom you regard as a *saint*', Bright admonished Cobden early in the second Palmerston government, 'is no more to be relied on than the rest.'[136] Similarly bitter observations by Bright are scattered through their correspondence. Cobden's more generous estimate was shrewder: 'The middle-class and a section of the aristocracy ... you must carry with you', he reminded Bright in 1861.[137]

Pragmatic habitually, often cynical, Palmerston cherished two genuine political passions. One was anti-slavery. An entry in Lord Stanley's diary for June 1864 depicts Gladstone talking very critically in Society about the way in which anti-slavery zealots welcomed the sanguinary American civil war.[138] He detested negro slavery; but he did not feel so strongly on this score as Palmerston.[139] That was the truth about his attitude to slavery. He did not believe it either right or feasible to destroy the Confederacy, which impressed him by the unity and determination of its white inhabitants; and he was fearful of social unrest in the Lancashire mill towns if the cotton famine persisted. His insistence on practicability; his anxious concern for class relations in Britain; his high, if not unqualified, regard for an authentic manifestation of nationality such as he discerned in the Southern States; and his scepticism of American democracy – all go to explain his partisanship during the Civil War.[140] While Palmerston sympathized with the South, he wanted to avoid putting Britain in a position where the effect of her action was to sustain slavery. When the cabinet decided, over the protests of Russell and especially Gladstone, not to authorize an Anglo-French initiative to bring about an armistice in America, Lewis recorded that Palmerston, who had endorsed the proposal, 'seemed not in reality to disapprove of the answer'.[141] In letters to Russell, Palmerston adverted to 'the difficulty about slavery', commenting pointedly: 'The French government are more free from the shackles of principle and of right and wrong...than we are.' Public opinion would not be with the government if it condemned slavery, he maintained.[142] Gladstone complained to his wife of the 'feeble and half-hearted support' that he had received from the prime minister.[143] Leaving aside 'a philanthropic minority', he thought the Northerners would not hesitate to adopt slavery if the economic and climatic conditions of the South were to obtain in their regions. He perceived in the democratic North 'the spirit of monopoly...the unquietness in the great towns, found in America as in all countries...ever ready for a row'.[144] Looking for a line of division between North and South in a cabinet memorandum of July 1862, he discovered it where there was 'a kind of aristocracy'.[145]

The other political passion of Palmerston's life was nationality, his own first. In Gladstone, this was as powerful as it could be in an intelligently devout Christian. When strongest in him, the emotion showed itself in conjunction with religion, as in his sympathy for the Hellenic nationalism and Greek Orthodoxy of the Ionian Islands,[146] and for anti-Papal sentiment in the Risorgimento. His *Quarterly Review* article of April 1859 on the Italian war singled out for eager speculation 'the fate of that hybrid Sovereignty, ever a marvel and now undoubtedly a monster, which...oppresses and enervates...and in the sacred names of the Gospel and the Saviour overrides every social right...'[147] His excessive admiration of Sardinia's limited constitutionalism stemmed from her quarrel with the Papacy.[148] He and Palmerston did not extend to the subjugated peoples of the British empire their solicitude for Greeks and Italians. It was partly this that brought them into dispute with the Tories' foreign secretary, Malmesbury, in 1859, who argued straightforwardly that Austria in Italy and imperial Britain were in the same position. 'I would ask the Emperor', he told the ambassador in Paris, 'how can we who have conquered Ireland and hold all India by the sword in common decency be the Quixotes of Italy.'[149] Palmerston's knowledge of Ireland made him well aware of her smouldering nationalism.[150] While Gladstone conceded in Parliament that the Indian Mutiny grew into a movement 'so much more formidable' than a military revolt, he took for granted the work of reconquest, distinguishing between necessary severity and atrocities.[151] Gladstone quite as much as Palmerston upheld Britain's Great Power status, to which the possession of Ireland and India was vital. He explained how he saw his country to an Italian acquaintance: 'The leadership in European politics legitimately falls, in my opinion, to the combined action of England and France, but both require to be kept in their proper places... the unity... and independence of Germany are necessary...'[152] International checks upon Britain were not to Palmerston's liking, but he, too, hoped for a stronger German Confederation.[153]

To regret the weakness of party was commonplace in the 1850s and early sixties. At times Gladstone imputed most political ills to the fact.[154] Palmerston asserted his belief in the dependence of British politics on the party system. He was not, however, a good party man. Nor was Gladstone. 'It is of course more convenient for a Government to have no united band in opposition to it', said the prime minister to his constituents in 1857, adding quickly that he did not deny it was 'in accordance with the constitution' to have an opposition.[155] Party was more resilient than he and Gladstone supposed. Remarkable testimony to its strength came from Malmesbury, a representative Tory. It was his habit each year to seek refreshment in those pleasures for which Paris is celebrated. During the peace negotiations there in 1856, he stayed away, lest he should compromise his party by being drawn into premature discussion. 'I even refused myself my annual lark at Paris', he proudly recalled.[156] On the Whig and Liberal side of politics, the cohesiveness of the Tories was the subject of envious comment. As Gladstone told the Queen in 1855, Toryism 'embodied one of the great fundamental elements of English society'.[157] In the absence of any comparable social basis, Liberalism had been held together by old associations and dislike of partisan Tory attitudes.[158] Palmerston, as prime minister, and Gladstone, as his colleague, gave the party a more substantial identity. Gladstone described it at Chester in May 1865 when he attributed to 'the party termed the Liberal party', in continuation of Canning's policies and Peel's, the removal of 'any occasion of... conflict between classes'. He linked the achievement with the name of Palmerston 'who has a world-wide reputation...whose admirable and popular qualities have given him a high place in the...affections of his countrymen...'.[159] For both men, the pursuit of class collaboration was far more important than party allegiances. The prime minister avowed in a debate of 1862 on legislation and the state of parties that his government would find support where it could: and would not conform to 'slavish, and I may say, jobbing principles...'[160] Gladstone declared at the 1865 general election that although 'a member of a Liberal government' and 'in association with the Liberal party', his views were 'truly conservative'.[161] Without undue optimism, therefore, Palmerston and Gladstone built into Liberalism an idea and a function, not by any means novel but so defined and emphasized as to take on a new meaning.

There ran through the politics of these statesmen a marked vein of pessimism. Palmerston included in his speeches a standard reference to the inescapable imperfection of all human institutions. Gladstone, in the customary speech of thanks after being returned for South Lancashire, considered it appropriate to reflect upon the pervasive operation of 'a principle of taint and corruption – a principle of lapse and decay'; the business of politicians was to counteract these forces.[162] Palmerston's understanding of human nature, in its essence, was Hobbesian. A lifetime in diplomacy and in governments faced with sometimes acute social tensions at home persuaded him that 'The love of quarrelling and fighting is inherent in man, and to prevent its indulgence is to impose restraints on natural liberty. A state may...shackle its subjects...'[163] He wrote that in 1861; it reveals what lay at the bottom of his policies. There are more ways than one of shackling a people. Gladstone's insight into human nature derived from his Christian beliefs. Among his papers for November 1864 is a theological meditation on 'the terrible mystery of Evil', which came to this conclusion: '...experience presented to me the difficulty...philosophy could do nothing for its solution, religion taught me the means by which at least each one of us might grapple with the problem...'[164] His experience of humanity collectively had been mainly political. If he subscribed to the notion of progress, it was in a restricted and consciously Christian form, envisaging a continuous struggle with resurgent wrong within the individual and the social conscience. The object of historical studies, another of his fragmentary meditations had it, was 'to fathom the nature that we bear in order that we may bear it worthily...'.[165]

Part II
At home

3

The politics of war and peace

Introductory

The Crimean war was seen on all sides as a test of Britain's institutions and of her standing as a Great Power. The main purpose of her governments then was to safeguard by the means at their disposal, including economic policy, traditional constitutionalism and libertarianism updated by the changes of the last thirty years. Britain's boasted superiority to American democracy and the authoritarian regimes of the Continent had not been seriously threatened in 1848, the year of revolutions, though there were grave misgivings. The first European conflict on a large scale involving Britain since the Great Reform Act was a sterner test. Those obscure exiles, Marx and Engels, did not observe the strains that war put upon this country more closely than did foreign governments at once attracted and repelled by the model for Continental liberalism. The Anglo-French struggle with Russia confirmed Britain's military limitations. On the other hand, it demonstrated her political stability, the strength of her economy, and the superiority of her finance. Palmerston had been the most determined advocate of war in the Aberdeen cabinet. The criticism of aristocratic politicians for mismanaging the campaign in the Crimea did not frighten him. As home secretary his direct responsibility was small; and as prime minister he was extraordinarily confident of being able to satisfy public opinion about the competence of his administration and its intentions. Parliament had difficulty in believing in a war for which the public was enthusiastic. To survive, Palmerston's ministry needed to balance one against the other: its success in doing so extended to the terms of peace. Neither his French ally nor his colleagues wanted to go on fighting for the different Europe which he had envisaged from the beginning. War had been declared for limited objectives, the attainment of which left the public with an inflated idea of British power. In developing an approach to politics that took more account of contemporary realities, Palmerston

45

naturally stopped short of telling his countrymen in wartime how little they could do, unaided, in Europe. They rewarded his prudence at the polls in the spring of 1857.

Party was not in abeyance during the war. The Tory leaders soon decided to attempt the overthrow of a weak administration almost entirely composed of its political opponents. They came very close to succeeding at one point: the sharpness of the reaction outside Westminster saved the government. A number of Tory backbenchers did not like these attacks on a minister who had taken office with a promise of no unpatriotic opposition from their leadership. Tory abstentions and cross-voting contained the unreliability of the Peelites and the disaffection of some radicals and others among the Liberals. Palmerston's lack of a majority was a constant incitement to his enemies on both sides of the House. In the aftermath of war, they fastened on the problems which came up abroad as offering the best chance of discrediting the prime minister; his domestic policy commanded very wide support. They failed to censure his handling of Anglo-American relations but defeated him over China early in 1857 on a motion by Cobden with support from Russell and Gladstone. On this occasion, the Tory defections did not save the government. Palmerston welcomed the opportunity for which he had waited since the fall of Sebastopol in September 1855. The delay enabled him to isolate the dissident Liberals and make the most of Tory divisions.[1]

War and its aims

Palmerston's real war aims were not the four points, on which the diplomacy of the conflict and its prelude centred. His vision ranged far more widely than the integrity of the Ottoman empire, and securities for its Christian tributary states in the Balkans and its Christian subjects elsewhere, for the freedom of the Danubian waterway, and for an end to Russian predominance in the Black Sea. He contemplated the territorial reduction of Russia by driving in her 'outposts', by which he meant broad lands – the Baltic provinces and Finland, Poland, the Crimea and the Caucasus.[2] Napoleon III shared these hopes, and to the indignation of the Queen and her husband, let it be known that France favoured Palmerston as Aberdeen's successor; his choice made use of that knowledge in forming the government.[3] While the Queen and the Prince were anti-Russian, they had no sympathy whatever with ideas that too closely resembled Napoleon's well-publicized aspiration to revise the European settlement made by the Congress of Vienna. As an extension of his plan to surround Russia with liberated nationalities, Palmerston wanted to persuade Austria, the leading German power, to give up her Italian possessions for the benefit of constitutional Sardinia, in particular, and accept compensation in the

Balkans at Ottoman expense. 'He would make a new map of Europe', said the Queen apprehensively at the end of January 1855, facing the prospect of a Palmerston ministry.[4] He had put his true war aims into a cabinet memorandum under Aberdeen, but he does not seem to have brought them forward again for collective scrutiny when prime minister. Most of his colleagues were no readier to consider these suggestions than they had been under Aberdeen. After Sebastopol fell, he talked to individual politicians of expelling Russia from her borderlands; they were equally unreceptive.[5] The influence he exerted over Clarendon at the Foreign Office helped Palmerston to keep up his pressure on France to continue the war: but when the Emperor decided that it was no longer in his interest to do so, the British prime minister acquiesced. The alliance depended on the French military contribution, much larger than the British. It was all Palmerston could do to hold Napoleon to the proposals drafted without consulting Britain and laid before the cabinet in November;[6] the banishment of Russia's fleet from the Black Sea was the only really significant improvement that she had won in the Four Points. They were practically the terms of the peace treaty signed at Paris six months later.

The public were unwilling to recognize the facts of Continental warfare. It was not only radicals like the historian George Grote who were fearful of the national mood, seeing in their country the emergent 'bully of Europe'. Lewis, the chancellor of the exchequer, had throughout regarded the war as mistaken, and reassured his friend: 'I told him', he confided to his diary, 'that the military prestige of England had been lowered by the war, and … its military weakness was believed to have been demonstrated.'[7] The heroism of Balaclava and Inkerman did not hide the truth from those who were prepared to acknowledge it. In a speech savaged by *The Times*, Lewis drew attention to the failure of the British in the final attack on Sebastopol, when the French took the fortress: unlike Britain, France had the manpower and organization for war on the required scale. The newspaper was incensed by 'ignoble exultation' on the Continent at the reverses to British arms. He did not 'feel with the people', complained *The Times*; patriotic emotion magnified Britain's part in the Crimean campaign.[8] Yet it was France that tired of the war; her finances felt the strain, the army suffered heavily from disease after the British had sharply reduced their mortality from that cause, and censorship could not conceal the unpopularity of a slow-moving war quite different from the brilliant operations of the first Napoleon. Another historian, H. H. Milman, drew an acceptable lesson: the war seemed to develop wealth and strength in Britain alone; preaching at St Paul's, he said she had stopped fighting 'just when … arrayed in the conscious panoply of might'.[9]

The prosperity that accompanied the war and gained from it underlay the feeling described by Milman. In the absence of conscription the

government was obliged to fight a limited war. Neither the army nor the
navy could raise the men they needed. The British ambassador told
Napoleon that conscription was all very well under a regime such as his but
in Britain 'there was not enough patriotism in parties to allow of such a
subject being actively discussed'.[10] In this the political parties were
representative of a country whose deeply rooted sense of personal freedom
contained the enthusiasm for war. It is not surprising that the French
thought they were being exploited by their ally. But Napoleon saw himself
as a liberal. The English alliance was an ideological necessity to him. The
Austrian envoy at his Court, Baron Hübner, was struck by his extreme
sensitivity to the British press; how the public opinion of liberal Britain
viewed him affected his claim to be no despot, appearances notwithstanding. 'C'est toujours la crainte de se dépopulariser en Angleterre qui le
retient', wrote Hübner.[11] Policy and inclination led Palmerston to make as
much as he could of the French commitment to a liberal Europe. His
speeches outside Parliament after Sebastopol depicted it as a victory over
a 'vast military empire', whose aggression threatened the whole world. The
'entirely disinterested' combination of Britain and France was directed to
establishing the liberties of Europe on a stable and lasting foundation. He
left no doubt that the two nations were fighting for much more than the
Four Points.[12] The British public identified eventual success in the Crimea
with the common cause. The government need not have worried about the
reception of the peace treaty; they were sufficiently concerned to bring over
Lord Cowley, the able ambassador in Paris, to testify that no better terms
were to be had.

British rejoicing at the peace proved to have been justified to a greater
extent than seemed possible at the time. Ministers underestimated the
severity of the war's demands on Russia. The reconstruction undertaken by
the new Tsar Alexander II exposed her internal weaknesses. In 1859
Clarendon dismissed this recuperating power, not altogether wisely, as
'that eunuch...Russia'.[13] The qualified victory of Britain and France was
a clear defeat for their opponent. Liberalism advanced visibly, not least in
Bonapartist France, where Britain's domestic showing in wartime made a
strong impression. Napoleon III was much influenced by his capable but
wayward cousin, Jerome Napoleon, who sketched his conception of the
future for European monarchy when sent to negotiate with the Hapsburg
Francis Joseph at the close of the war of 1859 between the two Emperors.
Francis Joseph found the very word 'constitution' objectionable, remarking
that he did not believe France was any more a constitutional state than
Austria. In practice, Jerome Napoleon conceded, French institutions could
not be 'très libérales', given the country's recent history. Nevertheless, if
France was not yet 'un gouvernement parlementaire à l'anglaise', he
hoped to see a genuine development of the representative system already in

place.[14] The Crimean war revealed the all-round inferiority of Russian absolutism – to the detriment of absolute monarchies everywhere. Palmerston had succeeded in his, and Napoleon's, fundamental purpose: to encourage the diffusion of what he understood by liberalism across the Continent where a reactionary Russia would no longer be in a position to inhibit political change as she had tried to do in the previous forty years. Sardinia's enlistment as a very junior partner of Britain and France in the conflict, and the British attitude to other Italian states at the Congress of Paris prepared the ground for French intervention at the end of the decade.

Parliament and public

The gap between the two was wider than it appeared when Palmerston took over the government. The Peelites and Tories supported the war without conviction. The Peelite resignations within the month could be traced to Gladstone's dislike of finding himself under a prime minister bent on prosecuting the war vigorously in accordance with the national wish and his own: 'to speak plainly and forcibly you doubt my views and intentions, and...think...I should be disposed to continue the war, without necessity for...objects unreasonable...or unattainable', Palmerston had written to him when forming the administration.[15] In May Derby decided to turn the ministry out; he commenced with an attack in the Lords, heavily defeated in that Tory-dominated chamber; and found many of his followers in the Commons equally loath to oust Palmerston, but almost put him in a minority on a critical division in July. The same month brought growing doubts in the cabinet to a head. Russell, once warlike, veered round to the sceptics. Despatched to Vienna to negotiate for peace while the fighting continued, he virtually gave away the allied case in agreeing to a formula that would have preserved Russian naval strength in the Black Sea; this had been the sticking point in the diplomatic manoeuvring before the war. On his return, he submitted the proposal to the cabinet but refrained from advocating it.[16] Napoleon's rejection in May of the terms on offer delivered ministers from having to accept what they knew would bring them down when explained to the public. Two months later, after Russell had criticized those terms in the House, he was shown to have agreed to them at Vienna. His resignation averted a vote of confidence which the government would certainly have lost. Yet it did not look as if Palmerston and the war could last. No progress was reported from the Crimea. Entries in Lewis's diary to September expressed a steady disbelief in the objects of the struggle which his finance was sustaining.[17] Lord Granville, who was a sounding board for his cabinet colleagues, wrongly supposed that the country would soon tire of a conflict 'in which the religious feelings and material interests of the nation are not concerned'.[18]

This interpretation of public opinion was widely shared, and inspired the resistance to the Turkish Loan Bill in July. The loan of £5 million with a joint Anglo-French guarantee was urgently needed to keep Turkey in the war. On the night of 20 July Lewis had to speak twice, and Palmerston three times, to save the bill from being thrown out on the motion of a Liberal backed by a very strong cross-section of the House. Disraeli, Gladstone, and Cobden took part in an assault which the government fought off by three votes, thanks to the presence of half a dozen Tories in their lobby. The Commons' behaviour, wrote Lewis immediately afterwards, reflected the inability to believe that there was 'a real national interest in supporting Turkey'. The public thought otherwise, and registered their disapproval so clearly that the second reading in the following week went unopposed, in spite of Gladstone's efforts. That rapid capitulation to opinion outside the House was indeed remarkable, as Lewis considered it.[19] The view of the war held by so many in Parliament did not change: Russia's encroachment upon the Ottoman empire seemed to be ordained by proximity and the difference in civilization; British intervention served only to delay the inevitable.

The capture of Sebastopol early in September transformed the scene. Palmerston had always maintained that the fortress would be taken that year, and it was; although only weeks beforehand the British commanders in the field predicted a continuation of the siege into 1856.[20] The Russian giant had been worsted on his own ground, and the preservation of Turkey from gradual subjugation was not an impossibility. Cobden 'amazed and disgusted and excited' at the spectacle of popular delight, hoped that Napoleon would use the triumph, as he did, to enforce peace with enough honour to satisfy his army.[21] Lewis seized on the implication for domestic politics; henceforth the Commons would be comparatively easy to manage. '…if the House proves intractable', he told Palmerston '…we cut down a stone which may be kept hanging over their heads until a real exigency arises.'[22] That stone was the threat of dissolution. The prime minister's opponents, Tory and Liberal, faced a weight of opinion in his favour that was now overwhelming. Even before Sebastopol fell, he was described as a dictator.[23] The imperative requirement when he took office had been for an effective war minister who could hold his own in the Commons; and there was no one else in sight. He brought to the higher direction of the war a purposefulness and a command of the business wanting in Aberdeen, who regarded the conflict with dismay.[24] The institutional reforms at the war office and other departments which Palmerston oversaw were less significant than the greater energy with which he infused a machine still familiar to him from his long tenure of the post of secretary at war. In the mid 1850s there was no Wellington in his prime to deploy the resources made available, and successive commanders in the Crimea were a disappointment. The secretary of state, Lord Panmure, was uninspired and hard to move. But the logistics of the campaign, which let down the expeditionary force so badly in the winter of 1854–55, were at least adequate within a few months. In strategy Palmerston was limited by the need to take Sebastopol before any further large-scale attack could be attempted. The overall impression of determination and competence went a long way towards allaying the anxiety behind criticism of Aberdeen's government.

Palmerston was much more than an energetic and capable war minister. He had to meet an upsurge of discontent that posed fundamental questions. The revelation in *The Times* of the troops' Crimean suffering provoked such a storm that for a short time there was widespread apprehension for the position of the aristocracy. Though superficial, the alarm was real. 'Cobden and Bright would be our ministers now but for their principle of "peace at all [sic] price"', said Delane of *The Times*, the most influential of contemporary editors, after the Peelite resignations in late February, which suggested that Palmerston's administration was on the point of collapse.[25] Prince Albert gloomily and inaptly likened the Common's insistence on the Sebastopol committee to the proceedings of the Convention in the French Revolution.[26] In this atmosphere, Bright believed it was in his power to upset Palmerston if he did not make peace. Some radicals, and Liberals with radical leanings, who were offered or retained in minor posts under Palmerston consulted Bright. Aberdeen let him know that he had counselled the three resigning cabinet ministers to 'act along with "the Manchester School"' in opposition. In a lengthy conversation with him a few days after those defections from Palmerston, Sir Erskine Perry and another similarly inclined MP, Danby Seymour, assured Bright of the imminence of great changes: 'no office, even [the] highest, to which I may not aspire', he recorded in his diary.[27] Cobden had a far better grasp of what was happening, perhaps in some measure owing to his reception at Leeds in January, where cries of '*Gammon!*' greeted his anti-war speech. There was, Cobden cautioned Bright, 'no out-of-doors support for the party of peace and non-intervention'; they would have to work through the House of Commons.[28] Working against them was the desire of the middle class generally that Palmerston should succeed.

He followed Aberdeen as prime minister because during his years at the Foreign Office he had acquired and nursed the reputation of someone who felt with 'the people'. When he set about restoring shaken confidence in the fitness of the landed class to rule an ever more urban, industrial and imperially minded state, he enjoyed the goodwill of a great many of the critics. One of the shrewdest middle-class Liberals, James Wilson MP, founder of the *Economist* and financial secretary to the Treasury under Aberdeen and Palmerston, was for a moment afraid that the war would

deal a 'death-blow' to the aristocracy.[29] Cobden could not persuade himself
that the breakdown of Aberdeen's ministry would have that effect: 'I am
not sure', he remarked shortly before the event, 'that it will so far raise the
middle class in their own esteem as to induce them to venture on the task
of self-government.'[30] There was a deep-seated conviction at that social
level, well advertised by those who spoke for it, that aristocratic government
responsive to the pressures of different interests served the country best.
Wilson's *Economist*, started as an organ of the Anti-Corn Law League,
had moved to a moderate Liberalism, like many of the League's leading
figures. In May 1855 it carried a reassuring article on the Administrative
Reform Association, newly established to make landed ministers and MPs
feel the strength of industry and trade in the clamour for changes in the
bureaucracy and the army that would give the taxpayer value for money
in war and peace. 'The gentlemen who inaugurate this movement do not
mean ... to attack the aristocracy', explained the *Economist*. '... the middle
classes ... have kept the democracy down ... for the aristocracy'. The
Association's organizers complained of exclusion from the heights of a
political system for which their class had to take the ultimate responsibility
under the 1832 settlement: 'They are its authors'. Moreover, the exclusion
was less complete than it might seem. The landed class filled the cabinet
and dominated the legislature: the middle class supplied some junior
ministers and, as a rule, the real administrators in the civil service.[31]

The speeches at the Association's first public meeting in June bore out
those comments. A. H. Layard, the ablest of several Parliamentary scourges
of inefficiency and nepotism called for a new party, 'not representing a
class', that would build on the demand for administrative reform. But he
repudiated the idea that the Association was aimed at the aristocracy;
denounced the advocates of a dishonourable peace with Russia as 'both un-
English and dangerous', and declared that 'if any man possessed the power
of effecting a change in the system ... it was Lord Palmerston'. The radical
shipowner from the North-East, W. S. Lindsay, a friend of Cobden's,
speaking after Layard, repeated the denial of 'desiring to wage war against
the aristocracy, as the aristocracy'. On the platform was an assortment of
MPs, with the Whig H. B. W. Brand, a government whip, sitting beside a
couple of earls and the Irish Catholic nationalist, J. F. Maguire.[32]
Palmerston easily contained the agitation by the offer of modest reforms,
and by the language in which he defended his order.

Parliament was more frightened than he was of the Administrative
Reform Association and the outcry that produced it, and more resentful.
Palmerston exploited the apprehension and the resentment. Emphasizing
the aristocracy's commitment to the war, and their sacrifices in the
battlefield, he defined the class more broadly than its enemies liked to do:
'we must include the gentry, for I hope the aristocracy includes them too'.

Replying to Perry, the moderate radical who was making up to Bright, he argued that such men misconceived the whole trend of contemporary society. The social process taking place was one of levelling up: 'I deny that it is a democratic movement. I say it is an aristocratic movement... I am delighted to see the humble classes raising themselves in the scale of the community'; if that phenomenon was democratic, he concluded, he did not fear it.[33] The longstanding acceptance of the claim to gentility advanced by richer businessmen and certain members of the professions made them highly susceptible to this line of argument. Moreover, the wealthy middle class had a vested interest in some of the practices that reformers wanted to end. As Panmure reminded the Court with their German predilection for an officer caste, the purchase of first commissions and promotion suited the quite numerous army officers who came from 'the commercial portion of Your Majesty's subjects'.[34] If Palmerston's extension of the term 'aristocratic' to the development of the lower middle and working classes strained the meaning, it was sound policy to proclaim the openness of his class and its diminishing distance from those below. The Commons closed ranks behind Palmerston in rejecting Layard's motion for administrative reform in June by the huge margin of 359 votes to 46. The prime minister was at once the best hope of reform and the reliable defender of the interests it alarmed.

Where Cobden and Bright differed sharply from other opponents of the war was in the tone of their references to the popular unrest to be expected if the economy deteriorated under the impact of higher interest rates, prices, and taxes. Bright warned the Commons in February 1855 that an industrial collapse was at hand. At Manchester a fortnight previously he said that if the substantial grain imports from Russia did not succeed in getting through, 'before two years are over, you will shoot your fellow citizens in your own streets'.[35] The *Economist* came down hard on Bright's 'frightful exaggerations', showing from Board of Trade returns that Russian grain continued to find its way into Britain through neutrals.[36] Britain had the 'good sense' observed Lewis, not to impose the comprehensive naval blockade of the French wars.[37] Prices rose nevertheless, and with them the hopes of those who were against the war. 'A bad harvest', Gladstone told his radical brother Robertson in August 1855, 'will produce... a more formidable state of things in this country than you or I have seen.' Palmerston watched price movements with the same care. Bread was an unusually deceptive indicator. There had never been a time when it cost so much with so little resulting hardship. The stimulus of war to production and the expansion of the forces reduced the normal pool of unemployed and stepped up wages. Interest rates went up, but not to the crisis levels reached in peacetime, fluctuating between $3\frac{1}{2}$ and 7 per cent during the war compared with 2 and 5 per cent in the five years before. Bright's stubborn predictions of economic calamity, in the face of all the contrary evidence, interrupted the attentive hearing which his oratory generally secured from that unfriendly audience.[38]

'Happily', stated *The Times* in its City column on 1 January 1856, 'the public are being gradually disabused of the vague terror that war and financial confusion are inseparably connected. A great nation making enormous annual additions to its capital from the profits... of industrial trade can carry on hostilities for any number of years without necessarily experiencing a moment of difficulty.'[39] While this article, and much similar comment, glossed over uncertainty in the markets, the Crimean war was a strictly limited conflict, for all that three Great Powers took part. Lewis's finance more than doubled income tax and increased indirect taxes, but the former did not exceed 1s 4d in the pound, 'the war ninepence': the rest of the expenditure was met by borrowing at low rates, under 4 per cent for £16 millions in April 1855. The British got the '*cheap war*' which Cobden maintained at the start of the year was a delusion.[40] 'That which has made the nation stick to the war', wrote Palmerston in its last months, 'has been... the fact that it has not... interrupted trade, nor added materially to... taxation upon the mass of the community.'[41] Cobden was so frustrated by political impotence that he was more and more inclined to seize on every scrap of rumour pointing to Britain's defeat and humiliation. 'I see no chance for us as a nation', he despaired in private, 'but through the furnace of tribulation.' Saner thoughts prevailed, as they almost invariably did with him, when he reflected on the uncontrollable consequences for property and order of probably indiscriminate popular fury in the eventuality: '*who* may escape the rage and ignorant excitement of that hour?'[42]

International problems after the peace

'England is struggling on the edge of social revolution', the fallen Austrian statesman Metternich assured the British ambassador in Vienna after the resignations of February from the cabinet. This was also Marx's hope.[43] Right and Left on the Continent believed that the more broadly based parliamentary government introduced in 1832 could not support the strain of war. Baron Hübner in Paris reported the view there that the change of ministry across the Channel was an unmistakable symptom of the greater change anticipated; the foreign minister, Count Walewski, was a reactionary with Russian leanings. Hübner himself warned against confusing the political 'coteries' at Westminster with the country: the British constitution was '*détraquée*' – out of order – but not about to perish.[44] After the peace, when his ideological preference for the British alliance had been vindicated, Napoleon opened his mind to the British ambassador Cowley, who enjoyed more of his confidence than other envoys. The emperor was at pains to impress upon him how much he regretted the need for a secret police in France and the unavoidable perpetration of 'unconstitutional acts', looking forward to the day when these features of his regime would be superfluous. 'I cannot say', commented the hardened diplomat, 'what an impression his words and manner in saying them made upon me'. The sources of Anglo-French tension discussed at this interview could not obscure the likeness between Britain and France. Napoleon's educated subjects, like the emperor himself, measured the regime against British standards of freedom and social discipline, and their conclusions filtered downwards. None of the other great powers possessed even the qualified sympathy that existed in Britain for Napoleon's France; to their rulers he was an usurper with revolutionary origins and intentions. Whatever Palmerston suspected, the emperor continued to regard Britain as 'the pivot of his policy'.[45] In Europe France was naturally the stronger partner, and British actions reflected the fact. Beyond Europe Britain's seapower and commerce made her the stronger: but French support was useful in China, and the want of it was felt in Anglo-American relations. The public opinion that saw Russia's defeat as a bigger victory than it really was, found satisfaction in the East.

Carrying out the provisions of the peace treaty in the Balkans gave Palmerston's government some anxiety. The domestic reaction was crucial. 'We are most narrowly watched and severely criticized at home', Clarendon informed the British minister at St. Petersburg, '...and we cannot plead a wish to be agreeable to the Russian people in justification of abandoning any part of the minimized conditions...settled at Paris.'[46] The landing of Turkish troops under the guns of the British fleet on Serpent's Island at the mouth of the Danube disposed of a claim that would have left Russia well placed to interfere with navigation on the river. The British attitude stiffened Napoleon to resist Russia's attempt to retain Bolgrad, with access by water to the Danube, in the Bessarabian territory added as additional security against her expansion. Palmerston celebrated this resolute diplomacy in his Northern speechmaking in November 1856.[47] In Italy the allies were less successful, and Britain's distrust of Napoleon made the embarrassment worse. The tension of years between Bourbon Naples and Britain came to a head after Clarendon deplored the political condition of Italy at the Congress of Paris in April 1856, and, more specifically, misrule in Naples and the Papal states. An Anglo-French note, a joint naval demonstration off Naples, and the withdrawal of ministers failed to elicit the intended response from King Ferdinand II, 'Bomba': he declined to be liberalized. The past and future Tory foreign secretary, Malmesbury, believed everyone must consider the possible bombardment of Ferdinand's capital 'an atrocity'. To his mind, 'a gentleman might as well strike a woman as fire upon Naples'.[48] This was the predominant reaction in Parliament. Outside, the righteous and aggressive Protestant nationalism so powerful in the middle class and the unenfranchised had no such qualms. As the *Leeds Mercury* of the devout Dissenting radical, Edward Baines, an old associate of Cobden's argued in a leading article of May 1858 that reviewed the continuing friction between Britain and Naples, 'There are two ways of making a request...one...the whining manner of the English beggar; the other...the manner of the Spanish beggar in *Gil Blas*, which though modest in tone, was rendered formidable by a loaded blunderbuss. This is the way in which it becomes a great nation to make its requests...'[49] Caught between parliament and public, the government had another reason to retreat: there was a French pretender to the Neapolitan throne, Joachim Murat's son, whose accession Napoleon frankly owned that he would welcome.[50] The British were hardly less afraid of a democratic uprising which did not put Prince Murat on the throne. They wanted the impossible, indeed the absurd: constitutionalism, and Bomba.

'The fact is', Clarendon emphasized, '...Bomba has rather got the whip hand of us by not yielding as we thought he would...we may be exposed to some ridicule which is...worse than criticism.' Palmerston acknowledged the setback where it mattered most, in the domestic context, '...very true...We are going to do too little, and some...may...ridicule...us for having gone so far and not having done more, but...we shall be more easily amnestied for having done too little than...for having done too much.'[51] The same public that wanted strong action in Naples was disinclined to risk another major conflict. In promoting British interests government was expected to act with discriminating vigour, and opinion showed itself extremely sensitive to official miscalculations. Hence a characteristic of Palmerston's policy: the extent of co-operation with France, on America, in Naples, China and other places. The reaction in Britain to the disputes with the United States in 1855–56 was significant. Palmerston's dislike of American democracy and his loathing of slavery disposed him to fight the Union, even during the Crimean war, over the two countries' longstanding rivalry in Central America and charges that the British minister at Washington and consuls had abused their privileges by seeking recruits under the Aberdeen ministry's Foreign Enlistment Act.[52] The danger to the British North American colonies did not deter Palmerston at first: 'If we are weak in Canada, the Americans are still more vulnerable in the slave states', he contended in September 1855, '...a British force landed in the Southern part of the Union, proclaiming freedom to the blacks would shake many of the stars from their banner...'[53] If few of his countrymen shared the American sympathies of Cobden and Bright, few were prepared for an interruption of the transatlantic trade vital to national prosperity. The cabinet agreed not to reply in kind to the British envoy's dismissal from Washington, and the naval commander in Central American waters was instructed to avoid anything that might be construed as provocation. The Commons approved this conciliatory posture by a large majority in July 1856. Such realism led several years later to acquiescence in the American demand that Britain should retire from her Central American territories with the exception of British Honduras.

Except in India, where he favoured large-scale territorial expansion until the Mutiny, Palmerston's preference was for influence through economic penetration backed by the intimation, and rarely the application, of force. Napoleon had his eye on the decaying empire of Morocco, and dangled the bait of Egypt before Britain as compensation for French aggrandizement. Palmerston would not be drawn. There was nothing to be gained by possession of Egypt, he told Clarendon, to offset a heavy liability.[54] British interests and those of civilization were best served by maintaining the native regimes in Egypt and Morocco, and opening both to trade as widely as possible. Britain's commanding lead in world markets made this excellent policy, intelligently self-interested and defensible before her rivals. She helped in two ways to preserve Moroccan independence. First, at Palmerston's instance, Clarendon called on the Admiralty to deprive the French of a pretext for intervention by curbing the depredations of Riffian pirates who undermined the Sultan's authority.[55] Secondly, the Anglo-Moroccan treaty of 1856 did away with almost all restrictions on imports, fixed the tariffs to which they were subject at 10 per cent, and regulated export duties. On the pattern of the Capitulations in the Ottoman lands, the treaty secured British residents the benefits of extraterritoriality.[56] It was the object of the war with China beginning that year to overcome obstruction to the implementation of similar arrangements in the Treaty of Nanking concluded in 1842, and to extend them to new areas of the empire. The action of the Chinese authorities at Canton in boarding the *Arrow*, a vessel of doubtful British nationality, and seizing most of the crew, happened conveniently.[57]

Britain, France, and the United States had been consulting about their next moves in the Far East. Within the cabinet Lewis submitted a long written protest against the design furthered by the incident at Canton. The whole idea of an 'armed negotiation', first with China, and then Japan, a country far less accessible to the West, was objectionable: the co-operation of France and the United States did not lessen the planned offence in international law. The obscurantism of Oriental states in resisting freer trade and the intrusion of resident Westerners into their closed societies did not breach that law; they were under no obligation to conform to alien practices. American proposals to seek religious freedom and judicial reform were subversive of Chinese sovereignty. Of France's solicitude for Catholic missionaries Lewis said it was not long since her own laws had exacted penalties not far short of death from Protestants.[58] The memorandum impressed Palmerston, but not sufficiently to counter the dismissive reply of Clarendon, Lewis's brother-in-law, that the restraints of international law need not apply to 'barbarous' states.[59] 'This doctrine may be made a cover for any aggression', returned Lewis. Britain had considered those countries bound by the same restraints as herself, 'so that when it suits our purpose we regard them as civilized...and when it does not...we treat them as barbarous'. Representing the Whig tradition at its most enlightened, he was too much of a party man to place his scruples above the fate of an administration which, with his help at the Treasury, had done well by any standards. He realized how eagerly his trading nation – 'all by fair means, and many by foul means' – wanted to see the Chinese market opened up: 'Public opinion will not be very nice on the subject.' In private, he was scathing about the men in the East responsible for the naval bombardment of Canton in October and November 1856; if the Russians behaved in this fashion to the Turks, or the Americans to the Canadians, 'we should be loud in our condemnation of so wanton an aggression'.[60]

Nothing that was said on Cobden's motion censuring the handling of events in China exceeded Lewis's confidential remarks in severity; he anticipated a bigger majority against ministers: 'All the argument is on the other side', he wrote after hearing Cobden and Russell attack.[61] On the morning before the division, the Liberal chief whip, Hayter, correctly predicted defeat for the government by a small margin. Accordingly, Palmerston's speech that night was angled towards his support outside Westminster. Sir John Bowring, Governor of Hong Kong and Chief Superintendent of Trade on the China Coast, the figure at the centre of the Parliamentary storm, appeared in Palmerston's defence as an example of middle-class achievement in the service of the state and the victim of factional politics. Bowring, a former radical MP, was 'essentially a man of the people', declared the prime minister, appointed under Aberdeen and once a member of the Peace Society to which Cobden belonged. Palmerston responded cleverly to Cobden's unwise taunt that the government had shrunk from fighting the United States the previous year because she was strong, whereas China was weak; he accused him of finding Britain cowardly when conciliatory, 'so much for the reasoning of this member of the Peace Society'. The Americans, too, had clashed with the Chinese at Canton; and they, said Palmerston, inverted the British approach by prefacing negotiation with bombardment. He charged Cobden, and by implication his allies, with ignoring the requirements contained in 'the foreign term "prestige"'.[62]

The speech did not convince in rebuttal of criticisms, from every quarter of the House, of the proconsular morality which the government endorsed: but it appealed to very different elements in his countrywide audience, and left his opponents in some confusion. The Queen and her premier agreed in the comparison of Gladstone's assault on the government with his ministerial responsibility for the Tory and Peelite continuation of Palmerston's China policy in the 1840s and earlier 1850s. 'We spoke', she wrote in her journal, 'of the wretched cant and humbug displayed in the debates.'[63] The City and the main provincial towns at once revealed the isolation of the victors in Parliament. The active membership of Lloyd's overwhelmingly signed an address to Palmerston. 'There is no class', observed *The Times*, 'more deeply interested in the legitimate progress of the commerce of the world and...the maintenance of respect for the British name than the London underwriters...the declaration is...one of the most important that could have been made.'[64] When the Court of Common Council passed a vote of confidence in the administration, exceptionally for a municipal body, one speaker hoped 'the shock which the late division in the House of Commons has given to the feelings of the people...call them prejudices if you like – will be sufficiently powerful to arouse their sleeping energies'.[65] So it proved. At Bristol two substantial Tory citizens got up an address, widely subscribed, expressing gratitude to the ministry for raising Britain's reputation, protecting her traders abroad and, too, its domestic record. The weighty Manchester Commercial Association was infuriated by suggestions in the Commons that British businessmen were 'a set of selfish individuals...regardless of all consequences, provided they secured their own interests'; it scorned the 'mock philanthropy and mock humanity' of MPs concerned for the Chinese.[66]

With his mercantile connections, Gladstone was uncomfortably aware of the likelihood of these reactions when he spoke on Cobden's motion. Professing his esteem for the class 'from which I am sprung', he went on to defy it: 'I utterly disclaim the notion that we are to bow to this species of authority.'[67] But his position, which was that of the anti-Palmerstonian coalition, involved no renunciation of expansion in the East, only the insistence that it must not be disfigured by acts which he found indefensible, like the bombardment of a great city. Everyone, even Cobden and Bright to some extent, acknowledged the inherent tendencies of economic and military power. As Gladstone's friend Sidney Herbert put it in a letter of December 1855 to Malmesbury: 'The stronger and more civilized necessarily absorb the weaker and more barbarous...The Russians encroach as we encroach in India, Africa and elsewhere – because we can't help it.'[68] The politicians of mid nineteenth-century Britain were realists, not cynics; they tried to ensure a balance between right and interest, which was what their public expected of them. Palmerston differed only in being readier to see things as they were. 'No powerful nation can ever expect to be really loved or liked by any other', he reflected that year. 'The interests and views of nations perpetually clash and men are apt to be angry with those who stand between them and the accomplishment of their wishes.'[69]

When he and his colleagues decided to dissolve instead of resigning, on being beaten in the Commons, the electors judged their performance primarily by reference to the ancient formula of national profit and power.

The parties and Palmerston

It is not easy, even after all that has been written on the subject, to appreciate the strength of parties which did not rest on the structures that developed in the last thirty years of the nineteenth century. Analysis of the Commons at the beginning of 1855 may leave an impression that the two-party division was less important than the discernible groupings and the independence of many members. Whatever ex-cabinet ministers like Gladstone and Graham asserted, generalizing from their Peelite isolation, most contemporaries never doubted that the names Liberal, or Whig, and Tory exercised an almost unbreakable spell. At elections only a very few failed to appear under the party colours of their choice. The ambiguity of 'Liberal Conservative', a designation favoured by Peelites but not exclusive to them, was usually resolved on the hustings, as Gladstone was forced to acknowledge.[70] A man did not change his party lightly. Palmerston had changed his once, and the Tories still hoped to retrieve him. The Peelites constantly discussed the permanent political home they knew they must find. Whigs and Liberals believed they would absorb the Peelites as they had absorbed the Canningites. Aberdeen himself regarded the coalition over which he presided as the means to Liberal digestion of his following. The three candidates – Derby, Disraeli, and Palmerston – to lead the succeeding coalition all assumed that it would also be dominated by one party or the other. Rule by party was too deeply entrenched for its replacement to be seriously considered.[71] Both Liberals and Tories wanted to make sure of Palmerston, without whom neither could sustain a government, even one joined by the Peelites.

From the moment of Aberdeen's fall the Carlton Club shared the general expectation that Palmerston would be his successor. It was enough for Derby that Palmerston would not join him. The two Peelites offered cabinet places, Gladstone and Herbert, also refused: but against their abilities had to be set Gladstone's unpopularity with his old party; his acceptance would probably have driven upwards of fifty Tories into rebellion.[72] Although Disraeli concurred in thinking Palmerston indispensable to a ministry in the circumstances, he blamed Derby for declining to risk office with an unsupported party and thus advertising their inability to govern. He blamed, too, Derby's confidant, Malmesbury, for not being present to stiffen their leader's nerve at that juncture. 'Disraeli is in a state of disgust beyond all control', continued the entry in Malmesbury's diary '... there can be no doubt, if the Russian war ends successfully and we take

Sebastopol...Lord Derby will have missed a great opportunity, and lost the glory and prestige...' Derby's judgement was better than that of his lieutenants. He knew the limitations of Toryism then, and his own. He had saved the party from self destruction in the crisis over the Corn Laws and afterwards, but only by adhering too closely to its Anglican and landed traditions; this comparative neglect of social interests not specially identified with Toryism had contributed to the paradox of its strength in Parliament and weakness outside. Moreover, he never learned to treat public opinion as Palmerston, and in his wake Gladstone, did. In Malmesbury's view, Derby was incapable of adjusting to 'the sudden growth and power of the '...press, for which he has no partiality...[a] feeling...reciprocated by its members'. Amid the excitement of those opening months of 1855, Derby shrank from exposing himself and the party to the fierce, though superficial, criticism of the political aristocracy, without the inclusion of Palmerston to recommend a Tory ministry to the country. Malmesbury believed Derby's courage had been undermined by protracted ill-health. The latter's fondness for going out shooting in mid-winter – 'no boy of sixteen could have enjoyed it more' – makes it unlikely that his gout was so debilitating.[73] It might be nearer the mark to see in him a clever man oppressed by the leadership of Toryism as it was at this time.

Derby realized how much the Tories would suffer from the refusal to persist without Palmerston. He suggested to the Queen and Prince that, although everybody knew he had been sent for, 'there was no necessity for making it appear...he had undertaken to form an administration'. They told him 'the best thing would be on all accounts to state exactly the truth as it passed'.[74] This was the course that Derby took in a Parliamentary explanation, 'a long speech praising his opponents and disparaging his friends', wrote Malmesbury. In spite of Disraeli's entreaty not to run down the party, Derby indicated quite clearly that he thought the Tories were in no condition to take office.[75] Short of ministerial talent, they were also divided – as he did not say in the Lords – over the war. Derby and Malmesbury wished to continue the struggle at least until it could be claimed that the Russians had come off worse: Disraeli leant towards the peace without victory advocated by Peelites and some radicals.[76] As a result, Tory backbenchers displayed little enthusiasm for overthrowing ministers when Derby went over to the offensive in May. The morale of the party and his restless condition drove Disraeli to encourage talk of his displacing Derby. Stanley's name was also mentioned in this connection; like Disraeli, he wanted to broaden Toryism's appeal.[77] Notwithstanding his mistakes, Derby's position was secure, such was the Tories' aversion to being again liberalized from within, their experience under Peel.

Between February 1855 and the dissolution of 1857, the government could rely on the votes of some thirty Tory MPs whose largely personal

hostility to Disraeli was stronger than their loyalty to Derby.[78] Dissidence
on the benches behind Palmerston did not display the same obduracy. The
setbacks that Russell met with promised to end a division among the
Liberals that went back to the breakdown of his ministry in 1851–52 as the
consequence of open antagonism between the premier and Palmerston. His
desertion of Aberdeen, his humiliating failure to form a government, and
his ineptitude at Vienna and Westminster over the peace negotiations
reduced Russell to the lowest point in a long career. The pronounced Whig
character of the cabinet after the resignations of February pleased that
element in the party. At Brooks's Club, the Whig stronghold, Milner
Gibson told Bright in the autumn of 1855, 'it is the fashion to denounce
Lord John Russell – and to say that his new wife has "softened his brain".
Palmerston is the idol, and the war is to be carried on "with vigour" until
Russia goes on her knees.'[79] Palmerston had 'no wish' to bring Russell back
into the cabinet, underrating his rival's considerable reserves of political
strength.[80]

The radicals, sharply split between opponents and supporters of the war,
gave Palmerston little trouble. To obtain a less unfriendly hearing for his
advocacy of peace, Bright informed the Commons that he counted himself
among 'the depositaries of the power and the guardians of the interests of
a great nation and an ancient monarchy'; Lord Aberdeen had been trying
to persuade the Court that this was true.[81] The feared radical worked with
a small number of high Tories whom Malmesbury termed 'pseudo-
Russians'[82]: General Peel, the statesman's brother, the Marquess of
Granby, who had once led the party in the Commons, and the recently
elected Lord Robert Cecil; an attack by the last on the morality of a Liberal
war outdid anything from Bright.[83] In this company, meeting the envoys of
reactionary states at Lady Alicia Peel's, wife of the general, Bright did not
pose a severe threat to the unity of the governing party.[84] The radical
supporters of the war directed their fire at Whig and Peelite ministers and
ex-ministers, but particularly the latter; Layard condemned Aberdeen for
having 'done more to destroy the Liberal party than any man who ever
lived'. Layard and Lord Goderich, whose radicalism was tempered by the
prospect of succession to two earldoms and over 20,000 acres, declared their
intention of standing by Palmerston so long as he had 'the confidence of the
people.'[85]

Radicals opposed to the war, and Peelites outside the ministry, were
anxious to maintain their links with the main body of Liberals. Both Bright
and Cobden attended a meeting of over 200 MPs at 10 Downing Street in
May 1855, as did Herbert and Graham; *The Times* reported it as a
gathering of 'all sections of the Liberal party' to hear the prime minister
vindicate his policy. While some of those present voiced their disagreement,
the continuing reality of the party was apparent.[86] The absent Gladstone,

who cast himself as the keeper of the Peelite conscience, held that without
the three members who resigned in February, the Palmerston cabinet could
do 'nothing good, but evil … very easily'.[87] Yet he did not vote consistently
against the government, and in the session of 1856 planned the return of the
Peelites to a Liberal administration, 'even with Palmerston as head'.[88] The
prime minister's speeches of November 1856 in the North arrested this
movement towards Liberalism: the reception given to Palmerston, wrote
Gladstone to his brother in Liverpool, 'may so inflate his spirit as to be the
cause of great evils'. Gladstone's dislike of much in government policies was
exacerbated by the alarming development of Palmerston's relationship
with extra-Parliamentary opinion. He subordinated everything to one
endeavour: 'putting out … Palmerston is the only question on which I even
pretend to see my way'.[89] Peelite votes, marshalled by Gladstone, supplied
the narrow margin by which the Tories, with the help of Russell and other
Liberals, carried Cobden's motion.

Central to the emergence of Palmerstonian Liberalism were those
steadily more numerous MPs, landed, business, and professional men, who
viewed themselves as Liberals because really uncomfortable with the dated,
aristocratic associations of the Whig name. They shaded imperceptibly into
the moderate radicals and complained, but not too loudly, of the hold
which the great, interrelated Whig families kept on political office and its
still extensive patronage. While the Gladstone of the 1850s attracted some
of these Liberals, they could not see him as a prime minister 'much less as
a dictator'; one of them called him 'an incomplete man' politically.[90]
Isolated from what others regarded as his natural party, Gladstone also
denied himself the authority which Palmerston increasingly derived from
public opinion. Lesser politicians were aware of what was taking place
beyond the Parliamentary arena where Gladstone excelled. 'I am not at all
sure that the public are not *setting up for themselves* in opinion more than they
have yet done', observed the aristocratic radical, C. P. Villiers, to Bright in
November 1855.[91] This junior member of the government did not know,
'candidly', whether the war was justified but was sure that it must not be
allowed to end in a way 'that is disgraceful or thought to be so by the
people'. After many months grumbling about Whig appointments to
cabinet vacancies, Villiers sought to persuade Bright that Palmerston had
earned his gratitude by bringing the war to an acceptable conclusion, and
was a changed man: 'It looks to me as if Palmerston is *in* for his life … I am
bound to say … I know of no one that I believe will be better or more
peaceful that could … fill his place. He has become far more careful and less
warlike than he used to be … far more attentive and able in … the House
than I ever thought possible.'[92] Villiers' old associate from Anti-Corn Law
League days, Milner Gibson, recognized the need to present radicalism in
a new light. In a speech at Manchester, delivered after consulting Cobden,

he said he would welcome a reform bill 'under the guidance of Lord Palmerston' and hoped to avoid having to vote against a government which he supported.[93] The unwisdom of challenging Palmerston with the war behind him and the promise of 'progressive improvement' ahead was shown when he dissolved in response to the defeat on Cobden's motion.

4

Party: Whigs and Liberals

The nature of party

The clarification of party lines after the 1857 general election was generally welcomed as a restoration of normality. The nature of that restored normality should not be misunderstood. Writing in the 1880s, Gladstone, singled out Erskine May's *Constitutional History* as the only book known to him which rightly explained the political history of the half-century from the end of the Napoleonic wars to the close of the second Palmerston administration. The first edition appeared in 1861, and he recalled how he had recommended it with the happiest results to a Liberal peer concerned about his heir's politics.[1] For May, as for Palmerston and Gladstone, aristocracy was the stabilizing element in the midst of 'so many classes... the encroachments of wealth – an expanding society, and popular influences'. Its leadership, however, was conditional upon going with 'the tide of public opinion'; else the different classes would cease to prefer its primacy to that of money or numbers. Its 'progressive policy' was instrumental to the continued deference accorded to aristocracy despite the competition from 'abler men of inferior social pretensions'.[2] Thus the landowners' material loss of direct electoral control following the 1832 Reform Act was not reflected in their influence. Party was simply a mechanism, if a very important one, ensuring the ordered and liberal functioning of a landed Parliament. Little divided the leaders of Tories and Liberals in 'policy and professions'; it was their partisans who cherished 'still essential diversities of political sentiment'. The popular attitude of 'comparative indifference' to mere party battles did not extend to the good, and 'progressive', government required from men of 'rank and station'.[3] May's is the classic rationalization of the paradox central to Victorian politics – the power of political endurance displayed by a class which on the face of it ought to have been in retreat before its nearest rivals.

On the contrary, it was quite evident to Cobden in March 1858 that 'during my experience, the higher classes never stood so high in relative social and political rank, ...compared with other classes, as at present'. The date is significant. Palmerston had just been overthrown on the Conspiracy to Murder Bill. Cobden did not believe it would be long before the fallen minister was back in office: 'How will you prevent his returning to power?' he asked.[4] The upset of February, he told Bright, had not really altered anything. If the Liberal party and press decided to retire Palmerston as 'the *popular minister*', it was committed, inside and outside Parliament, to his policies,[5] and remained what he had remade it by 1857, 'a national party'[6], which the Tories were not. As Lewis pointed out in his correspondence with Reeve of the *Edinburgh Review*, the Liberal party's disarray could not conceal the permanent majority for Liberalism in the House of Commons and the country.[7] Party in the sense of Liberal versus Tory was less important, therefore, than the personal and political considerations involved not only in bringing together Palmerston and those Liberals who had helped to oust him but in reinforcing the foundations of Liberalism. When Gladstone joined Palmerston in 1859, he did so hoping that Cobden would be in the cabinet. 'It was in his person', he wrote to Robertson Gladstone, 'that there seemed to be the best chance of a favourable trial of connecting his friends with the practical administration of the country.'[8] This was exactly what Palmerston had in mind. The principle that he applied in pressing Cobden to serve under him was to figure in Erskine May: 'When the aristocracy enjoyed too exclusive an influence in... government, they aroused jealousies and hostility: but when duly sharing power with other classes, and admitting the just claims of talent, they prevailed over every rival and adverse interest...' Palmerston's bolder and more constructive application of the principles on which aristocratic liberalism rested in Britain led this contemporary constitutional historian to signalize his 'wisdom and moderation' in domestic policy.[9]

Whigs and Liberals

Liberalism under Palmerston did not do away with the habitual and serviceable classification of its followers into these two categories and a third, the radicals. Those who, like Gladstone, styled themselves 'Liberal Conservatives' could be either Whigs or Liberals, if not Tories or, up to 1859, Peelites. Increasingly, Palmerstonians were to be found among men in each category, offsetting dynastic Whigs who had never forgotten Palmerston's political origins, and Whigs or Liberals and radicals who disliked his policies. The distinction between Whig and Liberal was hardly clearer to contemporaries than it is to historians. The Whig label had largely been discarded for public use by those to whom it particularly applied, seeming old-fashioned and exclusive, but others continued to employ it, as they did themselves in conversation and letters. When forming his first administration Palmerston divided the cabinet into Whigs and Peelites, reckoning an aristocratic radical as a Whig.[10] A younger man, Cornewall Lewis, used the terms Whig and Liberal interchangeably, but not always. Whigs in the ideological sense of conservative Liberals were never restricted to members of 'historic Whig families'; nor is it satisfactory to define them more widely as 'magnates, relatives, privileged associates, or clients of magnates'. Every county had a number of independent Whig gentry, and almost every Parliamentary borough men of property, in business and the professions, aligned with the Whig section of the landed class, without being dependent upon it. Subservience was not characteristic of political affiliation at those levels, or, indeed, lower down the social scale. Deference proved to be both critical and demanding of those accorded it. This was the social context of Palmerstonian Liberalism – and of Derbyite Toryism – within which Parliamentary politicians designated radical were obliged or content to operate. Whatever Bright and, less frequently, Cobden said, an electoral system reformed or, rather, modified in 1832 was certainly not supposed to negate public opinion.[11]

Palmerston had been a Canningite before he was a Whig. His management of public opinion as prime minister prolonged the life of the 1832 Act because it rendered another instalment of reform superfluous for the time being. He and Gladstone concurred in holding that people had no absolute right to the franchise: 'What every man and woman too have a right to is to be well governed and under just laws...'[12] That principle justified a carefully regulated suffrage underpinning in the position of the landed class; it was a Parliamentary aristocracy. The elasticity of the £10 household franchise, swelling the urban electorate with the growth of prosperity and population, took much of the strain off the system in its most sensitive area. Consistently with his record in the ministries of Wellington and Grey, Palmerston showed himself to be more liberal than the Tories, if still very cautious, in his attitude to both enfranchisement and re-distribution when Parliamentary reform was under consideration in this period. His religious, foreign, and imperial policies were more liberal, too – the last in a popular sense – than those of the Tories. The effect over a decade was further to liberalize the Whigs, and obscure the differences, such as they were, between them and the less aristocratic, less conservative Liberals who shaded into the radical element.

It has been argued that Palmerston's first administration was not a single party government. From the start, however, he hoped that it would become one. He needed the Peelites, but it troubled him that this element 'still endeavours to make itself a little separate section'.[13] On being invited to take the premiership, he had discussed with Lord John Russell the possibility of forming a purely Whig administration, and decided against it;

reinforced by the Peelites the opposition would have embraced 'more able men'.[14] The swift loss of the three leading Peelites from his recently formed cabinet drove him to consider a reconstruction which would have brought in two of the abler and definitely liberal-minded Tories: Sir John Pakington, a member of the Tory cabinet in 1852, and Lord Stanley, Derby's youthful and intellectual heir. 'The Cabinet wisely said no', commented Gladstone in a memorandum on events immediately following his departure from office;[15] they did not want to see the hold of party weakened still more by such a development. He told Prince Albert that the collapse of Palmerston's government was certain inside a year.[16] Its Whig replacements and a single, ardently pro-war Tory, the Earl of Harrowby, were no substitute for the retiring Peelites. Palmerston thought the same. Of these replacements, Russell had 'so lost caste' by his conduct in undermining the Aberdeen coalition from within that he had been shunned by most of his closest colleagues. Vernon Smith was agreed to be second-rate; and the inexperienced Lewis hesitated before consenting to succeed Gladstone at the Treasury after the Peelite Cardwell and the Whig Sir Francis Baring had refused. 'I have had a very harassing work', wrote Palmerston. 'It is so difficult to find men fit to be appointed and willing to accept...' The circumstances in which he came to power would, he anticipated, give him a breathing space necessary so far as Parliament was concerned. He contemplated a dissolution when he had got through the first session.[17]

Until he could appeal to the electorate, he had to rely on the forbearance of parties, his own included, more afraid of public opinion than he was. He appears to have been little worried by current strictures on his class, and his assurance was infectious. 'There has been a great outcry against the aristocracy, which the said aristocracy seems to care very little for', was how Cobden described the political atmosphere by mid-March 1855.[18] The eclipse of Russell in July, when ministers outside the cabinet demanded and obtained his resignation for mishandling and misrepresenting the peace negotiations at Vienna, increased Palmerston's authority over Whigs and Liberals. 'The party is not destitute of sufficient elements for a good government', he had stated on the day after he began to form his administration, unsure of any Peelite participation at that stage, '...I know...I have the country at my back, and that is a good foundation.'[19]

When he was left, almost at once, with a ministry heavily drawn from his party, and no longer really a coalition, the lack of an assured majority in the House made it vital for him to establish a personal ascendancy in the Commons on the basis of his admitted indispensability as the war prime minister. 'The House which was rather riotous at first is getting in to good order...', he told his brother in March; and by June he felt the position was relatively secure: 'The fact is that there is at present no other government possible, and people see that we are doing our work well.'[20] He was not remotely as complacent as this might suggest. Sebastopol had not been captured, and pending that still doubtful event, he was hard pressed to answer for the efficiency and resolution of the war effort. 'Between ourselves', the unsatisfactory war minister, Lord Panmure, informed the commander-in-chief of the Crimean expeditionary force, 'Palmerston is naturally nervous for the Army, and listens too much to the people.'[21] What Panmure regarded as failings in the prime minister saved the government and army from defeat.

His ministry remained short of talent, but Lewis quickly proved his worth: competent in finance; versatile in debate; and alert to the trend of opinion, winning Palmerston's friendship and trust: 'It is a great loss privately and politically', he wrote sadly on Lewis's premature death in 1863.[22] Lewis did not believe in the war; yet he made a significant and habitually intelligent contribution to waging it successfully on the home front, where his fiscal strategy was aimed at keeping the income taxpaying middle classes behind the government. Steeped in the history of a party to which he was quietly devoted, and editor of the *Edinburgh Review* for three years before entering the cabinet, he conceived of the Whigs' modern function in cautiously progressive terms. Rather less liberal than Palmerston in domestic politics, and much less so abroad, he was disinclined by tradition and temperament to court popularity.[23] He counselled Palmerston against dissolving to exploit the wave of patriotic emotion on the fall of Sebastopol, arguing that he had the House well under control already. The prime minister did not disagree. On the other hand he would not discount the threat from the opposition as Lewis did in saying, 'none of the other three parties...Derbyites...Peelites...Manchesterites are in good odour, or...good condition'.[24] The Tories, observed Palmerston, talked loudly against Disraeli in Society, 'but probably when it comes to a division they will go together into the same lobby like sheep through a gap'.[25] To promote a similar, underlying solidarity on his side of the House was difficult. In turning down Palmerston's approach in November 1855, Stanley was influenced by the consideration that acceptance required a change of allegiance 'from the stronger to the weaker...a sacrifice of permanent results for temporary distinction'. He thought Palmerston's hold over the Whigs uncertain, dependent on what Russell, as their real chief, might do; while 'the independent Liberal, or Radical section' – from which Stanley separated the few attached to Cobden and Bright – was fonder of the prime minister's foreign than of his supposedly negative domestic policy. It is quite clear that Stanley did not think he was being invited to join a coalition.[26]

Palmerston did not neglect home policy. In that sphere his choice of men and measures reflected a concern to build up his party. His address to the meeting of Liberal MPs of all shades in April 1856, urging unity after the war, was well received.[27] Since the preceding autumn he had elevated M. T. Baines of Leeds to the cabinet in December 'as representing middle-classes', something which he and Russell had discussed approvingly in February 1855.[28] Two Whigs in the classical mould, Henry Labouchere and Lord Stanley of Alderley, were promoted just ahead of Baines. The three came in for Canning, sent to India as governor-general, and the deceased radical Molesworth. If it was only a marginally stronger cabinet, the session of 1856 was marked by more than one attempt to emphasize the government's authentic liberalism. Ministers endorsed a church rates bill to exempt Dissenters, which passed its second reading. Although they did not ensure its continued progress through the Commons to certain rejection by the Lords, the bill served its purpose, namely, to demonstrate Palmerston's sincerity in his careful professions of goodwill towards a powerful interest. He told John Cheetham, the industrialist MP for South Lancashire, that his correspondent should not suspect any indifference to the wishes of Dissenters. This gesture to Dissent commanded only hesitant agreement among the ministers who decided upon it, Lewis noted.[29] The institution of life peerages took the cabinet by surprise. Palmerston acted independently to modernize the House of Lords by opening it to professional men – lawyers, soldiers, and sailors – without the wealth to endow a hereditary peerage. This infusion of new blood would, he said, do much to invigorate the Lords, whose political inferiority to the Commons derived from their social exclusiveness.[30] Palmerston's scheme foreshadowed that advocated in J. S. Mill's *Consideration on Representative Government* five years later,[31] and not realized until the Life Peerages Act of 1958. It was too far ahead of its time, and unduly pessimistic in its implied estimate of contemporary aristocracy.

The Tory Shaftesbury and the Whig Lewis were equally dismayed by what they deemed an unnecessary and dangerous innovation. The former did not doubt Palmerston's good intentions. Nor was he blind to the arguments for strengthening the Lords in that way. He shrank from a reform which 'brings under republican and hostile review the whole principle of hereditary succession, and has roused the democrats to hope and action'. He saw with relief that it was not popular, though applauded by those middle-class radical dailies with the largest circulations in the capital.[32] The intended beneficiaries, led by the Bar, received it no less critically, on the whole, than did the landed interest. Such was the social prestige of an hereditary peerage that they ignored an uncomfortable truth: 'the improper and … painful situation' in which ennobled professional men placed heirs who lacked the means to support their rank.[33] Under fire, the government tended to justify the initial creation of a life peerage for the judge Sir James Parke, made Baron Wensleydale, by stressing the need to keep the Lords provided with enough lawyers of distinction for its appellate jurisdiction. Lewis's diary shows this to have been a secondary motive, as Palmerston himself was to acknowledge. Lewis had no room in his conception of British political development for 'a sort of order of merit in the House of Lords, without reference to hereditary wealth'.[34] When the Lords voted to inquire into the validity of Wensleydale's peerage, the leader of the House, Granville, commented to the prime minister: 'You will see…that you were ignominiously beaten last night…It is not a bad subject to be beaten upon…'[35] The astonishment and indignation or, at the very least, profound unease of too many in both Houses killed life peerages; the Lords might safely rule against Wensleydale's patent, forcing the government to make him an hereditary peer. For all that, the episode, which Derby at once termed 'very grave…and a *coup*',[36] had considerable importance in establishing Palmerston's liberalism at home and refuting the familiar allegations of his disguised Toryism heard both from Disraeli and from radical critics.

As the session of 1856 moved towards its end, Disraeli reviewed 'the competitive emulation of great political parties' that continually went on before the public. Palmerston taunted him with the size of government majorities in big votes, which proved how little stomach the Tories had for a fight.[37] 'Disraeli made a mess of it', wrote Gladstone baldly in his diary afterwards.[38] Palmerston took pains to dissociate his ministry from the Toryism imputed to it. The prime minister countered, before it was uttered, Milner Gibson's temperately worded reproach that he had too readily given up liberal measures during the session: 'Failure, at first', said Palmerston, 'is an unavoidable incident of free discussion, of freedom of opinion and of the intercourse of Members… with persons out of the House, whose organs they must…be.'[39] Milner Gibson did not pretend that the old Liberal rallying cry of 'Peace, retrenchment, and reform' had yet recovered its pre-war popularity; but he advised the prime minister to base his policy on its revival.[40] Palmerston explained the minor defeats inflicted on the ministry to his brother as convenient 'for independent members to play with and boast of'.[41] The decline of party was a myth sedulously propagated by politicians out of office. It represented exaggerated hopes on the part of the Peelites and radicals unreconciled to Palmerston's leadership, or overdone fears on that of the Tories.

The sense of belonging to a party in better heart and order emerged among MPs when they spoke in the constituencies. At Plymouth the Liberal barrister, R. P. Collier, felt that Palmerston was 'peculiarly the man to take the direction of our affairs', but criticized the government's failure to persist with some of its domestic proposals. The ministry was expected to deal with 'many important social questions', such as church rates and law reform. He cited, however, the passing of the first Act to allow the widespread adoption of limited liability and the Cambridge University

Act enabling Dissenters to graduate there.[42] A radical businessman, Apsley Pellatt, one of the members for Southwark, likewise called for more to be done in different fields of reform. Of a sessional total of 120 public Acts, only two – one pensioning off the Bishops of London and Durham, and another giving the Education Department a salaried ministerial head – had excited 'any very great interest'.[43] Speaking at the Lord Mayor's banquet in November, Lewis met insistent criticism from MPs and the press with a sweeping promise that 'now...the House of Commons would...devote its entire attention to reforms...demanded by the voice of the people'.[44] The radical Whig, F. H. F. Berkeley, grumbled at Bristol that Palmerston was not enough of a Liberal: but since he believed 'Nothing will move the people to reform the Commons but great disasters', he did not seem dissatisfied with what Palmerston had to offer in peacetime. The other Bristol member, W. H. Gore-Langton, a safe Whig but 'no servile follower of Lord Palmerston', repeated Berkeley's acknowledgement of the prime minister's pre-eminent qualifications to rule: he considered the government would concentrate on 'social questions'.[45] Through these constituency speeches there ran the same broad endorsement of Palmerstonian policy abroad, sometimes confusedly expressed – Apsley Pellatt was for urgently reforming the Ottoman empire, a perpetual Anglo-French alliance, and non-intervention.

Palmerston's ministry began 1857 quite well covered by its performance and promise across the range of domestic issues, and best of all by its religious policy. The prestige of its foreign and imperial successes left a good margin for the American and Neapolitan setbacks. The Liberal party had been rehabilitated, and the Peelites partly absorbed. Opponents on either side of the House selected two aspects of Palmerstonian Liberalism for attack: military and naval expenditure, and overseas adventures as distinguished from legitimate action to protect British interests. With ample warning of what was being planned, the cabinet took a substantial slice off defence expenditure. Palmerston did not originally envisage cutting income tax sharply, disliked though it was. Its reduction by over half to the pre-war level became the centrepiece of Lewis's budget. The prime minister exerted additional pressure to trim spending a little more after the first day's debate of the new session. 'It is grievous to have to reduce our Estimates still further', he told Panmure, 'but necessity knows no law.'[46] The country wanted to be an imperial power – inexpensively. Even so, Lewis had a rough passage, and was grateful for Russell's help with the House at the critical moment.[47] The majority of eighty for the budget on 23 February, swollen as so often by Tories repudiating Disraeli's tactics, put the government in a strong position to dissolve when beaten on Cobden's motion by sixteen votes. Three days after that defeat, Lewis's budget survived a renewed challenge with another convincing majority, of sixty-two, on 6 March. 'Times are changed, and men!' wrote Gladstone on this rapid reversal of Parliamentary fortunes.[48] Palmerston went to the country knowing that he had his Tory, Peelite and radical foes at an insuperable disadvantage: the Commons had decisively approved his peacetime finance, with its hotly debated implications for foreign affairs and defence; while the electorate would approve his stand on events in China. The electors, he advised the House on 9 March, were 'too clear-sighted and too straightforward' for a different course to have any attraction.[49]

The 1857 election and its aftermath

The general election was fought on party lines and policies, too, although the Tories were in palpable disarray. The voting in the House on Cobden's amendment had followed party lines sufficiently for Palmerston to welcome a dissolution occasioned by a Parliamentary battle which enabled him to anticipate a reasonably well-defined conflict of parties at the polls: '...the Coalition has unintentionally rendered a great service to the Government', was his reaction to the momentarily triumphant majority against him in the Commons. '...the Government', he explained to the Queen, 'is more likely to gain strength by a general election brought about as the approaching election will be, than if...the dissolution had taken place without any particular event out of which a distinction between opposing parties could have been drawn.'[50] A few bitter opponents frantically tried to present the sudden contest as an unprincipled move to increase Palmerston's personal authority, indulge his love of power, and leave him freer to conduct foreign and imperial policy in the way censured by the House. 'Lord Palmerston...does not go to the country upon any question of internal reform', declared Cobden at a crowded meeting in London held to proclaim the union of Parliamentary and popular radicals. Layard, Roebuck, in the chair, and the Chartist ideologue, Bronterre O'Brien, also spoke.[51] Palmerston and his colleagues replied by using the China question to publicize the range of their policies. The attorney-general, Sir Richard Bethell, in his and Layard's constituency of Aylesbury, enjoyed himself 'vigorously satirizing the plea of humanity and religion, which, if good for anything, would compel us to abandon Canton altogether'. Continuing, he excused the prime minister for not having made 'more speedy progress in administrative and social reforms...the fault was not in Lord Palmerston, but in the timid, hesitating men at his side, or at his back...'[52] At the Mansion House on 20 March, Palmerston described ministers as 'instruments of the national will'. They stood for 'peace abroad...with honour'.[53] This was the unifying message of his campaign. 'Now is it correct to say that Lord Palmerston diverted the attention of the people from social improvement to foreign warfare?' asked Lewis in a speech delivered to his Welsh voters but really meant for the national press. He was disposing of the accusation as one that figured in Disraeli's election manifesto. Then he looked forward to an instalment of Parliamentary reform, congenial to government, broadening the occupation franchise 'very considerably' in counties without assimilating it to the less restrictive borough qualification. As for church rates, he affirmed his sympathy with the Dissenters' feeling of injustice, and warned the Church to compromise with them, or risk losing all her revenue from that source. Contrasting Disraeli's 'electioneering eloquence' on Britain in China with Derby's second thoughts on the subject, Lewis coolly observed: 'I am not called upon to maintain that Sir John Bowring's conduct was...immaculate'.[54] Echoing Palmerston in the Commons, Baines, the representative of the middle classes in the cabinet, extolled Bowring at Leeds as 'a man sprung from the people, having no aristocratic connections...raised...by his application and...extraordinary...knowledge...'. Bowring had been true to his Peace Society principles: 'He was on the spot and saw all...it sometimes happens...that we must engage in war to secure and perpetuate the blessings of peace.' Baines linked Bowring the former radical MP with the proconsul, associating himself with the plebeian hero: 'He is one of the most far-going reformers I ever met with'; while this cabinet minister still felt strongly upon Parliamentary reform, and believed there were 'many men of intelligence and moral worth' who might be safely and advantageously enfranchised. Under the same heading as these last remarks, 'the domestic policy of Lord Palmerston', he passed on to enumerate a variety of reforms, prospective or under way, to simplify legal procedure, follow out free trade principle and improve the administration of poor relief – his own department.[55]

Palmerston hoped the election would be a victory for what he designated 'the rational liberal party'.[56] His triumph fell short of that; but he humbled both the dissident Whigs in the person of Russell, and the radicals who either remained absolutely anti-Palmerstonian or converted too late in the day. For personal reasons, Palmerston did not wish Russell to be humiliated at the polls, but 'in a mere political view' his rejection by the City of London, his seat for sixteen years, could not be unwelcome. Palmerston did not like it when Clarendon put in a word for Russell with City magnates.[57] The foreign secretary was afraid of an ex-premier 'very sore and sour' at being relegated to a family borough.[58] Russell got back for the City, with the connivance of the Tories, and after drastically modifying his tone. To begin with, he returned a 'decided negative' to the question whether Palmerston should be supported 'irrespective of...principles... or...measures'. He ended by staying as close as possible to his rival: 'I quite allow that Lord Palmerston is a man...fit to preside over the councils of this empire. I think he deserves the support of the House of Commons and ... the nation.'[59] It was sufficiently humiliating for a statesman who had talked on the hustings as if he, and not Palmerston, embodied liberalism nationwide. He had had the assistance not only of Clarendon but of W. G. Hayter, the skilful chief government whip, who did everything in his power to help.[60] With this aid Russell retained his seat comfortably, although 'the merchant princes turned their princely backs upon me...'. On re-election, he stated his mind to Dean Elliot, disowning the stock charges against the prime minister but firmly resolved not to be submissive towards him: 'I do not agree with Graham that Palmerston is an old Tory of the deepest dye, or with Disraeli that his policy is turbulent and aggressive...I do think...these times...require a more forward and efficient policy at home than he is disposed or perhaps able to adopt.'[61] Russell regarded himself as the more liberal of the two, all things considered, and awaited the opportunity of proving it when men should rediscover his virtues.

At the same time, Russell was rather apprehensive of the new Parliament's disposition. 'I run the risk', he wrote, '...of being hurried further by the tide than I wish to go.'[62] The elimination of Cobden, Bright, Milner Gibson, Layard, and some lesser radicals went with a shift among Liberal MPs in favour of Parliamentary reform. This development, encouraged by Palmerston during the election, blurred the difference between Whigs and Liberals. The Duke of Newcastle still discerned in Parliamentary reform the issue 'which alone Palmerston cares about (and that in an *adverse* sense)'.[63] It did, intermittently, occupy the prime minister in home affairs for several years, but he was not opposed to it. His speech after being returned for Tiverton held out the expectation of 'progressive improvement'. Though he refused to give 'detailed pledges, or ... distinct promises', evasion of the issue was not his purpose.[64] That is shown by his letter of 26 April to Clarendon, discussing at some length what he had heard from 'so many intelligent men' around the country. The voters of the industrial towns did not, he was quite sure, want the £10 borough franchise lowered but, in common with most of the Liberal party and the electorate, disliked the idea of 'any considerable organic changes'. Parliamentary reform, however, was 'not an end, but a means to an end', the rule of 'property and intelligence'. There was a continuing requirement for flexibility in delimiting the political nation to take account of social changes. Palmerston did not think the existing system catered for the contemporary expansion in the professional classes. He was attracted to a professional franchise – separate from or additional to others that should embrace officers in the services, lawyers, all university graduates, registered medical practitioners 'and so on'. Like J. S. Mill, but not of course to the same extent, he wished to see 'intelligence' better represented. He was also prepared to revise the occupation franchise in the counties by substituting

£20 rating for £50 rental as the qualification. These suggested modifications of the 1832 Act did not arise from 'the slight stir' about its reform at the election; they were intrinsically desirable.[65]

Palmerston's calm approach contrasted with the anxiety of a steady friend in the cabinet to decide on a reform bill and its scope following the calls for one in the campaign. The cabinet having agreed not to mention the topic in the Queen's speech at the opening of Parliament, Wood put his case to Lady Palmerston and then to the prime minister. He implored Palmerston to announce that it was the aim of ministers to tackle Parliamentary reform: 'I have no object but to secure the well-being and existence of your government, and I confess I think that when you spoke of your fear of exciting an alarm of your intention being to do *too much*, you did not justly appreciate the feeling on this subject.' Wood wrote after conferring with M. T. Baines: members for Halifax and Leeds respectively, they could claim to know what the West Riding thought.[66] Palmerston made the announcement in general terms that night: but, replying to Wood, he pointed out that Baines had been 'acquiescent' when the cabinet determined to leave the question out of the Queen's speech. As to the contents of the bill, he did not mean to be 'forced, driven or hustled'; after the cabinet had gone into them fully, he would 'cheerfully' advocate 'whatever…may appear to me to be right, safe and useful'. Exceptionally, Wood's suggestion that the new Liberal majority might turn on him if he delayed and diluted reform made Palmerston angry with his colleague: 'I did not seek the position in which I am placed, I was brought into it by no ambitious intrigue or plotting. Being in it, I shall do my best to keep it so long as by…support from any quarter I may…do what I think right…' If he failed, others might assume 'the responsibility of doing public mischief for their private advantage'.[67] To Lewis, watching attentively, the statement appeared to satisfy the Commons; he had misgivings beforehand.[68] Wood and Baines both had to reckon with local activists of whose influence in their constituencies they were nervous. Their apprehensions were not generally entertained in the party.

The prime minister's estimate of the desire for Parliamentary reform was nicely judged. It reflected what had been said on the subject by his more radical supporters during the election. They outnumbered the righteous few of whom Cobden spoke despairingly at Manchester when fighting to save Bright's seat for him: 'Four, or five, or six, or eight, or ten – I could count them all on my…fingers who remained resolute and determined to maintain an independent course.'[69] In the great constituency of Westminster, the Crimean general, Sir De Lacy Evans, declared himself for a reduction of the borough franchise below the figure of £6 in Russell's bill of 1854; but zeal for reform did not conflict with his admiration of Palmerston: 'the greatest man had his faults'. The other member for

Westminster, Sir John Shelley, a baronet of ancient lineage and a bank chairman, stood for the ballot in addition to a wider franchise; he also upheld Palmerston's reputation as a war minister, and thought him 'deserving of every praise for the manner in which he appointed the recent bishops, although they did not suit the Gladstonites...'.[70] At Southwark, Admiral Sir Charles Napier, advocating triennial parliaments and the ballot, considered Cobden 'the only honest man' among the Commons majority against government on its policy in China; the Peelites were 'renegades' in politics.[71] A radical of a different type, the veteran reformer William Williams, told the electors of Lambeth in extenuation of his vote for Cobden's motion: 'All he could say was that...he had not the slightest idea of placing the government of Lord Palmerston in any difficulty or coalescing to bring in any other party...'[72] The important group of popular metropolitan constituencies was known for a leaning to radicalism, and a social composition that made it unwise for Liberal governments, especially, to alienate a highly politically conscious section of the national electorate. The voters in these seats included a large proportion identifiable as working class – the result of higher property values in London. The industrial structure of the capital fostered the convergence of middle- and working-class interests to an extent that completely defeated Chartism on vital and superficially favourable ground. Moreover, eight years after Russell gave up, during his premiership, the doctrine that the 1832 Reform Act represented finality, and against the recent background of wartime criticism directed at the politicians' initial failure to satisfy public opinion, it was not really open to Palmerston to follow another line from that which he traced for his party. One of his ministers, Sir Benjamin Hall, a liberal Whig, insisted on Palmerston's sincerity when speaking to his constituents in Marylebone: 'Nothing was more certain...than that no ministry could stand long on this country without bringing forward some measure of reform.' He maintained, to sceptical interruptions, that Palmerston had guaranteed the production of a Reform bill, which, as it turned out, was only a slight overstatement.[73]

The Whig radical, T. S. Duncombe, defended Palmerston at Finsbury by effectively combining the appeal of party and that of Parliamentary reform: 'Let them show...that they were enemies to a combination of factious Whigs, envious Tories, and those most amiable nondescripts – the Peace-at-any-price party...Lord Palmerston was entitled to the credit...of having introduced a more liberal system of government.' He answered Sir James Graham's attack on Palmerston's alleged Toryism during the election; Graham's ideas and Russell's had changed in the last few years: why should not Palmerston's? 'He is too good a tactician to be beaten by them in foreign or domestic policy.' Duncombe summarized the obligations of a Liberal prime minister as 'defending the rights of the poor, and the property of the rich, and…extending the freedom and liberties of mankind'.[74] These three broad aims comprised the fundamentals of Parliamentary radicalism, the creed of Cobden and Bright included. All other considerations were secondary. It was concern for the security of property that led Bright to confess: 'I am not myself very democratic…'[75] Nor did his and Cobden's talk of non-intervention imply indifference to the spread of constitutionalism abroad. Palmerston had persuaded the radicals that their aims overlapped his to a degree which they would be foolish not to concede. Clarendon's supposedly radical brother, C. P. Villiers, who held minor office, laid himself out to make that point in the industrial Midlands. 'Lord Palmerston', he said at Wolverhampton, his seat, 'was not quite the man that a Liberal and a Reformer would desire, but he was the best man that could be found.' For Palmerston really wanted to introduce reforms wherever needed; indeed Villiers claimed that 'there was not a man in power who had given utterance to a desire for limiting the possession of the suffrage by the people'.[76] The rich Manchester merchant and Anti-Corn Law Leaguer, Sir John Potter, who with J. A. Turner unseated Bright and Milner Gibson in his city, would have it that 'He had not left his old friends, but they had left him'; he saw nothing incongruous in being Palmerstonian and as much committed to Parliamentary reform as the defeated Milner Gibson.[77]

Lewis did not believe, after working on a reform bill with Palmerston for some months, that MPs were convinced of the requirement for one: 'however moderate…, that large majority of the House will be, openly or secretly, against it, and without more popular pressure than is likely…they will hardly be induced to pass it'.[78] Palmerston, who consulted him on the possible shape of a bill in September 1857, was initially reluctant to lower the urban franchise and to abolish the representation of even the smallest boroughs.[79] The cabinet committee on which the prime minister put himself, and which was subsequently charged with devising a measure, agreed to professional and educational qualifications for voting and to a revised occupation franchise of £20 in the counties. Beyond that point agreement was harder to reach. 'With regard to the boroughs', wrote Lewis, 'the impression was that the choice lay between a franchise of £8 rental or £6 rating – and a disfranchisement of about ten small boroughs.' £6 rating was roughly equivalent to £9 rental; £8 rental would therefore have been the lower qualification.[80] Nevertheless, the discussion moved forward to contemplate the elimination of Parliamentary boroughs having fewer than 300 voters, and grouping those with 300 to 400 in geographically dispersed constituencies like Lewis's own seat, the Radnor Boroughs. Most of the seats available for redistribution were to go to provide counties with a third member. The committee reported its ideas to the cabinet in December;[81] but Lewis's diary shows how the topic of

Parliamentary reform was crowded out by more urgent matters: the financial crisis of November 1857 and its aftermath; legislation for the transfer of India to the Crown as a consequence of the Mutiny; the grave anxiety over Anglo-French relations following the attempt on Napoleon's life, and the hurried examination of how far it was feasible to amend British law so as to discourage a recurrence; and, no light matter, the anger and dismay which greeted Palmerston's reintroduction of an old friend, the socially discredited Lord Clanricarde, into the cabinet, with his colleagues' assent. The Queen's speech at the early opening of the next session in December 1857 contained a mention in general terms of reforming Parliament. Despite the other claims upon its time and energy, the government was approaching a positive decision on a reform bill, and doing so from a position of some strength. The House rejected Disraeli's motion critical of ministers for their policy on the Bank Act by a majority of 178. This short, adjourned session of December 1857 appeared to Lewis to have 'passed off very satisfactorily for the Government'.[82]

Palmerston in opposition

After the event, Lewis briefly thought that the administration's overthrow by Liberal votes on Milner Gibson's amendment to 'the Colonels' Bill' in February should be attributed to the 'declining energy and increasing unfitness' of the prime minister for his responsibilities.[83] He did not, however, find the Tories, in as out of office, worthy of being a replacement for the Liberal ministry. The latter's fall, and the reason for it, seemed to him 'broad comedy'. Yet he felt bound to add: 'but I suppose…it will be treated as serious by the country, who see…they have made a mistake, and will not acknowledge it'.[84] He was right on both counts. The 'prevalent impression that…honour…had not been adequately sustained', which Lewis perceived in all parts of the House during the debate on the amendment, may have been absurd, given Palmerston's record and his disposition.[85] But it was a political fact, which only the international performance of the new government eroded. Besides, the Liberal party and the country could not acquit Palmerston and his ministers of other grave errors of judgement. Clanricarde's appointment before Christmas 1857 was one in which the cabinet 'acquiesced', so Lewis put it at the time. It elicited 'very strong' feeling on the Liberal side and 'set public opinion at defiance', as noticed in Lewis's diary over the ensuing weeks.[86] Likewise, the government's apparently crushing majority on its India bill only the day before its defeat on Milner Gibson's amendment lightly concealed dissatisfaction with the immediate prospects for the restoration of British rule in the vast area of the sub-continent affected. Palmerston's previous hesitation to commend Canning's performance in meeting the outbreak and spread of the Mutiny was shown to have been prudent, if nothing else, on 8 February. The unthinking insertion of the governor-general's name in a motion of thanks to the forces engaged in India provoked the utterance of 'many things…which must be very painful to Lord Canning', wrote his friend Malmesbury, and induced the prime minister to say that the resolution did not preclude a Parliamentary review of Canning's actions at some future date.[87] It remains that, in their journals and elsewhere, two good judges of the House on different sides – Lewis and Stanley – registered almost complete surprise at Palmerston's deposition.[88] If Russell's part in it did not come as a surprise, what had they missed?

A week later, Lewis assured himself that except on the issue raised by the fatal amendment, 'we possessed the general confidence of the country'; Derby leant to the same opinion.[89] Both men soon concluded that they were mistaken. Lewis persuaded Palmerston, who was impatient to resume office, that the Liberals should lie 'as quiet as possible and…avoid all appearance of faction'.[90] While amazingly resilient, Palmerston was under no illusion about the severity of the political blow he had received. It at once revived the fortunes of his old leader and rival. On the day after the vote against his ministry he feared 'John Russell, if joined by Peelites, might form a government and Liberals might take him up…'[91] The blunders of a Tory administration driven to court the Liberal centre and the radicals as the condition of survival did not automatically rehabilitate Palmerston and his cabinet. A hundred and twenty Liberal MPs assembled on 5 May 'to consider the present disorganized state of the…party'. They included Whigs and radicals but consisted predominantly of those who were neither. The lead at this gathering was taken by representatives of industrial towns. The barrister, T. E. Headlam, MP for Newcastle-upon-Tyne, put into the chair, stated that they had not met with the object of 'binding themselves…to any precise political programme', nor to concert support for Palmerston, Russell or anyone else. What they wanted to convey was the determination to see that the next Liberal government should have due regard to their political weight. M. T. Bass, the brewer and MP for Derby, proposed and W. E. Baxter, the Dundee merchant who sat for the Montrose Burghs, seconded a motion urging a Liberal commitment to 'the improvement of our institutions', indistinguishable in its cautious wording from Palmerston's 'progressive improvement'. More to the point, James Clay of Hull, seconded by William Jackson, railway contractor and MP for Newcastle-under-Lyme, moved that a new Liberal ministry should be constructed on 'a wider basis'. J. A. Turner, the Unitarian cotton manufacturer who had beaten Bright and Milner Gibson for one of Manchester's seats at the last election, and Locke of Southwark also spoke. It was decided to ask Charles Forster of Walsall to undertake the task, with others of his choice, of notifying 'the independent liberal party' when a question came up in the House that might demand its collective intervention. The sense of the meeting was not, however, in favour of dividing Parliamentary Liberalism but of 'promoting greater unanimity for the future'.[92]

These industrialists and successful lawyers were not aspirants to cabinet office: Headlam became judge advocate-general under Palmerston in June 1859; Jackson and Forster were to receive baronetcies and Baxter minor office from Gladstone. They were not hostile to aristocratic primacy, only perturbed by its failure to live up to recent expectations. They were restless because Palmerston had, in certain respects, disappointed the 'national party' which had emerged from his premiership and the 1857 general election. A batch of honours in January 1858, when Clanricarde's return to the cabinet was being indignantly talked about, dismayed Palmerston's supporters. *The Times* articulated their concern. A military courtier, Colonel the Honourable Charles Phipps, Prince Albert's secretary, received a KCB, the same honour that was conferred upon Brigadiers Archdale Wilson, 'the conqueror of Delhi', Inglis, the defender of Lucknow, and two other commanders who had won distinction in the Indian fighting. Moreover, Greathed, who marched to the relief of Agra from his exertions at Delhi, and Baird Smith, the indispensable chief engineer at the siege of the Mogul capital, were only made Companions of the Order. Unfortunately for the government, Phipps belonged to the family of the Marquess of Normanby, formerly ambassador to Paris, whose heir, Lord Mulgrave, was the new Governor of Nova Scotia. These Phippses epitomized the Whigs of radical and Tory legend, reputedly insatiable for all that the state could offer such privileged servants. Colonel Phipps's position with the Prince was another count against a prime minister supposed not to be unnecessarily anxious to please the palace: 'in this hour of the nation's trial and enthusiasm we...have elevated above its noblest sons...one...distinguished by... nothing but the favour of a Court', said *The Times*. The paper warned that 'the authorities are setting up their judgement rather too much in independence of national opinions and feelings'. It severely censured 'aristocratic favouritism' in different fields. In the exaggerated vein of some of its wartime editorials, it alleged that 'every appointment...high and low, is grasped at by the poorer members of aristocratic families with a greediness, an indecency, and a success beyond all precedent'.[93] Yet, *The Times* endeavoured to salvage as much as it could of Palmerston's reputation from the consequences of an abuse of political, ecclesiastical and military patronage which it considered had brought the ministry down.

The condition of Palmerston's recovery of power, according to *The Times* on 1 March 1858, would be to 'wash off his blue and yellow streak of caste, tear asunder the veil of superstition, and take half a dozen of the most shrewd and active Liberals he can find into his cabinet...' This was exactly what he did do in June 1859, recruiting five Peelites, the radicals Milner Gibson and Villiers, and cutting the proportion of Whig cabinet ministers to half the total. In his first ministry, Palmerston had undeniably proved himself to be 'something more than a traditional politician'; he had been able to utilize 'the excellence of our Parliamentary machine...prepared for legislation by the Press and by public discussion'. It was not enough: the ministry's Liberalism had been excessively concentrated in the premier to the advantage of Whig 'Levites...Brahmins', who preserved under him their hereditary status as a political priesthood.[94] *The Times*'s invective against the Whigs nevertheless presupposed that they would remain a major force. For Lewis the development of Britain's institutions, to obviate 'entire and organic change', was the historic and continuing Whig role. So it was not true, he insisted in September 1858, that 'the Whigs want *views* as well as *leaders*'.[95] Lewis realized very well that Whig reunion – meaning the reconciliation of Palmerston with Russell, whose stock had risen steeply – was only a stage in the Liberal party's reconstruction; but he was right in the importance he attached to it. Young men of the great Whig families had never ceased to feel for Russell a regard that persisted through his errors and setbacks. 'I am so glad', Lord Althorp, a new member in the Parliament of 1857, told his father after the first session, 'to see...Lord John...seems to have quite taken the lead again on great National questions...speaks admirably and treats everything in true statesmanlike language and spirit...'[96]

Russell's statesmanship in the summer of 1857 had been demonstrated in aid of Palmerston; when the Mutiny exposed the government to charges of underestimating the danger to imperial security in India before and after the outbreak. Palmerston, encouraged by Lewis, was ready and willing to accept Russell for what he had again become in February 1858, someone who could not possibly be left out of a Liberal ministry. On 7 March Palmerston, Sir George Grey, Granville, Wood, and Lewis discussed how best to handle their old friend. Lewis confided to his diary the delicate problem of rebuilding a good working relationship with Russell 'He wishes to set up for himself as leader of the Liberal party in opposition; he is extremely jealous of Palmerston, and much alienated from his former friends. It was agreed that we must do nothing which could make him suppose that we wished him to surrender his independence, and assume an inferior position with respect to Palmerston.'[97] On this basis, Lewis acted as the principal intermediary between the two ex-premiers. Meanwhile, Palmerston, in regular consultation with members of the late cabinet, took on the leadership of the opposition as a matter of course. In his correspondence prior to the change of government, Russell had sometimes been extravagantly disparaging of Palmerston: 'a prime minister with little knowledge to inform him and no principle to guide him...'. With his wounded pride restored in part by Palmerston's defeat, and his fund of good will towards the deposed premier replenished by Lewis's efforts, Russell came more easily to think, like the party man he was, that 'between Derby and Palmerston, I am inclined to prefer the Tory turned Whig to the Whig turned Tory'.[98] But Graham, to whom he had grown close over the 'Colonels' Bill', played on Russell's self-esteem to counteract the approaches from Palmerston's camp: 'he supposed the first condition would be that I should again serve under Palmerston. This I am determined never to do.' However, Russell wrote of his intention 'to steer in the same direction' as Palmerston, and '*in time* bring about a union of the Liberals'.[99] The implication here was that by then nature would have removed Palmerston from the scene.

Both Palmerston and Russell recognized the need for a broader choice in the next Liberal cabinet. Russell wanted Milner Gibson and the Peelites. 'Bright...would...upset the concern.'[100] Cardwell, a Peelite who had refused to be Chancellor of the Exchequer on Gladstone's resignation in 1855 and voted against Palmerston in the division of February, now enlisted under him in defiance of Gladstone. A notable acquisition, he was put up to open the motion of censure on the government over Lord Ellenborough's severity to Canning in an important dispatch, which was, in their view, brazen in seeking popularity by a renewal of the attacks on the governor-general. 'The government have overlooked the fact', commented Lewis, 'that a policy which is regarded as anti-national and unpatriotic cannot be popular.' Russell, Graham and Herbert promised their assistance, but Ellenborough saved the ministry by resigning.[101] Once Canning was secure, Graham promptly changed sides in the ablest speech that the Commons heard. 'Much troubled in mind about this sad Indian debate', Gladstone was torn between aversion to Palmerston and solicitude for Canning.[102] Russell stood by the opposition in one of his best speeches: but the Liberal backbenchers shrank from the inconvenience, expense and probable result of a dissolution after one year, to which ministers were prepared to resort if Ellenborough's sacrifice did not deliver them. Disraeli facilitated his opponents' retreat by responding to their final argument, concerted between Palmerston, Russell and Cardwell, that the government should affirm its confidence in Canning to repair his authority.[103] The withdrawal of Cardwell's motion clearly was not an ignominious reverse for Palmerston, as claimed at the time and since; nor was it entirely a wasted initiative in terms of the Parliamentary Liberal party's internal situation. At a meeting with 150 MPs, T. E. Headlam and others repeated for Palmerston the grounds of their discontent under his administration, 'particularly some of the appointments and an omission to consult the representatives of the large towns'. In reply, Palmerston undertook, if he

succeeded in replacing Derby, 'to attempt to comprehend as much strength
and ability as possible'.[104]

Palmerston knew that a dissolution would not be in the Liberals' interest,
at that juncture, whatever happened at the polls. 'I am quite ready to go
into harness again...' he told Clarendon, 'but... equally content to sit upon
the left hand side of the Speaker... As to a consolidation of the various
sections of the Liberal party, I see no prospect of it...'[105] His diary entry on
the conclusion of the debate read: 'This is of course a great triumph for the
Government, but relieved the minds of all. Those only who hoped for office
disgusted.'[106] The Liberals were not in a state to take over from the Tories.
Summing up his party's five months in opposition at the end of the session,
Lewis was too pessimistic: 'the disunion is as great... as it was'; personal
relations between Russell and Palmerston had improved, 'but the real
rivalry remains'.[107] Neither man would command the party loyalty he
enjoyed as prime minister. The speeches of Liberal MPs in the recess
suggested that Palmerston's domestic policies were better understood and
liked than his conciliatory attitude towards France, which, however, was
increasingly appreciated by politicians and public. He really had little
to fear from those urban members with genuine or supposed radical
leanings, of whom he was distinctly apprehensive in private after his recent
experience of their resolve to make themselves felt. This being so, the Whigs
might grumble but they would fall in behind him.

George Moffatt, an associate of Cobden and Bright, explained to the
Liberals of Ashburton why he, returned as a Palmerstonian, had voted to
kill the 'Colonels' Bill': 'not because it was... particularly offensive... but
simply because... introduced at the dictation of the Court of France'.
Moffatt was the type of radical whom Palmerston expected would press for
a dangerous reform of Parliament, and obstruct the unification of the
party. Instead, Moffatt repudiated any bill 'that shall make franchise of no
avail by bringing it down to manhood suffrage, or... shall cut the
country... into parallelograms and squares... This country has maintained
its character of representation... by the varied elements sent to Parliament.'[108] Another radical, A. S. Ayrton, the MP for Tower Hamlets,
said, 'while there were many things which he objected to in the proceedings
of the late Government, no one entertained a higher opinion of Lord
Palmerston personally than he did'. He had opposed the Conspiracy to
Murder Bill out of a conviction that France was 'deliberately and
persistently' gathering all her strength to attack.[109] Sir John Trelawny, MP
for Tavistock and the Liberation Society's Anglican spokesman in the
Commons, had voted in February to resist 'insolent menaces by a foreign
potentate'. He did not think the Derby ministry would last long, and
wanted to see Russell 'in its ranks' when the Liberal administration was
formed.[110] At Gateshead the local member, William Hutt, a veteran if

lukewarm radical observed that by imitating their predecessors the Tories raised 'few subjects for criticism or remark': but he advised ministers not to gamble on Parliamentary reform 'and include in their…bill all the points of Feargus O'Connor's charter, because I have considerable objection to some of them'. He thought the Conspiracy to Murder Bill had been a mistake, but defended the 'enlightened and generous' policy behind it. 'I believe the Emperor of the French will hold firmly to the British alliance…the best security for universal peace as well as for…progress and civilization', he said to significantly loud cheering.[111] Specially worthy of note were the speeches by Buchanan and Dalgleish, Glasgow's MPs. Buchanan considered that to have passed the bill that had undone Palmerston 'would have been an act of poltroonery, of national degradation'; but he regretted having helped to overthrow him, and intended to participate fully in 'rearing up again a strong…Liberal party'. Dalgleish did not regret the consequences of his vote against Palmerston in February; nor did he wish to have him back in office 'without certain pledges and measures…'.[112] W. E. Baxter of the Montrose Burghs recounted how he had been one of the Liberals who met in May under Headlam's chairmanship 'to protest against the constitution and policy of recent Whig Governments'. Those independent Liberals, he contended, had kept their identity to the end of the session, and numbered over a hundred. But he did not finish without recalling Palmerston's wartime 'faith in…this country, and…his firmness [which] maintained its reputation in Europe'. Baxter referred to Palmerston and his cabinet as consigned to 'their seats of penitence…until…they had time…to make up their minds to be liberal in deed as well as in words'.[113] Nearly all the Liberal MPs who argued on the same line resembled him in the evident presumption that there was no alternative to Palmerston as Liberal prime minister if he retained his health and vigour.

Conscious of the unpopularity of February that might revive if he seemed too deferential to Napoleon, Palmerston was afraid that acceptance of an invitation to visit the imperial court at Compiègne in November would jeopardize his political recovery. The decision to go reflected a growing confidence. Moreover, a calculated display of France's naval strength in August at Cherbourg, with its powerful new base defences, had widely impressed on Britain the advisability of attending to Anglo-French relations in the spirit he had shown at the start of the year. He wrote to Clarendon, who had also been invited and was professing great reluctance to accept: 'our being on friendly terms with him may be politically useful to us individually and to the country, if we should come into office again', and, in that event, a refusal 'would do us no good if we should…have to do business with him'.[114] Palmerston backed his own judgement in making the visit; and it was vindicated when Napoleon sprang the European crisis which he had been maturing with Sardinia since the 'Pact' of Plombières. Prince Albert's private memorandum of September reviewing the, to him, mysterious causes of Palmerston's 'extraordinary unpopularity' was outdated when composed, and anyway ludicrously inflated the 'phenomenon'. The reason why Palmerston was not 'in fact hated!', as the Prince would have it, appeared in Albert's wondering description of how the allegedly discredited statesman bore himself: 'Lord Palmerston... remains, outwardly at least, quite cheerful... seems to care very little about his reverses... speaks on all subjects, bids for Liberal support as before...'[115] At Compiègne Palmerston discussed, among other things, Napoleon's idea of limiting French manhood suffrage to married men, so forming a more conservative electorate from which the Catholic clergy would, however, be excluded. 'I observed', noted Palmerston, 'that property of some sort is the real basis...'[116] His ingrained suspicion of her expansionism did not blind Palmerston to the liberal element in Bonapartist France. He had already obtained a sympathetic hearing from Napoleon for his heartfelt concern about the scarcely disguised re-emergence of the slave trade under the French flag.[117] In contrast, Lewis expressed a view current in Whig circles, though not prevalent as at the British Court: 'We ought to lose no time in drawing closer to Austria and Prussia... A throne which rests on bayonets cannot ever have a firm foundation.'[118] All the Continental Great Powers were militaristic states; and Palmerston's preference for France was, on the whole, that of British opinion, with similarly extensive reservations.

A more friendly witness than Prince Albert, and a good one, the American historian and diplomat, J. L. Motley, saw Palmerston in June 1858, just after the Liberal challenge on Cardwell's motion had broken down. They talked at length about British politics and the affairs of the United States. Motley found someone 'not in the least like any picture... of him', and otherwise different. Palmerston's manner in conversation was 'very gentle, soft, and winning... it seemed difficult to realize that he was the man who made almost every night... those rattling, vigorous, juvenile, slashing speeches which ring through the civilized world...'. To Motley's question how he contrived to make 'those ready, impromptu harangues', Palmerston replied 'very quietly... it was all a matter of habit'.[119] The American was struck by the small amount of 'passion and rhetoric' in the Commons, which characterized Bright in that setting like everyone else. He noticed the weakness of the Conservatives, writhing under the condescension of dissident radicals and Liberals, on whom their continuance in government depended. 'It was quite amusing to see him patting Disraeli on the head from the Opposition benches', he remarked of Bright.[120] By the autumn, those dissidents were getting tired of propping up the Derby ministry. They ran down 'Whig arrogance, Whig exclusiveness, Whig jobbing and so on, even... at... the Reform Club', as an intensely disapproving James Wilson reported to Lewis: but, turning back to their party, they had to put away the notion that Whig leadership was – to quote a worried Wilson – 'not an absolute necessity to carry on government'.[121] If such men were loath to acquiesce in Palmerston's restoration, Russell or Granville were more narrowly aristocratic in outlook. Palmerston gained from Russell's sense of caste, which he thought a little ridiculous. Lord John did not hide his distaste for a man like Sir Erskine Perry, a Crimean war critic of aristocracy now prominent among the 'independent Liberals': 'Of course I do not agree with Sir E. Perry – I think a lord is as fairly entitled to justice as a middle class man.' 'In spite of Sir Erskine', he observed, 'there must always be Whigs in England...'[122]

Comprehensive Liberalism and power

When the eventful year 1859 began, Palmerston's position was strong enough for him to be his own man on the two great issues of the moment, the looming hostilities on the Continent and Parliamentary reform. He handled both questions, which created difficulties fatal to the Derby ministry, so as to prevent them from impeding the accession to power of the more comprehensive Liberal administration which he had promised a party meeting in the previous May to attempt. He was helped by the Tories, who dissolved in April 1859; and who imprudently gave as their main motive the divisions within the Liberal party unfitting it for the responsibilities of government, despite a clear majority against the ministers' reform bill. Gladstone called it 'this most blameworthy dissolution', coming when Europe stood on the verge of a war that threatened to involve Britain.[123] It was the crowning blunder of what Prince Albert, who was well disposed towards it, termed 'a weak and incapable...government'.[124] The election compelled the Liberals to fight together; they emerged resolved to settle their differences and oust the Tories. On Derby's resignation in June following defeat on the vote of confidence, the unsuccessful intervention of the Court to install Granville as premier enabled Palmerston to take office with added prestige in the eyes of his party, the legislature, and the public. The Prince's obstinate belief that the radicals hoped to govern through him did Palmerston no harm at all when it found expression in such an overt move.[125] The principle of comprehension on which he based his second administration was repugnant to some of his most loyal supporters. 'I do not think', wrote Wood to a Whig colleague excluded from the new cabinet, 'that we shall be very long-lived,...after that I shall make my bow under any circumstances, for I am heartily sick of it, and have taken the shilling with no heart in it.'[126] The experiment succeeded far better than he, or anyone else, anticipated. The real fusion of Whigs, Liberals, and radicals came about in the course of the government's life, and not at its inception.

'You are the best person to move in this matter', the ardently Italophil Russell told Palmerston in February 1859, anxious to see Italian freedom grow without incurring 'the calamity' of war.[127] There was little chance of avoiding war in Italy, Palmerston suggested. His speech of 3 February in the Commons had intimated as much; he did more than repeat long-held views on the withdrawal of both the Austrian and French garrisons which sustained the Pope's temporal power in Central Italy, and on the benefits to Austria of surrendering her North Italian provinces. He resorted to a studied lack of enthusiasm in conceding the legality of her claims to Lombardy and Venetia. The European treaties of 1815, whether 'right or wrong' in respect of those provinces, should be honoured for the sake of international order.[128] 'His policy' commented Lewis in alarm, 'though pacific in its terms, and in accordance with the Law of Nations, is nevertheless warlike in its tendency': a revolution must take place on Austro-French evacuation of the Papal States, spread to Lombardy, and draw in Sardinia, behind whom waited 'a band of five hundred thousand robbers with a despot at their head', that is, Napoleon and his army.[129] The House liked Palmerston's speech and its implications. He brushed aside the argument, so far deployed in private, which weighed heavily with Clarendon and Lewis, as with Malmesbury: 'if we are to engage in a crusade for oppressed nationalities', protested Clarendon, 'we shall find that the Austrians cannot be more hated than we are'.[130] 'What a libel upon England' exclaimed Palmerston, 'to say that our present position in Ireland and India is similar to that of Austria in Italy.' He was scornful, also, of the idea that Britain could somehow stop France from making war, 'with the navies of the two countries in the relative state in which we know them to be, with Cherbourg, Portsmouth and Plymouth in the condition in which they are'.[131] National self-interest and generosity coincided fortunately. From the revelation of the crisis in January, he rightly declined to believe that 'Parliament and the country would allow...war with France to maintain Austrian...dominion in Italy!'[132]

Austrian sympathies were stronger in the Liberal party than appeared on the surface. 'The cause of Italian liberty will be popular in England', admitted Lewis in January ' – and the utmost...we could accomplish would be neutrality.'[133] He was really fearful of entering a Franco-Austrian war on the side of Napoleon III. Palmerston interpreted British feeling correctly: it strongly desired neutrality in war, not in diplomacy; disturbed by the all too evident aggrandizement of France, it was yet favourable to Italian liberation through her instrumentality; liberation being understood, primarily, as freedom from the political Catholicism of Hapsburg and Pope. He exerted himself to calm the distrust of Napoleon, which he shared, and override the friends of Austria in his party: 'war must and will ensue', he informed Clarendon on the eve of its outbreak in April, '...public opinion here and everywhere will in the end turn against all those who have been deemed the upholders of the abominable system of misgovernment which oppresses ... Italy'. Moreover, he had before him an old vision of the entire peninsula freed from the 'diversified oppression', to which even the Emperor's plans to set up a Central Italian throne for his cousin, Prince Jerome Napoleon, and perhaps recover Naples for the Murat family, were preferable. However, what worked most to Palmerston's advantage, as he had foreseen, was the spectacle of the Derby ministry's anti-French policy in ruins, 'our government ... compelled to eat dirt, and stand by in ... inactivity and disgust'.[134] Freeing Italy was secondary to the shock to political and financial confidence inflicted by the government that April. A Palmerston administration offered some assurance against a repetition of isolation and panic. 'My conviction is that in the present state of foreign affairs, it is most desirable for the country that Palmerston should be in office', wrote Russell in the last days of May 1859, while persisting in the refusal to serve under him.[135]

A Palmerston premiership was 'a sufficient guarantee' of Parliamentary reform, Russell continued. He had not thought so until very recently. His attitude to the question was a proprietary one, understandably. He elucidated his conception of reform as it had evolved for Dean Elliot: 'I remain always of the same mind. A large extension of the franchise which will include the working-classes – but a very limited redistribution.' He considered the latter indispensable to safeguard the Lords from the overwhelming power of a more directly representative Commons; and advised the Dean, his unlikely channel of communication with the *Daily News* and other papers: 'It is quite true that I wish for a reform bill that will march with the House of Peers.'[136] For this reason alone, it was impossible for Russell to make common cause with Bright. Palmerston responded that, on the contrary, Russell would play into Bright's hands by proposing a £6 franchise in the boroughs: 'Would not the introduction of such a mass of ignorance and poverty', he inquired dismissively in January 1859, 'tend to alter that constitution in which he wants to give them an interest ... and for the worse.'[137] This was surprising of him: his cabinet committee in 1857 had arrived at a similar reduction – £8 rental or £6 rating – in the borough qualification. Palmerston seems to have been provoked by Lord John's culpable irresponsibility, as he regarded it, in maintaining contact with Bright. The radical's agitation had manifestly failed. No one could be unaware of an atmosphere of unreality surrounding the discussion of Parliamentary reform. Even Russell was prompted to tell the Dean: 'It is very odd that everyone says some boroughs must be disfranchised, and the suffrage largely extended, and at the same time that nobody wishes it.'[138] But Bright's recent campaign had made a greater impression on some Whig politicians than on their social inferiors. They felt a need 'to inspire confidence in Whig liberalism', answering not only Bright but Gladstone's 'impudent, insolent articles' in the *Quarterly Review* attacking the party's record under Palmerston.[139]

With that aim, Clarendon, Lewis and Henry Reeve of the *Edinburgh Review* would have liked to publish in its January 1859 issue 'a Whig manifesto' on reform which should not have 'the air of a Whig ultimatum'.[140] Palmerston and Russell independently chose to wait for the Derby ministry. Russell frankly wanted the credit of getting through a bill, writing 'I...keep myself...quite free to...condemn Derby, Bright and the *Edinburgh Review*', the last from resentment of the journal's criticism in his unhappiest hour after the 1857 election.[141] To Palmerston 'by far the best way' to dispose of this problem was a bi-partisan approach: to let the Tories bring in legislation, and amend it as the Liberal majority might decide. In that situation, the few radicals whom he feared would be much less able to turn party rivalry to account. On the appearance of the government measure, Palmerston saw first Russell and then Headlam and Charles Forster, representing their group, to concur in recognition of ministers' glaring omission in leaving the £10 borough franchise unchanged and to discuss a lower figure. Significantly, the two 'independent Liberals', like Russell, were satisfied with the minimal redistribution of fifteen seats in the bill, eight going to the counties. Their rejection of Bright was plain.[142] Palmerston stuck to his preferred tactic of amending the ministerial proposals when he spoke on the second reading. Derby said it was 'the most provoking and aggravating speech he had ever heard': naturally, since the cabinet meant to dissolve if beaten on Russell's hostile motion.[143] Beaten they were, however, by a margin big enough to have justified dissolution but for the developing international crisis. Ignoring the advice of Wood and Herbert, Russell could not resist expounding his alternative reform bill. Palmerston told the House that he was not bound by its 'details', thus limiting the Tories' capacity to use it against the Liberals with nervous voters.[144] Russell took Palmerston's manoeuvre in good part, looking ahead to the arrangement they were to reach when the election was over: 'I think you, like others, understand the line which separates Palmerston and me', he commented to Elliot, '...If he were to agree to my terms all personal questions would soon be settled'.[145]

Palmerston did agree to Russell's £6 borough franchise when it was safe to do so.[146] The concession, if that is what it was, deprived Russell of any but a personal pretext for staying out of the second Palmerston cabinet, and certainly made it easier for Milner Gibson to enter, who had decried the excessive conservatism of its head. War in Europe had pushed Parliamentary reform well into the background. The Liberals' preoccupation was with creating a majority administration so that, wrote Palmerston to Russell, 'this country and other countries should know in the present state of the world...the organ of Great Britain is a government...that...may have...weight...authority and...independence of action...'[147] No election since 1832 had seen fewer seats contested; unopposed returns were 15 per cent up on 1857. But this figure is attributable to the shortness of the interval since expenditure on the last election, not to apathy in the parties or the voters. In the City, Russell endeavoured to unite and conciliate, by his references to Palmerston, Liberals and Peelites. The ex-premier, he said virtuously, had been 'very much ill treated' when the Tories switched their votes on the Conspiracy to Murder Bill. He associated Palmerston with friendliness to Parliamentary reform, on which his opinions were 'of the utmost value'.[148] Russell's leading backer in the constituency, and colleague in its representation, Baron Rothschild, dispensed with such niceties; he asked the electors for 'a strong government', Liberal or Tory, against the background of 'critical' developments on the Continent.[149] It was Bright, however, whose two speeches at Birmingham on 23 April vividly acknowledged the comparative unimportance of other considerations beside those arising out of the confrontation in Italy, where fighting was imminent: 'nothing...he had ever said, or done,...approached...that which...would come if this country rushed into a European war', putting at risk a complex, industrialized economy and social stability with it. He branded as a 'traitor' the minister who despatched a single soldier or ship to war. Bright's unfeigned alarm amounted to an endorsement of Palmerston, though he tried not to see it as such.[150] There was no one better equipped than the object of his political loathing to reassure the public.

The subsequent exchanges between the Tory and the Liberal leadership turned primarily on the responsibility of ministerial diplomacy for the danger of British involvement against France and perhaps Russia if the fighting spread. The havoc wrought by rumour on the London Stock Exchange revealed the fears of property in the shadow of a conflict for which Britain was quite unprepared. 'Nineteen stockjobbers broke yesterday in the City', reported Lady Palmerston to her husband on 29 April, 'but in one way this...may be good...I believe the fright of war is against the Government...'[151] At Tiverton Palmerston found the Tories simply incompetent: their displeasure with France and then Austria was 'the anger of schoolboys – the anger of men...deceived by...want of foresight...want of intelligence...want of knowing what was going on...when it was their duty to know, and with common prudence they must have known...as they failed in their domestic legislation, so...they have failed in the conduct of these great European interests'.[152] Unfair in some respects, this was not mere electioneering but the verdict of an expert professional on honourable amateurs in statecraft. Lewis followed up Palmerston next day at Radnor by sceptically examining ministers' claims to have been in 'confidential relations' with the French government and underlining the menace already apparent of their 'mistaken information' to the 'mighty interests in commerce, investment, and speculation'. 'They are treading' he said with unwonted drama, 'on a mine ready at any moment to explode.'[153] The insistence of cabinet speeches, with varying emphases, that British naval and military intervention could not be ruled out – indeed, Disraeli's of 2 May at Aylesbury positively looked forward to it – undermined the Tory electoral strategy, which was to concentrate upon home affairs and Liberal disunity.[154] Disraeli's bitter critic in his own party, Lord Robert Cecil, declared that 'The question of war is now the dominant one in the English mind ... We ought ... for the peace of Europe and for the sake of our ... trade to take every means possible ... to preserve England from being drawn into the war.'[155]

Yet the Tories advanced far enough for Palmerston to think that the Derby ministry might survive a challenge in the new Parliament from what he gloomily called 'the disjointed fragments which make up the rest of the House'.[156] On the other hand, the Liberals had retained a comfortable, though diminished, margin over the Tories in England, which, added to their unchanged superiority in Scotland, gave them a reliable majority in the United Kingdom of thirty-one on the informed calculations of W. G. Hayter.[157] Russell estimated the Liberals in the Commons unfriendly to him and to Palmerston at some eighty each: but he did not attempt to compare the numbers of their respective supporters.[158] He had not wholly abandoned hope of becoming prime minister if Derby fell: but even Graham told him that he could look only to 'the old Whigs and the extreme Liberals', if to them; Palmerston's adherents in the middle were too many.[159] Russell was in the habit of consulting his brother, the Duke of Bedford, a personification of the old Whigs. Palmerston learnt from Wood that in a long talk the Duke had proved 'very satisfactory indeed. He is all for Lord John taking office under you.'[160] Russell's vanity was not insuperable; although he kept on saying that he would decline to join a cabinet 'of which I am not to be the head', he also insisted repeatedly that 'I am quite willing to see Palmerston prime minister'. What he required was a mark of 'large confidence from the party', against which he nursed 'a resentful feeling' that struck Lewis in their conversations all along.[161] To have Palmerston as prime minister in the Lords and Russell leading the Commons seemed 'the only possible form of a Liberal government which would offer any prospect of stability', wrote Lewis on 2 June.[162] Graham had anticipated him: but Palmerston objected to relegation to the upper House, and to the elevation of Russell. Graham was out to deny an old enemy the reality of his former position by means of Russell's agreement to 'making the apparent sacrifice ... to an old man ... but really removing him from the centre of power ...'. Lewis's motives were purely political: he thought Russell otherwise sure to wreck the projected administration from within or from the backbenches.[163]

By standing firm, Palmerston forced Russell to accept publicly a face-saving accord by which each consented to serve under the other, if the Queen sent for him. This was stated at the meeting of 270 to 280 Liberal MPs at Willis's Rooms on 6 June, addressed by Palmerston, Russell, Herbert and Bright, but not attended by Gladstone. 'Bright very moderate, owned he had sowed dissension among Liberals, but defended his former course. Result of meeting highly satisfactory', recorded Palmerston.[164] The theme of the speeches was that a united Liberal party in power 'might do much to bring about a restoration of peace', in Russell's words.[165] Three ineffectual dissenting contributions came from two radicals, Roebuck and W. S. Lindsay, and a temperamentally awkward Whig, Edward Horsman, who had their individual reasons for wanting the Tories to stay in. Bright confessed he would 'for the moment' have sacrificed his Liberalism 'if...confident...that the present government could and would preserve neutrality', but he was not. Herbert agreed with him. Replying to the discussion, which he had opened with a sweeping indictment of Tory failures, Palmerston sought to reassure those afraid of Britain's involvement in the war and said 'an alliance with France was...the most likely course to secure...peace'.[166] Unquestionably, the incentive to co-operation at Willis's Rooms derived principally from Britain's international weakness and peril. 'No consideration seems to have weighed more on the minds of the meeting', observed *The Times*, 'than the obvious inability of our foreign minister to give effect to his propositions and remonstrances, and the scarcely disguised contempt with which those propositions and remonstrances were put aside.'[167] In the debate that started next day on the opposition's motion of censure, deliberately couched in the most general terms, 'Liberals of all sorts', in Hayter's phrase, rallied to the appeal of its well-briefed proposer, the Whig Lord Hartington, to vote for 'peace and non-interference', certainly, but also *for* an 'increase in our armaments...an increase of taxation', with, unavoidably, 'discontent throughout the country'.[168] Bright voted for the motion, as did almost all those who shared his views to some extent.

Disraeli argued that if the government lost, it would be succeeded by a ministry not only anti-Austrian but really favourable to war.[169] No one believed the second charge. The truth of the first moved the Court to invoke its obsolescent prerogative on Derby's retirement and send for Lord Granville, bypassing Palmerston and Russell. There were Liberals concerned to succour Austria. Hayter conveyed to Palmerston late in May a warning not to forget the '*pro*-Austrian men in our numbers'; while on 3 June Shaftesbury grimly noted the agitation of Baron Rothschild, who was 'almost frantic, the loss of Lombardy to Austria is a loss of his rail roads and his dividends on his loan! ...Strange, fearful, humiliating, but so it is, the destinies of this nation are the sport of an infidel Jew!'[170] The Queen and the Prince hoped Granville would be, at any rate, more amenable to their concern for Austria as a member of the German Confederation. They neglected a previous caution from Lord Derby not to risk exciting by their partisanship 'an anti-German feeling…seriously embarrassing to Your Majesty'.[171] Told by the Queen of 'the bad effect that Lord Palmerston's name would have in Europe', Granville, though ambitious, doubted whether he could supplant him.[172] Clarendon, the most 'Austrian' of the potential ministers whom Granville saw, emphatically advised him to relinquish the attempt.[173] A courtly charade ensued. Russell conveniently took it upon himself to refuse office if he was not to be leader of the Commons, or prime minister himself, which saved Palmerston from offending the Court. Palmerston lost no time in informing the Queen that he felt it impossible to join a ministry too weak to meet his and Russell's aims in determining to combine their forces and call the Willis's Rooms meeting. '…it would be injurious to the interests of…Crown and…Nation, that on such an occasion an administration should be…destitute of the inherent strength necessary…'[174]

'Palmerston…will have no difficulty in forming a government', wrote Granville to the editor of *The Times*.[175] Nor did he, although it took him a fortnight, 'so great and incessant' was the pressure of correspondence and interviews with candidates for office.[176] Russell, given his choice of offices, excluding the leadership of the House, at once elected to be foreign secretary, eager to seize the chance of distinction offered by the post at that moment. There was a good deal of resentment among the Whigs as letters went out from Palmerston explaining why they had to make room for new men, 'independent liberals', associates of Cobden and Bright, and Peelites. Ten of the sixteen members of cabinet had not belonged to it in February 1858 – five Peelites, three Whigs, Villiers and Milner Gibson. From twelve seats, out of fifteen, the Whigs dropped to eight. In the lower ranks of the administration, they fared better, holding on to about half the posts outside the cabinet. One of the Whigs whom Palmerston had to leave out, Panmure, deplored the change from the last government 'composed of men well known to each other in…private life…and desirous, from motives of friendship as well as duty, to support you and each other'.[177] Panmure's remarks epitomized those Whig tendencies which Palmerston could not have afforded to indulge, had he wished. 'It became necessary in 1859', insisted Palmerston to a displaced whip, Lord Ernest Bruce, more than a year afterwards, 'to reconstruct the government upon a different principle and…out of a larger range of political parties. To have merely brought in the administration…turned out in 1858 would have been trifling with Parliament and the country.' A 'junction of parties' had been, and remained, his purpose.[178]

Palmerston was right to stress the role of public opinion in the ministry's origins, and Shaftesbury to find him indispensable to its survival, built as it was 'on a very wide basis', and containing 'elements of discord, rivalry, intrigue, ambition...' Always supposing that the premier was there to keep it together, Shaftesbury had a surprising confidence in the government's durability: 'if Palmerston were removed, the whole thing would be an agglomeration...of molecules floating in various, and even opposite, directions'.[179] A good sign was the delight of middle-class radical politicians with their place, though still a subordinate one, in the ministry. They entreated Cobden to take the seat in cabinet which Palmerston held for him until his return from a business trip to America. The offer was public knowledge; and on arrival at Liverpool an astonished Cobden received letters from Moffatt, Gibson, and a great many others urging him to close with it. Two leading lights in the Lancashire cotton trade and the politics of the region, Thomas Bazley, MP for Manchester since 1858, and Henry Ashworth, a personal friend of both Cobden and Bright, were signatories to an address exhorting him to accept. 'Indeed, almost without exception, everybody, radicals, peace men, and all, are trying to persuade me...it really seems to me that they must all have gone mad...' wrote Cobden to his wife.[180] He quickly made up his mind, however, to commit himself to support Palmerston's government so long as Milner Gibson continued to sit in the cabinet. Adamant, despite that commitment, in resisting the pressures on him to join the ministry he exposed the illogicality of his position at the interview with Palmerston and in writing to Ashworth: 'It grieved me to find...my own sense of duty and right conflicted with the views of yourself and my best friends in Lancashire... *How could I act otherwise?* With all my antecedents towards Lord Palmerston...the ardent and consistent assailant of his policy and principle, it was impossible that I should step from an American steamer into his cabinet without even a...week's quarantine!'[181] Yet he admitted that he had no answer when Palmerston put it to him that foreign policy, 'now uppermost', usually acquired its final shape in cabinet. '...why don't you come into the citadel of power...' asked the prime minister. In effect, that was what the Manchester men did, through Milner Gibson. The reaction of the businessmen who, to him, ought to be the natural rulers of Britain exacted Cobden's pledge to uphold Palmerston while Milner Gibson was his colleague; emotion, not reason, restrained him from serving in the same cabinet.[182] With the insight born of dislike and apprehension, Prince Albert perceived from this development of contemporary Liberalism in his adopted country that 'the English Government...a popular institution' was displaying 'chiefly the instinct of self-preservation' in the condition of Europe.[183]

The cabinet's early years

The history of the alliance between Whigs, Liberals and radicals in the
second Palmerston administration should not be written around Gladstone.
In its first years, Gladstone was soon oppressed by his comparative isolation
and friendlessness. Only when he was over the worst, because he had
reconciled himself to staying at his post on Palmerston's terms, did he follow
the prime minister in taking their common policies to the country. Liable
to be pulled up if he gave undue prominence to points on which he diverged
from Palmerston, Gladstone was worried by the radicals' inclination to
appropriate him politically, as the best potential leader for their not very
extreme purposes. Nothing but the deaths of Herbert and Lewis placed him
in the line of succession to Palmerston on the assumption, which was
debatable, that he had become a good party man. He himself was averse
to being one in a too exclusive sense, preferring, with Palmerston, to
broaden the appeal of the party to catch as many as possible of those who
accepted their fundamental aims of class collaboration and aristocratic
primacy. As the Liberals developed a coherence lacking before 1859, those
aims were kept at the centre and successfully contrasted with the narrowness
of the Tories. The identification of Liberalism with national security, so
rewarding in 1859, continued to be as advantageous as Palmerston believed;
the rational defence of empire, once recognized for what it was, made
converts of the former Peelites in the cabinet and of Milner Gibson with
others of his school. The government certainly appeared to live dangerously
in 1860 and 1861, under threat from its own side rather than the opposition,
but over five years it amassed political capital that carried it through the
discomfiture of Palmerston's foreign policy in 1864 to a convincing victory
in the general election a twelvemonth afterwards.

Palmerston described to the Queen, who was obstructing the inclusion of
an able radical MP in the ministry, the demands upon him of Parliamentary
management: 'Viscount Palmerston sits in that House four days in every
week during the session...from half-past four in the afternoon to any hour
however late after midnight...carefully to watch the proceedings...and to
observe and measure the fluctuating bearings of party and of sectional
associations on the present position of the Government and on its chances
for the future...' Those in 'higher regions' might not realize what was
entailed. Nor did the bureaucrats of the Foreign Office appreciate what it
meant to intrude upon his Parliamentary day with boxes unnecessarily
marked 'Immediate'. 'It is perfectly impossible for me to deal with such
things just as I am stepping into my carriage to go to the House', he
minuted in exasperation.[184] No more striking tribute was ever paid to
Palmerston's talent for handling men than by Cobden at Rochdale in
August 1859. The prime minister, he said, 'is of that happy nature that he

cannot create a personal enemy'.[185] This was not true; angry references to Palmerston recur in Cobden's letters to the end of his life. Palmerston, moreover, disliked him; and was insincere in saying, at their interview in July, 'even if there have been any personalities they never ought to be remembered for three months'.[186] But Palmerston could charm his bitterest enemies, and Cobden's warmth in his praise, though shortlived, was not forgotten. The prime minister did not relax his Parliamentary vigilance in the course of this government. With so small a working majority, he looked out for pitfalls. When the Queen's speech of 1860 was under consideration, he went through all the objections that might be raised were ministers to make it congratulatory on 'the satisfactory state of the great interests of the country'. If manufacturing industry was thriving, agriculture had had 'an indifferent year'; and if an approving mention was inserted of 'loyalty...at home and abroad', what about the indigo riots in Bengal and 'Papist treasons' in Ireland? The publicity given to recent murderous crimes, metropolitan pauperism, commercial distress in Nottingham and Coventry resulting from the Anglo-French commercial treaty were other possible sources of Parliamentary criticism which he foresaw.[187]

He did not in this letter to Lewis advert to relations with France and Europe. Its performance on that front ensured the survival of his government. It did what it came into office to do; preserved peace, stepped up rearmament, and soothed national alarm and indignation at Britain's vulnerability and her loss of influence with the Continental Great Powers. Palmerston's underlying distrust of France and her Emperor intensified when the two countries again differed over Italy. Napoleon's generosity in victory towards Austria, as previously towards Russia, suggested a design of enlisting them in carrying out 'his formerly declared intention of avenging Waterloo'. The prime minister was clear about 'our true policy' in the circumstances, and steadily pursued it. '...we ought to put ourselves into a state of defence by land and...sea...', he told the violently Francophobe Clarendon in September 1859, but 'without sacrificing interests or honour to maintain as long as possible our alliance with France'.[188] The second half of this policy was harder to sustain than the first: but sustained it was. A better free trader than Gladstone allowed, Palmerston concluded the Anglo-French commercial treaty, by which Gladstone and Cobden set such store, as a sop to the Emperor: 'It is...not easy for us to explain why we revert to the exploded system of a treaty about tariffs, without saying that it was the choice of the French government', he observed.[189] The cabinet yielded, wrote Lewis, 'a sort of hurried and reluctant support to the...treaty'; it had not been consulted before Palmerston authorized the negotiation.[190] The cabinet's unhappiness extended to that veteran of the Anti-Corn Law agitation, C. P. Villiers. Bright remarked on his private, and impotent, hostility to Cobden's

handiwork on behalf of the government: 'Villiers who is desperately and
absurdly anti-French ... talks ... as if to make a treaty were contrary to Free
Trade.'[191] There was not a majority in the Commons for the agreement on
its economic merits: but the House voted in its favour by 282 to 56. Like
the cabinet, MPs swallowed it in response to confidential pleas such as that
made by Clarendon to the Tory leadership: 'The treaty is thoroughly
unsound, and a great mistake ... I am sure ... rejecting it, making an enemy
of the Emperor ... would be a far greater mistake ...'[192] Liberal businessmen,
however, showed enthusiasm in addition to understanding; they stood to
lose most by war. 'As representing one of the largest manufacturing
constituencies in the kingdom', the pious and politically agile Edward
Baines said in the Treaty debate that 'political philosophy and ... historical
experience ... brought them to appreciate the old, simple and Divine
injunction, which might be attached as a motto to every commercial treaty:
"Thou shalt love thy neighbour as thyself".'[193]

Milner Gibson, supposedly Cobden's man in the cabinet, subscribed to
his hope that the treaty would damp down the clamour for rearmament
and check the excited rush to supplement the army, militia and yeomanry
by the spontaneous formation of volunteer rifle corps.[194] This did not
happen. Palmerston was determined from the start of his ministry that 'in
the activity ... and scale of our defensive arrangements ... we must not be
overreached by financial economy'.[195] Recognizing that the prime minister
had public opinion behind him, Gladstone fought to restrict defence
spending without much expectation of success: 'Parliament has been
encouraging ... expenditure and the country yet more egregiously has done
the same.' For some time to come there was no changing these political
facts, and he knew it. He did not propose simple economies, but the
redisposition of strength with the protection of these islands as its proper
role. 'We destroy our ... force at home by scattering it abroad', he
complained to the first lord of the Admiralty in December 1859.[196] Nor did
he set his face against paying for technological advance, though he queried
the pace of its implementation. 'It seems to me of the utmost consequence',
he stated, discussing the navy with Palmerston in November, 'that our
means of defence should be the most formidable and efficient which it is in
our power to employ.'[197] His main fear was of a fierce reaction to
overtaxation, eventually. He dwelt upon that prospect in a memorandum
written as he approached the brink of resignation in the summer of 1860
over large-scale plans for new fortifications at Britain's naval bases.
Palmerston and nearly all the cabinet were 'men who see ... nothing but a
certain cost ... who do not apprehend any political changes, any alienation
of the people from the Throne and laws, any disturbance of the relations
of class from the ... increase of financial burdens'.[198]

The risk was not imaginary; and it had to be met, as Lord Hartington indicated in his keynote speech for the Liberals on the vote of confidence in the previous June. Since Gladstone owned in this cabinet memorandum that he did not believe in the attainment of 'a tranquil sense of security, and ... possession of lasting peace', he virtually gave away his case.[199] If the outside world was such a dangerous place, the precautions on which Palmerston insisted were not unreasonable for a state with an expanding economy and healthy finances. In that context of growing national prosperity, the weight of taxation might safely be lightened by borrowing, and Palmerston overrode Gladstone's dogmatic objection to the expedient.[200] Even Bright cared for naval defence. He hailed the selection of his Whig friend, Captain Lord Clarence Paget, RN, MP for Sandwich, as secretary to the Admiralty; an advocate of a modernized navy, returning full value for money, whose views Bright commended to a Huddersfield audience.[201] Neither Cobden nor Bright wanted to see Gladstone resign in 1860: 'I think a change of government ... would bring us into many perils', wrote Bright to Cobden in Paris. They tried ineffectually to aid him by representations to members of the cabinet 'not hopelessly committed to fortifications'.[202] Gladstone found himself quite alone, in effect. His Peelite friends pushed him towards submission, which the Duke of Argyll dressed up as compromise; Aberdeen was wholly unsympathetic. Graham stripped Gladstone of any remaining illusions about the political value of his contemplated departure: 'The will of the nation is in favour of military preparation, quite regardless of expense ... the attempt to struggle against it is in vain.'[203] They forced Gladstone to understand how wrong he had been to hold that he was going '*with* the tide', running deep beneath the surface of events.[204]

Sardinia's cession of Savoy and Nice to France, accompanied by rigged plebiscites, confirmed national security as 'the master topic', if confirmation was required.[205] Bonapartist France had demonstrated her will to expand territorially. Palmerston and, more loudly, Russell, condemned the annexations in language as popular with their countrymen as it was annoying to Napoleon III, whom the prime minister nevertheless took continuing care to appease in that and other matters.[206] In this climate, Gladstone showed, again, that he was out of touch with public opinion by arguing in cabinet for the resignation of the ministry on the ground of its inability to steer the reform bill of that session through the Commons. Russell spoke for their colleagues in denying the existence of any pledge to enact Parliamentary reform.[207] Although the endeavour to pass a bill was not finally abandoned until February 1861, the question had never had, from the time of the government's arrival in office, the significance that Gladstone attached to it. Cobden deliberately discouraged hopes of reform in a speech of August 1859 delivered with Bright on the same platform: 'Everybody is for an extended franchise, ... upon my honour I think at

heart nobody likes it very much or cares much about it.' Of Bright's recent
campaign for reform he said, 'to speak frankly...I did not gather...there
was much spontaneous combustion in the country to help him in his
efforts'. It hardly sounded as if he really thought ministers would be
'suicidal and unwise' not to proceed with the bill that Russell wanted and
had publicized.[208] Palmerston's view was and remained that 'it would be
a good thing to get a bill passed', with the assistance of the Tories held out
to him through Baron Rothschild in December 1859. His uneasiness about
a lower borough franchise was echoed in the superficial cynicism of C. P.
Villiers with his experience of Wolverhampton, stretching back to 1832.[209]

As Palmerston's channel of communication with both Disraeli and
Bright, Villiers had his attention. He urged the prime minister that
December to make Edwin James, the opportunist radical MP for
Marylebone, solicitor-general, in spite of his dubious reputation at the Bar:
'the appointment of a man undoubtedly competent, of very popular
opinions with an exceedingly popular constituency would have more than
the usual effect...when we are about to meddle with the representation'.
He added: 'Our Parliamentary system must be taken with all its
consequences, some of which are, doubtless, *evil*...'[210] Villiers did not
persuade Palmerston to include James in his administration. The quality of
MPs after the enlargement of the urban electorate was the most disturbing
aspect of reform to the prime minister. He had a vision of numerous new
voters 'bribed by the rich or...swayed and coerced by their trade unions',
or worse, abandoned by 'the respectable and intelligent...a powerless
minority' to 'a small clique of socialist agitators'. Justifiably, he suspected
that current demands for reform were often the work of a few active
committee men in the constituencies.[211] When the government bill, with a
£6 rental franchise for the boroughs, came before the House the disparity
between a very limited redistribution of twenty-five seats and an electorate
increased to a size far greater than originally expected, and still uncertain,
was indefensible and a standing incitement to further reform and serious
agitation. In that context, the many hostile speeches on the bill from either
side dominated the debates. A notable one by the former Peelite, W. H.
Gregory, refreshed Palmerston's impression of the ruinous effects of
democracy in America.[212] Another by Bulwer Lytton invoked J. S. Mill on
plural voting and minority rights as someone 'yet more anxious than the
highest Tory to secure...a power that shall not be overborne by...
numbers': but, to Lewis's mind, its finest passage was on Napoleon III,
whose rule illustrated the affinity of democracy with absolutism.[213]
Villiers arranged the bill's demise, obtaining assurances that neither
Disraeli, nor Bright and others – 'some anti-reformers (that I saw in the
Reform Club)' – intended to attack the ministry for giving up.[214]

The opposition gave the reform bill an unopposed second reading, although in committee it joined Liberal critics of the measure. The Tories reserved their determined attacks for certain features of Gladstone's budgets in 1860 and 1861. They were bent on punishing a renegade, as he not unnaturally appeared to them, which was not incompatible with their desire to keep the government in office. Gladstone's abilities were such that Palmerston always meant to retain him, but not at the price of virtual independence for the Treasury. The prime minister's discernment and tact in dealing with his outstanding if unpopular colleague seemed exaggerated to begin with in the eyes of Lewis, for one, who remarked in June 1860: 'No man ever carried timidity and personal forbearance to a further limit.' Lewis thought it 'unaccountable' that Palmerston should have allowed the chancellor of the exchequer to have his way on repealing the paper duties when money was needed for defence.[215] That necessity was in fact the reason why Palmerston indulged Gladstone and generally treated him with extraordinary patience as well as, in the end, firmness. He knew his chancellor was no radical, and also really loath to resign. Gladstone had served notice in his Holyhead speech of October 1859 that his wish to reduce the imposts paid by the vast majority below the level of income tax was conceived in a long tradition of government finance, and was, moreover, conditional upon the willing assent of the rich and powerful, landowners and businessmen alike. Accordingly, in the strategic budget of 1860 he cut away several hundred indirect taxes, helped by the obligation to incorporate the provisions of the Anglo-French treaty in the British fiscal structure, but those – on beer, whisky, tea, and sugar – which bore most heavily on the people were too productive to be sacrificed, when income tax rose by a penny in 1860 only to fall by the same amount next year. The dislike of many Whigs and more Tories for Gladstone and the treaty found expression on the relatively minor topic of repealing the paper duties. It was practical politics to assail them without pretence or restraint, unlike the treaty and, as a whole, the connected budget of 1860 with its successor of 1861. The paper duties thus acquired an importance which they did not have when only Wood and Lewis opposed their abolition in the cabinet of 31 January 1860. As Bright told Cobden: 'Palmerston has no prejudice against repealing the paper duties; he says it is the right thing to do...and in this he is better than some others who oppose this particular remission from hatred of the cheap press, or from ignorance of its importance to the country.'[216]

The Tories used their majority in the Lords to throw out the bill doing away with the paper duties: selective action possible with a budget that consisted, according to usage, of a number of separate measures. The Lords were acting within the letter of their historic rights, which permitted them to reject, but not to amend, a money bill. However, this power of rejection had arguably fallen into desuetude. At the cabinet of 22 May 1860 two men of high character and recognized moderation, Herbert and Lewis, said they were ready to see the government resign in protest against the behaviour of the upper House, and so to bring on an authentic constitutional crisis: 'but' wrote Lewis in his diary, 'those who were most violent against the H. of L. did not appear to be prepared for resignation'.[217] Those in question, Gladstone, Russell and Milner Gibson – Peelite, old Whig, and Manchester School radical – actually sought nothing other than 'some means of visiting their displeasure upon the House of Lords', as Palmerston drily informed the Queen.[218] They let themselves be persuaded to refer the dispute to a Commons select committee, on which Palmerston, Sir George Grey, Lewis and Graham carried an anodyne report concerted with the Tory chairman, Walpole, over one employing stronger language and proposed by Bright which Gladstone and Russell supported.[219] The chancellor of the exchequer, and no one else, threatened to resign if the government contented itself with merely asserting the established position of the Commons in matters of taxation. He wanted a commitment to force a repeal of the paper duties on the Lords, but gave up for the moment, writing to Palmerston: 'I have little hope that the House of Commons, unless led by the Government, will vindicate its rights: and I do not desire...in debate...to bind myself to that course.' Nevertheless, on the following day in the House he invited 'action' against the Lords, unavailingly, while claiming not to dissent from Palmerston's declaratory resolutions.[220]

The prime minister's misgivings on party grounds about the paper duties had started to develop in March. Gladstone would not hear of postponing the bill for a year. It passed its third reading in the Commons on 8 May by the slender margin of nine; when Disraeli attacked Gladstone in a 'powerful and effective' way that reminded Lewis of his assaults upon Peel in the mid 1840s, and yet probably saved the bill from defeat by deterring several Liberals from being seen to vote with the Tories after an excessively personal attack on the chancellor.[221] The error was typical of Disraeli. Lady Palmerston thanked the leaders of the opposition who conveyed to her their desire to kill the measure in the Lords.[222] Gladstone did not try to work public opinion against the Lords, because unsure how he ought to react to their predictable vote. Answering an appeal from Granville 'not to let the House of Lords take an imprudent step', Palmerston refused to use his influence with Liberal peers, or countenance the delaying tactics suggested, which 'would give the Radicals time and encouragement for subversive agitation'.[223] Twenty-six government peers contributed to the opposition's majority of eighty-nine and another forty-four stayed away without pairing. The Commons were even less inclined than the cabinet to adopt an 'aggressive' stance towards the Lords. As for public opinion, the crucial factor, great provincial centres like Manchester and Liverpool, or their patriciates, approved of what the Lords had done.[224] The Tories hurried to assure the prime minister of their continued support if Gladstone and Russell left the government over the paper duties or Parliamentary reform.[225] The chancellor of the exchequer persisted in talking of resignation after his decisive interview of 6 June with Palmerston, but was, as Lewis described him, 'in a restless, excited state – stung by the vote of the Lords – disappointed at the want of sympathy in the cabinet – and perplexed by the falsification of his unreasonable expectations…He has to choose between staying in to eat his words…and going out alone.'[226] Palmerston made it easier for him by assenting to 'a childish condition' in the legislation authorizing a loan of £9 million to be raised over four years and spent on fortifying naval bases, namely, annual Parliamentary renewal of the power to borrow for the purpose. His triumph over Gladstone was nearly complete; he referred to the chancellor's months of 'ineffectual opposition and ultimate acquiescence'.[227]

After a mainly radical dinner in the middle of July R. J. Phillimore remarked how everyone present 'talked the strongest anti-reform conversation', and particularly Edwin James. Phillimore and a former Peelite whip turned Tory MP, Lord Alfred Hervey, sadly discussed the 'dead set' against Gladstone on the part of Tories and Whigs.[228] What the Liberal party as a whole cared about was the international situation; an end of session meeting at Downing Street cheered Palmerston's mention of the government's foreign policy. On the same day, the Commons passed by thirty-three votes a bill to align British and French duties on imported paper, as promised by the commercial treaty. Fearing 'no good could arise to the relations of the two countries from an adverse vote of the…Commons', Palmerston wished to seek French permission to drop the bill. Gladstone stood by the treaty, and this time had an almost united party behind him in the House.[229] It was a victory for the party much more than for Gladstone; who owed it to Palmerston's discreet intervention with Derby a few days later that his reintroduced savings bank bill got through the Lords.[230] In October the first of the prime minister's major provincial appearances during his second administration elicited Russell's sincere congratulations: 'Your progress in Yorkshire is triumphant…I am…much pleased to hear the trade in woollens and broad cloth is so right on foreign politics.'[231] Palmerston had written of Leeds and the West Riding as clearly disposed to round on the government 'if…we should be deemed to be…abdicating the position which this country ought to hold among the nations of the world'.[232] This was impressed upon him although he devoted his speeches at Leeds principally to class, and not international relations. He went there, the French ambassador heard from him, '*pour rencontrer des ouvriers*'. He did not find any evidence, he told Russell, of a desire for Parliamentary reform.[233]

At the cabinet of 17 November 1860, however, Palmerston was making another attempt to push through a government reform bill, leaving Russell to announce that it did not seem to be wanted, and to say, with irrepressible vanity, 'he was the last person...to complain of the country being satisfied with the Act of 1832'.[234] The cabinet was then unanimous in burying the question. Palmerston's letter of the day before to Russell suggests that he may have been testing opinion in the cabinet by his solitary advocacy of trying again.[235] When in February the cabinet considered what to do about reform bills introduced by private members, Palmerston voted in the minority of six with Herbert and Cardwell for blocking them, while Lewis, Gladstone and the three dukes figured among the ten prepared to let the House express a view.[236] Gladstone's third budget of 1861 was far more controversial: but his account of what took place in cabinet is misleading. There was little objection to the single unified finance bill which effectively nullified the Lords' anachronistic claim to reject a proposal for taxation sent up by the Commons. Gladstone carefully listed those speaking for and against the procedure; only two were 'keen' in their resistance to it, not including Palmerston, who was 'moderately' opposed: 'but if we had divided, of which I had fears, it might have gone wrong', concluded the chancellor of the exchequer's memorandum of that discussion.[237] Lewis's diary and letters pass over this episode in silence, but contain a full description of the questions that went to a vote in the cabinets of 11, 12, and 13 April 1861. Gladstone was meditating the threat of resignation well in advance on the score of defence expenditure. On 11 April he had a surplus of nearly 2 millions to report, contrary to his gloomy forecasts. At the meeting of 12 April he declared 'in the most resolute manner' that he would not present a budget to Parliament which did not cut taxation. Consideration of his remissions centred on repeal of the paper duties which he again put forward, amounting to just under 70 per cent of the sum to be relinquished. The cabinet voted on the proposition twice, first rejecting it overwhelmingly by fourteen to two – Gladstone and Milner Gibson. Eight favoured a penny off the income tax instead, and six a cut in the high duty on tea, which would effect a worthwhile reduction in the cost of living. From his 'dogged' air in the face of general criticism, Lewis expected Gladstone to resign. 'The cabinet then separated in...complete uncertainty', he wrote.[238]

On 13 April it was surprised to encounter a very different Gladstone, who had 'entirely altered his tone. He was extremely bland and conciliatory, and denied that he had ever insisted on anything – although his language was perfectly clear and...fresh in the recollection of everybody present.' To secure abolition of the paper duties, he accepted a penny off the income tax which he had not meant to concede. The cabinet 'acquiesced in rather than agreed to' the compromise; like Palmerston, it would have preferred a larger surplus 'to meet the many contingencies to which the unsettled state of Europe may give rise to'. Gladstone's original proposals would have left a surplus approaching £700,000, which the outcome of these cabinets halved. Lewis termed the budget 'reckless and hazardous, and intended mainly to discharge the bad political debts of the government'.[239] Gladstone's changed attitude between 12 and 13 April was brought about by reflections like those urged in the interval by Wood, who put two choices before him. Wood 'earnestly' hoped he would take the Palmerston line that 'in the present state of European affairs' there was no scope for returning any of the surplus directly to the taxpayer. Under cover of this argument Sir Charles offered Gladstone a way out of pressing for repeal of the paper duties, to which 'I think...*you* are to a certain extent committed.' '...this course is...honest to the public', he wrote. 'It relieves you from any appearance of inconsistency...It preserves our unbroken phalanx.' The other choice was for the chancellor to insist '*if* remission, then paper duty'.[240] Gladstone chose this alternative, and improved upon it. The budget as it stood, Palmerston told him on 14 April, could not be allowed to decide the future of the government. 'I assure you', replied the chancellor, 'that, reserving my own freedom, I never should have presumed to advance any such claim...'[241]

By taking a penny off income tax he won over a reluctant cabinet and party. Bazley of Manchester expressed this unequivocally on 25 April when the Commons debated the budget: 'The remission...was a relief to the wealthy classes...capitalists and landed proprietors.'[242] Hartington, for the more liberal Whigs, appealed to Palmerston to press the financial proposals on the House 'without flinching', and to dissolve if they were not accepted. Hartington welcomed Bright's approval of the budget as making up for his radicalism.[243] Gladstone imputed to the Tories a wish to devote the current surplus entirely to cutting income tax, 'and let the labourer shift for himself'. Yet repeal of the paper duties hardly helped the poor; and Gladstone thought the opposition's ideas of reducing the duties on tea and sugar fiscally irresponsible and politically unbalanced.[244] The Mancunian capitalist, Bazley, maintained that the House was bound to 'raise an equitable amount from each respective portion of the country'.[245] It was a principle to which Gladstone steadfastly adhered; he was adamant that 'so long as abnormal expenditure continued it was right that the labouring classes should...pay their share in the palpable form of...tea and sugar'.[246] The landed and business classes should not be expected to shoulder such a burden of taxation as would distort the working of a free economy, and encourage men of small property, and no property at all, to demand higher government spending and socially more discriminatory finance. The Tory amendment on tea was lost by eighteen votes; and the paper duties went down by fifteen in the great party contest of the session. Gladstone carried the budgets of 1860 and 1861 because they were in the prevailing tradition of intelligent conservatism at the top of politics, and made provision for what he called the 'abnormal expenditure' on defence.

Even so, he was indebted to Palmerston's hold over the party for the ability to overcome dislike of the Anglo-French treaty and paper duties repeal. Moreover, the prime minister's attraction for many Tories, whatever their leaders said and did, also rescued Gladstone from the consequences of their animosity, as in the final Commons division of 30/31 May on the paper duties, when Disraeli planned to defeat the government with the assistance of 'disappointed Whigs' and Irish Catholics, only to be thwarted by deliberate abstentions in his own ranks.[247] Palmerston stated the obvious to his difficult chancellor after the narrow result on Horsfall's amendment to lower the tea duty: 'many of our friends voted with us...simply and solely on account of their unwillingness to appear to desert the government'.[248] A sharp dispute in July over a small matter, the Law Courts Money Bill, gave Palmerston an opening to emphasize his authority as head both of the Treasury and of the government: 'I do not intend to be set aside.'[249] Gladstone's succinct answer to a letter of August from his friend Argyll proves that he was not tempted to deceive himself about his place in Liberal and national politics. Argyll did not rate highly the ministry's chances of living through another session: the Tory leadership was tiring of opposition, and no longer convinced of its unsuitability to govern. But, reflected Argyll 'after all, *Palmerstonianism* is the strongest element in favour of the present government, and...Palmerston's influence *out of office*...would be almost as great...perhaps even greater'. The Duke attributed that influence to the prime minister's foreign policy and, 'most essentially', to his insistence on preparedness against France. No other administration could spend much less; the grumbling at current levels of taxation was significantly muted. 'If therefore you have it in view to fight on this...', Argyll finished, '...pray be very careful of the definiteness and practicability of the ground you take up.' 'On what you say of the temper of this country, the position of the government, and the mainstay of its rather limited strength...I have only to reply that I agree', responded Gladstone shortly.[250]

He told one of the very few radicals prepared to belittle the Napoleonic menace that the French government was guilty of 'much falsification' in its statements. To allay 'the natural...mistrust' of Britain, the emperor should furnish incontrovertible evidence of his good intentions by balancing France's budget, revealing her real expenditure, and, lastly, proceeding 'I will not say to disarm, but to reduce.'[251] Scornful of what he deemed their opportunism and insincerity, Gladstone was not in the least inclined to see the '"Conservatives"' come into office.[252] While he considered the opposition was stronger than it had been, it lacked confidence, quite unable to

challenge the Liberals' demonstrable superiority in comprehending the
aspirations of different classes. A good number of Tories were determined
to behave like Conservatives, properly so called. A respected figure in the
party, General Peel, voiced this sentiment in the recess of 1861, and
reiterated a preference for Palmerston over a third Derby–Disraeli
administration. The General represented traditional Toryism and, he
argued, the politics of his late brother, since the party had long ceased to
be protectionist. As a Tory and an adherent of Sir Robert's conservatism,
he had great faith in the prime minister, relying on him to 'uphold the
power of the country and defend its honour'.[253] That summer, Shaftesbury
found the Tories quite unfitted to govern 'in conception, in boldness, in
appreciation of the dignity of the Empire, its position, its character, its
interests...'. 'The Palmerston party are not much better', he wrote: but
still better, under the one man who possessed the qualities enumerated.[254]

5

Peelites and radicals

Talent and potential

Two very small minorities, the unabsorbed Peelites and the genuine radicals, played an even more disproportionate part in politics after the 1857 general election than before it. During the interval of minority government in 1858-59 they were courted by both the Liberal and the Tory leadership. Neither of these little groups constituted a party in itself, but each preserved a distinct identity. At the polls in 1857 and 1859 the radicals fought as Liberals, as did most of the Peelites. In the Commons they assumed an independence of party less apparent among the Peelites in the Lords. This inconsistent and ungrateful behaviour, as it reasonably appeared, made them unpopular in the House. So did the imputation to themselves of political and personal virtues in which they found others gravely deficient. It did not help that Aberdeen, Newcastle, Gladstone and Herbert were men known for their devout and pure lives, and their aversion to the cynicism, superficial or otherwise, of a Palmerston or a Disraeli. Cobden and Bright were similarly blameless in private life, and insistent upon principle, if the latter's diary and correspondence show him to have been much less high-minded politically than is often supposed.

The moralistic politics common to Peelites and these leading radicals made for good relations and the friendly acceptance of profound differences. The Peelites were the most aristocratic of groupings, and believed in aristocracy wholeheartedly. Cobden and Bright believed, as sincerely, that the aristocracy was at best an anachronism, and at worst a social and political evil. Both men and their close associates had no option but to seek to influence the aristocratic politicians, Whig, Tory, and Peelite, whom they could not hope to displace in their time. In the circumstances, they were happy that the Peelites, with whom they felt an affinity, should acquire a share of power beyond their own reach. The Peelites might be unpopular, but they were respected in Parliament for their talents. While talent was the Peelites' strong suit, Cobden and Bright always commanded a hearing because the Commons appreciated their potential; if, or when, aristocratic government ceased to satisfy the country, they, or their political heirs, would be the natural successors, substituting middle-class for landed rule. By taking more Peelites and radicals into his second administration at the expense of Whigs, Palmerston secured the former's abilities, and channelled the latter's potential into regular and fruitful co-operation with the dominant landed element in the Liberal party. Peelites and radicals went with Palmerston, long the object of peculiar detestation to them collectively, in order to obtain some of the power which the party and public opinion gave him.[1]

The Peelites

Perhaps the most interesting account of how the Peelite secession from Toryism saw itself by 1855 is Newcastle's, in a letter to the Whig Granville: '*Peelism* – if I must still use the word, is really the more advanced form of liberal opinions', the Duke held, in the sense that it came between 'demagogic liberalism' and 'that oligarchic tendency of the old Whigs who wishing to extend freedom sought to do it by *making use* of the people instead of identifying themselves and their interests *with* the people'.[2] This also constituted the most important difference between Palmerston and the hereditary Whigs but, unlike him, the Peelites were averse to anything that smacked of populism.[3] The feeling against them ran deep among Tories and those Whigs of whom Lord John Russell was the embodiment. As late as 1860 Russell complained strongly: 'There is always a Peelite who stops the way in any distribution of patronage.'[4] On the formation of both his ministries, in which the Peelites' share of cabinet posts recognized their undoubted quality, Palmerston encountered the Whigs' jealousy and suspicion of men who claimed, like Newcastle, to have displaced them as the ablest exponents of aristocratic liberalism. For the Peelites were notably aristocratic; all the half dozen in the second Palmerston cabinet were peers – two of them dukes – or large landowners. Moreover, in the course of that administration, as before it, they cannot be said to have justified Newcastle's confidence that they were by definition better liberals than the Whigs; though Gladstone, at least, by following Palmerston's example acted out the Duke's idea of Peelism.

There were three stages in Palmerstonian Liberalism's assimilation of the Peelites. In the first, Argyll and Canning stayed in the cabinet when Gladstone, Herbert and Graham left it in February 1855, followed by nearly half the Peelite ministers outside that body. Argyll strove to convince Gladstone that 'in the present excited state of public feeling' there could be no adequate moral justification for the step he was taking: it might have the effect of permanently destroying that governmental ability to withstand popular pressure which almost everyone in the political nation believed was vital to the constitution. Argyll did not think the public would show much patience with 'sectional jealousies' in Parliament.[5] On that note, the two men parted company. The Peelites who thought like the Duke did not cease to be critical of war aims going beyond the Four Points. Canning, in a frank talk with Bright in April 1855, was 'evidently puzzled with the war, and the way to get out of it'.[6] Argyll himself told the prime minister in May that the Four Points went quite far enough: 'any enlargement...to territorial changes, "Nationalities", etc., etc., would be a policy unwise and injurious'. If this was not very different from what Gladstone was saying, the Duke carefully dissociated himself from his former colleague.[7] The measure of success that attended Palmerston's prosecution of the war confirmed the Peelites who had opted for his leadership in their choice, and drew others after them.

Palmerston began by accepting that his ministry should be a reshuffle of the preceding coalition, as Lord Chancellor Cranworth, for one, argued. The incoming prime minister fully appreciated the concentration of Parliamentary and administrative talent among the Peelites; and they were given five cabinet places instead of six, out of an unchanged total of fourteen: 'the...proportions cannot be deemed...unfair', he answered a protesting Whig colleague.[8] It was a notable tribute to the Peelites' quality, for they numbered only some forty in the Commons. When they split a fortnight later, the Peelites delivered Palmerston from both Whig and popular resentment of those in Aberdeen's government and his own who were held chiefly responsible for incompetence and lukewarmness in waging war. The Peelites remaining in office and in support of ministers benefited from the break, too, as the seceders attracted all the odium, and more besides, incurred by the undivided group. Palmerston looked out for able recruits from that part of it which had gone into isolation and irregular opposition. Herbert declined his offer: but Sir Robert Peel became civil lord of the Admiralty in March 1855, and J. S. Wortley, a friend of Gladstone, solicitor-general in November 1856. The prime minister estimated those Peelites who were 'steady opponents' at thirteen to fourteen by February 1857.[9] Herbert set Palmerston's failure over Naples against his successes over the disputed interpretation of the peace with Russia, and reached the conclusion that he was 'more popular and stronger than ever...To make Palmerston useful or even harmless his ministry should have been leavened, not opposed.' It seemed to him that the prime minister had broken the mould of party; he doubted 'if there is...or ever again will be such a thing as a party'.[10] Gladstone did not share the delusion. He warned a Tory acquaintance who considered standing as a Peelite in 1855 not to make the attempt: 'I know not whether there are any... returned by their constituencies for being such: the great majority came there *in spite of* their bearing that character. This is not pleasant: but it has been unavoidable.'[11] Gladstone aspired to reintegrate the isolated Peelites with one traditional party or the other. For want of historic roots or popularity, the Peelites could not be an effective third force, however high their calibre. Their natural home was Liberalism; Gladstone's description of Liberal government under Palmerston as 'surely..."an organized hypocrisy"'[12] expressed a frustration that drove him on to seek a fresh opportunity of deposing the prime minister and substituting, preferably, Lord John Russell.

Gladstone hoped to succeed by getting up 'an economical crusade' in conjunction with the Tories and radicals, but without committing himself and the Peelites to enter a Derby ministry. His attitude to party undermined these efforts; it came through in confidential negotiations and in the House. 'I care for no party,' he affirmed to Graham, 'except as an instrument of good government.' A spell in opposition, he inclined to think, would do the Liberals good, since they were wedded for the time being to Palmerston's foreign and imperial policies, with the financial implications.[13] His onslaught upon Lewis's budget in February 1857 failed, compelling him to return to the attack on ground unfavourable to Palmerston's assorted enemies – the latest developments in Anglo-Chinese relations. Their slender margin of victory over him on Cobden's motion was overturned at the polls, when Palmerston countered with a dissolution. Gladstone tried to induce Derby, in the face of certain defeat, to adopt an unequivocally anti-Palmerstonian programme on expenditure and foreign affairs. He used a revealing argument to the Tories' leader: 'it seemed to me it was high time for them to consider whether they would or would not endeavour to attract... such a strength of public opinion as would really put them in a condition to undertake the government... without which they could not be a real opposition'. Derby could not saddle his party with such a programme, offering a remote and doubtful prospect of popularity; although he – and Malmesbury, at his desire – solicited Gladstone's help during the election.[14] Contrary to the impression that he gave Malmesbury, the Tories got his aid, if at all, in a questionable form on the hustings in Flintshire. Gladstone did not run his brother-in-law, the mild Sir Stephen Glynne, as a candidate hostile to Palmerston, but called on his behalf for 'a government for the benefit of all classes that would support the Church, reduce... expenditure, extinguish... income tax, and keep taxation down generally'. Confronted with intense dislike of his and Sir Stephen's High Churchmanship, he was forced to stigmatize a follower of Dr. Pusey as 'a man who favoured the introduction of the Roman Church into the Church of England – a favourer of the Church of Rome'.[15] It was an ignominious experience for him. His charges against ministers of financial mismanagement and worse than recklessness in external policy went down badly. Before nomination day, Gladstone explained the niceties of the Glynne candidacy to his radical brother Robertson: 'I shall not...recommend Sir Stephen...as an *opponent* of Lord Palmerston's administration...he is not in political association with any...party but will act independently opposing Lord Palmerston in his bad measures...wars...extravagant expenditure...' In the circumstances his censure of the sitting member, for inconsistency in professions of Liberalism *and* independence did not come well from him.[16] The whole episode was a disaster for Gladstone.

Malmesbury attributed Tory losses in some measure to their attempted understanding with the unpopular Peelites.[17] In fact, of the three leading Peelite MPs, Herbert and Graham fought on the Liberal side; while criticizing Palmerston, they were not prepared to stand separately from the party under his leadership. Aberdeen regretted that Gladstone had not done likewise. The Peelite future lay with the Liberals who 'in this age of progress must ultimately govern the country'. 'Ultimately' was the operative word. Aberdeen argued that Palmerston's expected resistance to any but minimal Parliamentary reform might be the cause of a breach with many of the large new Liberal majority. In that event, he anticipated a realignment of parties, with Palmerston and Derby combining against reform and leaving Lord John Russell to head the Liberals, to whom Gladstone, Herbert and Graham should naturally adhere 'both from political affinity and private friendship'.[18] Gladstone, however, was prey to an internal conflict which he could not resolve for more than four years after his departure from Palmerston's first cabinet. Looking back in the 1880s, he distinguished between his 'sympathies' and his 'opinions' in the fifties, which had been with the Tories and the Liberals, respectively;[19] at the time of which he wrote, the division between emotion and intellect was less obvious. Yet whether leaning to one side or the other, or vainly seeking, in defiance of his own considered judgement, to reinvest the unabsorbed Peelites with a corporate existence, such as it ever was, finally ended by the 1857 election – he turned most often in the direction of Liberalism with or without Palmerston. While the election only cut down the identifiable Peelites to a possible twenty-six, it confirmed that they were no longer a coherent grouping, and virtually completed the break-up apparent in February 1855. In listing the members of the new Parliament, *The Times* put Gladstone down as a Tory, and Graham and Herbert as Liberals. The former Peelite whip, Lord Ernest Bruce, who had stayed in Palmerston's government and become his 'unhesitating supporter', selected for special praise the prime minister's grasp of economic matters: 'We had to thank that statesman for a reduction of taxation, for...taking off the [war] ninepence from the income tax, and for carrying out the principles of free trade.'[20] Bruce's merited tribute showed how awkwardly placed the government's Peelite opponents were. There was no popular issue which favoured them. The election rounded off the second, and irreversible, stage of the process by which Peelism came to terms with Palmerston. The third comprised the period to June 1859.

Gladstone was practically alone in trying to maintain that the Peelites retained a distinctive identity after the 1857 election. If it were otherwise, he contended, 'I have been deceiving both the world and my constituents: and … this deception has reached its climax within the … fortnight during which I have been chosen without opposition to represent Oxford [University].' Rather than submit to the inevitability of taking his place – a prominent one – in the Liberal or the Tory camp, he told Aberdeen, whom he revered, that he would 'in pain and distress endeavour to keep quiet: bow the knee I cannot'.[21] Aberdeen persisted in his view that Gladstone had in fact become a Liberal when the coalition of 1852 was formed. Nothing had happened since to change Gladstone's position; not even the serious disagreement with Palmerston: 'You have opposed the Government … but … as a Liberal.'[22] Herbert thought likewise. He now found the political lure of Palmerston hard to withstand for much longer: 'He has on his side … the strongest element in all human society, namely the public's national prejudices.' Herbert quoted George Canning, whose disciple Gladstone had been, on the importance of deferring to the 'non-sense' of the country, and added: 'Somebody said, give me the national songs and I will rule the nation.'[23] This was not the kind of reasoning that appealed to Gladstone, and it underestimated both Palmerston and British public opinion. Herbert was by nature a party man; his personal attachment to Gladstone kept him from his political home in the Liberal party until 1859. His bids for independence of Gladstone succumbed to the latter's emotional pleas for the separate existence of the Peelites: 'they enthrone again honesty and courage, the two English virtues, which England seems … almost everywhere to be trampling under foot'.[24]

In this phase, the inability of the scattered Peelites to make themselves felt collectively was screened by the continuing partnership between Gladstone and Graham. Sir James possessed a formidable talent for Parliamentary intrigue and manoeuvre; it was he who set the scene for the political drama of Palmerston's downfall on the Conspiracy to Murder Bill. Gladstone's oratory did the rest, in the sense that his was the decisive speech, swinging enough votes to topple Palmerston. Gladstone and Graham were obsessed with distrust and resentment of Palmerston's populism; but Graham was less principled and more rancorous. The chance denied them over China and India presented itself at last when the government, compelled to placate France, afforded its enemies the means of upsetting it with public approval. In 1863 Argyll described the essence of Peelism after Peel, guided by the example of Aberdeen, as 'the … spirit of generous resistance against all forms of popular injustice'[25] Argyll himself and Canning acted in that spirit within Palmerston's first cabinet, especially towards India; but they believed with another of their circle – Canning's predecessor in India, Dalhousie – that 'Palmerston was the only man who could command... the confidence of the country.'[26] The more influential Peelites remaining outside the government availed themselves of an opportunity to be both righteous and popular in February 1858; although Herbert recognized that the government had a case: 'we must not refuse to do right if it be right on the ground that we are asked to do it by a foreign country', he wrote to Gladstone.[27] They did not imagine that they had taken a turning which would lead Gladstone and Herbert, with Graham's blessing, to places in Palmerston's next cabinet.

The Divorce Bill was the memorable piece of legislation submitted to the shortened first session of the Parliament chosen in 1857, and brought Gladstone out of the semi-retirement to which he thought himself consigned by Palmerston's electoral triumph. His reputation suffered from the rigidly High Church position he took up, and his delaying tactics. Palmerston's prestige was further enhanced by the resolution he displayed in getting the measure through. An even lonelier figure now, Gladstone was inhibited by his loyalty to and concern for Canning in India, still a personal friend, from using the onset of the Mutiny to criticize ministers more aggressively than he did. Once Palmerston had consented to shield the Governor-General in his Mansion House speech of November 1857, Gladstone prepared to speak out, inspired by genuine anxiety. Reviewing the political situation in January 1858 for Robertson, he advised that important Liverpool politician, 'What is most serious of all is that the Indian prospects are really darkening, and that the slowness in sending out troops may prove to have made all the difference...'[28] His misgivings and hope of an opening to attack Palmerston were fully endorsed by Graham who observed grimly of the prime minister and the Indian crisis in August, 'we must await in patience that just retribution which sooner or later overtakes the wrongdoer'.[29] Their temper, and Herbert's, was not improved by Palmerston's unsatisfactory response, as it struck them, to renewed criticisms of Canning. Herbert felt the prime minister's references to Canning under Parliamentary pressure that February were 'low and deprecatory... I thought justice was not done him'.[30] Gladstone had been quick to put the worst interpretation on ministerial appeasement of the French after the British-based attempt on the Emperor's life in January: 'Will Palmerston truckle to Louis Napoleon and make proposals hostile to liberty in this country? It would not surprise me', he speculated to Graham.[31] The Conspiracy to Murder Bill's provisions were not of a kind to endanger individual freedom in Britain: Gladstone, however, treated them as symptomatic of Palmerston's insincerity in professing to uphold strategic interests better than any one else. His explicit statements to this effect were reserved for a contribution to the *Quarterly Review* in April 1858. He there depicted Palmerston's diplomacy as in reality 'Austrianism' in Italy and generally 'Gallicanism'; that is showing himself to be 'alike partizan and tool' of Napoleon III, rewarded by the Emperor with 'the honourable office of turnkey for life'. 'Such', he concluded, 'were the... results of the anti-national policy of Lords Palmerston and Clarendon.'[32]

The article's anonymity was as transparent as its immediate purpose was plain: to shatter Palmerston's reputation as a champion of nationality at home and abroad. He had written in his diary on the occasion of Palmerston's defeat, 'He is down: I must now cease to denounce him.'[33] He did not cease because it rapidly emerged that Palmerston intended to be an active leader of opposition bent on an early recovery of power while the Tories were at an insuperable disadvantage numerically and politically. Moreover, the Derby ministry disappointed him by its performance, as when it continued Palmerston's pro-Turkish and -Austrian stance in Rumania. He rejected Graham's advice in May to accept the Tories' latest overture, since temperamentally he belonged to them and 'your honest liberal tendencies would soon leaven the whole lump'.[34] Gladstone answered that 'his predominating political sympathies' were not with the Tories; nor did he see 'hope of my being able so to use that party as...to work greater public good'.[35] From May 1858 Gladstone's course took him towards Liberalism, if this was far from clear to contemporaries. The obstacle of Palmerston lay in his path. He tried to pretend it was not there; the ex-premier's ability to command the House, he told Robertson in June, had 'well nigh gone'.[36] He actually thought otherwise. The October issue of the *Quarterly Review* carried another fierce attack on Palmerston's record at the head of government: 'his stock-in-trade as a Peace Minister was... nearly null'.[37] 'His antipathy to Palmerston has become a sort of mania', remarked Lewis to Abraham Hayward, a correspondent licensed to spread political opinions through Society. 'It is quite ludicrous...to talk of Palmerston's ignorance of domestic questions.' In his diary Lewis noted Gladstone's seeming implacability: 'The election of 1857 is an inexpiable offence'.[38] He mistook the underlying purpose of these anonymous articles, which might as well have been signed, supposing them meant to pave the way for the author's reception into the Tory ministry.

Gladstone became ever more uncomfortably aware of his isolation. When he agreed to go to the Ionian Islands, it was a temporary escape from his predicament;[39] he was determined to be back in England for the Parliamentary trial of the Tory government's reform proposals, on which its fate would depend. On his return, the uncertainty resumed. While Gladstone took the ministerial side over reform, Graham worked for the restoration of a Liberal government. The general election of April–May

1859 convinced the latter that Palmerston could not be kept out of office. He so far overcame his notorious dislike of the lately deposed prime minister as to prepare Russell for acceptance of second place to his rival.[40] Gladstone owed a great deal to the loyalty of his Peelite friends, for unlike them he insisted on having it both ways during the period between his reappearance in Parliament and joining Palmerston's cabinet. He supported Derby in the division on reform in March that led to a dissolution, and in the vote of confidence in June. Meanwhile, he advocated privately a coalition between Derby and Palmerston as 'the only chance of a strong government', in which he would serve. However, he stipulated for the removal of Disraeli and Malmesbury from the leadership of the Commons and from the Foreign Office, respectively.[41] These were impossible requirements. He seems to have believed that Palmerston might be more easily controlled at the head of or within such a ministry. At the same time, he let it be known how strongly he disapproved of the Tory dissolution as premature, unconstitutional and dangerously irresponsible in the state of Europe. He was quite ready to vote in favour of censuring ministers on that score.

He was more consistent than many people thought: a 'good' and 'strong' administration was what he desired for the country and for the utilization of his own talents, and he waited on the emergence of the best and strongest to be had. He fully endorsed Palmerston's construction of the new ministry on the broadest basis compatible with liberal sympathies. He cared as little for Bright's radicalism as Palmerston did: '...what would agreeably surprise me' he had remarked of Bright in 1856, 'would be his showing any sort of attachment to our institutions on their monarchical and antique side'.[42] The explicit commitment of Cobden, if not of Bright, to the second Palmerston cabinet, through Milner Gibson's inclusion in it, was especially welcome to Gladstone and the Peelites. Graham had been active in securing their involvement.[43] The Peelites' apparently excessive representation in the new cabinet with five places, or six counting Argyll, out of sixteen, recognized both their individual quality and their acceptability to the other elements – Palmerstonians, Russellites, Manchester men and the balance – in the government and supporting it on the backbenches. The extreme informality of the residual Peelite connection made it easier to have its members forming such a high proportion of the cabinet. Of the five, or six, Argyll, Elgin and Cardwell had all previously gone over to Palmerston, if they did not cease to be Peelite at heart. Herbert and Newcastle would have joined without Gladstone. Palmerston, however, meant to enlist Gladstone, though not to give him the Treasury; for with him the government that was taking shape would be 'strong enough'.[44] At Gladstone's house on 26 May, Palmerston shook hands with R. J. Phillimore for the first time since the latter opposed him over China in 1857, a small sign of the impending realignment in politics. Phillimore's preference was Gladstone's, for the Derby–Palmerston solution; he did not like the idea of 'a new sort of Aberdeen government', Peelite dominated, resented by Whigs and Liberals on whose votes it would rely, and the object of Tory rancour.[45]

But Palmerston was not Aberdeen, and the representative radical in his cabinet, Milner Gibson, carried much more weight than Sir William Molesworth, an aristocratic and dated exponent of 'philosophic' radicalism had done in the Aberdeen and first Palmerston cabinets. The formation of this government saw the final absorption of the Peelites but it also vindicated Gladstone's claims for their abilities. While they might not be popular, they enjoyed the regard of informed opinion and, more grudgingly, of the House of Commons. A Peelite restoration, such as Phillimore feared, would not have been tolerated by the House or the public. Half a dozen Peelites in the cabinet, running their departments efficiently and separately, showing no wish or tendency to be a clique, but quite the reverse, were a different proposition, and an attractive one. For their part, the Peelites learnt not to pit an essentially Parliamentary strength against the sentiments of large constituencies which looked to Palmerston or Derby: 'it is no very cheerful prospect' wrote Graham, 'but if South Lancashire…Leeds and Kent will have it so, there is no alternative'.[46] Once they had entered, or re-entered, his cabinet, Palmerston gave them no cause to leave or to combine within it, thus isolating Gladstone. Remaining true to the spirit of Peelism, as described by Argyll, they did not encourage, although they acquiesced in, the systematic courtship of the enfranchised and politically conscious by both Palmerston and Gladstone, who adopted methods they deplored. To almost all the rest, as formerly to Gladstone, *public* opinion was suspect. In the same spirit, with the partial exception of Argyll, they did not take Gladstone's side in his budgetary battles of the sixties with the prime minister.

Radicals

At one end of Parliamentary radicalism stood C. P. Villiers, whose durable reputation as a radical derived from his participation in the anti-Corn Law agitation, and whose real politics were the same as his brother Clarendon's. At the other end were Cobden and Bright with a few trusted associates, the Manchester men of legend. In between came an assortment of individuals with some title to the name of radical. Mostly, they had no fundamental objection to landed government, but concentrated on specific weaknesses in its constitution and policies. Among their considerable figures, Layard served as Parliamentary under-secretary at the Foreign Office during the last days of the first Russell ministry in 1852, and held the post again under Palmerston from 1861. In the interval, he had been a leading critic of what he alleged was the systematic incompetence in the Army and civil service exposed by the Crimean war; and, while out of the House in 1857-60, had occupied himself with the foundation of the Ottoman Bank. J. A. Roebuck professed a sturdy impatience with aristocracy in general, which marked him off from Layard. His aggressive nationalism, however, set him apart from Cobden and Bright. Roebuck also had business interests that influenced him politically, in Austrian railways. Such radicals had a lot less in common with Cobden and Bright than with Liberals like the land- and coal-owning H. A. Bruce, a friend of Layard and prominent in the affairs of the Ottoman Bank, or G. J. Goschen, of the bankers Frühling and Goschen and member for the City, who said when seconding the Address in 1864: 'every country in Europe, America and even Africa has become tributary to our exchange'.[47] Radicals who were primarily representatives of Dissent also ranged from the advanced – Miall of the Liberation Society – to Baines of the *Leeds Mercury*, a convert to Palmerstonian Liberalism. There were, it should not be forgotten, scholars, soldiers, and the occasional man of exalted social rank – like Admiral Sir Charles Napier, General Sir De Lacy Evans, and Lord Goderich, heir to two earldoms – to whom the term 'radical' applied. There was no radical 'party', apart from Cobden, Bright, and a very few of their associates, who, according to Cobden in 1857, might be reckoned on his fingers.[48]

After the 1859 election, Graham put Bright's following – Cobden being absent in America – at thirty-five, but this figure comprised the supporters of a radical reform bill who did not agree with the Manchester men on other questions.[49] Hoping for a Russell premiership, Bright and Milner Gibson settled for Palmerston. Bright's diary lays bare his motives as he and Milner Gibson concluded the arrangements behind his appearance at Willis's Rooms on 6 June in the cause of Liberal unity. He tried unsuccessfully to stiffen Russell in his wavering resolve not to serve under Palmerston unless the prime minister went to the Lords and left him to lead the Commons. When he correctly foresaw that neither of the two cabinet places expected for his group would go to him, he was incensed: 'Blind fools!... this gang of aristocratic conspirators...' 'Whether we can break it up is not... certain', he added lamely.[50] The day after this entry he spoke as planned at Willis's Rooms, temperately requesting more attention to the opinions of radicals in future, and 'this – that all sections of the Liberal party should be fairly represented in the cabinet'.[51] A suggestion that he, Cobden and Milner Gibson should endeavour to obtain three seats in the cabinet 'as only a moderate representation' of their influence reflected alarm at his personal isolation. Gibson not only went in without him, but conveyed the unflattering message that ministers had 'something' in mind to console him – evidently a Privy Councillorship to which the Court objected.[52] Although, on returning from America, Cobden did not accept

Palmerston's offer, he completed Bright's rout by giving the prime minister a pledge to support the cabinet 'whilst Mr Gibson is in it, who represents identically my views, as I should if I were one of your government'.[53] Charles Gilpin, a staunch Quaker disciple of Cobden and Bright, became junior minister at the Poor Law Board under C. P. Villiers. Samuel Laing, according to Shaftesbury 'the chief of unsuccessful speculators', who had belonged to the 'Peace Party' became financial secretary to the Treasury.[54] *Dod* for 1860 listed the cabinet as 'Liberals', inclusive of Villiers and Gibson, or 'Liberal-Conservatives', the latter being the ex-Peelites, less Argyll. However much Cobden and Bright regretted having helped Palmerston back into office, they had been drawn into a more unified Liberal party than had hitherto existed. If their regrets posed a threat to the administration for at least a couple of years, they could not act to bring it down, as distinct from talking about the possibility, except at a political price sure to be high.

The cabinet-making in the early summer of 1859 was, therefore, decisive for the radicals; that is, for Cobden and Bright, who provided the measure of others' radicalism. While their altered relationship to the Liberal party fell short of the Peelites' integration, they had elicited from Palmerston an offer commensurate with their nuisance value, as he conceived it. Twice since March 1857 governments under him had been defeated on motions by the Manchester men. Neither China nor the Conspiracy to Murder Bill had been radical issues; otherwise they would not have produced a majority against the ministry. But when Tories, Peelites, dissident Whigs and Liberals ranged themselves behind the declared foes of aristocracy, they were tacitly expressing a belief in these radicals' special ability to sway public opinion. Bright's conviction that sooner rather than later his and Cobden's middle-class radicalism would put an end to the anomaly of aristocratic primacy was not seriously shaken, even by his electoral humiliation in 1857, until the undeniable disappointment of the campaign for Parliamentary reform in 1858-59. His angry confidence impressed MPs, especially after Palmerston's fall and the sudden eclipse of his popularity. Cobden, who had never been as confident, did not read too much into those developments. He told his friend and follower, W. S. Lindsay MP, in March 1858 that in the 1830s 'there seemed some hope of the middle-class setting up for themselves...now there is no such sign...'[55] By 1862 all he could say to another trusted correspondent was: 'I wish we could inspire the mercantile manufacturing interest with a little more self-respect...we have long passed the time when the prosperity of this country depended on its land...yet how little share this all-important interest claims in the government...'[56] He was unable to see any way forward so long as export-led profits continued to rise and kept businessmen from taking up politics in earnest. Nor did he fail to realize how this affected his own school and their power for change. He had been glad when Chartism succumbed to economic recovery and advance but perceived that 'radicals have been by the same process lulled into supineness, and Whiggery...into something hardly so good as Toryism'. There would be no reversal of the political trend without a major recession, 'from which Heaven defend us'.[57]

Bright's outlook was narrower and more partisan; that, in his heyday, of an intensely political animal. He thought with Cobden that Derby was preferable to Palmerston, but not for quite the same reasons. Cobden and Bright persisted in referring in their correspondence to 'the Palmerston imposture', on the assumption that he could not be anything but cynical in usurping the appeal, rhetorical and real, to a popular verdict which they regarded as their prerogative.[58] His reception in Manchester's new Free Trade Hall, commemorating the Anti-Corn Law League, during the Northern speech-making of November 1856 pained Bright: 'It is odd that Palmerston should have a glorification in it, before you *and* I have made an appearance on its platform!' he complained. It was also typical of both men that they should – privately – accuse Manchester's civic and business leaders of behaving like 'flunkeys as usual' to the prime minister.[59] Where Cobden and Bright did not think alike on the subject of Palmerston after the electoral experience of 1857 was in their estimates of what he had managed to do. Cobden believed Palmerston must soon regain the office he lost next year, but that it made little difference whether he or someone else now headed a supposedly Liberal government of 'half a dozen great families', so he maintained with Disraeli, to which industrial and commercial Britain relegated the conduct of national affairs 'when trade is prosperous and people are busy making money'.[60] Bright jibbed at paying the fallen minister the compliment of seeing him as having stabilized the political situation to that extent. He would not listen to Cobden's warning that 'the "popular" party have no grievance against Court, government, or aristocracy...The Reform Club is more responsible than the Horse Guards or the Carlton for...war and the...increase of our warlike establishments.' Were there, he asked, twenty radical MPs who shared Bright's views?[61] The materials existed in and out of the House, Bright contended in reply, for independent action against the old parties. With Cobden off the scene, and Gladstone the preserver of 'Oxford and tradition', there was 'no one to speak with any authority to the multitude', except Bright himself.[62]

The Derby ministry's intention of legislating on Parliamentary reform dictated Bright's initiative; he started an agitation for a radical bill to drive the government into abandoning or enlarging its rumoured proposals. His speeches had the additional, and not less important, purpose of checking Palmerston's political rehabilitation by endeavouring to discredit his foreign and imperial policies. Cobden felt he ought not to let Bright engage

Palmerston alone, but he shrank from the certainty of 'failure and rejection'. 'I consider that we as a nation', he confessed, 'are little better than brigands, murderers, and poisoners in our dealings at this moment with half the population of the globe – I would not care to take the "stump" and tell the people as much.... *Why should I do so?*'[63] The suppression of the Indian Mutiny and the war with China were too popular. Bright appreciated that he had an unequal fight on his hands. At the beginning of his campaign, he condemned the 'depraved, unhappy state of opinion' in Britain on the morality of overseas expansion, instancing the pressure from Chambers of Commerce that risked 'merciless and disgraceful wars'.[64] He had assured Cobden that he would be 'very moderate' in his speeches, and refrain from attacking named politicians:[65] but he unmistakably and repeatedly went for Palmerston. Referring to the 'Opium War' of 1839–42 as the origin of the recent Anglo-Chinese hostilities, he said: 'No man, I believe, with a spark of morality... no man who cares anything for the opinion of his fellow-countrymen, has dared to justify that war', which Palmerston had not been afraid to do. Bright dwelt on the setbacks to Palmerstonian policy in Europe, America and, not least, India, where in annexing Oudh 'we committed a great immorality and a great crime, and we have reaped an almost instantaneous retribution in the most gigantic and sanguinary revolt which probably any nation ever made against its conquerors'. Besides, the value of empire, territorial or merely commercial, was a delusion: 'the opening of markets, developing of new countries, introducing cotton cloth with cannon balls, are vain, foolish, and wretched excuses for war...'.[66] The obvious feature of these comprehensive speeches was defiance, of Derby as well as of Palmerston. His outline of a Reform bill did not go too far in a radical direction; the extension of the municipal ratepayer franchise to Parliamentary elections and the ballot were balanced by a £10 occupier qualification in the counties and a redistribution of seats, 'the very soul of... reform', not very different from that put forward by *The Times*. But he offered this package in a spirit calculated to excite strong antagonism as the continuation of 'a steady and perpetual war against the predominance and the power of the country gentlemen in Parliament'. The Established Church, the House of Lords and the Whig magnates also came under his lash.[67]

By giving such general offence, Bright virtually delivered himself to his opponents. When he saw James Wilson MP in December, well before the end of his campaign, he complained of having been sadly misrepresented. He succeeded in persuading Wilson, at any rate, that he had not meant what he said. '...he was carried away much further than he intended', Wilson informed Lewis, relaying Bright's anxiety to see the Tories turned out, his realization that it would be difficult to construct a Liberal ministry without the 'co-operation' of Palmerston and Russell, and his notion of the ductile Granville for premier.[68] It is quite clear from Bright's correspondence with Cobden that he had not been misrepresented or 'carried away'. The disappointing impact of his speeches at Birmingham and Edinburgh prompted his approach to Wilson. At Birmingham his furious attack on British diplomacy and the expenditure it entailed as 'a gigantic system of out-door relief for the aristocracy' had been met with 'great laughter'.[69] Wilson thought the crowded audience at Edinburgh attended principally from curiosity. What was more, the editor of the *Scotsman* had never had so many requests, before and after the speech, from people with seats on the platform to have their names left out of the published list of those so favoured.[70] These were the local '*influentials*' whose reaction had earlier seemed very promising.[71] Yet at Glasgow only days later Bright spoke in the same strain, missing, as Lewis foresaw, 'the right chord'.[72] He appealed for the union of middle and working classes to end the monopoly of government by 'a few families who enjoy all the emoluments and all the power', and to change the laws promoting concentrated landownership with 'the most pernicious consequences' for society.[73] Cobden had no stomach for, and no belief in the viability of Bright's direct appeal to the working class. 'There is more likelihood of a strike for [higher] wages throughout your district next spring than a rising for Parliamentary reform', he wrote on reading the provocative language at Glasgow. He was equally discouraging about redistribution, which Bright emphasized from the outset. Radical MPs like George Moffatt, a friend of Cobden, would find common ground with Tories in defence of their small boroughs: 'These are not times for carrying a disfranchising schedule through the House.'[74]

Bright, however, was convinced of having made a greater and more positive impression on politicians and the public. He sought an interview with Russell to propose working together on reform; despite the freshness of his animadversions on Whig dynasts, he always tended to discount the personal feelings of those whom he assailed. Russell described what passed: 'I could not help telling hem that if he had brought out his plan without its supposed levelling effects, he would not have created a quarter of the alarm he has done by his speeches...it would destroy all my influence with...the sane part of the community if I were supposed to have any connexion with his views and projects...' He liked Bright's candour, as well he might, since the circumstances of this application to him and the negative answer it was safe to return enabled the leadership of Whigs and Liberals to negotiate with radicalism from a position of strength.[75] After hearing from Russell, Lewis advised him not to leave Bright out of account in formulating a response to the Tory bill about to be revealed; for he agreed with Bright that 'some additional power' should be secured to business in its urban centres and provision made for a consequent, limited disfranchisement of small boroughs. 'But', Lewis was careful to say, 'because we are prepared to give him an inch, he must not take an ell.' The advice to treat Bright constructively in the hour of his discomfiture by public opinion, chiefly 'either indifferent or disapproving' did not move Russell, to whom the radical's scheme of reform appeared 'a complete subversion of the landed interest'.[76] As Palmerston was well pleased to observe, the general condemnation of Bright propelled Russell towards his old friends of the last government. Not quite fairly, but understandably, he remarked that 'the danger seen by Johnny lies not in Bright's subversive doctrines and republican aims but in his isolated position'. Palmerston reaped the reward of consistency in his attitude to a man 'who has now openly avowed those sentiments by which I have long seen that he is actuated, hatred of everything which forms the substance of our institutions...'.[77]

Wood, the loyal Palmerstonian to whom this letter was addressed, held that Bright had his price, and would have been tamed by office long ago: but he was not disposed to underestimate him. Throughout the industrial districts, wrote Wood, drawing on his experience of representing Halifax, there was 'a small but active' element that sympathized with Bright: 'they afford very serious matter for consideration to the leaders of the liberal party'. This element would nevertheless rally to a Liberal administration, but in its continued absence and with the party's leadership divided, they would grow much wilder. If the existing Liberal leaders did not resolve their differences, keep the party together, and guide it, a new one would probably emerge in due course which 'most of us old stagers' could not support.[78] Palmerston and Russell declined to accommodate Bright in the way suggested by Lewis: they heeded Wood's urgent advice to reunite against him, and they broke up his group as he hoped to break up the party. The reaction to his ideas of reform perhaps did more than anything else to unify the Liberals on a lasting basis. On 4 March when the contents of the Tory bill were known, Bright called on Russell to threaten him with the disruption of the party and the emergence of another within the year unless he got an endorsement of the ballot and a reduction of the £10 borough franchise to £4. To obtain these demands 'would give him all the rest', meaning that they would rapidly erode deference and compel redistribution. '...without a new policy', he told Russell, 'it was useless to take the government.'[79] Meeting shortly afterwards, Palmerston and Russell reached partial agreement on a minimum figure, and not a new one, half as high again for the vital borough franchise; enough to undercut the Tories on that point, without subverting, it was hoped, their very modest redistribution, which the two Whig statesmen wished to adopt. Whether £6, either rating or rental, or £8 rental should be the actual choice remained open between them.[80]

It had been thought that the Derby ministry stood to gain from Bright's verbal violence: whatever it came out with must be much more acceptable than his scheme and its presentation. The public lack of enthusiasm for the bill, and for the whole topic of reform, was a relief to all except the handful of MPs who genuinely desired change. Mild ridicule of the Tory bill predominated; Bright sounded out Wood late in March and found him treating reform 'with contempt: nobody wants Reform etc.'[81] Wood did not speak in these terms to the radical activists in Halifax, explaining to Palmerston that his advocacy of a £5 borough franchise on the hustings in April was personal and indeed local, designed to ensure an united Liberal vote, the precondition in the constituency and nationally of the party's victory. He was afraid lest Palmerston should commit himself similarly to a definite amount for the borough franchise, 'which might lead to the lower half of the party pledging themselves against your lead and thus rendering a strong liberal government impossible...'. There would have been little danger of a revolt if Palmerston had been more specific: but Wood wanted to eliminate the risk of its complicating the movement towards him for premier as a result of events in Europe. 'War and Peace have...entirely superseded Reform...There is no difference of opinion hereabouts as to displacing the...government...' was how he summarized the mood in all sections of the party in Yorkshire on 1 May, when he stated the urgency of 'compounding' a prospective Liberal administration before hesitation and rivalry supervened.[82] He and his radical colleague at Halifax, the younger James Stansfeld, used the developing European crisis to tell their constituents that foreign policy had to receive priority over reform, and that, with regard to the second question, 'those who entertain extreme views must give way'.[83]

In the election called by the Tories on the Commons' rejection of their unchanged £10 borough franchise, Bright attempted to build up Russell at Palmerston's expense. He depicted Palmerston as 'an eminent and aged statesman...leader of a small section in the House...latterly prime minister...I have never had...any kind of faith in the politics of Lord Palmerston'. He contrasted him with Russell who was willing to broaden the scope of the £6 figure by calculating it with reference to rental instead of rating, and whose supporters, he alleged, were more numerous. He could not suppress a note of high patronage when mentioning Russell, as at Rochdale: 'He was not born down there [but]...in a ducal palace...I say we must make allowance for him if he does not march quite at the speed which...all of us would wish.'[84] The issue of reform did not flourish in the early stages of the election. It weakened in the deepening shadow of war. 'They had one great question before them', he said at Birmingham on 23 April, '...a...struggle which...might end in bringing upon us discontent, disorder, and something approaching even to anarchy'. When his class fears came to the surface, the time was not propitious for expanding the electorate. His insistence on neutrality in 1859 took some more of the radicalism out of his posture; he was at one with Whigs and Liberals. The simultaneous deprecation of a well-armed neutrality, on the contrary, seemed doctrinaire folly. 'Do we require vast armies and...navies?' he asked at the end of April: cries of 'Yes' rose from a Birmingham audience.[85] Nothing was more expressive of Bright's accelerating political decline than Milner Gibson's speech on his unopposed return for Ashton-under-Lyne. Ranking next to Cobden and Bright among the Manchester men, he had never embraced their isolationism without reserve. He had already begun to separate himself from Bright upon reform in December by announcing that 'he would not be deterred from supporting a moderate measure, because it might not come up to...abstract theories of...the suffrage, being in the main what everybody...whether Tory or Liberal, must in his conscience hold'. In April he upheld a Palmerstonian concept of neutrality: 'He was not a peace-at-any-price man...war might be necessary...he was for such a...policy as maintained the dignity and independence of his own country, and...friendly relations with all other states'. As for reform, he alluded shortly to 'a more adequate representation of the entire people'.[86] After this speech, Russell thought him a distinctly good selection for a cabinet post.[87]

Milner Gibson defended the acceptance of office under Palmerston, of whose claim to head the party again he had previously been dismissive. He employed the arguments by which Palmerston had, without much trouble, won over his group: '...it is of no use to complain of governments being exclusive and aristocratic if when they open the door you won't enter...It is said...there have been great differences between Lord Palmerston and myself...Well, suppose there have been...It is the best government that can be formed out of the Liberal party at the moment.' The administration had been put together with the danger from the Continent in mind: 'a question far above all questions of internal reform', and especially menacing to an industrial town like Ashton-under-Lyne, vulnerable to the dislocation of its markets by a general conflict. To still continuing local criticism, he came back to the subject on his next visit and reinterpreted the past four years without apology: 'I am rather sick myself of governments, representing great parties, being broken up by mere dissensions and divisions, not upon...principle...' The differences that did exist with the cabinet were only 'matters of degree'; he did not believe they would turn into something more serious.[88] If Gibson's remarks did not destroy the credibility of his type of radicalism, they were bound to diminish its capacity to inspire the apprehension which Cobden and Bright exploited to make up for their weakness in other ways. *The Times* commented mockingly on the second speech: 'There is not one syllable...that would lead an old lady to put down her tea cup and appeal to the higher powers...'[89] Cobden

and Bright reflected that they had legitimate expectations of the ministry
to which they had palpably submitted. Bright awaited the outcome of the
promised instalment of reform, a Whig bill but better than nothing. The
negotiation of the Anglo-French treaty in 1859-60 absorbed Cobden for the
rest of the government's first year, and gave him a strong motive to ensure
its survival.

Cobden, Bright, and the Liberal government

Gladstone's financial legislation of 1860 embodied the Anglo-French
treaty; but Russell allowed the reform bill, which was peculiarly his, to die
in February 1861. With the treaty safe, and the bill clearly lost at the close
of the preceding session, Cobden and Bright began to think of encompassing
Palmerston's overthrow, and explored the possibility of Tory co-operation.
No help was then forthcoming from that quarter, and little from anywhere
else. 'It seemed towards the end of the discussion on reform', wrote
Cobden, 'that Bright was actually the only man who had anything to say
in its favour. What is the secret of men like Roebuck, Duncombe, &c.
taking no part in the matter?'[90] The answer lay in the breadth of
Palmerstonian Liberalism and its attentiveness to public opinion, which
compensated for its lukewarmness towards reform. Government policy in
the fields of religion; diplomacy; finance and the economy; empire – formal
and informal – satisfied too many of the radicals with special interests in
one or more of these areas. The possession of office by undisputed radicals,
and their continuing promotion to it, further detracted from the efforts of
Cobden and Bright to revive anti-Palmerstonian radicalism. Although not
one of their group, Layard re-entered Parliament in 1860 as avowedly
'what was called a radical' for a large metropolitan constituency with a
liking for radical sentiments. He combined 'the highest respect for Lord
Palmerston' with pleasure at the inclusion in his ministry of 'some
distinguished radicals', and specifically of Milner Gibson. He warmly
approved, as did his Southwark meetings, of Palmerston's foreign and
imperial record. At home he contended for the ballot, and the eventual
admission to the electorate of 'that large body of intelligent working-
men...now unjustly excluded'.[91] His appointment in April 1861 to be the
newly ennobled Russell's Parliamentary under-secretary and the Foreign
Office spokesman in the Commons, a step taken in the face of the Court's
strenuous objections, testified to the prime minister's determination to
build, very selectively, on the success of the experiment with Milner Gibson
and others. Palmerston told the Queen that Layard was 'of great
importance to the strength and stability of your...government'.[92]

James Stansfeld, junior, made civil lord of the Admiralty in April 1863,
was a radical justifying his move away from Cobden and Bright by
describing it to his electors at Halifax as an offer which it would have been
'moral cowardice' to refuse, 'when made to you explicitly as one of the

representatives of advanced Liberalism'. He established a reputation in 1862 by his motion for economy which Palmerston accepted in principle. Previous Liberal ministries deprived radicals of their identity by giving them office, but not Palmerston's, Stansfeld argued at Halifax: '...it was necessary for the advanced Liberals in their notions of policy to progress with the times. It was no longer a question of independence or of what... were too often futile pursuits....[but] of claiming their due share in the supreme management of affairs and in controlling the destiny of this country.'[93] The grandiloquent account of what his modest promotion signified was a good example of how eager most Parliamentary radicals were to go far more than halfway towards Palmerston if his policies made room for them. The policies were decisive: it was not enough to hand out minor, or cabinet, office. In his recommendation of Stansfeld, Wood pronounced him no radical in domestic politics, 'no democrat in any sense...'. His incongruous, if hardly exceptional, friendship for revolutionary liberalism and nationalism on the Continent should therefore be advantageous and without risk to a government that wished to bind radicals to it. 'He is in my opinion none the worse for the foreign radicalism', concluded Wood.[94] In the event, his old association with Mazzini gave the Tories a chance to force Stansfeld's resignation next year. Palmerston fought hard to save him and beat off by ten votes the opposition's endeavour to censure his past implication, however unwitting, in Mazzini's conspiratorial activities. The margin was too small in the circumstances. Stansfeld resigned in view of the disquiet persisting on the Liberal benches, where the episode fed a nervous mistrust of the government's relationship with radicalism. Palmerston could not find a replacement for a valuable ministerial link between his ministry and the radicals. 'Stansfeld's going loosens the connexion and is a great evil in that point', observed Wood.[95]

It was not easy to discover middle-class radicals with administrative ability matching that of the aristocratic and gentry politicians who perpetuated the leadership of their class. The former did not have the same hereditary experience of ruling at every level from the country magistracy upwards. The three radicals who did best and lasted longest under Palmerston had similar origins to those of their Whig and Liberal contemporaries in office: Villiers was brother to an earl, Milner Gibson a sometime Tory MP, and Layard the son of a Ceylon civil servant. They kept up with the radicals outside the government, so that the loss of Stansfeld was less serious than feared. Villiers's correspondence with Bright shows the minister consulting him and seeking to present the government favourably when the reform bill of 1860 was being discussed in a cabinet committee, 'as I am actively desirous if possible that you should not be estranged from us'. He tried to assure Bright of the cabinet's sincerity: 'there has been no sign of prejudice or sinister purpose...'. Villiers did not let him forget that ministers read the real opinion of the middle-classes differently, knowing this to be the weak point in all Bright's demands. '...the social relations between classes are more than usually friendly', Villiers reminded him. 'It is quite clear...there is nothing in the popular principle in England, as its development proceeds, that is at all subversive, I might say even democratic in character.' This was not what Bright wanted to hear, but it was true. Villiers rubbed in another truth, still more unpalatable. The prevalence of authoritarian regimes in the major European states and the troubles of American democracy left Britain 'after all...the freest...wealthiest...most orderly and progressive nation on the earth'. The country's refusal to be stirred up by all the talk of reform proceeded from rational causes, and not from the apathy and backwardness to which Bright ascribed it. Villiers invited him to submit 'your real and *calmly considered* views' on reform.[96]

On this topic, Milner Gibson had much less to say, and said it more concisely. 'My own *private* opinion', he informed Bright ahead of Russell's decision not to reintroduce his bill of 1860, was that the House and the public would not allow government to carry 'anything worth having'.[97] He rested quite happily on the principle stated in one of his Ashton-under-Lyne speeches in June 1859: 'the action of all governments must be controlled for evil as for good by the voice of public opinion'.[98] Bright nevertheless wondered at his willing compliance with ministerial policy in this and most respects, and finished by labelling him a Whig.[99] The two men did not, however, end their friendship. When Bright alluded to 'the *secret* cabinet of which you are not a member' in the context of the Anglo-American crisis over the *Trent* affair, Milner Gibson patiently replied that '*we*', the united cabinet, had been 'moderate and reasonable'.[100] On the subject of intervention in the Civil War, he sought to persuade Bright, with a trace of weariness, that *The Times* and other London newspapers did not speak for the government; and to defend Russell's handling of the question: 'he is far better than you fancy'.[101] He and Bright were in touch and on the same side, together with almost all the cabinet, over Schleswig-Holstein in 1864. Again, when the election year of 1865 opened, Milner Gibson sent his old leader a delightfully worded request: 'office seems to have caused a vacuity in my mind...*I wish you would give me a little hint* of the right thing to say at this time. I am serious.'[102] The speech he delivered at Ashton-under-Lyne afterwards renewed the handsome tribute that he had paid, since going to the Board of Trade, to Cobden's influence on the liberalization of Britain's overseas commerce; and wound up by restating his cautious beliefs as a Parliamentary reformer: 'He should be glad to see...such a measure as would, at least, have the effect, to a certain extent, of extending the political power of...unenfranchised working industry...' Had those possessing the vote applied the requisite pressure five years earlier, he remarked, the government would not have dared withstand it.[103] Although Gibson was treading in Gladstone's footsteps rather than Bright's, and dissociating himself from any incitement of the voteless mass, this passage, spoken after consulting Bright, sounded conciliatory. Conciliation was advisable to restrain the most eloquent of radicals from making more speeches in the vein of those he had made about the ministry, starting before his fury at the dropping of reform.

'Draw it mild', Villiers entreated Bright in January 1860, disturbed by his rhetoric: 'I say ... we should all march together and not ... divide society into hostile classes believing that causes for permanent antagonism exist.'[104] Bright denied in and out of the Commons that he had any desire to transform politics by fostering class conflict. During his campaign of 1858-59 he said that he wished it were possible to dispense with the terminology of class. 'I profess to be, in intention, as conservative as you', he said to an unfriendly but listening House in the subsequent debates on the Tory reform bill.[105] He was indeed conservative where property-rights were concerned. The conception of 'free trade in land' affected only the legal presumption of primogeniture and the power of entail. Yet the language in which he proposed this method of fragmenting the economic basis of aristocracy seemed to imply that he contemplated more drastic action. Both the respect for property and the animosity against landed pre-eminence were real, if the latter was to lose its edge when he sat in Gladstone's cabinets. He felt his exclusion from Palmerston's government more, and not less, as it survived and prospered; despite his objections to the policies which inspired recurrent, hopeful speculation that its days were numbered. Extreme though his attacks on the ministry sometimes were, after June 1859 they had little effect on the party. Whatever approaches he and Cobden subsequently made to the Tories, they would not have been able to contribute to the suggested alliance anything like the thirty-five MPs reckoned to sympathize with them on reform following the election. With the 'amalgamating' of the party, it was harder for so few to break away. Complaining to Disraeli in March 1861, Bright described himself as 'duped ... and ... alone, of all the prominent Liberals' who aspired to office, in being left out.[106] Cobden's dissatisfaction with the ministry related entirely to policy. He and Bright vented their frustrations and worked to radicalize Liberals in the constituencies against the trend fostered by Palmerston and Gladstone in speeches across the country. Villiers expostulated with Bright. 'Do not for *your own sake be anti-national*', he implored him during the *Trent* crisis, and then, the advice disregarded, strongly admonished him that to suppose Palmerston wished for war to ensure the continuation of his ministry was '*ludicrously malignant*'.[107] Quite unused to being addressed with such candour by associates careful of his notorious sensitivity, Bright was shocked into an infuriated answer: 'I never received a similar one from you', wrote Villiers, who returned to the theme of Palmerston's 'good temper and moderation' in cabinet. The prime minister did not like Americans but his loathing of slavery biased him against the South, Villiers told the fervently pro-Northern Bright. He also put the case for ministerial distrust of Napoleon with a similar mixture of vigour and reasonableness.[108]

Cobden did not differ from Milner Gibson and Villiers in that he too considered the political nation, at all levels, to be little interested in reform, and chauvinistic. Unlike them, he minded this condition of things very much: 'I wonder the working people are so quiet...Have they no Spartacus among them to lead a revolt of the slave class...?' he inquired of his friend, the Manchester businessman William Hargreaves.[109] The comparison of the British working class to the slaves of ancient Rome might have been preposterous: it did convey his moral revulsion from the unnatural submissiveness, as he saw it, of the people to social prestige and wealth. Feeling like this, Cobden was defeatist when he looked at the prospects of change. Agitating for Parliamentary reform was actually counter-productive 'by frightening a large part of the capitalist class into the arms of political conservatism'. There was no remedy for the domination of 'the feudal classes'. 'The misfortune for you and me', he wanted Bright to understand, 'is that the most potent section of the *middle class* is more inclined to see these matters through *their* medium than *ours*.' He was temporarily roused by the government's expenditure on fortifications to meet the contingency of a French assault upon Britain, exclaiming to Bright: 'I will only hold my seat in Parliament on the condition of being committed to the task of preventing the future existence of such a cabinet as the present.'[110] Cobden's disaffection from the society in which, paradoxically, he enjoyed an esteem not shared by Bright made him unusually sympathetic to Napoleon III's France, where 'an Emperor... dines with corporals and privates...millions...are landowners...every man of 21 has a vote...all sects are on a perfect equality and paid alike... primogeniture is abolished, &c., &c.'[111] He knew very well from negotiating the Anglo-French treaty how authoritarian the Bonapartist regime was; but the degree of propertied democracy achieved was as impressive to him as political liberty. Furthermore, increased defence expenditure devalued the treaty of which he cherished such hopes, as the best security to be had for peace and economy.

His resolution to take on Palmerston's government in open warfare cooled as he reviewed the obstacles in his path. There was Gladstone, who failed to resign over the fortifications. While being 'at heart a democrat of the purest type (I mean in his desire to serve the interests of the millions, not of a class)' – a conveniently broad definition of a democrat – Gladstone 'tried to serve God and Mammon', and contrived to please both masters too successfully.[112] There was Gibson: 'What are *we* to do? It is hard that he should be the buffer to prevent our hitting his chief as he deserves', asked Cobden in perplexity after eighteen months of casting about for ways – his basic pessimism notwithstanding – 'to convince the middle class that to allow Lord John or Lord Palmerston or the Dukes and Lords...in office to rule...is...against the interests of the industrial classes...'.[113] There was the appreciation – between spasms of optimism and indignation – of working-class political immaturity: 'The working classes may play their part hereafter', Cobden thought, 'but unless the employers are kept right now, we have no security against the combination of powerful interests...'.[114] There was, it had to be faced, very little prospect of Gladstone's agreeing to break with Palmerston, no matter what he said against him in private to Cobden and Bright. 'We have no support to offer him', wrote Cobden to Bright in October 1862. 'An invitation to adopt our views is tantamount to advising him to abandon office for the rest of his days.' The cause of their almost total impotence was the resilience of Palmerston's coalition: 'Let it be a warning to us never again to be parties to a political organization which shall profess to carry on government by...the union of all shades of opinion, from the intense aristocratic exclusiveness...of...a large majority of the cabinet, to the honest radicalism of Gibson, and the democracy of the Chancellor of the Exchequer.'[115] Coming from such a source, this was a high compliment to Palmerston's skill in rebuilding Liberalism on a surer foundation. Bright's more emotional nature exaggerated these truths. He referred to 'our friends in the government, if we have any', seeing Gibson as weak and Gladstone as calculating. Before long he had even less confidence than Cobden in the substantial middle class, predicting that its '*latent* power', when finally realized, would be inimical to their radicalism.[116] As for the working class, dependent upon the leadership of others, he did not believe it could be moved by his efforts and Cobden's. If 'some accident' were to bring down Palmerston for good, it might be 'the awakener' they sought. In the meantime, he concurred, '*we* are quite powerless...for it is...a "Liberal Ministry" among whose members is our friend Milner Gibson.' At moments he despaired: 'There is no longer politics – why the meetings, and why even members of Parliament?'[117]

Bright and Cobden, too, far outdid the Tories in criticism of the government to which their reinforced party ties bound them. They sounded a threatening note, as of old. In January 1860 Bright tried to raise the cooling temperature of politics, in a speech notable for its almost desperate boldness and the national indifference to it. He addressed a town meeting at Birmingham in support of the government reform bill, but deliberately exposed both its inadequacy and that of his own recent proposals: 'I want to ask whether England is to be the only country in which the natural and inalienable rights of Englishmen...should be denied to them? Can that

which is good in America ... Canada ... Van Diemen's Land ... the Cape ...
be evil in this country?' If manhood suffrage was the rule in English
settlements, the self-evident reason why it did not gain acceptance at home
lay in obstruction by those 'vast interests', aristocratic and warlike,
'...clinging round your Parliament...cabinet and...throne'. No friend to
trade unions, Bright acknowledged their uncomfortable strength in the
economic climate of the day, and suggested that it might be exerted more
profitably than in industrial disputes: 'Working men...can get up
formidable strikes against capital; sometimes...upon real, sometimes upon
fancy grievances...sometimes for things...impossible...I want to ask...
why it is that...these...organizations throughout the country could not be
made use of for...obtaining...political rights?' Frustration of the planned
instalment of Parliamentary reform in the coming session might be
countered, it was his express hope, by concerted trade union action. 'I
don't want for a minute to use the language of menace', he claimed
disingenuously.[118] The publicity which Bright's speeches commanded
served to advertise their lack of appeal. *The Times*'s full reports invited
comparison with the very different tone adopted by the two wealthy
Liberal businessmen who sat for Glasgow when they discussed the reform
bill that month: 'The members for that enormous borough...probably one
of the most democratic constituencies in these islands...touch the extreme
limit of moderation and conservatism.'[119]

Until the early summer of 1860 Bright continued with his attempts to
build up feeling for reform: 'Admitting the real representatives of the real
people to...the House of Commons' was the objective as he described it in
the Free Trade Hall at Manchester within the next fortnight.[120] Returning
to the same place in April, he tried to involve trade unionism again,
saying, to loud cheering, 'It has never yet been proved that trades unions...
or strikes are always bad.' He courted the unions with a more positive
statement that the strike weapon was both 'legal and moral' as a 'reserve
power', and not something he would renounce if he were a working man,
He then developed the suggestion of January that trade unionists should
organize nationally for Parliamentary reform; and advocated a delegate
conference mandated for a year to proclaim 'the opinions of the great
excluded mass', and to insist, without violence or the threat of it, on the
attainment of 'the just expectation...held out to them'.[121] By resorting to
these tactics, reminiscent of the Chartism he had feared, Bright condemned
himself to futility. He hit out wildly in reply when, in the April speech, he
called *The Times* 'Satanic'.[122] Outside Parliament, Cobden left him to fight
alone, except occasionally, for all the letters that passed between them
denouncing Palmerston and assuring each other that his ministry could not,
and should not be permitted to, last. He thought Bright was pursuing a lost
cause. While they could not give up Parliamentary reform, he told a mutual

friend, the chance to implement it came 'once in a century', when 'a generous fit' and 'great *common danger*' coincided as in 1830-32 to effect some redistribution of power.[123]

Before the next month was out, Bright had come to the support of government when the Lords saved the paper duties. Appearing before the council of the Lancashire Reform Union, he produced a depressing argument for not taking on the Lords with the weapon that had previously subdued them. A large creation of peers would not be in the wider interests of reform, 'because the commoner of today, who rises a peer tomorrow... usually becomes inflated with all those sentiments...inseparable from a privileged body...'. He approved, fulsomely, of the government's record to date, without trying to distinguish between different elements in the ministry: 'I know not when we have had a cabinet which has more honestly and fairly endeavoured to signalize its tenure of office by the benefits and advantages it has conferred...is it not our duty to stand by them?'[124] Whatever he said and wrote, Bright could not disown the government and party however fiercely he attacked aspects of Liberal policy and deplored the predominance of the landed class in and through both parties. If he was persuaded that ministers had embarked on their destruction and that of their class – '*Expenditure* will *destroy them*, and other Governments after them' – he felt obliged to warn Russell personally of the threat 'in all friendliness to the Government'.[125] He allowed, privately, that Palmerston's known opposition inside and outside the cabinet to repealing the paper duties stemmed from considerations of fiscal balance and not from obscurantism.[126] At Birmingham in January 1861 he appealed for realization of the certainty, as he viewed it, that the level of government spending must imperil the security of the throne itself.[127]

The twists and turns of Bright's political behaviour, in the open and behind the scenes, steadily reduced his credibility; while Cobden's reluctance to emulate his friend on provincial platforms, and his close association with ministers in negotiating the Anglo-French treaty and its detailed application, made him seem much less radical. The other member for Birmingham, William Scholefield, a local businessman and civic politician whose radicalism went back to the city's famous Political Union, repudiated Bright without actually naming him. 'A thorough reformer' still in advance, he said, of many citizens, he felt bound to condemn opinions which recurred in Bright's speeches: 'taking the House of Commons as it was, he could not hear anyone say that it did not fairly represent the people of England without expressing his opinion that such a statement was fallacious...no legislative assembly in the world conducted so large an amount of business...so fairly and honestly...Corruption was unknown there...he would undertake to find more corruption in the government of any other country...the despotism of...Austria, or...

republican America, in one day than could be found in the...Commons for
half a century.' The House was too conservative; it would have to accept
'great changes' in its constitution, and soon: but 'a more honourable body
of men did not exist'. He hoped to see the Commons' present character
maintained in a reformed House.[128] Scholefield did not aspire to office or
a title; his reputation in Birmingham was secure. He spoke for middle-class
radicals and Liberals confident of growing influence and well satisfied with
their country's position in the world. When Bright subsequently indited a
public letter to a Birmingham admirer, describing the Liberal party as
'enfeebled, debauched and humiliated', he exposed his own weakness,
frustration and changeableness.[129]

The radical or Liberal businessmen to whom the political future
rightfully belonged, so Cobden and Bright held, fitted comfortably into the
Palmerstonian party. Cobden mentioned half a dozen MPs from 'the
capitalist leading classes' in October and November 1861 as the nucleus of
a 'progressive' party. Neither his two personal friends among them – the
tea merchant and iron dealer Moffatt and the shipowner Lindsay, members
for Honiton and Sunderland – nor the rest – Baxter and Dalgleish, of
Dundee and Glasgow, Peto of Finsbury, and Bass, the brewer, who sat for
Derby – were nearly what he would have had them be in politics. His
complaint of Moffatt and Bass – that they let themselves be 'used' by
Palmerston – applied to all six; and, of course, to Baines, Stansfeld and
Gilpin. Cobden attributed this sore disappointment partly to irrational fear
of 'an anarchy of parties' in the national consciousness: but, as he
understood perfectly, stronger influences were at work.[130] After 1862 there
was little sign of the independent following with which Cobden and Bright
had been credited when the government was formed. When in their
Rochdale speeches of November 1863 the eminent pair indulged in more
disturbing criticism than hitherto of the landed class as such, they
discovered the extent, 'something almost incredible' of their loneliness. The
reaction made them appear, on Cobden's admission, 'impracticable
politicians...only not dangerous because nobody would have anything to
do with us'. He instanced the response of 'rich political boobies like
Crossley, good-natured weaklings like Scholefield', men who, he persisted
in thinking, should not have sided with the aristocracy.[131]

6

Toryism

Characteristics

Toryism was overrepresented in the Commons as a result of the 1832 Act and the pattern of subsequent demographic growth. It enjoyed a permanent majority of about two to one in the English and Welsh counties in the general elections of 1857, 1859, and 1865. Those proportions were inverted, or nearly so, in English and Welsh boroughs, despite the preponderance of small country towns in those seats. In Scotland the Tories did not win a single borough in 1857 or 1865, but held from two-fifths to half the county seats in the period: less than a third of all Scottish MPs. Their Irish performance, based on a relatively much smaller electorate weighted against the Celtic and Catholic population, gave the Tories from forty-four to fifty-five out of 105 members. Unless they could break the Liberals' hold on the boroughs or come close to eliminating the Whig county members of mainland Britain, the Tories had no hope of attaining power through the voters. By the early summer of 1855 they were no longer so afraid of taking on the government of a steadily more industrial and urban society, as they had been at the crisis in February. The stability and conservatism of national opinion, soon reasserted with Palmerston, emboldened them to attempt his overthrow in May and again in July. Later, in 1857, they recovered surprisingly quickly from a bad miscalculation and its electoral consequences. Yet they proved unable to evolve a set of broadly agreed policies with an appeal comparable to those of Palmerstonian Liberalism.[1]

In the first place, the association of Tories with the land and the Established Church was too restrictive. The Derby – Disraeli reform bill of 1859 did not merely try to safeguard the landed interest and rural Toryism but actually to increase their direct influence to the disadvantage of expanding urban constituencies. Nothing else would have been tolerated by the party in the Commons. As for religion, Shaftesbury encountered the active hostility of Derby himself in his efforts, so important politically and socially, to foster the mutual understanding of Church and Dissent. Another question on which the Tories presented a reactionary face was the admission of Jews to Parliament. It aroused strong feelings. 'The only thing which seemed to interest him was...the Jew Bill', wrote Lord Malmesbury in June 1857, after endeavouring to have a wide-ranging political conversation with Derby.[2] Tory anti-Catholicism was cruder, if not more intense, than that of Palmerston and his colleagues. These religious attitudes earned the party the reputation of being positively illiberal, and not just naturally resistant to change. In foreign policy insularity characterized the Tories through three wars: that of 1859 in Italy, the American Civil War, and the conflict between Denmark and the German Confederation. Unenthusiastic about the war with Russia, they were soon as apprehensive of Bonapartism as was Palmerston, but slower to recognize opportunities of reducing the tension between Britain and France where possible without subservience. The Tories felt, however, no greater sympathy with the old authoritarian regimes than did the Liberals. In the case of Italy, Malmesbury wrote to Derby of their common aversion to 'a strong *Codino* spirit...our traducers wish for nothing more than to identify us with that bigoted and unpopular set'.[3] Where the Tories differed from the Liberals was in their dislike of British interference to press constitutionalism upon countries doubtfully ready for it. A sharper difference separated the parties on the subject of empire. While anti-imperialism lost ground with the Liberal party, it remained a force in contemporary Toryism. This is only partly explicable by the minority support for the Tories in industry and commerce. They shared with the Peelites, Cobden, Bright, and some others a concern for non-European states and nations as intrinsically deserving of more respect than Whigs and Liberals generally extended to them. Before the Mutiny, Lord Ellenborough urged Canning, on his appointment to India, not to endorse the policy of absorbing native principalities in British-administered territory. Ellenborough, the Tories' spokesman on India, had been governor-general himself, and opposed the idea of a 'moral obligation not to permit the existence of a bad government within India...Depend upon it, more real security resulted from the confidence with which I inspired all princes who were faithful than I would have drawn from any annexation...' Suzerainty was the basis of Mogul rule, and the British would be unwise to discount 'an essential part of our system'.[4] China afforded a clearer instance of Tory distaste for the imperial expansion of the day. Derby deplored 'the reckless impolicy...of...war... not with a Government, but with a nation...'[5]

The great majority of Tory MPs adhered to their party because of what it stood for. The diary of Derby's son and heir, Lord Stanley, comments on the poor attendance of the Tory rank-and-file: but the Liberals were impressed by their opponents' turn out for significant votes on party lines.[6]

Tories in both Houses looked to Derby for leadership. What Malmesbury, who was no admirer of Disraeli's, called the party's 'stupid dislike' of him mattered less than it might seem to have done.[7] He was no more than Derby's lieutenant in the Commons; his authority derived entirely from his position as such. He would have liked to challenge Derby, but his unconcealed ambition in the mid 1850s failed to elicit a favourable response from any except a very few associates and his own weekly newspaper with a small circulation. Derby could safely observe with regret the extent of Disraeli's social and political isolation, which was so marked as to detract from his usefulness.[8] The Earl saw in him a competent Parliamentary technician, not an equal, and often communicated with him through Malmesbury. The latter had far more of the leader's confidence and deputized for him at need, to Disraeli's annoyance.[9] Stanley, who had been close to Disraeli, considered him a serious handicap to his party in Parliament and the country, knowing as he did that the suspicions of his old friend's integrity were well founded.[10] But Stanley was no Tory either: really a Liberal in outlook, he did not appreciate the moral strength of Toryism, which was proof against Disraeli's fondness for moves inconsistent with the party's tradition and sentiments. Derby and most of those who sat in the cabinet of 1858–59 were trusted as Disraeli was not. In the cause of helping the Tories into office, or to stay there, they were able to prepare measures which their followers did not care for, without exciting the animosity that met the leader in the Commons. The party's weakness was not so much a lack of appetite for power as consciousness of the electoral limitations dictated by the nature of Toryism. The diaries of Malmesbury and Stanley repeatedly mention the fear of a dissolution as accounting for Tory abstentions on important divisions.[11]

The Tories' habitual insecurity is central to their history in this period. When at the beginning of 1856 Bishop Wilberforce suggested to J. W. Henley, a member of the first two Derby cabinets, that Palmerston should be brought down without delay, he got the reply: 'No, social questions would rise and prevent that.'[12] The advent of peace calmed misgivings of that kind. But though the party's losses in counties and boroughs at the 1857 general election did not depress its leaders for long, the country gentlemen and others behind them did not forget a trying and, in their view, unnecessary experience which prompted many individual decisions on their part to appease the electors by proclaiming both staunch Toryism and 'an independent support' for Palmerston.[13] The Tory dissolution of 1859 made good some of the losses two years earlier; it was not a success in any other way. A man of great ability, Derby often thought he could do better than Palmerston, his cabinet colleague under Grey, having to his credit the containment of the worst Irish unrest between 1798 and 1918–21 while the Reform Act passed at Westminster. He sometimes gave the impression of not caring enough about public opinion. It was the affectation of a *grand seigneur*. Normally resident in industrial Lancashire, when Parliament was not sitting, he figured prominently in the life of the county where he owned nearly 60,000 acres, including extensive town property in and around Liverpool and lesser places. As the foremost territorial magnate in a manufacturing and trading environment, he eloquently analysed 'the happy fusion' produced, he said at Liverpool, by the rich complexity of classes and the mingling of their interests: for every man whose social status was clear, there were hundreds about whom 'two people would probably not agree whether they belonged to the higher, or higher-middle, to the lower-middle, or to the lower class'.[14] The politic exaggeration of this speech contrasted with his personal style: but it acknowledged a growing force in urban Toryism. Derby did not feel the same need to speak in the big provincial towns outside Lancashire. Disraeli preferred to address meetings in his county of Buckinghamshire, and delivered speeches tailored to rural audiences. He showed less awareness than Derby, and very much less than Derby's son Stanley, of the requirement for visits like those undertaken by Palmerston and Gladstone to industrial centres, if Toryism was to broaden its base. The character of the Parliamentary party inhibited such initiatives, and it was wanting in the self-assurance of an alternative government.

Land and Church

Lewis did not believe that the Tories could successfully launch a reform bill, as foreshadowed by Derby on taking office in 1858. 'Their reckoning will be with the gentlemen at their backs', wrote Lewis with pardonable relish of the new ministers' intention.[15] Stanley's ideal was to transform Toryism by a measure of Parliamentary reform issuing in 'a reconciliation and almost fusion of the landed with the town interest'; but he knew that was impossible to achieve: 'We cannot suppose that a... bill such as we shall pass will satisfy Manchester.'[16] At Hughenden in August 1858 he and Disraeli outlined to their own satisfaction a compromise: to disfranchise sixty to ninety seats and make the ballot optional, besides lowering the county to the level of the borough franchise, left unchanged, and introducing a variety of qualifications for plural voting. The third and fourth points were adopted by the cabinet. Stanley conceded that the second was quite unacceptable to Tories 'though in its real tendency Conservative'.[17] Redistribution ran into acute difficulties. At a late stage the prime minister was inclined to drop it. Disraeli, Pakington, Manners and other cabinet ministers in the House of Commons settled for minimal disfranchisement.[18] Stanley protested: 'It amounts to an assertion that... you see nothing to find fault with in the existing distribution of political power among the various constituencies...' He threatened resignation, but stayed; he had been beaten down in cabinet to between forty and fifty seats. Disraeli's fourteen – fifteen in the published bill – upheld 'the *status quo*... I neither think it can succeed, nor that it ought to...'[19] His father was a rather stronger advocate than Disraeli of the bill, it transpired. 'I confess I think you somewhat underrate the effect that would be produced by our failing to carry a Reform Bill', Derby told Disraeli. But everyone agreed, if not without initial reservations, on an aspect of the bill that predestined it to damaging failure. They were openly hostile to any reduction of the £10 householder franchise in the boroughs. Disraeli stated in the Commons debates on the bill that this step would undermine 'the social system'. He warned the House against 'sentimental assertions of the good qualities of the working-classes. The greater their good qualities, the greater the danger...'[20] To a leading country gentleman, Sotheron Estcourt, recently promoted to the cabinet in Spencer Walpole's place, it seemed 'a magnificent speech'.[21] Disraeli's was not the language of Palmerston or Gladstone, and it branded the Tories as reactionary.

Derby did not usually speak in these terms in Lancashire, where working-class Toryism existed in strength. The Tories in the Commons, however, knew little of industrial Britain. As it was, the cabinet lost two members, Henley and Walpole, who were particularly nervous of establishing the borough franchise in the counties.[22] Yet criticism of the bill in the House and at the subsequent general election compelled the cabinet to decide on its reintroduction with a cut in the £10 householder qualification to £6 or £8, which would have benefited the 'labour aristocrats' of whom Disraeli had so recently declared himself afraid.[23] Out of office before they could act on the decision, the Tory leadership got the worst of both worlds over reform, offending and frightening many of their backbenchers and, as Stanley predicted, very largely offsetting the political gains of the 'liberal spirit' displayed in other areas of policy.[24] The revised bill would still have retained a feature widely deemed objectionable: the removal from the county electorate of forty shilling freeholders living in Parliamentary boroughs, who were henceforth to vote there. Without the urban freeholder, the counties would be more preponderantly Tory. On the evidence furnished to the cabinet, the creation of £10 occupiers in the countryside was considered a reinforcement of rural Toryism: 'I am confident that this is the most Conservative provision in the bill', commented Derby, wholly disagreeing with Walpole.[25] The Liberals inevitably fastened on these electoral calculations, which could not be hidden, and used them effectively in attacking the bill for what it was, 'a party measure'.[26] Yet it should be remembered that intellectuals in the Tory party tended to arrive, by way of history and comparative politics, at the conclusions reached instinctively by backwoodsmen at Westminster: 'I

believe ... nothing has more saved England from mob leaders than the large
share in political life ... taken by persons of property, birth and refined
education', affirmed Bulwer Lytton in a long letter to Gladstone written
while Derby's cabinet struggled with the first Tory venture in Parliamentary reform.[27] Lytton and most of the cabinet – Stanley being the
obvious exception – did not have sufficient faith in the power of aristocratic
example over the middle class, let alone the working class, to risk a reform
that went anywhere near the professed aim of adapting the Act of 1832 to
decades of social change. The incoming Palmerston government had more
confidence. It was readier to expand the urban electorate downwards, and
not just laterally, but declined to outbid the Tories by modifying landed
representation.

The coolness with which the Liberal reform bill of 1860 was received
delighted the Tories. Stanley thought the apprehensiveness of working-class
enfranchisement among radical intellectuals especially significant: 'when
philosophers turn Conservative, there is real reaction'. He was mistaken,
not about the unlamented bill, but about the general climate, as he quickly
grasped.[28] Derby did not overlook the impact of what he rather sourly
termed 'Palmerston's ... repeated exhibitions in public' around the
country.[29] 'The towns', wrote Stanley to Disraeli in October 1860, 'are full
of money – and of Conservative opinion disguised as moderate liberalism.'
Palmerston's, and Gladstone's, oratory helped to ensure that a good many
of the substantial citizens seen by Stanley on his visits to speak in the
industrial North did not show a collective disposition to move towards
either radicalism or Toryism. Nor did the local Tories want to enter the lists
as the principal antagonists of Cobden and Bright, both of whom were
labelled demagogues by their contemporaries.[30] Stanley took a similar bi-
partisan line in his speeches. In the October after the Tory government fell,
Derby, Disraeli, Malmesbury, and Stanley all addressed a political banquet
at Liverpool; the provincial city where Toryism was predominant. Nearly
all the members of the late cabinet attended to hear Derby prescribe
responsible opposition as the function of the Tories, and cast doubt on the
prudence of reducing the borough franchise, 'in the interests of the lower
classes themselves', on whose corruptibility and ignorance he dwelt without
apology. Disraeli added that they must not expect the party in Parliament
to justify itself by inviting conflict: 'Great political questions should be rare,
and will be rare in communities which enjoy so salutary a political state as,
on the whole, England has long enjoyed.' Stanley struck a different note,
discussing class relationships without reference to party and claiming that
'The old breach between the landed and the mercantile and manufacturing
classes has been effectually and finally closed.' This statement must have
gone down well with the Liverpudlian patriciate, but it was not even a half-
truth so far as the Tories were concerned. He dismissed 'the masses' as

stirred only by economic discontent, which 'true Conservative policy' should always think ahead to prevent.[31] Derby had no illusions about the message of his speech, and Disraeli's on this occasion. He would have followed a different course had it been open to him on consideration of all the circumstances; and he looked out for the chance of toppling Palmerston.[32]

Derby hoped that the Liberals would succeed in passing a reform bill, although he was afraid of one. The £6 borough franchise which his own cabinet accepted as an option in May 1859 was '*very dangerous*', he wrote to Disraeli in January 1860.[33] He might talk, in private and public, of Palmerston's as a weak and divided government: but from the outset he perceived it was an abler and stronger ministry than a Tory replacement could conceivably be. In his major speeches to the party he compared the helplessness and vulnerability of minority government with the 'controlling and regulating power' which, he asserted, lay with the opposition. It was not a boast that he made in his political correspondence. 'I apprehend', he remarked to Malmesbury when contemplating the coming session of 1861, 'that our policy this year as well as last must be the "masterly inactivity" which was found so successful.'[34] Palmerston acknowledged his debt to the Tories, but they were not in a position to tell him what to do, if only because far more frightened of the radical element in Liberalism, which they habitually exaggerated, than he was. As Derby told a party dinner at the Mansion House in July 1863, the better part for Toryism in the Commons was 'to be held forth as a bugbear to the advanced Liberals by the heads of that party...'.[35] Even this implied a less passive role than the Tories actually filled. Palmerston did not employ them in the way claimed; he merely availed himself of proffered support that could not easily be withheld, as when introducing, and dropping, the 1860 reform bill. Derby assured his party that they did not face an indefinite future of self-abnegation:[36] but in January 1865 he cautioned Disraeli in the words that encapsulated the timidity and pessimism beneath his striking exterior: 'our course of action...I conclude must be that of "masterly inactivity"'.[37]

His one determined bid to oust Palmerston was staged in July 1864 over foreign affairs, a sphere in which he thought it might be safe to attack the prime minister in earnest when national pride had taken a knock. He did not wish to raise the temperature of politics on the complex questions affecting the Anglican Church: this in many ways worldly man was deeply attached to the Church.[38] When prime minister, he repelled with moving eloquence a proposal from the Evangelical Lord Ebury to have the Anglican liturgy redrafted with a view to closer unity between Church and Dissent: 'a more perfect liturgy I believe never was devised...a work of the utmost importance, and of the greatest beauty'; with the doctrinal truths it enshrined, it ought not to be handed over to the Royal Commission that

Ebury wanted, only to disappoint and embitter Dissenters, surely, if it were set up.[39] Living in an industrial county where Dissent flourished he could not but recognize the advisability of conciliation in such a question as church rates, which did not involve belief. His government of 1858–59 grappled with the problem. The Home Secretary, Walpole, in whom the Tory country gentlemen placed a trust they would not give to Disraeli, brought forward a scheme to exempt Dissenters from church rates and transfer the liability from the occupiers to the owners of property. Lewis observed the scene: the minister spoke 'in a tone of solemnity which bordered on the ludicrous. His plan... the... Conservatives did not seem to relish... highly but they cheered Walpole when he sat down, and are evidently prepared to support his measure.'[40] In cabinet, Lord John Manners, of Young England fame, had contended: 'As a Conservative and Church government we can't do better than struggle to maintain one of the most ancient and most equitable obligations on... property...'.[41] Stanley, typically, argued for submitting to the Liberation Society's demand for total abolition; it was too late for anything else, and the Dissenters too influential.[42] He did not share his father's affection and concern for the Church. Walpole's scheme was decisively rejected. In opposition the party gladly reverted to fighting the Liberation Society's bill without being impelled to vote for one of its front bench's devising. The refusal of militant Dissent to compromise created a situation which Derby uneasily let Disraeli exploit for all it was worth, and more: 'I doubt the policy of shutting the door beforehand against any overtures of our opponents.'[43] As he foresaw, the Tories profited by the Liberationists' intransigence to erode and finally overturn the Commons majority of several years in favour of their bill; while the Liberal cabinet treated it as an open question with Palmerston in one lobby and Gladstone in the other, for and against abolition respectively. The adversary of Dissent in the Lords when the Liberation Society's bills to do away with church rates or qualifying oaths came up was the same man that Wilson Patten, the veteran Tory MP for the county's Northern division, watched in the chair of the Central Executive Relief Committee during the Lancashire cotton famine. Derby's efforts received national publicity. Wilson Patten described to Sotheron Estcourt how 'Lord Derby has... by his character and influence done an immense amount of good which will be long felt. You would be amused to see him sitting in a c[ommitt]ee composed of all creeds and politics, cordially co-operating with men some of whom go even further than Bright.'[44] Derby epitomized, it may be said, the contrast in the Church between theoretical exclusiveness and practical tolerance and goodwill. Since he was the unchallengeable head of the party, these diverse attitudes of his had more meaning than Disraeli's politicking with religious issues.

The Church's exposure to charges of behaving like the spiritual monopoly it had once been, prompted those of her adherents who were politically wise to seek the elimination of the Jews' special grievance. Their exclusion from Parliament was a serious disability. By contrast, the complaints of Dissent looked small. Stanley suggested in cabinet that if church rates were abolished many political Dissenters might be sorry to lose a useful pretext for showing off their power.[45] The admission of practising Jews to the legislature raised a fundamental question: the Christian identity of the state. Palmerston resolved the difficulty conclusively for propertied Liberals of all sorts in that religious and nationalistic age. There was no danger that the few representatives of a small community would detract from the Christian character of Britain. Christianity and civilization were inseparable: 'The progress of mankind is governed by laws which admit of no retrogression. The Old Testament prepared the way for the New... but the New... will never lead us back to the Old.' The Jews' large stake in the country and the financial services of their great capitalists in the Crimean war surely entitled them to enter the House; shutting them out was 'the last rag and remnant of prejudice...'.[46] The Lords obstructed this change in the law for a quarter of a century, and took up their familiar stance in 1858. Disraeli's championship of admission over the years now threatened to disrupt a Tory cabinet fighting to survive. A liberal Tory, the fourth Earl of Carnarvon, Bulwer Lytton's under-secretary at the Colonial Office, came to the rescue with the idea of legislation enabling either house to admit religious Jews by passing a resolution that would last only for the lifetime of a single Parliament, unless renewed.[47]

Outwardly, the existing law would remain in force, but the Houses – that is, the Commons – might dispense Jews from taking a Christian oath, and substitute one in their form. Derby accepted the formula, which 'may save... dignity, and to a certain extent... principles'. He found it hard to differ from 'many of those with whom I generally agree... between whom and myself there is no difference on the merits of the question whether... a Jew should take part in a Christian legislature'.[48] Chelmsford, the Lord Chancellor, voted against the new bill, which by arrangement with Carnarvon was introduced by a peer who did not hold office – Lord Lucan, the Crimean general and Irish landlord, not a man suspected of liberal leanings. Malmesbury put the best face he could on 'a subject of great regret... a concession... made to a political necessity, and not from moral conviction'.[49] In spite of Derby's efforts, a large majority of Tory peers, including some in minor office, followed Chelmsford's example, or abstained. In the Commons, the split in the cabinet and party was painfully displayed: among cabinet ministers, Walpole, Henley, General Peel and Manners opposed the bill; Disraeli, Stanley and Pakington voted for it. Three of the four opponents from the cabinet went to the length of resisting the resolution under the terms of the Act just passed: Walpole, Peel and

Manners; together with Sir William Jolliffe, the chief whip, Cairns the solicitor-general, another and trusted whip, Colonel T. E. Taylor, and the two ablest of the younger high Tories, Lord Robert Cecil and Gathorne Hardy.

The Jews' Act dealt a heavy blow to Tory morale. Perhaps nothing did more to disillusion the party with minority government. A strenuous opponent of Jews in Parliament, Samuel Warren, MP for Midhurst, expressed to a sympathetic Bishop Wilberforce what he and others could not utter in their speeches: 'You saw … the fight I made to the last against the intrusion of the blasphemer … *Had you seen the air and gesture with which the Jew* [Baron Rothschild] *motioned away the tendered New Testament at the Bar of the House*, your blood would have run cold, as Hamilton [financial secretary to the Treasury] told me his did.'[50] Warren said in the House: 'the Conservative party in the country is … shocked and deeply hurt'.[51] Nor did Derby and those ministers voting equally reluctantly with him increase the respect in which they were held by critics of Toryism. Herbert was contemptuous of the way in which they yielded to the pressures on the government: 'Jews let in by men who think their own measure destructive of Christianity …'[52] It was probably true, as Charles Du Cane, for one, contended to the gentry and farmers in his constituency of North Essex, that resistance to the Jews' Act had been 'in accordance with the real feelings of the country';[53] but popular sentiment did not stir in reaction to a change imposed by a majority in the Commons with the co-operation, however grudging, of the prime minister. His administration depended on Tory unity and Liberal disunity. The Jewish problem exposed the limits of both. Beside Disraeli stood Stanley, to whom Carnarvon unfolded his solution. The Tories, they felt, could not afford to appear narrowly illiberal in the prelude to their main domestic legislation, the reform bill. 'Certainly, I did good service to the government', wrote Carnarvon in his private retrospect of the session.[54]

Anti-Catholicism united Derby and Stanley against Disraeli up to a point. Ministers still contrived to foster a disposition in Ireland which produced the only majority for the Tories in a general election there under the Union. State recognition of the Catholic university in Dublin was a delicate question. Disraeli wanted to bestow a Royal Charter on the university; it seemed easier than the modest land bill which nevertheless elicited a strong protest from the Irish viceroy and chief secretary. Stanley, who knew Ireland well, saw the danger in strengthening the clerical hold on the nationalist middle class. 'As to satisfying the Irish sacerdotal party, it is simply out of the question', he insisted. Concession only whetted the priestly appetite. It was not worthwhile, he advised Disraeli, to win over representatives of Catholic Ireland then in the Commons: those whom the proposal would alienate were likely to outnumber them. Stanley's dislike of

Catholicism stemmed from his secular philosophy: recognizing the university would not constitute 'a sound or liberal object'.[55] The Irish viceroy, Lord Eglinton and Winton, a much more conventional Tory, flatly rejected the suggestion: 'It is impossible that we can...give a charter to the R[oman] Catholic university. We should disgust our friends and the Whigs would turn against us on it...'[56] Disraeli was not deterred from dangling the prospect before Irish Catholics; Stanley drily adverted to 'the supposed inclination we have shown to negociate [sic] for their alliance'.[57] The Tories did, however, evince an unexpected solicitude for the Papacy in its contemporary predicament. Their relatively friendly attitude distinguished them, at the top, from the several elements that went to make up the succeeding Liberal administration. Malmesbury informed the ambassador in Paris of ministerial thinking: it was to volunteer 'moral and if necessary material assistance to establish another distribution by the Catholic Powers of the Pope's territory, or a forced improvement of the Pope's government...': but to do so only 'if we see hopes of improving the condition of the people without weakening the spiritual authority of the Pope'.[58] In the absence of Archbishop Cullen of Dublin in Rome, Cardinal Wiseman, the English Catholic primate of Irish origin, used his influence with the Church in Ireland to encourage the anti-Liberal trend that Eglinton and Winton discovered running 'in a most satisfactory manner' on his arrival in 1858.[59] In letters read out on the hustings in the general election, Wiseman stated that the Derby ministry had given Catholics in both countries 'more attention, more courtesy, and more ready assurance of redress...than we have experienced from others'. This was largely Disraeli's doing. The Cardinal cited the 'manly and unflinching' declaration by the strongly nationalist clergy of Meath that Irish electors must vote realistically. The feebleness and disorganization of constitutional nationalism at that period helped the Tories to their electoral victory in Ireland.[60]

Disraeli meant to build on his Irish success in opposition. Stanley besought him not to countenance in a 'direct or indirect' fashion the demands of the Irish Catholic hierarchy for unrestricted denominational schooling, which if pressed would be greeted with a storm of indignation in Britain: 'It will not do to have a No Popery cry raised against us, and to be in the wrong at the same time.'[61] The unpopularity of Disraeli's overtures to the Irish Catholics and crypto-nationalists in the House contributed to Tory abstentions on more than one occasion. After the most publicized of these votes, on Denmark and Schleswig-Holstein in July 1864, Derby decided to put an end to Disraeli's prolonged though rather furtive courtship of Catholic Ireland. An opportunity arose when the Established Church in Ireland came under Parliamentary attack in March 1865. Derby conferred with two formidable Protestant Irish lawyers in the Tory party, Sir Hugh Cairns and James Whiteside, and wrote to Disraeli about the impending motion: 'I feel sure... you will agree with me that it should be resisted to the uttermost... considering the great stress you have always laid upon Church questions.'[62] Derby and Malmesbury had previously signalled their indifference to Irish and Catholic opinion by attending, with Palmerston, Russell and Gladstone, a dinner for Garibaldi during the Italian's visit to London in April 1864. This tribute to a revolutionary nationalist upset the party. Malmesbury was alarmed, but not Derby.[63] His political judgement and religious outlook led him to accept the invitation in order to associate Toryism with the enthusiasm of his countrymen for Garibaldi, in which hostility to Catholicism loomed large. Just before the general election of 1865, Derby inserted an extraordinarily harsh passage in a Lords speech, distinguishing between the loyal English Catholic and his Irish co-religionist, 'a most vicious animal... nothing prevents his pulling you and me to pieces except the muzzle... round his nose', that is, a qualifying oath for office-holders which implied that Catholics could not be trusted to uphold the constitution. The Irish reacted angrily: the Tory majority from their country would have disappeared anyway, but the anticipated setback became a certainty. English Catholics liked this public drawing of a distinction which they were fond of making themselves. '... though my unlucky references to... "muzzling" *may* have lost us some votes', he replied to Disraeli after the election, 'our chief losses have been where such a cause could not have any effect.'[64] That was incontrovertible: the Irish immigrant vote in Britain had little significance before 1867; and their supporters among the quite numerous English Catholics in the Lancashire electorate had deserted the Tories only in the county's South West division won by Gladstone, who was on good personal terms with Catholic landed families locally, whatever he said and published in disparagement of Rome.[65] Derby's judgement was surer than Disraeli's. Worsening Protestant–Catholic and Anglo-Irish relations combined with Tory traditionalism at every social level to rule out even the very limited policy of conciliation applied in 1858–59, until the next interval of minority government.

Europe and America

The Tories desired a stable Europe after the Crimean war, but the extent to which peace depended upon Napoleon III irked them: and they thought Palmerstonian policy too personal and incautious, if not worse. The aristocratic radical, Lord Goderich, complained of 'the friendship with decayed despotisms which Dizzy advocates'.[66] In this Disraeli was scarcely typical of the Tory party. He made up to the first post-war Russian ambassador in London, Count Chreptovich, who Malmesbury was glad to see depart after an unusually short time: 'All feel that he hated us... and we therefore took care never to talk politics or mention India before him.'[67] Mindful of Bonapartism's liberal side, the Tories seem to have relied too much on it after the war. At least Malmesbury did. A regular visitor to France, he was connected by marriage with the old nobility. Their pragmatic reaction to the regime affected his estimate of the Emperor, based upon personal knowledge since Napoleon's exile in London. Standing in for Derby when the new Parliament of 1857 debated the Queen's speech, he gave 'judicious consideration to the different positions of France and England, geographically and constitutionally'. He alluded, less than judiciously, to 'a natural impatience on the part of the English people in consequence of their neighbour's not having a constitution as free as their own'. But he admitted that political arrangements in the two nations had the sanction of 'the popular voice... though differing in detail'.[68] The far-reaching implications of the Indian Mutiny were not, of course, lost upon the Tories. 'I would not trust the disposition of Powers more than the disposition of individuals', said Disraeli cynically in August, arguing in the Commons for bigger armed forces.[69] It was not an aspect of the crisis to which the Tories paid much attention at first. They gave little thought to the repercussions of the decision to switch their vote on Milner Gibson's wrecking amendment to 'the Colonels' Bill'. Malmesbury's printed and unpublished journals record the interviews with the French ambassador, Persigny, in which the gravity of the situation created by indulgence in the politics of opposition was borne in upon him. The anglophil Persigny was 'very violent' when told that the shaky Tory ministry was obliged to drop the bill which their party had backed on its first reading. His uncontrolled anger was excusable: Disraeli had assured him of 'uninterrupted support' for legislation heavily diluted in the Palmerston cabinet. Malmesbury consented to exchange draft despatches '*sub rosa*' with the Frenchman, who altered the wording of the one submitted to him, and after some days of further discussion between them and consultation with Paris permitted it to be sent.[70]

The Foreign Secretary submitted a highly improbable plea, that if ministers went on with the bill not only would they be forced out, but the next government under Russell, and including Gladstone, would pass a reform bill to make the House of Commons 'a revolutionary and unmanageable body'. Much more plausibly, he envisaged 'a *dégringolade* in England of aristocratic institutions' in the event of a war with France which his country was so badly placed to fight.[71] In effect the Tories threw themselves on the Emperor's mercy. He exacted a price for saving the ministry and sparing Britain national humiliation. 'I have not moved... without information, explanation, and invitation given spontaneously. I do not see how consistently with the honour of England I could have done more or shown more deference to an ally', wrote Malmesbury looking back in January 1859.[72] He was buying time for Britain, as he reminded the prime minister when she abandoned Portugal to French intimidation, despite the spirit of British treaty obligations: 'The moral of all this is that

with such a neighbour...if we are to hold our own, we must have more
ships at our command in the Channel. *Everybody* is for strengthening our
navy and I am sure you may do what you like in that way...' War had been
very close; throughout the government's short life, Malmesbury watched
the progress of naval rearmament with keen anxiety: 'If France had fired
a shot at Lisbon we must have gone to war...' He asserted Britain's
independence of France sufficiently to frighten Disraeli, the other member
of the cabinet in constant touch with developments on the Continent,
through his none too reliable private sources. 'Disraeli as usual alarmed',
noted Malmesbury dismissively after one meeting.[73]

It was only half in jest that Malmesbury observed to an envoy in a great
capital: 'Nothing can be more agreeable to a Foreign Minister though
perhaps not to an active mind like yours than the dormant state of politics
you describe. It is *my beau idéal* of human affairs...'[74] Hardworking and
vigilant, he did not neglect to put forward the British view as it became the
minister of a Great Power to do. His tone reflected an outlook different from
Palmerston's and Gladstone's in the impartiality which formed no part of
those statesmen's diplomatic philosophy. '...an absolute regime...' he
maintained of Bourbon Naples, 'had...the same privilege...as ourselves, of
self-defence against those who would overturn it.'[75] Answering Liberal
critics of his policy towards Naples, with whom he subsequently restored
the diplomatic relations broken off under Palmerston, Malmesbury said: 'I
believe it will be found that constitutional liberty is almost invariably the
child of peace and reason, and is seldom established by the sword...'[76] On
that principle, he worked, successfully, to resolve a dangerous dispute
involving Sardinia and Naples, which might otherwise have flared up into
an Italian, and then European, conflict.[77] Malmesbury also had a coherent,
distinctively Tory standpoint on nationality. He restated in the Lords
arguments for Austria's retention of her Italian provinces which had
incurred Palmerston's contemptuous anger when the Emperor let Granville
know the contents of the Foreign Secretary's letter of 7 December 1858 to
Cowley.[78] Austria held her territory in Italy 'by inheritance...conquest...
and treaty...the same titles by which Her Gracious Majesty holds...
Scotland...India...and some of the Colonial dependencies'. The Austrians
were Britain's 'very ancient allies...sharers in...events...recorded in some
of the most glorious pages in our history'. He professed to find French
intervention hard to understand, ascribing Austrian unpopularity to her
wide role of 'a constable' in the peninsula, which he thought should be
modified in her own interests. Sardinian expansion he condemned as
incompatible with her much-praised constitutionalism.[79]

Without that degree of trust on the part of Napoleon which Palmerston
had secured by his visit to Compiègne, or sympathy for the Emperor's aims
in preparing the war of 1859 in Italy, the Tories tried vainly to stave off the

conflict. 'I care for neither Austria nor France', Malmesbury confided to his diary in January that year, 'but Lord Derby and I are determined to use every effort to prevent war, which would cost 100,000 lives and desolate the fairest parts of Europe.' It was, he wrote to Cowley, 'the great duty of every honest man…to prevent the scourge which two or three unprincipled men would inflict on…mankind for their personal profit…'. Those adventurers were Napoleon and Count Cavour, the Sardinian minister.[80] Neither Derby nor Malmesbury considered Italians ready for unity and self-rule: 'Drive Austria out…and…Italy will become a second Mexico', which saw forty-eight changes of regime between 1821 and 1853. This, as Derby reassured a nervous Disraeli, did not imply that they were willing to go to Austria's aid: Malmesbury had warned the Austrian ambassador not to expect assistance.[81] The extension of hostilities to Germany would draw this country into the struggle to protect Continental markets. It was imperative to limit the war: 'France having always been a curse to Europe, we look upon it as the will of God and resign ourselves to the torment', Malmesbury told Cowley.[82] But by encouraging the German states to act together in restraint of France, Britain heightened tension. Partly to lend credibility to the government's diplomacy in recent months, which had not prevented the outbreak of war and insurrection in Italy, partly to confirm pride in their country as a Great Power still, Disraeli, Stanley and Pakington all mentioned during the elections the possibility that Britain might ultimately be drawn into a European struggle.[83] The result was quite other than they hoped. Malmesbury seems to have realized before then how irreversibly public opinion was moving. '…whatever might be the idea of individual ministers', he reported to the pro-German Queen on 3 May, 'not one in England would *dare* at present to leave a severe neutrality. There could be no doubt of the universal feeling on this point, which superseded every other question both with candidates and constituents… In fact it was the *only one*…ostentatiously expressed.'[84]

The elections and the ensuing vote of confidence were unfair to Malmesbury, in that he was the victim of Napoleon's duplicity, as of public alarm, and cast as the culprit for heavy losses in the war panic on the Stock Exchange. Derby had been circumspect in his allusions to Austrian rights and Italian unfitness for union and independence. It was Malmesbury whom Disraeli blamed for the ministry's downfall on the June vote of confidence.[85] But in 1860–61 the Garibaldian invasion of Sicily and Naples, and Sardinia's absorption of the Bourbon kingdom, along with the Marches and Umbria taken from the Pope, brought the Tory leader out in frank expressions of disbelief in united Italy and its serviceableness to British interests. He used a Shakespearean quotation in the Lords likening Italians to 'various dogs and curs'. 'If the quotation to which you refer could fairly be interpreted in the sense which you have ascribed to it, I must…admit…it was unfortunately selected', he conceded to a Liberal critic. '…I only sought…to illustrate the infinite variety of habits and feelings among the different populations…classed under the name of Italians.'[86] In another speech, he underlined the importance to Britain in Ireland and the empire of the Papacy's effective independence of political control, which he thought could not endure if, as the Liberals wished, France withdrew her military protection from the remaining Papal territory.[87] He cared little for the arguments that appealed to Liberals with their doctrinaire attitude to the Papal future. Derby, Malmesbury and Disraeli enjoyed questioning the liberalism of the Italian state in the light of its methods of repression in the unreconciled South. Why, asked Disraeli in 1863, were Polish rebels against the Tsar called 'patriots' and the pro-Bourbon insurgents in Italy 'brigands'? On the facts, the Tories had the better of these Parliamentary exchanges, but it did not help them politically. British public opinion was unreceptive to being told that the enlarged realm of Victor Emanuel II with 'the inevitable grinding conscription and taxation' was not an improvement upon the rule of the Pope and Neapolitan Bourbons, and that completing the unification of the peninsula would not be to everyone's advantage.[88]

The first principle of Tory foreign policy before and after the administration of 1858–59 was to keep Britain from being too closely involved in the affairs of the Continent. Yet Tory spokesmen did not think isolationism either feasible or desirable, while distrusting Palmerstonian assertiveness in Great Power diplomacy. 'That system of taking the lead in Europe, which used to be so rife at the Foreign Office', said Malmesbury in July 1863, 'is one of the most dangerous that can possibly be followed. It is averse to the present state of civilization in the country, to its sound state, and to its political interests.'[89] In government the Tories discovered how events propelled Britain far into the arena of European rivalries; in opposition they reverted to arguing for a position on its edge. The Tories agreed, though they did not like to say so, with Bright, who argued in the House when they held office: 'Is not prosperity Conservative? Is not peace Conservative?'[90] The official Tory line on British intervention on behalf of the rebellious Poles in 1863 foreshadowed that adopted by the party in the Danish crisis. Disraeli recognized in the Polish rising 'a national movement…a sacred cause', but advised against 'political sentimentalism', as did Malmesbury in the Lords. Neither humanity nor national interest, said the latter, would be furthered by incurring the risk of war for Poland, but quite the contrary. 'Putting the question on the lowest footing', continued Malmesbury, 'is there any commercial interest at stake?…I see none'.[91] When the Schleswig-Holstein dispute came to a head, he was quite clear how matters stood. 'The sympathies of our party are entirely with the Danes', he wrote. So were Derby's, who was 'much puzzled what to do', unlike Disraeli and Malmesbury.[92] Disraeli told Count Vitzthum von Eckstädt, the Saxon minister, that 'the integrity of Denmark was too insignificant an object to justify a European war'. Malmesbury considered the Prussian army alone more than a match for the combined land forces of France and Britain; that ruled out any prospect of Anglo-French action to restrain the German Confederation.[93]

In Derby's absence, laid low by gout, Malmesbury led the opposition to victory in the Lords by nine votes on a motion identical with Disraeli's in the lower House, condemning the ministry for Britain's discomfiture through Palmerston's encouragement and then abandonment of Denmark. Derby was nervous about the motion, and with reason.[94] In the Commons fifteen Tories were absent unpaired from the division, compared with nine Liberals; and six of the opposition went into the government lobby to swell the ministerial majority to eighteen, in spite of the desertion to the other side of eighteen Irish Liberals, all but one of them Catholics. Stanley believed that ministers were stronger for their ordeal. The Tory-Catholic combination gave offence to the party and the public. A good deal more unpalatable was the criticism voiced by Derby in a previous Danish debate in April. It sounded anti-national although that was not the intention. Derby reproached the government with having provided confirmation of 'the impression so prevalent in Europe, that we have ceased to be a great power, that our military and naval position has been made subordinate to our trading...interests; and that, however England may bluster...there is not the slightest danger of her interfering materially to exercise the slightest influence or control in...Europe'.[95] These complaints were obviously exaggerated and confused. Britain had not dropped out of the circle of Great Powers. Her wealth and the bigger, more modern fleet it sustained kept her there. As for the accusation of ignoble commercialism, Derby seemed to have forgotten the lesson of 1859, that no British government should appear to meditate hostilities without knowing the likely business reaction. Stanley hopefully interpreted the opposition's Parliamentary attack as aligning the party of the land with businessmen disinclined to let the approach of war jeopardize their contemporary profits.[96] Disraeli appreciated when he had lost. Perceiving 'the absolute necessity this year of attending the agricultural meetings', he went to talk to rural Tories of topics other than foreign affairs.[97]

While Palmerston and Gladstone had cautious confidence in the endurance, for their time, of aristocratic primacy at home and its applicability to newly or yet to be liberalized states, the Tories were more doubtful on both counts. This affected their outlook on Anglo-French relations. Malmesbury, with his Legitimist predilections, was particularly inclined to suppose Napoleon III bent on crippling Britain's power by employing his statecraft to discredit her ruling class in favour of the middle-class radicalism of Cobden and Bright. After an audience of the Emperor in April 1861, the Englishman concluded that 'he fears our aristocracy, whom he knows to be thoroughly English, and the most energetic of all the classes...he would like a Government who would diminish our army and navy, and...weaken our influence abroad'.[98] Palmerston thought much the same, but rarely lost sight of the need to maintain as good an understanding as possible with France. At Malmesbury's audience, his old acquaintance was 'very much prejudiced against the whole Tory party'.[99] Napoleon had some justification for his animus. 'I do not see', wrote Derby of the Italian question in January 1860, 'that we are in the least called upon to relieve L[ouis] N[apoleon] from his difficulties, which, great as they are, have been chiefly of his own making.'[100] It was not sensible to irritate the French government by conversations with foreign diplomats and Parliamentary utterances in this spirit. The Tory leaders realized the urgency of soothing France while Britain was arming; but it was a task they preferred to leave to Palmerston who had the stomach for it, and the Emperor's political respect. 'A change of ministers in an anti-French direction would involve serious consequences' reported Vitzthum, also in January 1860. 'Nobody is more persuaded of this than Lord Derby and Disraeli.'[101] Derby vigorously deplored the ministry's 'blunders' in diplomacy; but he did not as a rule press his criticisms to a vote: 'how far', he asked Disraeli in November 1863, 'are we prepared to take the responsibility of the consequences of success?'[102] The challenge over Schleswig-Holstein in July 1864 was exceptional, and unavoidable if the opposition were not virtually to abdicate its constitutional role.

The Tory like the Liberal party found that the American civil war cut across it, after the national unity of the *Trent* affair. Derby's exposure to the distress of the Cotton Famine might have been expected to bring him to the same conclusions as Gladstone. Both were afraid of violence in the stricken region. 'The prospects for the winter, especially if...severe...are fearful', Derby told Malmesbury in October 1862, 'and admirably as the people have behaved hitherto, it is impossible to say what continual and aggravated suffering may lead them to.'[103] But he did not approve of Gladstone's action in preparing the ground for recognition of the Confederate States in his Newcastle speech that same month. Derby's reasons were relayed to Palmerston by Clarendon, whose conservative Whig politics made him the recipient of Tory confidences. Derby based his refusal to take up either recognition of the Confederacy or European mediation between North and South, as he was repeatedly urged to do, on the peril of the first course and the futility of the second. To procure 'a single bale of cotton' meant breaking the Federal blockade of Southern ports; and it was certain that the mediating Powers would meet with uncompromising rejection. Derby's firmness in resisting the pressures on him derived from a total lack of Gladstone's conviction that Britain had a duty to succour the new nation whose cause and social character, slavery apart, elicited such sympathy from the mother country. Pakington had used language similar to Gladstone's. The Tory, said Derby, was expressing an individual view; but the collective responsibility of the cabinet covered Gladstone, unless he were known to have acted on his own initiative, and if so, 'anger in the North, false hopes in the South…speculation at home would have been very unnecessarily excited'.[104] Derby's stance helped the majority in the Liberal cabinet to turn down the imminent proposal of Anglo-French mediation. It was not easy for him. 'The feeling for the South is very strong in society', noted Malmesbury, who later heard from Napoleon personally how much he, too, wanted the South to establish its independence.[105] Meetings of former ministers in 1863 upheld Derby, when only Pakington, among those who had sat in cabinet, advocated recognition.[106] Bright selected Lord Stanley's moderation in the context of Britain and the American civil war for public praise.[107] The credit should rather have gone to his father, less expansive on the subject in his speeches, who kept the party, as such, back from open partisanship. Father and son gauged the strength and temper of the dominant Northern states shrewdly: 'The strongest American feelings are distrust of England, and belief in their own invincibility. Nothing can do away [with] the first – events only can dissipate the last', wrote Stanley, warning Disraeli against political temptation.[108]

Empire

The Tory government of 1858–59 left its mark on post-Mutiny India. Ellenborough's impatience with Canning cost him his place in the cabinet, but his policy survived him. The contribution of Bulwer Lytton at the Colonial Office to the development of empire elsewhere than in the subcontinent belongs to the history of a common approach to the colonies of settlement. The East, and Latin America, brought out the differences between Palmerstonian and Tory attitudes. The debates on Canning's proclamation dispossessing the rebel landholders of Oudh, where resentment of the kingdom's annexation to British India in 1856 had inspired a general rising in support of the mutinous soldiery, produced a direct clash. Shaftesbury, who had concerted his move with Palmerston and the late cabinet, opened the attack on Ellenborough for his leaked censure of the governor-general by quoting from the offending despatch: 'Your Proclamation', Ellenborough had written, 'will appear to deprive the great body of the people of all hope…while the substitution of our rule for that of their Native Sovereign has naturally excited against us whatever they may have of national feeling…We must admit that, under the circumstances, the hostilities…in Oudh have rather the character of legitimate war than that of rebellion.' '…make the case your own,' exclaimed Shaftesbury to an assembly full of Irish landowners. 'Suppose that…in Ireland in 1848 the exhortation had been addressed to the Lord Lieutenant: "Deal gently with the disaffected, because you must bear in mind that though…ancient governments were bad, they were at least native"!'[109] Ellenborough, who had already resigned, took him up on the Irish analogy: 'True, we have had confiscation in Ireland…But has the result been peace…prosperity? Do not all…who have considered the subject trace to confiscation all the disasters in that country?' It was not physically possible for Britain to enforce a measure unprecedented in Indian experience. 'You may have succeeded in wars purely political against Princes…I tell you…in a social war you will fail.'[110]Derby doubted whether Shaftesbury could still be a Tory, and wondered ironically how he would react to a decree expropriating his lands. Ellenborough called for an amnesty for the rebels. The government's defeat, said Derby, would signal to India the repudiation of 'a policy of mercy and toleration'.[111] Successful by nine in the upper House – a margin achieved despite a majority of votes given to the opposition by bishops appreciative of Palmerston's religious policy – ministers prevailed much more easily, even triumphantly, in the Commons where fresh evidence from India underpinned Ellenborough's arguments, but did not excuse his behaviour in making prematurely known his strictures on a proconsul engaged in the arduous restoration of imperial authority.

Palmerston was interested in the effectiveness of repression, present and future, and the substitution of the Crown for the Company in ruling India; quite happy to agree with Wood's observations: 'Your government in India will be a despotism.'[112] Derby settled on a more positive reaction from, at the latest, the autumn of 1857. He asked Ellenborough for his ideas, and wrote to Disraeli: 'I think myself that we have arrived at a stage…when, without laying ourselves open to any imputation of faction, we may fairly challenge the Government to vindicate the measures they have adopted in the East, including the forgotten China!'[113] The notion of a grand inquest upon Britain's Eastern policies did not materialize, but office afforded the Tories a chance to do something more than pass another version of Palmerston's India Bill. Disraeli's Commons speech of July 1857 had posed the question: 'Is it a military mutiny, or is it a national revolt?', and clearly implied that it was the latter, resulting from the menace of westernization to princely independence, titles to property in land outside the native states and the great religions of India.[114] Gladstone remarked to his wife: 'Disraeli made a speech in many points very clever, but…there was an absence of legitimate aim, and a risk of public inconvenience attending such discussions at this moment, which startled people.'[115] Malmesbury, on the other hand thought his colleague's '*tone* and *matter* were unexceptionable'. He grew alarmed when Disraeli's weekly paper, the *Press*, continued in the same tone as confirmation arrived of the deaths of British women and children at the hands of the mutineers: 'the atrocities ... have given another turn to the British mind ... to appear as the apologists, in the slightest degree, of the sepoy miscreants would be fatal ... to any party or their leaders'. Malmesbury was equally severe on Pakington's 'complacent palliatives of the rape, murder and infanticide of above a thousand of his nation – no wonder at his getting tremendously abused in society'.[116] It says much for Derby that in this atmosphere he was calmly looking forward to a significant change in the aims and methods of empire in the East.

The Court complained of Ellenborough after his resignation that, quite apart from the affair of the Oudh despatch, he had been 'writing letters of his own to all the most important Indian chiefs and kings explaining his policy'. The Queen and Prince correctly believed him to have been making Canning's position 'almost untenable' and the Government's in Britain 'very hazardous'.[117] But the cabinet were nearly as impressed with Ellenborough's case for amnesty and long-term conciliation as Lord Chancellor Chelmsford, that high Tory lawyer, asserted it was in the Parliamentary debates on the ex-minister's conduct: 'I am not afraid to confess ... I think great allowance should have been made for men ... drawn into revolt by some of the strongest motives which actuate the human breast.'[118] Ellenborough's successor, Stanley, was only a partial exception, more receptive to public opinion at home which lagged behind Parliament, and to the hopes expressed by British businessmen and planters.[119] The Royal proclamation issued to mark the ending of the Company's administration in India implicitly conceded that the Mutiny was, in a real sense, a national uprising. The princes received a solemn assurance that their rights and dignities would be safeguarded, as would native tenures, religion and customs throughout the empire. The draft proclamation went round the cabinet. After being revised to take account of detailed criticisms made by Malmesbury at the instigation of the Court and sent to the prime minister, it emerged as an imaginative piece of conservative political philosophy in the Burkean tradition, laying down guidelines for British rule in India over the rest of the century and beyond. Malmesbury told Stanley that his original draft read 'too much like a respectable Magistrate's notice after a parochial row'. 'There is not', he admonished him, 'half *bellows* enough in it for the personal address of a Great Queen to an Oriental Hemisphere ...'[120]

In the long period after 1859 as before, and often through Malmesbury who carefully consulted Derby before speaking, the Tories sought to curb the spirit of British expansion to the East of India and in Latin America. When in office, Derby declined the request of a powerful deputation of MPs

from both parties with businessmen from the City and the provinces that
his government should make Sarawak a British protectorate; the object of
the persuasive agitation by Sir James Brooke, the adventurer who had
acquired the principality for himself in the North West of Borneo. 'The
colonial dependencies of the country were already too numerous', Derby
told them, '... They were not additions of strength but of weakness.'[121]
Bright's reasons for opposing the absorption of Sarawak into the empire
were no different in essence, only more highly coloured. Stanley, who was
a shareholder in a big firm on the deputation, had tried to obtain a
protectorate for Brooke's territory, telling Disraeli: 'it is clear that whatever
we may think of the value of his conquest, public feeling will not allow
England to look on if the Dutch, or the natives, take it from him by
force...'.[122] For Stanley this consideration outweighed the cost; but Bulwer
Lytton, the responsible minister, demurred on financial grounds, and also
because Brooke wanted 'protection as an absolute sovereign by a
constitutional sovereign whose subject he is – a most false position'. Sir
James's ruthlessness in Sarawak, however profitable, had earned him a
reputation to worry the morally sensitive.[123]

The renewal of war in China stirred up equally uncomfortable questions
for the Tories. Their minority administration had little choice but to let
Palmerston's plenipotentiary, Lord Elgin, conclude the Treaty of Tientsin
in June 1858 without significantly departing from the instructions he had
been given by the Liberals. Besides formally sanctioning the opium traffic
and extending the British commercial presence in China, the treaty
imposed on the Chinese an intensely disliked provision for permanent
diplomatic representation at Peking, with the intention that it should
undertake the proconsular functions of British ambassadors at Constantinople. Derby and Malmesbury were both willing to modify the requirement
substantially by limiting the British envoy's stay in the capital.[124] The
resumption of fighting in the summer of 1859 over this issue of diplomatic
access to Peking followed the change of ministry. With evident relief,
Malmesbury dissociated the Tories from the use of force ordered by the
Hon Frederick Bruce, Elgin's brother and the British minister appointed
under the treaty, who acted on instructions sent by Malmesbury, but not
within them, according to the former Foreign Secretary. 'We are apt', said
Malmesbury in the Lords, 'to talk of the Chinese nation... and...
government as... barbarian... but the Chinese government is anything
but... barbarian... They are a very clever... very well educated people... I
believe they have nearly as much knowledge of what is going on as we have
ourselves.' Bruce had been too hasty; he ought to have waited on the
response to longer negotiation than the exchanges he had with the
Chinese.[125] Answering Malmesbury, Elgin defended his brother, and opted
for a stark realism. Britain had no interest in China except her trade, and

the present system there did not satisfy the wants of British merchants. Not a year had passed since the Treaty of Nanking without 'acts of war' perpetrated by individual consuls calling in the navy.[126] To such realism Malmesbury himself deferred, announcing Tory backing for the large Anglo-French expedition despatched to exact submission to the terms of Tientsin.[127] The bigger part played by the French in this last phase of the China wars of 1856–60 influenced the Tories, of course, but less than domestic public opinion.

The popular image of Palmerstonianism, and its feared effect on policy in regions experiencing British economic penetration and dominance, persistently attracted unfavourable comment from many quarters. Malmesbury scored with an apparently damning indictment of the rationale of gunboat diplomacy in Brazil: '*Civis Romanus sum*... of all the foolish misapplications of a dead language of a semi-barbarous country to a living and civilized nation, I never heard of a worse. There is not the slightest analogy between the circumstances of ancient Rome and the present...' The Roman citizen, master of the classical world and invested with privileges and immunities was not 'the prototype of the Englishman who has nothing in Europe but his own British islands... Heligoland, and the fortress of Gibraltar'. A British citizen might take legitimate pride, not in representing national power, but in belonging to 'a nation in the vanguard of civilization... founded on respect for municipal and international law'.[128] Once again these Tory sentiments were indistinguishable from those of Cobden and Bright. Lord Robert Cecil's scathing remarks on the morality of Brazil's treatment by Britain, made in the Commons and repeated in the *Quarterly Review*, do not add anything to Malmesbury's measured protest.[129] The Earl was able to impart a more distinctively Tory note to what he said by reproaching the government for weakening the one monarchy in Latin America, a constitutional state, 'a model for South American nationalities... the only country in that part of the world uncorrupted by democratic institutions'.[130] The opposition won this argument in the Lords, driving ministers to take refuge in a procedural evasion; an empty victory in a thinly attended House. There were Tory businessmen in the Commons who subscribed to the uneasiness of the landed politicians in their party and on the other side about the Eastward drive of the British economy and the inherent political risks. A prominent instance was G. S. Beecroft, the ironmaster who sat for Leeds. The pacification of India and the forcible opening of China more widely to trade gave 'ample scope... for British industry and... enterprise... there is... room for British prudence and... caution. It will be well to curb the spirit of excessive speculation... and second the persuasions of the missionaries by examples of Christian principle and commercial integrity.'[131] Beecroft carried his reservations to the hustings in Leeds, where he declared 'he disapproved of England bullying small states, and currying to large powers'.[132] The results of the 1865 general election indicated that, unlike their betters, the voters were not troubled by these apprehensions and scruples.

Intra-party tensions

In the months of reflections and discussions after the Tories' reverse at the polls in 1857, Pakington discerned two groups in the party's leadership; he put Ellenborough, Stanley and Bulwer Lytton with Disraeli and himself. 'I suspect', he wrote to Disraeli, 'that [we]...have little in common with Lord Derby...Walpole...John Manners and Henley.'[133] The first five did not, however, form a continuing, organized group, any more than the other four did. Neither Stanley nor Bulwer Lytton trusted Disraeli; Pakington fell out with him; and Ellenborough was too individualistic. Manners was a party loyalist, but Walpole and Henley placed their political ideals above party. Derby alone commanded the confidence that survives error and defeat, as both a man of principle and a practical politician. Disraeli's belief in party as an end in itself was not a source of strength, but the opposite. His consequent preoccupation with rewards and expedients offended a great many Tories. 'It is not becoming in any minister to decry party who has risen by party', he rebuked Pakington in December 1858, when the First Lord of the Admiralty passed over a Tory for the post of commander-in-chief, Portsmouth, which went to Palmerston's brother-in-law, Sir William Bowles, once a Tory then a Peelite MP.[134] 'In...your letter...you show that you misunderstand me', rejoined Pakington, '...I have no "fear of rewarding friends"...Nor do I "decry party". But I...disapprove of carrying party motives and objects into matters with which they have no legitimate connection.' He had consulted Derby, who preferred Bowles, about the political and the professional aspects of the appointment. 'I believe', ended Pakington, 'that the exercise of patronage with fairness... justice, and strict regard to the *public* interests, gives more real strength to an administration...' Disraeli's candidate was not only too junior but disqualified by poor eyesight.[135] This dispute, and the tone in which it was conducted, reveals how little authority Disraeli wielded, independently of Derby.

The Tory ministry of 1858–59 was a deliberate experiment in liberalization, seen by Derby as inevitable if the party were to hold office. A quick, and disastrous, start was made with the provision in Ellenborough's India bill of March 1858 for the elective representation of London, Manchester, Liverpool, Glasgow and Belfast on the new council to assist the cabinet minister in undivided charge of Indian government. The five councillors, out of eighteen, were to be chosen by the Parliamentary voters in each of these seats of industry and trade. Amazement greeted the prospect of such direct urban middle-class participation in governing an empire. Whigs and radicals viewed it as an absurd novelty in constitutional practice. Lewis described it as 'fantastic, extravagant, and unsound ... It is inconceivable how an entire cabinet should have agreed to so wild and foolish a scheme'.[136] Bright condemned it unreservedly.[137] Ellenborough's colleagues acquiesced in an obviously controversial proposal because told it would appeal to the middle class, who had always run India under the Company, subject to the ultimate control of landed ministers and Parliament from the late eighteenth century. The middle class proved to be mainly indifferent; and the ministry hastily gave in to its massed critics in Parliament and the press. Disraeli maintained that the rejected idea was sound. 'I cannot pretend', he said defiantly in the Commons, 'to compete for a moment with that power of sarcasm, that force of invective with which ... the great constituencies of the commercial towns have in this case been overwhelmed by the Liberal party.' Referring to the 'almost horror-stricken tone' in which an MP for a manufacturing town, the industrialist Thornley of Wolverhampton, inquired whether he 'really and seriously' intended that Liverpool, with an electoral reputation for venality and bigotry, should return a member to the new council, Disraeli countered by pointing to the constituency's choice in the not too distant past of George Canning, which could hardly be faulted by his political heirs, Liberal and Peelite.[138] The episode confirmed the unreadiness, asserted by its own representatives, of the middle class to rule.

Disraeli was nevertheless so shaken by his Parliamentary mauling that he temporarily lost his nerve: 'this must be the fate of all our measures in the present Parliament even if ... concocted by the Angel Gabriel ... we should not attempt to legislate ...'.[139] The expedient that got the Jews' Act through was not his. Parliamentary reform breathed fresh life into the Tories' liberalizing resolve. Malmesbury was sceptical, but stood by Derby; others were mindful of 'the great political truth: "It is easy to alienate your friends, impossible to conciliate your opponents"', which Manners stressed in a memorandum of 1857 on the courses open to what to him was 'the Country Party'.[140] The divisions within the cabinet on 'the most delicate' of all questions, as Stanley designated it in August 1858,[141] were to be reflected in those of after years. While General Peel and Lord Hardwicke did not leave the government with Walpole and Henley, they thought the reform bill went too far. Derby, Malmesbury and Manners occupied the middle ground. Among those who were liberal, or comparatively so, on the bill, there was less convergence of opinion. The sometime radical, Bulwer Lytton, had little belief in what they were seeking to do, worried as he was by the impact of a lower occupation franchise on his Hertfordshire electorate, and made more doubtful of the change by contact with colonial democracy. Naval rearmament had most of Pakington's attention. The one determined reformer was Stanley, whose possible resignation was a greater danger to the government than the loss of Walpole and Henley. 'Disraeli has behaved beautifully throughout', commented Malmesbury, 'trying to smooth all difficulties and faithful on all points to Lord Derby.'[142] Disraeli's fidelity to the prime minister was the condition of the bill's acceptance by the party. Over 200 Tory MPs listened to Derby on 1 March setting forth 'the pros and cons of the details of the measure'. Three notable figures on the backbenches, Palmer of Berkshire, Sir John Trollope of South Lincolnshire, and Newdegate of North Warwickshire, said they would have been better pleased with a £20 county occupation franchise; but all the speakers at the meeting fell in behind the bill. When forty-five Tory members had second thoughts, and deputed Palmer and Bentinck of North Norfolk to ask Derby to withdraw it, they were snubbed. Sotheron Estcourt recorded 'general dissatisfaction' with the bill by the middle of March. It was their respect for Derby, and the complete absence of any alternative leader, that so largely preserved Tory unity under this strain.[143]

As the ministry arrived at the last days of its existence, Malmesbury unburdened himself to Clarendon about Disraeli, '*who always lied*'. 'He was dead sick of his office which he only retained out of deference to Derby', wrote Clarendon to Palmerston, '...two-thirds of the party', he said, 'hate Dizzy intensely.' Malmesbury recommended the Liberals to avoid language wounding to Tory feelings; their reward would be considerable support for a Palmerston administration, on which it was in fact able to rely: 'his only wish was to see a strong government *quelconque*'.[144] The Derby ministry's defeats on the reform bill, church rates, in the election and the ensuing confidence debate, combined with the vulnerability in foreign affairs which brought it down, decided Derby and Malmesbury that they 'must help to keep these cripples on their legs', when their successors' tenure appeared precarious at the beginning of 1860.[145] A Palmerston government was preferable to a Tory ministry obliged to experiment with liberalization in ways for which it had no enthusiasm. The party blamed Disraeli, not very fairly, for a policy that exposed the limitations of Toryism. His perpetual quest for power by, it seemed, any means to hand, required to be checked, for his own sake as much as for that of the Tories. 'Disraeli is against the loan for the national defences', remarked Malmesbury in January 1860. 'If he opposes it in Parliament he is done for, both with his party and the country.'[146] Disraeli behaved prudently; Derby was firmly for the loan. Disraeli associated himself with Derby and Malmesbury in their unsolicited assurances of May the same year that the opposition would uphold Palmerston for the rest of the session, if he needed help to survive a conjunction of resigning cabinet ministers and radicals. Then in January 1861 Disraeli personally promised the Prince Consort that he, like his party, 'thought solely of strengthening the hands of the government in a patriotic sense' on the question of defence expenditure; he ascribed radical-inspired pressure for economy to 'intrigues...from the Tuileries'.[147] But by June

Pakington was angrily complaining that he had been left unsupported by Disraeli on the topic, 'of such extreme importance to the country', of Anglo-French naval rivalry. Disraeli, the letter went on, was 'our recognized leader in the...Commons' but ought to consult his colleagues on the front bench in that House, a practice he too evidently did not care for. Pakington entered a solemn protest: 'I cannot admit...that we should have neither voice in the course of action to be taken, nor knowledge what the course is upon which you have determined.'[148]

Actually, Disraeli had made a show of retirement from the Tory leadership in the lower House at this juncture by staying away briefly after the Tories failed to get all their men into the lobby against Gladstone's abolition of the paper duties. He was tolerated as an unpalatable necessity, and knew it: '...glad to see...you had resumed the seat to which you have so well asserted your claim', Pakington repeated that 'support and confidence can be neither permanent nor useful unless...reciprocal'.[149] It looks very much as if Disraeli's neglect to consult his principal colleagues in the House reflected his profound indifference to Toryism as a creed when he was not inclined to ridicule at least one of its doctrinal pillars – religion. No one could rival his assiduity and skill in the day-to-day management of opposition in the Commons under the remote but definitely effectual control of Derby; no one, it seems, wanted the job.[150] The misunderstanding and conflict that easily arose came out in the Tory reaction to the radical Stansfeld's motion for economy in June 1862. Disraeli saw a chance to put the government in a minority. He was always drawn to combination with radicals, as the most readily detachable section of the Liberals. The Tory party never relished the prospect, and especially not when the issue was spending on defence in the shadow of Napoleon. Only 186 out of more than 300 MPs gathered at Derby's summons and cheered his speech asking them to vote for a Tory amendment to Stansfeld's motion, ostensibly separate but couched in similar terms, which Disraeli hoped would attract enough radicals and Liberals to be carried.[151] Derby had previously called twenty MPs, members of his last government and influential backbenchers, to his London home for a discussion of tactics. He approved of an amendment to display Tory concern for the taxpayers, but was 'most anxious to avoid treating it as a motion which, if carried, must lead to the overthrow of the Government'. '...it would not be decent', Stanley was clear, 'to use the votes of the economico-radical party as a means of defeating Lord Palmerston in a party division.' General Peel and Pakington, who had headed the War Office and the Admiralty respectively, did not want to countenance any reduction in expenditure, which must result in lower naval and military estimates.[152] Prompted by his inveterate opportunism, Disraeli had also come under the progressive influence of his ex-Peelite protégé, Sir Stafford Northcote, a Devonshire baronet once private secretary to Gladstone at the Board of Trade. Northcote pressed him to embrace Anglo-French co-operation wholeheartedly: 'is it not conceivable that the intentions of France are as pure as our own?'.[153]

More Gladstonian than his old master, Northcote took his argument for mutual trust between the two countries to the length of suggesting that Napoleon might legitimately put his disturbing moves in recent years down to British incomprehension and unfriendliness: 'we have declined to... make sufficient allowance for his difficulties...'.[154] Northcote had the high-mindedness of the Peelites but without much political sense. He did not possess the wider knowledge of opinion that would have enabled him to judge correctly the reception of a plea for economy in estimates which Gladstone had himself agreed with the spending departments. Northcote brought the latter's speech at Manchester in April to the notice of Disraeli as proof that there was 'serious discontent' at the levels of taxation. But a Tory drive for economy, he acknowledged, had to be managed carefully: 'our friends should see that we are not trying to get Cobden and Bright to join us in an onslaught on Lord Palmerston, but that we are delivering our testimony upon matters which we regard as of high national importance'.[155] Thus the Tories went forward to a fiasco in the debate on Stansfeld's motion. Their amendment was entrusted to Walpole, who had no sympathy whatever with Disraeli's ambitions and Northcote's pacific reasoning. Palmerston threatened the opposition and the partisans of economy behind him with a dissolution; and secured a crushing majority, Liberal and Tory, on the main motion after a debate emptied of real interest when Walpole at once withdrew his amendment, saying that the prime minister's announcement created a new situation. Stanley thought Disraeli's speech reproducing Northcote's points was his ablest for a decade; but its merits were quite lost upon his side, where Malmesbury set down the prevailing impression of his performance derived from its finale: 'Disraeli got up again to deliver the most vindictive diatribe against Mr. Walpole, to the disgust of almost all the Conservative party.'[156]

There is a good account of this confusion, as felt by an MP not yet admitted to his party's inmost circle, in the diary of a rising man among the younger Tories, Gathorne Hardy, Walpole's under-secretary at the Home Office in 1858–59. '...his...thoroughly Conservative tone and repudiation of alliance with the radicals carried the meeting', he wrote after hearing Derby address the disappointing attendance of Tory MPs before the debate. Hardy then described how 'as soon as we began to think it over, our misgivings arose...'. He believed Walpole had been right to withdraw the opposition's amendment; had it gone to a vote, the result would have been 'division within exposed'. 'I am delighted', Hardy concluded, 'that we are out of the whole affair, which appeared...a sham and humbug.' He accepted the force of the prime minister's warning that the Tories would be humiliated in a general election.[157] The Speaker, J. E. Denison, found it 'altogether a most singular evening', in which Palmerston disabled his opponents by showing again that he could make 'a better and more effective speech than any other man, taking the House between wind and water with wonderful skill'.[158] Gladstone, the real target for many of the Tories unwilling to oust Palmerston, took pleasure in 'A scene as notable and a rout as complete' as he remembered the Liberals' unsuccessful attack on the Tory administration in May 1858 to have been: 'I sat on velvet throughout', he remarked of this occasion.[159] Stanley surmised that Walpole had been led to provide the government with its victory by his strong-minded wife, who loathed Disraeli personally and had not forgiven him for the Jews' Act. According to Stanley, ministers had prior knowledge that Walpole did not intend to persevere with the amendment, and the prime minister devised his counter-stroke in the light of that information.[160] No convincing evidence exists for either statement. Nor was such knowledge necessary when Palmerston and the cabinet decided on their tactics; they were aware of Derby's and his followers' limited aim, no secret after their party meeting of the previous day, 'rather to damage and disparage the Government than to turn them out'; and they suspected Disraeli's ambitious design. Palmerston was hugely satisfied with the effect he achieved in resorting to the menace of a dissolution: 'This fell like a bombshell on opposition. Walpole staggered...The triumph was great'; but he did not deceive himself about its extent.[161]

Called on to restore an approximation to harmony among his colleagues in the lower House, Derby wrote to Disraeli: 'I will do my best to smooth matters: but I fear it will require time to reunite the party.' Walpole was 'very sore'; while Sotheron Estcourt complained of the Tory *Morning Herald*'s interpretation of Walpole's amendment, published on the morning of the debate, as designed to evict Palmerston from office. Derby, who had interpreted the amendment to exclude that meaning, saw the *Morning Herald* article, 'so injudicious', on its appearance; and alerted the former Tory chief whip, Jolliffe, who was with him, to the danger it presented.[162] It was plain to Lewis from Disraeli's speech that he had envisaged a challenge to the government's existence.[163] The implication of Derby's letter, not obscured by a scathing reference to his correspondent's political wounds, was that Disraeli had only himself to blame if he had inspired the newspaper, and further alienated the Tories when he spoke. Disraeli subsided into a long spell of relative quiescence, broken by such reminders as this from Derby in January 1863: 'As our Parliamentary campaign is about to begin, it is high time that we should have a conference on the general state of affairs.'[164] It seemed to Stanley that Disraeli was losing some of his interest in the political game.[165] The leader in the Commons certainly took up a more conservative attitude for the remainder of the

Parliament. His entry in *Dod* at the time of the abortive Tory reform bill claimed that he was a champion of 'those popular and aristocratic institutions which had made power a privilege within the reach of all who exert themselves to deserve it'. In the 1865 edition of *Dod*, he figured simply as one who would 'uphold our constitution in Church and State'.

Defensive politics

As so often with him, Disraeli went too far in the opposite direction when he decided to change course. At the National Conservative Registration Association dinner of June 1863, where Malmesbury, Walpole, Henley, Manners and General Peel were among those present, he delivered what was intended to be a major policy speech. There was no community of purpose, he averred, between Tories and Liberals, but a profound antagonism: 'The Liberal party are of opinion that the...franchise ought to be democratic. We are not. The Liberal party are of opinion that the union between Church and State should be abolished. We are not. Our colonial empire...the national estate...which gives to the energies and abilities of Englishmen an inexhaustible theatre – the Liberal party are of opinion that the relations between the metropolis and the people of the colonies...ought to be abrogated...We are not....Through all the most considerable features of our social and political system...the... differences...exist really and in theory between the two great parties...'[166] This grotesque caricature of Palmerstonian Liberalism obliged Derby to refer to it within days on a brilliant party occasion, a banquet to him at the Mansion House. If Disraeli's contrast applied to 'at all events...the advanced Liberal party', yet they were 'for the most part...very well satisfied to leave their favourite projects in abeyance' under Palmerston. 'We, as good Conservatives', he declared, 'were...satisfied for the present with that arrangement.'[167] Henley was blunt in his relief at the position they had reached in Parliament and the country. 'On political subjects, thank God', he said to his Oxfordshire constituents with one of the Tory magnates, the Duke of Marlborough, beside him, 'there is nothing for us to say...we are at peace with the world, and...at peace with one another... Other countries seem willing...to fight...but I hope we can keep out of it. I see no English interest mixed up in it.'[168] The last two sentences conveyed a rebuke to those Tories who would have liked Britain to intervene, somehow, between North and South in the American Civil war. General Peel had preceded his leader and colleague by a couple of years in expressing a similar view of Tory strategy.[169]

In his Mansion House speech Derby reiterated, but more emphatically, the theme of strong, responsible opposition which he had sounded four years earlier, and to which he had returned in the interval: '...there can be no greater misfortune than that the Conservative party should obtain office with a majority, if...any majority at all...day by day at the risk of any... combination...that might be formed...by the various elements...sure to agree well enough to oppose them'. Derby habitually thought of most Liberals, many Whigs included, as 'Radicals'. He did not forget his own Whig past, but he mourned 'that great...party...of Grey...Brougham and Mackintosh'; he had been proud to belong to it. He regretted that their successors were prepared to compromise with policies and men, 'of which and of whom in private they would not hesitate to speak in the most deprecatory terms'. He deplored Gladstone's supposed readiness to be 'the Coryphaeus and mouthpiece', not of the government, but of a pro-American radicalism discredited by the 'approaching dissolution' of the United States.[170] But while Palmerston lived, Derby was practically resigned to his rival's success in presiding over a party which the Tory leader did indeed consider fundamentally disunited and only kept in a semblance of order by Palmerston's talent for manipulation. Derby avoided answering the question that his political analysis begged. How was it that Palmerston controlled the genuine radicals, as the Tory gave him credit for doing in this speech? Understandably, Derby did not choose to sap the morale of Toryism by dwelling on its failure to make more headway in the towns. Until the Liberals alienated some of their middle-class voters, the Tories, he realized, could not attain power, distinguished from the experience of place which they had twice had for short periods in the fifties. Derby appreciated the Palmerstonian policy of class collaboration without wanting the party to change its identity. He would not tolerate in Disraeli a rival with a different approach to current politics.

'As I can never hold any office but the first, so neither can I be the head of any but a *bona fide* Conservative government':[171] this stance of Derby's after 1859 did not survive Palmerston's death within months of his last victory in the general election of 1865. The Liberalism refashioned by the dead man withstood proposals of fusion from the Tories to selected Whigs. To compensate for this frustration, Derby's third minority administration gambled on a reform bill that far exceeded the limits of the Russell–Gladstone franchise and redistribution measures defeated by Tories and dissident Liberals in 1866. The first of these measures would have added fewer voters to the electorate than its predecessor of 1860. The Tory bill of 1867 passed because, with the Liberals in confusion and public opinion more receptive to legislation on the subject, Derby and Disraeli raised the bidding. But its passage demoralized and discredited the party to a much greater extent than was apparent from the polls next year. Gladstone came in with a cabinet full of men who had served under Palmerston at that level or in junior ministerial posts. The advent of Gladstone surrounded by good Palmerstonians was widely seen as a return to the stability and 'progressive improvement' of Liberal governments between 1855 and 1865. The outcome might have been foreseen, if the Tories had not professed to think that neither Palmerston nor Gladstone was a liberal conservative in the spirit of Canning, but, respectively, a cynical reactionary and a crypto-radical. Stanley, for instance, was sceptical when in July 1864 Gladstone vigorously asserted his unchanging conservatism in private conversation as on the platform.[172] It is difficult to resist the conclusion that the Tories were in some degree taken in by their own propaganda; whether like General Peel and Henley, they applauded Palmerston's supposed pre-dilection for immobility, or, like Disraeli in the 1865 election, built up the always disturbing figure of Bright to frighten the electorate: 'a member of the House of Commons second to none in ability and reputation...he has never disguised his objects. He says we must change the tenure of land... He is opposed to ecclesiastical institutions in connexion with the state.'[173]

Northcote's letters to Disraeli reveal the Tory predicament in the face of a Liberal administration which so many of the party did not want to disturb. Disraeli referred in the speech just cited to the regular defectors from the outwardly imposing total of over 300 Tories in the last Parliament, 'whenever the Conservative leaders made an appeal...on any important question of party'. He put the number of these defectors at about fifteen; there were rather higher estimates, but not all the fifteen to twenty-five members 'invariably' voted with ministers. He had to admit, in the midst of the election, that Palmerston's was 'an able and successful govern-ment'.[174] In recent sessions Northcote had filled the role of a zealous, capable and sympathetic lieutenant, supplying one of Disraeli's greatest needs. Sir Stafford too, looked for 'a line of our own'. To Disraeli's advantage, however, the upright and devoutly Christian Northcote was more sensitive to the moral conflicts inherent in Parliamentary opposition. The best that he could suggest to distinguish Toryism in foreign and imperial policy was 'a mean between a fussy interference and absolute indifference...'. It was not obvious that the Palmerston cabinet had generally failed to strike that balance. For Russell's proneness to 'strong language and weak action' characterized the foreign secretary and not, ordinarily, a prime minister seen to dominate his colleague, as he did Clarendon before him.[175]

7

Religion and politics

Objectives

Palmerston's religious policy reflected his concern to improve and stabilize class relations. Protestant Dissenters were predominantly drawn from the skilled working class with relatively high earnings. A small but authoritative middle-class element, varied in size between the major sects, strongest among Baptists and Congregationalists, weakest in Primitive Methodism. A little under 5 per cent of MPs elected in 1865 belonged to Protestant Dissent.[1] The figure is deceptive and should be adjusted to take account of Quakers and Unitarians whose doctrines made them questionably representative of their fellow-Dissenters. Much the largest of the sects, the Wesleyan Methodists, dissociated itself, as a whole, from agitation against the Established Church and her intimate relationship with the ruling landed class. If Dissenting political attitudes were otherwise far from easy to define, they generally incorporated two conflicting tendencies, hereditary loyalty to the Whig/Liberals and impatience with subordination to them. A better understanding within Liberalism depended as much upon inter-denominational goodwill as upon a broad community of secular aims. While Palmerston sought to diminish tension between Church and Dissent primarily for political reasons, his personal inclinations were involved, too. He told Gladstone's wife, who approached him early in the life of his second administration to convey her husband's disquiet about the distribution of ecclesiastical patronage, that the nature of the appointments represented 'his *political* duty'. The prime minister reportedly 'disclaimed altogether any religious duty' in that respect.[2] In fact, he professed a low temperature Christianity; what he liked in a preacher was 'sound common sense', and it appears to have been mainly in Low Churchmen that he discerned this supreme quality.[3] No Evangelical, he approved, as did so many others then, of the demonstrable success that Evangelicalism had with practical religion, and especially in promoting the co-operation of Churchman and Dissenter.

167

His governments benefited in all major areas of policy, internal and external, from the encouragement of religious solidarity. They sought more determinedly and extensively than their Whig predecessors to redress the grievances of Dissent over church rates, qualifying oaths, and education. The preference for Churchmen whom the sects found congenial was still more effective in disarming radicalism. The dry Erastianism of Russell, personifying a less flexible Whiggery, was dated. Palmerston's anti-Catholicism, perhaps the strongest feature of his personal beliefs, reinforced party and national unity in foreign and Irish affairs. Urged on by Disraeli, some Tories paid Palmerston the high compliment of trying to centre the struggle of parties around his religious policy. More significantly, Gladstone revised his political, if not his theological, objections to Palmerston's handling of religion.[4]

The prime minister and Shaftesbury

Palmerston's views and his past, like Disraeli's, unfitted him for the ostentatious championship of religion. Unlike Disraeli, he did not cast himself for an unsuitable public role. Instead, he took judicious advantage of his family connection with the greatest of the Evangelicals, Lord Shaftesbury, whose diary shows how conscious he was of not exercising that domination over the prime minister's mind with which he was widely credited. If Shaftesbury had Palmerston's ear, he rightly thought it was 'always ready to be tickled by liberal flourishes' – liberal, that is, in the theological sense – and deplored the countervailing advice of William Cowper MP, the prime minister's stepson.[5] For the key bishopric of London in 1856 Palmerston selected A. C. Tait, a choice that gave Broad Churchmen a leader and real weight within the Establishment. The historian and future Dean of Westminster, A. P. Stanley, perhaps the broadest of the school, heard with delight the report of Tait's preferment: 'Lord Palmerston would have done more to put the Church on a liberal and efficient footing than anyone in his generation', he wrote to his cousin in the cabinet.[6] After seven years in the see, Tait composed a private memorandum listing his chief preoccupations. Apart from his uncontroversial solicitude for the dechristianized urban poor, he had set himself to reassure the middle classes, 'whom the High Church development seemed fast alienating...I feel convinced that its prevalence would end in the denationalising of the Church of England...'. Of still greater moment, he considered, was the continuing attachment to the Established Church 'of the vast body of thoughtful and somewhat religious persons in the upper classes, who are influenced neither by the *Record* nor the *Guardian*', the leading Evangelical and High Church journals, respectively. If unable to retain a firm hold on the upper classes, the Church would not stand, 'its nationality...surely gone'. 'I have always thought it was a special part of my mission to prevent the alienation of these...', he said.[7] Their almost solid Anglicanism distinguished them from other social classes; the English Catholic aristocracy and gentry were too few and unassertive to count. Where Palmerston differed from the Broad Churchmen was in his awareness of their limitations. While by no means universally popular, the Evangelicalism of the Low Church certainly had a wider appeal than competing types of Churchmanship at this time. The Evangelicals' lay genius, Shaftesbury, noted in his diary for June 1855, 'Under God, I have no hope but in publicity.'[8] The organizational and journalistic activity of Evangelical Christianity enabled the religious message with its social and political content to infiltrate and unify classes as well as denominations to an extent impossible to quantify with any precision but obviously substantial.[9]

According to Gladstone's friend and confidant, the sometime Peelite MP, R. J. Phillimore, Palmerston gave 'a sort of promise' to eschew 'extreme appointments' when he came to power in 1855.[10] Apprehension that he would nevertheless discriminate against High Churchmen in favour of their Evangelical and Broad Church opponents turned out to be well founded. Towards the end of the following year, his cabinet colleague, Wood, who was staying with Sidney Herbert at Wilton, advised him of the now 'great dissatisfaction' in High Church circles excited by the latest Evangelical preferment, a dean for Carlisle. Wood, who described Gladstone as 'the antipodes of my opinions in Church matters', thought it would be wise to heed the High Churchmen's plea 'to try and find a man who will not be obnoxious to them' for the vacant see of Ripon.[11] A decided moderate was Wood's own preference but the prime minister went for an Evangelical, Robert Bickersteth, thereby incurring royal displeasure at his insistence upon a partisan, yet another one.[12] 'Your letter touched upon a great difficulty', replied Palmerston to Wood. For him, the decisive factor in making these contentious appointments was their impact upon Dissent. The religious census of 1851 enumerating attendance at places of worship in England and Wales, revealed virtual parity between Church and Dissent on that basis. Palmerston dismissed the subsequent claim of ardent Dissenters to numerical equality in the English and Welsh population, the majority of whom had not attended church or chapel on census Sunday.[13] With other evidence, marriage statistics – a more reliable guide to religious loyalties than Sunday observance in a random week – indicate that Dissenters who would have nothing to do with the Establishment formed a much smaller proportion than he supposed. In 1861 the Church performed 80 per cent of marriages in England and Wales, compared with 84 per cent ten years earlier, including those of numerous Dissenters who freely chose an Anglican ceremony for the event. Nevertheless, Dissenters of all kinds constituted a formidable presence, increasingly aware of the fact as the sects' middle-class leadership grew in prosperity and political experience. They were a principal source of middle-class radicalism, a brand of politics in which religion played an important part; and to which prudence dictated that the respectable working class should not be attracted in greater strength. The more pronounced clericalism and sacramentalism of the contemporary High Church, so visibly enhanced by the Oxford movement, faced a corresponding antagonism from Evangelicalism which in a little over two generations had strikingly raised the level of belief and practice. High Churchmen were suspect as crypto-Catholics, and the trickle of conversions to Rome from their ranks intensified the suspicion.

The advisability of making Evangelical bishops, deans and canons on an unprecedented scale may be seen from the swelling hostility at this epoch to one of the outstanding High Church parish clergymen, W. F. Hook, Vicar of Leeds, and from his reaction. Such was the mood of the town's strong Dissenting community that he momentarily despaired, after more than twenty years in Leeds: 'The case is now hopeless', he lamented to Wilberforce, his leader in ecclesiastical politics, 'We must unite our forces with the Evangelicals, unless your Lordship, and others, will come forward in the cause of sound Church of England Protestantism...' He had been warned, moreover, by 'several of our Yorkshire squires – men who could do much for the Church...that it is impossible to maintain our ground... confused...with the Romanizers'.[14] Wilberforce answered this and similar pleas by attacking Roman Catholicism even more vigorously than was his wont, while maintaining that the Church was both essentially Catholic and faithful to the Reformation.[15] Palmerston might safely tell Mrs Gladstone that 'an anti-Romanist distribution of ecclesiastical patronage' was a political obligation, however unpalatable to her husband.[16] There could be no denying the friction between High Church prelates, on the one hand, and Low Churchmen and Dissenters, on the other; nor that, although High Churchmen joined heartily in detestation of the Papacy, and sincerely recoiled from certain features of Catholic devotion, they did lean 'towards Popery', to quote Palmerston's language in private. For all their severe criticism of its medieval and modern development, they gave priority to the rediscovery of Catholicism in doctrine and discipline over their Reformation origins. Low Church bishops were 'forbearing towards...their High Church brethren and...at peace with the Dissenters', argued Palmerston, plausibly as regards Dissent. No one could say that Wilberforce bore himself meekly in his diocese or on the national stage. Filling more sees with men like him, the prime minister felt, 'would raise a flame throughout the country...'. Deeply prejudiced against the Tractarians, he had no difficulty in perceiving a governmental and class liability in them.[17]

It may be hard to appreciate the resentment aroused by Palmerston's elevation of a few Evangelicals before the 1857 election. The scope of his policy was, however, clearly perceptible in attempted and successful legislation: his government's qualified support for the Liberation Society's position on church rates came into the first category; into the second fell a measure to pension off the Bishops of London and Durham. This Act of 1856, passed in the absence of any regular provision for episcopal retirement, was fiercely assailed by Wilberforce and Gladstone on its way through Parliament. Both denounced it as simony, bribing the prelates concerned to resign in order to place their sees at Palmerston's disposal. 'We have been utterly smashed on the second reading of the Bishops' Bill', wrote Gladstone dispiritedly to his wife.[18] The voting saw Cardwell desert the Peelites for the government lobby, although Walpole broke away from the Tories to join Gladstone. The opposition of the two last, prominent University members representing distinctively clerical constituencies, was eloquent of the Evangelicals' unpopularity with a majority of the Anglican clergy, amongst whom their overemphasis on a common Protestantism struck many conventional Churchmen, not at all High in outlook, as undermining the Establishment. Its evident success fed the dislike and fear of ministerial populism in religion. Shaftesbury congratulated himself, in his diary for August 1856, on the 'undoubted popularity' accruing to Palmerston when the prime minister acted on his recommendations for preferment.[19] Lord Derby complained angrily in the Lords, after the dissolution of 1857 had been announced, about the use to which Palmerston and his political friends had put the Church. He did not relish Parliamentary discussion of church appointments, and 'how much less should they be made the subject of bitter...contest in the crowded arena of the hustings...amid all the ribald feeling and cries which often distinguish these election saturnalia?' The government's well-advertised predilection for one wing of the Church must prove harmful both to the Establishment and to the state. Carefully repudiating any suggestion of animus against Dissent, he criticized the Evangelical tendency 'for the sake of a false peace and...a false union' to minimize differences between the Church and the sects; and he affirmed – 'thank God' – the will and ability of the former to uphold traditional claims. To protect this declaration of Tory fidelity to Anglican supremacy from a fatal misinterpretation, he prefaced it with an unsparing condemnation of the High Church: their exaltation of ecclesiastical authority was anachronistic, and could not be tolerated; their innovations in the externals of religion 'if they assume any further meaning' implied 'more than an approximation...to a creed...religiously corrupt and politically dangerous'. A better Christian than Palmerston, Derby was, if anything, rather more anti-Catholic.[20]

The most remarkable feature of Derby's speech was his scathing reference to an alleged election cry which proclaimed 'blasphemously, at least irreverently, "Palmerston, the Man of God"'. He credited the *Record* with this folly, which the journal had not perpetrated.[21] The Evangelicals were thankful to have Palmerston at the head of affairs: but their regard for him fell a long way short of the sanctification imputed to them by Derby. They knew the prime minister was not attached to their puritanism, any more than Derby was. When it suited him to do so, Palmerston made it quite clear that he complied with their wishes only from political calculation. The 'Great Band Question' of 1856 was such an episode. An united front of Evangelical Christians in Britain demanded and secured the cancellation of Sunday concerts in the London parks by military bands, as a profanation of the Sabbath. Palmerston gave way, accepting the existence of a serious Parliamentary threat to his government, of which Shaftesbury urgently advised him.[22] At the same time, he received plebeian deputations seeking the continuance of what had been deliberately initiated as blameless popular recreation. He sympathized warmly with their complaints, and was at pains to assure them of his esteem for, and confidence in, the working classes, for whom they spoke. The behaviour of the metropolitan crowds had been exemplary in the face of provocation, as he plainly considered it, by the sabbatarian lobby of their social superiors, but only 'such as any man…at all acquainted with the character of Englishmen…would have expected,… especially those who have watched the progress of the working-classes in industry, intelligence, morality, and good order'. The 'innocent' concerts, 'no desecration of the Sabbath' were intended to draw people into the open air, out of unwholesome conditions of life and work. While he held that 'in a free country like this' government should not take sides in religious disputes, his administration had been forced into that position, caught between two great bodies of opinion, one of which had inevitably prevailed. '…it was not', he said, candidly, 'the duty of the government to run counter to…so large a number of the community…entitled to respect'.[23] In other words, the organized electoral weight of Evangelical Christianity must carry the day. More specifically, it was the attitude of Dissenting activists in the borough constituencies, and of Scottish members in the House of Common itself, that influenced the ministerial retreat.[24] The 'Great Band Question' and its outcome exaggerated the power of Evangelical pressure group politics. They were able briefly to unite Low Churchmen, Dissenters and Scottish Presbyterians of more than one kind on an issue unusually promising for them and awkward for government.

The Sunday trading riots of the previous year in London, protesting against a sabbatarian bill introduced by the Evangelical Lord Robert Grosvenor, had been welcomed by *The Times* as a warranted rebuff to puritanism. Grosvenor was compelled to withdraw his measure. 'It was a got-up thing', alleged Shaftesbury, quite mistakenly, '… *The Times* approves ... this lynch law ... millions on millions of Christian people should meet to "pray down" that paper ...'[25] Compared with a threat to the freedom to buy and sell on Sundays in the places that catered for them, the interdiction of bands in the parks was an annoyance, not a hardship. In 1855 Palmerston himself had been the target of popular anger because of his association, through Shaftesbury, with dedicated Evangelicals; and particularly with the aristocratic element, personified by Grosvenor in this instance, which took the lead natural to its class. The bands were an idea to put the formidable London crowds in a better humour with government. Politically conservative Evangelicals, like the High Tory Shaftesbury, saw here a further, dangerous concession to irreligious democracy; others were simply provoked by official concern to indulge old English mob rule at the expense of new, self-confident godliness. Never again did Shaftesbury and the Anglican Evangelicals manage to combine with the sects to such effect. The loyalty which bound most, not all, Low Churchmen to the Establishment inhibited a similar display of unity, except in the agitation for a more definite policy of christianization in post-Mutiny India. Then it was Shaftesbury who pulled back to save Palmerston's government from perilous embarrassment.[26]

The cultivation of Dissent

The Dissenters' religious independence was compatible with eager deference to Shaftesbury's exposition of the social and political dimensions of faith, an unending task in which lesser men of his rank assisted him. These devout aristocrats assumed a central role in the network of societies, generally the creation of Evangelical Churchmen, designed to bring Anglican and Dissenter together in varied Christian endeavours. They were also invited to preside over Dissenting societies, being significantly favoured by the foreign missionary organizations of the sects, at which their appearance provided gratifying confirmation of Dissent's acceptability and standing. The High Church *Guardian* dismissed a characteristic Dissenting grievance – exclusion from a share in the control of endowed grammar schools – by saying 'the dignity of Dissenting notabilities is wounded'.[27] It was an inadequate comment, and an unwise one. Shaftesbury strove to enlist those notabilities on his side. In his religious labours, he seldom allowed himself to lose sight of closely related objectives. Too intelligent not to realize that the political nation must steadily expand, however alarming the prospect, he described the action to take in a speech of April 1858 to an Evangelical gathering in the City: 'Whether we will or not, this and every other country was gradually sliding into democracy ... a healthy public opinion would become the only safeguard ... Hence the great importance of a ... process in the mind of the people, whereby it might be well seasoned and taught...correct views,... to regard all subjects in a religious aspect. Only by this could we be preserved from disturbances which might even occasion a disruption of social order.' It was binding on all Christians, to do 'their utmost' towards the realization of this aim; the press would not fail to mirror their achievement.[28] Despite the pessimism inherent in his type of pious Toryism, he discerned real hope of the trend he postulated. Its furtherance depended on the exertions of Church and Dissent; in 'a generous and moral rivalry', they should agree on the principle that: 'For many operations the simple teaching of Evangelical truth was necessary– the Word of Christ and nothing else.' Appearing at Exeter Hall in May 1860 with Edward Baines MP, Shaftesbury cited the interdenominational special services begun several years earlier. Amid the censures of opposing Churchmen, they were aimed at 'the hungry masses'. The Dissenting audience at this annual meeting of the London Missionary Society expected something more in purely theological justification of a joint approach to those not in regular, or in any, contact with institutional Christianity. They enthusiastically applauded his unequivocal declaration against the High and the Broad Church, 'Tractarianism and Neology would not do'.[29]

On a simple doctrinal basis, Shaftesbury proceeded, time and again, to impress upon receptive audiences the unifying force of true religion on the nation's mundane purposes at home and abroad. Class collaboration stood first in the order of priorities. The speeches at the South London Working-Classes Industrial Exhibition of 1864 illustrate the convergence of Anglican aristocrat and Dissenting industrialist in recognition and encouragement of skilled workers as a distinct and rising interest in the social hierarchy. Shaftesbury, who took the chair, was supported by John Bright; the devout Baptist Sir Morton Peto MP, a well-known railway contractor and a baronet of Palmerstonian creation; the Congregationalist Samuel Morley, of the Administrative Reform Association and the Liberation Society; and the Reverend Newman Hall, the famous Congregationalist preacher of the period. Peto, from his knowledge of the district as an employer, avowed his satisfaction at working men's 'rapid progress ... in elevating themselves in the social scale'. Bright was more controversial; working men were too low down that scale; 'temperate and provident habits' would help their advancement. He stressed 'the necessity of a closer connection and co-operation between the different classes...to elevate the masses...to bridge...the gulf which...so widely separated them from their richer brethren'. Shaftesbury echoed Bright in deeming Parliament morally bound 'to remove...every impediment that prevents the working classes from having full and fair play', and also in saying 'it would depend upon their individual exertions to gain many of those political rights which a most justifiable ambition made them desire'. Like Bright, he held up the self-discipline of temperance, thrift, and education as instrumental to their betterment. Of the two, the Tory Earl sounded more confident that working men would in fact display the responsibility for which he appealed.[30] A prey to acute recurrent anxiety about the results of an extended franchise, he yet hoped and believed his brand of religion could render it safe. In 1856, he told the wealthy and influential Church Pastoral Aid Society, which existed to diffuse Evangelicalism within the Establishment: 'although I am anything in the world but a Parliamentary reformer...if...an ordained minister and his curate...should constantly inculcate among the people...the Gospel, I should have no more fear of granting universal suffrage than I had of assenting to the enfranchisement of the £50 renters in the Great Reform Bill'.[31] It was a visionary goal. Strong inside the Church, Evangelicals remained a minority there, which enhanced the value to them of the links with Dissent. The societies in which Low Churchman and Dissenter combined to undertake an exhaustive range of activities gave institutional expression to a spiritual kinship. Shaftesbury's unique position in the Evangelical Christianity of the country allowed him to use these bodies as a political medium with a directness and frequency that others could not emulate to the same effect.

As the largest and most widely spread of the organizations common to Church and Dissent, the British and Foreign Bible Society afforded him an obvious platform. In the troubled year of 1860 he reminded the Society that 'the word of God may be regarded in two different aspects...spiritual... [and] political...'. No one should be indifferent to the dangers besetting them, which he discussed from the angle of Protestant nationalism, so congenial to the religious public. 'Who can be blind', he exclaimed, 'to the fact that there are many who desire the empire we possess – who can doubt...there are many who look with hatred upon the civil and religious liberty...we enjoy?' Britain's strength lay not in any Continental alliance, but in herself: in her government's defence policy, in new and powerful weapons, in the Volunteers, above all in free institutions rooted in Biblical religion. This vindication of a prime minister under fire from Gladstone in his own cabinet, from some Parliamentary radicals, and from the opposition was not out of place, since the religious dimension of foreign policy meant more to public opinion than it would seem to have done from diplomatic documents and the private correspondence of ministers and envoys.[32] Two years later, Shaftesbury spoke to the Society in unstinted laudation of Palmerston, whose administration had lost some ground with Dissent. Announcing a handsome subscription from the prime minister, he said, 'You may well cheer (Renewed cheering). Let me tell you...a more patriotic...a more thorough Englishman never lived', one, moreover, who thought their Society an 'admirable institution'. The president of the Methodist Conference got up to reaffirm Wesleyan devotion to the Bible Society and its interdenominationalism, deprecating 'controversy...

division...separation among you'. As proof of the protection that a simple
and scriptural religious education furnished to counter a revival of
'Chartist agitation', he instanced the 'remarkable resignation' of the
unemployed cotton workers, 'their failure to rebel against their rulers
and...complain of authority'.[33] Shaftesbury told the Church Pastoral Aid
Society next day that 'the great body of persons, devout and learned men,
to be found in the ranks of the Nonconformists' admired the Church of
England. Secure in the knowledge of that powerful Dissenting sympathy
with Evangelical Anglicanism, he rebuked militant Dissent for lacking 'the
elements of good breeding or Christian charity'.[34]

The words just quoted express the value he placed upon educating
Dissent in its responsibilities. He did not exclude the most feared of
Dissenters from his concern, counselling Palmerston to invite Bright into
the cabinet of 1859 when Cobden declined to join on its formation. Bright
would have been the first English Dissenter to sit there, and by his accession
have provided a triumph for the radicalism of the sects at its most
aggressive. At the start of his Reform campaign the previous autumn, he
had caused great offence by describing episcopal representation in the
Lords as 'that creature of – what shall I say? – of monstrous, nay, even of
adulterous birth'. Shaftesbury opined that Bright's many enemies would
acquiesce in his promotion, even so. He considered that whether or not
Bright accepted, the offer would administer a 'Quietus'.[35] Shaftesbury
judged his man shrewdly. Bright's diary shows him to have been tempted
by the thought of high office, in which he later proved to be innocuous.[36]
Shaftesbury had little direct contact with the outwardly formidable radical,
but by association with other Dissenting politicians he helped to isolate
Bright. The impression Shaftesbury made on those men was primarily due
to his and their Evangelical beliefs, between which and Bright's Quakerism
there stretched a theological gulf. They responded to Shaftesbury's patent
sincerity in deploring the view, which Palmerston came close to holding,
that the Established Church and religion itself should be supported 'as a
great political engine' with 'no higher motive'. He recoiled from 'the low
aspect of conservative principle'.[37] A Christian conception of nationality,
puritanism's sense of English destiny intensified by contemporary experience, reinforced the spiritual bond uniting Evangelicals of his rank and
middle- and working-class Dissenters. On the political level the religious
awareness of empire did much to reconcile articulate and prosperous
Dissent to a still distinctly subordinate place in the life of the country, one
not commensurate with its gains from industrial advance in the regions of
its densest concentrations. 'I believe', said Edward Miall, the founder of
the Liberation Society, in a speech during the Mutiny, '...it is necessary
that the British supremacy in our Indian empire should be maintained...
at any cost...' When he and his creation, representing the organized

militancy of Dissent and its ultimate aim of disestablishment, took that line, it lessened the force of complaints about the 'large and splendid hierarchy' in church and state at home. Chairing the Society's triennial conference in 1859, Edward Baines disowned any seeming aggression on the part of Dissenters; their posture was 'in reality...of a defensive nature'.[38] By personally endorsing the abolition of church rates, first for Dissenters and then altogether, Palmerston improved upon Shaftesbury's efforts on his behalf, and facilitated the concentration of Liberationists' attacks upon Toryism. They soon forgave him for not making abolition a cabinet question, recognizing that he had gone too fast to unite his colleagues behind him in doing away with what was, after all, principally a symbolic grievance.

The closer integration of political Dissent with the Liberal party and the consequent dilution of middle-class radicalism may be followed through the growing Palmerstonianism of Edward Baines. As editor and proprietor of the *Leeds Mercury*, which was to the industrial West Riding what the *Manchester Guardian* was to Lancashire, he felt himself 'most powerfully driven by the evidence of fact', he explained to Cobden, to put his newspaper behind the Palmerston government during the Crimean war.[39] With good reason, Cobden saw in the elevation to the cabinet of M. T. Baines, Edward's Anglican convert brother, the prime minister's desire to make sure of the *Mercury*.[40] On the fall of that government, the paper vindicated Palmerston: 'we think he was moving with a firm step in the paths of reformation and improvement'; nor could anyone else unite the party in Parliament. These political virtues excused 'the gaiety [which] may sometimes have bordered on levity', and a foreign policy too bellicose for the *Mercury* after peace with Russia but not, it observed, too aggressive for the public.[41] Baines appealed locally, to a party gathering, for 'abiding union' between landed and business Liberals in the Riding, 'those two vast interests, those two equally important interests – important constitutionally, socially and industrially'.[42] Thus he repudiated Bright's class, sectarian and personal hostility to the minister whom the latter had just helped to bring down. The claim to equality with the landed class was not, however, one that Baines wished to press nationally. The *Mercury* considered it enough, on the eve of Palmerston's visit to Leeds in 1860, that there should be a 'a new feature of the age... the *intercommunication of classes*'. The essential distinction was that between class, which 'has always existed and probably always will exist', and '*castes*... the offspring of pride and folly'.[43] Under Palmerston, Baines's newspaper displayed a warm admiration for aristocratic politicians who had guided the development of a thriving, ordered society, a model to less advanced and fortunate countries. Dissenting respect for a liberal aristocracy, nevertheless, afforded only partial protection for Anglicanism, which savoured too much of caste.

Baines, ironically designated 'the master of twenty legions' by Lewis, exploited the second Palmerston government's tiny majority and dependence upon extra-Parliamentary opinion to force the withdrawal of a proposal that would have permitted the Establishment to demonstrate that the 1851 census overstated its weakness.[44]

The ministry intended at the next census to ascertain religious allegiance in the course of the normal house to house inquiries, instead of taking a count at places of worship. The obvious gain to the Church from such ostentatious confirmation of its preponderance was arguably inconsistent with the conciliatory trend of Palmerstonian policy; and Baines conveyed the reaction to a move which provoked the Evangelical Dissenters he represented to a convincing show of strength. The Dissenting MPs and men of substance who determined the effectiveness of the Liberation Society now made it the instrument of undisguised coercion, directed against Palmerston himself. '…it is very lowering to the character and authority of a Government to give way to the unreasonable bidding of a central cabal wielding an organized hypocrisy', wrote the prime minister angrily in a cabinet minute.[45] But give way he did: when even Wesleyan Methodism joined in objecting to the projected question in the census, the pressure was too great to risk defying. In the House, Palmerston confined himself to saying that ministers deferred to feeling which they thought unjustified. His colleague, Lewis, usually so temperate, spoke the government's mind. He compared the Dissenters' resistance to the obscurantism of Eastern peoples confronted with the enumerator. British experience in India, he suggested cuttingly, showed that 'progress…and the increase of intelligence may lead to the removal of prejudices which, at a given moment, are invincible'.[46] Lewis's rationalistic Christianity went with the consciousness, traditional to Whig and Tory, of religion's social power and its indispensability to the state. 'I suppose the Church may be disestablished, but I should expect to see a republic in ten years', Russell remarked a little earlier.[47] This signal defeat of Church and State at the hands of combined Dissent taught the second Palmerston administration to persist with the religious policy of the first. The Peelite High Churchmen readmitted to the cabinet in June 1859 and solicitous for the Establishment on high doctrinal grounds had aroused Dissenting suspicions. In cabinet discussion of the inquiry excised from the 1861 census, Gladstone commented that to his clerical constituents it seemed 'a claim of justice', which, regrettably, it was inadvisable to press. The Gladstone of 1860 perceived no mitigating circumstances in the surrender: 'the Government may suffer from offending the Dissenters but cannot by merely conciliating them retain the…strength necessary for its credit'.[48]

The episode stands out in the history of Palmerston's two administrations as the sole instance of a complete breakdown in relations with political

Dissent. The disharmony was shortlived, to the immense frustration of Bright who had been delighted to see 'the Government...cutting its own throat'.[49] His victory on the census set up Baines for the rest of this period as Bright's equal, at least, in the eyes of the Dissenters without whom Parliamentary radicalism would have been a disparate collection of individuals. In contrast with Bright, he sincerely wished to turn his achievement to the advantage both of Dissent and of a social order in which he found so much worth preserving. Insistent on the validity of the 1851 census as evidence of real denominational strengths, he maintained 'it did so happen that there was something approaching a balance between...the Establishment and the Nonconformist sects'. The conclusion he drew was, 'that fact should teach them to respect the power of each other, and the efforts each was making to advance the grand cause of religion and the welfare of the country'.[50] After the dropping of Russell's measure, it was Baines rather than Bright who kept reform and its central issue alive by the bill he regularly submitted to effect the same reduction in the £10 borough franchise of 1832; but his intention was hardly radical: to pre-empt the revival, which must otherwise occur, of an unruly demand for reform and by timely action to secure that 'so long as human nature and the structure of society remain what they are...we need not fear that...Parliament will ever be composed of lower-class men, or fail to contain the foremost men in the kingdom'. On the hustings in Leeds at the 1865 election, Baines declared 'he was not prepared to vote for anything that would diminish the influence of the Church as a religious institution...he would not, at the expense of a revolution, sanction anything violent in this country'. If disestablishment were to come, it should be with the consent of Parliament, the people and the Church.[51] Militant Dissenters opposed to Baines's stance tended to despair of the foreseeable future, as Bright did when receiving a Baptist deputation in February 1865. He sought to impress upon them the 'uselessness' of moving against the privileges of the Establishment, by means of a public petition or a Parliamentary inquiry. '...the State Church', he advised, 'can only come to an end by explosion from within or from political and democratic changes in our representation and government.'[52] In their different ways, Baines and Bright bore witness to the vigour and attractiveness of Palmerston's politics, to which religion was not less important than economic growth and the diffusion of its benefits.

Redress of grievances

The amenability of Dissent was conditional upon concessions, or the hope of them, when they were obstructed in Lords or Commons, like the many church rate bills. One change took the form of an administrative act by the Committee of Council for Education. From 1863 the Committee refused building grants to Anglican schools having a monopoly of parochial teaching, unless they allowed Dissenting parents to remove their children from religious instruction. The *Guardian* suspected the Committee of Council of enforcing 'a method of construction which leaves...schools open to the possibility of being absolutely secularized'.[53] While it was an exaggerated fear, Robert Lowe, the Vice-President of Council responsible for education, put forward the suggestion that Church Schools should limit general religious instruction to the Ten Commandments, the Lord's Prayer and the Apostles' Creed, reserving specifically Anglican teaching for those children prepared for the rite of Confirmation at the close of their brief elementary schooling.[54] Behind Lowe were the considerable figures of Russell, Granville and Argyll, interested in broadening, if not in doing away with, the denominational character of grant-aided, Church-run schools attended by three-quarters of the children who received some elementary education with state help. These three grandees, and others, patronized the predominantly Dissenting British and Foreign Schools Society, which advocated Christian but undenominational education. Russell's plan of 1856 for expanding the coverage of elementary schools had Palmerston's approval, although heavily voted down in the Commons. It envisaged creating a system of education districts in England and Wales, locally administered, subject to central inspection, by the elected representatives of those paying a school rate. There was to be provision for Scripture reading and such additional teaching of religion as each local committee might prescribe, with the right of removing children from those classes. 'Unfortunately', said Palmerston, 'religious instruction is the... great difficulty.'[55] The Newcastle Commission a few years later tried to solve the problem by recommending a similar organization of schools in receipt of public funds but with the preservation of denominationalism. Addressing the British and Foreign Schools Society in May 1862, Russell referred to the 'bitter contention' between Church and Dissent which adoption of the Commission's proposals would have entailed: that was why ministers had not sought to implement the scheme.[56] The Dissenters were themselves divided over the state in education, against which their voluntaryist minority, headed by Baines, protested with diminishing force as the schools' need of government money to help them educate an increasing population became harder to dispute. But whether voluntaryists or advocates of undenominational, even secular, education under a degree of state control, Dissenters were appeased by the evident ministerial concern that Anglican elementary schools assisted from taxation should not be conducted in a spirit of ecclesiastical dominance. '...the educational bureau reserves its aggressions for the schools of the Church', wrote the aggrieved *Guardian* in 1860.[57] With certain exceptions, the Endowed Schools Act of that year declared the mostly Anglican grammar schools open to Dissenting pupils. It was another move to prevent the Church's tremendous educational influence from weighing too oppressively upon the sects.

The Tory majority in the Lords blocked legislation on qualifying oaths repeatedly passed by the Commons to relieve Dissenting office-holders from the requirement to disavow any intention of subverting the Established Church as such. The oath, inserted in the measure of 1828 repealing the Test and Corporation Acts, was very often ignored in practice, but it rankled, as a reminder of the Dissenters' inferior status in law. Palmerston's first administration had seen Cambridge degrees opened to Dissenters, following those of Oxford in 1854; fellowships remained closed to them. In 1862 he did not think the entrenched Anglicanism of the ancient universities any longer desirable in theory. 'If they had to commence *de novo* with Oxford and Cambridge', he reflected to a deputation, 'he should be sorry to see established the system on which they had...been founded.' Once again, he was in advance of Gladstone.[58]

The rich Dissenters' appetite for recognition was sparingly fed: but the sects were easily gratified. The admission of prominent figures to the lowest hereditary rank with baronetcies for the Baptist Morton Peto, the Congregationalist Francis Crossley and David Baxter of the Free Church of Scotland, was 'highly popular'; as Shaftesbury confidently predicted in soliciting the honours for the last two from Palmerston.[59] 'Lord Palmerston has displayed much of his characteristic wisdom in advising Her Majesty to raise to the baronetage...such...men of the people', said Shaftesbury's organ, the *Record*, in due course, citing the satisfaction of the provincial press. Peto and Crossley were, moreover, MPs in the forefront of the movement to whittle away legal discrimination against Dissent. Elevating a man like Peto to the aristocracy made him apologetic when inviting the House to redress a Dissenting grievance: '...he disclaimed all ulterior designs...he believed sincerely that the Bill, so far from weakening, would tend to strengthen the Church of England...', ran his speech of 1863 on the sensitive question whether Dissenters should lawfully be able to bury their dead in parish churchyards without Anglican rites.[60] It was the language of Edward Baines. The aristocratic embrace largely succeeded in stifling the radical inclinations, such as they were, of wealthy Dissenters. Minor office enticed Bright's co-religionist and political associate, Charles Gilpin, and the Unitarian James Stansfeld, junior. In Gilpin's case, Palmerston disregarded a warning from Shaftesbury that the most radical appointment to the new ministry forming in 1859 was a speculative businessman.[61] Stansfeld, who did not join the government until 1863, belonged, as an Unitarian, to the 'the aristocracy of Dissent', one of the reasons adduced for promoting him by Wood, his colleague in the representation of Halifax.[62]

Sir John Trelawny – the Cornish baronet who, although an Anglican, took charge of the Liberation Society's church rate bills – ridiculed Tory apprehensions of political Dissent in 1863: 'he could hardly think... Members opposite... sincere in their horror of the... Society', which certainly aspired to separate Church and State, 'but what' he asked, 'was its power of effecting it?' Trelawny revised his old radical views on the subject, and now perceived the Church, in good Whig fashion, as being 'in the nature of a corporation under the authority of the civil power... he should be extremely sorry to extinguish the control they possessed and exercised...'. His sponsorship of church rate abolition continued with the genuinely restricted purpose of getting rid of an irritant. His conversion stemmed from the acknowledgement that 'a large section of the Dissenting classes... were highly favourable to the Church... and... should be taken into account'.[63] Without Palmerston's adoption of a considered religious policy, helped by Shaftesbury, the situation would have been very different.

Wesleyan Methodism furnished the bulk of Dissenters who upheld the Establishment along with their own sectarian independence. Presiding at a Wesleyan function in the North-East, Sir William Atherton, attorney-general in the second Palmerston administration, described the mainstream of Methodism as 'never an opposing force to the Church... rather... an auxiliary army... with a peculiar fitness for... disseminating the truths of the Gospel among the multitudes of the lower classes'. After paying tribute to the Wesleyan inspiration of reinvigorated nineteenth-century Anglicanism, he spoke of the implications which the alliance between Churchmen and Wesleyans had for domestic politics and Britain's international repute: 'We might say, without vanity... that we were the light of the world... Providence had favoured us... defended by our insular position... blessed with a free constitutional government.' When, not if, he said to loud applause, a reform much to be desired brought them a 'considerably greater' electorate, 'buildings like that in which they were assembled – erected for the worship of Almighty God and for... religious education – were the means by which the people must be trained to exercise a higher and more extended part in the government of the State'.[64] *The Times* reported this speech of October 1861 without comment. What Atherton said was significant precisely because unremarkable. The Wesleyan laity indeed, if not the clergy, still evinced a marked tendency to vote Tory, chiefly out of respect and affection for the Established Church. Miall's *Nonconformist* momentarily allowed itself to depict matters as they really were towards the end of the Palmerstonian era. It compared the collaboration of Church and Dissent in urban and industrial areas with the 'frightful disadvantage' at which rural Dissenters too often had to live. The 'melancholy indifference' of the first to the flagging offensive against the Establishment appeared in their avowed liking for 'easy and friendly intercourse' with Anglican laymen and even clergymen; and, more seriously, in their interpretation of the divergence from Anglicanism as amounting to no more than 'varying shades of religious belief, or taste, or modes of worship' between the sects. 'They see nothing at stake', wrote the *Nonconformist* bitterly of Dissenting complacency about the leakage into the Church of those who had risen higher socially; not a new phenomenon, but the loss to Dissent of natural leaders was absolutely and relatively greater.[65] Where Dissent had acquired local power in important places, its historic sense of inferiority was assuaged by the experience of ruling a town like Leeds through its ratepayer democracy under the Municipal Corporations Act of 1835, but necessarily in partnership with Anglican Liberals, from Whigs to radicals. At that level, as nationally, Church Evangelicals played an unifying role, which in Leeds, for instance, was directed by the Reverend William Sinclair, Vicar of St George's, who earned a mention in the *Dictionary of National Biography*. The son of a Scottish baronet and son-in-law of a prominent Whig politician, Sinclair's birth and connections stood him in good stead with the civic patriciate; and in his special work of reconciling Church and Dissent his labours counteracted the ill-feeling stirred up by the High Churchmanship of W. F. Hook.[66]

The Catholic minority

Sinclair and Hook in their major provincial town, Shaftesbury and Wilberforce to the nation at large, preached an anti-Catholicism that was as much political as religious. Whereas the Bishop and Hook attributed to the Established Church, above all else, the grandeur, freedom and prosperity rooted in British Protestantism, the Earl and Sinclair gave Dissent its due. Catholicism was linked with Continental reaction and Irish rebelliousness in the public mind. Speaking in his own neighbourhood but to a wider audience, Lewis ascribed Anglo-French tension after the Crimean war to 'what might be called the High Church party in France – the ultra-Catholic party – who, from ... repugnance towards this country on account of its Protestant religion and also from ... dislike of its liberal principles and free institutions, regard us with ... animosity'.[67] The comparison of French ultramontanes and reactionaries to English High Churchmen made by a senior cabinet minister, and one so moderate in most respects as Lewis, came from the heart of Liberalism then. All Wilberforce's attacks upon Rome could not dispel suspicions that the High Church was anti-national. Catholicizing the Church of England, to Wilberforce and his school, meant ecclesiastical autonomy, impossible to square with the lay domination of institutional religion inseparable from British constitutionalism. The ultramontane Catholicism strengthening its ascendancy over the Roman church was not merely populist but democratic in Ireland and among the expatriate Irish; and simultaneously the mainstay or prop of absolutism on the Continent. It did not seem at all strange to British Liberals, and many Tories, that democracy and absolutism should ally with Catholicism personified by Pius IX, for they conceived of all three as illiberal. In a speech delivered a year before that just quoted, during the critical months of the Indian Mutiny, Lewis adverted to the exultation in Britain's difficulties of some Irish and Continental newspapers which he identified simply as 'ultra-Catholic'. Against this enmity, he set the friendliness of French, German and American papers which gave the view of the civilized world.[68] After another crisis, that over Denmark in 1864, one of the cabinet radicals, Milner Gibson, condemned Disraeli's readiness to avail himself of Irish Catholic votes in the Commons division of 8 July: 'such a combination...was not one that could, or ever ought to, govern England; or...ever could promote the cause of civil and religious liberty'. He extended the condemnation of Disraeli to embrace his circumspect support of a reconstructed final court of appeal for the Established Church more or less in accordance with High Church thinking. Milner Gibson felt 'afraid...such a tribunal savoured of a kind of Holy Inquisition and...would put an end to all freedom of thought and intellectual activity among the clergy...;' so extensive was the distrust of anything that bore a distant resemblance to Roman claims and practice.[69] Even Bright could not forbear to celebrate the Papacy's losses in 1859–60 and Britain's anti-Papal diplomacy after the change of government in June 1859. '...to despoil the monarch-priest of Rome of...almost all...his territories...has given wonderful pleasure' he said to the working-class reformers of Leeds, 'not to you only – not to the middle-classes only – there are members of the aristocracy who have spoken of it with apparent satisfaction.' He praised Russell's reaffirmation of classical Whig doctrine in foreign affairs in his despatch of 27 October 1860 to Turin; this at a time when he was losing patience with ministers over their handling of reform and economy.[70]

The numerous Irish immigrants in Britain took literally violent exception to the government's anti-Papal policy, goaded by its popularity. Palmerston traced the blame for the Irish riots of 1862 in London to Napoleon III. By securing Pius IX in what remained of the Papal States and so contributing to perpetuate his spiritual authority the Emperor had encouraged 'a standing feud in many parts of Europe', of which the disorders in Hyde Park were a manifestation.[71] The French ambassador, the Comte de Flahault, to whom the prime minister addressed his complaint, replied that the turbulent Irish Catholics would be angrier if France abandoned the Pope to his fate.[72] Palmerston wanted to begin reversing the progress of the Roman Catholic Church in England and Wales through Irish immigration by inducing the Papacy not to fill the vacant primatial see of Westminster on Cardinal Wiseman's death in 1865. He hinted at a repetition of the outcry against 'Papal Aggression' when a Catholic hierarchy was restored fifteen years previously, if a successor to Wiseman were appointed.[73] '...the Catholic Church here', Russell reminded him, 'is *libera chiesa in libero stato*.'[74] Palmerston's reluctance to face the fact of a sizeable Catholic presence in Britain was typical of his countrymen. The immigrant response was to assert their despised religion and nationality. The Fenian organization of Irish revolutionary nationalism from 1858 allocated three of the seven elective places in its supreme council to the areas into which it divided Britain: Scotland, the North and the South of England. Except by some native Catholics such as Bishop Robert Cornthwaite, the diocesan of Yorkshire, the spread of Fenianism through the Irish communities, and the extent of their participation in the movement, went unrealized for years. As happened in the United States, the immigrant Irish discovered in expatriate nationalism an escape from, and the hope of permanently overcoming, their depressed condition. The independence of Ireland, won by a national uprising supplied with funds, arms, and recruits from the Irish abroad, would raise the status of Irish people in the countries of emigration, so it was credibly supposed. One aspect of the pervasive, if inevitable, injustice from which they suffered must suffice by way of illustration: a prolonged Commons inquiry into the working of the Poor Law during the first half of the 1860s showed how guardians openly violated the statutory safeguards for the religion of adults and children in workhouses. The civil servants of the Poor Law Board and their political master, the radical Villiers, could not or would not prevent the abuse. The middle and lower middle classes controlling poor relief in the industrial towns where the Irish settled thickly far outdid landed politicians in Protestant zeal. A Bradford guardian thought it right to deny the last rites to a dying girl of ten: 'All Catholic children are to be educated as Protestants till they are able to judge for themselves.'[75]

The dream of a close Tory-Irish alliance which Disraeli entertained had no chance of being realized in the atmosphere of Anglo-Irish conflict on either side of the water. He chose to overlook, among other factors, the mutual disesteem of English and Irish Catholics. Writing to the Roman Curia in 1856, Archbishop Cullen of Dublin, the ecclesiastical statesman who was to sustain constitutional nationalism in Ireland in opposition to the Fenians, charged the native English clergy of the Catholic Church with indifference to the pastoral needs of the immigrants with whom he believed the future of the Church all over the English-speaking world to lie.[76] English Catholics were accustomed to take aristocratic leadership for granted, and its increasingly organized usurpation by bishops and priests in Ireland incurred their disapproval. They resented and feared Irish Catholic nationalism as patriotic Englishmen, and as jeopardizing the tolerance which the possession of rank and wealth, in addition to devoted loyalty, had obtained for them. The attitude of English to Irish Catholics had the effect on which Cullen dwelt in his Roman correspondence of the mid-1850s: 'The sentiment of nationality cannot be suppressed', he wrote, 'nor indeed can it cause surprise when one remembers how Ireland has always been treated by England – not only by Protestant England but Catholic England also.'[77] It would be wrong to leave the impression that English Catholics did not try to do their Christian duty by the immigrants: but they did it with misgivings for themselves, confronted by the swollen majority of alien Catholics in the aftermath of the Great Irish Famine. Lack of money was not the only reason why the importation of clergy from Ireland fell a long way short of the requirement. What English Catholics wanted, with J. H. Newman in his *Apologia* of 1864, was to build upon Pius IX's restoration of a national hierarchy, of 'a church of our own... our own habits of mind... our own tastes, and our own virtues'. What they actually got was a divided Church, the structure of which Palmerston seriously thought of starting to dismantle.[78]

The Tory response to Palmerston

Disraeli's flirtation with political Catholicism persisted: but at no time was it central to his strategy. The Established Church lay at the heart of Toryism. In the Parliament of 1859–65 he decided to rally a disgruntled party with the historic Tory cry of 'the Church in danger'. This he could not do without deliberately misreading the Palmerston administration's policy. He failed to convince almost all his principal colleagues that 'in internal politics there is only one question now, the maintenance of the Church'.[79] They knew him too well to be edified by the spectacle he presented in championing the Establishment. Wary of provocation to Dissent, they did not think the Church endangered. The party outside Westminster, however, liked the look of Disraeli's '*vrai cheval de bataille*' – Lord Derby's description.[80] Constituency Tories may not have been gravely worried for the Church, but they were irritated by what they saw as the presumption of Dissent, encouraged by government. They were less enthusiastic about the incongruous association between Disraeli and Wilberforce. The two men needed each other to campaign against the government's treatment of the Church. The Bishop had lost Gladstone to the Palmerston cabinet, and Disraeli welcomed the ablest and most eloquent of Victorian prelates to his side. It would have been better for the Church, Disraeli himself conceded, if Gladstone had returned to his old party in 1858. His lieutenant Northcote, a devout High Churchman, clung to the hope that Gladstone might still furnish 'some positive evidence of his continued earnestness in the cause of the Church'.[81] Reviewing nearly five years spent in opposition at a provincial party dinner, he implicitly admitted the superior ability of Palmerston's government to protect the interests of the Establishment: 'never...was there...a ministry possessed [of] the advantages which the...Ministry possesses; never has a Ministry had a...better opportunity of coming forward and proposing a satisfactory settlement of questions which it is dangerous to leave unsolved.'[82] The message and its urgency were unmistakable. Disraeli's initiative had disappointed: worse, it brought out the antagonism to High Churchmen that Wilberforce invited by his combativeness.

The Tory newspaper with the largest circulation, the *Standard*, severely criticized the episcopal exercise of authority and patronage which the High Church valued. 'How is it possible', asked Wilberforce of Disraeli, 'that with our organ printing such things the Church can ever heartily support us?...What can the Church do without its leaders, and what can the leaders do if they are the base wretches that article over and over states... them to be in its long tissue of falsehoods?'[83] Disraeli excused such attacks, which he did not like to censure as Wilberforce wished, by reference to the political facts. Wilberforce was especially vulnerable through his connection with the *Guardian*, a journal 'peculiarly distasteful to the great body of the Tory party'. The *Guardian's* Peelite sympathies were not forgiven, 'one of the unhappy consequences of the unfortunate disruption of 1846', wrote Disraeli half a generation later.[84] Stanley, who was not a religious Tory, set down the reaction of some Evangelicals and High Churchmen in the party – 'ultras' in his terminology – to the Disraeli–Wilberforce axis. They planned a stillborn coup, replacing Derby in the Lords by the seventh Duke of Marlborough, an actively Evangelical magnate, and Disraeli by Lord Robert Cecil, the future prime minister and an ardent High Churchman. The plotters evidently contemplated breaking away from Disraeli's identification of the party with the exclusive tendency in Anglicanism. Marlborough's refusal to have any part in it demolished the conspiracy.[85] Stanley did not know Cecil's response, if he was sounded: but, replying to a previous inquiry as to where he stood, Cecil had written with pretended irony, 'I have long regarded Dizzy's leadership as an irreversible chastisement'; Disraeli's parade of English Churchmanship struck him as a 'senseless affectation of Saxonism', offensive to Low Churchmen.[86] If the Duke was not a warm partisan in politics, though a conscientious parliamentarian, he had a surer awareness than Disraeli of what made his country 'politically great'. On the Bible Society's platform in 1860, with Shaftesbury occupying the chair, Marlborough said: 'It is not the Queen who governs England...not...Parliament...not the Ministry...but the power of self-government in the people, the national genius...nourished, strengthened and confirmed by...the Christian religion...political objects... can always be effected when the voice of public opinion is raised and brought to bear upon…Government.'[87] Disraeli underrated the socially unifying element in English religion. The very few leading Tories who came out equally strongly for his endeavour to challenge Palmerstonianism in this sphere had their reservations. Walpole remarked at High Wycombe in October 1862, where he appeared with Disraeli and Wilberforce, that there was no other battle than that of the Church in which he would rather fight beside Disraeli.[88] Stanley's diary records Walpole's cautious encouragement of the 'ultras' against Disraeli.[89]

Gladstone's course

Gladstone began his six years in the second Palmerston cabinet within a High Church, Peelite group of three, and ended, religiously isolated in cabinet, by being ousted from his seat for Oxford University after nearly two decades owing to doubts whether he was a good Churchman by any standard. Palmerston did not ignore the anxiety of the three that his ecclesiastical appointments should be seen to register their accession to office, and several did. 'I cannot help imploring you', Newcastle told the prime minister, 'to raise to the Bench a prelate of a different stamp from those…recently appointed.' The elevation of Bishops Wigram and Waldegrave, and the translation of Bishop Villiers to the great see of Durham had, Newcastle pointed out, disturbed more than one section of the Church. It was naturally the High Church that pre-occupied him. Its clerical adherents, he claimed, viewed Toryism 'as a stone round the neck of the Church', and hoped for the incentive to switch their political allegiance. Knowing how Palmerston felt, Newcastle assured him that he was 'no ultra-churchman…not what is foolishly called a Puseyite'; his choice of incumbents for livings in his gift would furnish the proof. Newcastle's apologetic tone could hardly have softened his operative sentence about those for whom he pleaded: '…often and often I have heard them say that if the highest places in the Church are to be filled by very inferior men merely because they take in the *Record* newspaper and speak in Exeter Hall, they can only look to Lord Derby for fair play'.[90] The language travestied a grievance, and must have hardened Palmerston's dislike of the High Church. The Duke's protest followed on Gladstone's and Herbert's. Herbert stressed his own moderation, and thought 'a fairer participation without going to the extreme of either party…the best for the Church in the long run'.[91] Palmerston saw a successor in him; they drew closer over this and most other questions.[92] At that stage of the party's development, the distribution of patronage, simply as such, retained a good deal of its significance in Palmerston's youth. But the bestowal of bishoprics, deaneries and canonries involved considerations of principle above those of place. While Montagu Villiers benefited from being Clarendon's brother, he was an exemplary parish clergyman of the Evangelical school. Lesser, but sometimes lucrative, patronage, in the form of Crown livings, was distributed in a more secular spirit. 'I have a living to dispose of', wrote Palmerston to George Denman, the Whig who sat for Tiverton with him, 'and I believe you have a brother without a living; shall the two be brought together?' The preferment was 'of average emolument'.[93] '...my chief means of giving employment are confined to the Church' he explained to another Whig, 'and even these means are very limited...'[94] Hence his insistence that all church appointments, of whatever rank, under the Crown were a prime ministerial prerogative. He had no patience with his sovereign: '...the Queen...fancies, poor woman, that she has peculiar prerogatives about [sic] the Church because she is its head...'[95]

His second administration gave the Convocation of Canterbury, the ancient clerical assembly revived with Peelite help in the earlier 1850s as a deliberative body, a conditional right to legislate. The rebirth of Convocation in the Northern ecclesiastical province of York followed. The High Church led the way in restoring Convocation in North and South, thus keeping the prime minister on the watch to restrain the institution's further exploitation by Wilberforce's clericalism. Palmerston made sure that the assemblies would not be allowed to go on growing in scope: 'My opinion is that unless kept very right and within the narrowest bounds convocations could become a nuisance...I should not...consent to any alterations which would tend to give them a more real and practical existence.'[96] In this political climate, Gladstone remained a High Churchman spiritually but adopted politically, halfway through the government of 1859–65, a near-Palmerstonian attitude to the problem of Church and Dissent. To Pusey, the saintly inspiration of the High Church, as to Wilberforce, its leader, he issued a warning: '...we are in the early eddies of the whirlpool for University and Church alike...what I fear is that tenacity to all extremes and at all hazards of temporal privilege will more and more compromise interest of a higher order'.[97] He and Palmerston had voted in different lobbies on church rates as members of the same cabinet: but from 1862 Gladstone became seriously dissatisfied with the outlook of the Anglican clergy, and not of High Churchmen alone, on their legal rights. He told the Reverend W. M. Mayow, a regular correspondent, that they paid too much attention to the 'social and conventional incidents of their office'. His obligation as a Christian statesman was 'to study the means of producing harmony in their relations to the community of the State at the expense of everything but the essentials of faith and discipline'.[98] Translated into political action, this meant speaking and voting for Peto's Burials Bill next year to the perturbation of many Churchmen and his Oxford constituent in particular; and otherwise persuading Dissent that he was a friend, not to be classed with the unbending Wilberforce. There was little more to it. Even so, he felt constrained to warn the Reverend Newman Hall of the Congregationalists, that 'the exclusiveness of the University and...the Established Church...may in the abstract be infringements of religious equality...but religious equality...is a principle to be applied according to times and circumstances'. Its application to Oxford was 'distant', as he clearly preferred it should be.[99]

The change from being the political hero of High Churchmen was too marked. He had reached the conclusion that the Church's contested rights in matters like burials and church rates, marginal to its existence as an establishment, would be ceded in practice where Dissent prevailed, if not abolished by Parliament. 'This is the way', he wrote to a Cornish vicar, 'in which the affairs of the Church of England have been arranged since the Revolution [of 1688]: and woe betide them who attempt to manage them in any other manner.'[100] Palmerston allowed a mellowed Gladstone to nominate the chairman of his election committee at Oxford to a major see. The prime minister wished him to hold on to his seat there, retaining one of the two clerical constituencies for the party and preserved from the excitement, to which he was allegedly susceptible, of a less conservative electorate.[101] In approaching Palmerston, Gladstone certified Dr. Jacobson as free from any taint of the High Churchmanship and Toryism present in his Oxford committee: 'He has never been a party man: in his general opinions he may be described as mildly liberal...'[102] Palmerston's letter to Gladstone approving his candidate was sent after Shaftesbury had been consulted. The Earl deemed Jacobson not the best choice but 'a good man...belongs to no exclusive school of theology...you could safely and conscientiously appoint him'.[103] By contrast, Gladstone went against the spirit of Palmerston's advice and excited anti-Catholic and anti-Irish sentiment in both parties when he suggested in March 1865 that the Established Church of Ireland was really no longer defensible, while supposedly taking on its Parliamentary defence. This cost him Oxford, as he realized it probably would.[104] In the short term, it did him little good on the national scene. He heeded the pressing advice of the Liberal chief whip, 'in the common interest', not to widen the damage, and postponed indefinitely his first visit to Ireland.[105]

8

The factor of confidence

The role of government

The state shouldered heavy obligations in economic affairs which it could not, and did not, seek to escape. The limitations of *laissez-faire* were better understood then than they have often been in retrospect. Immediate responsibility for the value of the currency carried with it ultimate responsibility for the stability of the money market and the availability of credit, as was strikingly demonstrated in the banking crisis of 1857. In the circumstances, it was impossible for the state to observe the self-denying ordinance in Peel's Bank Charter Act of 1844 which restricted the note issue to ensure convertibility with gold. The experience of suspending that Act in 1857, as in the previous such crisis ten years before, confirmed the necessity of intervention. It also showed how quickly and smoothly financial order could be restored. Peel's Act survived unamended. It was thought, on the whole, to work well as a curb upon overlending and over-speculation that fell short of an acute crisis; and suspension was widely considered the simplest and most effective means of action when, across the country, solvency, employment and the public peace were under an intolerable threat. Given the Bank of England's central importance in the market, Gladstone aspired, without success, to lessen its independence of the Treasury at times of anxiety. The Bank made good use of its power as the lender of last resort to influence interest rates with the overriding objective of maintaining at a prudent level its stock of bullion, which provided the foundation of the currency, of credit transactions and of so much else. The blame for what happened in 1857 could not convincingly be attributed to a failure of judgement at the Bank. As Sir James Graham predicted, the entire 'money interest,'[1] led by the privately owned Bank and its directors, would stand up to a reforming chancellor. There was, however, a close relationship between the Treasury and the Bank with its historic agency for and management of government securities which had

191

dominated the Stock Exchange from its beginnings. The price of Consols reflected the political and economic health of the country, and affected it, too, in some measure.

The rapid increase of British prosperity and its global ramifications called for higher defence expenditure: to Palmerston's mind this was as much an investment as the huge sums sunk in industrial growth. The public agreed with him; and so did Gladstone, if he was reluctant to believe that the link between commercial confidence and national security had not been exaggerated. Everyone accepted the vital connection between economic and foreign policy. There were no uncompromising isolationists in the front rank of politics, and few anywhere else. Neither Cobden nor Bright could be reckoned among them. The diffusion of free, or freer, trade was incompatible with isolation and weakness. Palmerston brought this out more clearly than his assorted critics, who obscured the point by assaults on his personality and style. It was Britain's combination of riches and strength that impressed Napoleon III and moved him to lower French tariffs: a notable tribute to the soundness of British policy which was not altogether appreciated by the insular neighbour worried by his Continental domination. The peaceful international co-existence that trade was supposed, with some justification, to encourage depended more on mutual respect for power between major states than on the conviction that idealism and profit could be simultaneously pursued among nations. It followed that empire, preferably informal rather than formal, was unavoidable and best secured by working with the European Great Powers and the United States. Such co-operation, never easy, would be doubtful unless Britain were strong enough to elicit it as a matter of common interest. At stake was the domestic standard of life and all that its rising level meant for the social balance. This was the Palmerstonianism that appealed to the City, to industry and commerce, and to the large urban constituencies.

In his *Considerations on Representative Government* of 1861, that most conservative of radicals, J.S. Mill, inserted a passage specially relevant to an understanding of what the Palmerston governments tried to do. Mill was critical in many ways of those who constituted the political nation and entertained a distant vision of a fully democratic, and socialist, society. Yet he did not think the propertied classes' behaviour in so largely excluding 'what are called the working classes' from the franchise should be misconstrued. They were wrong not to open up the electorate, but they did not harbour 'any intention of sacrificing the working classes to themselves'. The reverse was true. 'They willingly make considerable sacrifices, especially of their pecuniary interest, for...the working classes, and err rather by too lavish and indiscriminating [sic] beneficence; nor do I believe', he concluded, 'that any rulers in history have been actuated by a more sincere desire to do their duty towards the poorer portion of their countrymen.'[2] Fiscal policy was an instrument of social concern, and acknowledged as such. Gladstone shared Mill's view that the working class paid relatively too little rather than too much in taxation: Palmerston did not; but the need to keep taxes down as far as possible to satisfy electors and non-electors alike was undisputed. While land, business and the professions, subject to income tax, would not tolerate it, in practice, above the level of tenpence in the pound reached for a single year of peace in 1860, they desired, out of prudence and humanity, to see cuts in the burden of indirect tax on the unenfranchised. Confidence in the complex and delicate machinery of credit and safety from foreign attack were helped by the unprecedented recession of 'class jealousy', on which the austere *Banker's Magazine* commented gratefully in 1862, saying: 'We have literally nothing to fear.' It stressed the indispensability of private charity to this atmosphere.[3] The magnitude of the contemporary charitable effort emerged when it was concentrated in relief of the Lancashire cotton famine. Exceptional state assistance, which was inadequate to the emergency, came in the form of loans to shore up the poor law and fund public works in the localities affected. The intervention of the state to mitigate some more ordinary hardships of industrial life was another aspect of heightened concern, and one with which Palmerston associated himself. However, such legislation had only marginal significance compared with budgetary measures designed to maintain the growth of industry, trade and agriculture. Limited liability, forcefully advocated by Palmerston, provided the framework for orderly expansion and new opportunities for the investing public. Then as now, the first priority of economic policies was growth. Without it, the fast increasing population would have exacerbated the problems of poverty and social control that politicians could not forget for long.[4]

Confidence and credit

Walter Bagehot once remarked on the anomaly that with free trade triumphant in deregulating the economy banking still had to work within the constraints of the 1844 legislation. Credit was so liable to get out of hand that the flexible restriction on the Bank of England's note issue appeared salutary to him when reviewing its operation. By law the fiduciary issue was limited to between £14 and £15 millions; the security for notes in excess of that amount consisted of bullion in the Bank, which adjusted its rate of interest to prevent disruptive outflows of precious metal. The situation had twice arisen, and would inevitably recur, when the restriction itself became disruptive. Bagehot quoted Lewis: 'Peel's Act does incalculable good, except for one week in ten years, and during that week it does so much harm that we doubt whether the previous good is an adequate counterweight...' Bagehot's solution was an amended Act, enabling the

Bank to meet exceptional demands by issuing notes above the limit.[5] This tidy suggestion did not find favour in influential quarters. Lewis, advised by Bagehot's father-in-law, James Wilson, had encountered a good deal of opposition to suspension of the Act in 1857; a step taken with Palmerston after the chancellor of the exchequer decided that 'every hour's delay... was dangerous'.[6] Their action, which followed discussion in cabinet the previous day, required a statutory indemnity, voted by a large majority. Wilson, the founder of the *Economist* and Lewis's financial secretary to the Treasury, seems to have had misgivings after the event: 'The more one sees, the more one is convinced of the folly of attempting to guide so fine and intricate a machine as commercial relations in all their bearing and especially in connexion with monetary affairs.'[7] Lewis had no such feelings when he looked back on those fraught days. The 'wonderful rapidity' with which the crisis had been dispelled demonstrated the case for government interference: critics of the resolute and highly successful action did not realize the scale of the disaster averted.[8] 'Constitutional liberty is an excellent thing', he replied to Lord Overstone, the enormously rich currency theorist, whose banking fortune was safely invested in land, 'but circumstances may arise to justify the proclamation of martial law.' The impending destruction of 'mutual confidence' in the world of business had compelled government to intervene, and would probably do so again.[9] The episode illustrated the state's central role in economic affairs, and the impracticability of evading it.

The crisis was American, not British, in origin. The calamitous breaking of a transatlantic boom that tempted participants to reckless irresponsibility put intense pressure on many houses heavily involved with America, as so many were, and their bankers. Lewis stood aside, consulting the cabinet, until big provincial banks succumbed; he regarded them as casualties inseparable from the working of a free market. The inability of a prominent firm of bill brokers in the City to meet its commitments apprised him of the extreme seriousness of the position: the discounting of paper, 'even of sound bills, representing real transactions', practically came to a halt in London, leaving the Bank of England to supply a demand for money which drained its reserves. The Bank's rate of interest was higher, and the reserves lower, than in the crisis of 1847.[10] Lewis's memorandum written on the day the Bank was told it might ignore the limit on its note issue, referred to the certain result of inaction: massive unemployment as credit dried up; at Glasgow, where two banks had stopped payment, the preservation of order was already in some danger.[11] Afterwards, Lewis asked Overstone to contemplate the chain reaction that would have taken place in the City if legality had not been breached: the complete collapse of bill-broking, the flight of deposits from the London joint stock banks, and the exhaustion of the Bank of England's remaining bullion. Overstone, and others, held that there should be no tampering with the currency for the sake of rescuing those who were imprudent, or worse. The chancellor thought it was doubtful morality to confuse 'the innocent...with the guilty in the far-reaching consequences of the insolvency of large firms'. The desperate applicants at the Bank had good securities to offer: they were not the victims of their own folly.[12] On the other hand, *The Times* asserted, two-thirds 'at least' of those who went under got their deserts: 'purging commerce for a time of the most pestilent beings...'. As for the rest, they had not exercised proper care: 'neither these nor society...can talk of undeserved misfortunes'.[13]

Delane gave qualified approval in his editorial columns to the suspension of the Bank Act. Privately, he was inclined to think that the government had overreacted; the additional credit released into the system seemed unnecessarily generous. He mocked the despatch of troop reinforcements to Glasgow: 'as for Scotland', he wrote, 'I will be bound they never had a million sovereigns in the country before. No wonder they require extra troops there to prevent the people from scrambling for them.'[14] In its usual long article on the first City page of January reviewing the year just ended, *The Times* contended that the crisis of 1857 occurred because 'according to experience it had become due'.[15] The speculative impulse so powerful in an expansionary climate was hard to resist. Overstone and the journalists writing on the City in *The Times* knew their world. It was one in which the desire for profit overcame caution and scruples. The newspaper compared high finance, to its disadvantage, with the friendly societies fostered by legislation. The membership of those humble bodies, *The Times* believed, had probably done as well for themselves as their social superiors. There was more honesty, 'the great essential', among the general population than in the proceedings 'at almost every meeting of great companies'.[16] Periodic crises were not only economic corrections, but also morally cleansing. This detached and severely righteous attitude was out of the question for government, as indeed for *The Times* in the hour of decision. In the cabinet, Granville, whose income derived largely from his Midlands ironworks, was particularly sensitive to the consequences for industry of the money market's difficulties. Half his neighbouring ironworks failed. But, he, too, felt the shake out would prove salutary. 'If we manage to hold on, it will do us good in the end', was his comment on the national economy a fortnight after the government stepped in.[17] The demise of weaker firms, lacking in judgment and under-capitalized, was in fact a healthy blood-letting. Industrial production fell by $7\frac{1}{2}$ per cent between 1857 and 1858, but reached a new peak the following year.

The over-extension of credit, though a recognized peril, had grown with its geographical spread. '...the whole world was indebted to us, and that was the chief reason why our own capital was so exhausted', observed

James Wilson.[18] As the crisis of 1857 came to a head, Lewis set down the elements of trouble overseas; 'The crash in America...Speculation in France and the Indian disturbances.'[19] Complaints that the Bank Act was too rigid and did not take account of this external pressure, the volume of which in a few years' time had not been anticipated in 1844, were superficially plausible. Added to the increasing home demand for credit, however, the scale of commitments abroad strengthened unwillingness to amend the Act. Its simple mechanism for ensuring that there was sufficient bullion in the Bank to underpin the currency and the swelling market in credit stood the test of changed conditions. The movement of its interest rate replenished the supply gold in its vaults, safeguarded the note issue, and damped down excessive activity in the market. Sound money was a prerequisite of free trade's achievements, which would have been impossible without flourishing credit and confidence in economic and political arrangements. '...money,' declared *The Times* in 1861, 'is the most important mercantile commodity...England owes an immense portion of her influence and trade to the manner in which her capital has been scattered.'[20] 'A high rate of interest not a necessary cause for anxiety' was the title of an article in the *Economist* that year. Eight per cent at the Bank did its work in reversing a temporary outflow of gold; the rate was not long in falling to 3 per cent. The passing cost to business was worth it to avoid 'the least danger of a recurrence of the terrible events of 1847 and 1857'.[21] Although long intervals often separated his meetings with the governor and deputy governor of the Bank, Gladstone assured an audience of Liverpool businessmen in 1864 that it was his practice as chancellor to watch the London money market 'from day to day...with the closest attention'. The Bank Act had not been replaced or amended but it was being worked differently, with speedier intervention to ensure security and stability. He hinted at his dissatisfaction with what the Bank had attempted.[22] His own ideas of how to improve on its handling of the system under strain never saw the light. They embraced great flexibility, stiff interest rates and a sharing of functions with the Treasury – a technically debatable scheme and politically contentious. Like their counterparts elsewhere, the substantial Liverpudlians who heard him regarded *The Times* commentary on money matters as 'their daily prayer book'.[23]

The rewards of this financial discipline were visible in the pace of economic expansion over the decade commencing in 1855. Cheaper credit than would otherwise have been available was reflected in the production of coal and iron, up by half, and in the growth of the railways with the length of track up by rather more than half, to mention the most prominent examples of industrial advance. Only less important than finance for industry on attractive terms was the part played by credits from British houses in swelling the flood of raw materials that poured into the country at favourable rates of exchange. The investment of capital overseas in stock and share issues, estimated to have been between 53 and 65 per cent of total investment through that medium, bore witness to the capability and strength of financial institutions, as it did to the wealth generated by manufacturing, trade and land. A feature of the City in this period was the creation of overseas banks, facilitated by the coming of limited liability. If many of them did not endure, the names of others are evidence of that desire to find new outlets for capital which is reckoned to have more or less doubled Britain's investments abroad in the ten years under discussion. The return on these investments also doubled; and it accounted for around three-quarters of the surplus on the balance of payments. Foreign and colonial governments from both hemispheres came to raise money on the London market. Its subscriptions to their loans have been put at a minimum of £40 million in 1860–62; when another £40 million went into securities issued to finance railways overseas.[24] The ordeal of the autumn of 1857, when the government kept its nerve and averted a general collapse from which recovery would have been slow, had a lot to do with the eagerness to risk ever larger amounts of capital abroad from a secure base.

As in the spring of 1855 when Lewis raised £16 million in Consols for the war at a cost of under 4 per cent, government borrowing, which Gladstone liked to deplore, helped to stabilize the money market. It drew off politically embarrassing liquidity while keeping money in the country at rates not high enough to inhibit growth of the domestic economy or of overseas investment. Gladstone had a point: in 1859 servicing the debt absorbed almost £29 million out of a government income of some £65 millions. But when he was first elected to Parliament in 1832, the figures had been £28 and £50 millions. Industrial production had since risen two and a half times and was gathering speed. Thus there was scope to borrow, and an unfailing appetite for government stock, the annual yield on which averaged a little over 3 per cent, year after year, despite some sharp fluctuations in price. Gladstone gave himself away when, having attacked Lewis for peacetime borrowing, he 'calmly' approved of Disraeli's resort to the expedient in his budget of 1859.[25] The funded debt was what it had been for generations, easily the favourite of investors, and very widely held. The £900 million of British funds dwarfed any other category among the £1,600 millions, at nominal values, of securities quoted on the Stock Exchange in the mid 1860s; although the figure for all other securities had doubled in ten years. An investment of such proportions and its numerous holders responded quickly to anything that promised to influence national fortunes. The price of Consols was a benchmark for the Stock Exchange, and something more for the whole country. The rise and fall of Consols signalled reactions to foreign policy and war, the prospective or actual change of ministry, and to questions of equal moment, or less. *The Times* called these price movements 'the barometer of the opinion of the prudent and intelligent classes'.[26] Investors in Consols had put their money into the biggest enterprise of all, the state. Their outlook and that of dealers on the Exchange, were together a potent factor in maintaining confidence, and in exposing its fragility.

Confidence and national security

'CONFIDENCE – the life of trade', said *The Times* in January 1860, had come through another crisis in the past year when the tensions intensified by the conflict between France and Austria seemed to threaten Britain's peace in Europe. The second Palmerston administration's plans for spending on defence had served 'to warn off all aggressors'. That expenditure was in fact 'pecuniary gain'; without the reassurance it provided, apprehension would have undermined British prosperity.[27] They were Palmerston's views exactly. Answering a railway chairman who complained of taxation when the prime minister opened a new line in 1864, Palmerston told him in front of an approving crowd: 'it is the public revenue which produces that security at home through which the great developments of railway industry have been made profitable...'[28] It was a reaffirmation of what he had been telling the public with a new urgency since the dangers to Britain's international position had become clearer from the time of the Indian Mutiny, and before. '...surely a manufacturing and commercial nation like this', he argued confidently in his Sheffield speech of 1862, '...is peculiarly interested in...those means of defence necessary, not only to protect our hearths and homes, but to render safer to our trade...every ocean.'[29] His emphasis was always on defensive measures. He ruled out competition with European Great Powers and their conscript armies: 'It would not be wise, it is not desirable that Great Britain should imitate their example'; the structure of society and of the economy dictated the strategy, in which the navy, operating from well-guarded bases, 'must redress the balance'.[30] Palmerston had always thought the world a dangerous place. Effective self-defence, he suggested to the Commons in 1859, should be considered an obligation making for peace. Rivalry and instability were constants in the behaviour of states. He painted a disturbing picture of the situation in which Britain then found herself, based on his theory of international relations: 'England with so much wealth to protect...in every part of the world...has no right to rely for her safety on the mere forbearance of powerful states. It is not even fair towards them... conflicting interests are at work...complicated by passion and prejudice... we can scarcely expect that foreign nations should, out of forbearance and friendship...abstain from giving effect to...superior power.'[31] They were the ideas that informed his policy. In the contemporary setting, free trade

was broadly interpreted according to this perception of reality, which
blunted the criticisms of Palmerston. Those who objected felt for him the
respect and dislike which are the portion of those who see things too plainly
for comfort.

The regular Victorian deficit on visible trade, from now on steadily and
impressively offset by the surplus from invisible earnings in which the
return on overseas investment figures prominently, was a structure that
made an open economy very sensitive to the threat of disruption by large-
scale war. The concentration of the struggle with Russia in the distant
Crimea left 'the Continent of Europe...practically at peace', gratefully
observed the chancellor of the exchequer, Lewis.[32] It was too much to hope
that another war between Great Powers involving Britain could be waged
in such a convenient fashion for her; the economic results of those hostilities
were decidedly advantageous. Moreover, the excess of imports over exports
doubled under the Palmerston governments, as did the surplus from
invisibles and, within it, the return on investment abroad. The country was
growing richer, but more vulnerable. Palmerston's speeches on defence and
foreign policy, were a triumph of political education in that he did not
conceal the unpalatable truth about Britain's inherent weakness even when
the level of preparedness had been raised to dispel nervous fears of invasion.
An attempt to enlarge popular comprehension of the national interest
featured in the remarks he made at Tiverton in March 1857. The voters
were warned against mistaking the nature of British power, or what he
stood for, in the patriotic mood of the moment: '...we wish to be at peace
with all the Great Powers of Europe'. It did not matter to Britain whether
the Powers were 'despotical, monarchical, or constitutional...That which
concerns us...is that...free or enslaved, commercial intercourse shall not be
interrupted, but shall be as free with respect to tariffs as the prejudices of
these different nations may permit...' This section of the speech was
overshadowed by his references to the war in China.[33] The public was
impatient, then, of the distinction between Europe or the United States and
the Orient. Many who voted for him in 1859 did not comprehend, and
certainly did not relish, his overt appeasement of the Bonapartist regime
next year. It took the alarm of 1857 and the spectacular damage caused on
the Stock Exchange for his realism to be accepted. The failure of British
diplomacy to preserve Schleswig and Holstein for Denmark he explained,
consistently with the past pronouncements, by saying: 'Our object is
defence – not aggression...this...does not allow...great sacrifices...of men
and money.'[34]

The Palmerstonian approach to countries strong enough to be a
potential, if not an actual, menace to Britain was questioned as
overstatement and attacked as cynicism. To the last Gladstone thought the
public's idea of the perils surrounding his country was inflated; and, he told

him, he held Palmerston responsible. '...you misplace cause and effect', came the reply, '...I have rightly understood the feelings...of the nation.'[35] If Palmerston was too modest, Gladstone knew, and had known since he re-entered the cabinet, how little could be done to change the national outlook, once formed. In 1860, wanting some economies in the army and navy estimates, he presented his colleagues with an excellent reason for declining to comply: 'It is not the object of this paper to counsel any sharp resistance to public feeling.'[36] As a Liberal politician, he did not hesitate to correct his brother Robertson, the radical businessman, who identified 'pacific and economical' tendencies with the middle-classes.[37] Those classes were not to be defied when their collective mind was made up. At times in his speeches, Gladstone seemed to echo what he had condemned and still deprecated in Palmerston; it is difficult to read any other meaning into these passages. The rapid accumulation of wealth, he was quite aware, tended to produce a 'full-blooded, heady, and wanton' disposition in the fortunate nationality.[38] Shortly after the exchange with Palmerston on the influence of his popularity, he spoke at a Volunteer dinner of the 'high and strong hand' which Britain should always be ready and able to show, at need, in her dealings with the rest of the world.[39] Where Gladstone and Palmerston did not agree was on the sort of expenditure requisite for such strength and its assertion. They argued over the timing, number and type of warship orders, and, angrily, over the fortification of naval bases. Palmerston linked finance, the economy, and security, unanswerably: 'if the French had command of the sea, they would soon find means to make a full Exchequer empty'.[40] In a speech of 1862 at Manchester Gladstone himself demolished the crude notion of the commercial treaty with France as 'an infallible specific'. Admirable though it was, it would not transform Anglo-French relations: 'It is not given to us to alter the fundamental conditions of human society', he said; a favourite reflection with Palmerston.[41]

In addition, while the chancellor contended all along for powerful sea and land forces at and near the centre of empire, he proposed applying the principle of 'ships where there is service' strictly, outside home waters and the Mediterranean. Retrenchment was not obviously the primary motive for this proposal. There remained his objections, which he modified, to methods employed beyond Europe in the pursuit of trade. 'To send a minister with a fleet...was a positive mischief', he complained, mildly now, when he touched on China in this cabinet memorandum. The slave trade, piracy and 'actual violence' warranted a naval presence; vessels might be detached from the main fleets to deal with contingencies. Ships permanently on station in remote waters gave British representatives of lowly rank and inexperienced naval officers 'virtual powers of peace and war, greater... than are possessed by the cabinet'.[42] The first lord of the Admiralty's subsequent memorandum described the genuine requirements of British business. In the Far East, wrote the Duke of Somerset, the need was not merely for protection but also for control of traders with their propensity to stir up trouble for themselves; Gladstone had not realized this aspect of the problem. Latin America was a far larger market – Britain's exports to it were more than twice those to China in the middle of this period – but one plagued by incessant revolutions in its component states.[43] In such conditions, British property had to be safeguarded and claims for compensation supported by a show of naval force, and its occasional use. As the Duke remarked, corvettes and sloops sufficed to watch over trade and 'give countenance to...consuls'. That was why Palmerston in 1859 envisaged building warships of all classes.[44] Gladstone in 1864 still criticized the Duke and the government for having ships *all over the world...* to multiply causes of quarrel', when steam and the telegraph made it possible to summon them for distant stations.[45] It was not a realistic view to take, particularly for someone who saw the necessity of employing power in the service of trade.

If there was so little to choose between Palmerston and Gladstone in their understanding of how free trade and security were related, Cobden's doctrine of non-intervention definitely took second place to practical politics in the last six years of his life: 'I think power, wherever it is...gives the real rank in the world', he said and repudiated the persistent suggestion that he was opposed to a strong navy.[46] By that date, March 1863, non-intervention was a receding ideal. When news of war in Italy, and the rumoured imminence of its spread, reached him in the United States four years earlier, he felt near despair: 'another Buonaparte playing over again the game of his uncle...And yet we are told that we live in an age of progress'; had he been younger, he would have left Europe to its fate and settled in America.[47] For him, as for Palmerston and Gladstone, the danger to Britain came from France and her ruler. Cobden was as alive as anyone to the damaging effects of uncertainty on the economic climate, noting it with approval when Napoleon's minister, Fould, said of the proposal for an Anglo-French commercial treaty that something must be done to allay uneasiness in the financial and commercial world.[48] The Treaty was a less than satisfactory experiment. 'It is a sad conclusion to have to come to', he observed on the day he signed the agreement as a plenipotentiary for Palmerston's government, 'that the merchant's ledger is to do more than the Bible to carry out the Christian precept of peace and goodwill...'[49] The poverty of economics uninformed by religion and politics was not lost on him.

In the course of further negotiations to work out the detailed application of what had been argued, Cobden indicated his rethinking of non-intervention in a letter to Bright. Palmerston was too evidently right in doubting whether the treaty could be squared with free trade principles; it had to be placed in the context of solicitude, on both sides, for the health of the alliance. How 'safe and simple' it would be were Britain to give up any responsibility for the good behaviour of her neighbours, wrote Cobden, but even then 'strict justice in…international relations and a good example' would stand in the way.[50] He covered himself with the unanimity of the Commons in supporting the maintenance of British naval superiority over any other country, and recommended ministers to build more ironclads.[51] Nor did he evade the issue of force in aid of commerce with China and similarly unequal trading partners. 'When you have established your English merchants everywhere', MPs heard him declare in 1862, 'you are bound to protect them…and their property to the utmost…of your power.' He asked only that they should consider whether it was to the national advantage to let traders set up where the local reaction promised a 'vast sacrifice' of taxpayers' money.[52] No government, as he well knew, had the authority to stop British businessmen from entering these new markets; nor could it withhold the expected protection; nor had the consequent use of force been expensive. The closeness of his views to Palmerston was a source of embarrassment and irritation to him; but there was no help for it. If Bright displayed much less political sense, his attitude to India, about which he entertained few of Cobden's reservations, combined with his eagerness for a good Anglo-French relationship to dilute his professed isolationism. 'I do not think it would be possible to select a minister who could better carry out a policy…most just to France, and most beneficial to ourselves, than the noble lord', he said at the outset of Palmerston's second ministry.[53] It was avowedly reluctant homage to the statecraft which he regularly assailed.

At the close of his life, Gladstone denied that Palmerston was an authentic free trader because he did not give the same weight to the moral as to the economic reasons against protectionism.[54] In practice, they both accepted that free trade must be about power. But Palmerston apprehended, as Gladstone did not, the intensity of the conviction in, for example, the states of the North German Zollverein, that in preaching free trade 'our object was to inundate Germany with British commodities, and so to extinguish…German industry in all its branches…'. 'Disabusing Europe' would take time. He nevertheless claimed to believe in the possibility. Glancing at the debatable link between freedom of trade and international harmony, he drew the Commons' notice, with undisguised irony, to the thriving British export of armaments.[55] The dismantling of protective tariffs in Britain had been justified by the overall result: but it was unilateral free trade which soon inspired misgivings in quarters where the strictest orthodoxy might have been assumed. A deputation from the Manchester Chamber of Commerce, no less, was sent away from an interview with Palmerston, disconcerted at his sweeping refusal of comfort: 'Well, you know we have nothing to give, we have given all we can in repeal of duties... and we cannot go to market with nothing to sell.'[56] For Britain's remaining imposts on foreign trade were revenue duties; she had nearly divested herself of bargaining counters in commercial negotiations with industrializing countries. The divestment had been taken to those lengths by the cabinet decision to extend changes in duty under the treaty – reductions and removals – to British imports from other states. The budget that incorporated the changes went further, leaving forty-eight items out of 419, and those at lower rates. Appearing before a Commons select committee in 1864, the foreign secretary, Russell, gave 'Imperial considerations' as having determined the cabinet.[57] He did not elaborate but Gladstone expounded the government's motives in rounding off free trade thus completely to an Italian friend. Protectionism set 'class... against class, and classes against the common unity'. Regulation of the economy by natural instead of artificial laws made for the acceptance of class differences, for the fullest employment ever seen, and 'an almost equal blessing', for stability of employment. 'Our Queen rules, as we believe, over the most attached and loyal population in Europe.' In foreign affairs, he noted how self-interest checked the assertiveness which these remarkable developments bred; at least, it did so where British trade was largely involved.[58]

In the end, the economic performance of the state was judged by a simple test, one that Cobden used to furnish Napoleon with an argument to quell his protectionists. The comparative figures he offered for the industrial standard of living in Britain and France delighted the Emperor: 'What an answer to those people!' Cobden's statistics were incomplete, referring only to 'operatives', but adequate for the purpose. The British working class outstripped the French by a conclusive margin.[59] France, however, retained tariffs of up to 30 per cent on British exports after the 1860 treaty. While Continental states appreciated the discipline of competition, they declined to allow it free play, afraid for their industry and power. As it was, they could not escape the sometimes uncomfortable influence of Britain on their economies: 'when English commerce suffers, European commerce cannot be in perfect security', a leading Parisian newspaper put it judiciously. The conduct of London as the world's unquestioned financial centre was a subject of admiration and complaint: 'The Anglo-Saxon... a bold and fearless speculator' tried nerves on the money markets of his neighbours; but he supplied 'endless' capital to clients outside Europe, indeed too much for the good of European borrowers, who had to pay more for their money.[60] The Continental disinclination to imitate Britain's abandonment of protectionism gave an added impulse to the flow of Britain's trade and investment towards the Americas and the East. Milner

Gibson at the Board of Trade, deplored the lack of reciprocity in Europe, except for the Turks, the Dutch and the Swiss; 'the liberality has been all on our side', he said in 1865.[61]

The search was for markets capable of sustaining the rate at which the British economy was growing. One, it was thought, lay in China, which quickly proved to be a disappointment. France's co-operation with Britain there, like that of the United States, was based on recognition of the preponderant British interest in the Far East. Gladstone hoped the two countries' joint action would 'draw us together'.[62] As in Europe, the old antagonism was subordinated to mutual advantage, economic and political, if not always with the same relative amity between governments displayed in this instance.[63] India did not disappoint. British exports to the sub-continent rose by over 70 per cent in the five years to 1860, when they comprised over one-eighth of all domestic exports, and continued to rise almost unchecked. Moreover, four years later, Britain imported twice as much from India to supply her industry as she exported to her. The expansion of Anglo-Indian trade was looked on as vindicating the national attitude in the darkest days of the Mutiny. In the absence of information from India, dealings were almost at a standstill on the Stock Exchange in late July 1857. *The Times*, on its City page, dared to suggest that if the British were driven out, Anglo-Indian trade would nonetheless recover and flourish.[64] This was what Cobden believed, but not, emphatically, the British public. Lewis, who leant to Cobden's view, knew 'the people of this country will never consent to lose India...and will go on playing Double or Quits until they win'. They could afford to be resolute. The home government, he confirmed to Palmerston after the fall of Delhi, had so far spent a 'trifling' amount on suppressing the revolt, the cost of which throughout was borne chiefly by the East India Company and the Indian administration that succeeded it.[65] Palmerston refused the assistance of troops from the Continent, proffered in the name of European civilization to subdue a barbaric enemy: these allies would be likely to outstay their welcome.[66] A rich market was retained for Britain without incurring awkward obligations to Europe and at small continuing expense, since India met the bill for a considerably augmented white garrison. The post-Mutiny expectations of British business ran so high that Palmerston and his Indian secretary, Wood, endeavoured to restrain them. Nothing they said was calculated to modify seriously the idea which the intelligent and humane W. E. Forster, for one, expressed to a political meeting in Bradford: 'the prosperity of the working-classes...rested upon...our Indian empire'.[67] If India's importance was often overstated she made a significant contribution to the climbing real wages of the period.

In 1855, for the first time, the East from the Levant to further Asia took more British merchandise than the United States. This change was part of

Palmerston's inheritance on becoming prime minister, as was the position that Britain enjoyed in Latin America, where her exports showed an increase of 80 per cent in 1855–65. His policy at the Foreign Office had fostered trade which now accelerated. The steep fall in exports to the United States at the start of the civil war, and their slowness to make up the loss before its end, put pressure on government to assist with the removal of obstacles to British trade in the Eastern and Latin American markets. The railway promoter Samuel Laing, one of the 'Peace Party' during the Crimean war, Gladstone's financial secretary to the Treasury in 1859–60, and subsequently finance member of the Viceroy of India's council for two years, preached to the converted in speeches given full coverage by *The Times*. He criticized the 'shallow theory' of free trade's incompatibility with the imperial spirit. While India stood 'first in the list', the colonies of settlement, when combined, already rivalled her as an outlet for British goods; but Britain's attraction and authority came through in other ways, pervasively. Sterling as the commanding medium of global exchange held sway over 'the Indian ryot, the Egyptian fellah, the Chinese coolie'. The 'wild Somali' coaling ship and loading cargo at Aden, whose patient toil Laing compared to that of the Irish docker in London, was a symbol of British economic primacy, if not, as this businessman–politician would have it, witness to the heathen's preparation for 'a purer...religion' through the civilizing agency of commerce.[68] Europe still accounted for a constant proportion of growing British imports and domestic exports, about 40 per cent of the former and a third of the latter, as well as the great bulk of her re-exports; little short of half the grand total for exports and re-exports. These facts put into perspective Milner Gibson's charge of illiberality against the Continent, as they do the dread of war with France or a general European conflict, and Palmerston's determination that this country should have the armed forces needed to save her from being drawn into either through feebleness.

Confidence and the classes

The surest element in confidence was the political integration of classes. Bagehot in his articles on 'The Money Market' in the *Economist* for 1864 quoted the Parisian banker who said of the risks that his brethren in London took as a matter of course in extending credit, 'Ah! You do not know what 1848 was in Paris; *I do*. If you knew how suddenly a revolution may come, and how much money it makes people ask for, you would be as cautious *as I am*.'[69] The thought of social revolution was present to British minds. Industrial property had more reason than land to be afraid. It had been in the front line when Chartism confusedly menaced the propertied classes. Employers in industry had a great deal to lose, and little to gain, by

opposing the continuation of landed primacy in a country whose economic
character had been, and was being, so altered. They shrank from placing
themselves at the head of popular agitation that would disrupt and imperil
their businesses. Broadly typical of contemporary industry were the
Lancashire millowners who depended on bank credit, their historian has
written, 'to aid both survival and growth'.[70] The extent to which cotton
and other firms were internally financed did not insulate them against a
crisis in the money market, if it helped them to weather the storm. The
experience of such crises had taught them what to fear from a loss of
confidence inspired by well-founded alarm for domestic political stability.
'Your landed estates', said the cotton master John Bright in a landowning
Parliament on the Tory reform bill of 1859, 'are much more permanent as
property than...our manufacturers. Any convulsion in the country, any
violent action of the democracy would be infinitely more perilous to us than
it could possibly be to you.'[71] Here is an important part of the explanation
for the hesitation and ambiguity perceptible in his radicalism. Again, the
politically mature Bright acknowledged that it was normal and desirable
for successful industrialists in the North and Midlands to buy land for the
'great social position and great political influence' it conferred, as the
possessors of fortunes made in the City and commerce had long been
doing.[72] Although his attacks on land and its anachronistic hold on
government and Parliament were notorious, he disliked and feared the
reality of a class society.[73] Cobden, too, was reluctant 'to recognize the
necessity of dealing with working men as a class'.[74] Palmerston and
Gladstone met that reality with fewer evasions, less frightened of its dangers
while never complacent. For the two radicals class consciousness was a
weapon against aristocracy, and otherwise something to be deprecated.
Palmerston's social strategy, which became Gladstone's, assumed the
legitimacy of class and tried to utilize it positively, taking account of
change.

In one obvious respect, order was fragile. There were only 23,000
unarmed police in Great Britain for a population of 23 millions, compared
with 12,500 of the para-military Irish Constabulary for under 6.5 millions,
or Napoleon III's 25,000 gendarmes, part of the army, in addition to his
civil police. The troops – regulars, yeomanry and militia – no longer had
the same police function that had been theirs when Palmerston was
secretary-at-war under Perceval and Liverpool. The newly formed
volunteers were never intended to have it. Faulty though his judgment
often proved, Clarendon was not wrong when he told the Duke of Bedford
in 1858: 'We do not fight in the streets like the French, but we can give
ourselves a new constitution by law more effectively than by violence.'[75]
The machinery of physical repression was inadequate and, more to the
point, unusable. The rulers of Britain, like most rulers, relied upon

consensus; Marx's variable theories of class behaviour discerned its existence and, after a fashion, its structure. The catalyst of change at an unwelcome pace in the early 1830s had been economic discontent, leading to a temporary decline in deference. This remained a latent threat. The larger problem was more subtle, the nineteenth-century difficulty of transition at a critical stage. Palmerston saw and advertised the significance, in this context, of skilled workers, artisans whom Chartism had failed to recruit in sufficient numbers. They had the potential not only to revive popular radicalism but to make it, without resort to self-defeating extremism, more formidable than it had ever been. Technological progress, then, swelled the demand for skill in bigger units of manufacturing industry as in numerous small workshops, often engaged in sub-contract work, where a craftsman could aspire to be his own master. In either sphere, the artisans had an economic value that invested them with real bargaining power under favourable circumstances, and therefore with an independence that also represented the perpetuation of ancient craft traditions adopted by new trades when they emerged. Their wages were, in general, twice those of the unskilled, and might equal, as in the iron works of Middlesbrough, the pay of a field officer in the Army. They were usually literate when the illiteracy rate in England and Wales, measured by the simplest test, was around one in three, though falling. Trade unionism was theirs in origin and substance, legalized before the 1832 Act. Artisans would be the natural leaders of the working class if it developed an autonomy dreaded by land and business. Without their participation, no movement from below against established institutions could pose the threat freely talked about but unrealized.[76]

Cobden regarded the artisans as an extension of the middle class, socially comparable to small shopkeepers.[77] Today it has been argued that they evolved a 'sectional culture', breaking up such working-class unity as had existed but not susceptible to 'just the old style control from above'.[78] Their improved status, evident in the patronage of mechanics' institutes, savings banks, temperance, friendly and building societies, and their insight into the workings of society itself, the subject of impressed comment, made them unreceptive to radicalism of Cobden's kind, or Ernest Jones's. Trade unionism worried Palmerston, as it did Bright or Baines: to him and to them, it was still an instrument of class conflict rather than a legitimate means of exploiting market forces in the interests of labour. The truth was that skilled workers, like the middle classes, were divided by political and religious loyalties shared with those above them. This was the assumption on which Palmerston proceeded. He relegated to the past the supposition of mutual antagonism between employers and workers in industry, and between land and business. Real wages, adjusted for the unemployment in the nineteenth-century economy were approaching the top of a rise, put at over 25 per cent, from the mid-fifties to the mid-sixties, with the skilled minority of the working class faring distinctly better than the majority. '...a live minister...you will see...is very much like one of yourselves', he said in his Scottish tour in 1863 to the applause of a specifically working-class assembly in Glasgow, composed of artisans and others. The burden of his speech was the intelligence and the rewards of mutual respect and dependence: landowners, manufacturers and working men were all vitally interested in the continuing growth of industrial and agricultural incomes and production. Working men contributed increased skill, for which they should be paid commensurately; and by their rational attitude to investment and profits they helped everyone, but not least themselves: 'without...accumulation of capital there never could be...increasing employment'. He dwelt on the opportunities which social mobility afforded: the country was full of 'immense wealth' amassed from humble beginnings.[79]

Palmerston contrasted the 'almost impassable' social barrier found under authoritarian regimes with the openness of Britain, enjoying 'popular representation'.[80] Some, observed *The Times*, would think the prime minister daring for his inclusion of the working class, 'in a sense', within the community of those to whom government was directly answerable, but that class was 'on the natural way' to the franchise.[81] A good many artisans were qualified to vote, under the provisions of the Reform Act, by uneven and rising rateable values. Bagehot in the *Economist* had no doubt of Palmerston's readiness to accommodate the working class: 'If they *would* have power, he would let them have it.'[82] Palmerston refused to anticipate the demand; to move prematurely would be to play into the hands of 'the directing agitators' in control of the trade unions, who, in the metropolis, were indeed flirting with Continental socialism.[83] The speeches he made were intended to encourage, in advance of the irresistible enfranchisement, the strong working-class tendency to identify with constitutionalism, property and aristocratic government. His success with the working men of Glasgow characteristically appeared 'singular and inexplicable' to Cobden, who nevertheless accepted its genuineness.[84] The budgets of Lewis and Gladstone had social objectives in keeping with Palmerston's, which gave more emphasis to the workers, as such, during his second administration. It should not be forgotten, however, that Gladstone held very conservative ideas on taxation.[85] After five years at the Treasury, he estimated the average share of personal income paid in indirect taxation at one-fourteenth but 'in the higher class...decidedly less: and in the lower decidedly more'.[86] Five-sevenths of central government revenue derived from taxes on consumption. It was an imbalance that he did not wish to see altered, he said in the House towards the close of his stewardship, 'so critical' were the risks to the landed class.[87] The language of both

Palmerston and Gladstone about social solidarity and equality of opportunity, sometimes exaggerated as in the former's address to Glaswegian working men, sought to compensate for this admitted fiscal discrimination against wage earners.

Economy was thus a political imperative to protect the landed interest and spare the working man. If income tax in peacetime went to thirteen or fourteen pence in the pound, argued Gladstone to the cabinet, it should be considered an 'experiment...neither safe nor right'; were it to be tried, he expected a clamour for varying rates according to the type of property.[88] Bright had propounded a 'heavy' tax on the returns from 'realized property', so exempting businessmen and farmers, a rural middle class in England, both of whom, he conceived were engaged in creating the wealth off which landowners, mortgagees and investors in the Funds lived. Later, he substituted a proposal to tax the capital value of property, very moderately, producing four times the current (1857–58) yield of income tax and allowing indirect taxes to be slashed. His target was the landed estate with fewer borrowings than business to set against tax, or so he imagined; he wilfully overlooked on this and many other occasions the extent to which businessmen were doing on a large scale what they had always done, and acquiring land.[89] 'Bright's finance would be more ruinous than his Reform', wrote Lewis, who attacked the scheme in the *Edinburgh Review*.[90] Harder to withstand was the plan of J. G. Hubbard, a Tory MP and ex-governor of the Bank of England, for differentiation of the existing tax between incomes arising from employment and those from invested property, at the expense of the latter. The cabinet were equally divided over Hubbard's motion for a select committee; they decided to oppose, but lost in the Commons by four votes. Gladstone sat on the committee, where Hubbard's 'unimpeachable justice', as J. S. Mill designated it, to the business and professional taxpayer went down to defeat.[91] The Tory's persistence in bringing forward his plan, with its undeniable attractions, next session, elicited an unsparing condemnation of such irresponsibility from Gladstone: 'I must tell him...he is treading upon far more dangerous ground than he is aware of...coming near to questions that cut deep into the foundations of social order.'[92]

Gladstone continued to regard himself, 'at least', as pledged to managing the national finances with the aim of giving Palmerston the opportunity to abolish income tax, if he so wished.[93] He feared the tax, rightly in the very long term, as subversive of his social ideals. He had some embarrassing allies, like Mill in his evidence before Hubbard's committee, who objected to the tax, in principle, as one on saving. Gladstone, the architect of the modest succession duty in 1853, would have nothing to do then with Mill's suggestion that, instead of a tax on income, a higher levy on capital at the point of death was the 'most unobjectionable' way of arriving at equity in taxation under the conditions prevailing in society.[94] To make up for this determined fiscal conservatism, Gladstone rearranged indirect taxes, relying on a few that were extremely productive to stabilize the absolute contribution of customs and excise to the revenue as incomes and purchasing power grew with the contemporary expansion in economic life. Compassion and the self-interest of the propertied directed his financial planning. 'Why all this idle talk about economy?' he asked in his budget speech of 1864, given the 'enormous development' of the country's wealth, which he had been describing. He did not believe, any more than Palmerston did, in the elimination of dire poverty by the industrial capitalism that generated such riches: 'You have...and will always have an enormous mass of paupers', over three-quarters of a million being relieved by the Poor Law, 'the last necessity', and an unknown number dependent on private charity; distress in Lancashire only aggravated the normal indigence. Paupers or not, the great majority of their fellow-countrymen endured 'a struggle for existence', if at a level somewhat better than they had experienced until lately. The betterment lifted expectations, to which MPs might not safely be blind. Though falling, the incidence of taxation for all those millions was not low, and must not be permitted to climb.[95]

Gladstone's difficulties were largely of his own making. Neither Palmerston nor Lewis was similarly afraid of the income tax. On the contrary, they were apprehensive of the reaction should it be given up. It was easy to denounce the tax, said Lewis in 1858, and get a cheer in the House; but its abolition and partial replacement by higher taxes on consumption, would have to be vindicated before 'assemblages of a very different character', overwhelmingly composed of people, voters and non-voters, who did not pay tax on their earnings.[96] Not that Palmerston and Lewis were unworried when the rate exceeded Peel's seven pence in the pound, at which it stood until the Crimean war. The sensible alternative to rates that might 'cripple enterprise...derange industry, or interfere with the ordinary distribution of capital' was to borrow, as Palmerston and the cabinet forced Gladstone to do in the sixties.[97] The cost to the taxpayer was so much less that Gladstone's financial purism isolated him. He may have occupied firmer ground in resisting the prime minister's desire to reduce indirect taxation rather than let the chancellor go on cutting income tax from six to four pence at that stage. Growth, he pointed out, meant that a fourpenny rate would yield more than the seven pence of Peel. Palmerston consented to the lower rate; but the chancellor halved the tea duty, from a shilling to sixpence per pound.[98] In 1857 the official calculations available to Lewis estimated that the working class accounted for 44 per cent of the tea consumed in England and Wales, and 40 per cent of the sugar.[99] Those percentages had since gone up. Gladstone reduced the duty on sugar by nearly a third in 1864, and tea was next in line. His reasoned preference for taxing consumption was modified by Palmerston's common sense.

The Lancashire cotton famine seemed exaggerated to Palmerston, always mindful of the deprivation ordinarily around him. The local guardians, he noticed in November 1862, were then giving the family men among millworkers on relief a weekly sum equal to, or in excess of, the wages on which an agricultural labourer in Southern counties supported his dependants. In Palmerston's reasonable view, the overproduction of 1860 and 1861 would have resulted in serious distress, if not on the same scale.[100] He was actively concerned to prevent the spectacle of Britain's greatest industry in profound depression from obliging the state to make a substantial grant in aid of the laid-off workforce, so setting an expensive precedent. His impression of conditions in Lancashire reflected the uncertainty about them. Visiting Preston, a place he knew well, Stanley saw 'not a sign of suffering or distress' but was not deceived by appearances.[101] Palmerston braced himself for the impact on public opinion of 'Cobden's speeches and…*Punch*'s pictures'.[102] To the prime minister's surprise, Cobden was true to his economic principles and expressed 'horror' at the thought of a government grant: 'who will care about its frugal expenditure?'.[103] Ministers legislated for a rate in aid of the worst affected areas, to be collected from other unions in the country. Cobden would have preferred a national rate, shutting his eyes to the inconsistency with the principle of local accountability. The Union Relief and Public Works (Manufacturing Districts) Acts of 1862–64 empowered the unions of the cotton region and, in the case of the Public Works Acts, the municipal authorities as well to obtain loans from government. The unsuitability and aversion of the millworkers for heavy manual labour made these works of little use in alleviating unemployment.[104]

Private charity organized itself to maintain the level of income disapprovingly mentioned by Palmerston, which had to be compared with family earnings, in an industry employing men, women, and children, that accustomed a household to spending several times as much on food alone as it did after being thrown out of work. Thus it was not the help from the state but what Villiers, president of the Poor Law Board, called in a private letter to Palmerston the 'unceasing solicitude of the wealthy and benevolent' that left its mark on cotton operatives.[105] The operatives were a section of the working class whose wages in good times put the highly paid on a par, in some respects, with the 'labour aristocracy' typified by the artisans. The élite of the mills, the spinners, were, however, more subject to the control of employers than were skilled men in many other trades; indeed the degree of their skill has been questioned. The experience of the cotton famine tied them closely to their benefactors. The cotton masters resented the initial censures of landed politicians and the press for failing to see where duty and interest lay; but they followed, so far as they were able, the powerful lead given by Lord Derby and lesser landowners in the county, particularly the Liberal Sir James Kay-Shuttleworth, the first baronet distinguished as an educational administrator, and Colonel John Wilson Patten MP, Derby's friend and political colleague. If the limits of entrepreneurial philanthropy were exposed, the workpeople received a tangible assurance of class collaboration from the traditional leadership of society. Derby chaired the central executive committee co-ordinating relief in Manchester; Kay-Shuttleworth was his vice-chairman, and officials from the Poor Law Board, placed at their disposal, checked information from local committees. This aristocratic intervention commenced in June and July 1862 with meetings at the London house of the Earl of Ellesmere, a Lancashire magnate. From setting up the Bridgewater House Fund, Derby and Kay-Shuttleworth quickly graduated to the positions described, a natural assumption of responsibility not disguised by the Earl's vindication of the cotton masters' sense of social obligation.[106]

H. B. Farnall, the senior of the Poor Law Board officials working with the central executive committee, and a member of it, was criticized for some of his actions and the quality of his reporting and advice. So, too, were civil servants in another field by Palmerston. Those in the Board of Trade and the Home Office, he alleged, had always sided with the employers on legislation 'which I am very much for', extending the Factory Acts to women and children in bleachfields and dyeworks. He exhorted Lewis, the minister concerned, to stand by the majority for the bill on its second reading in the Commons and not to countenance damaging amendments at the prompting of his advisers. Palmerston thought the outlook of masters in the trade on the employment of children no better than that of slave-owners.[107] Lewis found the subject 'tedious'.[108] Whether routine, as apparently with Farnall, or principle infused the bureaucracy with what to Palmerston was 'the...genuine spirit of narrow-minded Red Tapeism', widely present in government departments, the slow trend towards social legislation gathered a certain momentum under his administrations.[109] There were civil servants who furthered the movement; but they laboured in an uncertain climate and needed the friendly influence of Palmerston at the centre. He both understood and believed in 'all the sanitary questions',[110] as well as extension of the Factory Acts and the place of the state in education. The last had implications for confidence to which Palmerston referred in a speech at Leeds in 1860, besides its recognized value to an industrial economy in want of literacy and numeracy. He spoke with compassionate realism of irremediable poverty and its dimensions, sure to grow with the size of the population on his projection of the capitalist future, even more pessimistic than Gladstone's. His recommended method of social control over this huge mass below the artisanate and the semi-skilled operatives, miners and the rest – was simple religious and moral instruction in the elementary schools which government helped to support: 'Teach them betimes the...importance of rules, regulations and order.'[111] There was no other way in practice. He protested in his second cabinet against the reduction effected by the adoption of the Revised Code in the modest amount which the state devoted to educating 'the lower classes'. '...we have,' he argued, 'its full value in the improved intelligence and good conduct of those classes'.[112]

During his first administration he reminded the industrialists of Lancashire, in the context of high profits and low taxation, that the workers, 'the foundation of the social fabric', were not 'machines to produce so much profit to yourselves but...rational beings', on whom a great many of their betters and the government spent a lot of money 'to raise them in the scale of society...and in their own self-respect'.[113] The working class of his speech was not the same as that of which he talked at Leeds, but the skilled and semi-skilled in regular work. These speeches of 1856 and 1860 displayed a sensitivity to what was happening absent from Gladstone's memorandum on state aid to schools written soon after he returned to the Treasury: he represented the education vote, less than 2 per cent of government spending, as an 'evil [that]...swells with such rapidity from year to year'.[114] After 1862 when, in palpable imitation of the prime minister, he really started taking policy to the country, he showed more insight; although the reduction of expenditure on schools went ahead. The wisdom of Palmerston's political sermons and then Gladstone's came through in middle-class censure of, and working-class indifference to, Cobden's attack on the landed interest in November 1863, outspoken, unexpected and seconded by Bright. Land was blamed for the abject condition of the agricultural labourer, and, with rich businessmen, for poverty and illiteracy everywhere, ill-concealed by national prosperity and strength: he swept aside 'your army and navy, your exports and your imports – it is no use telling me you have a small portion of your people exceedingly well off'. Without Parliamentary reform there could be no improvement: political power was the means to economic and social change.[115] It sounded as though he was trying to revive the Chartism he had opposed. He was, naturally, attempting to promote a moderate reform bill by scaring property into submitting to it for fear of worse. They were Bright's tactics in 1858–59, when Cobden disapproved of them. From time to time, the latter's emotion mastered his intellect; the deference of his compatriots to the landed, which he habitually exaggerated, incensed him: 'It is not to be found in any other country to the same extent – *outside of Asia*.'[116] The tone and wilful inaccuracies of his speech earned it a chastening reception in most of the press, metropolitan and provincial.[117]

The Stock Exchange united upper- and middle-class investors as never before; while limited liability opened up business far more widely to the direct participation of many previously deterred by the risks. The nominal

value of quoted securities, other than British Funds, rose in ten years to
£700 from £460 millions. A hundred millions of the increase was in the
funded debt of foreign and colonial governments, three-quarters of it
foreign. Many such securities inspired a perilous enthusiasm, *The Times*
thought: 'foreign loans do not form fitting investments for families, or for
many persons to whom loss would be fatal'. Yet in one period of nearly nine
months, Egyptian and Turkish 'adventures' furnished the Exchange with
its most conspicuous profits, adverse publicity notwithstanding. Official
encouragement to invest in certain loans added to the attraction of this
section of the market, and underlined its connection with the authority and
stability of British governments; Palmerston as prime minister was good for
its speculative stocks.[118] As for quoted equity capital, it profited from his
keen advocacy of limited liability; but the effect of that change reached
much further. The number of companies incorporated annually with
limited liability went up from a couple of hundred in 1856, when the statute
broadening its applicability was enacted, to over a thousand in 1865. Some
opponents of the measure were radical businessmen and MPs, but they
subscribed to the arguments of Lord Overstone. He entered an injured
protest at the behaviour of the government and 'especially the head', who
had 'fanned a popular cry for the purpose of pulling down a small
minority...'.[119] Palmerston had said that 'this contest lies between the few
and the many'. It was, and he resolved to win; if Parliamentary obstruction
prevailed, 'the country shall at least see with whom the fault rests'.[120]

The 'great capitalists' opposing him looked, he suggested, very like
'"monopolists"...an odious and offensive term', in the light of the
imputed desire to refuse the investing public a chance to share in the
rewards of sizeable undertakings without exposure to prohibitive risks. The
telling line of attack that Palmerston pursued was enjoyable as retaliation
for charges of monopoly in land levelled against his class – and unfair.[121]
Overstone and those who thought as he did were afraid of fictitious
concerns, raised by the demon of speculation; they saw 'a most flimsy
sophistry' in Palmerston's arguments that limited liability was a legitimate
development of free trade.[122] The prime minister understood the dangers,
but proclaimed the advantages of setting free the capital of small investors.
The people he had in mind were middle class.[123] If they retained their
preference for the Funds, railways and foreign loans, this and subsequent
Acts to 1862 erected a legal structure for expanding business that, with all
its well-advertised imperfections, was a good expression of ordered
liberalism. The men of substance who inevitably gained more from the
company legislation received another lesson, if it was required, in the ability
to govern of a landed Parliament, ably led. 'The more prosperous...the
greater their servility to the ruling class', lamented Cobden.[124] In so far as
that 'servility' was purchased, competence in economic policy made up a
large part of the price.

9

The political nation and the people

The myth of inaction

The one serious attempt to challenge the government in the session of 1862 was prompted by the success of its foreign policy. The opposition sought to exploit the radical Stansfeld's motion for economy in the absence of conflict in Europe, and were spectacularly discomfited. Lewis described the beginning of the Parliamentary year as 'flat and without excitement'[1]: and the Commons gave the government whips little trouble during the rest of it. A prominent Liberal member, John Walter, the proprietor of *The Times*, was not displeased to remark that it had been almost impossible to get up 'a party fight'. 'To keep the peace abroad', said the chief whip in his constituency, was the main responsibility of the House elected in 1859, and preparedness the key to security.[2] Against the background of uncertainty on the Continent and war in North America, this settled purpose went far to explain the stability of an administration with a very small and seemingly precarious majority but with admitted strength in foreign affairs. The debate of July 1864 on the diplomatic reverse suffered over Schleswig-Holstein took place amid realization of the public sympathy that Palmerston commanded in his embarrassment. Such comparative freedom from Parliamentary upsets had another side to it. This was not the 'provisional government' depicted in the *Economist* of March 1865, after which the domestic climate was going to change.[3] Change was already under way. Cobden attributed the 'political torpor' to Palmerston's manipulation of the middle and working classes.[4] In doing so he implicitly conceded the existence of the social understanding which featured in the prime minister's speeches as the basis of progress, and not only in living standards. Palmerston's reception when he spoke outside the Commons showed that he was not popularly identified with the exclusion of classes from their legitimate influence in politics.

There was no question of blocking Parliamentary reform. Individual

215

ministers discussed the scope of the next bill; its timing would depend on public opinion. The organized demands in the industrial North and London for an extension of the franchise had a limited impact because those who voiced them were pushing at a half open door.[5] One of the ministers who regularly returned to the topic of reform, Layard, told his Southwark constituents that 'indirectly, our working classes exercised more political power than the same classes in any other country in Europe'.[6] American example was at a discount in the years of civil war; besides, it had never enjoyed the unmixed admiration of working people with their widespread family experience of emigration to the United States.[7] The expanding sub-culture of working-class institutions in Britain, fostered by business and property, reinforced the structure of society. If trade unions were often seen as a threat, leaders and members were keen to establish their respectability.[8] The working class, and particularly its 'aristocracy', had a sense of participation in local and national affairs that was acknowledged in the language and conduct of those higher up. The ideal of 'progressive improvement', which Palmerston held up on his first prime ministerial visit to the North in 1856, depended very much less on the actions of governments than on those of individuals and classes. The typical fondness of Gladstonian Liberalism for socially unifying rhetoric followed Palmerston's skilful use of it.

The political nation and those without a vote were conscious of a general advance, not of stagnation outside economic life. Education in rights and responsibilities through the medium of the newspapers was undoubtedly as effective in tempering progress with popular conservatism as Gladstone claimed it was in 1864, reviewing a decade of rising circulations.[9] By then such figures as J. W. Henley and E. B. Pusey, not usually credited with democratic tendencies, were letting it be known that they were unafraid of household and manhood suffrage, respectively. Even more surprising to those who had mistaken the meaning of Palmerston's tenure of power was Pusey's endorsement of his religious policy: the Church was stronger, and Dissent better disposed towards her.[10] The election of 1865, like the noisier one of 1857, was a triumph for Palmerston. The electorate voted on his record: he had maintained peace and, Schleswig–Holstein apart, prestige, while his domestic statecraft, authentically Liberal, appealed to so many.

The confirmation of Palmerston's ascendancy

A good idea of Palmerston's influence on domestic politics during his last four years may be gained from the diary of Sir John Trelawny. Independent and well regarded on the Liberal backbenches, Trelawny was neither a Whig nor a Palmerstonian; he had voted against the prime minister in the division that brought him down in February 1858; but like many others similarly situated in the party, he appreciated its leader's enhanced stature. Palmerston's 'extraordinary energy and readiness on all occasions' was decisive in sustaining the administration. That individual authority was much more than the sum of his Parliamentary skills. Trelawny, a political friend but still a critical one, saw in him a 'dictator by general consent'.[11] A highly intelligent enemy, blinded by hostility, Wilberforce professed to see in his command of the House the looming extinction of 'the slight remains of constitutional government which exist amongst us'.[12] The recognized ability to read public opinion and direct it gave Palmerston his hold over the Commons. He had, wrote Trelawny, 'the happy gift of saying tonight what no one expects but a great majority will agree to tomorrow morning'. His speechmaking tour in Scotland over the Easter recess of 1863 brought an enthusiastic comment in the diary: 'Fine old fellow! What a slave to his duty! and how he shames our Spanish aristocracy and political Aztecs!' The political nation responded to Palmerston and so, evidently, did the people, defined as those excluded from the franchise. In the Commons of these years, he did not discount party, but often contrived to transcend it. Wilberforce accused him of 'debauching' the House by obscuring the distinction between government and opposition, while Trelawny felt it was 'not quite satisfactory... to reflect that the personal qualities of one man carry everyone captive'.[13]

Few really doubted that the prime minister was a better, that is, a cleverer, conservative than Derby or any of his lieutenants; a more convincing Liberal than the pure Whig and Peelite traditions could boast; the best guarantor of peace without forfeiting Great Power status; and a prudent imperialist. 1862 was the turning-point in his second ministry. 'A great event for the country', wrote Lewis on the settlement of the *Trent* dispute in Britain's favour with French help; as he anticipated, it invigorated the government and subdued the opposition at the start of the new session.[14] The Tories then tried to exploit the relaxation of tension in foreign affairs which combined with the cotton famine to stimulate the demand for some reduction in defence spending. Gladstone, speaking at Manchester in April, practically invited taxpayers to seek 'material' economies. They were not to suppose, he said, that these had been obstructed by the government or its head: current expenditure, 'right and justifiable' with reference to national needs and 'called for by the public voice', would be cut if and when the country decided it was time. He did not envisage a return to pre-Crimean war levels of taxation. At Cobden's instigation, Henry Ashworth asked Gladstone for more than he suggested in his speech.[15] The chancellor had done enough for Palmerston to elicit an explanation. It amounted to continued acquiescence in the prevailing policy.[16] Palmerston had never been indifferent to economy; keeping taxes

as low as possible was fundamental to the health of the British political
system in all his long experience. The advocates of more thrift were stronger
in the House than with the electorate. The prime minister had used that
fact to allay the anxiety of his chief whip: 'I am quite sure that a nation
which has turned out 150,000 volunteers will back up a government
resolved to maintain it in a state of sufficient defence.'[17] It lay with his
critics to show what would be sufficient, and much cheaper. Neither
Gladstone nor Stansfeld on his motion for retrenchment from the Liberal
backbenches in June, lengthily discussed in cabinet beforehand, could do
so. The Tories were in the same uncomfortable position.

Gladstone agreed with the prime minister in their correspondence of
May on this subject that it would be 'mean and guilty... to hold out...
promises of vast retrenchment'; he had avoided doing so at Manchester.[18]
Palmerston told the cabinet of 24 May that they must take account of both
the desire for economy and the concern for defence.[19] The emphasis was on
the latter. Stansfeld, with others, approached Gladstone and Brand, the
chief whip, representing that this motion should be considered friendly to
government and accepted. The chancellor, very properly, said only that he
had to apprise Palmerston, who answered the radical through Brand: if the
motion was mutually acceptable, it would look like collusion and injure the
Liberal party. Ministers undertook, Brand ended, to say 'all we dare' for
retrenchment. Stansfeld's motion was couched in apologetic terms,
reserving 'the safety, independence or legitimate influence of the
country'.[20] The Tory amendment drafted to attract radical and moderate
Liberal votes contained rather more of aggression. Brand reckoned on even
numbers if all the Irish members, for reasons having nothing to do with
economy, joined Cobden, Bright and their associates in the opposition
lobby. The cabinet 'without difference of opinion' authorized Palmerston
to treat the amendment as a question of confidence, his mere announcement
of which routed the Tories.[21] The House divided on Stansfeld's motion and
rejected it by a majority that topped 350; the minority of sixty-five included
only a scattering of Tories and Irish Liberals. Cries of disbelief greeted
Cobden's claim that they were debating the fiscal rescue of depressed
Lancashire and 'if the cotton industry falls, everything else will fall with
it'.[22] Palmerston's real victory was over the doubters and dissentients in his
own party. Trelawny, who voted for the motion, wished after hearing him
that Cobden had retired from political life 'or got out of the groove of...
peace-at-any-price principles'; while Stansfeld's unsatisfactory generaliza-
tions were not what the Commons expected of someone aspiring to give an
important lead.[23] Lewis deemed Palmerston's speech 'masterly'. It
demolished the motion and Tory amendment, without giving anything
away. It affirmed that both economy and security had been and remained
Government objectives.[24] Cobden was frustrated in his hope that

Parliamentary attacks on the prime minister might diminish his appeal when he took politics to the country after the House had risen.[25]

Between the fiscal years 1859–60 and 1865–66 government expenditure declined from its peak under Palmerston and Gladstone of close on £73 million in 1861–62 to £66.5 million. In addition, there was an extraordinary saving of some £2 million on imperial wars after the relatively costly expedition to Peking. Even without this item spending on national defence fell by nearly £4 million from its highest point; while everything comprised under the heading of 'civil government' declined by little more than half a million. The Liberals, the traditional party of retrenchment, laid out 4 millions more on defence in 1865–66 than the Tories in 1858–59. As a percentage of total expenditure, the cost had risen from thirty-two to thirty-seven since Gladstone arrived at the Treasury, roughly the same proportionate change upwards as that downwards in debt charges.[26] He knew very well that the country was not likely to be 'possessed with a really strong spirit of economy'. In 1863 he put a figure on his aim for reduced defence spending, then still climbing: £3.25 million; a target comfortably exceeded by 1865–66. He looked ahead, with Palmerston, to the next general election.[27] The decisions that accounted for £2.5 million of this fall were reached amicably between prime minister and chancellor in the winter of 1863–64. Their last such dispute in the following year involved a smaller sum, which Gladstone found disappointing, no doubt because he had not had to struggle for the larger cut. While Gladstone provoked him to reply at length, this final conflict does not seem to have worried Palmerston, as those of 1860 and 1861 had done. The chancellor put forward a quite unrealistic suggestion although the order of his true expectations was known, and over-played his hand: he treated a return to the defence expenditure of 1858–59 as a serious proposition: 'That is the statement of an historical fact...not a political argument...if argument it can be called', rejoined the prime minister. The requirements of defence should be assessed with reference to the state of international relations, to changes in naval and military technology, to improved conditions of service in line with the general rise in the standard of life, and to what the people wanted.[28]

'I am not aware', protested Gladstone, 'of having used the words that there ought to be a considerable reduction of Army and Navy...'[29] This is an illustration of the casuistry for which he is famous. It was wasted on the prime minister. He dreaded the clashes with Palmerston; the nervous strain made him 'sensitive, fretful and impotent', he admitted in November 1864: 'I am not by nature brave. I am always between two fears, and...more afraid of running away than of holding my ground.'[30] At the end of his second administration, Palmerston was what he had been from the start, the stronger of two strong men. Lewis's death put Gladstone in line for the leadership after Russell: but only if he did not diverge from the policies of the government. The qualified approval that Cobden and Bright extended to him, an asset in so far as it broadened his appeal, was a liability in that it perpetuated, among many Liberals, the doubts of his soundness originally inspired by the Peelite past. His mishandling of Parliamentary reform seriously embarrassed him; and he protested his innocence of radical sympathies. The upshot of that episode was to commit him firmly to a Palmerstonian approach to eventual legislation.

Gladstone came from behind to take his stand with those in office – Milner Gibson in the cabinet, and Layard outside it – and on the back benches who had not let the topic drop when Russell gave up the attempt to pass the bill of 1860. The subject was not one that would die, and nobody expected its demise. Charles Neate, professor of political economy at Oxford and MP for the city, said aloud what others thought on being returned for the constituency in November 1863: to democracy 'we must come at last'. He defined himself as a conservative Liberal, who wished to proceed slowly down that road.[31] 'The truth is', wrote Palmerston after a by-election defeat the previous December, '...Radicalism is out of fashion... and if Government candidates *go the whole hog*, they run the risk of being beat by disgusting many Liberals...' Moreover, he told Brand, should such a candidate, strongly pledged, be elected, he might prove 'an inconvenient auxiliary'. Palmerston said he had no objection to 'bit by bit reform' when he spoke on the radical Whig Locke King's bill to establish a £10 franchise in the counties in 1858, which he had opposed the year before, preferring a figure of £20.[32] In 1861, however, he would have liked to sidestep the next important division on this constantly reintroduced measure by resorting to a procedural device. The cabinet decided otherwise in a discussion of the merits of piecemeal reform, going against advice from the chief whip that Palmerston accepted: 'the House and the country look upon reform as a disagreeable dose. They know it must be taken, and they would prefer to take it at one gulp...at the fitting time.'[33]

Accordingly, the prime minister supported Locke King's bill with his vote. It failed, more decisively than the margin suggested. Another instalment of 'bit by bit reform' passed, on which the cabinet had decided separately.[34] The representation of two small Southern boroughs disfranchised for corruption in the 1840s and 1850s was to be transferred to the industrial North and the metropolis. Palmerston had the two cabinet radicals on his side in adopting the proposal. The minority of six – Russell and Gladstone among them – did not want to pre-empt redistribution under a comprehensive reform bill.[35] The Commons amended the legislation to give all four seats instead of three to the North: two to the West Riding, one to South Lancashire, and one to Birkenhead, a new constituency. This recognition of its political influence took the edge, for the time being, off the justified complaints of under-representation in that great and growing belt of population and industry. When Baines introduced his Borough Franchise Bill in 1861, he drew on the evidence of upper working-class prosperity and respectability in the region. His immediate aim was limited to enacting the £6 franchise in the government's own reform bill of the previous session. Gladstone's supposed boldness on this measure three years later does not bear examination. Five of his cabinet colleagues joined him in voting with Baines, together with Brand and other office-holders; Palmerston, Wood and Sir George Grey did not vote. When the bill came up again in 1864, Gladstone made the celebrated remarks, misconstrued, he rightly maintained, as a declaration of radicalism. He did not vote on that occasion, perhaps to cover himself from the instant criticism, while Wood, Grey, Cardwell, their two radical colleagues, Brand and the rest went with Baines. Next year, Gladstone supported the bill, like all those just named, leaving Palmerston, who was convalescent, as the only cabinet minister in the Commons not to have recorded his approval. This time it was a cabinet decision, taken in Palmerston's absence, to back the bill.[36] Wood, Grey, Cardwell and the chief whip were not men to be suspected of radical tendencies.

In Palmerston's judgement, the case for reform was weaker than it had been. Speaking on Locke King's bill in April 1864, he said that its sponsor would have done better not to persist. Parliamentary reform was not an end in itself but a means to 'great alterations and improvements', many of which they had seen Parliament achieve without the 'organic changes' that its further extensive reform involved. Public opinion had shifted as a result. It was affected too, by the experiences of other countries, a reference to America.[37] His isolation on the issue of reform was more apparent than real. '…looking to the integrity of the Liberal party and…our attitude on the hustings', Brand urged upon him in the following May the need to identify the government before an election with the spirit of its attempt to legislate in 1860. Baines's bill provided the opportunity.[38] Ministers were unafraid of reform and glad to reassert the principle of a reduction in the franchise, said Grey in the House a few days later on the reappearance of that bill.[39] In reality, as he told Palmerston beforehand but after the cabinet had agreed their position, Grey strongly objected to the bill and was reluctant to speak. Why he did not intend to vote with the Liberals openly opposed to Baines 'I confess…is a question I cannot answer very satisfactorily'. He would have preferred to abstain. There was no good argument for not voting against except that the government could not very well escape the consequences of putting forward the identical franchise in 1860.[40] But the cabinet had not bound themselves to a particular figure. The prime minister successfully insisted on the avoidance of any such commitment. He privately regarded £6 as a qualification rather too low for the comfort of property and education.[41] On the other hand, his search for some way of broadening the electorate without swamping it was genuine. He shared Mill's doubts about the fitness of the working class for admission to the political nation and, largely, his belief that they must not be alienated from it, but not his readiness to propound an impracticable solution to the problem.

Mill wanted to discriminate, still on the basis of class, by weighted educational and occupational qualifications substituted for property.[42] The attitude of Palmerston and the government to working-class electors anticipated the warning that W. E. Forster gave from the backbenches: 'If they are excluded as a class and feared as a class, they will agitate as a class and demand admission as a class.'[43] Any other attitude would have been self-defeating; from the time that he first came to power, Palmerston's whole policy was directed towards improved class relations. Artisans enfranchised through higher property values in London by the passing of the 1832 Act and elsewhere, much less numerously, by the rising standard of life since the mid-century, showed little inclination to political independence, let alone subversion. In so far as this artisan vote was radical, it followed the lead of its betters locally. The political consciousness of labour's aristocracy now represented a development of, and no longer a potential threat to, the public opinion hitherto expressed so largely by the middle classes. If that was less certain than it is with the benefit of hindsight, Palmerston made the assumption in his oratory. There was no alternative. The reception he got at Glasgow in 1863 demonstrated the rewards of crediting the working class with a maturity of which he was unconvinced. The evidence of his popularity induced near despair in Cobden and Bright.[44] Palmerston relied on the knowledge of his influence over the country and the classes to maintain himself in office as by-election losses reduced his precarious majority of June 1859 to vanishing point. 'these defeats', he wrote to Brand at the end of the session of 1863 '...will not materially affect the stability of the Government', which lay 'not simply in the balance of votes...in the House of Commons but mainly in favourable public opinion and the division of sentiments in the Conservative party.'[45] Public opinion determined his cautious, though always flexible, line on Parliamentary reform.

Gladstone's 'Chartist speech', as Trelawny designated it, on Baines's bill strengthened the prime minister all round.[46] The offending passage did not advocate democracy, but its extemporized wording placed the burden of proof on those, himself included, who contemplated a popular franchise with apprehension.[47] The reaction to Gladstone's mistake laid bare unease at the movement towards integrating the working class politically, between which and a simple extension of the franchise Palmerston was careful to distinguish, since the 'legislative machine' should represent interests and not numbers.[48] The Tories' astonishment and perturbation at what Gladstone seemed to say were reflected almost throughout the House. Trelawny, who was considered a radical, set down his thoughts: 'Rousseau is, apparently, in communication with our chancellor of the Exchequer through some medium. Will Gladstone go further and throw upon owners of estates the onus of showing their titles to exclusive possession? I suggest no arguments against his views; I merely inquire how far he would carry them.'[49] Like Stanley, he surmised that the House had seen a bid to change the course of politics.[50] Gladstone dispelled the speculation by repudiating its cause; 'I agree in your denial "That every sane and not disqualified man has a moral right to vote"', he replied to the prime minister with obvious sincerity. The impression of flawed judgement remained. Palmerston pointed out to him that the figure of £6 had been the undoing of the 1860 reform bill.[51] That was indisputable. For the hostile majority that Baines encountered in May of that year was significantly larger than in 1861 and 1864. The 1865 election imparted little, if any, urgency to the question.[52]

The perception that derives from loathing informed Cobden's references to Palmerston in correspondence with his circle. He knew his enemy, and admitted that Palmerston had spoken better since reaching the premiership at seventy than before. He was not disposed to read a great deal into a manifestation of support for Parliamentary reform when the prime minister visited Bradford in August 1864. '...too much...of a sickening and discouraging kind' marked the proceedings, and showed how susceptible to Palmerston the middle classes were everywhere. Those classes were the source of power; all that working men had done at Bradford was to save themselves from 'the stigma of having altogether joined in prostration...' In moments of overstrained indignation, eminently quotable, Cobden and Bright tended to depict Palmerston as a political necromancer. They assured each other that he owed his deplorable prestige to the total absence of principle with which he exploited the inveterate servility of their middle-class countrymen – a weakness unparalleled the world over, declared Cobden. They had, of course, no difficulty in understanding the success of his policies: 'Are *we*', Cobden asked Bright, 'the proper leaders for a generation which follows Palmerston?'[53] They did not, in fact, attempt to provide regular leadership under the conditions that applied after the emergence of real Liberal unity in 1859. Whatever he said to them, Gladstone aligned himself more closely every year with a statesman whom he had once extravagantly denounced, and under whom he never felt easy. What bound him to the prime minister was the latter's central achievement, to which he paid public tribute, in making the Liberals the party of class collaboration.

Class and government

The politicians of this period continually talked about class. The interdependence of classes was a cliché. Without a novel prosperity the social tensions of two generations would not have dwindled so rapidly: but that prosperity was not enough by itself to effect a transformation, which went forward through political education in the widest sense. The politicians spoke to a country well prepared for their message by organized religion, the press, and other agencies. The community of interest between different orders and an imputed equality of esteem were traditional declarations, now adapted to classes in an industrial society. They had a greater, and a liberating, impact after the growth of middle- and upper working-class numbers, independence and contentment. The life of industrial towns where the environment seemed hostile to deference was found to be increasingly compatible with landed government at the centre. As a result of the close attention that ministers and Parliament paid to urban interests and opinion, the towns' legitimate grievance of under-representation in the Commons lost much of its force. Cobden recalled how in 1849 the radicals in the House mustered nearly a hundred votes for a ratepayer franchise at Parliamentary elections, the ballot and uniformly sized constituencies. In 1865, he commented bitterly, Baines's £6 figure was the most that could be proposed and then only with the certainty of rejection.[54] At the same time, the decline of agitation for Parliamentary reform, the expiry of Chartism, and the encouraging aspect of the working class led to intensified speculation that household or even manhood suffrage might prove no sort of threat to existing rulers but the reverse. Charles Greville, for one, the confidant of leading Whigs, had the possibility strongly in mind when he pondered the implication of the enthusiasm that greeted the Queen on her visit to Chartist and radical Birmingham.[55] To capitalize on the promise of those who could not be indefinitely excluded from the political nation, while retaining the confidence of the landed and the middle classes, was the aim of virtually all Liberals. The Tories were less sure of their course.

A matter of weeks before his death Lewis published a *Dialogue on the Best Form of Government*. The little book was far from being the intellectual exercise suggested by the unoriginal title. Its academic guise permitted Lewis to enunciate political truths which were not for open discussion by a cabinet minister.[56] The imaginary debate took place between contemporary Englishmen. The participant expounding Lewis's own views held that the monarchy was politically dead, though still important socially. 'It may not be a democratic republic', 'Aristocraticus' was made to say of his country, 'but it is a republic, nevertheless.' Ministerial responsibility implied the powerlessness of the Crown; its prerogatives were empty of meaning.[57] The doctrine of 'Aristocraticus' on British constitutional monarchy was hardly exaggerated compared with the language that Palmerston used privately. 'The sovereign...', he wrote to the Duke of Somerset, 'has of real power little or none...' Queen Victoria's belief that she was not a figurehead seemed pathetic to the prime minister.[58] Yet he advised the Duke as first lord of the Admiralty, to humour the Queen in naval concerns: 'the less the sovereign has in substance, the more tenacious the sovereign is about forms'.[59] The dignity of the Crown was inseparable from respect for the social hierarchy and had to be safeguarded. Ministers sought to protect the Queen and her family from themselves. Her necrophilia embarrassed them but not, they were surprised to discover, the public. Lewis referred to the projected memorial to Prince Albert as 'this puerile monument'; but he recognized that the House of Commons did not share the cabinet's reluctance to provide a substantial grant for its erection.[60] The cabinet's original figure was £16,000 or £18,000; it went to £30,000 and, after the chief whip reported on the mood of the House, to £50,000.[61] More generous financial provision for the Prince of Wales and his bride than Gladstone thought was quite prudent also won immediate acceptance.[62] The Queen's younger children were a problem from the start, and particularly the princes. 'It is puzzling', mused Palmerston, 'to know what to do... to make them respectable and... keep them out of mischief.'[63] Gladstone entertained the notion of sending Alfred, the second son, to Ireland as viceroy, such was the aura of royalty in Lewis's crowned republic, if not among the Irish.[64] What the public minded was the Queen's seclusion in widowhood and her Germanism. *The Times* rebuked her for self-pity; the neglect of her representational duties was politically as well as personally harmful. Her German sympathies caused greater anxiety: fearing a surge of popular anger at the imminent fate of Denmark in 1864, Brand believed it would be directed against the monarch.[65]

The state of another institution raised doubts. The wealth and influence of the House of Lords were declining in relative terms. Granville, leader of the House in the two Palmerston ministries, came to appreciate the need for fresh blood 'in some proportion' to the swelling riches and population of the country. He wanted to sustain the credibility of the aristocracy as an estate that was not exclusive.[66] Palmerston actually embraced the ideal, which could not be said of Granville, despite his acquiescence in the abortive experiment with life peerages in 1856. The leader of the Liberal peers used his authority, that same year, to dissuade the prime minister from giving hereditary peerages to a couple of Northern industrialists, R. H. Greg of Manchester and J. G. Marshall of Leeds. The precedent would have opened the House to provincial fortunes; the City was already represented there.[67] In 1865, although worried by the Lords' decline, Granville remained sure that nothing could be worse than to 'swamp' them

with new creations that set different standards for ennoblement. His sense
of caste got the better of him. Another Whig peer in the cabinet, Stanley
of Alderley, described the House as 'the Palace of the Dead', so little
animation was there in a chamber thinly attended as a rule.[68] The better
known Lord Stanley concluded from a detailed examination that three-
quarters of the peerage lived in obscurity. He astonished himself by his
findings.[69] They were deceptive. Respect for the House of Lords was bound
up with the local standing of its members. Peers who did not rate a mention
in Stanley's list played the part expected of them in their districts.
Gladstone made such criticism of the aristocracy a target of his speeches, as
at Halesowen in the industrial Midlands when he spoke in the course of
celebrations marking the coming of age of his nephew, Lord Lyttelton's
heir, in October 1863. The position of the peerage, derived 'partly from...
direct interest and power...much more from the place it had...in the
hearts of the people', was earned by continuing leadership and responsibility. The 'signal instance' of the Lyttelton family in Worcestershire
illustrated a general truth.[70]

Attendance in the House of Commons, too, was very often thin. Its work
was effectively done by fewer than 200 members drawn, wrote Stanley,
from those presently or formerly in office and from 'liberals of the middle
class'. According to him, only one Tory backbencher without experience of
office made a regular appearance, and that one an octogenarian provincial
banker, not a landowner. The attitude of the landlord class to its wider
responsibilities exercised thoughtful Liberals and Tories. Stanley recorded
conversations on this topic with Wood, Edward Ellice – chief whip under
his brother-in-law Lord Grey and still an MP – and Spencer Walpole.
They all believed there had been a falling off in the readiness of their class
to perform its many unpaid duties. If continued, the trend would not
permit a satisfactory answer to the question, '"What is the use of a class of
rich men and large landowners?"'[71] J. S. Mill, whose *Principles of Political
Economy* commanded general respect, allowed that British landlords could,
on the whole, justify their aggregations of property 'in an economical point
of view'.[72] Their real value to society, however, lay in the uses to which they
put their wealth and leisure. In the wake of attacks on the class made by
Cobden and Bright with a violence reminiscent of the Anti-Corn Law
agitation, *The Times* offered a conventional but unusually well-expressed
defence. 'Today', it said in February 1864 on the eve of a new session,
'there will meet what has often been called a parliament of landowners.
Fortunately, these landowners are very often something else; fortunately to
be a landowner implies a good deal more...land is the beast of burden on
which everything is placed in this country. All local and social obligations,
religion, charity, order, peace, all rest on the land... The greater the
income...the loftier the position of a landowner, the more exigent and

multifarious are the claims...on his money, his influence, and his time.'[73] The eulogy was broadly deserved. The remarkable concentration of landownership – the New Domesday of 1873 revealed that fewer than 7,000 people owned four-fifths of the land of the United Kingdom – would not have been sustainable as industry and the towns steadily overshadowed the countryside but for the landed tradition of gratuitous service.

Unsalaried legislators and magistrates administering the counties who cost the ratepayers nothing enjoyed a better claim to deference than they would otherwise have done. Elections were sometimes dearly won, or lost; other calls imposed heavier burdens. Stanley spent nearly a third of his entire income over twelve years to 1863 on charities and 'public objects': but he, described by Lord Clarendon as 'a sort of political monk', was unrepresentative.[74] It is estimated that on the great estates which comprised a quarter of England's acreage from 4 to 7 per cent of gross income, perhaps, went on charities, excluding significant contributions to Church schools. In many, if not most, cases the expenditure represented a considerably higher percentage of net income. On the middle-sized estates that accounted for 30 per cent of land, the figure was 1 or 2 per cent of the rental before outgoings.[75] While the teachings of religion formed the social ideals of both classes, the ethos of the landed, titled and untitled, was a model for business wealth. At this date the largest fortunes were still based on land[76] and, on a national scale, the munificence of their possessors overshadowed the generosity of even the richest businessmen. Below that level, however, something like parity existed between land and business in the ownership of substantial wealth and provision for charity, education, Church and chapel, but not for long: business profits were rising more than three times as fast as rents.[77] Sir Bernard Burke, the contemporary expert on family and status, opined in 1861 that a baronet should have at least £500 a year and a peer £2,000 to maintain their rank.[78] No one, Ellice told Stanley, ought to sit in the Lords by hereditary right without a qualifying annual income of £3,000 or £5,000 after deduction of other charges. It was barely enough when, as Stanley discovered with amazement, a Lancashire industrialist paid his senior managers £1,500, the salary of an under-secretary of state.[79]

'I am not', wrote Lewis in his *Dialogue*, 'a believer in the infallibility of aristocracy.' He used the term in a wide sense to denote a patrician class, not necessarily landed on the British pattern. He rejected the idea of the House of Lords as an essential part of the 'aristocratico-democratic representative constitution' which Britain enjoyed; it was only the best second chamber yet devised. The influence of aristocracy, so defined, derived from property and the beneficial control exercised by public opinion.[80] The intellectual level of aristocratic government in Britain was little higher, Mill complained, than that of a democracy like the United

States. The element of truth in this characteristic exaggeration was not a source of weakness but the reverse. Without views and prejudices common to rulers and ruled, the system of representation, 'oligarchically constituted', after as before 1832, would not have produced what was, on Mill's admission, 'a popular government'. Britain had in her landed class 'an open aristocracy'.[81] Bright, so resentful of the primacy of land, felt obliged to welcome the investment in it of fortunes made in Manchester, Leeds and Birmingham. It was 'a natural...advantageous, and healthy thing' for the buyer to seek the social position and political influence that went with an estate.[82] The acknowledgement detracted from such force as his pleas for free trade in land contained. The new men of the North and Midlands were not eager to see legal obstacles to the disposal of landed property removed when they could afford to take their place among the gentry and might hope for a baronetcy. The political complexion of the middle class or classes was not fundamentally different from that of the landed. Pollbooks show that the professions voted Tory by a margin of two to one in the constituencies on which the fading hopes of Cobden and Bright for middle-class independence of the landed rested; so did at least a third and as many as two-thirds of businessmen, shopkeepers, artisans, and labourers.[83] Although Derby and Disraeli neglected to foster this urban Toryism as they should have done, it underpinned the Palmerstonian tendency of Liberalism in those seats. There was no adequate base for anti-aristocratic radicalism in the middle and working classes. In the circumstances, Lewis and his colleagues could afford to be fallible, within reason.

Cobden and Bright ascribed the preference of their own kind for being governed by Liberal and Tory landowners to a want of self-respect, as well as of confidence. At the same time they accused Palmerston of pandering to the self-importance of the class.[84] A contradiction still more damaging to the case they made against landed primacy was the use of language which they deplored in the context of industrial society. 'I wish we had no such terms, or...some better terms', said Bright when talking of classes.[85] The property to which he and Cobden addressed themselves recoiled from playing at class war to coerce another kind of property into sharing power more equally. The argument that an extension of the franchise would assist the social integration of the working class, evoked a much more favourable response. It was consistent with Palmerston's recognition, notably in his speeches of 1862–63 at Sheffield and Glasgow, that skilled, literate workmen must be treated as politically mature, although their admission in large numbers to the electorate was not to be hurried: 'the noble lord knows a good deal of the character of the people', Bright allowed.[86] The voteless majority had 'no very great grievance', Sir Francis Crossley, the industrialist MP for the West Riding, told supporters of Parliamentary reform, of whom he was one. It was a public response, carefully weighed, to the Rochdale speeches of Cobden and Bright in November 1863, in which they ascribed the mental and physical deprivation they saw all around them to the restriction of the franchise. The middle classes declined to be frightened into reform. Astonishment as much as anger constituted the reaction.[87]

The Tory proportion of the existing artisan and labour vote was indicative of essential moderation in the working class from top to bottom. Artisan radicals were as always a minority.[88] The remarkable circulation of *Reynolds's Weekly Newspaper*, stridently democratic and republican, notoriously owed more to its sensationalism than to its political ideas.[89] Gladstone knew of nothing 'so conservative' – with a small 'c' – as the further expansion of the London and provincial press that followed the removal of the paper duties within a few years of the abolition of the newspaper stamp. Indulging in politic hyperbole, he saluted 'the press of the people' that was 'nearly perfect' on every issue. It offered 'loyalty to the Throne...confidence in the legislature...profound attachment to the institutions and affectionate love of the country'.[90] It was true to say, more prosaically, that the newspapers' attitude reflected as well as inculcated the broad acceptance of aristocratic government throughout the population. The *Beehive*, which established itself as the voice of London trade unionism, denied any intention of promoting class warfare. So did the Reform League of the metropolitan unionists. 'We seek not to overbalance political power by the substitution of one class influence for another', wrote George Howell, the League's secretary, in an open letter published in the *Beehive*. Manhood suffrage was the means of ensuring that Parliament provided for the needs of labour. It would not change the voting habits of working men. The paper gave prominence to Gladstone's encouraging remarks on the observed disinclination of working-class electors who were £10 householders to act as a body.[91] It did complain, however, of 'colour blindness...to class rights and wrongs', and chose Bright with his dislike of trade unions and factory acts as an example of that disability. As between Liberals and Conservatives, the *Beehive* said, 'we feel...our judgements are with the one, and our likings with the other'. The Liberals' performance did not match their professions of friendship for the working class; they listened to businessmen unfriendly to the unions. The Tories were only 'kind under correction'; they had not yet come to terms with a changed society. What the *Beehive* sought for the working class was a greater realization of the social partnership that figured in Palmerston's speeches. The economic objective was reassuring to property: to see working men, secure in well-paid employment, become 'capitalists in their degree' through savings banks and co-operative societies. For the rest, the paper took pride in the Indian empire under the administration of Lawrence, a popular hero; in the 'citizen soldiery' of the volunteers; and in the birth of 'our little prince', the future Duke of Clarence.[92]

Marx complained of the British workers' 'servile, Christian nature'.[93] To the persistent disappointment of Continental exiles like himself, the sympathy of most working-class activists for revolutionaries abroad did not differ in kind from that of their betters. Garibaldi's visit to London in April 1864, which upset the Court, many Tories and some Liberals, furnished 'a proof of the community of feeling among all classes of the nation'; Palmerston was able to reassure the Queen, pointing to the aristocracy's controlling part in the arrangements.[94] The enthusiasm of Garibaldi's reception was for the ally of Victor Emanuel II in 1859–61 and the implacable enemy of the Pope's spiritual and temporal authority: 'You know what ardent Protestants we are!' wrote Cobden afterwards.[95] Palmerston had wanted the visit to be strictly private. He saw almost at once that this would be impossible; nor could the government dissociate itself from the welcoming publicity.[96] The crowds that greeted the Italian in London were estimated to number half a million. In the capital city where extremists were sure of asylum, Garibaldi met Mazzini, Herzen, Ledru-Rollin and Louis Blanc; there was a disturbing suggestion of that 'European revolutionary conclave' which Palmerston hoped to prevent, fearful of its effect on Britain's relations with the Powers in the midst of the Schleswig–Holstein crisis.[97] The organizers of the reception in London were anxious that the proceedings should not confer respectability on Garibaldi's own political creed, for which there was no room in the new Italy, or in Britain. It was to be a festival of constitutional liberty, as defined by the existing order in those countries. At the public meeting to complete preparations, R. W. Crawford, in the chair, G. J. Goschen, also an MP for the City, and the Reverend Newman Hall, representing Nonconformity, all insisted on that limiting purpose: '...it could not be urged too strongly', said Newman Hall, 'that they were not met to discuss the question of Democracy *versus* Monarchy'.[98]

Granville believed that the participation of the aristocracy, including Derby, Stanley and Malmesbury, had taken 'the democratic sting (as to this country) out of the affair'. Malmesbury supported Derby reluctantly, afraid that 'we have made a mistake and...our party are disgusted'.[99] Disraeli held aloof, equally unconvinced and much more vulnerable to Tory censure. Gladstone was careful to put the responsibility for government's actions in the matter on Palmerston: 'you will lead...and we shall follow suit'.[100] Garibaldi obliged his aristocratic hosts by eulogizing the society over which they ruled. The comparative absence of the apparatus of coercion integral to Continental states – liberal and reactionary – astonished him; from that angle, he understood the strength of a practical freedom divorced from his egalitarian ideals. Before an audience of over 20,000 at the Crystal Palace, he said that he had seen a lot on his visit 'but one great thing – half a million people kept in order by a dozen policemen – plain, simple policemen; and when I speak of English policemen, I take off my hat, for these are no *gendarmes*, no *mouchards*... They cannot live in...free air.' Many more than a dozen police, of course, had been on duty for the procession through the streets of London. Nonetheless, the contrast with the atmosphere and structure of united Italy was remarkable; he gave the few ultra-radicals present no encouragement. His compatriots had still more to learn: 'Let...Englishmen...be a lesson to us. Let us imitate them, and admire their splendid institutions and their... liberty. England is envied by every country.' It was intensely gratifying, not only to his hosts but also to plebeians congratulated on standing 'so proudly at the head of the admiration of the world'.[101]

Yet when the Reform Club entertained Garibaldi to lunch, forty or fifty members let it be known that they objected.[102] A junior minister, Stansfeld, had just resigned after being attacked for his links with Mazzini and Italian republicanism. The threat from that quarter to Napoleon III's person and policy ensured a sharp French reaction to Stansfeld's indiscretions as well as Liberal and Tory condemnation of a ministerial association, however well intentioned, with the extreme Left on the Continent.[103] On Garibaldi's arrival, Palmerston had promised to interrogate him 'as if I was an Old Bailey counsel' about his part in revolutionary designs on European regimes. When the Duke of Sutherland, with whom Garibaldi stayed in London, brought him to see the prime minister, he was advised not to renew his attempt of 1862 on the remaining Papal territory, garrisoned by France, and to leave Austrian-held Venetia alone. Although Garibaldi said at his interview that he did not choose to join 'the party of action' and therefore had little influence over them, he saluted Mazzini as 'friend and teacher' when he met him some days later.[104] By then Gladstone, acting on behalf of the government and seconded by Shaftesbury, had induced him to cut short his visit. The indignation excited in Paris, and other capitals, by the marks of honour that Garibaldi received from Palmerston and his colleagues, as much as by the popular demonstrations, was too great.[105] His sudden departure, on the transparent pretext of health, elicited loud protests from the Working Men's Reception Committee and others. Out of the Committee's protest the Reform League arose: but the retrospect of the past year in the *Beehive*'s first issue of 1865 alluded to the row over the termination of Garibaldi's stay as 'an unfortunate misunderstanding...it will soon be forgotten...if not already'.[106] The Italian's harmlessness in domestic politics was quite evident. '...there is no people in Europe among which Garibaldi's real ideas have made, or are likely to make, less way' wrote Stanley when the visitor was being fêted.[107]

The *Beehive*'s survey of 1864 selected the Wimbledon meeting of the

Volunteers for enthusiastic mention; it had been 'a really glorious gathering of the citizen soldiery'.[108] The Volunteer movement was, the politicians recognized, more important for its civil than for its military results. Militia and yeomanry represented the old England, and the Volunteers the new. The corps that proliferated from 1859 drew heavily on the skilled working class, which did not aspire to the yeomanry and was not attracted to the militia.[109] They were officered very largely by the middle class who thus added another dimension to their urban leadership.[110] The local initiative responsible for raising the units brushed aside doubts whether it was prudent to arm working men.[111] There was no hint of a challenge to landed primacy. The Tory Lord Ranelagh and the Peelite Lord Elcho were prominent in the movement, which had a strong supporter in the radical Whig Earl de Grey, as under-secretary and then secretary of state for war. Noblemen were in demand as commanding officers of units; the Volunteers' eagerness for aristocratic participation excited mild ridicule. John Bright saw the zeal of industrialists in the West Riding and Lancashire to put themselves at the head of battalions and companies as one more sign of their 'inveterate flunkeyism'. Even W. E. Forster, of whose advanced liberalism Bright had hopes, erred in that way, 'which does not say much for his penetration'.[112] There were very few who shared this jaundiced view. De Grey spoke of the advantages, social and political, to the nation of teaching so many men 'the benefits of being under disciplined authority'. The theme was constantly re-echoed. Employers were clear that Volunteers made better workers.[113] Lord Robert Cecil, in his high Tory phase, found it immensely reassuring that the people could be trusted with arms, 'unreservedly'. The Volunteers were a manifestation of the real unity beneath superficial party disagreements, and a pledge for its maintenance.[114]

If Palmerston was deeply pessimistic about the feasibility of improving the condition of the large under-class which he considered to be inherent in an economically advanced society, he regarded upward mobility as indispensable to political health. The Tory *Saturday Review* was acid in reproving him for gross exaggeration of a working-man's chances of rising when he spoke at Lambeth in April 1865. It was wrong that the prime minister 'should palm off false and unreal notions'; wrong, too, that 'his listeners should be so weak as to like them, when all the time they knew them to be false'.[115] In the criticized speech, Palmerston credited the respectable working class with greater intelligence and maturity than the *Saturday Review* suggested. He did not imply that everything lay within the reach of enterprising men such as those he was addressing; far from it. In the nature of things, rich prizes went to a very few: 'You may not become full generals or admirals...chancellors or archbishops...members of the cabinet – but...you will raise yourself in the social system of your country.'

Two complementary 'aristocracies' were 'essential ingredients' of the system; neither was exclusive, in gratifying contrast with the position abroad. That of wealth was open to the ambitious and determined working man; and while entry into that of rank was even harder, it did not form a closed caste. For those who failed to rise, there was the 'conscious satisfaction' afforded by family life, continuing self-education, and a common pride in national 'dignity' and well-being. As at Glasgow in 1863, Palmerston claimed to be in a sense, a fellow worker. What he told the London artisans was cordially received because he recognized in them an extension, downwards, of middle-class attitudes.[116] The inclinations of the upper working class – and not least the trade unions that Palmerston, like Mill, distrusted – were pervasively bourgeois.

It was widely assumed that when aristocratic politicians courted working men in their speeches, they were indulging in humbug. Palmerston's 'air of apparent conviction' puzzled the *Saturday Review*, compared with Gladstone's 'peculiarly unctuous' manner on these occasions. The prime minister believed in the necessity of saying what he did.[117] Gladstone felt less certain of his own judgement, as his private correspondence with Palmerston shows. The condition of future harmony was the steady development of a middle-class outlook among working men. Nothing, perhaps angered Palmerston more than the attempt to radicalize the middle class and with it the country. Writing to Gladstone, Palmerston expressed intense irritation, in the last year of his life, at the inverted snobbery of Cobden's attacks on the aristocracy: 'knowledge of the practical working of our constitution' should have taught him not to ignore the plebeian origins of a string of statesmen, commanders and ecclesiastics; titled families did not enjoy the alleged monopoly of place.[118] Palmerston's objections to admitting the working class indiscriminately to the franchise differed little from Mill's in the *Considerations*. Mill ruled out the admission of illiterates and paupers; that drastically reduced the numbers after enfranchising women who were otherwise qualified. The voting power of the literate and self-supporting should be graded by education and occupation: a single vote for a labourer; two or more votes for electors higher up the social scale, starting with artisans. Finally, the 'privileged' electors should, by some unspecified arrangement enjoy half the total voting power of the electorate. Mill's idiosyncratic definition of democracy rejected the domination of one class, 'even the most numerous'. He was quite as much opposed as Palmerston to the 'class government' that would assuredly be the outcome of 'too low a standard of political intelligence'.[119]

The similarities between Palmerston and Mill are instructive of the national consensus cleverly fostered by the statesman and reflected in the thinker. The socialism which the latter distantly foresaw was going to emerge without confiscation and violence, he imagined,[120] from its adoption as their goal by 'the very *élite* of the country', the enlightened middle class, whose spreading influence would be decisive.[121] The abolition of prerogative and entail, the policy of free trade in land dear to Cobden and Bright, was also Mill's way of assisting economic logic in a slow redistribution of landed property to small working farmers. As for industry, the moral and economic appeal of co-operative ownership was such, to his mind, that it must eventually displace private capital. The era saw the rise of successful industrial co-operatives beside the growth of the historically better-known retail co-operatives.[122] The inspiration of these enterprises, like that of the trade unions, was improvement within the accepted social framework. The thoughtful artisan radicals in the leadership of co-operatives and unions were attracted to Mill's gradualism, so much more realistic than the urgency of Chartism. His patriotism with its grasp of imperial necessities recommended his ideas to the interested working class.[123] Some of them believed as he did that the democracy of the United States was not worthy of imitation. They perceived what Benjamin Moran, the American secretary of legation in London, conceded in his diary: 'it is folly to say people don't starve in the... States, as the facts are otherwise... voting don't get people work and prevent them being cheated'.[124] Mill held, with Palmerston, that it was wrong, and perilous, to treat the franchise 'as a *right* and not a *trust*', and, with him, resisted the ballot. 'The English', wrote Mill to Mazzini, 'are at bottom, in all their feelings, aristocrats... They do not dislike to have many people above them as long as they have some below them.'[125] The working class was stratified, and part of 'a complex society... as tessellated as an old Roman pavement'.[126] If government is usually a matter of continuous improvisation, Palmerston's administrations were no exception. From the time that he first came to power, however, the process of levelling up was extolled in his oratory. It was, he said, an 'aristocratic' trend;[127] an insight shared with Mill and others that eluded many. By annexing the trend politically, and suppressing his doubts, Palmerston allayed the fears and directed the hopes that might else have made social change divisive rather than unifying. The *Daily News*, a Liberal paper often critical of him, concluded that he had 'devoted more time and ability to the work of understanding the people than any democratic politician of his age'.[128]

The general election of 1865

The Liberals came out of Palmerston's last election with a majority doubled since the previous trial of party strength. There was virtually no change in England: the Liberal gains were made in Scotland, Wales, and Ireland for reasons special to those parts. As in his triumph of 1857, a large number of

Tory candidates found it politic to state that if returned they would offer 'no personal or factious opposition' to the prime minister.[129] The struggle was far quieter than it had been eight years before, though a few more seats were contested. Palmerston's victory was anticipated; it seemed fore-ordained by the course of events following the Tory rout on Stansfeld's motion in June 1862. The one chance subsequently of overturning the government, presented by its inability to save the duchies for Denmark, only strengthened Palmerston: the narrow margin of his Parliamentary survival was deceptive; he noted how the crowds gathered outside cheered him each day when he arrived at Westminster for the long drawn out debate.[130] He was master of the issues in the subdued election campaign of 1865. They were foreign policy, religion and Parliamentary reform, in that order. The theme of class collaboration was sounded. Palmerston's health confined him to the minimum of electioneering, but it was enough. He went forward as '"the safe man *par excellence*"', at home and abroad.[131] Party, for him as for Gladstone, was not an end in itself. Without party spirit, however, politics would become 'vitiated and corrupt'. The clash of parties was essential to attain political truth and to work free institutions. These conventional observations of his were designed to counter suggestions that he was above party; if it had taken hold, the idea would have weakened him and the Liberals.[132]

Disraeli was not in the habit of paying compliments to his opponents. He did so, obliquely, when he said in September 1862 that this country had 'solved the most difficult problem of politics, and...combined not only freedom and order, but progress with tradition'.[133] The Tories had not contributed to the solution by overthrowing Peel and, for a little while, Palmerston. Disraeli's enemies behind him were delighted with the calm that descended upon the House of Commons for the year and a half after the overwhelming defeat of his bid to exploit Stansfeld's initiative. Those Tories mistook the nature of Palmerston's Liberalism. Cecil told his constituents that it would be impossible for him, 'even if he were to try', to deliver a political speech when almost the whole of his party had voted with ministers in that division. Henceforth, he remarked with pleasure, 'party politics are, as it were, the occupation of our leisure time'. Northcote was more discerning. The opposition had to 'do violence to their feelings' in finding fault with the government, he confessed on the same occasion, but the party conflict was 'harmless, or even beneficial', provided it did not involve 'collisions between class and class'.[134] Cecil's confidence in the government did not last. His *Quarterly Review* article on the imminent election in 1865 alleged it was 'painfully apparent' that Palmerston no longer had any effective control over members of his cabinet: the public ought not to be led to suppose, as they were being encouraged to do, that they would be voting for him. Cecil's genuine alarm on this score was not shared by Derby, who did not doubt that Palmerston remained in charge.[135] Gladstone gave conservatives in both parties cause for anxiety: but Palmerston was 'well satisfied' with his colleague's performance during the election.[136]

The prime minister's address to the voters of Tiverton took credit for peace, economic progress, sound finances, preparedness for war, Canadian loyalty and growing Indian prosperity. On the hustings he drew attention to the contrast between Britain's 'sufficient defence' and the armies of Continental Powers, the size of which indicated a propensity for aggression.[137] Mill, whose candidacy for Westminster received full coverage in the press as a radical portent, outdid Palmerston in his distrust of foreigners. He did not think Britain should lower her guard 'in the presence of the great military despotisms of Europe, which regard our freedom through its influence on the minds of their own subjects, as the greater danger...to themselves'. Tory gibes at double standards in international relations that allowed the government to purchase glory cheaply by making war on non-European peoples, failed to register.[138] For one thing, even Cobden said after the Parliamentary challenge to ministers over Denmark in 1864 that they should not have been made the target of censure when the Tories were really more to blame, because more strongly pro-Danish, for national delusions about Britain's ability to help the small kingdom.[139] The tribute of the *Nonconformist*, normally unfriendly to Palmerston, showed how he had educated less ungenerous opponents than Cobden or partisan Tories. It praised the skill and honesty he had displayed as prime minister in avoiding war, seeing in him a 'political expert' whose equal it would be hard to find in modern European history.[140] He taught the political nation to comprehend the limitations of British policy if it was to be successful and in doing so to appreciate his achievement in quite a different way from their admiration of 1857. The double standard of which some complained seemed sensible and right to the great majority. They now accepted, from Palmerston, that the political costs of a European or an American war were prohibitive, and that it was not for their country to seek one. With Palmerston, they nevertheless believed she should not adopt a low profile unbecoming to her as the exemplar of liberty. On the last point there was little disposition to listen to Cobden, who claimed that in the interests of peace he and Bright had refrained from 'publicly supporting this nationality or that'. The broad agreement on foreign and imperial questions was a solid electoral advantage for the Liberals which Gladstone's opening speech of the campaign exploited; he spoke of Palmerston's international stature: 'almost wherever the name of England is known, his name is known along with it'.[141]

Malmesbury noted with surprise that the most famous of High Churchmen, E. B. Pusey, had declared for Palmerston and Gladstone in the coming election.[142] The significance of this was not lost on the diarist. The Tories were endeavouring to give priority to the Church's fears and discontents, where they believed the Liberals to be more vulnerable than on other issues. Pusey was not politically active like Wilberforce but High Churchmen revered in him the spiritual eminence of the Catholic revival within Anglicanism since Newman's conversion to Rome. 'Puseyite' was a pejorative term, and Palmerston used it as such in private. Yet his distribution of ecclesiastical patronage after 1859 led Pusey to write in the columns of the *Churchman*: 'Lord Palmerston has, in some important respects, deserved the gratitude of the Church. His own ecclesiastical appointments have at least been religious...we owe him more on this ground than may generally be suspected.'[143] Pusey and Shaftesbury had made common cause against the spread of a rationalistic outlook in the Church. Evangelical bishops appeared to be a lesser evil, in a subtly changing climate of faith, than Broad Church prelates.[144] The Tories were not better able to unite the Church. Derby was a rather old-fashioned Churchman who cared as little for the heirs of the Oxford movement as he did for the Evangelicals. Disraeli's agnosticism was too widely known or guessed, and his opportunism blatant. On the opposing side, Gladstone's presence in the Liberal party was a powerful, but by no means an irresistible, attraction to High Churchmen. To other Churchmen it was an actual disincentive to vote Liberal. Consequently, Pusey appealed to the clerical electors of Oxford University, where Gladstone was facing defeat after eighteen years, not to lend themselves to an attempt to disturb Palmerston's government by rejecting their unpopular member. Cecil in the *Quarterly Review* asserted unconvincingly that Pusey's arguments were not representative.[145]

The Economist thought the position of the Church was 'the great question of the next age': neither the Liberals nor the Tories had an election cry that made much impression.[146] If so, it was not for want of trying on Disraeli's part. His address conjured up a vision of 'the corruption of nations and the fall of empires' enacted in Britain, should the country fail to uphold religion, identified with the privileges of the Establishment. Translated, this urged continued resistance to church rates and burials bills. The characteristic hyperbole invited demolition. His front bench colleague Stanley obliged 'I have never raised the cry of the Church in danger', he said at King's Lynn, 'nor would I ever support it...I do not believe that the Establishment,...in England, is in any danger whatsoever.'[147] However, there was an insidious threat, not to institutional religion, established or unestablished, but to the integrity of belief. Cecil in the *Quarterly Review* was less afraid of militant Nonconformity than of 'the latitudinarian assailants of the Church'. They were Churchmen, who wanted an Establishment 'purged of dogma' but still influential for social purposes: 'devoting all its energies', wrote Cecil with journalistic licence, 'to the foundation of mechanics' institutes...'.[148] Stanley was just such a man, although Cecil naturally selected his examples from the Liberals. For the uncompromising, Palmerston's preference for the Evangelicals in his ecclesiastical promotions, as a matter of political judgement, did not excuse his sympathy with the theological views against which High and Low Church combined. The *Churchman*, which printed Pusey's letter, disagreed with him: it could not easily recall a government that had treated the Church worse; it denounced Gladstone for his changed politics, and it insisted that voting Tory was the test of religious allegiance, except where the candidate was thoroughly Erastian. The enemy was Erastianism.[149] Disraeli's flirtation with this kind of High Churchmanship only harmed his party. The South-West Lancashire Tories gave Gladstone the seat in 1865 immediately after rejection by the clericalism of Oxford freed him from an increasingly uncomfortable association.[150]

'In the recent contests', wrote Gladstone, 'the strength and determination of party laid me prostrate, but the kindness and liberality dwelling in the bosom of the same party raised me up again.'[151] Another High Church journal, the *Guardian*, approved of Gladstone's powerful contribution to the national campaign in which he based the claim of the government to re-election on their success in uniting social classes.[152] Referring to the cross-voting in South-West Lancashire, the Honourable Algernon Egerton, one of his fellow-members for the constituency, interpreted that support as confidence in Gladstone's will to resist a 'democratic invasion and great constitutional changes', including any threat to the continuance of the Establishment.[153] When Gladstone discussed Parliamentary reform in his speeches during the election, it was explicitly with a view to preserving 'the political and social equilibrium' achieved under Palmerston. He defined Liberalism as trust in the people, Toryism as 'mistrust...only relieved by fear'.[154] These definitions acquired meaning and force from insistence that the Liberals were mainly responsible for 'the progress and...union of class to class' which the Palmerston years had seen. As Palmerston had done at Sheffield and Glasgow, Gladstone addressed the artisans specifically and appealed to their sense of occupying a recognized place in the hierarchy of classes; there were 'many...below them as well as many...above them'. Levelling, he said to loud cheers, was 'a mistaken and abominable doctrine'. The painstakingly built and ordered society of which they were part would meet with 'ruin' if one class became dominant.[155] But the position of the middle classes was crucial and must not be jeopardized. Such unexceptionable views reassured those, and they were numerous, who remembered his unwisely worded remarks on Baines's bill the year before. All Gladstone wanted was 'some sensible... liberal...safe extension of the franchise'. He was concerned to keep in step with the prime minister and to warn off Disraeli. The Tory, he believed, favoured giving the vote 'rather freely' to the unskilled.[156]

Bright told his constituents at Birmingham that for the last two or three years he had avoided attacking Palmerston, though he could not bring himself to praise the object of his detestation. He warmly denied, speaking at Rochdale, that there was no difference between Whigs and Tories, whatever he had said in the past. The great changes of the recent decades were the work of Whig governments. They had 'saved the country from anarchy and its people from all the dreadful consequences which attend political convulsion'. The mass of the people, too often neglected by governments, owed to the Whigs higher wages, increased employment, improved literacy and the provision of cheap newspapers: 'they felt themselves...slowly, but...steadily and certainly, rising to a better state'. In that popular feeling lay national salvation. The applause that interrupted him was significant.[157] It was to this Rochdale audience that Cobden made the speech in November 1863 which Bright had echoed and now, in effect, refuted point by point. Complaining still of Palmerston's disinclination to further Parliamentary reform, Bright could not pretend that the prime minister had not made a major contribution to the Whig achievement. The resistance to 'broad democratic doctrines' was stronger than ever. Hardly anybody in the manufacturing districts, or elsewhere, was ready for working-class predominance in the electorate.[158] Parliamentary reform was not a topic that held the voters' attention. It was simply taken for granted that an instalment of change in the structure of representation would not be long delayed. Palmerston had done nothing to discourage the idea. Even Clarendon wrote to Henry Reeve of the *Edinburgh Review* that June urging him to depict the Whig attitude to reform as 'liberal and progressive'. It was a natural result of Palmerston's opening of 'the citadel of power' to moderate radicalism on the formation of his second government. Milner Gibson was only the most prominent of those who had never allowed the subject of reform to drop.[159]

Mill, standing for Westminster, offered a definition of his 'advanced' politics that placed him well within the ambit of Palmerstonian Liberalism. Pragmatism was all: 'I...accept a reasonable compromise which would give me even a little of that which I hope in time to obtain.' Trust in the people should be 'limited only by prudence', he said, quoting Gladstone. The first article of Mill's creed was the freedom, equality *and* responsibility of the individual, the second, that social progress – which should be understood, by 'diligent study' as organic, growing out of history, and not breaking with it – was not to be hurried. This was the teaching of his essay *On Liberty* and of the *Considerations*; he stuck to the detail of the latter when he talked about the franchise. One class must not be able to outvote the others. Nor should men, or women, become electors without passing a test in reading, writing and simple arithmetic. As for the ballot, they did not need it; if any one did, it was the shopkeepers whom they could coerce by withholding their custom.[160] However much Mill impressed the voters of Westminster, they returned a Grosvenor with him, by a larger majority. Family and party were a winning combination in the metropolis as in both the newly created divisions of the industrial West Riding. *The Saturday Review* saw no reason for Tories to be afraid of a Liberal party 'heavily ballasted by money, or land'. This was in reply to the misgivings that Disraeli expressed; he made use of Bright as a 'bogey', notwithstanding the latter's freshly discovered esteem for the Whigs.[161] It was even more improbable when Robert Cecil discerned in the coming struggle for Parliamentary reform 'the great controversy of modern society, the...issue upon which the hopes of...civilization depend'.[162]

Gladstone was 'a little surprised' by the outcome of the elections; he had not expected them to be so favourable to the government. The 'Conservative reaction' much discussed by political commentators in the last few years failed to materialize in a party sense and, arguably, any other sense.[163] Palmerstonianism was not reactionary but evolutionary in its social purpose. The charges of inertia and opportunism levelled at Palmerston, usually by the same people, lacked substance, He did not make high intellectual claims for his policy of adjustment to irreversible trends, domestic and external. It might be said that he left them to Gladstone whose political education he completed. Except on Ireland, Gladstone's policies as the Liberal leader were essentially Palmerstonian in conception, and in execution. He, too, was a lifelong believer in the natural superiority of aristocratic government, 'whatever control a good system may impose by popular suffrage'. Experience of Palmerston in opposition and in cabinet taught him what he had previously been unwilling to concede, that the courtship of public opinion was not subversive of Parliament but a condition of its survival as the preserve of 'the leisured class'.[164] Caution marked his approach to Parliamentary reform in 1866–67 and subsequently; it was Derby and Disraeli who took advantage of the more secure climate inherited from Palmerston to venture on household suffrage.[165] Though Gladstone handled the Lords roughly at times, he retained his reverence for their order. Nearly twenty years elapsed before he resolved to ennoble businessmen, and he did not revive the proposal to create life peerages which he had deemed unconstitutional. He had the Peelites' preference for undiluted aristocracy. In the extremely important area of ecclesiastical reform, his break with the past in disestablishing the Irish Church was the most radical thing he did. For the rest, he maintained continuity with the practical, Whiggish view that the Church in England should be divested only of those rights that made more trouble than they were worth. His High Church sympathies and appointments, however, cooled relations between the Establishment and Dissent, never better than under Palmerston. As a peace minister, his practice followed Palmerston's closely. His ministries asserted Britain's Great Power status in Europe and the world, while avoiding a major conflict. Naval and military expenditure did not fall to levels that would have satisfied fanatics for economy and non-intervention. The emotions and interests of Empire he described as 'part of our patrimony'.[166] Radicals who anticipated that Gladstone's liberalism would be quite different from Palmerston's were disappointed.[167]

'His party was his period.' This comment is taken from one of the editorials that reflected on Palmerston's premiership after his death. The *Daily Telegraph* did not think it would be useful yet to decide whether he was really a Tory, or a Liberal: 'We must do that...when the time comes that we can thoroughly comprehend how, being what he was, he remained what he was.' It was generally argued by the leader-writers and obituarists that the Liberals owed more to him than he did to the party. To say that he had imposed 'a compulsory truce' on the parties was patently untrue.[168] No mistake was commoner, observed *The Times*, than to suppose that 'the whole secret of his power' resided in a combination of personal address and political tact. He was a creative politician whose ready improvisations derived from a well thought out strategy: to identify and influence public opinion was his basic preoccupation.[169] *The Times* contrasted him with the other great figure of British politics in the last two generations: 'Sir Robert Peel gave up his principles; Lord Palmerston merely relinquished his party.'[170] When Palmerston left the Tories to join Lord Grey's cabinet in 1830, he retained his Canningite outlook and conviction that public opinion was ultimately supreme in the working of the British constitution, even then.[171] The Canningite influence on Gladstone was not so strong.[172] If Palmerston supported the Reform Act from necessity, he adapted to its consequences as they unfolded. He personified the balanced liberalism that reconciled progress and tradition in a class society to the envy of Europe.

Part III
Abroad

10

The revision of Britain's Great Power diplomacy

The conditions of foreign policy

Even before the serious British diplomatic failure to maintain the connection between the Danish monarchy and the duchies of Schleswig and Holstein, J. T. Delane, the editor of *The Times*, told a senior member of the cabinet: 'I think this country has passed through the warlike phase of its character... and could never again support a great war.' 'You must', he advised Wood, 'keep us out of war as we shall soon lose that great fictitious reputation on which all our power is based. We might manage one in India, but in Europe or America we should soon see our real weakness exposed.'[1] Four years previously, during the crisis of the Risorgimento, Napoleon III's ambassador in London, Persigny, recommended his master to allow Britain a say, which she would not otherwise have, in determining the future of the Italian peninsula. In contrast with Delane, Persigny believed in the latent power and will of Britain to make war. He assured the Emperor that while he would be as glad as any other good Frenchman if 'Waterloo, Poitiers, Crécy...Azincourt' were to be avenged, they must not underestimate Britain's economic strength and her possession of the resources – iron, coal, shipyards, a large seafaring population and the taxable wealth necessary to increase her existing naval superiority quickly. Nor should they blind themselves to the patriotic energy and unity of purpose in her industrial classes, ten times as numerous as France's. Moreover, wrote Persigny with privileged frankness, the British, on the defensive, would have the moral and political advantage of opposing 'le drapeau de la liberté à celui du despotisme'. It was undeniable that the absolutism of Russia, Austria and Prussia resented Britain and would rejoice in her humiliation whenever it came, as it did with the crushing of her protégé Denmark. She did not, however, threaten their security as her neighbour did, 'la France victorieuse, c'est l'indépendance de toute l'Europe qui est menacée'.[2] Persigny's arguments reinforced Napoleon's inclination and judgment.

Jeopardized, also, by an Anglo-French struggle would be the uncertain stability of the Bonaparte dynasty, whose internal enemies Persigny enumerated. Britain and France should each expect to fight alone: but the latter stood to risk more. It remained that from the time of the Indian Mutiny Britain was in no position to engage in Continental warfare for the rest of this period and long afterwards, with or without a major land power as her ally on the classical pattern of British intervention in the past. Before the upheaval in India, she had 40,000 troops stationed there, compared with the force of some 70,000 deemed necessary in the 1860s to overcome the peoples of the sub-continent. Deducting the garrisons wanted for Ireland, the colonies of settlement, the imperial strong-points in the Mediterranean, elsewhere round the world, and an absolute minimum at home, the Army could not find an expeditionary corps, of a size deserving the name, for European service. A much bigger standing army was ruled out by the cost of the fleet, on which it was dangerous to economize, and by the domestic political requirement for low taxation.

In these circumstances, Palmerston insisted that Britain should practise an assertive diplomacy while reflecting that for good reasons it would not lead to war with her main rivals. 'I do not think', he wrote to his first foreign secretary, Clarendon, on New Year's Day 1858, 'it is a dignified course for a country like this to depend on the concurrence of other and jealous powers, whether we shall or shall not complain of what we consider an infraction of our rights, ... I do not think that such a doctrine would be acceptable to the House of Commons.'[3] To complain was safe when, as he commented subsequently to the same correspondent, 'in spite of conflicting interests which might place England at variance ... with France and the United States, the ties of commercial interest are too strong to be broken'.[4] Malmesbury at the Foreign Office in May 1859 dreaded the loss of access to North Sea and Baltic ports in the event of a general war between France, aided by Russia, and members of the German Confederation coming to Austria's help: 'the blockade ... must eventually drag us into ... war, as our trade would be ruined, and this is the only question besides the Turkish one that would do so'.[5] The fate of the Ottoman empire likewise involved both economic and strategic considerations. Following the Crimean war, Britain supported the Sultan with her money and her fleet, resisting Napoleon's suggestion that the Turkish dominions were ripe for partition. In this area, Malmesbury pursued the same policy as Palmerston, but in a markedly more conciliatory fashion towards France, when Napoleon joined Russia after the war in encouraging the Porte's Christian subjects in Balkan tributary states to defy their Moslem overlord. Malmesbury shrank from the certain horrors of racial and confessional strife,[6] and Palmerston took a more narrowly British view of the need to defend Ottoman territory and jurisdiction.

The compassion he felt for the victims of negro slavery was not matched by his solicitude for those of admitted Turkish misrule. Persigny, in common with other anglophils, saw in Britain the standard-bearer of freedom. Palmerston's liberalism abroad, however, was selective – on principle. Prince Albert remarked in 1861: 'The Englishman does not believe in Germany nationality, for his eye is met by extravagances on the part of professors and students...'[7] What Palmerston looked for in Continental liberalism was leadership broadly comparable to that of his own class in Britain. He found it in Italy, but not the Balkans or Germany. This was convenient for British policy. Yet Prince Albert was not justified, as a result, in accusing his adopted country and the Palmerston ministry of political cynicism. Answering Disraeli, who thought Italian Whiggery a delusion, Palmerston said: 'there is a great Whig – a great constitutional party in that country... [which] has... made head... against Republican and Mazzinian... subversion and convulsion... Though no Brooks's [Club] exists there, I should be very glad to see one established...' Such was his ideal of 'rational and moderate freedom... the only solid foundation of happiness'.[8] An English Catholic champion of the Pope's temporal power, George Bowyer, MP, sought to impress on Bishop Grant of Southwark the aristocratic involvement in the Italian national movement. 'That', he told the Bishop with reference to British opinion, 'is a point difficult to be *met*.'[9] Russell claimed Cavour and Gino Capponi in Italy, Thiers and Guizot in France, the Prince Consort's brother, Duke Ernest II of Saxe-Coburg-Gotha in Germany as Whigs: 'They exist all over Europe.'[10] It was they who enjoyed the active sympathy of Palmerstonian Liberalism, where they were strong enough.

They were not strong enough, however, to offset considerations of power. Palmerston was no crusader for constitutionalism abroad, trusting to time and example to diffuse the influence of British institutions, helped by quietly confident advice, usually in private conversation with foreign envoys and distinguished visitors, as when he reminded another French ambassador that 'the word constitution all over Europe means a Parliament'.[11] He was justifiably apprehensive lest the British traditions of freedom should be so abused as to discredit her true political self: 'We are... deemed the deliberate... protectors of revolutionists and assassins, pretending to shield ourselves under constitutional difficulties, but in truth actuated by a base desire to reduce other countries to confusion and anarchy under a notion that our prosperity and relative power would thereby be increased.' Nor was it only the 'ignorant and vulgar' as he hoped, who viewed him and his country in this light.[12] To an intelligent, well-informed reactionary like Prince Alexander of Hesse, brother-in-law of his namesake the Tsar and a general in the Austrian service, Palmerston, encountered at Windsor in 1863, was the 'notorious prime minister... the cunning old rascal' with 'the most inconceivable ideas' for an autonomous and parliamentary Russian Poland. Alexander of Hesse also visited the French Court, where: 'I said much the same thing to the Emperor Napoleon as...to Palmerston and Russell,...making the most of their mutual suspicion...' He conveyed the impression that Palmerston would be glad to see France fighting Russia and the German Confederation over Poland. Napoleon replied similarly that 'these English' had first held out to him the prospect of advancing France's Eastern frontier to the Rhine if he went to war for the Poles against Russia and Germany, but had then remonstrated at the peril of being themselves drawn into hostilities by the manner of his intervention with the Tsar in response to purely French pressures. Britain's Polish policy certainly lent itself to the interpretation that Palmerston wanted 'the privilege of deciding on his own actions according to the issue of...war'.[13]

The Continental Great Powers were weaker than they seemed from a comparison of Britain's widely scattered regulars with their conscript armies. Their rulers' sense of insecurity before the future exceeded anything felt by such confirmed pessimists as Clarendon in British politics. Alexander II wrote to his trusted Hessian relative: 'Uncertainty, friction and doubt paralyse everything. These are the principal weapons of the party which seeks the dissolution of Europe.' Conscious of 'living at a time when government is very difficult, revolutionary principles are gaining ground, and finding more and more following among the masses', this autocrat was as anxious to avoid a war that would feed the internal dangers to his empire as he was determined not to relax his grasp upon Poland.[14] Francis Joseph of Austria agreed with the Tsar; he, too, located 'the chief breeding-ground' of the 'revolutionary party' in 'so pernicious an instability...in the relations between the Powers'.[15] Vitzthum von Eckstädt, the long-serving Saxon minister in London, remarked that 'in the England of the present day the monarchical principle has become a matter of form. Her people are standing wholly on revolutionary soil.'[16] He was right from his point of view when a member of the cabinet, Cornewall Lewis, could publish a pamphlet arguing that the British monarchy was in reality impotent and should be seen 'as properly belonging to the class of republics'.[17] Lewis's distinction between democracy and what he designated 'the aristocratico-democratic representative constitution'[18] of Britain appeared insubstantial to someone like Vitzthum, who considered Prince Albert too liberal. This German diplomat was worried by the activities of exiled German revolutionaries in Britain: 'under the leadership of the well-known Marx...working openly for war...'. But Derby, for one, is believed never to have heard of Marx, which illustrates the remoteness of this country, where Bright frightened men, from the political experience of her neighbours on the Continent. Nevertheless, Marx and his associates correctly assessed another factor: 'England will only bark, not bite...'[19]

The London capital market was a force to reckon with in diplomacy. No foreign government stood much chance of raising money in Britain if investors looked on it as unfriendly to her. Two of the four Continental Powers, Austria and Russia, had open recourse to British finance. Reacting to the menace of a general war over Napoleon's thrust into Italy in 1859, Tsar Alexander's consort found comfort in some indications from the City: 'I hope it is a good omen for peace that negotiations are going on with English bankers for a railway...in which a large mount of capital...has already been sunk. God grant that it may be realized. Rothschild...also... is anxious for peace...he has subscribed 50 millions [roubles] to our loan.'[20] Palmerston told the Russian ambassador that if another country's aim was 'to secure a good understanding with England, they ought to liberalize their commercial system...'.[21] The export of capital did not necessarily help industrial profits and employment at home, while assisting the post-war recovery and progress of Russia. Palmerston, moreover, distrusted the independence and volatility of financial markets. 'Of course', he observed sardonically on the approach of war in 1859, 'it is perhaps on the whole better that Italy from the Alps to the Straits of Messina should continue to groan under diversified oppression rather than that 3 per cents and *Credit Mobilier* and railroad shares should fall...'[22] The case of Britain and France brought out the efficacy of trade as a way of lowering tensions fraught with the gravest peril to both states. The inherent precariousness of Napoleon's plebiscitary and militaristic empire once led Palmerston to say: 'As to what is to take place in France two years hence none but the gipsies at Epsom Downs tomorrow [Derby Day] can pretend to foretell.'[23] It was equally true, and Palmerston never lost sight of the fact, that 'if we choose our allies according to the mischief they might do us...and according to the advantage we should therefore desire from having them as friends instead of foes, Austria would do us no possible harm, France would injure us seriously'.[24] On his principles of foreign policy, he could not but welcome, if with less than enthusiasm, the Emperor's resolve to conclude the Anglo-French commercial treaty of 1860. Present friendship, like old enmity, had relatively little to do with sentiment. 'Governments and nations', Palmerston laid it down in November 1859, 'are less influenced by resentment for former antagonism or by gratitude for former services than by considerations of present or prospective interest'.[25]

The Anglo-French alliance was central to the policies of Palmerston and Napoleon. The Englishman always believed that the logic of Bonapartism made his country a likely target for French aggression one day. At the same time he did everything he could to placate France without being submissive. His first rule, hard to observe consistently, was 'to accept as *argent comptant* all the friendly assurances...and to betray no suspicion of her intentions against us in any way but in active and efficient preparation of defensive means'.[26] Secondly, he recognized in France 'the best ally for England'. As

Palmerston's admirer and former cabinet colleague, the historian Macaulay, explained to an American, in the French empire 'Liberty has gone, but civilization has been saved': Napoleon was the salutary outcome of the conflict with revolutionary democracy in 1848.[27] The Legitimist alternative did not appeal to Palmerston, especially because of the 'ultra-Catholic opinions' of its supporters.[28] Not only were Catholic Austria and Orthodox Russia inferior in civilization, as Macaulay and his public understood it, to France, but, wrote Palmerston: 'I cannot see the use of representing the French emperor as a deep deceiver...an inveterate enemy...he professes the fixed desire of being our faithful ally.'[29] He gave measured public expression, therefore, to his concern about French ambitions, and asked the imperial government to put the best construction on that declared anxiety: 'distrust has not been accompanied by the slightest...hostility...and is purely and entirely a feeling of a defensive character'; for Britain to plan an European coalition isolating France would be 'insane'. 'What possible hopes would anyone have of success?' he continued, assuring Napoleon and his foreign minister of the British cabinet's 'great wish to maintain the closest relations of friendship...with France'.[30] Austria was too weak and unreliable, Prussia not strong enough, besides being exposed on the Rhine, and Russia's co-operation too improbable for any or all these Powers to be a substitute for the French alliance.

Like Napoleon, Palmerston acted to give these professions of friendship binding force, wherever practicable, 'without sacrificing interests or honour'.[31] The idea of an Anglo-French commercial agreement with nicely calculated mutual tariff reductions did not commend itself to him; he preferred a simpler move towards lifting restrictions on trade. The French suggestion of such an agreement as was concluded four years later attracted Clarendon in 1856.[32] The cabinet was discouraging, and Lewis met another approach next year by flatly rejecting the possibility of lower British duties on wine; the effect on the volume and structure of taxation seemed unacceptable.[33] By 1859–60 Palmerston hoped, with Russell and Gladstone, that 'They could rely on their influence *with*...and *over*...L[ouis] N[apoleon]'.[34] Setting aside his doubts on the subject, therefore, he told the British ambassador in Paris to assure the Emperor that 'I will attend to his wishes...about the commercial treaty'; although he wondered how he was going to explain his actions in the matter to Parliament and public opinion.[35] In the event, he was able to return a confident answer to Malmesbury's complaint, through Clarendon, that: 'The Government... have got the H[ouse] of C[ommons] and the country in a very unfair and false position with France.' 'It remains to be seen which party has formed the best judgement of the feelings...of the country...' Palmerston replied, 'I would back the convention...against the anti-conventionists.'[36] The Tories, and many troubled Liberals, acquiesced in the treaty and the consequential provisions in Gladstone's budget of next session. There was no gainsaying the reluctant advice that Malmesbury had from Clarendon, who considered the terms agreed to be one-sided and fiscally undesirable, but thought it imperative to avoid offending the Emperor.[37] Palmerston had misgivings about the strategic imbalance between commodities affected. The guaranteed duty free supply of coal to France struck him as 'under the garb of reciprocity...obviously a concession made by England alone';[38] but he did not persist in the objection.

It is all very well for a modern English historian to write scathingly of Napoleon as the chief of 'gangster followers' and morally distinguished from them only by his superior resolution. The Emperor's habitual mendacity in the transaction of diplomacy created acute problems for the European state system, and not least for France.[39] Yet Mr A. J. P. Taylor's 'demagogue–dictator' aspired to the gradual introduction of a liberalized monarchy, bearing a strong resemblance to Britain's, and initiated the process as early as 1860, without, apparently, taking any of the ministry into his confidence, apart from his kinsman Walewski. The British ambassador described the ministerial reception of the changes: 'The general exclamation from everybody except Walewski was that "it was a Parliamentary Government which he was instituting, and that if that was intended it would be better to say so candidly".'[40] Napoleon's liberal aspirations help in understanding why he attached such significance to British reactions. The latter were influenced by his acceptance of an unitary and liberal Italian state as well as of a territorially much diminished Papacy, by the satisfactory operation of the Anglo-French commercial treaty, and by France's helpful attitude in the *Trent* affair. In that context, the reforms of 1860 enhanced the Emperor's stature with Liberal politicians and the public in Britain, if not with Palmerston and most members of the cabinet. The behaviour of those present at a dinner given by a hundred MPs to Rouher, the French minister of commerce, surprised and disconcerted Lewis in July 1862: 'The health of Louis Napoleon was received with repeated cheering – as if he had been the successful candidate after a contested election. This was remarkable – considering that the company consisted of the party most active in turning out Lord Palmerston's government on the Conspiracy Bill.'[41]

That bill had been Palmerston's undoing in 1858. The House of Commons narrowly overthrew his ministry when it was evident that public opinion had come out against the measure. Palmerston appreciated the depth and conceded the justice of France's response to the nearly successful plot to kill Napoleon and his empress, the latest and worst act of political refugees enjoying the security of Britain while they prepared to strike: 'These feelings are perfectly natural and would have been ours in as great a degree if attempts and outrages of the same kind had been repeatedly

committed in London by criminals issuing from Paris.' 'A greater evil' was
the effect on France's historic anglophobia; she might indulge it to the
extent of declaring war 'with a plausible and avowable cause which all
Europe will admit to be just'. The insularity of colleagues heavily defeated
his proposals to cabinet for legislation enabling the home secretary to
deport foreigners suspected of designs on 'the internal tranquillity of any
friendly power or...life of any...sovereign'. Parliamentary scrutiny of
deportations was to mean a committee to hear government's reasons in
secrecy and confirm or reject their validity.[42] Lord Chancellor Cranworth,
for one, argued complacently that the activities of refugees had nothing to
do with the matter: 'the real ill will in France, so far as it exists, is...
founded on...deep seated jealousy of our power and superiority'. Argyll,
for another, referred dismissively to the 'natural but illogical indignation...
now pressing upon us'.[43] The cabinet, however, were correct in assuming
that the plan could not be carried through Parliament. The change in the
law of conspiracy adopted instead was so limited as to persuade its
opponents that ministers did not take the danger from France seriously
enough to warrant such an unpalatable gesture.[44]

On taking office the Tories were caught between two fires. In order to
survive as a government, they dropped the Conspiracy to Murder Bill,
while knowing that 'if unfortunately any more attempts are made on the
Emperor's life by refugees from England, war will inevitably result'.[45] The
Derby ministry was driven, for some time, to outright appeasement of
France. It was open to Palmerston, without fear of being accused of
pusillanimity, to restate his views on the nature of Anglo-French relations.
The Queen and her husband, attended by Malmesbury, the first lord of the
Admiralty and the Duke of Cambridge, commander-in-chief, were invited
in August 1858 to see one of the regime's additions to French naval and
military capability: the modernization of Cherbourg to accommodate an
army and a fleet with Britain as the obvious target. Palmerston put the
question of the moment to Algernon Borthwick of the *Morning Post*, 'what
is the moral for us?' and supplied a long, considered answer quite free from
irrational belligerence. He thought that Napoleon contemplated, not war,
but the liberty to use 'high language' and dictate policy to Britain if she
declined into 'palpable inferiority'. Palmerston felt there was no reason for
panic: his government had provided for a naval reserve, and the militia
'well organized and maintained' stood behind the army. He professed to be
more worried by whom and what might follow Napoleon's demise. He was
for defence 'costing as little as possible consistently with its efficiency when
not wanted'. This assessment of the situation ought to be 'soberly placed
before the reflecting part of the nation', who, appreciating his middle
course, would ignore 'the foolish counsels of the Peace Party and
economists', and refuse 'to be drawn by...alarmists into needless expense',

but would sanction further expenditure on defence that gave value for money in the much improved fortification of naval bases, as displayed at Cherbourg, and in the organization of reserves.[46]

Written to indicate the way in which the relationship between Britain and France should be handled in the press, this letter appeared rather complacent. When Palmerston saw the Emperor later in the month, Napoleon encouraged him to be complacent, saying quite disingenuously that 'the French would build *no more large ships*'. Palmerston was not taken in. In their conversations, the Emperor showed himself 'very inquisitive' about Britain's reaction should France and Austria fight over Italy. He also brought up Russia's general intentions, and the irredeemable condition, to his mind, of the Ottoman empire. On these two points, Palmerston welcomed Napoleon's recognition that Russia was indeed crippled after the Crimean war, and contended for the immense strides made by Turkey since the early 1830s. The Englishman told his country's ambassador in Paris that 'if words are to be trusted…there is no danger…with respect to us'. France's overtures to Russia had been exciting concern in Britain from the close of the Crimean war. It was now clear to Palmerston that the French did not expect too much of Britain as an ally, and would like to be sure of her goodwill in a struggle with Austria. On that crucial question of Italy, 'everything would depend on the cause of the quarrel', he advised the Emperor. The implication was plain enough in the light of Palmerston's long held convictions on the subject of Austria's presence in Italy.[47] The French government had not hidden its regret and indignation at Palmerston's fall from power; and its partisanship was confirmed by Napoleon's talks with him in the summer and autumn of 1858. On his side, Palmerston's speech of 3 February 1859 at the beginning of the Parliamentary session was a signal to the Emperor. Its apparently reasonable and familiar plea that both Austria and France should withdraw their garrisons from Central Italy amounted, given the prevailing atmosphere there, to supporting a revolution in the Papal States and the duchies which must spread to Lombardy, entail Sardinian intervention and allow France to return in force.[48]

There were times when Palmerston believed war with France to be in the offing. But active co-operation proceeded over the latent antagonism near the surface. Napoleon, however surprisingly, meant what he said in 1862 to the Paris Rothschild on his dealings with the Powers: 'Je regarde l'Angleterre comme ma femme, les autres comme des maîtresses.'[49] He admired Britain, and did not admire the others. His attitude, of course, presupposed a Britain willing and strong enough to stand up for herself, with whom it would be worth France's while to work. There was no question of sacrificing French interests to British. After the Crimea, the two countries co-operated in using force against the Chinese and Japanese empires, and the anarchic Mexican republic. Britain's establishment of the Glücksburg dynasty in Greece after the 1862 revolution would not have been feasible without the Emperor's acceptance that he must not seek to impose his views in a question which bore on the continued existence of Turkey. The French intervention of 1860–61 in Syria was limited in scope and time for the same reason. Palmerston never gave Napoleon enough credit for restraining the natural desire of Frenchmen to make difficulties for their ancient enemy. Of the alliance in China he wrote: 'These combined operations are full of evil, though sometimes they are unavoidable or are the means of avoiding greater evils.'[50] The store which France set by Britain's diplomatic support over Italy was demonstrated 'in the most frantic way' by the Comte de Jaucourt, of the French embassy, and the Sardinian minister, Marchese d'Azeglio, in the lobby of the House of Commons when the Derby administration lost its vote of confidence in June 1859.[51] Palmerston expressed his gratitude more discreetly for France's assistance in bringing the *Trent* affair to a successful conclusion. The French foreign minister, Thouvenel, hoped in vain that this significant help would dispel the distrust of the Emperor and his government. Palmerston neither liked nor admired France and her ruler; he merely preferred her under Napoleon to the conservative Powers of Europe, and to American democracy. In the last weeks of his life, he welcomed the French navy's goodwill visit to Britain for the 'additional stability to peace' and continued: 'These meetings will also have a most wholesome effect in Yankee land, where they will be taken as indications of a closer union than in fact...exists, and...will thus tend to disincline the Yankees from aggression upon us.'[52] By then Britain's discomfiture over Schleswig-Holstein, much enjoyed in France, too, had underscored the lesson of Poland in 1863: there was no alternative to a good understanding with the Emperor if British diplomacy was to avoid a repetition of such European failures. It is an indication of Palmerston's stature in home politics that these reverses had no lasting effect on the fortunes of his government.

Britain and German national aspirations

John Morley in his biography of Cobden referred to the known 'Germanism' of the Court in the Prince Consort's final years, a sentiment cherished by his widow.[53] 'National hatred between these two peoples is a real political calamity for both', wrote Queen Victoria to Palmerston about the British and Germans in 1861.[54] She and the Prince were far more discerning, in this at least, than Palmerston and, it seems, his colleagues. Anglo-German relations leading up to the demonstration of Germany's nationhood in her war with Denmark may be approached through the vain endeavours of the Queen and her consort to bring the politicians round to their ardently pro-German outlook. A startled Gladstone confided to his wife in December 1860: 'The Chancellor says (keep this from view) that Albert said to him at Windsor, "We Germans have no boundaries – our only boundary is the Quadrilateral," i.e. fortresses in the heart of Italy.'[55] It was hardly a secret in political circles that the Queen and her husband had wanted Britain to intervene on the Austrian side in 1859. Their sympathies lay with Prussia in the rivalry between Hohenzollern and Hapsburg for the leadership of Germany, but the partial loss of Austria's possessions in Northern Italy was deeply felt by most German patriots. The Prince's assertion revealed how his Germany identified herself with the medieval Reich at its apogee. In deploring the neutrality of Prussia in 1859 and her restraining influence on lesser German states, the Queen and Prince reproached British politicians of both parties with their exertions to secure that result.[56] The Prince, whose ascendancy over his wife was complete, acknowledged with pain a divided national loyalty[57] which affected the Court's relations with ministers, Liberal and Tory, always liable to strain over differing interpretations of a constitutional monarch's functions. In Albert's view, the Crown's undeniable right to be consulted by ministers involved a more positive surveillance, amounting to a degree of control, than the politicians were ready to accept. Their appreciation of what the Prince had done for the monarchy under a Queen, whose Hanoverian tendencies to emotional and mental instability he and they had reason to fear,[58] did not extend to his ideas on the British constitution or British foreign policy. Their unwillingness to let him have statutory precedence immediately after the Queen, displacing the Prince of Wales and his other sons, reflected the feeling expressed by his admirer Gladstone in 1855, that the position which he had made for himself was arguably unconstitutional when it came between the sovereign and her 'sworn advisers'.[59] The Palmerston cabinet 'unanimously disapproved' in February 1857 of a bill drawn up by the Lord Chancellor to give effect to the Queen's importunity on behalf of her husband.[60] Its members submitted their collective advice in a formal minute, of Lewis's composition; they deprecated 'the shock…to…the people' if legislation arbitrarily demoted the Prince of Wales in favour of his father during his mother's lifetime.[61] For the opposition, Derby had already warned the Queen that the House of Commons and the country would suspect 'some unavowed and objectionable design' in such a bill.[62] With more directness, the cabinet minute referred to the unstated conclusion of her argument; the emergence of Albert as 'King Consort' was out of the question.[63] Gladstone made the same comments when, through Aberdeen, he saw an early outline of the 'Prince Consort Bill', casting doubt on its prudence, especially with reference to the clear implication of a kingly, not a princely, title.[64] In the end, the title of prince consort was conferred by letters patent without prejudice to the Act of Henry VIII governing precedence.

As German liberals, Victoria and Albert were sincere in wanting a Russian defeat in the Crimean war that would put an end to her active encouragement and protection of absolutism in Central Europe. The desire of husband and wife that Albert should have 'a legal status in the English hierarchy'[65] was more than personal and dynastic: it had a political motive. While Britain recognized in him only the younger son of a Duke of Saxe-Coburg-Gotha, it embarrassed him in the practice of a royal diplomacy which formed his main interest. Taking the part of his elder brother, the 'Red Duke' Ernest II, against the conservative rulers of Germany, Albert worked not only for a more unified country, but for one in which rulers and parliaments would share authority on the model of their uncle Leopold I's Belgium, where the monarch had a positive role irrecoverable in Britain. Albert was sensitive to such foreign mockery of the existing federal structure in Germany as appeared in a *Times* editorial of February 1858: 'What is the Germanic Bund?...a mysterious, half-fabulous phenomenon. It is... like... the last Mammoth splashing about in his...mud-bath.' The newspaper counselled the member states of the Diet not to interfere in Schleswig and Holstein: 'The Great Powers of Europe have settled that question...'[66] To Albert, the Diet was 'simply the representation of Germany'.[67] 'I am for Prussian hegemony', he wrote to his daughter in Prussia, 'but *Germany* is for me first in importance, Prussia *qua* Prussia second...'[68] Palmerston did not find the Prince Consort's dearest ambition credible: he consistently underestimated German nationalism.

The British Crown's revived claim to a greater share in the making of foreign policy in the first months of the new Palmerston government was, the prime minister considered, put forward by the Court to cloak their real objection to anything that tended to impede the restoration of Hapsburg princes to the Central Italian territories from which they had just been expelled by their subjects. When he and Palmerston talked over the constitutional dispute and its origins, Albert, 'the prompter in these matters',[69] did not dwell on the Austrian record in Italy but confirmed his position 'as siding with a German Power against Italian interests'.[70] More deferential in language and manner, Malmesbury had been equally firm in withstanding pro-German pressure from the Court earlier that year.[71] 'Queen alarmed but not so German as when Prince [Albert] there', he noted after a worrying discussion. It took nearly a month to modify their view of the situation. In the second half of May he found her 'very jealous' of his efforts to localize the conflict, and wholly under her husband's influence: 'She and prince evidently anxious not to stop the war but to let Germany go at the French...' Their eldest daughter, wife to the Prussian

Regent's heir, went further at a Buckingham Palace dinner, seeking active British participation: 'Queen touched the same string...', commented Malmesbury.[72] But at the end of May Victoria and her husband admitted the impossibility of British intervention, much as they would have liked to see it.[73] They still wanted the Queen's speech at the opening of the new Parliament in June redrafted to avoid wording which 'contains a public apology for arming, and yet betrays fear of our being attacked by France'. Derby and the cabinet would not consent to insert the hint of belligerency suggested.[74] The attitude of the Court mattered abroad, where it was well known, and had its effect on the Austrians as well as the French. Given his distrust of the Prince's family, and their Orleanist connexion, Napoleon could not accept that behind Malmesbury's attempted organization of diplomatic opposition to France's Italian venture there lay only a determination to stay neutral until Britain was caught up in spreading hostilities. The consequent apprehension made him impatient and thankful for Palmerston's arrival in power. After receiving Malmesbury's special emissary, the British Court's favourite diplomat, Cowley, the Emperor Francis Joseph let his good friend the Crown Prince of Saxony know that 'even though... we may not be able to get any promises, we may yet count upon England in the event of a big war'.[75] In this belief, Austria did not wait for France to strike the first blow.

This was the background to Palmerston's disagreement with the Court over England's part in the critical period after the Peace of Villafranca. At length, the prime minister won easily enough on the main issue by threatening the sovereign with the government's resignation if the Prince, and through him the Queen, continued to be 'very tiresome'. 'We must come to a clear understanding with the Court one way or another', observed Palmerston to Russell in September 1859.[76] Albert composed a rancorous memorandum for his own use in which he accused Palmerston of intolerable behaviour in sacrificing Britain and Europe to Napoleon by a false neutrality: 'if impeded by... the Queen... he is violent and over-bearing... cheats and tricks'.[77] The prime minister maintained, for his part, that 'The Queen might rightfully say... she insists upon her own German policy... and... we must either resign or adopt it...', but he added that, since she had not chosen to do so, the ministry ought to be free to carry out 'an Italian policy' without encountering persistent objections.[78] Such was his interpretation of what royal confidence in ministers signified: he understood it as defined by his old master Lord Liverpool under George IV. Albert was the innovator. The Queen and Prince were within their rights in querying the formulation and execution of policies, but Albert's hard and informed work on her boxes, supplemented by the habit of engaging members of the government and foreign envoys in political conversation, did little for his beloved Germany.

Clinging to the hope of a liberal Prussia, he realized its improbability. Vitzthum von Eckstädt reported on a talk with him that took place when Germany was savouring the acute frustration of the disunity blamed for France's victory over Austria: 'Pure Prussianism is as distasteful to Prince Albert as to the majority of Germans. In his opinion, however, the feeling of humiliation and weakness in foreign relations would overcome the popular hatred of Prussia.' The lesser German dynasties, Albert said, must follow the Prussian lead if they were to be perpetuated within a reorganized German federation.[79] Palmerston was not opposed, any more than Gladstone, to the growth of an united Germany in the abstract: he thought it very unlikely in practice. 'The Prussians and the smaller German states are selfish and foolish, the Austrians pigheadedly blind...'[80] 'Ah, si l'on pouvait seulement amener cette véritable union en Allemagne', he replied, without insincerity, to her representative's defence of Prussia's German ambitions.[81] The advantage to Britain was obvious of a power appreciably stronger than Austria and Prussia together and situated between Russia and France. The likely disadvantage was Prussian leadership in Central Europe, reaching into the Balkans: 'Prussia sets public opinion in England against her', wrote Palmerston, 'by her aggressive policy against Denmark... her anti-English policy all over the world, and by the rudeness and roughness of all the people employed... by the government or... railroad companies' – the last point being a reference to an incident which had recently excited the British press.[82] Albert was only relieved that the Prussian regent was not a Victor Emanuel, and that there was no Cavour among his ministers. The Duchy of Coburg would not suffer the fate of Parma, Modena, and Tuscany. He was tied to the Hohenzollerns by the marriage of his daughter, and by his enmity to Austria's pretensions to lead Germany, where he regarded the Hapsburgs as 'a tool in the hands of the Austrian Jesuits, who... keep down all progress and check every healthy development in the bud'.[83] Anti-Catholic though he was, Palmerston preferred Austria as co-operative with Britain in the Ottoman empire; and in his view the best available barrier, failing reform of the German Confederation, to French and Russian expansion.

When Albert died in December 1861, the Queen's limitations made her less of a nuisance to government in foreign affairs. On the other hand, as her prime minister tartly remarked, she indulged her 'Germanism' in a way that the Prince had the sense not to do.[84] The consequence was an unpopularity deeply felt by Victoria, who artlessly told her daughter, the Crown Princess of Prussia, 'I really speak with more thorough impartiality than anyone... my heart and sympathies are all German... and... in war can only be with them! So it was in Italy – with beloved Papa and me.'[85] She was writing as Austria and Prussia moved on Schleswig, the duchy with a mixed population, for which the Danes stood and fought, whereas they had retired from German Holstein on the entry of federal troops. When it was virtually all over, Palmerston owned to Gladstone that 'the Danes... were wrong in the beginning, and have been wrong in the end but... the sympathies in the majority of the House and in the nation are Danish'.[86] More than a year before fighting began, Hammond, the permanent under-secretary at the Foreign Office, a loyal and intelligent Palmerstonian, concluded 'it... is high time to wash our hands of this petty squabble'.[87] It had been put to the prime minister by the Prussians earlier still that they had to act with and for Germany in seeking to make Denmark fulfil agreements preserving the status of both duchies and the German identity of the inhabitants. 'Ah' answered Palmerston lightly, 'c'est toujours votre position en Allemagne.' To this dismissive observation, Bernstorff, the envoy in London, retorted that Britain loudly approved of Sardinia's national policy in Italy between which and Prussia's in Germany there existed 'une certaine analogie'.[88] '... all things considered', Palmerston held, 'dualism is the only arrangement possible in Germany', by which he envisaged no institutional change in the Confederation, but encouragement of the practical tendency for minor states to gather round Austria or Prussia, so that 'there would be two strong bodies to unite against a foreign foe'.[89]

The prime minister nevertheless attached due significance to the German claim, voiced by Bernstorff, on Schleswig as a part of the national territory, which Holstein always was, belonging as it did to the Confederation under her king–duke.[90] Palmerston had unsuccessfully supported a partition of Schleswig when Foreign Secretary under Russell, after the first round of warfare between Germans and Danes was stopped by the intervention of Russia and Prussia to save dynastic right from being sacrificed to nationalism. The Treaty of London in 1852, signed by all the Great Powers, vested the succession to the duchies in the Danish Crown, and regulated the descent. The Confederation was not a signatory and therefore un-committed, although Holstein's membership of its body was underwritten by the treaty. The Dano-German agreements relating to Schleswig were made separately with Austria and Prussia. Several years of rising tension were ended by the open conflict of 1863–64 on the promulgation of a new Danish constitution that incorporated Schleswig in a unitary state.[91] Palmerston outlined British policy in 1860: 'We must on general principles wish the Schleswickers to be well treated, and we have an interest in maintaining and keeping together the little monarchy which holds the keys of the Baltic and... is already weak enough.' He would have liked to see Schleswig, and Holstein too, merged with Denmark, but knew this to be quite unacceptable to Germany. His cabinet memorandum of 3 December 1863 recognized that the Germans had a case, initially, for reacting as they did. The danger all along had been that, given the pretext, they would set about dismembering the Danish Crown territorially.[92] Palmerston's verbal assurance to the Danes in the House of Commons that July was intended to warn off a predatory Germany.[93] The victim might be, and was, plausibly deemed the aggressor, as Queen Victoria insisted. The Diet of the Confederation upheld a rival claimant to the thrones of Denmark and, more importantly, of the duchies. Its forces occupied Holstein with the participation of Austrian and Prussian troops who subsequently invaded first Schleswig and then Denmark proper to compel the performance of Danish engagements to the two German Powers. Prussia's real object was annexation of the duchies to herself. She did not, therefore, question the Danish king's title to dispose of Schleswig and Holstein in defeat. Nor did Austria acknowledge the rival claimant.

Both the Austrian Emperor and Palmerston saw the invasions of Schleswig-Holstein and Denmark as over-reaction. To avert the attack on Schleswig, the Danes fruitlessly offered to revoke the integration of the duchy as quickly as the necessary legislation could be enacted. 'Should we have admitted', asked Francis Joseph, 'that Germany – as in my opinion – had entered upon an unjust war?' To have taken that stand would not have ensured peace for his empire. It must have compelled Austria and Britain to fight Prussia and a majority of the Confederation, with France coming in to renew the Anglo-French partnership of the Crimean war, naturally a prospect unwelcome to the Hapsburgs. 'Such a thing would have been impossible, and we were therefore bound to join Prussia', he wrote.[94] Gladstone echoed Palmerston's condemnation of Germany, and of Prussia in particular. He disliked even more strongly Prussia's motives for embarking on war: Bismarck's planned capture of national sentiment to gain the upper hand in his constitutional struggle with the liberals and in intensifying the contest with Austria.[95] There was little hope that France would intervene. Napoleon's foreign minister pointed out that France, fighting on land, would face Germany 'levée comme un seul homme'; while Britain could only sail her fleet up and down the Baltic without an enemy to fear.[96] Palmerston was angrily convinced that the Queen had fostered the belief in Germany that the Court could prevent Britain from going to Denmark's assistance.[97] Bernstorff compared Victoria to 'une digue insurmontable' should her prime minister persuade the cabinet to sanction the use of force.[98] The cabinet was inclined to think, like Gladstone, that this was not, and should not be permitted to turn into, 'a serious war'.[99]

Vitzthum, sounding out the Tories, made the most of the view to which Gladstone gave private expression. The Count urged Lord Derby not to lose sight of 'the insignificance of the object'; the Ottoman empire might rate a great war, but not 'the Danish succession, the "integrity" of an empire of two millions and a half'. The Treaty of London was regarded as the outcome of 'foreign dictation', to a then helpless and divided Germany, by Tsar Nicholas I.[100] Nevertheless, Palmerston tried to rescue something for Denmark. 'This', he considered, 'is just one of those occasions...when one determined will carries with it the hesitation of others...we have... truth, duty, engagements and European interests on our side.' When Austria and Prussia crossed into Schleswig, he examined the possibilities of action by Britain, and at that early stage effectively agreed with Gladstone. It was impracticable to despatch a British expeditionary force of 20,000 men to meet 200,000 or 300,000 Austrians and Prussians, besides the contingents from smaller members of the Confederation. Next, sending the fleet would not have much effect unless understood to be a first step. He questioned the wisdom of actually inciting France to expand into the Rhineland, 'an evil for us and...Holland and Belgium'. Lastly, he doubted whether either the cabinet or public opinion were ready to take on 'all Germany'.[101] He had summoned the Austrian and Prussian representatives in London to tell them that the 'guilt for all the bloodshed and loss of life would be on their two governments'. There was little else he could do.[102]

The cabinet blocked a naval demonstration, for what it was worth; and Palmerston persisted with the idea of a conference, embracing the signatories of the Treaty of London. It met in the British capital at the end of April, while an armistice was arranged during the negotiations. The obduracy of the Danes finished by exasperating Palmerston, who did not care for their frequent reminders of Britain's obligations and appeals for help in arms. They rejected the Austro-Prussian offer of a strictly personal union between the Crown of Denmark and the duchies. 'They are not an intelligent race and very *borné*', said the prime minister to the Queen, complaining of their unwillingness to swallow so small a change from the situation prior to 1863.[103] Palmerston's problem was, and had been for months, public opinion, not the monarch or the cabinet. It suited him to play on its pro-Danish sentiments as they became more marked with the stiff resistance put up by the Danes on the battlefield. He cautioned Delane against pacific editorials in *The Times*. 'The only check we can have upon them [the Prussians]', he explained, 'is the indefinite notion that public opinion here is getting irritated against them...'[104] Bismarck was unmoved. He feared his own public opinion more than Britain's: 'it was better for Prussia to run any risks from a foreign enemy than from revolutionary movements in Germany' while France remained neutral, which he felt assured she would do. By revolutionary he meant liberal, but was none the less in earnest. Hostilities with Britain alone, he informed her ambassador in Berlin, must be restricted to the sea and futile: the British fleet was safe from Prussia, and Prussia hardly vulnerable to maritime blockade.[105] At the ensuing cabinets on 24 and 25 June, it was decided by eight votes to seven that only if Copenhagen was in danger of occupation would Britain reconsider non-intervention.[106] It was a recognition of weakness in line with the prime minister's better judgement, formed as far back as February. In old age Gladstone regretted the failure of Franco-British co-operation which might have stopped Austria and Prussia by deploying all its strength, and altered 'the whole course of... European history'.[107] At the time he had no illusions about the prospect of succouring the Danes in that way: 'there is none'.[108]

After a period of joint occupation the Convention of Gastein in August 1865 allotted Schleswig to Prussia and Holstein to Austria. Palmerston took understandable pleasure in the Queen's perturbation at this outcome. '... now that the example is... set of extinguishing petty states like Coburg', the prime minister observed, 'her sense of right and wrong has become wonderfully keen... her mind revolts at... consequences which flow naturally from the proceedings she approved of.' Palmerston was in no doubt that the strengthening of Prussia was more satisfactory than the independence of the two duchies under Frederick of Augustenburg, the Confederation's claimant and favoured by the Queen. He did not condone the manner of Schleswig's acquisition but 'there is a future as well as a present and a past'. The balance of power needed the stronger Germany, not an addition to her *Kleinstaaterei*.[109] When he counselled Bernstorff to maintain a good understanding with Austria, he remarked 'd'une certaine bonhomie' on its efficacy in circumstances most unpalatable to himself, at which they both laughed.[110] The French embassy in London reported that Bismarck had nothing to fear from Palmerston, severely critical though he was of the German statesman's character and methods.[111] In Germany, Bismarck affirmed his indifference to British public opinion.[112] The perception of the Schleswig-Holstein crisis as a victory for Continental reaction, from which the opposition at home could take almost as little satisfaction as the government, worked decisively in Palmerston's favour.

There was no question of Britain withdrawing from the affairs of Europe: but Russell spoke for Palmerston in saying to the French that Britain would imitate their professed intention of not interfering in Germany, between Austria and Prussia, or with the Confederation.[113] The prime minister foresaw that Austria would be a loser by her participation in the coercion of Denmark: 'being made a fool of by Bismarck, she will have her fingers burnt'.[114] He did not foresee that France would be the ultimate loser. He looked upon her as did Wood, who 'thought the power of France, already enormous, would reach a proportion... appalling for the rest of Europe, which by its perpetual blundering had played into the Emperor's hands...'.[115] That was one lesson of Schleswig-Holstein for Britain. The other was eagerly reported in a letter of Gladstone's to his correspondent, the French minister of finance, Achille Fould: 'Our two countries have an incredible mass of common interests; and those common interests are the interests of the world.'[116] Spurred on by its intense hostility to the Papacy, the Palmerston government did not cease to argue for the completion of Italian unity. British ministers tackled the Emperor on his liberal side, and their importunity had 'some effect'[117] – all that Palmerston expected – on the decision to pull his troops out of the last territory remaining to the Pope in 1864; although they were obliged to defer to his conservative side in cutting short Garibaldi's visit to England that same year. In the eyes of the voters at the general election of 1865, the success of British diplomacy in Italy more than made up for the reverse sustained in defence of the Danes.

The Queen's Germanism was modified by her shocked indignation at the division of the Duchies between Austria and Prussia.[118] She had pressed on the ministry what she devoutly imagined would have been Albert's wishes. He might have been more reserved in his commitment to Germany, disturbed as he was by her anti-constitutionalism and unquiet militarism.[119] However, his liberalism did not go deep, by English standards, and he was on principle antagonistic to parliamentary control of armies. When the Indian Mutiny caught Britain unprepared, he remarked scathingly to his teacher and friend, Baron Stockmar, on 'the utterly decrepit state of an army which rests upon civil government and the press...'.[120] Yet it is certain that he would have tried to prevent the Court's pro-German sympathies in 1863–64 from becoming common knowledge, as he did over Italy in 1859 and subsequently. A privileged member of her household, Lord Torrington, whom Albert had liked, ventured to tell the Queen's private secretary, General Grey, that the Court was '*unacquainted* with public opinion and feeling', which the Queen had just offended by accepting from William I of Prussia the order of the Black Eagle for her son, Prince Alfred. Torrington's protest secured him an interview with the Queen who addressed herself through him to Delane of *The Times*, one of whose sources he was. She expressed her resentment of *The Times*'s language about the German decoration for her son, and defended it, naively, as 'a mark of the King's desire to be on good terms with her and the family in spite of...English feeling'. Her strongest sentiment was dynastic; she declined to recognize what Torrington had written to Grey: 'family feeling could now have nothing to do with a great national question'.[121] Her response to the shock of the Duchies' absorption by Austria and Prussia, to the exclusion of the Confederation's candidate, was to marry her daughter Helena to the disappointed pretender's younger brother, Christian of Schleswig-Holstein-Sonderburg-Augustenburg.

The Great Powers, Italy and the Papacy

French arms opened the way for the creation of a unitary state in Italy which did not feature in the Emperor's plans. It was Britain that proceeded

to identify herself closely with the sudden huge expansion of Victor
Emanuel's liberal kingdom in the North. The social and political character
of the Risorgimento enabled Russell to utter his famous boast likening it to
the Glorious Revolution in his own country, and signalizing it as a defeat
for democracy.[122] To the conservative Powers of Europe a revolution was
hardly less abhorrent for being liberal instead of democratic. While the
Holy Alliance of Tsar Alexander I was incapable of resurrection, said
Prince Gortchakov, the Russian foreign minister, the Continental Powers,
France included, had a common interest in combating 'les idées de
désordre'.[123] For Napoleon III was an absolute monarch, whose liberal
vision could only be gradually realized. 'I am accused of having two
distinct policies. It is true!' confessed the Emperor to the Austrian
ambassador when discussing Italy in December 1860, 'I am obliged to have
two, because my origin forbids me to be reactionary, and I dare not be
revolutionary...'[124] By that date he had ended Austria's domination in
Italy, leaving her to rule the single province of Venetia; but he had failed
in his aim of an Italian federation, under the presidency of the Pope, as a
symbol of legitimacy, which was to have combined a kingdom of Northern
Italy for Sardinia with one of Central Italy for his cousin Jerome Napoleon,
and perhaps a Murat restoration in Naples. Italian nationalism, delivered
from Austrian hegemony, foiled this sweeping extension of French and
Bonaparte influence. As the Emperor stated to Austria's unsympathetic
ambassador, he was unable, without losing his credibility as a progressive
ruler to arrest by force the advance of Sardinia towards Italian unity on her
terms; although a French squadron, inhibiting a blockade from the sea for
some weeks, enabled the last Bourbon king of Naples, Francis II, to hold
out a little longer in the coastal fortress of Gaeta, surrendered in February
1861. Conversely, Napoleon might not, without incurring domestic political
risks, withdraw his military protection from the Patrimony of St Peter –
Rome and the districts historically connected with the city under the
Papacy – where he had sent troops in 1849 to overthrow Garibaldi's
Roman republic and bring Pius IX back from exile. The Emperor feared
a very serious reaction in France from an ultramontane church and the
powerful Legitimist party attentive to clerical wishes, if he removed his
garrison and left the Pontiff to seek refuge abroad. At the beginning of
1861, he was still assuring Lord Cowley, the British ambassador, that 'the
unity of Italy...he believed...to be an impossibility'.[125] The previously
arranged cession of Savoy and Nice to France by Sardinia early in 1860
afforded some compensation for his frustrated ambition and fears, but not
enough. Garibaldi's part in the conquest of Sicily and Naples angered and
dismayed him, as much as other princes from Tsar Alexander II to Prince
Albert. The revolutionary democrat was the more alarming for the support
he received from a strong element of the nobility, and from his relations

with the Sardinian monarchy, culminating in his entire submission to it. The new kingdom of Italy was born of revolution, first in the centre and then in the South, after France had driven the Austrians into Venetia.

It did not impress the conservative Powers, or Napoleon in his 'dynastic and anti-revolutionary' moods,[126] that only 2 per cent of the population enjoyed the right to vote in elections to the Italian legislature, while France had manhood suffrage. Bonapartist France was a long way from being a genuine parliamentary state, which Italy definitely was, although Victor Emanuel both reigned and ruled. Russia had aided and abetted the French attack on Austria in Italy by measures short of war; under a secret treaty she ordered intimidatory troop movements on the Russo-Austrian border. The Tsar and his advisers had regarded the war as one of straightforward aggrandizement, on France's part; and, so far as Russia was concerned, vicarious revenge for Hapsburg policy during the Crimean conflict. Russian legitimism could not stomach what followed the cessation of Austro-French hostilities. The peace or armistice of Villafranca in July 1859 not only limited Austria's loss of sovereign territory to Lombardy, but restored the ruling dynasties, Hapsburg and Bourbon, to their Italian duchies and the Romagna to the Papacy, against the wishes of a majority of the politically conscious inhabitants and within the framework of a federation that made room for Venetia under the Hapsburgs. Subjected to pressure from Sardinia, from Italian nationalists who had seized power in the areas to be returned to their old governments, and from Britain, Napoleon went back on this provisional settlement, the interpretation of which the Treaty of Zürich in November finally entrusted to a European congress that never met. The duchies and the Romagna voted overwhelmingly for annexation to Sardinia in manipulated plebiscites of the adult male population. There ensued the Garibaldian and Sardinian invasions of the rest of Italy. To these events the conservative Powers reacted with profound indignation. From London Bernstorff reported to his royal master that the Prince Consort fully subscribed to the widespread condemnation of Sardinia on the Continent. Albert blamed the British cabinet for having done everything it could to nullify the agreement reached between Francis Joseph and Napoleon; he was convinced that, without Britain's interference, those terms might have been carried out.[127] Italy, remarked her minister in London, d'Azeglio, had no reason to regret the Prince's death in December 1861.[128]

Albert's and the Queen's concern for Austria in Italy, as representing Germany, and for legitimacy there left little room for the anti-Catholicism typical of the royal couple; although the Prince's general criticisms of France included her policy of 'acting...in a purely Catholic, not a Christian, sense',[129] Palmerston never lost sight of the Italian problem's religious implications. He approached Italy with 'English and Protestant

interests' in view. Under the European settlement at the Congress of
Vienna, Britain was a party to the apportionment of Italian territory which
war and revolution swept away in 1859–61. Palmerston was happy to
distinguish between signing treaties and enforcing them: 'We have a *right*
to require the stipulations... to be observed, but we are under no *obligation*
to do so.' He busied himself with proposals to divest the Pope of nearly all
that remained of his states. 'I believe', he reminded his foreign secretary,
unnecessarily, 'that the more his position, spiritual or temporal, is lowered
the better for us in all respects.'[130] The native statesman who promoted the
unification of the peninsula with such agility, Cavour, made use of this
British preoccupation, as when in 1859 he pointed to the encouragement
that Irish Catholic nationalism, which had made the Papal cause its own,
must derive from the return of the Romagna to its former ruler: 'If the
Pope should obtain a victory in Italy, the presumption and pride of the
Cullens and McHales would swell beyond bounds...'[131] Those members of
the Liberal cabinet who did not applaud Austria's defeat were reconciled
to all its consequences by the blows that fell on the Pope and the Church:
'...without being at all fanatical about Italian liberty and nationality... I
conceive... the ascendancy of the Roman Church has been the curse of
Italy... anything which tends to weaken it, I look upon with unmixed
satisfaction', explained Lewis in December 1860 to a kindred spirit.[132]
Gladstone, indeed, put the removal of the Papacy's temporal power, as a
British objective, above the enlargement of Sardinia.[133]

Garibaldi was anathema to most European governments, with the clear
exception of Britain, where the leaders of the Tory opposition joined in
paying tribute to him when he came to London in April 1864. The
principle of revolutionary nationalism which he embodied did not
commend itself to Victor Emanuel and Cavour; they used and discarded
him after the collapse of the Neapolitan Bourbons. The British, reassured
as to the nature of Garibaldi's conquest, had declined to employ their naval
power in co-operation with France to prevent him from crossing the Straits
of Messina in August 1860.[134] Russell put their appraisal of the situation to
the French ambassador, Persigny, in June: '...the King of Sardinia is the
only man who can keep order in Italy... the King of Naples is not likely to
keep up his authority, or to keep down the democratic party...'. He
advised Persigny of Metropolitan Police reports on the current talk of the
uncompromising revolutionaries, followers of the doctrinaire republican
Mazzini, among Italian exiles in the British capital: 'The Emperor may
despise it, but it would not be fair to conceal it from you.'[135] Napoleon and
his foreign minister, Thouvenel, listened because they really believed
Britain capable either of inspiring and taking part in war against France by
a coalition of the other Powers determined to end Bonapartist aggression,
or of embarrassing her by encouragement of '*une grande explosion des*

sentiments révolutionnaires' in Italy.[136] As Persigny had always seen, Britain's authentic liberalism was potentially a dangerous enemy to the Emperor; it could confer respectability on reaction or democracy, his foes at home and abroad. Palmerston was very well pleased with the outcome of Garibaldi's operations and his submission to Victor Emanuel as king of an united Italy. Fortified by local opinion, the British prime minister wrote from Leeds in October 1860 to emphasize his confidence in Garibaldi who had enabled the Bourbon monarch's subjects 'to exercise a free choice as to their present condition and…destiny'. Much later, discussing the Italian's announced visit to Britain, Palmerston considered that 'we ought to view him as the man who gave Sicily and Naples to his King…', a truer description of what Garibaldi had achieved.[137]

For the Palmerston government, its Parliamentary following, and the public, the unification of Italy and spoliation of the Papacy outweighed France's annexation of Savoy and Nice – her lowest price for defeating Austria and consenting to Sardinian absorption in stages of nearly all the peninsula. Malmesbury believed Palmerston's indignation at the transfer of Savoy and Nice to be simulated. According to his information, the British prime minister had been told of the arrangement for their cession when, out of power, he visited Napoleon at Compiègne in November 1858; made privy to the Emperor's 'whole plan' for Italy, he 'entered into it completely'. Clarendon, who accompanied him, was not let into the secret of the Franco-Sardinian agreement reached at Plombières in July: but he did learn of the Emperor's '*ideas*' about Italy to which he gave a critical hearing. 'Thus from the beginning', stated Malmesbury in his unpublished diary, 'Palmerston connived at this baleful act' – the surrender of so much Sardinian territory – 'and never resisted it till he saw the disgust it inspired in Parliament and the country.' If Malmesbury's facts were correct, it was no wonder that Persigny, incensed by Russell's outspoken attack on a move ominously reminiscent of the first Napoleon, should have reminded Lady Palmerston before a score of witnesses at the Austrian embassy that 'her husband had always known of the intended annexation, and…the Emperor had never concealed from him his views…'.[138] Palmerston's Commons speech of 13 March was a conscious effort to calm the excitement both in France and among his countrymen. Russell's unwise threats were uttered a fortnight later. Britain, he said, would have to look to a common front of the Powers against French expansion. The prime minister recalled Napoleon III's famous speech at Bordeaux in 1852 heralding the restored empire and declaring that it meant peace, not European war. 'I do not hold', argued Palmerston, 'that…what took place in Italy last year…was any departure from that principle…France undertook a noble enterprise… freeing Italy from foreign domination – aye…French domination included…' Regrettably, he admitted, the acquisition of Savoy and Nice detracted from the French achievement, which otherwise he presented in a most flattering light.[139]

As before, Palmerston was striving to preserve good Anglo-French relations. To help Napoleon accept Sardinian possession of the Italian duchies and the Romagna, he had urged on the cabinet in January a defensive alliance with France and Sardinia in the event of an Austrian attempt to re-establish the status quo in the duchies and that part of the Papal States. In the memorandum he wrote for his colleagues the prime minister represented the proposal as a move to apply not unwelcome pressure on the French Emperor. The risk of war, he considered to be small; and were it to occur, Britain's share would be almost entirely naval: probably no more than a squadron in the Adriatic. The projected treaty was a way of ensuring that Napoleon's liberalism got the better of his conservative inclinations. Personally, he had always found the Emperor consistent 'in regard to freeing Italy from Austrian domination and curtailing the temporal sovereignty of the Pope' – carefully chosen words. An aspect of the Italian question on which he laid great stress was the opportunity it presented of buying goodwill and time from France for the completion of British rearmament which 'once accomplished would put us comparatively at ease as to future contingencies...' It was his belief that Parliament and public opinion would approve this degree of involvement in the affairs of Europe 'upon the double ground of its own merits, and of its tendency to avert a rupture with France...'.[140] Gladstone gave Palmerston his backing 'in every particular'; although he did think that 'the improbable... war' would be more serious if it came, and that a grave misunderstanding with the French could not be excluded after, and as a result of, the agreement. What was decisive for him seems to have been the behaviour of 'the Papal party' throughout Europe rallying to the defence of the temporal power.[141] Russell, the Manchester School radical, Milner Gibson, and the Duke of Somerset were the only other members of the cabinet to support such a departure from the principle of no armed intervention in Italy to which the ministry was pledged.

Mainly interested as they were in divesting the Papacy of as much as possible of its traditional influence, a large number of his colleagues nevertheless disagreed with Palmerston over the treatment of Austria in Italy. The permanence of her withdrawal from Italy beyond Venetia was not 'a real English object', Wood cautioned the prime minister; and Argyll tendered his confirmation that 'the reluctance shown by the cabinet... is but a reflexion of the feeling of the country' about fighting in and for Italy, beside France.[142] Palmerston did not act on a threat to resign if the cabinet prevented Britain '*altogether*' from allying with France and Sardinia against the despatch of Austrian troops into the territories supposed to take back their exiled rulers under the terms of Villafranca and Zurich. 'What virtue may be in this *altogether*, I know not', commented Lewis. He found out next day, when without further discussion of the controversial proposal, ministers were invited to authorize negotiation of the Anglo-French commercial treaty, already begun through Cobden's agency, and also a British call on both Austria and France to eschew military intervention in Italy outside Venetia where the legitimacy of the Austrian presence was recognized. To that there could be no objection, remarked Lewis.[143] The mauled Hapsburg state had decided not to aggravate its post-war difficulties.

The Emperor in person explained the history of his Italian annexations to Cobden, who in writing to Bright blamed Count Cavour for having tempted Napoleon into war by the promise of them. The audience and Napoleon's language at it were indications of his anxiety to dispel British fears. Cobden was an idealist, but not a political innocent: 'the mercantile...manufacturing and mining interests had the power and the determination to keep the peace', he replied to the Emperor's inquiries about the depth of anti-French sentiment in Britain.[144] Quite aware that Napoleon entertained ambitions to redraw the map of Europe, Cobden believed in his attachment notwithstanding to the British alliance: 'He has nothing to gain and everything to lose by war with us.'[145] Yet he could not disguise from himself the menace to be seen in the military and popular celebration, which he watched in Paris, of the dynasty's repossession of Savoy and Nice, lost to France on the fall of Napoleon I. However much the democratic basis of the regime appealed to him, he was compelled to reflect that 'we do not insure ourselves against the conquering propensities of despotic sovereigns by transferring the supreme power to the masses of the people'.[146] It was a Palmerstonian thought. Countrywide protests obliged Palmerston to make a show of exerting moral and diplomatic pressure on France to hand back what she had acquired, but he had Persigny informed that war was out of the question.[147]

Some intemperate observations were made on the French side, too, by the Emperor in front of the diplomatic corps and by Persigny, who having listened to it at the House of Commons exclaimed that Russell's spirited condemnation of Napoleonic aggrandizement was not to be borne.[148] 'What has England to do with Savoy?' said the Emperor sharply to Cowley. He reproached him with France's very different attitude when her ally suddenly occupied the islet of Perim opposite Aden in 1857 to avert any danger to her position in the Red Sea and the Indian Ocean if it should pass into foreign, meaning French, hands. Later in the evening Napoleon apologized to the ambassador: 'I must recollect...that he had not spoken of the Government, but of those who attacked him.'[149] The conciliatory behaviour was ill repaid by Russell in his speech. That was why Palmerston had to make good the damage, without appearing to truckle to Napoleon. He felt able to tell Persigny, coolly, that the French were too much given to dealing with matters 'sur le terrain d'amour propre national'.[150] Both sides were, in fact, justified in their soreness. The Emperor did not act on his own suggestion that the Great Powers should be consulted: 'It is not likely', he assured Cowley with bland insincerity 'that I should act against the advice of Europe.'[151] Nor did he cede to the Swiss, for the better security of their frontier, two adjacent districts of Savoy neutralized by the Congress of Vienna, as he led them and others to expect. Palmerston asked Persigny whether justice, generosity and honour did not counsel France to meet Switzerland's claims.[152] On the other hand, Palmerston and Russell had incurred the scandalized disapproval of their own monarch for advising Napoleon III to ignore the spirit, if not the letter, of Villafranca and Zürich.[153] They, and their cabinet colleagues, were not well placed to lecture the Emperor on political morality.

In the middle of 1861, after Victor Emanuel II had become King of all Italy except Venetia and the Patrimony of St. Peter, Napoleon could still tell the Austrian ambassador that an Italy divided into three suited him best, namely, Venetia as well as Lombardy, the former duchies and the Romagna joined to pre-1859 Sardinia, less Savoy and Nice; the Papal States otherwise restored to their sovereign, but administered, subject to his authority, by laymen instead of ecclesiastics; and a revived Kingdom of Naples and Sicily, with Francis II put back on his throne. It is in the context of these 'dreams', as Napoleon liked to call the potentially explosive thoughts which he was used to revealing on international issues in order to create a climate for their possible realization, that Britain's Italian policy, anti-Papal and self-interested first and pro-Italian second, should be placed. A central Italian realm for Jerome Napoleon, a Murat for the Two Sicilies – hopes reluctantly discarded – were perhaps less disturbing than the suggestion of a Bonaparte Pope in the person of a clerical cousin of the Emperor's who was destined for the cardinalate.[154] The Roman question raised in its most acute form yet the division among Napoleon's closest advisers. The Empress Eugénie and Walewski, another cousin, were Catholic and conservative in their sympathies. Jerome Napoleon, Persigny, Achille Fould and Rouher wanted to strengthen the regime's appeal to liberals. The liberal cousin, Jerome Napoleon, solicited a representation from the British government to strengthen the case for withdrawing the French troops stationed in and around Rome. 'A word from us may do good...to the Emperor without offence', Palmerston told Russell. 'If he really wishes to get out of Rome, it may help him. If he really wants to remain, it may be less easy for him to give plausible reasons for doing so.'[155]

Napoleon tried to allay Palmerston's suspicions by a personal message sent through a reliable intermediary: '"Tell Lord Palmerston to trust and have confidence in me".' Napoleon's intermediary reported his professions of sincerity as to evacuating Rome without seeking further territorial compensation from Italy.[156] The Emperor and his ambassador in London both tried to convince the prime minister that the French government, too, had to reckon with a public opinion sensitive to the appearance of foreign dictation.[157] Palmerston was quite unreasonably sceptical, though mindful, as usual, of the need to avoid provoking Napoleon.[158] He adhered to the view, for which there was much fresh evidence, that Napoleon had not ceased to think of stepping in, should Italy's fragile unity give way, to organize 'division and federation'.[159] In fact, Napoleon's hesitation between policies was deceptive. He had to have regard to France's increasingly vigorous Catholicism with its ultramontane focus. 'If Rome is to be evacuated', his Protestant finance minister, Achille Fould, explained to Cowley, 'it must be…without prejudice to the Pope's position…'[160] Napoleon was indeed so anxious to extricate France from her Roman imbroglio that after the fall of Gaeta he suggested pulling out his troops, in return for an Italian promise not to incite an immediate uprising, followed by intervention, in the wake of the French departure. Cavour, however, refused to lend himself to the transparent pretence that France would thus bear no responsibility for completing the destruction of the temporal power; he preferred to explore the chances of reconciling the Papacy, which he well understood was integral to Italian life, to the new order.[161]

The Emperor felt his way towards a settlement.[162] Britain offered the Pontiff asylum in her devoutly Catholic island of Malta, a calculated initiative publicized by the French for quite different reasons; few Frenchmen, of whatever political colour, could contemplate with equanimity the Pope's reduction to the status of a British dependent in a colonial outpost.[163] The 'Convention of September' in 1864 was the eventual outcome when Victor Emanuel II renounced the aspiration to make Rome the capital of Italy and undertook to safeguard, to the best of his ability, Papal rule over the territory from which France agreed to withdraw her garrison.[164] This result was a considerable improvement for the Pope on earlier proposals, particularly on one, of which Britain approved, to dispose of the problem by an arrangement close to that currently prevailing under the Lateran Treaty of 1929.[165] Garibaldi's bid in the summer of 1862 to overrun the Patrimony of St Peter helped, by its failure, with the Franco-Italian compact two years afterwards. Napoleon acted decisively by intimating that he would stop the nationalist hero if Victor Emanuel did not allow his conservative generals to take action.[166] The British ambassador expressed official satisfaction with the Convention of September.[167] In 1862 Palmerston had described such a solution, outlined by the French foreign minister of the time, as 'quite inadmissible' by reason of the odium which the Italian monarchy would incur internally, if it tried to uphold the Pope on terms of that kind, or externally, if it 'inevitably' broke the agreement.[168] Britain and France were now equally keen that this treaty should work, against the odds, and let Italy turn her attention to establishing justice and sound finance within the kingdom. French-occupied Rome had been a base for the ex-King of Naples's activity, such as it was, in support of the backward South's popular revolt against the modernizing centralism of North Italians. The British had considerably exaggerated the scale of Neapolitan Bourbon operations across the Papal border, and of French complicity which amounted to little, if anything, more than turning a blind eye as a way of inducing Victor Emanuel to be more co-operative in resolving the Roman question.[169]

Palmerston's old aim of getting Austria out of Italy, which featured in his sweeping private plans for the reconstruction of Europe during the Crimean war, had always been subject to the proviso that Austria should be strengthened, and not weakened, as a result. The straitened and disordered finances of the Hapsburg empire after the war of 1859, and the encouragement that Hungary derived from Vienna's military defeat to agitate for her lost autonomy under the imperial crown, presented him with a good opportunity of urging his double aim on the Austrians. It was suggested that they should sell Venetia to Victor Emanuel II and spend the proceeds on consolidating and, later, extending their dominions in Central and Eastern Europe. The idea seems first to have come up among ministers in November 1859.[170] Moved by solicitude for 'the cause of European peace', Cobden quite independently went to the Austrian ambassador at Napoleon's court in January 1860, and apprised him that if there were a nationalist rising in Venetia suppressed with heavy civilian casualties, it would be very difficult for any government in England to resist a public demand for armed intervention.[171] The cabinet did not consider a detailed proposal from Russell until late November and December 1860: Austria was not only to receive a price for Venetia, but a Prussian guarantee of her frontier with Italy, and a British guarantee of the long Adriatic coastline remaining to her. The cabinet objected to the risk of being drawn into a war for Austria; it was eventually decided to ascertain what the French emperor thought.[172] Palmerston's ultimate purpose was unchanged, an end to Hapsburg rule in Italy; he believed its survival in Venetia could only be temporary. He brushed aside the misgivings of the pro-Austrian Clarendon, outside the government, in a letter of December 1859: 'The refrain of the Austrian song to us is, If you love us and have any regard for us or for making us happy, do for Heaven's sake help us to continue to tyrannize over the Italians and to make them as unhappy as we have made them for the past.'[173]

The similarity between Cobden's arguments in tone and content and those of Palmerston was striking. Cobden, too, recommended the sale of Venetia as true wisdom, on Austria's part. The way in which she had accepted the territory of the conquered Venetian republic from Revolutionary France in 1797 was a continuing outrage upon the European conscience. Austrian resistance to cession ran counter to contemporary trends, and would prove quite useless, while a price of 20 or 30 millions sterling, easily financed, might be effectively employed in promoting reform in the older Hapsburg lands. The Austrian ambassador, Prince Richard Metternich, pointed out what Cobden chose to overlook, like Palmerston when he wished, the nature of the empire as a collection of nationalities, plainly vulnerable to the implications for her inevitably more artificial unity of being prepared to sell off Venetia.[174] Napoleon discussed the removal of this understandable objection by inducing debt-ridden Turkey to sell her Balkan provinces of Bosnia and Herzegovina to Austria, who could hope to obtain twice as much from the Italian purchase of Venetia; altogether better for Hapsburg power and prestige. Palmerston was appreciative of a clever bargain, although he deemed one province, Herzegovina, enough for Austria. Her government constituted 'an odious tyranny' for Italians, but it would be 'more enlightened and less arbitrary' than that to which the Slavs of Herzegovina were accustomed under the Sultan. The French emperor, however, did not think that Austria was ready to abandon finally her Italian presence.[175] Palmerston kept the solution in view, with growing doubts as to its feasibility. The British and the Austrians suspected Napoleon of the intention to use the latter's continued occupation of Venetia as a pretext for the general war they feared.[176]

Cowley, whose highly professional objectivity exposed him to charges of being pro-Austrian and pro-French under the second Derby and Palmerston administrations, respectively, submitted a long, cogent memorandum in January 1862 discounting these fears. Napoleon was mindful of the narrow margin by which the French army under his command had beaten the Austrians in 1859. In common with Francis Joseph and the Tsar, if not to the same degree, he lacked the funds to embark on a great war. Cowley ruled out higher taxes in France and doubted whether it was practicable for Napoleon to demand a war loan on top of an anticipated one to offset accumulated deficits. As for their ally of 1859, the French had no confidence in the fighting qualities of Victor Emanuel's troops; they were not in a state to take the field. Nor was the new Italy in any condition, financially, to enter a war. Cowley felt certain that the Emperor and his army did not desire to attack Austria again and, with her, Germany.[177] The quest for glory almost continuously necessary to the regime was carried on by his reckless diplomacy, by admitted anti-Hapsburg and anti-Ottoman intrigues in Hungary and Rumania, and by the Mexican venture on which it had just embarked. The public opinion of France, like that of Britain, did not want to pay dearly for cutting a great figure in the world. Italy provided both countries with a stage on which to indulge limited ambitions.

The French expended blood and treasure; the British contented themselves with advertising their international right to take a hand in the involved diplomacy, acting with and trying to influence the stronger side. Even a Tory such as Lord Augustus Loftus, the British envoy at Vienna, reacted with something close to contempt when the Austrian foreign minister, Count Rechberg-Rothenlöwen contrasted Britain's support for the nationalists of the revolted Italian duchies – two of them belonging to branches of the House of Hapsburg – with her uncompromising firmness towards rebellion in India, Ireland and the Ionian Islands. 'I replied to him that there was no analogy', reported Loftus in a despatch printed in the Blue Book, '...In India Great Britain had lately suppressed a formidable mutiny with her own strong arm without foreign intervention. If the Italian Archdukes...had remained at their posts, and could thereby have maintained their authority, Europe would no doubt have applauded them; but they had unfortunately pursued another course.'[178] His words illustrate Britain's consciousness of herself as a Great Power.

11

The extension of realism in foreign affairs

Introductory

'A portentous mixture of bounce and baseness': with this description of Liberal foreign policy Lord Robert Cecil associated himself with European contempt for the Palmerston governments. The contempt was there, but mingled with envy and respect. The despised qualities are not very much in evidence when the record is examined. Cecil was brilliantly unfair – as so often in his early career – in these frequently quoted attacks, comparable to Bright's habitual rhetoric in their severe moralizing. He recognized the dependence of any ministry on public opinion, but censured the Liberals for giving in to it. '"Cheap war"', he wrote scornfully after the German conquest of Schleswig and Holstein, 'is the cry with which, if our age were not too respectable to speak its mind, members would return to their constituencies.' There was no cheap war to be had in Europe or North America. While this realization acted as a curb on the middle and upper working classes, something of which a landed cabinet and Parliament were glad, the politicians and those to whom they were answerable expected an active but not a reckless diplomacy from government: behaviour commensurate with being a Great Power. Many years away from his long tenure of the Foreign Office, Cecil scorned, because he did not yet properly grasp, the reasons for avoiding a major conflict, if it was at all possible without incurring greater present or future harm. To him it was demeaning to confine the translation of big words into action to cases where it 'does not send the Funds down and only stimulates the iron trade'.[1] Such patience made excellent sense in the light of those grave social realities underlying prosperity to which Palmerston drew attention at Leeds in October 1860.[2] The demands of national sentiment and of the economy guided Britain's course in opting for more or less intervention in the Ottoman empire, the American civil war and the Polish tragedy of 1863 as in the struggles for

Italy and the Danish duchies. The Anglo-French relationship was likewise a source of difficulty and of strength.

The Ottoman empire and Russia

Napoleon III made no secret of his impatience with Britain's protection of Turkey after the Crimean war, when he was courting Russia preparatory to the attempt at driving Austria out of Italy; he really thought the Ottoman state was past redemption. Its partition between interested nations seemed perfectly reasonable; it would contribute to lessening European tensions. To these ideas Palmerston was resolutely opposed, and the Emperor did not force the issue, although he never allowed it to rest for long. Napoleon promoted Balkan nationalism at the expense of the Sultan; sent troops to the rescue of the Christian minority in Syria endangered by Druze and Moslem violence through Ottoman weakness and connivance; and talked openly of breaking the links between Constantinople and the Moslem tributary states in North Africa as a step towards their acquisition by France and Britain. As he did elsewhere, he took note of the British response, usually one of alarm, and sought an understanding. It would not be true to describe Palmerston as Turcophil, in the sense of his collaborator and sometime critic, A. H. Layard, a founder of the Ottoman Bank and an able Parliamentary under-secretary at the Foreign Office from 1861. He did not possess the faith in a reforming Turkish nationalism that his successive ambassadors to the Porte, Lord Stratford de Redcliffe and Sir Henry Bulwer, professed. By this period, Palmerston's defence of the Turk had become a holding operation, essentially, against Russia and France; with an eye, always, on political and religious feeling in Britain which he knew might override the country's concern for her strategic and economic stake in the ailing empire of the Caliph. The succession of a reactionary ruler, not at all amenable to management by Britain and her ambassador, would probably bring on the apprehended Franco-Russian conquest and division of the spoils. The British government would be powerless to intervene in a war arising from the flagrant oppression of Christian minorities.[3]

Westernization was, then, the means of saving Turkey from herself and from her enemies, and more urgent than it had been in the days of Sultan Mahmud II (1808–39), to whom Palmerston looked back with a certain regret. The British were as eager to foster a modern national consciousness in the Turks as they were afraid of doing so in India. Not the least of the obstacles they confronted in their efforts to work out the client empire's salvation was the rapacity of their own countrymen. In the early 1860s Bulwer told Layard that British merchant houses in Constantinople were borrowing at 5 per cent in the London money market to lend it at 30 per

cent to the Ottoman government.[4] Such ruthless exploitation was bound to
end in the ruin of some of the speculators. Bulwer was unwilling to reveal
all he knew to the public: 'Turkish finances...are all in all both as to
Turkey...and to those...who wish to support her.'[5] As chancellor of the
exchequer in the second Palmerston cabinet, Gladstone had to overcome
his hostility to the oppressor of Eastern Christians, and help with the
wearisome endeavour to transform the fiscal habits of the Sultan and his
ministers. 'It would appear', he wrote acidly in a memorandum of 1863,
'...that the Ottoman mind has not as yet ascertained the true meaning of
the words surplus and deficiency...' In so far as the Turks understood their
combination of old ways and new promises, their conduct attained the
height of budgetary irresponsibility, diverting to normal expenditure the
proceeds of a loan for another purpose.[6] He, like Bulwer, was appalled at
what might happen in the event of a financial crisis in Turkey, when
everything would come out. France, with her numerous investors in
Ottoman loans, would have good cause to turn on the British who had
traditionally taken the lead in striving for order and improvement in the
Sultan's administration of his revenues.[7]

Gladstone favoured the appointment of a virtual overseer, 'a competent
person from England, who would have no administrative powers whatever,
but whose word would be...final in this country upon any question of fact
relating to the Ottoman revenues'.[8] It was a development of the principle
involved in the advisory mission of Lord Hobart and M. H. Foster, civil
servants from the Board of Trade and the Treasury, sent to inspire British
investors with confidence in the large loan of 1862.[9] Gladstone's suggestion
would have considerably strengthened British influence in the affairs of
the empire, so dependent was Turkey on foreign loans and the City of
London. He had been called on in May 1863 to answer Cobden, in
Palmerston's absence, when the radical delivered an effective indictment of
British protective intervention in Turkey as utterly wasteful of the public's
subscriptions to Ottoman loans, for more serious reasons than the
apparently ineradicable Turkish disregard for financial probity. Almost
certainly, Britain could not prevent an uprising, fatal to the empire, of the
Christian majority of the Sultan's subjects: Cobden considered 'the wisest
thing...is...so to arrange matters that the civil war in Turkey shall not
spread...'. To clinch his argument for leaving the Turks to their deserts, he
read out a letter received by the Secretary to the Society for the
Propagation of the Gospel on the depravity of the race. Gladstone dealt
with him by claiming that the government was equally committed to non-
intervention: 'Only we must understand what is meant by non-
intervention.' 'Let us firmly adhere to the ancient policy', he said, of aiding
Turkey to resist 'foreign intrigue and...aggression.' The real alternative
was to head a crusade against the Ottoman empire; a course sure to do

more harm than the one he was defending.[10] He informed Bulwer privately
that he had been unable to speak '*up* to the rather sanguine tone of Lord
Palmerston' on Turkey, present and future: but the differences between
him and the prime minister were clearly slight, despite the statement in his
diary that he had spoken 'reluctantly'. '...an attack on you is an attack on
the Government', he assured Bulwer.[11]

Unlike his predecessor, Stratford de Redcliffe, Bulwer was not free from
any suspicion of using his position at Constantinople for personal profit.[12]
But the Turks trusted him; and he went far towards identifying himself with
them in defiance, finally, of British public opinion. His intimacy with the
Ottoman statesman, Aali Pasha, allowed him to put forward unpalatable
truths without great risk of offence. He warned the Pasha of the imminent
risk of a damning exposé of Turkey's fiscal ills and the causes: 'on fait sortir
le manque de bonne foi...les déficits perpetuels, les dépenses inutiles; la
corruption des employés, etc., etc.' He implored his correspondent – for it
was late in the day – to lose no time in setting on foot a scheme of reform
'*assez radicale*' to establish Turkish credit on foundations 'réels et
rationels'.[13] He thought it prudent to vindicate his criticized attitude to the
Turk in letters to that influential gossip at home, Abraham Hayward: 'I
don't really care about the East, save when English interests are combined
with it, and I am then for maintaining those interests where they are
vital – *coûte que coûte*.' He realized the Turks's ability to surprise their many
enemies in Europe who had written them off too soon: 'they don't take into
account that the whole of the Turkish people are as one man, and that their
fighting power *quoad* the races they are intermingled with are [sic] those of
wolves or dogs amidst sheep'. '...all our policy', he added, 'is comprised
in a few words. There is no race settled in those countries who can govern
if the Turks can't, and we are not at present prepared to have any foreign
race govern here.'[14] There was much more to British policy. Malmesbury
had replaced Stratford de Redcliffe by Bulwer to please Napoleon:[15] but
the new ambassador, although personally acceptable to the French
emperor, continued where the old left off.

In modernizing Turkey, Stratford de Redcliffe held, '*a force from without
to keep up a steady...pressure...can alone constitute* – if even *that* can – a
durable and efficient *principe moteur*'. The drawback was the absolute
requirement for Russia's co-operation, which he spelled out to Clarendon.[16]
His ascendancy over Sultan Abdul Mejid could not compensate for French
dissent from his aims. On his official farewell visit, after Bulwer had
succeeded him, Stratford de Redcliffe wrote an important, and pessimistic,
state paper. 'There is no magic in diplomacy' observed this eminent
diplomat. He had obtained from Abdul Mejid in 1856 the Hatti-
Humayum, a charter of liberties admitting Christians to equality with
Moslems in the empire without diluting the Sultan's autocracy in other

respects. The ambassador's vision of the former embraced, besides the correction of manifest abuses, 'the fusion of classes, the development of resources, liberty of conscience and improved intercourse with foreigners irrespective of religion'. Outside 'the department of material improvements' in which Western businessmen were actively negotiating for railways, telegraphs and loans, progress was disappointing. He recurred to the indispensability of European direction: but he saw that 'to be available it must be consistent in spirit, and, as far as possible, in form, with the rights of national independence'.[17] Bulwer took on from that point: the Turks evinced 'an insuperable repugnance' to Western supervision, which he ascribed to their permanent irritation at the Capitulations investing foreigners with the privileges of extraterritoriality. That regime increasingly undermined government in the host country, as more traders, concessionaires and missionaries from the West joined members of Eastern Churches, natives of the empire and immigrants, who in one way or another contrived to remove their cases from Ottoman to foreign jurisdiction. Bulwer advocated a gradual modification of the Capitulations to a sceptical Russell: 'The Turkish Government is called independent… there is not the smallest Vice-Consul who does not pretend to control it… in the simplest action of life a foreign hand intervenes to prevent the national authority from … administering justice according to its own usages and laws.' The least of South American republics and the King of the Sandwich Islands were not so humiliated. The objective of a Turkey 'sufficiently Europeanized to look Europe fairly in the face' would remain incapable of achievement unless she were free to employ Westerners on terms impossible under the Capitulations.[18]

Russell was unmoved: the Capitulations, he replied, 'rest on the principle that Turkish rule and Turkish justice are so barbarous that exceptional privileges are required'.[19] These exchanges between foreign secretary and ambassador were published, leaving no one in any doubt that Bulwer's strenuous championship of Turkey did not accurately represent thinking at home, inside and outside the government. Palmerston was a good deal less hopeful than Gladstone imagined. In conversation with Napoleon he had naturally depicted the Ottoman empire in the best possible light.[20] He summed up Abdul Mejid on his death in 1861 as 'a good-hearted and weak-minded man who was riding two horses to the goal of Perdition, his…life and that of his empire…luckily his…life won the race'. Reform and progress existed chiefly 'on paper'. His expectations of the new Sultan, Abdul Aziz, were little higher.[21] Russell deplored Abdul Aziz's indulgence in sensual pleasures, and fixed his hopes on Aali Pasha: 'He must endeavour to save the Sultan from his insidious flatterers and pimps.'[22] The foreign secretary simultaneously admonished Bulwer against engaging with too much vigour in the struggles around the throne for ministerial office at the inception of the reign. Palmerston stepped in to correct Russell's ignorance of Great Power diplomacy at the Porte: 'Your caution is very just in itself; but in a place like Constantinople one is sure that somebody or other will be trying to influence such changes...the Frenchman...the Russian...some Turkish intriguer...All we can really wish is that our ambassador should use his influence for the purpose of getting good and honest men employed, if such...are to be found.'[23] Bulwer, even with his venal Greek mistress and debts, was a good choice, bringing to the post conviction and skill.

Palmerston, while upholding him, conceded to the Greeks in November 1862 that if the Turkish empire crumbled they might expect to gain, provided they first put their own house in order.[24] For Bulwer considered the young, small and disorderly Greek kingdom's probable destiny was to break up into statelets: 'Athens and Sparta minus the slaves and the literature.'[25] To consolidate the Greek monarchy under a new dynasty following the revolution of 1862, Palmerston would have liked Turkey to cede Thessaly and Epirus, or to hold out the prospect of cession at some future time. A less dissatisfied and more stable Greece, he reasoned, might refrain from making war for fifty years on Turkey, the hereditary enemy.[26] He was soon compelled to explain just where Britain stood in response to an enquiry on this aspect of the Greek succession made by one of the stronger candidates, the Queen's brother-in-law, Ernest of Coburg, who wanted to be king of a bigger Greece. '...if the question means', wrote Palmerston, 'are we prepared to help Greece forcibly or by revolutionary intrigues to detach...portions of the Ottoman empire...such is not our intention.' Whoever assumed the Greek crown lost by Otto of Bavaria must be neither pro-Russian nor pro-French: 'Either...would be a...certain danger to Turkey and to the peace of Europe...'[27] The French Empress pushed the claims of a candidate, the Duke of Leuchtenberg, the descendant of Napoleon's stepson Eugene Beauharnais and nephew of the Tsar; but the Emperor did not suggest a prince unacceptable to the British, recommending instead the Coburg – not Duke Ernest – whom Queen Victoria and her ministers unsuccessfully tried to persuade of his duty to the family and to Europe. The Greeks' desire for a British prince was such that they proceeded to elect the Queen's second son, Alfred. Britain met their importunity with an unalterable refusal, although Palmerston had had Alfred in mind for the job. Filling it entailed a lengthy British survey, verging on the absurd, of Continental candidates, one after another of whom was found to be personally or politically unsuitable.[28] The process held the critical attention of *The Times* City page on behalf of investors in Greek bonds. Greek motives were hardly less financial than political. In arrears to their bondholders, the Greeks were after a further loan; and they looked to draw Britain away from Turkey.[29] Accordingly, they took the first

Glücksburg monarch – the Princess of Wales's very youthful brother – with a territorial sweetener in the shape of the Ionian Islands ruled by Britain since the Napoleonic wars. Neither the bondholders nor the Greeks, it should be said, got their money.[30]

Napoleon behaved helpfully over Greece, letting the British attempt to instil some idea of responsibility through the medium of a selected 'liberal' king. The Emperor thought it a futile undertaking 'when constitutional principles are applied to people who have no moral principles and no education'.[31] He distinguished, however, between constitutionalism and nationalism with a clarity that did not come easily to the British. Political backwardness did not preclude the resurgence of subject peoples in the Balkans as Turkish power waned and Western notions of nationality and its rights had an impact on their traditional leaders. The Austrians, nervous of consequent unrest among the Rumanian and Slav minorities they ruled, sided with the Turks. Prince Metternich at Paris told Vienna that there was no changing Napoleon's policies in that quarter: he could not withhold the support of his 'sympathy and convictions' from the Christian peoples who invoked his protection.[32] Russia's historic involvement in Ottoman Europe was much greater: it obliged her unyielding domestic absolutism to indulge the propensity of her co-religionists and fellow Slavs to adopt constitutions that were liberal in appearance, if not in operation. After the Crimean war, she worked in the Turkish dominions as she did generally, within the limits imposed by her defeat. The experienced Russian ambassador in London, Baron Brünnow, approached Palmerston in November 1862 to remind him that only in Persia and Turkey were British and Russian interests possibly antagonistic, and to discover how he saw them. The prime minister had no complaints about Russia in Persia; but he was outspoken on Brünnow's dissimulation as to Turkey: Russian agents were undermining the Sultan's authority and their government was encouraging every rebel. Arms were reaching the rebellious principality of Servia in such quantities via Russia that the supply could only be an imperial initiative. Palmerston referred pointedly to Russia's internal difficulties, 'enough to engross the whole attention of her government', and to her comparative isolation internationally.[33]

He boasted prematurely in a minute on a despatch from the ambassador at St Petersburg; the comment lays bare in its crude exultation the significance for him of the diplomatic battle over Turkey in Europe: 'The French and Russians are no doubt deeply mortified and... provoked at the signal failure of their anti-Turkish intrigues in Servia, Montenegro and the Herzegovine and at the success of English policy'.[34] Russell in a declaration sent to Bulwer and printed in the Blue Book on Servian affairs announced the presence throughout the European part of the Ottoman dominions of 'a conspiracy, scarcely concealed... to substitute... a Sclave... [or] a Greek

Empire…all look to plunder…power…revenge, and…bloodshed'. He summoned the Great Powers that had guaranteed the integrity of Turkey at the Congress of Paris to honour their commitment.[35] Greeks and Orthodox Slavs, both, dreamed of driving the Turk back into Asia and of enthroning the Tsar or a Greek ruler at Constantinople. While the dream was eternal, no concerted enterprise was practicable. Instead, there was a local erosion of Ottoman overlordship, accompanied by rising discontent in directly ruled provinces. The Christian principalities in the Balkans were in a particularly favourable position. 'Servia governs itself as completely as Belgium',[36] Bulwer assured Hayward, with some exaggeration. A tributary state, Servia also had Turkish soldiery and dependent civilians in Belgrade and certain other towns, under treaty arrangements prohibiting military interference in the country. France and Russia put themselves behind Servia's resolve to be rid of these vestiges of Turkish occupation. The intensified friction resulted in a crisis when the Ottoman garrison bombarded Christian Belgrade in 1862. All the British and Austrians were able to secure, in the event, was the retention of four of Turkey's garrisons after the evacuation of her civilian population. As for Montenegro, she had stubbornly resisted Turkish domination in her mountain fastness, inflicting a major reverse on Ottoman forces at Grahovo in 1857. Malmesbury had expostulated vehemently with France for backing the Montenegrins. He was afraid their success would set the Balkans ablaze. If that were to happen Britain could not interfere:[37] it was one thing to protect the Ottoman empire from France and Russia, and quite another to go to her aid against a general revolt of the Sultan's Christian subjects. Palmerston entertained the same fear.

The popular nature of Balkan nationalism, compared with the aristocratic liberalism uppermost in Italy, disturbed British policy-makers. Russell's published despatch to the chargé d'affaires at St Petersburg in August 1862 warned the Russians that they were playing with fire. Michael Obrenovic, the Prince of Servia, and those about him wished, so Russell believed, to take the principality into 'a great Confederacy of the Danube…to rise from the ruins of surrounding empires' – Ottoman and Hapsburg. 'Russia ought not to be indifferent', he went on '…it was not in the interest of any of the Great Powers to favour this democratic movement.'[38] Bulwer, from his knowledge of them, did not credit the Christians of the Balkans with the capacity for union: they hated each other more than the Turks whose rule was preferable to anarchy.[39] Not inhumanity, therefore, but a humane realism accounted for Palmerston's satisfaction that the Turk had mastered a Serb rebellion in Herzegovina, and for the refusal to contemplate Montenegrin access to the sea and easier communication with Turkey's enemies. Montenegro, he observed, was described by the British proponent of the unacceptable suggestion as barren and unproductive; she could not make the pretence of developing trade.[40]

Palmerston had been ready to see Wallachia and Moldavia, the Ottoman tributary states in emergent Rumania, transferred to Austria. That was in the context of large territorial gains for Turkey elsewhere, all part of his Crimean war aims; but the idea kept its attraction. The Austrians in Rumania would be a serious obstacle for Russia when, rather than if, she resumed her drive against Turkey. Napoleon espoused the cause of Rumanian union, subject to the retention of Ottoman suzerainty, before the Congress of Paris, where it was decided to establish an international commission that should reorganize government in the principalities. France and Russia worked for union; Britain and Austria sided with Turkey in resisting it. Thus encouraged, the Turks manipulated a consultative vote in July 1857 to produce an anti-unionist majority in Moldavia. The British ambassador, Stratford de Redcliffe, incited them to it, since the end, preserving Ottoman authority at an exceptionally vulnerable point, justified the means.[41] Napoleon seized the chance to expose Britain's weakness with India in revolt: 'completely spoilt by...adulation...from Continental potentates...it galls him to see that we do not equally obey his behests', warned Cowley from Paris.[42] Following France's lead, Russia, Prussia and Sardinia severed diplomatic relations with the Porte over the elections in Moldavia. It was outwardly a striking demonstration of Europe's hostility to the Turk and irritation with Britain and Austria for befriending him. Russia and Prussia were, however, scarcely credible champions of an oppressed nationality to French and British eyes. Napoleon's orchestration of this European movement did not conceal its superficial nature, certainly not from himself. 'He knows...that a rupture with us would shake his own throne', advised Cowley. The Emperor came to Britain, angry to learn that Palmerston did not welcome his advent.[43] At Osborne in August, conferring with the British prime minister and foreign secretary, Napoleon 'utterly scouted' the imputed switch to a Russian in place of a British alliance at the centre of his intricate policies.[44]

He meant to secure Rumanian union, while saving Britain's face. 'We might undoubtedly have staved off the Union', Clarendon explained to the ambassador at Vienna, 'but Russia and France would have stirred the Principalities into open rebellion, and there is no knowing what the consequences might have been of that.' The Moldavian elections were to be annulled and the '*cooked*' roll on which they had been held revised, steps to which the Sultan duly consented.[45] Although the 'compromise' reached on the main issue was deliberately not spelled out, Palmerston's version of it for the succeeding Tory ministry in 1858 showed how far the British yielded: 'we said we should be willing to agree to any common administrative arrangement, which without trenching upon the political separation of the two provinces might conduce to the general interest of the people of each...'. In return, Palmerston and Clarendon understood that Napoleon was pledged to the maintenance of separate hospodars, native rulers, in Moldavia and Wallachia. 'I am quite certain that when these things are brought to the attention of the Emperor, he will remember them', Palmerston assured Malmesbury, going on to recount the French objection to a signed record and full public knowledge of what had been talked through.[46] This informal and secretive agreement provided the basis for an international conference at Paris, from May to August next year. The distinct Moldavian and Wallachian legislatures under the resulting constitution lost little time in electing the same hospodar, an ardent admirer of Napoleon, Alexander Cuza – a proceeding excluded by Osborne but within the letter, though not the spirit, of Paris. The Emperor's duplicity was transparent; but it cannot have been unexpected. In 1856 he would not hear of French 'influence and ascendancy' when discussing the Principalities with Austria's ambassador. After the war of 1859, he offered, in conversation with Metternich, to put a Hapsburg in Cuza's place: 'an Archduke might be invited by the Rumanians, if the matter was handled carefully', he blandly suggested to the astonished diplomat. Austria, he indicated, would be getting compensation for recent losses in Italy and a strategic position in anticipation of Turkey's collapse.[47]

On receiving the news from Osborne, Lord Wodehouse, the British minister at St Petersburg, argued that Rumanian unity promised to erect a national barrier to Russian expansion; and would be compatible with continued nominal subjection to the Porte.[48] This approach to the question appealed widely, to Napoleon and to Gladstone, who pleaded for it in a Commons debate of May 1858, unaware of the extent to which real union had been conceded at Osborne.[49] For the secrecy surrounding that agreement was really more helpful to Palmerston and Bulwer than to imperial France.

Malmesbury's Toryism could not resist the thought that Palmerston must have felt 'a bitter pang' in bowing to the demand for fresh elections in Moldavia.[50] To have revealed, besides, the significant concession of principle on union would have been a grave embarrassment to the government. By the time the Tories entered office in February 1858 their eagerness to conciliate the Emperor exceeded anything that Palmerston had ever shown, fearing as they did Napoleon's legitimate displeasure with their tactics on the Conspiracy to Murder Bill before and after they turned the Liberals out. What seems to have happened at Osborne is that Palmerston undertook a diplomatic exercise in conjunction with Napoleon, Walewski and Persigny rather than a competitive negotiation. According to the prime minister and Clarendon, the Emperor besought them not to break silence on his retreat from advocating complete union of the Principalities, alleging his fear of the reaction in France. What he ensured was the freedom to persist in moving towards his aim without so discomfiting the British at any stage that they would take serious offence.

The claim of Palmerston and his colleague that, in the former's words to Malmesbury, they had 'gained a substance while the Emperor gained only an appearance' was hard to believe from their own detailed accounts of the meeting.[51] 'I confess I never could look upon the question of "Union" or "non-Union" as possessing all the importance attached to it', replied Wodehouse calmly to Clarendon's typical letter, at once boastful and alarmist.[52] That was true; but Palmerston had to think of Turkish morale and British public opinion, and Napoleon III's sudden visit to Osborne confirmed his estimate of the alliance even when Britain was distracted by the uprising in India.

French designs on Ottoman territories in the Levant and North Africa aroused in Palmerston a determination to thwart them that had no parallel in his handling of the Principalities; those Christian tributary states were peripheral, in every sense. The landing of French troops at Beirut in 1860 to succour the Maronites of the Lebanon and the Christians of the Syrian hinterland was effected under a convention to which the five Great Powers of Europe were parties, Britain reluctantly. 'I am heartily glad to have got the French out of Syria, and a hard job it was', commented Palmerston on their withdrawal.[53] He had no hesitation in attributing the outbreak of bloody fighting in the Lebanon between the Maronites, Uniate Catholics, protected by France, and the Druze, whom England favoured, to the intrigues of the French. Admonishing Cowley for his failure to penetrate the Emperor's intentions, he told him that France had supplied arms to the Maronites with one of two objects in view: a victory over the Druze for their clients, or a pretext for intervention should they lose. 'The French never anticipated', he allowed, '...a catastrophe...it would have been difficult for us...hearing of such atrocities to have absolutely refused consent to the French expedition.'[54] The British member of the Five Power commission that went out in the wake of the French army, Lord Dufferin, was appalled by the sight of the Christian quarter in Damascus, the scene of arson, pillage and massacre: 'Such a monument of human wickedness and sorrow I have never beheld.' The Turkish authorities had let their soldiers participate in the destruction of life and property, as they had let the Druze sweep through Maronite country, killing thousands, with the difference that the Christians of Damascus were an inoffensive, largely defenceless community. At Dufferin's insistence, the high-ranking Turks sentenced to death for complicity in the slaughter at Damascus were shot. But British ministers would not endorse his plan for giving Syria a generous measure of independence from Constantinople under a virtual substitute for the Sultan, in whose appointment Britain and the other Powers would naturally have a say.[55]

It was not the business of Britain's commissioner to weaken the Ottoman empire further. Policy and his marked inclination coincided in the

Lebanon, where the trouble had begun and would begin again unless the administration of the area were satisfactorily reconstructed. Acknowledging their 'most horrible crimes' Dufferin felt for the Druze. The Maronites' Catholicism, even more than their enjoyment of French patronage, set the British firmly against them. '...the tyranny of a half-barbarous, Maronite...necessarily...a mere puppet in the hands of a fanatical priesthood', objected Dufferin to France's proposal for vesting . the authoritarian rule of the Lebanon in one of her protégés; who though chosen by the Porte was to be irremovable except with the sanction of the Five Powers. France and Britain compromised: the Lebanon came under a Christian governor, but one brought in from outside, immediately subject to Constantinople, and removable after three years.[56] The rest of the Turkish province of Syria lay beyond the scope of this arrangement. Napoleon was evidently speaking the truth when he told Cowley in January 1861 that while he wanted to order his troops home, he could not evacuate until some sort of government was established.[57] His foreign minister, Thouvenel, asked the ambassador in London whether Palmerston understood that should the Christians again be the victims of atrocities, the future of the Ottoman empire would be in doubt: '...l'indignation de l'Europe l'emportera sur tous les calculs de la diplomatie'.[58] Wodehouse, now Parliamentary under-secretary at the Foreign Office, had expressed, when in Russia, a common British distaste for Eastern Christianity, Orthodox as well as Catholic, which was an element in his country's cool reaction to the bloodshed in the Lebanon and Damascus: 'I wonder they can find anyone not a born Russian, or Greek, willing to conform to the ludicrous mummeries and superstition of "Orthodoxy"', he had written.[59] Britain's aggressive Protestantism thus helped to separate her from the other Great Powers, among whom Protestant Prussia treated her sizeable minority of Catholics with a consideration usually absent from British policy towards Ireland and the Irish. Yet the French were genuinely surprised by Palmerston's attitude to their salutary action in the Near East. 'La passion que Lord Palmerston met á cette question tient de la sauvagerie', remarked Thouvenel, contrasting the prime minister's intemperate suspicions with Cowley's quite different response.[60] Palmerston thought Cowley was in the grip of 'a moral...French influenza'; and gave himself credit for having prevented the occupation of Syria by the French.[61]

If Palmerston was too distrustful of Napoleon III, even to the extent of sometimes making himself ridiculous in the eyes of the Emperor and his ministers, he did not err similarly in his reading of French national character and traditions. 'This policy is not of his invention', observed the British prime minister of Napoleon's long-term ideas for the Ottoman territories; 'it was that of his uncle, and of the Bourbons, and will be that of all who follow...'[62] The Emperor learnt from Algeria the enormous demands, financial and military, of a conquest which, as he described it to Cowley, was 'not a colony...but an independent Kingdom...nobody knew how to govern'.[63] He had to reckon with a feeling in his army exemplified by the young officers who asserted to Lady Dufferin that the French force sent to the Near East meant to prolong its stay, if necessary by stirring up the animosities it had been directed to repress.[64] Napoleon had no intention of falling out with Britain over an empire generally believed to be nearing collapse from within. Besides, on the Moslem shores of the Mediterranean, and especially in the Levant, Britain had the naval capacity to prevent, or at least to impede, French operations. The continued connexion of Tunis, Tripoli and Egypt with Constantinople as tributary states was very important, if not essential, to the Sultan. The maintenance of that link depended on the superiority of the British fleet in waters of such strategic value that the Duke of Somerset, in a memorandum accompanying the navy estimates of 1860, considered the Channel and Mediterranean stations to be, in effect, one.[65] No matter what he said to the contrary and how often, Palmerston conceded, as in a letter of January 1865 to Layard on the subject of France in the Mediterranean, that 'the French Government, though bent upon encroachment and acquisition, will always wish to avoid a rupture with England unless it be unavoidably forced upon them'. Resistance in kind to France's pushful diplomacy in the Sultan's North African tributaries did not, therefore, carry with it a serious risk of armed conflict; and was imperative if French diplomats and entrepreneurs were to be kept from establishing their country's dominance, sure of approval from the Emperor and his government, whatever Paris said in deprecation of their zeal on receiving British complaints. 'Our business', Palmerston would have the Foreign Office realize, 'consequently ought to be to unravel their plots, to see through their intrigues...to defeat their schemes by counteraction steadily and systematically applied...'[66]

French influence had been strong in Egypt since the days of Mehemet Ali; and the memory of the first Napoleon's occupation remained in Palmerston's mind. De Lesseps's Suez Canal project aroused his liveliest fears. These were, however, quietened, although by no means dispelled, as the result of firm denials that France wanted to detach Egypt from Turkey, and of a most reassuring talk with Said Pasha, the Egyptian ruler, when he came to London in 1862. Palmerston was apprehensive lest Said, struggling to meet obligations to mainly French capitalists, should have gone so far as to threaten the viability of his state by the economies made; another way of exchanging vestigial subjection to the Porte for complete dependence on France.[67] Said's explanations were lengthy and satisfactory: he was not pro-French; Napoleon III had never raised the question of independence from Turkey with him; Egypt would be out of debt by 1864; and, finally, he was not afraid of colonization by the French in a climate unsuited to white labour and in the face of the fellaheen's objection – insuperable, he was convinced – to working for Europeans.[68] Said was too optimistic about his finances, while Palmerston did not cease to worry over the Suez Canal. It seemed to him an undertaking of such magnitude that it would very likely lead to a French ascendancy,[69] whether or not the waterway was actually constructed, that would endanger Britain's two enduring interests in Egypt, freedom to trade and freedom of transit.[70] His anxiety was not baseless: Said had admitted to being more deeply involved in de Lesseps's enterprise than he wished.[71] The undertaking as a means to French domination of Egypt was what Palmerston feared, not the canal itself, in the commercial success of which he did not believe.

The key to Britain's ability to sustain the Ottoman empire was financial power. Without the City Palmerstonian policy in the East would not have been possible. Looking back, during the Eastern crises of the mid-1870s, Lord Salisbury described that policy as 'introducing the Turk with a sort of quasi-guarantee to our stock markets and then leaving him to his own devices'. He felt that Britain should have pressed the services of the ablest Englishmen on Turkey after the Crimean war, and taken a stronger line with France, Russia, and indeed the other Great Powers who exploited Ottoman weakness and the Capitulations.[72] As he tended to do before he learnt better at the Foreign Office, Salisbury overrated Britain's strength, especially under Palmerston. It had not been open to her to behave with sufficient forcefulness against the Powers. Britain had bowed to their concerted action, less Austria, in the dispute over the Rumanian principalities in 1857; when the differing Anglo-French approaches to Turkey came close to bringing about a diplomatic breakdown between the two Western Powers in that quarter. Thinking that time was on her side, France did not give the fate of the Ottoman empire a high priority. Her various preoccupations, with the state of her finances, with Poland, with her Mexican adventure and with the Roman question disposed her to be accommodating, while Russia had become less unfriendly, for the moment, distracted by internal problems. The field was comparatively clear, wrote Bulwer later, for the politicians and financiers in his country whose calculations were based on the alignment of Ottoman and British interests. These men knew what the Turkish minister must understand: 'le Public chez nous est maintenant le Gouvernement'; and investors were part of the public.[73]

While Turkey had her strong supporters, as well as her enemies, in Britain, Bulwer overstepped the mark when he asserted of the Porte that 'Looking at things reasonably, it is but just to observe that this Government, at this time, is about the most tolerant in Europe' in the behaviour of the ruling religion to others.[74] His moral relativism incensed the missionary lobby already upset by his opposition, on political grounds, to the proselytization of Moslems in the heart of the Caliph's own territory. But no one could pretend that Russia held out even such limited early promise of liberalization as Turkey offered. The half-Russian Sidney Herbert confirmed from his special knowledge that 'Russia is not in these days a possible ally for us, in the sense in which you use the word when talking of a French alliance'. For him, regretfully, as for Palmerston, who had no such feeling for Russia, she obstructed 'the progress of good government in Europe'.[75] Gladstone noted with amusement that his *Letters to Lord Aberdeen* of 1851 condemning the misrule of an absolute monarch were still banned by the Russian censorship nearly three years after the kingdom of Italy was an established fact.[76] Palmerston was caught between his appreciation of Russian power, valued as a check on Napoleonic ambition, and his personal and the national aversion to Russia, which the treatment of Poland brought out again when the Poles rose in 1863. On the one hand, he reminded Russell in April that year of 'the feeling at this moment strongest in the middle and lower classes in this country...intense interest in favour of Poland'. On the other hand, he had begun by resisting the idea of a formal protest to the Russians by Britain and France, or by Britain alone: 'These poor Poles are almost sure to be cut...and shot down...to have their homes and villages burnt, any representation to be useful to them must be friendly and informal.'[77]

He was not willing, as he had been in Italy shortly before, to see the treaties of Vienna set aside. In them, he explained to the aristocratic Polish exiles who sought his help, lay the sole effective source of international assistance they could hope for.[78] There was provision at Vienna not simply for the separate kingdom of Poland under the Tsar but also for a constitution recognizing the Western outlook of its political class. The constitution had been abrogated after the previous Polish revolt in 1830–31, when Palmerston was first foreign secretary and showed, in the words of a cabinet critic, 'squeamishness...if not sheer pusillanimity' in opposing British diplomatic support for rebels.[79] British public opinion had been too much for him then. It now drove the Palmerston government from a declared inability to tell the Tsar how he should govern his subjects to an official request for return to the Polish constitution of 1815 and an amnesty. This move was followed by action jointly with Austria and France, seeking the territorial enlargement of Congress Poland through the inclusion of wide historically Polish tracts in Russia, together with a detailed agenda of reforms for a conference of the Powers on the kingdom.[80] The Poles' military performance, and their claims for it, gave some reason to think that Russia might be induced to negotiate, particularly if the liberalism stirring in Russian society affected her army. As it was, Palmerston indulged in further diplomacy to keep up Britain's reputation in her own eyes and abroad: 'The only thing for us to do seems to be to make such proposals...as we can...with credit to ourselves...' He did not really move any distance from the policy indicated to the Commons ahead of the revolt.[81]

On that occasion, he had compared his ministry's careful indifference to a recent thronged political funeral in Dublin with the Russians' authoritarian over-reaction to a similar event in Warsaw: 'it would have been an act of folly on the part of the Government to have interfered... In the same way the funeral at Warsaw might have been permitted to pass...quietly.' To this counsel for the Russians, he added advice for the Poles and their numerous British sympathizers. Russia after the Crimea was going through 'a great social and political change...a change which cannot be single'. He looked on Alexander II's emancipation of the serfs as perhaps the boldest social reform ever undertaken with such speed. 'Does any man believe', he asked, 'that...emancipation...must not, sooner or later, lead to some extension of political privileges and power...to the Russian nation?'[82] The Poles might expect to benefit when the time came. The insurrection of next January and the Russian reply to it elicited Palmerston's confirmation in Parliament of his Polish sentiments. He also pleaded for comprehension of the Tsar's unenviable position in Poland, 'an inheritance of triumphant wrong...so fatal a bequest'. The passion for liberty in men was matched by that – 'I doubt whether it is not as strong' – for oppressing another nationality. This latter emotion held Russia fast and, necessarily, her ruler.[83] His arguments commanded the House, which was, he reported, 'unanimously Polish', but swayed by 'prudence as to taking matters out of the hands of...Government'. The Tories did not differ from the prime minister.[84] Cobden, typically, scouted the notion of a resort to force, putting Russia as a supplier of grain to Britain above the fate of Poland.[85] The need was to persuade the public that ministers had done their best for the Poles, short of war. Asked to speak by Palmerston, Gladstone joined in expounding the uncomfortable nature of international politics. Poland reborn would no doubt be 'a great safeguard and a great glory to Europe': but the amputation of Russian provinces required a courage wanting in the British administration of the day and any likely successor. He sought to refute the analogy between Poland and Italy by arguments which he had to admit 'would not materially edify...us': no ministry ought to commit itself except in a righteous cause; and no cause was really righteous for governments, 'unless the objects contemplated are practicable and attainable'. It must be faced that long-established political wrongs were too often irremediable: 'Italy...has perhaps been a peculiarly happy case.'[86]

Russia was convalescent during Palmerston's second premiership. Her recovery and growth until she came to resemble ancient Rome in extent and influence – the Muscovite dream – appeared unstoppable to Palmerston, always provided that she was able to build an 'enlightened' fiscal structure. Then 'mistress of all Asia except British India whenever she chooses to take it...her command of men...enormous, her pecuniary means gigantic...her power of transporting men over great distances most formidable', she could be restrained from westward aggression only by a powerful Germany centred on the Prussian state. The peril, a commonplace like the defence envisaged, was acquiring a fresh seriousness with the post-Crimean reconstruction and expansion of Russia.[87] A few months previously Palmerston had sent a cross minute to the Foreign Office on Russia's steady penetration of Central Asia. The repeated denials of territorial ambition issuing from St Petersburg did not merit the slightest confidence.[88] It was the denials rather than the fact of expansion that irritated him. Britain might escape Russia's domination, as she did France's, behind her navy. Palmerston observed the modernization of the Russian Baltic fleet, and brought it into the constantly renewed discussion of relative naval strengths.[89] He responded cautiously when the king of Sweden and his heir, visiting Britain in 1861, begged for an annual cruise in the Baltic by even a single gunboat. The Swedish royalties contrasted the Royal Navy's absence with the regular calls of Russian warships at their ports. The pressing request received a temporizing answer. The Swedes' ambition, to add Denmark to Norway, which had been handed over to them in 1814, was discussed but it was not one that the British wished to countenance by any gesture. Nor was it expedient to encourage Sweden in her desire, also put to Palmerston by Charles XV and his brother, to retrieve Finland from Russia.[90] Nevertheless, the prime minister did eventually ask his first lord of the Admiralty for a frigate and a couple of smaller vessels to afford the 'alleged...great moral support' against Russia.[91] He and his ministers expected Russia's influence everywhere to remain unfavourable to constitutionalism, whatever hopes to the contrary he might publicly voice.[92] Moreover, the character of the political ferment that very quickly developed under Tsar Alexander II deprived it of much appeal to those British observers who understood how little social basis there was in Russia for the liberalism they knew. '...it is frightful to consider the immediate results of a revolution in a country organized as this is', Lord Granville had written from Moscow in 1856.[93]

The disturbances of 1861 in Russia's state universities presented *The Times* with an opportunity to comment on the reasons why 'learning... freedom...any other characteristic of university life' were compatible in Britain with the conservative politics of Oxford and Cambridge. There students were 'some of the most contented specimens of a contented nation...taken from well-to-do and satisfied classes'. '...it is the blessing of this country', the newspaper went on, 'that such classes, instead of being confined to a caste of nobles, pervade society from top to bottom.'[94]

Idealistic members of the British landed class were not, therefore, driven to advocate the sacrifice of their social interests in order to free and elevate the people.[95] Differences of that sort partly account for the tensions close to the surface of Anglo-Russian diplomacy. Russell's broadcast despatch of 27 October 1860 celebrating the forcible unification of Italy as a 'revolution... conducted with singular temper and forbearance' gave deep offence.[96] Baron Brünnow said contemptuously, and mistakenly: 'Ce n'est pas de la diplomatie, c'est de la polissonerie'.[97] The moderation of Italian liberalism in victory rendered it more, not less, threatening to the Russian autocracy, vulnerable, if at all, only to the persistence of such liberal ideas among the nobility through decades of repression. The Russians took comfort from Britain's failure to avert Denmark's defeat and the total loss of the Duchies, because the episode cut Europe's one great liberal state down to size, in purely military and diplomatic terms. The Russian embassy reported with pleasure Bismarck's disregard for the British public's hostility; yet Gortchakov, the Tsar's foreign minister, had made overtures to the British after the Franco-Russian entente of the late 1850s crumbled under the pressure of events in Italy and Poland.[98] Palmerston exaggerated Russia's isolation at that point: perhaps Gortchakov, successively disappointed by France, Austria and Britain, in his quest for an 'intimate alliance', would turn to Turkey or the equally feeble German Confederation, he minuted sarcastically in September 1863.[99] He passed over the Russians' closer relations with Prussia when Bismarck assumed the direction of her policy. Cemented by Prussia's almost embarrassing support in the Polish revolt, these relations were to provide the Russians with the satisfaction of contributing to Britain's discomfiture in the outcome of the Schleswig-Holstein crisis. However, the decline in co-operation between France and Russia helped Britain in the Ottoman empire; although Palmerston was swift to warn the Foreign Office against underestimating the tenacity of the Russians' political and religious commitment in the Ottoman lands.

America

The approaching disruption of the United States by civil war was not a certainty until the eve of the conflict. Her Southward expansion into Latin America seemed a stronger possibility, and not an unwelcome one to Britain. To Palmerston it was predestined that the Spanish and Portuguese Americans – racially degenerate as he considered them – should succumb to the Anglo-Saxon stock of the Northern republic attracted by vast territories with populations incapable of creating and sustaining the political conditions for their proper economic development. Although in other respects an unpalatable prospect, this would benefit British trade by the improved order, stability and fair dealing to be expected of the superior race.[100] It was also believed likely that the dispute between slave and free states within the American union would be exacerbated by the predicted annexation of Mexico, which must at once raise the question whether or not to recognize slavery in the new acquisition. The break-up of the United States was compatible with the advance of her successor republics on the Latin South. Obviously, the bigger America promised to become, the more desirable her division appeared to the British, and to the French. The principled dislike of American democracy shown by Britain and Continental Europe was perhaps surprisingly marked in Napoleon III, whose bid in the 1860s to convert Mexico into a monarchical French client state had Palmerston's approval. Britain possessed a further interest in the anticipated American expansion: its direction was away from her Canadian colonies. For these reasons, in addition to the increasing pressures of commerce, investment and migration, the second Palmerston government, like the preceding Tory administration, carried appeasement of the United States to lengths scarcely imaginable in the very recent past. If the advent of civil war, or at least of secession, had been awaited without misgiving, it was to cause Britain moments of serious anxiety and embarrassment for a couple of years. Not the least of her problems was Gladstone's Southern partisanship; he did everything he could to convert the government, of which he was a leading member, to full recognition of the Confederacy.

In the two Palmerston cabinets, Lewis exercised an important influence on Britain's policy towards the United States. Standing up to her in Central America would only serve to prolong the life of a union which he held was destined to fall apart unless its aggressiveness were indulged by foreign war. The savage physical assault on the radical Republican Charles Sumner in the United States Senate by a Southern member of the House of Representatives signified much more to Lewis than the brutishness of democracy. 'To me it seems the first blow in a civil war', he wrote presciently of this event in 1856. 'I see no solution ... but the separation of ... slave and free states into distinct political communities.'[101] In such a political climate, 'playing with edge-tools' was his description, at different times, of diplomacy which endangered peace between Washington and London.[102] When Palmerston was out of office in 1858–59 Britain made a major concession, exceeding anything to which she had resigned herself in Central America during his first premiership. The United States obtained from the Tory minority government the practical suspension, where merchant ships going under the American flag were involved, of the maritime right of search on which British efforts to stamp out the slave trade largely depended. Speaking in the Commons, Palmerston pointed to the inherent advantage that the United States enjoyed with France and Russia: 'There are three great ... powers ... so far independent of naval warfare that even a naval reverse does not materially affect them ...' He publicly welcomed the civil war in that it offered hope of overcoming, by agreement, American resistance to a more effective anti-slavery patrol: 'possibly the spirit of the North would prevail over...the spirit of the South'.[103] Let the North prove its abhorrence of slavery by enabling British warships to detain suspected slavers going under the American flag, he told his foreign secretary.[104] The proof was forthcoming; the Anglo-American treaty of 1862 agreed on a mutual right of search and mixed commissions to adjudicate upon arrested vessels.

Palmerston's care not to provoke America reflected the discernment of British public opinion. The surrender of the Mosquito Coast and the neighbouring Bay Islands to Nicaragua and Honduras in 1859–60, evoked a last ditch protest from the colonial secretary, Newcastle, on behalf of the islands' population, couched in language which Russell at the Foreign Office called hardly decent between cabinet ministers. Newcastle put in a strong, and inconvenient, plea for 'the rights of...British subjects... which...ought not to suffer' because Britain had accepted the American contention that there should have been a withdrawal from the islands under the Clayton–Bulwer Treaty of 1850 binding both her and the United States not to acquire or, in Britain's case, to retain territory in Central America, British Honduras excepted. The Duke did not seek to prevent Russell's intended confession of '"usurpation and...violation of the... Treaty"'; although unable to stop himself from adding, 'if wrong has been done'. All he wanted Britain to attempt was to mitigate the hardship of the inhabitants handed over to Honduras.[105] The other Peelite duke in the cabinet, Argyll, had also lately reflected on the virtual impotence of a ministry whose policy in distant regions did not convince at home. At issue then were the small but awkwardly located San Juan Islands lying on the marine boundary between British Vancouver Island and the American state of Oregon. Argyll pressed the foreign secretary, who naturally did not wish to give way to the Americans almost simultaneously in the Caribbean and the Pacific, to remember that 'the people of this country will never allow any government to run the risk of a contest on a matter which concerns them so remotely'. His advice to Russell was to soften the wording, in exchanges with the United States, of 'our *value* for', as carefully distinct from 'our *right* to', the islands.[106]

Argyll emphasized Washington's conciliatory tone: 'Bullying has been disavowed by the American government.'[107] Public sensitivity in Britain to the parade of America's latent strength was the one thing that could make the political nation care about faraway places, which were insignificant for imperial security and a liability to flourishing Anglo-American trade. Lewis had been apprehensive of that conceivable British reaction in 1856.[108] The regular army and the navy of the United States were so small before the civil war that it was easy for a British government to look ignominiously weak in yielding to her. Aware of this risk, the Americans rightly thought it was outweighed in British minds by commercial considerations. 'Commercially no doubt we should gain...but politically...that is no reason why we should not try to keep our own', Palmerston had said in forecasting irresistible United States expansion Southwards.[109] By 'our own' he meant no more than the British West Indies: he would gladly have let America take Mexico if she wished. Clarendon, as foreign secretary, and Napoleon concurred in regarding the step as natural, and no great addition to American power.[110] Chronic disorder in Mexico demanded intervention by someone. To Clarendon Mexico was 'a den of wild beasts and should be treated as such if we only knew how'.[111] Malmesbury noted that annexation by the Americans would do something else besides promote British commerce; it would bring the pro- and anti-slavery struggle in American domestic politics to a head, resulting in the end of the union: 'The Yankees know this...so well that they hesitate...'[112]

The Anglo-French-Spanish expedition to Mexico in 1861–62, to exact payment to their citizens with claims on the republic, was a strictly limited enterprise for the British, and the Spaniards. Palmerston thoroughly approved, however, of the French purpose in staying on after the other two countries withdrew their contingents, leaving Britain's creditors unsatisfied. 'If the North and South are definitively disunited and...at the same time Mexico could be turned into a prosperous monarchy, I do not know any arrangement that would be more advantageous to us', he told Russell firmly; for his colleague had comprehensive doubts.[113] The foreign secretary had previously minuted that the Americans would do their utmost to prevent the establishment of a Mexican empire.[114] Britain eventually furnished Napoleon's choice for Mexico, the Hapsburg Archduke Maximilian, with the 'moral support and countenance'[115] that Palmerston wanted, and restored the diplomatic relations broken off under the republic in 1860. Palmerston associated both absolutism and republicanism with illegality and force. The American civil war was confirmation, he had the satisfaction of informing the American historian, J. L. Motley, that the once United States, like Latin American republics and European despots, could not avoid sliding into 'all sorts of violence without regard to law... spies and police and martial law'.[116] A Mexican empire might be an object lesson to all the republicans of the New World: but Palmerston, too, found it hard to credit optimistic statements about the acceptability of monarchy made by Mexicans and Napoleon's court. He was not prepared either to help the French in arms with the creation of the empire, or to guarantee their Archduke's retention of its throne. He fell back on the argument that, if it did succeed, the experiment would surely favour the trade of Europe with Mexico. This was several months after the battle of Gettysburg in July 1863, an awesome demonstration of the North's resources and will to impose unity.[117] It must be said that he had, from the beginning, a deeper reservation about a foreign enterprise to confer political civilization on the Mexicans: 'a better government...might possibly grow out of these operations, but its growth should be spontaneous and not the result of... dictation'.[118]

Palmerston even entertained, fleetingly, the hope that the Confederacy would discard its cherished American institutions in favour of monarchy, on the slender evidence afforded by the talk of officers on a Southern warship calling at British ports. At no time, however, did he feel inclined to overlook the South's defence of slavery. In the opening months of the civil war, he suggested to Russell that suspected slavers flying the confederate flag might be stopped and searched without ceremony.[119] He remained as opposed to Southern slave owning and trading as to Northern democracy. A minute of October 1861 set out his pragmatic attitude to the war in America. It was 'in the highest degree likely' that the North would be unable to suppress the rebellion; it was clear that the Confederacy, once allowed to go its own way, would offer a valuable and extensive market for British manufactures, with industrial competition from the Northern states of the former union curbed; but the military position, 'too indecisive', made it premature to accord the South diplomatic recognition.[120] There was another aspect of policy which he kept before him: the value of a good Anglo-French understanding in the situation created by the civil war. On the outbreak of hostilities, he received a welcome overture from Flahault, Napoleon's ambassador in London, who unfolded a plan that was to work well, and very well for Britain. The government in Washington should be left in no doubt as to the futility of trying to play France and Britain off against each other, when the two European Powers contemplated saying or doing anything that the North deemed unfriendly. The best way to persuade Washington of this was for the French to assume a more prominent role in the concerted statements and actions of the two Powers, thus depriving the Northerners of the natural American reliance on France's historic jealousy of her neighbour. 'I said I could see no objection to this division and allotment of parts', Palmerston informed Russell.[121]

The *Trent* affair at the end of the year tested the arrangement. The removal of Confederate envoys to Europe from the British ship of that name by a Northern man-of-war made the prime minister talk of fighting: but he was less warlike than a shocked and indignant public. The seizure of the two Southerners was interpreted as an act of aggression towards Britain; and the ministry could not have supposed otherwise. The City was particularly loud in its clamour for the assertion of British power. The official tone to Washington was indeed 'peremptory and unconciliatory' before being 'somewhat mitigated' by both the cabinet's and the Prince Consort's redrafting.[122] Such utterances, however, were for publication.

Palmerston apprehended that President Lincoln and his secretary of state, Seward, were in danger of being driven into a corner by their public opinion: 'It is difficult not to come to the conclusion that the robust hatred of England which animates...almost all the Northern newspapers will make it impossible...to grant our demands.'[123] Lewis expressed the same fear, but took comfort from the thought that there were other powerful forces in the Northern states:'the banking and commercial interests, who will surely make themselves felt, cannot be so insane.'[124] Cobden, in his letters to Sumner, chairman of the Senate committee on foreign relations, warned him against the instinct of the press on both sides of the Atlantic 'to envenom the affair', and against mistaking the strength of feeling behind the British government.[125] The cabinet heard with approval how Lord Lyons, the minister in Washington, had worked on Seward, known for a combative dislike of Britain, to convey his country's intention to fight if the prisoners from the *Trent* were not released. Lyons had striven to accomplish this 'without using the language of menace' in the frankness of privacy.[126]

In Lewis's view, the French communication of support for Britain was a very, if not the most, important factor in bringing Washington to give up the men: 'It cast away all hope of assistance from that quarter.'[127] Palmerston preferred to attribute the American decision to his government's determined stance and well-advertised preparations for war.[128] He thanked the French Embassy for what he termed, more than a little ungenerously, the Emperor's good offices.[129] Napoleon's foreign minister had written to Flahault in the last days of December: 'j'espère que notre attitude...inspire quelques remords à Lord Palmerston et à Lord John Russell, et que nous ne venons pas de rencontre de sitôt les défiances contre lesquelles vous avez eu à lutter.'[130] The gratitude of Palmerston and Russell was transient. They felt no remorse for their unceasing mistrust of Napoleon, which did not diminish. Lewis did not, of course, leave a third factor out of account: the compulsion on the North not to divide its forces in the presence of the Southern enemy.[131] There were others that operated on Britain: vulnerability of the Canadian colonies to Northern attack, and Britain's thriving trade with the North, which, countrywide, helped to offset the harm done by the Federal blockade of Southern cotton ports. The Queen and the Prince 'spoke much...and in the anti-Northern sense' about the *Trent* when Gladstone discussed what had happened with them on 28 November: they were, nevertheless, concerned, like their ministers, to prevent the incident from developing into a mutually damaging Anglo-American conflict.[132] 'It is obvious', *The Times* correspondent in America, W. H. Russell, had told Delane in September 1861 '...that the North will succeed in reducing the South...'[133] If not many agreed at the time, on any sensible reckoning the Northern states were a formidable force. The City was hot against the insult to national honour: but Consols fell. 'All the commercial interests are thoroughly conscious of the debt they owe to Lord Palmerston', stated *The Times* City column when news arrived of the North's consent to hand over the two Confederates.[134] The British public wanted a victory, and on this occasion it was ready to pay a high price. A painless triumph delighted Britain. Palmerston's reactions were the same: pleasure at having made 'that low-down fellow, Seward...eat the leek', without incurring 'a large expenditure...much embarrassment to commerce...painful sacrifices of lives and blood'.[135]

In the handling of this shortlived crisis, Palmerston did not depart from the principle laid down months ahead of the civil war: 'Nothing could be more undesirable than for us to interfere in the dispute, if it should break out.'[136] Interference might take other forms besides war with Washington. There was the full recognition of the South for which Napoleon and Gladstone worked; and, as a long step towards it, the offer of mediation between the combatants. The French and Gladstone argued, with much force, that the Northern blockade of cotton exports was doing intolerable damage to the leading industrial economies of Europe. Gladstone conjured up the spectre of social disruption in Lancashire; it would oblige Britain to intervene without any decent pretence of acting in 'the general interests of humanity and peace'.[137] France's less mature economy and her recent terrifying experience of proletarian revolt made her government impatient of British caution: 'pour bien des motifs, le malaise de nos classes ouvrières ne nous laisse pas aussi froids que nos voisins', observed her foreign minister.[138] The main motive behind the Emperor's policy was not economic. Napoleon 'could not forget the overbearing insolence of the United States...in its days of prosperity and hoped that they might receive a lesson'. He was prepared to help the South, if it were possible, meaning that any moves should be undertaken jointly with Britain.[139]

Gladstone's dislike of the North, as 'the more genuine representatives of American democracy', was similarly strong but rather different in conception. He was unequivocally for liberalism of the British variety, and construed it to sanction the Confederacy's bid for a separate existence. 'I hear you quoted...saying you think the Southern States most in the right...I do not believe it', exclaimed his Whig confidante Harriet, Duchess of Sutherland.[140] He was frank with the North's best friend in the cabinet, Argyll, dismissing the celebrity Mrs Beecher Stowe's anti-slavery arguments on behalf of the North with the assured comment that: 'She has lost what may be termed her intellectual integrity.' There was not, he opined, 'a tithe of evidence' to confirm her view of the civil war as primarily one against slavery. The South was really fighting for its freedom from Northern domination. The North's answer to secession, 'which Mrs Stowe finds sublime...in my eyes is tumultuous', he went on. Admitting that the Northern states' 'strong instinct of national life' had merit, he still rated it lower than other, less worthy incentives for trying to keep the union alive. The jealous protectionism and aggressive urban democracy of the North were more important causes of a struggle which he considered to be 'the perpetuation of horrors without the prospect of good'. Secession furnished an irrefutable demonstration that the United States was not a 'homogeneous political society'. Not only had the Northerners exceeded 'the bullying disposition of my own countrymen' abroad, they were guilty of 'incredible and unexampled injustice' to Britain in attacking her want of sympathy with them. They would be glad to make war on her as well. This fear explains his anxiety that the government should avoid provoking Washington unnecessarily over the *Trent*. The Northern states had it in their power to hurt Britain but not, he was sure, to subdue the Confederacy.[141]

Palmerston watched the progress of Southern arms with a satisfaction tempered by his personal and political sensitivity to 'our great difficulty... the question of slavery'. He had told Gladstone in their critical encounter of June 1860 that the extirpation of the slave trade, an aim unattainable while slavery itself lasted, was one of the 'two great objects always before him'.[142] Gladstone did not pretend that Britain was as pro-Confederate as some supposed when he urged international mediation in the conflict upon the prime minister. He predicted an irresistible tendency to involve Britain deeply with the cause of the white South 'heroically struggling against... a much larger number' to vindicate their rights as free men. The admitted evil of slavery ought not, therefore, to rule out intervention in a frightful war which was, moreover, so damaging to other countries. In order to wield 'every moral influence with a view to the mitigation, or if possible... removal of slavery', Britain must stand well with the Southern government when its independence was achieved. To delay interference, he concluded, was not to help the slaves. To Argyll he wrote that mediation would open 'a road of retreat' for the North: 'There is much nonsense talked in the papers about the propriety of remaining neutral *to the end*.'[143] 'I am not disposed in any case to take up arms to settle the American war by force', Russell assured Lewis after reading this memorandum of Gladstone's. Palmerston was unwilling to contemplate recognizing Southern independence – not fighting for it – until the Northerners should have suffered 'a very complete smashing' in the field and have refused to negotiate a permanent separation from the South on Anglo-French advice. He was not inclined to underestimate the danger of a diversionary attack upon Britain and her Canadian colonies by the Northern states.[144]

President Lincoln's proclamation of 22 September 1862 announced that his administration would proceed to abolish slavery throughout its reunited territory. At the same time the North succeeded in checking the Southern advance. With undiminished confidence in the South, Gladstone tried to propel the cabinet into acceptance of Anglo-French mediation by saying publicly at Newcastle on 7 October what he had been saying in private: 'Jefferson Davis', the Confederate president, 'and his comrades have made a nation.' He believed the prime minister was with him, and counted on Palmerston's popularity, 'as high as at any former period'.[145] Palmerston did think his colleague 'not far wrong' in anticipating the independence of the South;[146] but he disowned what the protesting American minister hardly doubted was Gladstone's personal initiative.[147] It is evident from his letters to Russell that while Palmerston seized on the Confederate failure to make the expected, conclusive breakthrough, he was more affected by uneasiness about making a diplomatic move as welcome to the slaveowning South as it was unwelcome to the finally abolitionist North. Following Lincoln's proclamation, he repeatedly came back to this point: 'slavery... was from the beginning the obvious difficulty in our way as mediators'. He approved of the Conservative leader for objecting to recognition of the South or mediation between the combatants, and allowed Derby to know what he thought.[148] At the cabinet of 11 November, when mediation, commencing with an armistice for six months, was discussed, Gladstone found himself alone in determinedly advocating it; and complained of having been let down by Palmerston and Russell. He had some reason to feel sore. Although Palmerston spoke in support of the armistice, he conveyed that its rejection did not displease him. For the eleven members of the full cabinet who voiced their opposition, 'some in a very strong and decided manner', had been impressed by two memoranda from Lewis.[149] The Whig Sir George Grey and the radical Milner Gibson were quick to call on Lewis, and left telling him that they agreed with the case against mediation as he stated it in the first paper. He disposed of the illusion that Britain could help the South without compromising herself intolerably: 'if England were to undertake the function of a peace-maker... to suggest... terms... what are those... to be? If our scheme maintained the institution of slavery in the Southern states, we should be virtually giving the guarantee of England for its maintenance.' The resumption of Lancashire's blockaded cotton supplies – 'this philanthropic proposition', in his words – was outweighed by the risks to Britain as a whole and to the government: a country divided and discredited; her flourishing and varied trade with the North and the safety of Canada both exposed to desperate Federal counterstrokes.[150]

Lewis did not omit to record in his diary the public's backing for the cabinet line when it became known.[151] Gladstone clung to his hopes for the South, trying to persuade himself that Britain had not decisively excluded the possibility of joint action with France.[152] Palmerston referred, when necessary, to the view in which the cabinets of 11–12 November had confirmed him: British opinion would not allow ministers to have anything to do with a negotiated peace in America that perpetuated slavery, a condition on which the Confederacy would insist.[153] He was more than ever anxious not to provoke the North, as by sending larger reinforcements to Canada in 1863 than were actually despatched. He seemed almost resigned to a Federal attack on Britain in that quarter, and not optimistic about the chances of beating it off. Within days of this letter, after seeing the Law Officers' preliminary advice that the export of warships building on the Mersey for the South was legal, he suggested buying them for the Admiralty to prevent their delivery to the Confederate Navy.[154] The government took possession of the vessels and later bought them; no ship was delivered to the Confederacy after the famous raider, the *Alabama*, left the Mersey in July 1862. Gladstone's partisanship gave way to realism: by February 1864 he was asserting to the Northern Senator Charles Sumner that: 'I have neither fears nor prejudices in respect of America.'[155] Both he and Palmerston had the Anglo-French relationship in mind when considering the problems posed by the American civil war, as did the rest of the cabinet. Gladstone naturally wanted Britain to fall in with Napoleon's wishes. Lewis and others were opposed to their country becoming involved with the Emperor's personal antagonism to the United States.[156] On his side, Napoleon blamed Britain for keeping him back from recognition of the Confederacy. Willing enough to take the lead, he was, reported the British ambassador at his Court, determined to take no step without her. It therefore suited Palmerston to be overruled by the cabinet in November 1862, after which he disclosed an 'insurmountable objection' to mediation. Any move favourable to the Confederates should be preceded by consultation with France, he reminded Russell in the summer of 1864 when it looked as if they might be able to hold their own in a war of attrition.[157]

J. L. Motley was sure that only the announcement of slavery's impending abolition would enable the British government to withstand Napoleon's pressure by putting a very large part of the British public behind ministerial resistance to being forced into war beside France and the Confederacy.[158] Gladstone did not believe, until the last moment, that Lincoln would issue his proclamation against slavery.[159] Motley exaggerated the Palmerston administration's deference to the Emperor; and at first gave it much too little credit for sharing the widespread aversion to negro enslavement. He soon saw the improbability that Palmerston, 'all his life a consistent hater of African slavery', was in a hurry to acknowledge Southern nationhood while he had the option.[160] Lewis's dispassionate analysis of the conflict between North and South as it commenced was representative of British liberalism, with a small 'l'. His *Edinburgh Review* article of April 1861 anticipated that the North would go along 'the higher track of social freedom' leaving to the South commercial freedom under the regrettable necessity of continuing slave labour, dictated by geography. He did not think the South could be expected to commit economic suicide, when British experience in the West Indies had shown that a free negro workforce was an unsatisfactory substitute for slavery where climate precluded the employment of whites as field-hands on the plantations. Slavery was admittedly a greater evil than the protectionism of the union on which an independent South would turn its back, so Europe was led to believe. But the establishment of free trade in that wide and prosperous region nevertheless seemed to Lewis a contribution to 'the progress of mankind and rational liberty'. The conventional anonymity of this article was easily penetrated. Its distinct preference, coming from such a source, helped Washington's case. The North was credited with a moral edge over the South, even though Lewis pronounced their separation to be 'the "manifest destiny"' of the United States.[161] To reinforce this significant advantage in Britain was an important reason for the timing of Lincoln's proclamation.

Gladstone and Bright were the only British politicians of their standing to take sides with conviction in the civil war. While his cabinet colleagues restrained the one, the other had less latitude than he cared to suggest. Cobden's personal, and costly, knowledge of American business disposed him to adopt a brutally realistic view of its political friends in New York, the financial centre of the union and as such strongly disliked in the South: 'Is it not commercial gain and mercantile ascendancy which prompt their warlike zeal for the Federal government?', he asked William Hargreaves, an influential Manchester figure. '...the North will learn moderation and modesty in the school of adversity', he wrote to the same correspondent not long afterwards, repeating his prediction, made to Sumner and many others, that Europe would intervene to raise the blockade of the cotton ports before the middle of 1862, if the North did not lift it first or demonstrate the certainty of Southern defeat. As for the negroes, they would achieve a better status 'somehow', but not in the near future when he assured Hargreaves that European recognition of the Confederacy was almost bound to come.[162] Cobden was in touch with the French government, and did not disapprove of its American policy. Like Gladstone, he wanted his country to work closely with France, which he pretended to himself was not a Palmerstonian course to take. The famous radical considered Lincoln's proclamation 'a quaint, droll affair. Not a word about the war or its victims... [but] homilies on slavery'. Yet he granted that the President had met Europe's criticisms of the North in 'about the most effective' fashion.[163]

Bright complained, in his correspondence with Hargreaves, that Cobden 'had...entirely forgotten the negro'.[164] From within the cabinet, after the decision not to embark on mediation with France, Milner Gibson wrote to him making it clear that in their pro-Southern statements, *The Times* and other London newspapers did not, as was so often assumed, speak for ministers.[165] Gibson was Cobden's designated representative inside 'the citadel of power':[166] but he and practically all his colleagues were nearer to Bright on the question of the hour. Bright had some difficulty in adjusting to this political truth. Cobden warned him that 'we may...see Palmerston claiming your support as the friend of the North'. The South's best friends, he advised him not to forget, were the men named in his letter of December 1862: W. H. Gregory, W. S. Lindsay and J. A. Roebuck; a Peelite and two radicals on the Liberal backbenches. He further attempted to sway Bright by the argument that good radicals like themselves ought to concentrate on domestic problems, 'and not...be diverted on a false scent...we must avoid being thrust into the attitude of...champions of the Federal party'. The Foxite Whigs had been crippled by sympathizing with the 'violence and folly' of the French Revolution to the extent that they did, instead of simply trying to maintain non-intervention. It followed that '*we*' should not risk being compromised by an imprudent defence of the North if, for instance, the proclamation against slavery were to bring on a slave rising and 'excesses which we may deplore'. 'What really constitutes your safeguard against forcible intervention', he informed Bright, 'is the naval strength of the Americans.' The Northern navy's expansion and technological advance must soon deter European nations from sending their fleets to enforce a settlement. That this was really a matter for regret on Cobden's part, whatever he said to create a different impression, comes out in a previous letter to Bright: 'I know the men at the head of affairs on both sides', he told his ardently Northern friend 'and I should say that in energy of will...comprehensiveness of view...habits of...command... knowledge of economic and fiscal questions, Jefferson Davis is more than equal to Lincoln and all his cabinet. I dread the consequences of his incapacity more than the power of the South.' Washington's obstinate protectionism over the years, economic mismanagement in wartime and undivided America's abrasiveness. to which the North was heir, diminished the South's inherent weakness, slavery.[167]

Bright's Parliamentary success and the discomfiture of Roebuck in June 1863 could not be ascribed, commented the American minister, to sympathy with the North – something particularly wanting in the Commons. It was due to Roebuck's misjudgment of the situation.[168] He asked the Commons to override ministers, and comply with Napoleon III's desire to recognize the Confederacy. Bright appealed to the dislike and apprehension, always near the surface, of the Emperor; who, if he sought to impose his will in America, as well as in Italy, Mexico and the Far East, would confirm suspicions that he had 'more ambition than Louis XIV, more daring than the first of his name'. 'Not in the habit of defending gentlemen who sit on that bench', Bright followed this disclaimer by putting the government case better than Gladstone. Arguing that the South was strong enough to hold out, he drew attention to the anti-British record of Southern politicians before the civil war. They might well dominate a reunified America such as he depicted. After an interval of separate existence, the South and the 'humiliated' North would be impelled to come together by a common desire for American greatness; and on a possible basis of 'Southern opinions and ... the Southern social system' which were likely to win the acceptance of wealthy businessmen and the immigrant Irish in the North, the free negroes' competitors for work in the cities where both collected. Then, warned Bright, Britain in Canada, France in Mexico, the two countries in the West Indies, stood to be overrun by 'a great state built upon slavery and war'. This speech, which pleased the anti-slavery sentiment of Britain, did not differ in its practical conclusions for British policy from the lately dead Lewis's views. Gladstone, put up for the government on this occasion, did not retract his belief in the South; and questioned the hold of unbending abolitionism on public opinion in Britain, censuring its leading adherents – who, of course included Bright – for wanting an end to slavery 'although they could only travel to it by a sea of blood'. However, he now acknowledged 'the strongest reasons' why Britain and France should not commit themselves in the way that Roebuck advocated. Britain's enormous interests in the American continent, France's presence in Mexico, disqualified them from acting with the impartiality necessary to prevail.[169] Bright's was, effectively, the speech for the government, and, as such, the Commons found it convincing.[170]

In the Commons, Bright made a disparaging reference to wealthy businessmen the world over as being 'from the uncertainty of their possessions and the fluctuations of their interests ... always timid and almost always corrupt'.[171] It was not an estimate of the class to which he gave prominence in his public statements elsewhere; since it undermined his alternative leadership to aristocracy: but it was realistic. He hoped that pro-Northern agitation, such as it was, could strengthen the 'rational section' of the cabinet on America; to succeed in doing as much would be 'a great thing'. *The Manchester Examiner and Times*, the newspaper on which he relied in its industrial region, disappointed him: 'It is neither for nor against the North – which means in reality, for the South', he wished those who set its tone to know in November 1862. The Palmerston government's collective judgment of how Britain should react to the civil war was sound in terms of its own national opinion, well stated to Bright by an unquestionably liberal MP, in both senses, whose business fortune was immune to the volatility of the raw cotton market. If Bass the brewery magnate was no supporter of the Confederacy, he did want 'two American nations, as being less powerful than one', yet without having believed for a long time – this was August 1863 – in a Southern victory.[172] The collective judgment of Palmerston and his ministers was also sound in terms of the future Anglo-American relationship. J. L. Motley, oppressed by the danger of British intervention in 1861–62, did not allow enough for a factor mentioned in the advice he sent: 'There are many in England who do not love us, but who, for selfish reasons, would deprecate hostilities if they can honourably be avoided'. Triumphant in April 1865, the North had grounds for resentment against Britain, but they were more than offset by the knowledge that she had been instrumental in restraining the French Emperor. The published American diplomatic documents contain the timely account of an interview in July 1863 between Washington's representative at Napoleon's Court and his foreign minister. The Frenchman confirmed his master's answer to Roebuck and another radical, W. S. Lindsay MP, when they sought to persuade him to force their government's hand by announcing his intention of recognizing the South in advance of the debate on Roebuck's motion. Napoleon recalled how Britain had rejected his initiative for joint action, and told the radicals that he declined to act independently of her, 'more especially' where America was concerned.[173]

The Anglo-French understanding

'Now in seeking for a general or first principle which should rule our foreign policy, I think that the first fact to be realized is that *England stands outside the cycle of organic changes...going on in Europe*', wrote the rising young diplomat, Robert Morier, in March 1864 to the Marchioness of Salisbury, a lady whose intellectual appreciation of such matters, added to her position in Society, made her the recipient of unusually interesting letters from a wide circle of able men.[174] The combination of liberalism and nationalism was securely established in Britain under conditions dissimilar to those evolving on the Continent. The foreign minster of Austria down to the war of 1859, Count Buol-Schauenstein, treated the British envoy to an analysis of the insular state's differences from the Hapsburg empire and, by implication, the other European Powers. International relations, said the Count as the conflict approached, had a dimension which he labelled social: 'You have your ideas of liberty, of constitutional government, of religion, all in opposition to ours.' He did not, therefore, expect Britain and Austria to converge at that level of feeling. The international dimension still seemed more important. Britain, he asserted, had no choice in the event of an assault by Napoleon III upon the independence of Europe: 'You would – you must...go with us'. The best hope of peace that he could discern lay in the preoccupation with financial gain that characterized some of the Bonapartist regime's major figures: 'la Bourse est notre meilleur allié'.[175] The stock exchange, and all that it represented in a period of spreading industrialization, did not save Austria and France from war. Napoleon, however, refrained from pursuing the same career of conquest as his uncle. His restless speculations about frontiers and nationalities continued; but he was, in reality, quite well satisfied with the Continental primacy that was his after the defeat of Russia and then Austria. His imperial ambitions beyond Europe were of secondary though increasing concern. They nevertheless had the effect of strengthening the reservations entertained by the most earnest British advocates of Anglo-French understanding. 'There ought to be no more partnership with France in our operations in China. France has no trade there, and therefore no interests in common with us. If we are to have an ally there, it should be the United States...', Cobden told the millowner Henry Ashworth as early as July 1860.[176] This remark, which would have surprised most of his contemporaries, illustrates the validity of the principle that Morier described. But Britain could not afford to offend France without sufficient cause in the way suggested by Cobden. The social aspect, so to call it, of Great Power diplomacy noticed in Buol's conversation influenced her much less against France, their old enmity notwithstanding. A persistently anglophil Bonaparte continued to build on that uncertain foundation, with more help from Palmerston than was, and is, realized.

Observing the Parisian crowds out in force when the authorities invited them to rejoice over the absorption of Savoy and Nice, Cobden was depressed by the scene. He reflected in his journal on the fact that there was nothing to choose, it seemed, between the French, British and American peoples in their politically immature susceptibility to nationalist emotion. Democracy was still unsafe everywhere. Although certainly not free from uneasiness about the Emperor's plans for Europe, Cobden credited him with doing his best to prevent a war between the two historically antagonistic nations. For the Emperor to adopt any other course would be self-defeating, to Cobden's mind.[177] Palmerston needed to trust the Emperor, but was often full of doubt. The language in which he gave vent to the deepest anxiety of his second administration is eminently quotable.[178] He did not share Cobden's belief that Napoleon was unable to risk an attack upon Britain for fear of bringing the other Powers to her aid, glad to unite in his overthrow. Neither those conservative states nor Palmerston would forget what the Emperor had said and done to harm them. Yet the Continentals looked on Palmerston as Napoleon's accomplice, or little better, who had taken fright at the aggrandizement of France: 'We have no idea in this country of the accumulated amount of hatred that exists towards us on the Continent' wrote Clarendon to Lewis. He and Lewis both accused Palmerston and Russell of 'conduct instigated at every turn by personal motives' in wanting to create an anti-French alliance. The prime minister and foreign secretary were prompted, according to Lewis, by resentment at Napoleon's embarrassing assertion of French interest in Italian policy, and by a wish to ingratiate themselves with the Court.[179] It was true that Russell had written to Palmerston stating his conviction that 'we cannot maintain our Quaker position any longer...the way of coming out of it must be worthy of us, and have the sympathy of Europe – but above all of England'. The Queen and Prince appalled Cowley when he saw them in April 1860 by their 'violence and indiscretion against the Emperor and everything French – they want to push things to extremities'.[180] Palmerston, though troubled, was not ready for a break with France.

His extended review of the situation in June was written to comply with the Queen's desire for a formal minute of advice from the cabinet. Its conclusions did not fulfil the Court's hopes of a diplomatic revolution. He went over the reports of France's intended expansion into the Rhineland, into Spain to the line of the Ebro, and into Morocco, with Turkey next on the list for intervention when Italy had been settled. These accounts were upsetting Europe; he himself could not lightly dismiss what had been said by the prominent French banker Laffitte while visiting this country: that Britain was impotent to stop France from acquiring, as would happen, the left bank of the Rhine and Belgium. Palmerston recommended consultation with Austria and Prussia to agree on 'a common policy and common objects' to counter French designs. 'This', he at once explained 'should not be an agreement for joint action'; for Britain traditionally avoided tying herself down. It was unnecessary to enlarge the planned increase in Britain's military and naval strength, but prudent to make sure of 'the means of rapid augmentation if...events should render augmentation indispensable'. Palmerston did not propose to weaken the basis of his domestic policy by lending substance to current allegations of over-taxation. Britain's Great Power status was not to be measured solely by the immediate ability to deploy physical force; a state such as she was 'If known to be strong within itself, and capable of exertion when required... will command attention and...often powerfully influence the course of events.'[181] Put before the cabinet, this draft attracted the critical comments of Lewis, Wood, Granville and Sir George Grey. They all considered that the suggestion of restricted co-operation with Austria and Prussia would incur the Emperor's active displeasure,[182] and give him good cause to excite French feeling.[183] An arrangement of the kind suggested between the three Powers would merely encourage a closer Franco-Russian relationship, to Britain's serious disadvantage in the Ottoman empire. The authors of these criticisms pointed out that Austria and Prussia were hardly likely not to inform Britain of any threats from France; the agreement would, therefore, be superfluous as well as a dangerous irritant to Napoleon. Granville believed the Emperor, undeterred by such a limited understanding might exploit it to influence public opinion both in France and England.[184] The open indignation of Cobden and Bright at the prospect of British collaboration with reactionary states befriended by the Court, so nearly resembled what Palmerston thought, and continued to think, that Russell's recent Commons speech airing the possibility[185] and the prime minister's confidential submission struck the cabinet as highly questionable. Its members were afraid of the national mood; rightly, Persigny told his government, when *The Times* said that anyone mad enough to come out for war over Savoy should be locked up.[186]

The cabinet's reception of Palmerston's draft minute, and the terms in which these good Whigs dissented from it, gave him full support for the uneasy maintenance of Anglo-French understanding. The Emperor and his advisers, like everybody else versed in the transaction of international politics, distinguished between Russell's judgement and the prime minister's. On 1 August *The Times* carried the text of a letter from Napoleon to Persigny insisting on his regard for Britain, his hope of peace among the Powers, and his concern to reassure the British statesman whom he admired: 'Lord Palmerston knows me and when I affirm a thing he will believe me', the ruler of France informed anyone who read *The Times*.[187] The letter struck diplomats as extraordinarily conciliatory, and evidence that the Emperor was apprehensive of British participation in a common front that might even include Russia.[188] Palmerston felt free to make the private suggestion that the people of a liberalized empire would be more amenable to Napoleon's declared friendship for Britain than they were under an authoritarian regime. The lack of the absorbing political life that the British enjoyed perpetuated in France 'les passions haineuses de nos guerres'.[189] This was a tactful way of saying that Bonapartism must change its outlook, and not just modify its political structure, for peace to be lasting. To help the Emperor with the diplomatic problems of the moment, and the Italians too, Palmerston got the Queen to concede the inexpediency of a meeting between herself and Francis Joseph of Austria in the round of monarchical encounters then going on and directed against France: 'it might lead to much talk and…many rumours which might do harm'. Napoleon had little cause to be dissatisfied with Palmerston.[190] The prime minister treated as 'very cock and bullish' the Portuguese minister's story of imperial complicity in a Spanish plot to annex the Coburg kingdom of Portugal. Yet his distrust of French national sentiment, and its susceptibility to the inherent expansionism of the Bonaparte dynasty, remained unabated. He enumerated instances of official French soundings and propaganda in sensitive areas like the Walloon provinces of Belgium, and Ireland: 'Of course, we laugh at these things, as Leopold does…but…though unimportant in themselves they are…the trifling tremulous motions which sometimes precede the explosion of the volcano.'[191] The best insurance available against an eruption was Napoleon himself who, after his victories in the Crimea and Italy, had a strong incentive to restore French finances, attend to the economy and initiate, cautiously, domestic political reforms. It was consonant with his aspirations for France to heed Britain's plea and preserve 'that commercial confidence...which ultimately forms the happiness of nation'.[192]

The sight of Francis Joseph, the Tsar and the Prussian regent gathering at Warsaw in October 1860 to concert their policies towards France offended British opinion, little though the conference achieved. Before the Warsaw conference, Napoleon gave a superfluous warning that if Palmerston failed him he would be 'turned out...by a coalition of Tories and radicals upon the cry of Peace, against what they could represent [as] a policy calculated to bring about a war...'[193] In his quest of an opening to regain office, Disraeli had been suggesting to the Emperor that he would find the Tories more to his liking on their return.[194] Palmerston was not afraid of being displaced by an opposition that took its orders from Derby, nor by the still more improbable alternative of a Gladstone–Cobden ministry.[195] Yet his diplomatic philosophy precluded the more relaxed approach to Napoleon's intentions urged by Lewis, who could not be accused of a predilection for the Emperor. Lewis had cast doubt on a favourite maxim of the prime minister's, that in international affairs as in medicine , prevention was better than cure. Palmerston hoped Lewis had been guilty of 'a conversational paradox, and not a deliberately adopted theory'. 'Timely vigour in negotiation' it was his belief, would so often have served to arrest a slide into war. Such vigour must be accompanied by adequate preparations, should 'Inkshed' have to give place to 'Bloodshed'.[196] He was quite confident of the backing inside and outside Parliament for an inherited and expanded programme of defence expenditure, and especially of naval construction.[197]

For him, mutual suspicion between states that were natural rivals was predestined; during his first administration, he had advised a far less intellectual politician, Clarendon, that 'intimate alliance cannot long subsist between equal powers. Those relations can be lasting only between a stronger and a weaker state when the weaker allows itself to be guided by the stronger...we will not submit to an Emperor, the Emperor...does not like an equal.'[198] In the light of his general principles, Palmerston continually referred to the potential menace from Napoleon under the twin pressures of his own ambition and that of his people upon him. In the event, the inevitability of armed conflict, which he sometimes assumed, receded. 'We fulfil our duty', he told Russell pessimistically in February 1861, 'as long as we...by negotiation and management...avoid rupture and open collision...' The Emperor joined in containing Anglo-French rivalry within what Palmerston termed 'the shackles of diplomatic trammels'.[199] The minutes of the prime minister, Wood and Gladstone occasioned by a speech from Napoleon's cousin, Jerome Napoleon, display the same realism. The prince's reaffirmation of the Bonapartist wish to redraw the map of Europe and do away with the Continental settlement, still largely intact, at the Congress of Vienna was belligerently expressed. Jerome Napoleon liked to patronize restless nationalities in the Romanov, Hapsburg and Ottoman empires independently of his relative, but not without his knowledge, as the British ambassador heard at an imperial audience.[200] Palmerston commented that they could not ignore the prince's 'hatred and resentment' of Britain as a victor in the wars of the French Revolution and the first Napoleon. 'I cannot say', wrote Wood, 'that the speech...made the least difference in my opinion.' He concurred with Palmerston, however, in believing that they must improve national defence as much and as rapidly as possible. Gladstone also argued that Jerome Napoleon had not exceeded 'what is warranted...by the traditional rivalry': but he disagreed with his two colleagues in refusing to admit to the corollary of permanent hostility.[201] The danger of overreaction in Britain seemed greater to him. He gave fuller reasons for being thus optimistic in a letter to Lord Brougham. Cowley had been reporting from Paris on the reality of the Emperor's difficulties with his legislature after allowing it to discuss his Italian policy, or policies. The debates evinced a papalist tendency openly critical of Napoleon, and a serious embarrassment.[202] 'When we read the generality of the opposition speeches', observed Gladstone, '...we form a mean opinion of the bulk of his adversaries and this works in favour of the present government of France.' The House of Commons 'surprised and delighted' Gladstone by its contrasting acceptance, if with varying enthusiasm, of the new Italian state.[203] Catholic and Legitimist attacks on the Emperor in the nominated Senate and ostensibly democratic Corps Legislatif undoubtedly had an effect in reconciling politicians and public in Britain to his uncomfortably powerful international position.[204]

The impact of the Macdonald affair in the early sixties on Britain and Prussia furnished confirmation of the relative friendliness between British and French at government level and below. A Captain Macdonald, travelling in the Rhineland, had been forcibly removed from the train and detained, following a dispute with railway officials. *The Times* assailed what it considered to have been the excessive and quite unwarrantable authoritarianism displayed in the incident. The matter became one for the attention of both governments, and generated further ill feeling. The Queen and the Prince traced to this episode 'that tone of virulence, which could not fail to produce the deepest indignation amongst the people of Germany'. The royal letter included an extract from one of Clarendon's, warning that the Prussian army was particularly offended by *The Times* articles, which were conceivably harmful to their daughter, the Crown Princess.[205] The prime minister acted on the Queen's appeal to restrain *The*

Times but he sent her the editor's insouciant reply, in which Delane ascribed his newspaper's latest offence by way of 'that most cruel of inflictions – good advice', to the 'surprising anachronisms' upon divine right pronounced at his coronation by the conservative William I of Prussia, previously regent for his brother. Palmerston told the Queen, not for the first time, that *The Times* was primarily a large commercial enterprise; that such criticism sold better than the opposite; and that foreign governments were safer targets than any other for violent attacks. 'A dull paper is soon left off', he wrote.[206] He was heeding his own counsel to Russell that in dealing with the monarch they should not try 'to improve her political principles more than may be...necessary for...our... course'.[207] Delane's remarks about divine right echoed those which Palmerston had made to her in the past.[208] The Prussian foreign minister blamed 'our travellers...vulgar people'. Palmerston reflected that his countrymen of the same sort caused very little trouble in France, where they proliferated, though there was much more national antagonism between English and French than between English and Germans.[209] While he rightly linked the behaviour of Prussian officialdom generally with the policies of the government towards Britain, he did not realize the full extent of German, and not just Prussian, dislike for unconcealed British scepticism of Teutonic destiny. Moreover, if the Prince Consort was not quite right in his assessment of the nature and likely development of the German national idea, he grasped its necessary connection with liberalism. Writing three months before his death, he still assumed, like nearly all those in Britain concerned for Germany, that Prussia's leadership of a stronger federation of German states was dependent upon a steady commitment to liberalism in his, not the Palmerstonian sense.[210] Bismarckian conservatism might overrule liberal institutions: it was careful to perpetuate and extend them.

There can be no doubt that Palmerston exaggerated the animosity of France as much as he discounted the threat from resentful Prussia and Germany. At the time when the scare about Britain's defences, which gave the Volunteer movement such an impetus, was at its height, Lewis's permanent under-secretary at the Home Office came back from Paris saying that he had observed nothing to suggest peculiar hostility to this country, and echoing the French view that the British press was responsible for the fright.[211] Yet Cobden, negotiating the commercial treaty, was aware of 'a secret instinct for...war and isolation' in the imperial mind, which he earnestly hoped to counteract by his methods.[212] The insecurity was pervasive. On passage to the East in 1860, a Tory diplomat, E. B. Eastwick, noted an encounter with a British naval officer at Naples; the sailor regarded the Royal Navy's threatened superiority over the French as already lost, and thought its loss better admitted.[213] These professional fears had enough substance to redouble the anxieties of shrewd listeners, from the prime minister down. Clarendon, prone to inflate a foreign or domestic menace, retailed news from Cowley of the French military's anger at Russell's reference to the possibility of a European coalition after France had proceeded to take Savoy and Nice.[214] There was the dreadful possibility that the new British ironclads were technically inferior to the French equivalents even if the rate of construction ensured that they were numerically superior.[215] To Palmerston it was the most urgent of questions: ' I am haunted by a vision of the deplorable state of one of those ships after a quarter of an hour or twenty minutes long engagement with the *Magenta* or *Solferino*...'[216] Cowley, in his otherwise soothing memorandum of January 1862 on Napoleon's intentions, conceded that a cut in the French navy seemed unlikely: 'There, jealousy of England comes into play... I believe the nation would sooner see its military than its naval establishment reduced.'[217] Though British naval expenditure fell by £1.4 million to £10.4 million over the five years from 1860 to 1865, this is misleading: modernization required almost a fifth fewer seamen and marines. At the end as at the beginning[218] of his stewardship of the national finances under Palmerston, and notwithstanding the counter-arguments he had deployed, Gladstone recognized that 'the transition to iron ships and new armaments is justly argued as a cause for increased charge in building ships'.[219]

Anglo-French relations recovered from their lowest point in 1860, when Malmesbury learned of the contingents' mutual hatred in the joint expedition to Peking.[220] Prince Albert detested '"l'élu du peuple"' to the last; and alleged that he was deliberately trying to discredit parliamentary institutions in Britain and Prussia by the budgetary struggles to which greater defence spending led.[221] Cowley mentioned the 'large speculations... abroad' of French investors as inhibiting war with Britain. France's overlarge forces were, he put it to Russell, a diplomatic instrument and a psychological necessity for the Emperor.[222] How far the French army, and Napoleon, were content to rest upon their Italian laurels appeared from the British military attaché's findings in February 1864, when his government would have liked to hear that France's soldiers were spoiling for a fight – against Prussia and her allies. 'I never remember such an absence of warlike symptoms', he reported. A war of annexation for the Rhine frontier would be immensely popular at any time: but France was not 'morally' prepared for it. The not so tame legislature and the country were 'most decidedly' pacific. Colonel Claremont was a good observer, and he did not think Napoleon would contemplate a move of that importance contrary to public opinion. The French army had no love for Prussia, and was as friendly to Denmark as the rest of France, its master excepted. If the soldiers were indignant at the Germans' abuse of their strength, the army was 'a machine and... does not originate anything'; a more informed judgment than that prevailing in Britain.[223] These were the years of the

Second Empire in which profits continued to climb and real wages recovered from their decline in the 1850s to advance living standards significantly.[224] The Emperor had a good deal to lose, on every front, by going to war after 1859 – with Germany, or Britain.

Napoleon neither wanted, nor could he afford, to give up his European pre-eminence. He had no illusions about the outcome should he ever be defeated in war: 'If I am beaten, who will come to my assistance, or even pity me?' he said to Cowley in February 1864. The Bonapartist legend, which overshadowed him, demanded victory. The Polish rebels of 1863 elicited what a Prussian diplomat ventured to suggest was 'a very cheap form of sympathy', when the Emperor admitted his people's unwillingness to take up arms for Poland.[225] A Continental war was impossible, Napoleon had earlier told Cowley; although the Empress Eugénie endeavoured to persuade her husband otherwise, with a grandiose plan for a redistribution of territory between the four land Powers in return for an all but independent Poland under a Russian grand duke. Partly to compensate for the ill success of France's Polish diplomacy, Napoleon formally proposed a congress of Europe to revise comprehensively the work of that held at Vienna too long ago. The wording of the announcement left no doubt that the liberal principle of nationality was to guide these collective deliberations; but not to the exclusion of self-interest with power behind it. Cowley learnt without surprise from the French foreign minister that if this theatrical invitation came to nothing, the Emperor counted on being able safely to devote himself to France's internal development; for he would have exposed the apathy of Europe.[226] Palmerston naturally thought the proposal called for very serious consideration. Britain might accept, decline or inquire what would, and would not, be on the agenda; though he was doubtful of any considerable result in the event of a congress.[227] His distrust of Napoleon was such that he preferred, on reflection, to '*rest* without being thankful' – a reference to Russell's complacency in a recent well publicized speech.[228] Palmerston seems to have been conscious of a missed opportunity, as when seeking to persuade himself, after the British rebuff to France, that the chance to have what was left of the Pope's temporal power removed with European consent was probably only one of the traps laid by Napoleon for countries that trusted to his good faith. The prime minister imagined a disagreeable dilemma for the British government on the Roman question alone: either the attainment of its longstanding and avowed objective would excite the Catholic Irish, something he admittedly did not want to do as the next election drew near, or it could be pressed by the assembled states into recognizing and guaranteeing the legitimacy of Papal rule.[229]

Palmerston did not like the French foreign minister's suggestion, made to allay disquiet, that the congress might limit itself to amending the Vienna

treaties in the light of subsequent changes, mainly those arising from the
war   of 1859, and reaffirming the original agreements with those
modifications. He had, of course, no objection to the changes in Italy:
undeniable violations of the Vienna settlement, 'they were the will of the
people'. His language here, addressed to the Queen's uncle, Leopold of the
Belgians, showed how close his thinking was, sometimes, to that of the
French emperor, when Napoleon followed his liberal bent. Drouyn de
Lhuys's gloss on the imperial communication failed to please the British
prime minister; all it offered was 'an improved title' to territories whose
retention he considered wrongful – Savoy by France; the free city of
Cracow by Austria; and, not least, the Patrimony of St Peter by the
Pope.[230] In the circumstances, it was ironical that the other three
Continental Powers should have turned to Britain for a lead in replying to
the Emperor's move. Refusing to undertake this responsibility, she was
effectively saddled with the burden by the terms of Russell's despatch and
its publication before the French received it. Russell was unnecessarily
dismissive, and Napoleon commensurately indignant: Cowley described his
tone as 'more angry than I have ever known him to assume'.[231] The Tories
did not dissent from the substance of the government's answer; they were
frightened by the idea of the congress: 'Probably England would be
required to give up Gibraltar', wrote Malmesbury. That same fear of
Napoleon prompted Derby's comment that the style of the despatch was
hard to excuse.[232] The Queen predictably approved of the snub
administered to the Emperor: 'This Congress is…an impertinence.'[233] It
was not the end of the Anglo-French alliance, to which Napoleon protested
his fidelity as Denmark faced defeat at the hands of the two German Powers
with the Confederation behind them. There was every reason for him to say
of his country at that juncture that she preferred peace and tranquillity to
an increase of territory.[234]

The alliance was naturally based on the appraisal of each partner's
interests. The British had no compelling interest in the duchies of Schleswig
and Holstein, at least so long as the kingdom of Denmark itself survived, if
not in its entirety. That was the significance of the cabinet's narrow vote on
25 June not to consider intervention unless the Danish capital were directly
threatened.[235] Charles Villiers, a supposedly radical member of the cabinet,
insisted on the danger to international morality from breaking treaties: but
he responded more encouragingly than Derby to Vitzthum von Eckstädt's
argument that preservation of the Danish Crown's rights was 'a mere
phrase', meaningless for Britain. Villiers told the German that he was going
to resist the prime minister's 'warlike policy' in cabinet; and that he did not
believe in the plan of a conference on the duchies between interested
parties. To this observant diplomat, British priorities were clearly indicated
in August 1863. Then *The Times* paid more attention to the engineer and

arms manufacturer Sir William Armstrong in his presidential address to the British Association for the Advancement of Science than it did to the congress of German princes at Frankfurt to discuss greater unity within the framework of the Confederation. Armstrong's speech had gone into the ever-growing national value of the coal industry. Coal and its derivatives, said *The Times*, 'have exercised a far more important influence, even in political matters, than the King of Prussia or the Prince of Lippe-Detmold'.[236] It was Britain's economic strength and consequent military potential rather than her actual unpreparedness for European war which made the public so tolerant of diplomatic setbacks that pleased the Continent, and were deeply humiliating to Lord Cowley's professionalism in his capacity as the country's leading, and hitherto successful, representative abroad.[237] The Gallic *Schadenfreude* of which Cowley complained was understandable, but it did little damage. At the audience he gave to the Prussian ambassador in August 1865 Napoleon wanted the Prussian ruler, whose standing had been enhanced by the war with Denmark, to announce a genuinely liberal programme for Germany. The Emperor deplored, with the British, the acquisition of Schleswig by Prussia, and Holstein by Austria, regardless of the inhabitants' wishes, including those of the Danish minority in Schleswig. The fundamental response to 'this sad affair of the duchies', as Napoleon described it, was similar on both sides of the English Channel.[238]

The Emperor's cousin, Jerome Napoleon, whose assertion of France's right to expand despite the alliance with Britain was the subject of cabinet discussion in 1861, had long seen in British institutions the source of inspiration for a reformed empire. Two years after that controversial speech, he had acknowledged, in a letter to his illustrious relative, the reduction of the old difficulty for French liberals holding his views: British hostility to France. '... there exists in that country', he wrote of Britain, 'a background of sincere liberalism which is having greater weight every day on her traditional policy... The distance travelled by public opinion... is immense.'[239] The Palmerston ministry had shrunk from affording France its full backing in the diplomatic moves to help Poland: but politically conscious people in the two Western Powers were equally outraged by Russia's extreme severity to the rebellious Poles. When he commented on the strong reaction among all classes of Frenchmen to Russian sharpness in rebuffing Napoleon's, and Britain's, efforts on behalf of Poland, the permanent under-secretary at the foreign office, Hammond, picked out the report of the naval attaché at the Paris embassy. The French navy at Cherbourg, the base for operations against Britain, did not conceal its wish for war with Russia, evincing great indignation.[240] Since the French also sympathized with the Danes, the British visit of their fleet in 1865 went so well that Palmerston, though glad of the advertisement that Britain was not

isolated, became nervous. He instructed Cowley that the display of amity
should not be mistaken for complacency or weakness on Britain's side. This
warning, however, was not to be construed as 'hatred of France and…
everything French, but solely… that watchful care… which… is the duty of
every government…'.[241] On good terms with France, Britain had less
reason to be afraid of the United States; while the French were
understanding, if a little scornful, about British reluctance to cross Bismarck
again. When he died, Palmerston was more worried by the thought of what
Russia would be one day than by his constantly reiterated suspicions of
Napoleon.[242]

12

Ireland

Race and religion

Palmerston's estimate of Ireland's importance to the British empire[1] is set forth in a letter of October 1857 to Lord Clarendon. He told Clarendon, who regarded the contemporary Indian mutiny with the liveliest alarm, that 'the smallest outbreak' in Ireland would 'go further to shake the impression of our power than all that can happen in India'.[2] It was not that Palmerston agreed with Lewis, who avowed to the House of Commons in a debate of February 1858 on India his scepticism 'whether that empire is of the value which is attributed to it',[3] Palmerston simply thought Ireland mattered more than India, valuable though British dominion over the sub-continent was, economically and politically. As a constituent part of the United Kingdom, Ireland was integral to British power. In a confidential memorandum written during his second ministry, Palmerston compared the Anglo-Irish relationship to that between Austria and Hungary under the Hapsburgs. 'The question we have to determine', he stated, 'is whether we shall conciliate a third … of the United Kingdom, or make the same mistake about it which Austria … is making with one third of her empire, Hungary, and alienate and irritate an important element of our … strength.'[4] The Austro-Hungarian tension could only be contained by the *Ausgleich* of 1867. Such a solution was not open to the statesmen of mid-Victorian Britain. In Palmerston's case, it was precluded by his realistic, if hostile, understanding of Irish nationality. Some of his colleagues in government considered he was exaggerating a conflict of nationalities, the reality of which they nevertheless acknowledged with discomfort. The rebirth of revolutionary nationalism in Ireland after 1858, and the nature of the response it elicited from the great majority who did not enrol in the movement, confirmed Palmerston's fundamental belief in the resilience of Ireland's nationhood. That belief conditioned his whole Irish policy. It stiffened his well known resistance to land reform, and reinforced his

aversion to the Catholicism, at once ultramontane and national, of the Irish
church. It underlay his objection to recognizing a Catholic university, as
such, which he rightly foresaw would be a centre of separatist feeling. In
general, that belief confined within narrow limits the various concessions he
was prepared to offer those constitutional nationalists like J. F. Maguire,
MP for Dungarvan and the last leader of the independent Irish party, who
were obliged to take the Liberal whip at Westminster in the later 1850s and
the 1860s. For prevailing circumstances made the effort to maintain a quite
distinct Irish parliamentary presence seem vain for the time being.
Palmerston's dislike for the necessity of securing their votes, and the way in
which he repeatedly questioned it, are extremely revealing.

It suited Palmerston to emphasize, as he did in parliament, the religious
rather than the racial divide. He explained this to Cardwell, his Irish
secretary of the moment, when they were discussing the advisability of
permitting the formation of volunteer corps in that country during the
wave of enthusiasm for amateur soldiering that swept over Great Britain in
1859–60. Distrustful of their political reliability in Ireland, Palmerston
wrote: '...without placing our objections to such corps upon any doubt of
the loyalty of the Irish people, we might well put it upon the violence and
acrimony of religious differences and a doubt whether means given for
defence against an outward enemy might not be used in internal conflicts
against fellow countrymen.'[5] There was nothing to be gained, and much to
be lost, by admitting publicly the extent of Irish disaffection. The reaction
of Catholic Ireland to the recent imperial crisis of the Indian mutiny had
been so unfriendly as to draw from Palmerston the unambiguous statement
that Britain must not fail to have on hand there 'a sufficient Saxon force to
make any movement on the part of the Celts perfectly hopeless, and sure to
bring immediate destruction on those who take part in it.'[6] The correlation
between religion and racial origin, and between religious and national
allegiance, justified Palmerston's attitude from a British standpoint. He
never succumbed to the partial complacency of Lord Carlisle, viceroy of
Ireland in both his ministries,[7] let alone the over-confidence of Mill in his
Considerations in 1861.[8] The Irish constabulary's role in close support of the
British army was one that he wished to preserve at a high level of efficiency,
telling Carlisle's successor in 1865 to select for the vacant post of inspector-
general 'some military man who will keep the force in a good state of
military organization'.[9] The able and influential permanent under-
secretary at Dublin Castle in Palmerston's time in Downing Street, Sir
Thomas Larcom, was also a soldier. When Sir Robert Peel, the Tory prime
minister's son and a favourite with Palmerston, was Irish secretary in the
1860s, he and Larcom began each day in Dublin by seeing the inspector-
general together, and checking on the operation of 'the present system of
active surveillance' which constituted the Irish constabulary's other main

function.[10] The suspicion and vigilance that Palmerston urged went far to frustrate the plans of Fenianism at that epoch.

When Palmerston spoke, in the memorandum of August 1861 cited above, of the Irish contribution to British strength, he had in mind, among other things, an aspect of the Union which later declined in significance. Irish Catholics then accounted for almost 30 per cent of the British army and the Royal Marines, compared with roughly half that proportion on the eve of the 1914–18 war.[11] The requirements of Indian and imperial garrisons elsewhere could not have been met without recourse to Irish manpower. Irish like British recruits enlisted primarily owing to the pressure of poverty:[12] unlike their British comrades in arms they were no more than mercenaries, which is not to imply an adverse judgment of their martial qualities. In the aftermath of the Mutiny about a third of the army was stationed in India as an insurance against repetition of the shock Britain had sustained in 1857. While Irish Catholic soldiers, comprising well over a third of British infantry, could be relied upon to fight unquestioningly against Asiatics, Palmerston and his ministers had no illusions about the risks involved in deploying them where the enemy might plausibly appeal to their national sentiments. Before 'military Fenianism' gave rise to anxiety in the army, Palmerston advised that regiments sent to defend Canada in the event of an American or expatriate Irish invasion should be 'more English or Scotch than Irish'.[13]

Palmerston thought that the problems posed by Irish Catholic nationalism would be lessened by furthering the political and administrative integration of Ireland with Britain. The office of lord lieutenant, or viceroy, of Ireland appeared to perpetuate and legitimize a sense of identity subversive of the Union. For that reason, Palmerston wished to abolish the viceroyalty and transfer its duties to the Home secretary, or to an additional secretary of state. He concluded, however, that no British government headed by himself would profit by the change until the mood of Catholic Ireland had been made more receptive by an amicable settlement of the Roman question.[14] There was no prospect of settling the question in a way acceptable to British and Irish opinion alike. Palmerston did not merely want to see the papacy divested of its temporal power: he held that, ideally, it should be reduced to the position of the Eastern Orthodox ecumenical patriarchate at Constantinople.[15] This was popular in Britain; but, always a realist, he knew quite well that the spiritual and moral authority of the papacy, and hence its political influence, was growing despite, and also because of, the reverses it had experienced and with which it was threatened in Italy. He did not think it either possible or desirable to come to terms with ultramontane Catholicism, just as he could envisage no trust between British and Irish nationalism. Of the calculated but energetic protests from the Irish hierarchy, led by Archbishop Cullen, against government policy towards Ireland and Italy, Palmerston commented: 'These Catholic priests are no less cunning than encroaching.'[16] His second ministry conceded rather more than his first to Catholic Ireland, helped forward by warnings such as those from its chief whip. Brand successfully sought to impress it upon Palmerston that 'you cannot carry on a government with a whole nation against you', asking him, '...is it safe in the present state of Europe to inflame Ireland...?'.[17]

The land question

Palmerston had a substantial stake in Irish land, receiving a large slice of his income from estates in County Sligo. Parliamentary weakness drove him at the outset of his first ministry to countenance the attempt to give the Irish tenant compulsory compensation for improvements to the holding. He would never consent to any advance on this concession; and declined to go even so far in the legislation placed upon the statute book in 1860 in a bid to affirm the futility of continuing to agitate for land reform.[18] A good landlord, he did not act upon his celebrated aphorism that the tenant-right of Ireland was 'equivalent to landlord's wrong'.[19] Joseph Kincaid, of Stewart and Kincaid, the leading firm of Dublin land agents who looked after Palmerston's Irish interests, with continual reference to the owner, explained the practice on the Sligo property to the Devon Commission. Answering the question, 'Is there any tenant-right, or right of sale by the tenant, recognized on the estate?' he said: 'Not at all to the extent that it is in the North of Ireland; at the same time, if a tenant came to the agent, and stated that he had sold his farm to another person, and that person was approved of by the agent, there would be no inquiry as to the amount... given for it.' Asked whether the landlord on taking farms into his own hands would pay the occupiers for their tenant-right, as in Ulster, Kincaid replied that he would, or else resettle them on another part of the estate.[20] Palmerston's refusal to sanction the statutory enforcement of tenant-right owed less to abstract principle and more to the fact, particularly evident in the years of recovery and betterment after the Great Famine, that his tenantry were virtually co-proprietors of the soil already, exercising the practical freedom to dispose of their holdings by sale or bequest. Investing tenant-right with the force of law would have gravely undermined the landlord's restricted control over a typical Southern Irish estate, as happened under the Gladstonian land legislation. The reduction of very small tenants on Palmerston's property in Sligo was achieved by laying out a considerable sum of money, aided by the country people's assimilation of the harsh economic lessons of the Famine. When prime minister, Palmerston defended Irish landlords and tenants from the often ill-informed criticism current in Britain of the former's social responsibility and the latter's industry and economy.

He claimed that the exertions of Irish landlords for their tenants surpassed those which English landlords made, or needed to make. He rebutted the charge that Irish tenants were lazy and improvident. The Irish land question, he declared, should be seen in its historical context, 'of rebellion; of confiscation; of wholesale and violent transfers of land from class to class; of penal laws; of the exclusion of the largest class of the nation from the ordinary privileges of social existence ... of laws which exaggerated those animosities which political and social inequalities were, of course, of themselves calculated to produce'.[21] He thus acknowledged in parliament the reality of that popular feeling of dispossession which had no counterpart in Britain, and the intensity of which distinguished Irish agrarian politics in Western Europe. Given this historic temper among the people, Palmerston strongly deprecated the imprudence as well as the inhumanity of wholesale evictions. But he told the House of Commons that such drastic action might be necessary to counteract the power of Ribbonism; that is, of the widespread peasant secret societies which were exclusively Catholic and bound by an oath breathing fierce hostility against landlords and Protestants.[22] Episcopal condemnations of these societies as incompatible with the Church's teaching appear to have had little effect. The attitude of the parochial clergy to agrarian violence was more significant. In December 1863 the younger Sir Robert Peel reported to Palmerston 'a very remarkable change for the better' in this respect, on the evidence of remarks that parish priests addressed to their flocks from the altar. The two previous years had seen 'bitter denunciations of a shocking character against landlords and against British rule [which] were of most frequent occurrence, a very powerful source of enmity in country districts...'.[23] The change was almost entirely due to clerical concern at the resurgence of revolutionary nationalism, which, following the lead of Archbishop Cullen, they considered as sure to result in failure and repression. The revival of constitutional agitation for land reform at this date, with strong clerical backing, was an initiative launched, in part, to channel support away from Fenianism.[24]

The Encumbered and Landed Estates Acts of 1849–58 had been intended to attract British capital investment in Irish land by compelling the sale of heavily mortgaged estates on the creditors' petition. The buyers of encumbered estates turned out to be mainly Irish residents, including a good number from the Catholic middle-class, whose acquisition of property in the Landed Estates Court was on a scale large enough to disturb Palmerston. The displacement of his own kind by 'Catholic middle-class men' must – if it went on, as it did – loosen their hold on Irish land, for which the Union partly existed, and on which it partly depended.[25] The security of landlords was a major preoccupation with Palmerston. After the government had moved against Fenianism in September 1865, he felt that 'it would be prudent for the gentry of the South to send their families and valuable property to Dublin as soon as any outbreak takes place.' He was anxious to have cavalry patrols out to protect country houses and their occupants, believing that the Fenians' best plan would be to strike at these isolated but eminently worthwhile targets.[26] In the event, the Fenians, although disorganized by well-timed arrests, persisted with the more ambitious tactics that were to fail in 1867. If Palmerston was the truest friend the Irish landed class ever had, he could not prevent the gradual erosion of their position by the working of the Encumbered and Landed Estates Acts. The breach in landlord defences made by the Acts was not one that he could have repaired, had he wished to try. The legislation commanded the slightly regretful approval of the British landed interest as well as embodying the wholehearted convictions of Manchester School radicals. Irish landlords had few friends in Britain, where their unpopularity, as a class, with the tenantry often seemed hard to understand except by generalizing from the sins of individuals; so different was the British experience of landlord–tenant relations.

The government and Catholicism

Palmerston thus saw the greatest threat to British rule in the growing Catholic middle class in town and country. He believed he had the measure of the Catholic clergy. Resenting their hold over the popular mind, he yet did not consider the clergy capable of placing themselves at the head of an organized, effective national movement.[27] Nor, steeped as they were in the O'Connellite tradition, did the clergy aspire to do so. Hence his unwisely contemptuous dismissal of clerically dominated rallies held to denounce his Italian policy. 'Let these poor priest-driven Catholics in Ireland assemble, make violent speeches... The fate of the Pope will in no degree be influenced by the ravings and rantings of Irish demagogues.'[28] Several years afterwards he was cautioning the foreign secretary, Lord John Russell, not 'to take openly a position hostile to the Pope and distasteful to our Catholic fellow-subjects'.[29] Loath to concede anything in response to her political pressure, he did not seek to annoy Irish Catholicism gratuitously. On the contrary, his government passed the Party Emblems Act of 1860 in a fruitless attempt to restrain the customary provocation of Northern Orangemen, whose 'factious turbulence' he deplored.[30] He personally stood up for the continuance of the state grant to Maynooth. He did not pretend to approve of the political ethos inculcated at the seminary. He argued, first, that abrogating the grant would involve 'a breach of faith towards the Irish nation'; and secondly 'upon a broader ground...for considerations connected with the interests of the British empire'.[31] Withdrawal of the grant would have plunged Ireland, and the Irish overseas, into an uproar, so long as parliament upheld, with him, an Anglican establishment in a predominantly Catholic country.

The most famous Englishman to live and work in Ireland during this period, J. H. Newman, rector of the infant Catholic university in Dublin, shared Palmerston's grasp of the Irish clergy's objectives in political life, but with a discriminating sympathy absent in the statesman. On the one hand, Newman remarked in 1856, 'no small portion of the Hierarchy and clergy of Ireland think it...a misfortune that they have any of the upper or middle classes among them...in fact...they think that then only Ireland will become again the Isle of Saints, when it has a population of peasants ruled over by a patriotic priesthood patriarchally'.[32] On the other hand, Archbishop Cullen and many of the bishops wanted to give the middle class a Catholic and national formation. Of this clerical aim Palmerston really was afraid. As rector, Newman assumed that the institution had a basic political purpose, set out in his address of November 1858 to students attending evening classes at the university. He discerned in the Catholic middle class of Ireland 'the depositaries of increasing political power'. It was their destiny to guide 'the increase of political power in the Island of Saints'. He prophesied that the Catholic Ireland of a mature middle class which had enjoyed substantial access to higher education would arraign his own country before 'the tribunal of the European populations' on either side of the Atlantic; obtaining 'retribution...for past crimes in proportion to their heinousness and their duration'.[33] Newman's address is in itself explanation enough of the Palmerston government's reluctance to foster the Catholic university by state recognition. The most that ministers would hold out was a supplemental charter to the Queen's University empowering it to examine and confer degrees upon the candidates not educated in one of its component colleges. To Palmerston the demand for a chartered Catholic university, to be inevitably followed by a clamour for it to receive public funds, represented a very serious threat. He counselled the viceroy, Lord Wodehouse, to use 'much circumspection' in handling this question. '...what the Catholic priesthood want', he summed up, 'is that their Catholic college should be the only place of education for the young Irish Catholics, and that it should be like Maynooth a place where young men should be brought up to be bigoted in religion, to feel for Protestants theological hatred and to feel political hatred for England.'[34] In the fullness of time, the Catholic university, under the title of University College, Dublin, featured prominently in the phase of revolutionary nationalism that succeeded in erecting an Irish state.[35] The weakness of the middle-class element in early Fenianism was perhaps as severe a handicap as the disinclination of the countryside, under clerical guidance, to participate more actively.

Constitutional and revolutionary nationalism

The first Palmerston ministry had no majority before its triumph in the 1857 general election; and the second's margin over the Tories sometimes appeared precarious in the extreme. This was the setting of Palmerston's unenthusiastic play for the votes of Irish members, and of Disraeli's pursuit of an alliance between the Tories and the Irish Catholics. Stanley's diary has several interesting references to the alliance.[36] Disraeli, who never set foot in Ireland, dreamed for twenty years of something more, of a 'union'.[37] How little he understood the Irish question was embarrassingly clear to Stanley who visited Ireland a number of times. He was familiar with conditions on the family property in Tipperary and Limerick, where his father had been worsted in a trial of strength with his tenants at the end of the 1850s.[38] 'D[israeli] says', wrote Stanley, '"Ireland is agricultural, aristocratic, and religious: therefore Ireland ought to be Tory", but he does not allow enough for the antipathies of religion and race.'[39] Tory gains at the 1857 and 1859 elections, giving them over half the Irish representation, proved to be a disappointment. Catholics in the small, less than free electorate who decided to support Tories on this scale were not undergoing the conversion for which Disraeli hoped, but signalling an obstinate detachment from British politics. Repelled by the anti-Catholic and anti-national stance of Palmerston and Russell, these temporary Catholic allies of Toryism had no other means of asserting themselves so widely at the elections; since the independent Irish party was far gone in its decline. Even if Archbishop Cullen had not determined to put an end to it, the alliance, such as it was could not long have withstood Tory resentment of Disraeli's characteristic desire to transform another of his party's traditional attitudes. Stanley noted the Tory discontent on this score in June 1861.[40] Shortly after, one of Palmerston's senior cabinet colleagues, Granville, described the state of mind among Tories in Ireland, where he had accompanied the Queen on her visit that summer; they liked Palmerston's foreign policy, unsurprisingly, and they preferred him to Disraeli, whom they did not trust.[41]

Their loyalty, however, was to Derby. Derby's reservations about Disraeli's Irish strategy were no secret. Granville assured the prime minister that Irish Tories could not be induced, so long as Derby lived, to take the government side in party politics. Granville was endeavouring to dispel an idea that Palmerston found very attractive and had put to him, as to other ministers.[42] The need to conciliate Catholic Ireland tried the prime minister sorely. He perceived, or imagined, an escape from that compulsion by uniting Irish Protestants behind him. Irish Tory landlords, whose class owed him much, ought to be won over by the favours that were the small change of politics. Under the existing electoral system, the unified weight of the landlords would be formidable indeed. Palmerston nursed a hope, too, of making headway with the popular Toryism of Protestant Ulster. He was infuriated by the ingratitude, as it seemed to him, of Catholic Ireland when his government had incurred a certain risk to appease her. 'It is no doubt a good maxim of human conduct that we ought to return good for evil', he admonished Carlisle, whom he suspected of being soft with the Catholics, 'but the application of this principle to the practical affairs of this world admits of some qualification, and especially in cases in which other persons return evil for good.'[43] Looking back over the generation since Catholic emancipation, he persuaded himself, in his indignation, that Britain had 'heaped benefits and favours on the Irish Catholics'. The statement in his letter that 'We have relieved them from all their civil and political disabilities' – which was, of course, untrue – is a specimen of his claims for Britain's record. He was writing five days before he composed the memorandum of August 1861 in which he showed himself alive to the charge of exasperating the majority in Ireland. In the interval came Brand's warning, to the impact of which Palmerston alluded. Yet he could not bring himself to implement his own conclusions with a good grace. He hankered after the policy of courting the Irish Protestants.[44] In November of the same year there was speculation that the replacement of Cardwell as Irish secretary by Sir Robert Peel, and Peel's prompt display of antagonism towards the Catholics was 'a well planned design on the part of his chief' to gather the Protestants of Ireland round a government afraid of their hereditary enemies. While Stanley deemed Peel incapable of such premeditation, he thought Palmerston might be letting an impulsive, outspoken man, warmly anti-Catholic, have his head 'without being told why'.[45] What Palmerston actually wanted to be able to do at this juncture was to lean in the Protestant direction but to avoid setting the Catholics more against his government. This, he informed Carlisle, was the policy he favoured with the concurrence of some of his colleagues. There was to be no question of overt enmity to the Catholics, or of wooing the Toryism of Ulster. '…we might', he suggested, 'throw enough of coldness in our bearing towards, and dealings with, the Catholics to make them feel a difference, without giving them any stateable ground for complaint.'[46]

It was an impracticable suggestion. The 'Liberal Protestants',[47] whose importance in that country Palmerston exaggerated in his search for political materials, and the 'considerable body of Catholics, who are aware that your government is a good government', alleged by Granville to exist,[48] could not furnish a basis for ministerial independence of 'the Catholic party'. 'The Catholic party' was the expression that British Liberals and

Tories used to designate a reality in Irish politics in the chronological gap between the independent Irish and Home Rule parties. Archbishop Cullen infused this party with a moral unity and purpose which Palmerston's government might not ignore. J. F. Maguire was not quite representative of the nationalism of a party which had no formal existence. In common with Cullen, whom he would have been glad to see involving himself more closely in political warfare, Maguire had been a repealer when repeal seemed attainable, and remained one at heart. Of thirty- two Catholic MPs from Ireland at Westminster in July 1864, when Palmerston's second ministry was put to its severest parliamentary test, a single Tory MP contrasted with thirty-one Liberals, eleven of whom had sat as adherents of the defunct independent Irish party. Deducting two English Catholic landowners from the total, the remaining twenty-nine Catholic Liberals were pretty evenly divided between members of established landed families and men from business or the professions, inclusive of businessmen's sons.[49] The attraction of the Union for wealth, old and new, was patent in either of these broad categories. Nevertheless, the 'party' did respond, if uncertainly, to Cullen. His tactics were a continuation of the independent Irish party's: but his vision was clearer, and his tenacity greater. He did not believe in British friendship, Tory or Liberal. '...it is necessary for us to steer between the two parties and to get as much as we can expect from enemies', he wrote to The O'Donoghue MP after Palmerston's return to office.[50]

The constitutional nationalists feared the perennial appeal of an uprising against British rule. The *Cork Examiner*, Maguire's newspaper and the most influential Catholic and national journal outside Dublin, carried an article in December 1860 intended to dissuade its readers from hoping for French intervention in Ireland, as a result of deteriorating Anglo-French relations. The article quoted Robert Emmet at his trial, when he said of the French and their treatment of other nations: '*They promised them liberty, and when they got them into their power, THEY ENSLAVED THEM.*' Napoleon III, continued the *Examiner*, would rule Ireland 'on the Paris model' before eventually handing her back to 'an enraged and vengeful England'. The paper held up the Emperor's current duplicity in the affairs of Italy as proof of his unscrupulousness.[51] Sending a copy to Palmerston, Lewis observed that it would do more for the government than any prosecutions for sedition, 'which are always double-edged tools'.[52] The prospect that Britain would exact a price too terrible to contemplate from a rebellious Ireland haunted Cullen and those who thought like him when Fenianism took hold. He and they were not less ardent patriots for that. 'On our side is Erin and truth. On theirs is the Saxon and guilt', ran the Archbishop's simple analysis of his country's plight in a private letter to Major Myles O'Reilly MP, another moderate nationalist sitting as a Liberal.[53] It is noteworthy that Cullen expressed himself in racial terms, as did Palmerston, when he dropped his reserve.

The leading Catholic politicians and newspaper editors looked to Cullen. The O'Donoghue MP, whose behaviour Palmerston called 'unadulterated treason',[54] flirted with revolutionary nationalism; but he, like Maguire, pressed the Archbishop to intervene more in politics.[55] Cullen himself realized that 'Nothing can be done now without letting the Fenians into it.'[56] The Dublin *Freeman's Journal*, edited by the Protestant nationalist, Sir John Gray, reflected Cullen's ideas. Gray's knighthood, bestowed in 1863, recognized this newspaper's standing as the principal organ of 'the Catholic party'. Cullen revived O'Connellite nationalism when no successor to the Liberator could be found. Maguire, The O'Donoghue and J. B. Dillon were not remotely comparable figures. By the middle of 1861 Palmerston was having to face up to the disagreeable fact that 'scarcely any supporter of the Government would be returned at the present moment by any Irish constituency'.[57] If Catholic nationalists who were only nominal Liberals had to be reckoned as enemies, the parliamentary outlook for the government was uncertain. It was still more uncertain taking into account clerical and nationalist pressure upon genuine Liberals occupying Irish seats. Sir John Acton, the historian, is an instance of the second class. The near impossibility of finding a constituency in his own country prepared to return a Catholic led him to approach Cullen with due humility in search of an Irish seat.[58] Cullen's good offices, and those of the Archbishop's venerable uncle, Father James Maher, enabled Lord Granville's stepson to represent the borough of Carlow.[59] The electoral organization of the clergy, exemplified in the archdiocese of Cashel under Cullen's collaborator Archbishop Leahy,[60] induced the government to treat 'the Catholic party' with outward, if not with inward, respect. Brand told Palmerston in July 1861 that he would not be able to rely on ten out of nearly fifty Liberals returned by Ireland in any test of the government's stability, unless he adopted a more conciliatory posture towards the Irish Catholics.[61] The vote of censure in July 1864 on Palmerston's foreign policy, arising out of his undeniable mishandling of the Schleswig-Holstein question, demonstrated the potential of constitutional nationalism in Ireland to make itself felt through the British parliament. Out of the twenty-nine Irish Catholic Liberals, only eleven supported the government: two office-holders, an aspirant to legal office, the governor of the Bank of Ireland and, among the remaining seven, five substantial members of the landed class. Three Irish Catholic Liberals abstained and fifteen sided with the opposition, as did several of the other Liberals from Ireland, Acton included.[62] The ministry's margin of survival was eighteen. Tory votes and abstentions saved it. '…there is one thing certain', Cullen remarked '…the people of Ireland are heartily tired of Lord Palmerston and Sir Robert Peel…they are persuaded no justice or fair play can be expected as long as they are in power.'[63]

Abroad

Palmerston and Gladstone

The sharp lesson was not lost upon ministers. Palmerston continued to query and resist concessions to the majority in Ireland: but Gladstone was not alone in letting it be known that there were those within the government ready to review the big issues on which Palmerston had taken a firm stand. Having publicly indicated his conviction that an Anglican establishment in Ireland was an anomaly, and spoken at Manchester of the state of Irish feeling as discreditable to Britain, Gladstone joined cabinet colleagues in obtaining the prime minister's agreement to a select committee of inquiry into the land question. 'We *persuaded* Lord Palmerston', he wrote in his diary.[64] Although Palmerston ensured that the committee's composition and terms of reference rendered it innocuous, the cumulative impression made by these ministerial initiatives was favourable. 'The Catholic party' threw its influence behind the government in the general election of 1865. The outcome was only superficially a victory for Liberalism. Liberal candidates of one kind or the other took fifty-five seats to the Tories' fifty. The government also did better in Britain, so that the menace of an adverse vote by Irish Catholic Liberal MPs in conjunction with the Tories was diluted but by no means removed. H. A. Bruce, the junior minister in charge of education, explored the implications of the result when in Ireland after the election to negotiate the future of the Catholic university. He did not suppose that the election had settled anything between the two countries. It still remained to 'restore the Liberal party to its natural position in Ireland', as he put it to Lord Granville. Surely 'restore' was not the right word. At any rate, there was no doubt in the opinion of this very mildly radical British Liberal, a large landowner and coalowner in Wales where he evinced a sympathetic insight into a Celtic people, that some attempt must be made to place the Anglo-Irish relationship on an altogether better footing.[65] He did not minimize the difficulties. No stranger to Ireland himself, he told his daughter: 'You would be surprised to see how very different things are here from in England. It is like a foreign country, and in fact no foreign people in Europe are more utterly unlike the English in their views and habits of mind.'[66] He saw the Irish malaise as primarily political and religious; he did not try to separate these causes of unrest. He was prepared to risk 'the even ostentatious abandonment of our old policy of distrust and exclusion'. He retailed the bitter complaint of Thomas O'Hagan, solicitor- and attorney-general for Ireland from 1860 to 1865 before being made a judge, and men like him, the handful of Catholics in politics who had completely identified themselves with the British connection. Their consuming grievance was the common one: political control of Ireland by Englishmen and Protestants. In these last months of Palmerston's premiership the viceroy, the chief secretary, the permanent under-secretary, and the inspector-general of constabulary were all Englishmen. The lord chancellor of Ireland and the two law officers were Irish Protestants. It was irrelevant that the Irish judiciary had a Catholic majority, in striking contrast to the magistracy. Bruce went on, reporting what he had heard: 'This exclusion gave life and strength to that conviction which the Church Establishment had long since implanted, that they were kept systematically in... political degradation.'[67] The one Irish Catholic currently serving in Palmerston's government was, symbolically, a whip: the wholly anglicized Lord Castlerosse, heir to the earldom of Kenmare and over a hundred thousand acres of Irish land.

Palmerston's answer to O'Hagan's complaint had been given earlier, in letters to Chichester Fortescue, the MP for Louth and heir to his brother Lord Clermont's 20,000 acres in that county, who was a junior minister at the Colonial Office. O'Hagan, then attorney-general, had put his case to Chichester Fortescue. Writing in September 1864, Palmerston dwelt on the proportion of Catholic judges, which he argued was a security for even-handed administration of the law; but he insisted that Irish Catholics 'while professing a desire for religious equality, aim at nothing less than political domination.' He referred to Fortescue's dependence on Catholic votes in Louth, and reminded him that he, as prime minister, had to think 'imperially and not locally'.[68] After Palmerston's death, there began a period of wider reforms than he had been willing to carry out. Yet the essentials of Gladstonian policy did not differ markedly for many years. The Irish Church Act of 1869 did away with what had become a liability in British politics. The 1870 Land Act, in the version that Gladstone did not get through the cabinet and in that passed through parliament, was designed to leave the landlords sufficient of their legal rights to allow the class to continue figuring prominently in Irish life.[69] No Irish Catholic sat in a Gladstone cabinet. O'Hagan, promoted lord chancellor of Ireland after the law barring Catholics from the office had been changed, found himself excluded by Chichester Fortescue from the shaping of the 1870 Land Act.[70] In one respect, Gladstone was more Palmerstonian than Palmerston. Palmerston had briefly thought to perceive a 'breach... beginning to open between the priests and the laity of the Irish Catholics', which his government might exploit.[71] It was not an illusion that lasted for very long. Gladstone fought so hard in Britain for the Irish Church and Land Acts, especially the latter, that his emotional commitment fed an extraordinary notion of their significance. He conceived of the legislation as 'winding up the great chapter of account between the state and not the Roman Church or priesthood but the people of Ireland'.[72] He anticipated that his measures would drive a wedge between clergy and people. He subscribed, indeed, to Palmerston's view of 'ultramontane disloyalty'[73] in the clergy towards Protestant Britain. The land bill's failure to meet with popular acquiescence, let alone acclaim, seemed monstrously ungrateful to him, and he laid the blame on the Church. Until then, lacking Palmerston's vein of innate pessimism, he expected the Irish people to appreciate the limitations within which an imperial statesman had to work, and which he was as disinclined as Palmerston to overstep. For Gladstone, too, Irish nationality was a fact; but to both men the interests of Britain and her empire were paramount. This is also true of Gladstone's altered policy in the late 1860s.[74]

13

Empire

The scope of imperialism

The empire was integral to Britain's improving economic and political condition, as to her position in the world. At £25 million, her exports to the United States had risen by £7 million between 1855 and 1865, while those to India were up by 80 per cent at £19 million. Imports from India trebled over the same period to comprise 13.5 per cent of all imports against a figure of 6 per cent for Australasia and British North America but, collectively, the colonies of settlement were overtaking India as a growing market for British goods. On one estimate, India and the colonies of settlement took a third of new British investment abroad through the issue of quoted securities in the early 1860s. Nor was the remainder of the empire commercially negligible. Yet three-quarters of all exports went to foreign countries in 1865 along with two-thirds, or a higher proportion, of external investment through securities on offer in London.[1] Some foreign trading partners are reckoned to have constituted an 'informal' empire. The nature and extent of British investment in this notional empire can easily be exaggerated. Britain then neither ruled nor aspired to rule any part of it as Lord Cromer was to rule Egypt, after the Gladstonian occupation of 1882, in the name of the Khedive and under the vestigial authority of the Porte. Influence, not control, was Palmerston's aim. Nor was it exclusive influence that he wanted; it would have been politically unwise and economically unnecessary. He did not see the Anglo-Chinese war of 1856 to 1860 as such; those significant events in imperial history were limited operations, which left Britain at peace with China South of the route to Peking from the mouth of the Peiho river: 'we and the French are only exerting a *friendly pressure*'. His war minister, Sidney Herbert, cautioned the commander of the British expeditionary force in 1860 not to disturb the uninterrupted flow of commerce at the treaty ports. Palmerston, he wrote, supported an advance on the capital because satisfied that it would not result in the

331

collapse of the Manchu dynasty and 'by plunging everything into confusion destroy our trade'. 'Our object in going to China is to trade', stressed Herbert.[2] In common with Gladstone and other Peelites, Herbert had come to terms with the situation in the Far East since challenging Palmerston's policy in 1857. There and elsewhere, in countries similarly placed in the contemporary scale of civilization, economic penetration, backed by diplomacy and the judicious use of force, was Britain's method and her interest. Palmerston pursued the elimination of the traffic in negro slavery, his humanitarian passion, by like means.[3]

If the economic motive for maintaining and strengthening territorial empire, as for extending the range of imperialism outside the limits of formal possession, was very strong, it cannot be isolated from different considerations, in both instances. 'Despotism is a legitimate mode of government... with barbarians, provided the end be their improvement', stated J. S. Mill flatly after the Indian Mutiny, summing up a lifetime's experience of Indian administration from the London end.[4] It was a truism, although following the Mutiny Palmerston decided that the vaunted professionalism of the East India Company's administration had been found out: they should be put under the direct control of 'statesmen with large and general views...'.[5] Those views, said Gladstone in the House, ought henceforth to include a clearer perception that Indians possessed 'their own institutions... ideas... history... civilization'; it was quite wrong to suppose 'we had nothing to do but to walk into their country and proclaim the superiority of the Anglo-Saxon race'. This did not mean that it was possible to govern India otherwise than despotically, but that measured conciliation should accompany firmness.[6] Sir Charles Wood's adherence to such a line when he took the India Office in the second Palmerston ministry caused Bright to protest, with many businessmen, that he had thrown away the chance to effect 'an entire revolution in the condition of India', to the economic benefit of conquerors and conquered.[7] Palmerston preferred Wood's approach. 'The result... makes England a bright example for other countries', he told him with unfeigned pleasure. 'What a pity that you cannot take the Russian empire and the Poles in hand for a couple of years...'[8] The colonies of settlement, under responsible government by 1859 except for South Africa and Western Australia, were also a source of pride. One of the constellation of dukes in Palmerston's cabinet, the colonial secretary Newcastle, talked in 1862 of the settlers' freedom to sever their ties with Britain at will, and of his confidence that they would not break away. The Canadians had 'as one man' upheld 'the honour of our common flag' during the *Trent* crisis, defying the risk of an American invasion. The Australians' 'democratic spirit', though, worried him. On the same occasion, Lord Stanley, more of a liberal than the Peelite duke, described Australia as the setting for a trial of democracy under ideal conditions. If successful there it 'would not only raise a magnificent empire, but...do much to mould the political organization of the world'.[9]

Scattered round the globe were a number of imperial strongpoints. Bright attacked the retention of Gibraltar as 'contrary to every law of morality', and suggested, like someone who thought he knew a good bargain, that its return to Spain might be used to obtain the conversion of her tariffs to revenue duties.[10] For Mill, such places created no moral problem; they existed for 'the convenience of the governing state'. To him, as to Palmerston and public opinion, Britain was 'the Power which, of all... best understands liberty – and whatever may have been its errors in the past, has attained to more of conscience and moral principle in its dealings with foreigners than any great nation seems either to conceive as possible or recognize as desirable'.[11] Coming from whom it did, when it did, it was an effective endorsement of Palmerston's policies. On this view, his determined efforts to eradicate the slave trade harmonized with his actions as a whole. It is arguable that anti-slavery was a way of salving the national conscience for Britain's treatment of India and China. If so, there were those who regarded this lifelong commitment as a useless and dangerous indulgence, antagonizing France and America; *The Times* contended it was exactly that in a succession of editorials appearing in 1858. The newspaper was, however, 'painfully aware' of Palmerston's strength in domestic policies on this issue.[12] His motives and the public's may have been mixed: but his and their hostility to the slave trade was real; it helped to bring round Napoleon III and encouraged the opponents of slavery in the United States. *The Times* erred badly in its sarcastic observation that other countries lacked the 'moral elevation' to appreciate this peculiarly British cause.[13] Humanitarianism, trade and force were rarely quite separable in the regions subjected to European domination in one form or another; hence the cynicism of some contemporaries and historians about motives. The principle of extraterritoriality, a prominent feature of the treaties now concluded with Morocco, China and Japan, was applied more widely than in the past to take the strain of expanding commerce, or in anticipation of it. Without the framework built on that principle, which was not uniquely British, opening up the East would have resulted in greater instability and conflict. Extraterritoriality was a civilizing principle, inapplicable to Latin America, where the Monroe doctrine inhibited it, or wherever native governments were too primitive to accommodate it, as in most of black Africa.

India

The Mutiny presented the most serious challenge to Western dominance in the East that the last century saw.[14] This aspect of the rising was soon clear, and explains the surprising amount of sympathy for Britain in Europe and the United States, enhanced by revulsion at the massacres of white men and their families, although the numbers involved were small. News of the outbreak did not dismay Palmerston; in a sense, he welcomed it: 'distressing by reason of the individual sufferings and deaths, but...not really alarming...it may lead to our establishing our power upon...a firm basis'.[15] He was very slow to realize the gravity of the revolt, which, in his eyes, was not a 'real war'. On the fall of Delhi, he looked forward to 'a widespread tiger hunt' as the military rebels dispersed.[16] He did not expect the emergence of a 'partizan war', waged with the popular support undeniable in 'chronic insurrection' over huge areas of Northern and Central India. That was how the situation appeared to the commander-in-chief in India, Sir Colin Campbell, in the middle of 1858. It compelled the Derby ministry to act on pressing representations from India that the war had taken this turn, 'of all struggles...the most difficult to deal with'.[17] Sir John Lawrence asked for a thorough change of policy to avoid a long and debilitating campaign, unwinnable, he feared, for want of British manpower. Campbell held much the same language to the Duke of Cambridge at the Horse Guards.[18] Lawrence's achievements in the Mutiny were such that no one could accuse him, as the governor-general, Canning, was accused, of weakness and poor judgement. The Sikh and other Punjabi troops raised by him had proved indispensable; their realization of the fact was another threat, to which he pointed. The Tories carried out Palmerston's intention of terminating Company rule, and drafted at home the Royal Proclamation of November 1858 announcing the conditions on which it was proposed to govern India. Besides a generous amnesty for the rebels, limits were set to Westernization: the fabric of Indian society was guaranteed against disruption. Gladstone, following where Disraeli had led, said in June what he thought from the outset: the rebellion was no 'mere military mutiny'; it stemmed from the tendency of the British 'to destroy, in a great degree, not from any vicious purpose but from necessity, the whole upper class', quasi-autonomous princes and the superior landholders in directly administered territory.[19] This policy, to the extent that it had operated, was reversed to nearly unanimous approval in Britain. Even Bright concurred: only subsequently did he feel that economic change was being impeded by an excessive concern for native interests; and then it was the shielding of the peasantry that drew remonstrances from businessmen in Britain and India, with which he broadly agreed.[20] The growth of the Indian economy rated a high priority after the Mutiny; not the highest; since to make it that was considered incitement to discontent.

The Proclamation read like an implicit admission that the Mutiny was a national uprising. The rebels' immediate focus, planned or unplanned, had been the formerly imperial Mogul dynasty at Delhi, pensioners of the East India Company with unforgotten claims to suzerainty over the sub-continent, and until quite recently in receipt of marks of allegiance from their paymaster. Some native princes continued to strike coins bearing the superscription of the King of Delhi until the Mutiny. Under the last, westernizing governor-general before the Mutiny, Dalhousie, it was finally decided to put an end to this embarrassing reminder of the origins of Britain's presence in India: the octogenarian Bahadur Shah II learnt, a matter of months ahead of the rebellion, that on his death the kingly title would lapse and the family would be moved out of the ancestral palace. The aged king played a central, if passive and unwilling, role in the ensuing historical drama. The forbearance that had enabled him to do so excited Palmerston's indignation: 'Our policy seems to have been to keep a... sovereign, a...capital...and army' – the royal guard under a British officer – 'and then we wonder that all of a sudden on a tempting opportunity a violent attempt was made to turn all this into a reality.' Bahadur Shah died a prisoner in British Burma; two of his sons and a grandson were summarily shot after the city fell. Thus was Britain's legal standing in India drastically assured. Palmerston contemplated the destruction of every secular building in Delhi evocative of Moguls' greatness.[21] Vernon Smith at the Board of Control was attracted by the idea of razing the city to the ground. Canning argued against 'the great loss and injustice' of such indiscriminate severity, but promised to employ 'every device that can be invented to crush and obliterate the Mogul dynasty and recollection of it'.[22]

The unification of India's double government under the Crown was a measure to which Palmerston proceeded in the belief that the Company could not be left in place after what had occurred.[23] Wood – an 'energetic', his own word, president of the Board of Control in Aberdeen's ministry – considered that policy, supervised by the Board and its cabinet minister from the end of the eighteenth century, was to blame rather than administration, the Company's preserve. The insensitive westernization that bred a 'general disposition to revolt' against British rule, reflected the outlook of the House of Commons. Changing the form of government would do small good. Palmerston was right in his judgment of the situation. The India bill had so large a majority on its second reading in February 1858 that the Tories were not in a position to drop the reform of Indian government. Working the new system, as a distinguished secretary of state, brought Wood to a balanced conclusion that might have surprised those, and they were many, who thought him overbearing in the discharge of his responsibilities: but it hardly differed from what he told Palmerston when the takeover from the Company was in prospect. India was not better managed in London. The cabinet and his department should confine themselves to ensuring 'an even tenor of conduct' in 'certain great questions'.[24] They were, however, questions in which he had done much to lay down policy. The reduction of the native army, the removal of its artillery, and the substantial permanent increase in the number of British troops stationed in India at Indian expense were obligatory precautions, in the circumstances. Sir William Denison, governor of Madras, who came to the presidency from the complete contrast of New South Wales, objected to the plans that Canning had put in hand for associating native notables with the British under what became the Indian Councils Act of 1861, for improving the status of the 'gentry' in the localities, and for providing them with more openings in the army suited to their social rank. They were, to Denison, schemes irrelevant and potentially harmful in a country like India 'which we may fairly be said to hold by the sword'.[25] India was held by the sword: but it could not long be retained by 'any possible army of occupation', as Wood warned Palmerston in September 1857. To enlist their active sympathy, the natives must somehow be given more prominence in the structure of power without its being weakened. How this might be done perplexed him: 'I confess...I do not see my way at present.'[26]

Canning showed him the way. Dalhousie's anti-aristocratic bias aroused the strongest feelings, after the Mutiny, in his successor, who was bent on demonstrating that 'we look upon a native gentleman of family and property as something more than a coolie'.[27] Dalhousie favoured the school of Indian civilians who took the part of the cultivators; he regarded the superior landholders as 'false, oppressive and corrupt'.[28] Over a very wide area, this attitude influenced the operation of the land settlements, traditionally protective of the ryots in intention, which were a feature of British rule. Wood had misgivings about the 'levelling process involved'.[29] In the North-West Provinces and Oudh, where the Mutiny was centred, the resulting alienation of the 'gentry' did not, it turned out, imply a grateful peasantry. The ryots followed their natural leaders in preference to their British benefactors. Significantly, in Madras, the presidency least affected by rebellion, the feudal element was weakest; under the prevailing settlement there the ryots held immediately from the government. As Gladstone said, the policy embraced by his fellow Peelite, Dalhousie, was not 'vicious' in its moral purpose but destructive in its social logic. Its most controversial aspect, the absorption of native states into British India proper, had disturbed Wood. The pretext – failure of direct heirs, or the incorrigible abuse of princely authority – might or might not stand up to the examination of right in every case; the political wisdom displayed was certainly debatable. The states, covering some two-fifths of the country when the Mutiny broke, but with only about one-fifth of the population, perpetuated an India free from British administration; although their treaties with the Company, its residents at their courts and the British officers with their contingents made dependencies of the biggest of them, Palmerston looked to their eventual disappearance from the map.[30] The fateful decision to annex the large kingdom of Oudh, lying between Bengal and the North-West Provinces, went to the full cabinet in November 1855;

where Wood, then at the Admiralty, alone had reservations in the light of war in Europe but did not go to the length of opposition. Vernon Smith kept his doubts to himself.[31] The outbreak of revolt convinced Wood that the princes must remain, and have their fears of annexation dispelled. It was clear to him that if all Indians were reduced to 'the uniform level of our subjects', they would make common cause against the British.[32] Already, before the Mutiny, Canning had taken his opportunity to restore confidence among native rulers. He personally told Scindia, one of the most important, that 'we would very much prefer to see his people well and happily governed by him to governing them ourselves'. This change from Dalhousie's attitude may well have influenced the behaviour of leading princes in the Mutiny, as Canning believed.[33]

The governor-general brushed aside Vernon Smith's anticipation of 'great embarrassments' in rewarding princes for varying support of the British. He recommended the territorial concessions and, where possible, the relaxation of treaties, limited but reassuring measures, which he carried into effect between 1858 and 1860.[34] He was even more concerned to build up a native approximation to the British landed class. In order to assess the feasibility of a project that he made peculiarly his own, selected individuals in Oudh and the Punjab unexpectedly got 'the status and trust of gentlemen associated with – not severed from – the ruling power of their country'.[35] They were invested on their lands with the jurisdiction and functions of British administrators. Overall, settlement officers and their chiefs now tended to be more even-handed between superior and inferior landholders than in Dalhousie's day. Thus far, Wood backed the changes, sure that to have moved in the opposite direction would have been 'unnatural'. It was only sensible to 'conciliate to our rule the existing state of society'. With that aim, he accepted the inclusion, proposed by Canning, of Indians in the reformed viceroy's legislative council, as in the legislative councils restored to Bombay and Madras and newly instituted for the lieutenant-governor of Bengal.[36] Canning's closest adviser and Wood's regular correspondent, Sir Bartle Frere, advocated it 'under the idea that, as the Indians must rule...sometime or another, we had better begin to teach them to do so'. Denison had no patience with this very far-sighted view, disclosed in their exchanges. Britain should not think of relinquishing, at however distant a date, what was hers by conquest and reconquest: to have a native sitting in council, 'as a *quasi*-representative of India is but a sham'.[37] This was the voice of predominant sentiment, British and Anglo-Indian. Wood, who had hesitated over Indians in the councils, retreated into deliberate ambiguity. Native representation, literally interpreted, was 'simply and utterly impossible'; on the other hand, he said of the princes and the magnates to be chosen for the councils, 'they will no longer feel as they have...done...excluded from the management of affairs in their own country'.[38] He reckoned the Indian Councils Act was a crucial piece of legislation, 'a great experiment' in its shift away from 'the old autocratic government'.[39] Seven Indians served on the viceroy's legislative council in 1861–65. Their contribution bore out, on the whole, Denison's forecast that these legislators could not but be aware that they were 'only there on tolerance'.[40]

The Mutiny came from below. Indians of high rank, like those later put into the councils, seem to have had little to do with the disaffection in the army of the Bengal presidency. Princes and large landlords, though resentful of their treatment by the British and uneasy about the future, stood to lose greatly by supporting rebellion. The King of Delhi and his family, the deprived royal house of Oudh, the Nana Sahib denied the pension paid to his adoptive father, the last Peishwa, and the Rani of annexed Jhansi, had obvious incentives to foment unrest and give the mutineers the leadership they needed as and when they rose. Yet even in Oudh, the taluqdars so recently mulcted in the review of tenures after annexation, did not fully commit themselves until the failure of the first bid to raise the siege of Lucknow. The Company's mutinous troops, westernized to the point of feeling that they were a match for the British soldier, made the rising credible by their early successes, their convergence, whether spontaneous or inspired in the beginning, on Delhi, and their continued resistance after the fall of the city and the capture of Bahadur Shah deprived them of those unifying symbols of a resurgent India. Scindia and Holkar, a prince of similar standing in Central India, were unable to prevent their men from joining the rebels. Decades previously an eminent Anglo-Indian authority had predicted that 'the spirit of independence' would surface first in the native army.[41] The sepoy was, it has been well said, 'a peasant in uniform',[42] but one imbued with the confidence derived from Western training and discipline. The corps of native officers promoted from the ranks and accustomed to commanding a company or a troop in the frequent absence of the British officer allotted to it, held units together in mutiny and took them into battle with a standard of efficiency flattering to their erstwhile masters. The Bengal army, with few exceptions, revolted or had to be disarmed. The mutinies preparing in the Bombay army were nearly all scotched because government had been alerted by those in Bengal, which may have been triggered prematurely; but the evidence of complicity between the two armies was alarming. Nor were the troops in the Madras presidency exempt from the influence of subversion. Had the Bengal army, with the capital and the representative of the Moguls in its power, succeeded in overrunning the British in the North and centre, the sympathetic reaction in Bombay, Madras and the native states, notably Hyderabad, might have been uncontrollable, driving the foreigner back to the seaboard, as feared at the time. '...the...mass of the community would rise against us if they dared', observed Denison two years after the fighting had ended. 'I do not go this length', replied Canning, '...I admit that we cannot trust the *mass* of the community anywhere.'[43]

The princes were safe with Canning's successor; but he knew that should Lawrence become viceroy, a title introduced to mark the end of the Company in 1858, the policy of '*actively*'[44] identifying the native gentlemen with British rule would receive less emphasis. His proclamation dispossessing the rebels in Oudh, so vehemently criticized at home, was intended to lead, as it did, to the replacement of the land settlement imposed after annexation. That had failed politically; superior landholders were to recover many of the rights too extensively lost to the cultivators. However, Canning, who left India in March 1862, had not meant to deprive inferior landholders of the protection so recently given to their occupancy-right.[45] Its removal was the work of C. J. Wingfield, chief commissioner of the province from 1859 to 1866. Canning's conviction that the Indian social order should be strengthened and turned to account by government was transformed under Wingfield into an insistence on making British landlords out of the taluqdars, to the best of his ability and in conformity with 'the natural laws of society'. He construed Canning's exceptional grant of permanent ownership to them as excluding subordinate rights. The question was decided for Wingfield on the analogy with the United Kingdom, where full proprietorship admitted of no interference between landlord and tenant: 'every attempt to legalize it under the guise of tenant-right in Ireland has been defeated in Parliament, and the idea of limiting the power of the landlord as to...rent...or the choice of a tenant has been denounced as Communistic by an eminent...living statesman'. The statesman was Palmerston, whose language in Irish land debates Wingfield echoed to defy Lawrence, a firm friend of the ryot throughout his career.[46] Wood felt increasingly doubtful about the justice of reducing the Oudh ryot to a tenant-at-will; but he hesitated to upset a supposed part of Canning's arrangements without evidence of discontent. Where there was actual discontent, or good reason to be afraid of it, he came down on the side of the cultivator.[47]

The indigo-growing districts of Bengal presented him, from 1860, with a collision between the ryots and British planters, behind whom were the merchant houses of Calcutta; a combination able to enlist powerful allies among Indian civilians and at home. Comprehensive legislation of 1859, in theory, protected the Bengal ryots, and did encourage them to stand up to the planters. Feeling the effects of quickening economic expansion, they were reluctant to deliver indigo at the old price to masters who, for several generations, had bought or leased the rights of native zemindars. The crop was grown against advances by the planters, whose arbitrary behaviour, though habitual, now provoked disturbances that stopped well short of rebellion and were not aimed at government. Canning and his advisers appointed a commission of inquiry, which exposed the abuses of which an illiterate peasantry had been the victims, and passed a temporary measure compelling the ryots to fulfil their manifestly inequitable contracts, lest they should abandon indigo for a food crop saleable at a market price. Wood refused in 1861 and again in 1862 to countenance a lasting change in the law making breaches of contract directly or indirectly punishable as a criminal offence in order to facilitate the delivery of agricultural produce. The indigo disturbances were serious enough for Palmerston to list them among his ministry's problems at the beginning of 1861.[48] Wood said the home government 'had done their duty...by holding the scales as impartially as possible between...ryots and planters'.[49] He claimed no more than that, knowing how Canning had yielded to the alliance of officialdom and capital, united by racial prejudice and financial interest in a bad cause. The issue was soon revived in the shape of proposals for the 'specific performance' of contracts to be enforced by civil proceedings. This variant of the amendment to the law originally put forward did not prosper, either. Lord Elgin and Lawrence both thought it was the ryot and not the planter who needed protecting. Wood was more anxious to avert unenforceable legislation and its consequences.[50]

The law member of the viceroy's council from 1862 was the jurist, H. S. Maine, who, consistently with his already famous thesis, advocated a gradual transition in India to the supremacy of contract and competition.[51] Nevertheless, Wood's caution struck him as exaggerated; quickly established as an influential figure in the politics of Indian administration, he could tell the secretary of state: 'You are...too much influenced by...the antagonism of race and...the supposed analogy of Ireland.'[52] Wood's long, and discerning experience of Irish unrest taught him the impolicy of asserting 'strict legal right' when a large majority rejected it; he mentioned the Tithe War of the 1830s and its outcome, the shooting of Irish landlords and the bitterness of the evicted tenant in America, 'a feeling of which we have not seen the end yet'.[53] The decline of indigo planting in Lower Bengal, hastened by the ryots' unwillingness to grow it, went some way towards proving his point. In their predicament, the planters tried to coerce recalcitrants by trebling or quadrupling rents. 'The Great Rent Case' that ran for several years elicited a definition of fair rent under the relevant legislation as the market value. The judgement by Sir Barnes Peacock, chief justice of Bengal, confirmed Wood's worst fears. It removed an essential safeguard of occupancy-right. Its principle, if upheld on appeal, would spread from Bengal and revolutionize the tenure of land outside princely territory, giving 'the superior white race'[54] what it must not have, a binding claim on government to exact submission to the British who had invested in India. The strength of the ryot lay in custom and its official recognition since Lord Cornwallis's settlement of Bengal in the 1790s. To break with these traditions would be extremely unwise: 'What is, should be preserved', Lawrence was glad to hear from Wood, who told the viceroy that he did not want to seem to extend tenant-right in India when ministers were resisting it in Ireland.[55] The reversal of Peacock's ruling by the full Calcutta high court, when the chief justice was isolated among his fourteen colleagues, came as a relief to the secretary of state. Maine expected the decision on appeal. His rationalization of statutory tenant-right, for Indians, was simple and uncontroversial: on the subject of current litigation, he thought the existing law set 'much the same bar against rackrent which social and political considerations place between English landlord and tenant'.[56] This was the spirit in which Indian land legislation had been framed: an application of inveterate British paternalism, whatever help the anti-landlord theories of Utilitarian economists afforded.

Yet, writing to Wood after the high court had decided, Maine favoured the prospective abolition of the rights just mentioned. Hard to defend from home criticism, those rights conferred by occupancy should be restricted to existing tenants, and so phased out.[57] A specimen of the criticism was *The Times*'s attack on the final verdict in the Great Rent Case. Its editorial came from the pen of Robert Lowe, articulate and formidable on the Liberal back benches, who doubled as a leader-writer.[58] The article called for the legislative reinstatement of Peacock's overturned judgment, and invoked for both Ireland and India Maine's doctrine in his classic on *Ancient Law* that custom could not withstand the inevitability of a free market.[59] Wood bore in mind something else that Maine had said in a letter to him. Ireland and New Zealand, too, where the war between settlers and Maoris had lately flared up, illustrated how 'all real dangerous disputes with masses of population...arose out of land questions'.[60] The secretary of state had not hidden his distrust of British settlers, if settlers they were, in India, quoting in the Commons Mill's *Considerations*: '...the individuals of the ruling people who resort to the...country to make their fortunes are...those who most need to be held under powerful restraint...Armed with the prestige and filled with the scornful overbearingness of the conquering nation, they have the feelings inspired by absolute power without its sense of responsibility.'[61] There was plenty of sympathy where it mattered with Wood's hostility to the freedom loudly demanded by men eager to exploit India's resources. Shaftesbury headed a long list of signatories to an address thanking him for his refusal to let the criminal law be employed to compel the fulfilment of contracts for indigo and other produce; an example of the great Evangelical's practised use of pressure-group tactics. The address dwelt on the certainty that a hold, unknown to English law, over the contractor would be abused.[62] Samuel Laing accused the signatories of inverted racialism and of transferring to India an old prejudice against the employer; he praised Canning and his councillors, of whom he had been one, for trying to remove before the cotton famine 'defects in the way of bringing European capital into direct contact with the native cultivator'.[63]

The intemperance of Laing's charges damaged his cause; but the government and Wood were vulnerable to the clamour for cotton during the American civil war. 'I am much obliged to you for... early intimation of my warning to quit', wrote Wood to Delane on the topic, '...But... consider that the ryots are small people like the Irish tenantry.' The simplest and fairest method of inducing them to grow cotton was '*price...* all that is needed' with the provision of improved communications already in hand. Government agency and purchase to stimulate cotton would be cumbrous, expensive and superfluous.[64] He was sardonic about free-trading Lancashire's importunity for state intervention to help obtain its raw material.[65] The waste land resolutions passed by Canning and his council in October 1861 and designed to further British investment were unacceptable as they stood to Wood, out of the same concern for the ryot. Edmund Ashworth of the Manchester-based Cotton Supply Association, a close friend of Bright, said that the 'keystone' of cotton cultivation must be ownership in fee simple, quit of the revenue due to government, as the successor of native rulers, on all land. The nominal Tory, Stanley, was sympathetic, when secretary of state, to the Association and to the promotion of British colonization in climatically suitable areas.[66] Canning's resolutions gave land to buyers very cheaply, and permitted redemption of the revenue on the basis of a low imputed assessment. Wood objected to the financial loss entailed upon India's government and taxpayers. The amended regulations for sale and taxation did not prevent a 'company mania' that inflicted speculative casualties.[67] Even the alienation of these unoccupied tracts in thinly populated hill districts troubled Wood; he stipulated that the assertion of prior claims to the lands should not have to be made almost at once but within the normal limit of time in law. Discussing waste lands at length in his correspondence with Delane, he adverted to Lawrence's views, a stronger version of his own: 'nothing is so likely to create a combination against us, and a general discontent and rising as interference with their land'.[68]

Tea and coffee, but little cotton, was grown on the plantations thus acquired. Lancashire was not prepared to make the investment; although the Manchester chamber of commerce protested to Palmerston at the dilution of Canning's resolutions.[69] British millowners only wanted Indian cotton, Wood told Delane, so that they might have access to an alternative source of supply when they could not get American cotton at the right price, or at all; when they could, he was afraid that India's crop would be left on her hands.[70] Bright's plea for a five-year exemption from assessment for the revenue wherever landholders turned to cotton was risible to Wood in its palpable self-interest.[71] Nevertheless, he pressed the Indian authorities not to delay spending the money allocated to a large programme of railways, roads and irrigation, mixing state with private capital. The expenditure would reassure the House of Commons of his determination to pursue the economic development of the sub-continent, benefiting not merely Lancashire but all the industries represented in a huge delegation from chambers of commerce that waited on him in February 1861. Quite as much as Wood, Palmerston understood that Britain's best interests would not be served by the wholesale sacrifice of India to the impatience of such recent converts to imperialism as George Hadfield, the Non-conformist radical MP for Sheffield.[72] It needed the prime minister to contain the belief concisely stated in the *Leeds Mercury* of Edward Baines, another Anti-Corn Law Leaguer who had adjusted his vision of the world: 'India is not a military position, nor a benevolent undertaking', declared the *Mercury* in August 1860, 'it is a great commercial adventure...our main object, as a people, is not to civilize or to Christianize...We hold India, as a nation, for the sake of opening up its commerce, and so of extending... our own.'[73] This was the negation of the Cobdenite ideal of universal progress by means of unfettered industry and trade.

India paid for her subjugation and contributed to her development by the imperial power. To the ordinary expenses of Indian administration were added those of putting down the Mutiny, of support of the increased British force stationed in the country, of investment in public works, and of accumulated debt. Government's chief source of income was the land revenue, widely subject to periodical revision. While Wood sanctioned a permanent settlement of the revenue in principle to reap the political and economic benefits that its proponents anticipated, he effectively stopped its implementation, for financial reasons. This was a debate about the long term. In the mean time, on either view, the ryots' ability to pay had to be supplemented. A low income tax, with a limited life, was brought in to reach men and classes above the ryot. Low differential tariffs – 5 per cent in the case of cotton goods – were standardized at 10 per cent; as the Indian deficit shrank, the rate went down to 5 per cent again on cotton good in 1862, and 1 per cent on imported iron in 1863, and $7\frac{1}{2}$ per cent generally in 1864.[74] '...it was a remarkable thing', George Hadfield complained, 'that the conquerors of India were made the tributaries of that people.' He and his constituents resented the 10 per cent on Sheffield's engineering exports to a country for which Britain had shed 'her best blood', and which he alleged did not subscribe 'a single farthing' to the Treasury. Anxiety mingled with resentment in the assembled cotton masters listening to him at Manchester. Thomas Bazley, a cotton spinner, MP for the town, and yet another veteran of the League, estimated labour costs in India at a quarter of Lancashire's. On top of that advantage, the higher tariff amounted to protection; he envisaged a native textile industry arising 'extremely injurious to us'. There was a 'duty to sympathize with the labouring classes' in the grip of the cotton famine. The Hon. Algernon Egerton, a Tory MP for the county, argued that British investment in India would be diverted from cotton growing to manufacturing: 'Nothing...could be more suicidal.'[75] It was an imperial, and not a purely Indian, question. Palmerston treated it as such. India taxed herself heavily to meet the expenditure on the British and native armies; he advised the impressive deputation with its thirty MPs from both parties to take 'the rough and the smooth together'. But the Indian government reduced the objectionable tariff on cotton goods that year.[76]

The 'rough' was a transitory irritant. The 'smooth' was reflected in the statistics of Indo-British trade and the returns on capital invested flowing homewards. The state-guaranteed dividend of 5 per cent on money put into railways ensured the great popularity of those undertakings with British investors, if it cost the Indian taxpayer dear. As Wood predicted, the ryots did grow cotton at the prices prevailing during the American civil war, and the feared competition from Indian mills did not materialize in the shadow of the British industry. Bombay, the centre of the boom in raw cotton, witnessed an extraordinary fever of speculation, and a correspondingly dramatic collapse when the American crop came back on to the market. Every sort of corporate venture was started, 'getting shares afloat to gamble with', wrote Denison from Madras. 'They say that everybody at Bombay is bankrupt, officers civil and military, judicial and ecclesiastical.'[77] The repercussions of the crash were to be felt in London. The striking expansion of the Indian economy since the Mutiny received a check; it was, in the event, no more than that. Facing a meeting in his industrial seat of Halifax, Wood had said that he did not govern India for the well-being of Lancashire, or for the 50,000 whites in the sub-continent, but for the 180 million natives. He proclaimed the greatest happiness of the greatest number as his criterion of good government: 'That was the true policy.' His remarks concluded soothingly, however, after a defence of the refusal to exempt land under cotton from liability to the revenue; of the modifications to Canning's waste land resolutions – both vindicated as simple justice to the huge majority; and of the pace at which public works were proceeding. India ruled in the way he considered right, would not fail to yield more 'wealth as well as...glory to the English nation'.[78] Not that he placated Edmund Ashworth, who asserted he was an obstacle to progress with whom the Ottoman Sultan compared favourably.[79]

Absolute property in land and an exceptional contract law, Ashworth claimed were requisite for investment 'in safety in a country like that'; putting money into cotton growing was not advisable on any other terms.[80] He and his fellow Quaker Bright put the interests of British businessmen and planters in India first, as the instruments of economic change without which there could be no progress in other respects. Theirs was a sincerely held view, although Wood and his colleagues thought it a dangerously exaggerated, and to that extent a selfish, delusion. When the India bill of 1858 was before Parliament, Bright sought a government 'not for civil servants... but for the non-official mercantile classes from England and... the... natives'. In practice, he only wanted to see 'two or three at least... intelligent natives' on each of the councils of the five presidencies, immediately answerable to London, into which he advocated redividing India on grounds of manageability from home. Official and non-official British members should be sure of a large majority of council places; self-rule for Indians was out of the question for anything between fifty and five hundred years.[81] Such insistent pressure from business amid the Mutiny's legacy of worsened racial antagonism prompted plain speaking by Wood in the House. He reinforced his strictures on the character of the British who went to India to make money by setting forth the general theory of race relations which he endorsed: 'All experience teaches us that where a dominant race rules another, the mildest form of government is a despotism.' Were the British settlers, so called, to be indulged in their natural wish for a considerable say in government, this popular element would be certain to abuse its position. In fairness, he noted the hardening of racial attitudes among the higher ranks of the military and the civil service. The relationship between 'civilized and less civilized' seemed to him the most serious problem of the age internationally and within territories that were, or had been, the scene of conflict. Grave in the United States, the British colonies of South Africa and New Zealand, the situation was nowhere more critical, he believed, than in India.[82] Wood kept unofficial British members on the councils under the Act of 1861 to a minimum: 'I do not think them very fit to legislate for other people, whom they despise or hate, or whose interests are totally different', he wrote to Frere.[83] Neither the secretary of state nor the government of India could stop the misuse of economic power over the native population, but they limited it.

The Mutiny's religious aspect gave rise to expectations in Britain which ministers had to disappoint. While the fusion of Moslem and Hindu in the rebellion under the Mogul figurehead indicated its essentially political nature, the British were identified with their religion by the rebels. A combination of westernizing disregard for native *mores* and greater missionary activity than the Company had previously countenanced, although not by any means on a large scale, fed the smouldering unrest. The notorious issue to Bengal regiments of cartridges greased with a mixture of beef and pork fat, and therefore offensive to Moslem and Hindu, was the occasion of revolt, or a pretext. In a real sense, the survival of

Christianity in India depended on the outcome of the struggle that followed: but the survival of Islam and Hinduism did not. The reliance of the British on uncertainly loyal native troops, princes and landholders of influence to fight for them, or not to fight against them, precluded a crusade even though the reconquest was widely seen as one. The government's embarrassment lay in resisting the orchestrated clamour for the abandonment of official neutrality towards Christianization, the old stance of the Company. A junior minister, W. N. Massey, under-secretary at the Home Office, called for a complete reversal of policy: toleration was, by definition, religious freedom for Christians, and stretching it to comprehend superstition 'a gross abuse of the term'. Maladministration there might have been, but he discovered the outbreak's primary cause in the wrongly tolerated native religions, the devotees of which imputed the authorities' restraint to 'fear...subserviency and...want of...faith in the...truth...of the Christian revelation'.[84] Massey was a highly educated man, a historian of some repute and later finance member of the viceroy's council; whose 'imbecile display' in this speech Mill lashed in *On Liberty*.[85] No intellectual, the Baptist preacher and rising star of Evangelical Dissent, C. H. Spurgeon, interpreted religious liberty with the same righteous narrowness to his popular audiences at the Crystal Palace, and said that the British government ought in conscience to have suppressed 'the vile religion of the Hindoos'.[86] Shaftesbury, the Broad Church Bishop of London, Tait, Bishop Wilberforce for the High Church, and Miall of the Liberation Society all rejected any sort of coercion to spread Christianity. They were not less inclined to denounce its competitors.

Lewis convinced himself, his diary shows, that the Mutiny was religious in origin.[87] Yet, libertarian that he was, he preferred not to see it as a conflict between Christianity and its Indian rivals but as an episode in the struggle of 'civilization against barbarism'.[88] With more perception, Tait depicted a clash of civilizations. A classical education created a predisposition to sympathize with 'refined heathens', until the atrocities that disfigured the Mutiny revealed 'what a refined heathen is...in a moment he can be transformed into a raging beast...impelled by a spirit of demoniacal wickedness'. There was no longer room for illusions about non-Christian religions. Conversely, the Bishop rejoiced in examples of heroism furnished by the British in India; proof of 'the reality of Christianity'. 'A polished Brahmin, or a polished Mahometan, is a savage still', concurred Wilberforce.[89] Miall spoke of Islam's duty to propagate itself by the sword, and of the 'absurdity...impurity, and...cruelty' of Hinduism. Shaftesbury condemned 'false religions' but ascribed what had happened rather to the workings of original sin, unchecked by christianization.[90] The Evangelical *Record* attacked Canning, Vernon Smith, Derby and Ellenborough, for uniting to retard the diffusion of the Gospel in India, and hoped that

Palmerston would not 'imperil his just popularity' for the sake of the first two.[91] The High Church *Guardian* criticized the 'indifference or cowardice' of Stanley, when he was responsible for India, in declining to sanction even voluntary Bible classes in the schools and colleges run by government.[92] Palmerston and Wood also refused to take the risk of offending Moslem and Hindu susceptibilities on this minor symbolic departure from traditional neutrality. Shaftesbury supported ministers in the Lords when they saw to it that nothing came of a motion censuring the Bible's exclusion.[93] The British were content with the political salvation of their empire. They accepted the comfortable argument, restated by the *Economist* at the height of the religious excitement in Britain, that 'our railways...our steam vessels...our system of equal taxation...our scientific physics...prepare the way for a spiritual faith' by erosion of the moral and intellectual foundations of superstition.[94]

When he discussed the suppression of the Company with Palmerston in September 1857, Lewis opined, with some reason, that they had been saved from disaster by the division of the native army into three self-contained establishments for Bengal, Bombay and Madras.[95] The dreaded contagion of mutiny shaped the reorganization of that diminished army. The native artillery, often well handled during the recent battles, was disbanded. The lately conquered Sikhs of the Punjab gave a lead to the Moslems and Hindus who had lived under their dominion; they formed the core of Lawrence's troops and fought for the British as the lesser of two evils, to defeat the threat of being ruled from Delhi, the object of their ancient enmity. 'Seldom', observed his biographer, 'has the somewhat sinister maxim, *divide et impera*, been acted upon...with...more triumphant results.'[96] The reconstruction of the native army was based upon the same principle as that which Lawrence had skilfully applied in the crisis. 'If all India was to unite against us, how long could we maintain ourselves?' wrote Wood to Canning's successor, Elgin, on utilizing racial differences in the recruitment and distribution of native regiments. With the thought of another mutiny always present, Wood did not wish to have an efficient war machine: the clear inferiority of the native to the British soldier was to be desired.[97] For Lawrence, viceroy from 1864, the 'good humour' of native troops took precedence over the enforcement of discipline to the standards of the British service. The secretary of state defended the viceroy to the Duke of Cambridge. Lawrence's patriarchal ideal of an Indian regiment should not be sacrificed to 'mere discipline'. In the pre-Mutiny army the 'inevitable separation' between British officers and sepoy had gone too far: the tendency must be reversed, 'if we are to preserve our rule'. Government was really powerless, Wood believed, to halt the deterioration in the racial climate that surrounded the British settler. It was all the more urgent to foster better relations within the native army.[98]

This protracted debate started with adoption of the irregular system of regimental organization for all native units as a result of the Mutiny. The number of British officers to a regiment was lowered from a theoretical twenty-four to seven, who did not usually command a formation smaller than a wing.[99] The enhanced status of native officers in permanent command of companies, troops and squadrons, with the possibility of direct entry for those of 'high birth and fair fortune', supplied almost the only opening under government to 'congenial and honourable employment' for the cadets of Indian feudalism, argued Canning: 'No native dynasty has ever neglected...that...We have done so, and have no reason to be proud of it.' 'How many native dynasties have been deprived of their thrones by successful feudal dependents?' riposted Denison.[100] It was generally agreed that the attractions of the irregular system were great for British officers able to stamp their personalities on regiments organized to reflect the commander's personal example and initiative; to Canning they were 'the very best servants that England can have in India'.[101] Such commanders proved their worth in the Mutiny, especially with Punjabis; but the Ambala campaign on the North-West frontier in 1863 revealed that the average native regiment could not do without a stronger British cadre, as Canning had foreseen. Whatever the state of the native army's morale, Britain's ascendancy over the sub-continent rested on security through white soldiers maintained by the Indian taxpayer, and on the figure she cut in the world. Canning ought to have taken more notice of the warning signs before May 1857. Prior to his departure for the East, Ellenborough, who had been governor-general in the forties and remained perhaps the best informed of British statesmen about India, sent him concerned letters. They dealt with the effects of annexing Oudh, and of further reducing 'by one man' the white force, depleted by the calls of the Crimea. Ellenborough forwarded, too, the remarks of William Edwards, a particularly discerning Indian civilian, on the setbacks in the Crimea, 'the lamentable absence of all which the natives term "Bundobast"', roughly translatable as good management, were very damaging to British prestige. In the bazaars, the eventual fall of Sebastopol did not compensate for previous loss of face.[102]

Bright's suggestion for abolishing the central government in India and making the presidencies independent of each other was not original.[103] Lewis put the idea to Palmerston before they knew Delhi had been regained: 'without carrying too far the maxim of *divide et impera*, there was no reason why we should destroy those elements of separateness and mutual repulsion which already existed, and were not...our creation'.[104] Superficially tempting, the extensive development of a tried policy that he recommended did not go with the grain of history. The British could not destroy the unity they had fostered, a considerable advance upon that of the Moguls, nor govern in what they themselves knew to be a narrowly selfish spirit. The ruthlessness displayed in the heat of vengeance and repression was seen as a passing, and frightful, necessity: 'in exacting a tremendous retribution we are doing our duty, and performing an act of mercy', argued Macaulay in his journal; he nevertheless realized the corruption, personal and political, of legitimate savagery.[105] So did Canning, who was blamed for trying to check these excesses, and the Evangelical Lawrence, who was not.[106] Delane, whose newspaper had been loud for severity during the critical months, said later that he had striven to keep the details of British atrocities 'from the public of Europe, as...discreditable to the national character'.[107] The repression endured in the folk memory, as it was designed to do.

In this setting, Palmerston, and Wood beside him, played down the role of the home government when it suited him under pressure. The prime minister sometimes talked as though India enjoyed the independence of control from London that the colonies of settlement did. It was also a way of protecting her from home opinion, the intrusion of which in the sub-continent Mill deplored.[108] For the experience of the Mutiny, recollected on the other side of the world, did not necessarily make for prudence at the highest, or any other, level after the restoration of order. A cabinet minister, the Presbyterian Argyll, surveying Indian policy in the *Edinburgh Review* for 1863, found the scrupulous respect for native worship promised by the Royal Proclamation of 1858 inconsistent with social progress. British rule must inexorably encroach upon 'the habits...customs and legal principles of a barbarous religion'.[109] As a result of withstanding the demands of different lobbies, the concept of trusteeship emerged more clearly; it was interpreted conveniently and genuinely to mean solicitude for 'the timid Hindoo' and firmness towards 'the bigoted Mahommedan'.[110] Conventional wisdom perceived the natural enemy of the victors in the latter for decades after the final overthrow of the Mogul dynasty. It would be long before products of the universities set up at Calcutta, Madras and Bombay in the year of the Mutiny became a greater danger than the mutinous sepoys, ambitious princes and discontented landholders, large and small. For Palmerston the government of India were only officials, he said to the Manchester chamber of commerce when it tried to rely on the viceroy against the secretary of state.[111] 'A controlling authority at home... competent, vigilant, and strong' owed its establishment to Palmerston's political will, on which Wood was able to count.[112]

The colonies of settlement

Outwardly, the settler colonies drew a fraction of the interest and concern that India attracted, but in the aggregate they were hardly less significant.[113] The first Palmerston administration inherited the com-

mitment to responsible government, and did not stand in the way of its
enlargement. Economically, the arrangement served the mother country
well. The onset of protectionism in the colonies did not prevent the growth
of British exports, which benefited from the dominance and security of
British investment in this field. Politically, there were divided reactions at
home, cutting across party. Palmerston did not want to lose the self-
governing empire's contribution to Britain's place among the nations. The
public was equally appreciative, without any need for the display of
emotion called forth by the Indian Mutiny, of these and of expanding
settlement under its flag. In the second Palmerston administration,
Gladstone was loath to believe in the depth of the colonists' attachment to
Britain as justifying a continued obligation to take care of their external
defence. 'If Canada desires to be British and to fight for [the] British
connection as men fight for their country', he eventually admitted, 'I do
not think we can shrink from the duty of helping her.'[114] The ethnic
Britishness of the colonies was undeniable, French-Canadian and Cape
Dutch minorities apart. In many minds, however, a question mark hung
over the outlook of relatively egalitarian societies, where a rude grasping
democracy, as it seemed, rejected the ordered politics of its British origins.
Accordingly, Gladstone's friend, the Hon. Arthur Gordon, when
lieutenant-governor of New Brunswick in 1863, considered that the people
were 'essentially foreigners'. Gladstone fastened, too, on the fact that the
settlers enjoyed a higher standard of living than the poor of Britain, 'who
form my flock'.[115]

Palmerston was scornful of 'theoretical gentlemen' who argued that the
colonies were a drain on Britain's resources. The economics and politics of
the subject were, as usual with him, interdependent. The passing of British
North America, Australasia and the Cape into foreign hands would inflict
'a loss of character...reputation...power...which England would not
easily nor soon repair'.[116] Lewis, at the Treasury, explained on frankly
commercial grounds the advantages that the colonies secured from the
home government and Parliament; legislation guaranteeing a loan to New
Zealand was before the House.'...by preventing them from pursuing the
policy of independent nations...excluding English manufacturers...
establishing high prohibitory duties', he said, 'an immense commerce...
was ensured to this country.'[117] The resented Canadian tariff of 1859 gave
the despised theorists an extended opportunity to attack the political and
military links between Britain and the settlers in the context of the North
American colonies' increased exposure to invasion by the United States
during the 1860s. 'The alpha and almost the omega of the subject', thought
Gladstone, was to make those colonies primarily responsible for their
landward defence, leaving Britain to take maritime action.[118] Something of
an armchair strategist, he proposed an impossible task for the inhabitants.

They could supposedly rely on British regulars, assisted by the colonial militia to hold invaders somewhere North of the Great Lakes, while the Royal Navy sailed against America. The cabinet agreed to foot the bill for fortifications to be put in hand at Quebec, and the Canadians to meet the cost of making ready other strong-points in the anticipated campaign. Writing to Gladstone about Cobden, who believed British North America neither could nor should be defended from its neighbour, Palmerston commented, without optimism, that invasion by the United States was 'not necessarily equivalent to conquering...'.[119] Absolute deterrence was out of the question, and defeat more likely than victory in the event of hostilities. The British ran the risk, as Bright warned the Commons with unaffected apprehension, of being humiliated by America, should they persist in maintaining a connexion offensive to her. 'Great national harm' would flow from a disaster avoidable if the Canadians were told to go their own way, whether it led to an independent confederation of the colonies or to entry into the American Union.[120]

The risk was one that Britain had no option but to accept. To appease the United States by severing ties with free colonies would involve a worse humiliation than a lost war. Lewis, at the War Office since July 1861, perceived that 'any great exertions' could not be expected of the Canadians, who counted on Britain to defend them and, failing the looked-for response, were resigned to being absorbed by America: 'at present they do not contemplate independence, with its responsibilities and obligations'. So long as the colonies of settlement formed part of the contemporary empire, their defence must fall mainly on its centre, no matter what 'abstract formulas' the House of Commons had endorsed in March 1862 to divide the burden more evenly.[121] It was obviously right that these prospering dependencies should do more to help themselves. When the settlers of Victoria, however, asked for a small permanent naval force to guard its harbours, at the shared expense of Britain and the colony, they set off an interesting discussion in Whitehall and the cabinet. The Colonial Office favoured joint control of the vessels. Somerset and the Admiralty thought it better to vest control in the colony, to which Newcastle objected that to encourage the development of colonial navies would lead to 'speedy independence'. The Whig duke was less alarmist and more liberal than the Peelite. As the colonies grew, so would their demands on the Royal Navy, already stretched. The cost of a small fleet should make a colony reflect on the price of complete independence. The prospect of a useful saving on the British naval estimates harmonized with the 'wise' principle of allowing the 'greatest liberty' to self-governing colonies. Palmerston leant towards Newcastle 'for many reasons, domestic and foreign'.[122] The imperial responsibility for external representation and defence was an effective means of retaining, or rather strengthening, the allegiance of settlers. In

time, this reliance would diminish, until, as Cardwell, colonial secretary in
succession to Newcastle, invited the Commons to foresee, Britain called on
the colonies for help in her turn.[123] Palmerston did not propose to
jeopardize a slow and mutually beneficial transition for the sake of minor
economies sought by Gladstone or any other minister

The perceptible doubt whether Britain had a natural affinity with
colonial society, in spite of the racial and economic bonds, had to be faced.
In an article published in January 1862 to offset the report that appeared
from the select committee on defence spending in the colonies, Lewis
claimed that if their governments were 'too democratic', it was the fault of
Parliament: 'the mother-country would not be justified in visiting the
colony with a punishment for the results of her own policy'.[124] It was not
an entirely convincing plea. The quality of colonial politicians repeatedly
exercised British ministers, and occasionally startled them. The Tory
administration of 1858–59 shrank from knighting the mayor of Melbourne
when threatened with 'a storm of accusations' about the involvement of the
candidate, and his wife, in brothel keeping.[125] The Court was keen to
bestow an appropriately graded hereditary honour, a baronetcy, on
selected colonials in order to 'assimilate their feelings and usages with ours',
in the words of the Queen to Palmerston in 1856.[126] A model recipient, Sir
Alan MacNab, ex-premier of the largest Canadian colony, attempted a
transfer to British politics, standing as a Tory in the 1859 election. His
example was not encouraging, remarked Derby, for the hereditary principle
in a colonial environment.[127] To a worrying extent, wealthy settlers tended
either to abstain from political activity, or leave for home. Nothing,
reflected Bulwer Lytton to Gladstone in this context, had done more to
preserve their country from the mob and its leaders than the pre-eminence
in her life of an hereditary political class fit for its role. Writing in the late
fifties, Lytton believed he discerned a 'more aristocratic' trend in Australia,
where in fact the squattocracy was soon to lose much of its influence.[128]
Newcastle, a couple of years later, rated the Canadian colonies 'infinitely
superior in every way' to the Australasian. If there was too much jobbery
in the former, local politics had achieved respectability through the
participation by educated and public-spirited men. The flight of Australia's
rich not only inhibited the emergence of a 'natural aristocracy'; it
condemned her to be ruled 'for the sole gain of the few of what would be
in England the *middle* classes'.[129] As Lytton remarked to Gladstone, a
gentry element was present in British North America from the beginning;
he singled out Nova Scotia, but other colonies possessed it.[130]

'Whatever may be the wish of the colonies will meet with the concurrence
of our Government and Parliament': the quotation from Cobden refers to
the most ambitious project for the empire of settlement then, Canadian
confederation;[131] and shows why his anti-imperialism found little purchase

in the relationship between Britain and her free dependencies. Both sides had every incentive not to let the disagreement end in conflict and rupture. The Colonial Laws Validity Act of 1865, passed without debate, confirmed the wide legislative autonomy that had speedily evolved. Of the reserved powers under responsible government, as originally conceived, the amendment of colonial constitutions, the disposal of publicly owned lands – a vital question in countries of immigration – and the regulation of external trade had been given up in practice. They were unenforceable without the local population's goodwill. So far as defence and foreign affairs were concerned, the unwillingness of settlers to assume these responsibilities, and Britain's substantial acknowledgment of what she and they regarded as her duty, reinforced the colonists' identification with her. The enthusiasm with which they adhered to an imperial identity surprised Newcastle when he crossed the Atlantic in attendance on the youthful Prince of Wales. Reporting on that royal tour, the first of its kind, the Duke thought Canadian loyalty was assured 'for some time'.[132] Soon afterwards, Lewis's regular correspondent, Sir Edmund Head, governor-general of British North America from 1854 to 1861, was pessimistic about the colonies' readiness to contribute largely to the expenditure if war broke out between Britain and the United States.[133] It remained true that, as Newcastle informed Palmerston, Canada did not want independence, 'much less a change of masters'.[134] Representing the authorities in London who chose them, the governors of 'monarchical republics'[135] – Bright's apt description – knew that the connection which they embodied expressed both the 'moral supremacy' and the 'material supremacy' of Britain.[136] 'Do your best always to keep up the pride in the mother country', Lytton advised a new Australian governor. Colonial nationalism was in its infancy and its maturity could not be forced.[137]

The priorities of life in the settler colonies left governors with more authority than that of a constitutional monarch in matters other than defence and external relations. Sir George Bowen, sent to Queensland on the partition of New South Wales to create another self-governing colony, told how 'I was an autocrat...without a single soldier...without a single shilling.' He organized a police force on the model of the constabulary in his native Ireland, and borrowed from the banks to augment the seven pence halfpenny in the colonial treasury. '...liberty began here at the wrong end', suggested Bowen, discussing the weakness of Australian institutions in a letter to Cobden. The naval and military governors of early days bequeathed to democracy a tradition of centralized administration, which lent itself to abuse by the localities in pursuit of their different needs. The staple of Australian politics was the rivalry between districts for the funding of public works so necessary to small, scattered communities in a developing country.[138] Bowen's analysis, though oversimplified, was an

improvement on Denison's private denunciations of responsible government to Labouchere, colonial secretary in Palmerston's first cabinet:
'Responsibilities...clap-trap...devised by the unscrupulous as a means of
deluding the unwary, meaning nothing but the right of the majority to
make fools of themselves without let or hindrance.' Yet Denison, in
deference to his instructions, helped to make the fundamental reform he
deplored work on its introduction into New South Wales. Subsequently, the
first legislature elected by manhood suffrage saw a ministry whose
inexperience added to his weight in the councils of the colony. 'The
anticipations of those who hailed...a political millennium have been
grievously disappointed', he commented with satisfaction, looking back on
the opening years of responsible government.[139] The disenchantment was
widespread, and counteracted Bright's allusions to colonial democracy as
illustrating the welcome shape of the future.

   Gladstone called the practice of appointing governors to free colonies
from home, considered as 'vital or important' to British interests, 'one of
the old superstitions not yet exploded'.[140] Its durability throughout his
lifetime and beyond proved him wrong. In his opinion, this manifestation
of an imperial presence retarded colonial initiative. If Britain could not
leave Canada to defend herself, the use of British troops in the Maori wars
was highly questionable. The settlers' encroachment upon aboriginal lands
provoked the recurrent conflict. G. A. Selwyn, the Bishop of New Zealand,
an old friend of Gladstone, lamented the transfer of power to a 'colonial
oligarchy' unprincipled in its methods.[141] Gladstone expressed sympathy
with the people of the colony, white and coloured, but put the British
taxpayer first. The fighting in New Zealand had cost 'poor John Bull'
getting on for three million pounds. That responsible government should
entail such expenditure for internal security seemed to him 'a perfect
caricature of political relations'.[142] By the middle of 1865 it was safe to
enforce an end to advances from Britain's Treasury to the colony in the
latest Maori war: the settlers could pay for themselves; although British
regulars stayed in the field.[143] There had been disquiet in the Commons for
several years about the natives' treatment. The Tory ex-cabinet minister,
Walpole, denounced 'an unrighteous war' in the House. 'It sounded to me
like music', wrote the Liberal Trelawny, who was active on the Maoris'
behalf: 'Similar phrases fall from many. Consciences are awakened.'[144] He
was too sanguine. The British government simply left the Maoris to their
fate when they had ceased to pose a serious menace. The experience of New
Zealand affected policy in South Africa where the black tribes heavily
outnumbered the colonists. Newcastle opposed autonomy for the Cape
Colony, 'leaving with the Home Government such a shadow of
responsibility as shall support a claim to have...wars carried on at Imperial
expense'.[145]

An apparent exception to the general rule of non-interference in the internal affairs of colonies enjoying responsible government, was the smallest, Prince Edward Island. Its absentee landlords, who included Palmerston's brother-in-law, were protected from the efforts of the land legislature to expropriate them on its terms: 'a flagitious attempt' the prime minister told Newcastle, '...to do what has been...frustrated in Ireland, namely, to transfer property from the lawful owner to the dishonest tenant'.[146] Under Palmerston's eye, the Colonial Office used its residual powers during his two ministries to disallow island laws subversive of landed rights. Even so, Newcastle recommended a compromise to the landlords: 'not just or legal', but the best they might expect. Little Prince Edward Island underlined the lesson that free colonies would go their own way when sentiment and interest did not turn towards Britain.[147]

Promoting Canada's unification was sensible in view of the expansion and temper of the United States. Similar schemes for Australia and South Africa were, respectively, a matter of indifference and full of risk. The technique finally employed in Canada was the carrot and stick. The settlers were made to understand that they must demonstrate the political will to remain separate from their giant neighbour. In return for movement towards confederation and a larger colonial contribution to defence, Britain continued to hold her shield, rather nervously, over Canada, hoping for 'a powerful moral effect' on the United States from limited measures.[148] The anti-imperialism that wanted no such liabilities broke down on the claim, voiced by Bright, that the Canadians were already a distinct nationality.[149] It was not credible. Even those officials in the Colonial Office biased against the retention of obligations to self-governing colonies, men who figured in Palmerston's dismissive references to opponents of his policy in this field, recognized what their country must be prepared to do against the odds. Sir Frederic Rogers, the permanent under-secretary, went 'very far in the desire to shake off all responsibility'; but confessed to a more extreme colleague that leaving Canada to fend for herself would strike him as ignominious, bound 'somehow or other' to incur retribution in time and indicative of resignation to national decline: 'There is something beyond philosophy, or at least my philosophy, in such doings.'[150] Nor were the Tories likely to acquiesce in the retreat suggested by a vocal few, had the Liberal ministry, inconceivably, acted on advice so unpalatable to the country. If ever Disraeli thought with Cobden and Bright on the whole question of settler colonies, he did not miss a chance to accuse the Palmerston government of not caring enough about Canada under threat from the United States: 'a great empire, founded on...freedom and equality', he said, 'is as conducive to the spirit and power of a community as commercial prosperity or military force...'.[151] The first Gladstone ministry's withdrawal of nearly all the imperial garrisons from Canada,

Australia and New Zealand, was feasible because Britain had seen the Canadians and New Zealanders through periods of tension and danger. It did not imply any radical change of policy from the Palmerstonian era: colonials still looked to Britain for external defence and international representation as their natural guardian in that century.

Trade, humanitarianism and force

The belief in a civilizing mission beyond Europe was not special to Britain. She was merely better placed than the French or the Americans to carry it out. The historic application of force to penetrate China and Japan, its minimal use or, much more commonly, its advertisement in Latin American waters and on African coasts necessitated a cautious approach, despite allegations to the contrary. To lessen the corrosive envy of her influence and prosperity and to avoid clashes that could not be localized, Britain increased her co-operation, when Palmerston was prime minister, with the other two naval powers whose ships ranged as widely as her own, or nearly so, although there were fewer of them. The incident of the *Charles et Georges*, discussed below, compelled the British public to recognize how Anglo-French, like Anglo-American relations, circumscribed the action of their government in distant regions where they expected the dominant power to prevail. It was often in the interests of France and America to work closely with Britain. Trade united the three nations because it was British policy to seek unity of commercial purpose, usually under her leadership, in such regions. Humanitarianism had a divisive effect until the Emperor Napoleon and then President Lincoln realigned their countries with Palmerston's drive to extirpate slavery, which had faltered before a resurgence of the traffic helped by political attitudes in Washington and Paris. The export of slaves from the West coast of Africa had practically dried up by Palmerston's death. Success on the East coast, where conditions were different, took longer. The least controversial aspect of informal empire, so called, was not the suppression of slavery but the richly profitable relationship in which Britain stood to Latin America. In China, Japan and Morocco, extraterritoriality accompanied economic penetration, establishing or enlarging an *imperium et imperio* modelled on the Ottoman Capitulations. This was informal empire at its most developed.

'...even the threat of naval action against these Spanish American states will generally bring them to their senses', minuted Palmerston in 1857.[152] The wealth and potential of Latin America held an overwhelming attraction for British trade and capital; chronic political instability made tempting targets of foreign businessmen and investors. Mexico alone underwent forty-eight changes of regime in thirty-two years. On the other hand, the weakness of authority allowed British diplomats and consuls, able to call on the navy's modest strength in those latitudes, to take a strong line. Indeed, they were obliged to do so in the ordinary discharge of their functions, such, Palmerston did not let them forget, was the innate propensity to injustice and to the victimization of foreigners. If hints of forcible intervention seem to have been standard, actual resort to it was infrequent. To prevent Britain from being drawn further into the internal affairs of states like these, where she had to consider the reactions of rival powers besides all the other disadvantages of being enmeshed, Palmerston had laid it down when at the Foreign Office that British holders of foreign government securities must not normally look to their own country for redress in the event of default, a common enough occurrence.[153] Nevertheless, they persisted in asking for help, 'beyond endurance in their roguery and impudence', wrote Palmerston in 1856. The Latin Americans received warnings that Britain might be compelled to come to the bondholders' aid. It was in Palmerston's mind, as prime minister, to use force if it could be done without setting an universal precedent.[154] The peculiar iniquity of the delinquents suggested that it could. The real obstacle was the reluctance of British industry. 'I remember', commented Palmerston a little later, 'that we were always brought up by the question, what can we do in the way of coercion?...a naval blockade...is always objected to by...Liverpool, Manchester and Sheffield.'[155]

Britain's shortlived participation in the international expedition to Mexico in 1861–62 was, briefly, a victory for the City, which mounted a strong agitation on the topic of Mexican bonds. The holders were to have been among the beneficiaries of the compensation extracted; together with British traders and residents subjected to robbery and outrage, on whose undisputed right of appeal government was accustomed to act positively, after due inquiry. For these bondholders had their claims backed by agreements to pay interest and arrears concluded between naval officers on the spot and the Mexican authorities. Such agreements were an idea that attracted Palmerston in 1856, and were obviously intended to prepare the ground for enforcement.[156] The officers had been authorized to negotiate and sign: 'The British name is something', noted the foreign secretary, Russell, in defence of consequent intervention.[157] His under-secretary, Layard, experienced in business and politics, had pointed to the Tory attacks from Stanley, with his Lancashire connexions, and Sir John Trollope, a spokesman for the squires, on government collection of '"bad debts"' abroad.[158] Palmerston satisfied himself that 'public opinion is with us' before Britain joined France and Spain. It was not sufficient, he told Russell, to say 'we are quite right'.[159] Yet the failure of the Mexican experiment, owing to France's larger ambitions, put an end to the policy in the Dunlop and Aldham Conventions. Layard pronounced the funeral oration with relief, and no kind words for the bondholders.[160] His

Palmerstonianism was not in doubt; he relied on arguments to which the
prime minister adverted: the virtual impossibility of making Latin
American offenders honour their engagements, whatever was done. They
would survive 'trusting for indemnity...to distance and the mutual
jealousies of...powers', until the United States swallowed them.[161] It was
the weakness of Latin America that embarrassed Britain. Under
Palmerston, she tried, on principle, to minimize liabilities arising from the
expansion of trade and investment where the rule of law applied so
uncertainly.

Yet a condition of expansion, in the circumstances, was access to
diplomatic and consular assistance, with the navy in the background.
Home-based investors in Latin American bonds were restricted, before and
after the two abortive Conventions with Mexico, to the good offices of
diplomats and consuls, who sometimes acted as their agents with the debtor
governments. This degree of help usually produced results, when combined
with the desire of states not to be excluded from the London capital market
by the operation of business judgement. The British resident in, or trading
to, the republics and monarchical Brazil might expect fuller support for
authentic claims in accordance with international practice and the
persistence of commercial treaties, where states oppressed or patently
neglected the duty to protect foreigners. '...until a sloop of war appears...
our diplomatic representations will be of no avail', remarked Russell in a
typical minute on Peru.[162] Brazil provided the best instance of force applied
to secure redress. In 1863 the Royal Navy detained Brazilian shipping off
Rio de Janeiro against compensation for the plunder of a wrecked British
merchantman and the murder of her crew. Palmerston compared Brazil's
submission, under protest, to the conduct of a 'Billingsgate fisherwoman...
she feels the strong grip of the policeman and...goes as quiet as a lamb
though still using foul-mouthed language at the corner of each street'.[163]
The response in Britain was mixed. The only monarchy in Latin America
had more political friends than all the republics. Cobden begged the prime
minister to remember the adverse reaction from the British mercantile
community in Brazil. Britain's 'vast' stake there was in jeopardy; but he
asked its proposer not to divide the House on a motion critical of
government. Layard had made an effective speech in which he emphasized
the connection between the settlement imposed in this case, and the
position of the British as creditors generally throughout Latin America. If
the Commons were to disapprove, it would be taken to signify the
establishment of a coveted freedom, to repudiate debt of all kinds,
extremely damaging to British interests. No rigid separation existed
between debts that were collectable by force and those that were not;
Palmerston's Foreign Office circular of 1848 reserved the right to intervene
on behalf of bondholders which it announced was inconvenient to exercise.

Failure to exact reparation for the cargo and crew of the SS *Prince of Wales* would have been damaging, if not to the extent that Layard alleged for the purposes of debate.[164]

The nature of the perennial difficulties with Latin America was too well understood to excite much controversy. Palmerston's suggested reply to the Brazilian minister on the impending rupture of diplomatic relations read: 'My good fellow, put your despatch in your pocket...go home with it, and let us hear no more about the matter.'[165] The problems of the Far East, relatively unfamiliar to Parliament and business were of a different magnitude, and did not permit such insouciance. China and Japan fitted better into Palmerston's general scheme of 'the usual and unavoidable stages of the intercourse of strong and civilized nations with weaker and less civilized ones': initial willingness to accept a commercial treaty, succeeded by breaches of faith and violence that evoked protests and reprisals by the civilized party or parties to broken agreements until the final 'successful display of superior strength'.[166] Latin American states had not been reluctant to conclude treaties of trade and navigation which dated from the 1820s and were still being extended to the smaller republics in the 1860s. These guaranteed the private rights of British subjects coming to trade and settle as well as most favoured nation treatment for British goods. While the working of the treaties was a source of friction, in no sense were the states closed societies, deeply alien cultures, like China and Japan. The hostilities begun in the autumn of 1856 led to the Anglo-French occupation of Canton and capture of the Taku forts on the Peiho. The great anxiety of the Chinese in negotiations was Western insistence on permanently resident envoys in the capital; well aware of the foreigners' underlying intention, the imperial government resisted, as long as it could, the erection of what was conceived as 'a sort of diplomatic protectorate'. Elgin, the British plenipotentiary agreed to waive the permanent residence of envoys at Peking in practice, though not as a right. They would visit the Court from a mission stationed in the provinces. The concession offered won the approval of the British and French governments, but the Chinese were obdurate. Renewed fighting and the advance on the capital, which fell to nearly 20,000 men from two Western powers, had to take place before ratification and slight enlargement of the Treaty of Tientsin by the Convention of Peking in October 1860.[167]

The principle of extraterritoriality, already operative, was expanded. The number of treaty ports increased from five, after the first Anglo-Chinese war, to fourteen where the customs effectively passed out of Chinese control; and the interior was opened to trade and travel. The representatives of the treaty powers, firmly ensconced at Peking, and especially the British minister, watched over the implementation of these and other provisions. The master treaty was Britain's; the fact reflected her pre-eminence in China. France, Russia and America concluded versions of it. The resumption of war in 1859 had hardened Palmerston's outlook; he dismissed apprehensions that the fall of Peking might subvert the Chinese empire, and disrupt trade.[168] The aftermath produced his public conversion, in language greeted with incredulity: Britain was morally bound to rehabilitate the central authority she had undermined; hence the deployment of her troops to counter the Taiping rebels.[169] It should not be forgotten that Lewis's argument against the coercion of both China and Japan in 1857 impressed Palmerston. The *de facto* protectorate that Lewis feared became a reality, while the Indian Mutiny inspired profound misgivings at the thought of responsibility for another huge Oriental dependency. The Chinese empire was appreciably weaker than the Ottoman, but as in the latter, a network of interlocking agreements spread the burden among Western nations, and restrained others from too much interference harmful to Britain's local economic superiority. Although Japan's external trade was a fraction of China's, Palmerston attached similar importance to international co-operation there, when it came to bombarding the Japanese into compliance with the letter and spirit of agreements which granted extraterritoriality and designated treaty ports on the Chinese pattern. The Anglo-Japanese treaty of Yedo could not be directly attributed to force, unlike that of Tientsin in the same year, 'unless', observed Lewis drily, 'the Emperor of Japan is influenced by the example of his brother of China'.[170]

The fiercer Japanese reaction to Europeans coming among them resulted in a succession of Western naval operations, the largest of which assembled seventeen warships – eight British, the rest French, American and Dutch – to silence the batteries guarding the Straits of Shimonoseki at the entrance to the Inland Sea.[171] The United States Navy was represented, owing to the civil war in America, by a small vessel under the command of a junior officer, for whom Palmerston wanted the Order of the Bath that was to be conferred on senior allied officers in the action. A beneficiary of China's defeat at the hands of Britain and France, the United States had not, after all, been a belligerent power in the conflict; although units of her navy did come under and return Chinese fire. Her insignificant naval participation at Shimonoseki should be marked, the prime minister argued, to draw her into more active promotion of 'the common cause'.[172] The civil war growth of the American fleet, and speculation about its future employment, reinforced the case for partnership with her in the Far East, where her traders and missionaries were busy. Co-operation helped to disarm critics at home. Cobden and Bright found it difficult to attack the United States, while Gladstone hoped their joint efforts in China would offset Anglo-French discord in Europe.[173] Interrogated by a friend, he confessed to the 'misery...it is not too strong a word' of having to endorse decisions that flowed from a policy and the commencement of war which he still condemned: 'Often have I tried to cure or mitigate the system of parading force which I conceive to be the root of the evil.'[174] Later, when the question of coercing Japan arose he asked only that the resort to force should be '*short*'.[175] The British bombardment of Kagoshima, which unintentionally burnt down the town, revived moral unease in Parliament. Ministers, said Layard in his successful explanation, conformed to the wishes of backbenchers, 'who were forever telling the Government that it was their duty to open fresh markets all over the world'.[176] The Kagoshima debate 'went well', wrote Gladstone in his diary, reconciled, politically, at any rate, to the element of violence in commercial empire.[177]

Lord Elgin, who recorded his distaste for much that he had to do in the Far East, put it to Gladstone, doubtfully, that compulsion on the Chinese to follow their strong trading instincts without hindrance amounted to liberation of a sort: 'This may hardly be a justification of such force, but it affords some grounds for a new and better order of things.'[178] Trade improved; but little else. If legalizing the import of opium into China from India, to whose finances it was so important, ended abuses connected with smuggling the drug before 1858, that legality did not still the prickings of conscience, even in mercantile circles handling the commodity. The value of opium was still about twice that of imports from Britain in 1865, evidence of China's intractability to Westernization, as of India's in a lesser degree. The illusion of trade as civilizing in itself had begun to fade by then. Palmerston was conscious of the subtle change and its damaging implications. To call British policy in the Far East 'selfish' was to misunderstand its main concern, fundamentally the same anywhere, the accessibility of markets. Government had an absolute duty to expand the nation's trade 'by every means in its power...and so to render our own people happy and prosperous at home'. That great purpose was not to be confused with the sectional interests of British merchants overseas. Those who challenged his definition of the national interest in global commerce were 'doing their best to take the bread out of the mouths of our working-classes'; a statement that wrung a cry of protest from Bright. 'I do not admit', said Palmerston, '...that our policy has been a selfish one in the sense in which the word is sometimes employed.' The welfare of the country and the classes could not be sacrificed to international altruism which had no place in the real world.[179]

Morocco,[180] unlike China and Japan, produced talk of resignation in the cabinet. The Anglo-Moroccan commercial treaty of 1856, which broke down the country's isolation, had a strategic motive. Unable to prevent Spain's invasion in 1859–62, warranted by the attacks of Riffian tribesmen on her enclaves in the North and supported as it was by the European Great Powers, Britain came to the Sultan's rescue with diplomacy and finance. She objected to any significant cession of territory and arranged a loan for him in London towards the indemnity on which the Spanish evacuation of the fortress city of Tetuan was conditional. The cabinet twice considered guaranteeing the loan to attract investors, and decided against it.[181] Russell, with some encouragement from the prime minister, proposed to ignore the collective opinion after his colleagues had dispersed. He or Russell, Gladstone believed, might have to resign; but the foreign secretary dropped the idea for the time being. 'So that is over', the chancellor told his wife in January 1861.[182] Later that year he had second thoughts, and ideally wanted a joint Anglo-French guarantee: 'Thus... mutual jealousies would be neutralized.'[183] There was reason to fear France behind Spain. Morocco's trade, which Britain dominated, could not compare with that of Turkey. The case for a loan was far more political and military than economic. The cabinet refused to see it in November 1860 as '*preventive*', afraid of taking on, at a difficult juncture in the affairs of Europe, a tangible commitment to the preservation of Moroccan independence.[184] Gladstone did not contest Palmerston's insistence on the value of her independence to the British position in Gibraltar, and therefore in the Mediterranean. Neither man thought it probable that Parliament would agree to a loan on its security, which it regarded jealously.[185]

Layard, who arrived at the Foreign Office in the summer, acted as intermediary between the government and the City, relaying Baron Rothschild's advice that 'a virtual guarantee' would be needed to get the money on the right terms.[186] Palmerston wrote a long memorandum on the arrangement that Rothschild wanted. According to the prime minister, it involved only 'a shadow of responsibility' and avoided recourse to Parliament.[187] In fact, it involved a substantial responsibility without Parliamentary sanction. Under the convention with Morocco, a British commissioner, whose duties the minister resident and consuls discharged, received half the total customs revenue on which the loan was secured; subtracted interest and sinking fund payments; and returned the surplus to the Moroccans. Gladstone felt the additional functions given to Britain's representatives might very well lead to further interference in the country and Anglo-French dissension.[188] Lewis disliked the evasion of Parliamentary sanction by the absence of a formal guarantee, when investors supposed, as they were meant to do, that government would not see them lose their money.[189] In his memorandum, Palmerston anticipated that if the Sultan failed to meet these obligations, 'we as a maritime power... have ample means without trouble or exertion... to compel him to stand by his bargain'.[190] The cabinet reluctantly agreed to the convention; 'an impolitic measure',[191] Lewis called it. Parliament, apparently, had few questions. The City was distinctly pleased with the loan, four times oversubscribed, 'both as a political and a financial operation'. With official British sponsorship, the Sultan paid 5 per cent on his bonds; without it, the Pasha of Egypt had recently had to pay 10 per cent.[192]

Palmerston's personal crusade against the slave trade finally succeeded when it did only because states too powerful to coerce abandoned policies that would have ensured its defeat. Secession, civil war and Lincoln dispersed the Southern lobby in Congress. France's revival of the traffic under the guise of 'free emigration' lent it a veneer of respectability. Slaves purchased on the coasts of Africa landed in French sugar colonies as indentured labour, with the prospect of freedom to go home, in theory, on the expiry of their contracts. France wanted to be able to tap the supply of coolies available from India to British territories as voluntary substitutes for freed negroes. Britain's objections rested on her regulations governing the supply of indentured labour and its treatment, and on the partial diversion of the flow that was none too large from her own sugar colonies. The French were, they made it clear, driven to the expedient of 'free emigration' from Africa.[193] Talking to Palmerston in November 1857, Napoleon's minister of state, Fould, maintained, not altogether disingenuously, that their captives or subjects were all that African chiefs had to sell in exchange for European goods. They certainly had nothing else so valuable. Fould did not deny, speaking privately, that his country was dealing in slaves. The French government, throughout, contended otherwise; this official pretence exasperated Palmerston: 'it is not a question of law but of common sense', he remarked.[194] Disturbing in themselves, the open activities of the French emboldened clandestine slavers of various nationalities. French vessels engaged in recruiting 'free emigrants' were fitted out as slavers. Two earned notoriety. The human cargo of the misnamed *Regina Coeli*, lying off the West African shore, staged a bloody revolt, known to the world after the ship was found drifting and taken into Freetown harbour. When Palmerston, out of office, saw the Emperor and Walewski in Paris some months later, they talked about the revived French slave trade, exposed for what it was.[195]

Within weeks, two French battleships entered the Tagus and secured the release of the *Charles et Georges*, arrested in Mozambique waters and brought to Lisbon, whose captain alleged that he had been picking up 'colonists'.[196] The British were severely embarrassed by their inability to help Portugal, whom they stood treaty-bound to aid; but they left her to suffer for having carried out the general anti-slavery policy adopted at Britain's instance and overseen by her. Malmesbury, the foreign secretary of the moment, consulted Palmerston, and instructed Cowley at Paris to transmit what he had said to the ex-premier, soon to visit the Emperor at Compiègne, about the danger of war and France's neglect of arbitration over the *Charles et Georges*. The British ambassador was enjoined to tread delicately, 'but we cannot pass over the event in silence'.[197] Napoleon lost no time in moving towards the British, and exploiting the nervousness of the Tory government. Negotiations on the availability of coolie labour had been initiated in January 1858 when Palmerston was still prime minister and following the candid discussion with Fould.[198] 'The French are, I believe, excessively anxious not only to get the thing done, but to get it done *immediately*', wrote the civil servant who had talks with Persigny, the ambassador in London, that were cut short by the change of ministry.[199] The Emperor's public letter of 30 October to Prince Jerome Napoleon, his minister for the colonies, avowed that 'the independence of the national flag' was the motive behind the retaking of the *Charles et Georges*. That said, he went on to reveal his moral discomfort: if the controversial system of finding negroes for the French colonies was slavery under another name, he dissociated himself from it. Negotiations with Britain for coolies, instead, should be restarted. On the eve of his Italian enterprise, Napoleon was anxious not to alienate the support he might expect in Britain. Palmerston believed it was a matter of recovering goodwill lost through the imperial government's 'slave trade operations'.[200]

Malmesbury, playing for time in which to strengthen the Royal Navy, drew Bishop Wilberforce's attention to the imperial letter. He hoped Wilberforce, fiercely opposed to the French activities, would use all his influence, in part hereditary, to create the climate for an agreement on which the foreign secretary believed peace with France depended, as well as an end to the thinly disguised traffic in slaves. Malmesbury, that humane and underrated man, did not think the substitution of indentured coolies for captured negroes was a perfect solution: but if 'there may be suffering more or less, because all the securities against it cannot be obtained ... we are sure that the aggregate of crime and misery will be vastly diminished'. The British had a good friend in Jerome Napoleon, who issued a decree prohibiting recruitment on the East coast of Africa, although the ban was ineffectual.[201] The two conventions with France, signed by the restored Palmerston administration in 1860–61, sought to protect labour recruited in India from abuses inherent in its migration, and specified that its welfare was the proper concern of British consuls; the latter provision being one extracted from the French. To the last Napoleon III kept up the public pretence that his regime was not guilty of permitting slavery; a declaration to this effect accompanied the 1861 convention.[202]

Britain under Palmerston and for some time afterwards, had no wish to do more in black Africa, above the extreme South, than police her anti-slave trade treaties with European states and native rulers while promoting legitimate commerce as an alternative, and for its own sake. Unlike the French, especially in the Far East at this date, Palmerston did not favour a missionary presence that entailed the assistance of the state. The interior of the continent, he advised Archbishop Longley of Canterbury, was no place for an Anglican prelate. The government, though unable to protect him, would have to face 'the just indignation of the British nation', if he came to any harm.[203] On the East coast, Britain lacked the resources to put down the slave trade; even after the French honoured their agreements to suppress the traffic. Britain's treaty of 1845 with Seyyid Said of Oman and Zanzibar, exempted the movement of slaves within his dominions.[204] Layard wanted to close a loophole of such dimensions on those coasts. Russell refused to ask for the redistribution of warships from the West to East African waters: 'I am persuaded that if we do so, we shall fail in both.' Following the break-up of Seyyid Said's empire, pressure upon the Sultan of Zanzibar, whom the British upheld in 1859 against an attempted dynastic coup mounted with encouragement from the French on the scene, was precluded by his weakness and indispensability. It was no use, wrote Russell, to offer this Arab potentate compensation for the extinction of the slave trade if Britain did not have force enough in the vicinity to back him up in the eradication of an evil built into the foundations of the state.[205] Moreover, British hopes of developing other trade in the region north of Mozambique to the Horn of Africa depended on the stability of Zanzibar.[206]

'Informal' empire, for the British, was a set of attitudes and practices designed to minimize imperial burdens. It put a premium on persuasion and collaboration in dealings with other countries, whether they were rivals or the objects of international improvement. The domestic priority of cheap governments was a salutary check on adventurers. If the national conscience made too many allowances for them, it remained lively and was a powerful determinant of policy. The Palmerston governments acted to restrain businessmen, and not only to secure and widen openings for them. While Layard acknowledged the prudent and responsible behaviour of leading merchant houses, he sharply criticized 'the host of little traders', whose 'preposterous pretensions' were a constant liability to their country abroad.[207] Britain could not stem the diffusion of her trade; the economy and its social dictates were too strong. She did try to exercise some control over the global consequences. The strong-points of empire afforded facilities for surveillance and protection besides being centres of regional exchange. Their strategic value in relation to the Mediterranean and India might be more or less significant, or of no significance at all. The pre-emptive occupation of Perim at the entrance to the Red Sea in 1857 safeguarded Aden; though directed against France, Napoleon found it a natural precaution.[208] The acquisition of Kowloon in 1860 enhanced the usefulness of Hong Kong. The annexation of Lagos next year signalled Palmerston's determination to stamp out the slave trade on that coast and foster substitutes for it. When the seaborne traffic in slaves was in terminal decline on that side of the continent by the middle of the decade, the retention of the West African settlements, unhealthy, troublesome and economically disappointing, seemed hard to justify. It was barely possible to maintain that they had a commercial future, and an influence for good on the tribes of the hinterland. Prestige in itself was not, under Palmerston, the factor it later became: Britain gave away territory to appease the United States and gratify Hellenic nationalism.[209]

Epilogue: a genius for adaptation

Palmerston represented the liberal strain in the Pittite tradition that runs through nineteenth-century British politics. Looking back in the 1880s, Lord Salisbury summed him up dispassionately as 'the type of an astute and moderate leader',[1] whose genius was for adaptation to realities at home and abroad.'People must in this world take things as they find them, and deal with them as best they can', wrote Palmerston of political life in the early 1850s.[2] His foreign policy after the Crimean war, and indeed before it, was based on a lucid perception of Britain's strengths and weaknesses, in both of which, as prime minister, he sought to educate his compatriots. His comment on the mistakes of a former colleague – the Peelite governor-general of India, Canning – is applicable to himself with a change of tense: '...he might by going along with public opinion have guided and governed it'.[3] Palmerston does not have a reputation for constructive statesmanship rising above the continuous improvisation of which government largely consists. His administrations are seen as an interlude between the aristocratic ministries that worked the 1832 settlement and the democratic politics that arrived with the reform bills of 1866–67. In fact, his governments were a conscious introduction to the new era. This is not to say that he welcomed the advent of democracy: it is impossible to find any politician of note who did not have serious doubts that it would work well. The 'monarchical republics'[4] – Bright's expression – in the settler colonies with their wide distribution of property in land and high wages for unskilled labour were not a reliable guide to the democratic future in Britain; in some ways, their experience was the opposite of reassuring. Irresistible in those colonies, democracy was bound to come at home: Palmerston accustomed the country to the idea of it before the extension of the franchise. The skill and sureness with which he did this explain the tributes at his passing. They were not such as are paid to someone whose chief talent has been for procrastination. 'Death has laid low the most towering antlers in all the forest', wrote Gladstone,[5] who completed his political education under Palmerston.

Appendix 1

Cabinet ministers in the Palmerston governments

	1855–58	1859–65
First Lord of the Treasury	Viscount Palmerston	Viscount Palmerston
Lord Chancellor	Lord Cranworth	Lord Campbell Lord Westbury (June 1861) Lord Cranworth (July 1865)
Lord President of the Council	Earl Granville	Earl Granville
Lord Privy Seal	Duke of Argyll Earl of Harrowby (Dec. 1855) Marquess of Clanricarde (Feb. 1858)	Duke of Argyll
Secretary of State for the Home Department	Sir George Grey	Sir George Cornewall Lewis Sir George Grey (July 1861)
Secretary of State for Foreign Affairs	Earl of Clarendon	Lord John Russell (created Earl Russell, 1861)
Secretary of State for War	Lord Panmure	Sidney Herbert (created Lord Herbert of Lea, 1860) Sir George Cornewall Lewis (July 1861) Earl de Grey and Ripon (April 1863)
Secretary of State for the Colonies	Sidney Herbert Lord John Russell (Feb. 1855) Sir William Molesworth (July 1855) Henry Labouchere (Nov. 1855)	Duke of Newcastle Edward Cardwell (April 1864)

Chancellor of the Exchequer	W. E. Gladstone Sir George Cornewall Lewis (Feb. 1855)	W. E. Gladstone
First Lord of the Admiralty	Sir James Graham Sir Charles Wood (Feb. 1855)	Duke of Somerset
President of the Board of Control (Secretary of State for India after 1858)	Sir Charles Wood R. Vernon Smith (March 1855)	Sir Charles Wood
Chancellor of the Duchy of Lancaster	Earl of Harrowby M. T. Baines (Dec. 1855)	Sir George Grey Edward Cardwell (July 1861) Earl of Clarendon (April 1864)
Minister without Portfolio	Marquess of Lansdowne	
Postmaster-General	Viscount Canning Duke of Argyll (Nov. 1855)	Earl of Elgin Duke of Argyll (May 1860; also Lord Privy Seal) Lord Stanley of Alderley (August 1860)
President of the Board of Trade	Lord Stanley of Alderley (Nov. 1855)	T. Milner Gibson (July 1859)
President of the Poor Law Board		T. Milner Gibson C. P. Villiers (July 1859)
First Commissioner of Works	Sir William Molesworth (until July 1855)	
Chief Secretary for Ireland		Edward Cardwell (until July 1861)

Appendix 2

The electoral showing of parties in the United Kingdom, 1852–1865

| | Votes cast and percentage of total vote[1] | | | | Seats | | | | | | | |
| | | | | | Unopposed returns | | | | Totals | | | |
	1852	1857	1859	1865	1852	1857	1854	1865	1852	1857	1859	1865
Conservatives and 'Liberal Conservatives'[2]	311,481 (41.4)	239,712 (33.1)	193,232 (34.3)	346,035 (39.8)	160	148	196	142	330	264	298	289
Liberals	430,882 (58.4)	464,127 (65.1)	372,117 (65.7)	508,821 (60.2)	95	176	183	161	324	377	356	369
Chartists	1,541 (0.2)	614 (0.1)	151 (0)		0	0	0	0	0	0	0	0
Others		12,099 (1.7)				4[3]				13[3]		
House of Commons membership									654	654	654	658

[1] Adjusted for multi-member constituencies

[2] Peelites: their numbers, difficult to estimate with anything like precision, have been put at 45 in 1852 and 26 in 1857. Blake, *The Conservative Party from Peel to Churchill* (London, 1970), p. 96

[3] The Independent Irish Party: Dr B. M. Walker's figures in F. W. S. Craig (ed.), *British Parliamentary Election Results, 1832–1885* (Aldershot, 1989), pp. 698, 700–1

[Source: F. W. S. Craig (ed.), *British Electoral Facts* (Aldershot, 1989)]

Appendix 3

The economy: selected statistics, 1853–1866

Year	Index of Industrial Production (exc. building) (1913 = 100)	Index of Wholesale Prices (Rousseaux) (average of 1865 and 1885 = 100)	Real Wages (allowing for unemployment) (1850 = 100)	Bank Rate (highest and lowest points in each year)	Government Expenditure (Gross) (£m)	Standard Rate of Income Tax in the £ on incomes over £150
1853	28.0	112	107	5 and 2%	55.3	7d
1854	28.4	125	97	$5\frac{1}{2}$ and 5%	55.8	7d
1855	27.8	125	94	7 and $3\frac{1}{2}$%	69.1[1]	1/2d[1]
1856	30.6	124	95	7 and $4\frac{1}{2}$%	93.1	1/4d
1857	31.9	127	94	10 and $5\frac{1}{2}$%	76.1	1/4d
1858	29.8	111	94	8 and $2\frac{1}{2}$%	68.2	7d
1859	32.6	115	104	$4\frac{1}{2}$ and $2\frac{1}{2}$	64.8	5d
1860	34.2	120	105	6 and $2\frac{1}{2}$%	69.6	9d
1861	33.6	115	99	8 and 3%	72.9	10d
1862	31.6	120	100	3 and 2%	72.3	9d
1863	33.3	121	107	8 and 3%	70.3	9d
1864	34.6	119	118	9 and 6%	67.8	7d
1865	36.9	117	120	7 and 3%	(67.1)	6d
1866	38.4	120	117	10 and $3\frac{1}{2}$%	(66.5)	4d

[1] For year ending 31 March from 1855 onwards

[Source: B. R. Mitchell and P. Deane, *Abstract of British Historical Statistics* (Cambridge, 1971)]

Notes

ABBREVIATIONS

In the notes the normal conventions in a book of this kind are employed. Citations of the Broadlands, Gladstone and Russell Papers, which are used extensively, have been shortened to BP, GP and RP, followed by the remainder of the standard reference.

1 INTRODUCTION

1 E. D. Steele, 'Liberalism', in M. A. Riff (ed.), *Dictionary of Modern Political Ideologies* (Manchester, 1987); W. E. Gladstone, 'Notes and Queries on the Irish Demand', *The Nineteenth Century*, February 1887, p. 81.

2 J. S. Mill, *Considerations on Representative Government*, Everyman's Library edn (London, 1954), p. 209.

3 Sir T. E. May, *The Constitutional History of England since the Accession of George the Third, 1760–1860*, third edn, 3 vols. (London, 1871), I, p. 165.

4 P. J. V. Rolo, *George Canning: Three Biographical Studies* (London, 1965), p. 187, quoting Canning's speech at Liverpool, 30 August 1822; GP (BL Add. MSS 44535), Gladstone to the Ven. T. B. L. Browne, 22 July 1865; K. Bourne (ed.), *The Letters of the Third Viscount Palmerston to Laurence and Elizabeth Sulivan, 1804–1863*, Camden fourth series (London, 1979), p. 97, Palmerston to Laurence Sulivan, 24 December 1807, where he refers to Burke as bearing 'the palm of political prophecy'.

5 A. J. P. Taylor, *Essays in English History*, Penguin edn (London, 1976), p. 114.

6 J. R. Vincent, *The Formation of the Liberal Party, 1857–1868* (London, 1966).

7 The quotation is from A. D. Macintyre's notice in the *English Historical Review* (1988, p. 524) of P. J. Jagger (ed.), *Gladstone, Politics and Religion* (London, 1985), where ch. 2 below first appeared. The view that Palmerston was little, if anything, more than a 'supremely professional politician' is most clearly set out in N. Gash, *Aristocracy and People: Britain 1815–1865* (London, 1979), pp. 278–9.

8 Vincent, *The Formation of the Liberal Party*, p. 146.

9 J. Morley, *The Life of Richard Cobden*, 2 vols. (London, 1896), II, p. 350, Cobden to Bright, 29 December 1859.

10 Recent studies of party in this period include A. Hawkins, *Parliament, Party, and the Art of Politics in Britain, 1855–1859* (London, 1987); J. R. Bylsma, 'Party Structure in the 1852–1857 House of Commons', *Journal of Interdisciplinary History* (1977); V. Cromwell, 'Mapping the Political World of 1861: a Multidimensional Analysis of House of Commons Divisions Lists', *Legislative Studies Quarterly* (1982); R. M. Gurowich, 'The Continuation of War by Other Means: Party and Politics 1855–1865', *Historical Journal* (1984).

11 BP (GC/BR/28), Palmerston to Brand, 14 August 1863.

12 Cobden Papers (BL Add. MSS 43651), Cobden to Bright, 21 November 1861.

13 Morley, *Cobden*, II, pp. 228–34, Cobden to his wife, 30 June, to Sale, 4 July 1859.

14 H. Perkin, *The Origins of Modern English Society, 1780–1880* (London, 1969), ch. 9.

15 At Sheffield and Glasgow, *The Times*, 11 August 1862, 1 April 1863, and Lambeth, *Daily Telegraph*, 3 April 1865.

16 *Leeds Mercury*, 27 October 1860.

17 *The Times*, 24 August 1864, 2 May 1859.

18 *Churchman*, 27 April 1865.

19 *The Times*, 29 March 1863, 5 January 1865.

20 O. W. Hewett (ed.), '...*And Mr Fortescue*'. *A Selection from the Diaries from 1851 to 1862 of Chichester Fortescue, Lord Carlingford* (London, 1958), p. 117, entry for 3 December 1857.

21 The diary of Sir John Trelawny, Bt, MP, Bodleian Library, Oxford (MS Eng. hist. d 414), entry for 15 May 1863; A. R. Ashwell and R. G. Wilberforce, *Life of the Right Reverend Samuel Wilberforce, D.D.*, 3 vols. (London, 1880–3), III, p. 91, Wilberforce to the Hon. Arthur Gordon, June 1863.

22 Trelawny diary (MS Eng. hist. d 413), 1 August 1862.

23 [Sir George Cornewall Lewis], *A Dialogue on the Best Form of Government* (London, 1863), p. 82. The anonymity of this provocative little book by a cabinet minister was not seriously meant.

A selection from the lives of Palmerston must begin with Sir Henry Bulwer (Lord Dalling and Bulwer), *The Life of Henry John Temple, Viscount Palmerston, with Selections from his Diaries and Correspondence*, 3 vols. (London, 1870–74); vol. III was edited by Evelyn Ashley. Ashley continued the unfinished work in his *Life of Henry John Temple, Viscount Palmerston, 1846–1865*, 2 vols. (London, 1876). This century has contributed H. C. F. Bell, *Lord Palmerston*, 2 vols. (London, 1936); D. Southgate, '*The Most English Minister...*' *The Policies and Politics of Palmerston* (London, 1966), a political life written from the printed sources; J. Ridley, *Lord Palmerston* (London, 1970); and K. Bourne, *Palmerston: the Early Years, 1784–1841* (London, 1982), the first volume of two. The short study by M. E. Chamberlain, *Lord Palmerston* (Cardiff, 1987), is a good introduction to the larger works listed.

24 E. D. Steele, 'Palmerston's Foreign Policy and Foreign Secretaries, 1855–1865',

in K. M. Wilson (ed.), *British Foreign Secretaries and Foreign Policy: from Crimean War to First World War* (London, 1987), esp. pp. 65–75.

25 The first volume (1856–65) of S. Walpole, *The History of Twenty-Five Years*, 4 vols. (London, 1904–08), is still useful.

26 Morley, *Cobden*, II, p. 399, Cobden to William Hargreaves, 7 August 1862; Salisbury Papers (HHM/4M/387). Salisbury to Lord Cranborne, 22 February 1881.

27 This section is based largely on the sources listed in n. 23 above.

28 Bourne, *Palmerston-Sulivan Letters, 1804–63*, p. 213, Palmerston to Laurence Sulivan, 14 August 1828. Sir C. Webster's classic, *The Foreign Policy of Palmerston, 1830–41: Britain, the Liberal Movement, and the Eastern Question*, 2 vols. (London, 1951) was supplemented and extended in time by the documents and commentary in Bourne, *The Foreign Policy of Victorian England, 1830–1902* (Oxford, 1970). Bourne, 'The Foreign Office under Palmerston', in R. Bullen (ed.), *The Foreign Office, 1782–1982* (Frederick, Maryland, 1982), describes Palmerston's habits of work, running of the department, and relations with his diplomats abroad.

29 Bourne, *Palmerston-Sulivan Letters, 1804–1863*, pp. 299–300, 304, Palmerston to Laurence Sulivan, 24 February, 28 September 1852.

30 R. Bullen and F. Strong (eds.), *Palmerston: Private Correspondence with Sir George Villiers (Afterwards Fourth Earl of Clarendon) as Minister to Spain, 1833–1837*, Prime Ministers' Papers Series (London, 1985), p. 105, Palmerston to Villiers, 11 February 1834.

31 A. D. Kriegel (ed.), *The Holland House Diaries, 1831–1840* (London, 1977), p. 418, Lord Holland to Melbourne, 7 July 1840.

32 Hansard (third series), LIII, cols. 704–20 (7 April 1840); quotation from col. 719.

33 Bourne, *Palmerston-Sulivan Letters, 1804–1863*, p. 275, Palmerston to Laurence Sulivan, 27 November 1842. W. C. Costin, *Great Britain and China 1833–1860*, new edn (Oxford, 1968), chs. 1 and 2.

34 A. C. Benson and Viscount Esher (eds.), *The Letters of Queen Victoria*, first series, 3 vols. (London, 1908), II, pp. 67–9, Palmerston to Melbourne, 26 December 1845.

35 Bourne, *Palmerston-Sulivan Letters, 1804–1863*, pp. 285–6, Palmerston to Laurence Sulivan, 6 September 1844.

36 A. J. P. Taylor, *The Italian Problem in European Diplomacy, 1847–1849* (Manchester, 1934), esp. pp. 4–5 and *The Struggle for Mastery in Europe, 1848–1918* (Oxford, 1957), ch. 1.

37 Hansard (third series), CVII, cols. 807–15 (21 July 1849); ibid., CII, cols. 204–17 (2 February 1849); quotation from cols. 206–7.

38 Russell's side of the story is in S. Walpole, *The Life of Lord John Russell*, 2 vols. (London, 1889), II, ch. 23; see also J. M. Prest, *Lord John Russell* (London, 1972), ch. 14.

39 Benson and Esher, *Letters of Queen Victoria*, II, p. 329, n. 1.

40 Ibid., pp. 235–7, memorandum by Prince Albert, 3 March 1850.

41 Quoted in Chamberlain, *Lord Palmerston*, pp. 71–2.

42 M. R. D. Foot and H. C. G. Matthew (eds.), *The Gladstone Diaries*, vols. III and IV (Oxford, 1974), IV, p. 221, 25 June; J. R. Vincent, *Disraeli, Derby and The Conservative Party: Journals and Memoirs of Edward Henry, Lord Stanley, 1849–1869* (Hassocks, Sussex, 1978), pp. 21–2, entry in Stanley's journal for 25 June 1850.

43 Hansard (third series), CXII, cols. 380–444 (25 June 1850); the closing sentence includes the famous reference to the claim '*Civis Romanus sum*'.

44 Bourne, *Palmerston-Sulivan Letters, 1804–1863*, p. 305, Palmerston to Laurence Sulivan, 31 December 1852.

45 Ibid., pp. 307–8, Palmerston to Laurence Sulivan, 11 January 1854.

46 K. Martin, *The Triumph of Lord Palmerston: a Study of Public Opinion in England before the Crimean War*, new edn (London, 1963).

47 Benson and Esher, *Letters of Queen Victoria*, II, pp. 80–2, memorandum by the Queen, 31 January 1855.

2 PALMERSTON AND GLADSTONE

1 K. Bourne, (ed.), *Palmerston-Sulivan Letters, 1804–1863*, p. 195, Palmerston to Laurence Sulivan, 18 August 1827.

2 Harpton Court Collection (3572), Lewis's diary, 2 August 1858.

3 (PRO 30/22/13C), Russell to Elliot, 6 April 1857.

4 Kitson Papers, Leeds City Archives, Herbert Gladstone to James Kitson, 24 November 1884. Kitson was president of the National Liberal Federation, 1883–90.

5 Glynne-Gladstone Papers (box 28/6) St Deiniol's Library, Hawarden, Gladstone to C. Gladstone, 25 May 1961.

6 Gladstone rejected an urgent plea from one of the two Peelites remaining in the cabinet: '…may not the Committee be the best safety valve for a very excited state of public feeling…?', G.P. (BL Add. MSS 44098), the eighth Duke of Argyll to Gladstone, 20 February 1855.

7 E.g. 'I always think Thomas à Kempis a golden book for all times…' Gladstone to Harriet, Duchess of Sutherland, 5 March 1861, J. Morley, *The Life of William Ewart Gladstone*, 2 vols. (London, 1905), I, pp. 812–20.

8 Glynne-Gladstone Papers (box 29/1), Gladstone to C. Gladstone, 29 January 1863.

9 'He saw nothing but evil in Lord Palmerston's supremacy. That was his unending refrain.' Morley, *Gladstone*, II, p. 566.

10 Ibid., II, pp. 583–6, Gladstone's memorandum of 22 May 1858, submitted to Lord Aberdeen and Sir James Graham.

11 GP (BL Add. MSS 44263), Gladstone to the fifth Duke of Newcastle, 30 January 1857.

12 *The Times*, 19 October 1865.

13 Hansard (third series), CLIII, cols. 1154–5 (2 March 1859).

14 B. Connell (ed.), *Regina v. Palmerston. The Correspondence between Queen Victoria and her Foreign and Prime Minister 1837–1865* (London, 1962), pp. 186–7, Palmerston to Queen Victoria, 9 October 1855.

15 *The History of The Times*, 5 vols. (London, 1935–52), II, ch. 16.
16 Hansard (third series), CLVIII, col. 77 (7 May 1860).
17 Cobden Papers (BL Add. MSS 43652), Cobden to Bright, 29 December 1862).
18 Ibid. (BL Add. MSS 43650), Cobden to Bright, 26 December 1858.
19 *The Times*, 7, 8 November 1856.
20 Aberdeen Papers (BL Add. MSS 43071), Gladstone to Aberdeen, 10 November 1856.
21 Glynne-Gladstone Papers (box 9/1), Gladstone to R. Gladstone, 12 November 1856.
22 Wodehouse Papers (BL Add. MSS 46692), Wodehouse to the fourth Earl of Clarendon, foreign secretary, 22 November 1856, 14 February 1857. Wodehouse is better known as the first Earl of Kimberley.
23 Connell, *Regina v. Palmerston*, Palmerston to the Queen, 18 October 1857, pp. 228–9.
24 Quotations in this paragraph are from the speeches at Salford and Manchester Town Hall, *The Times*, 7 November 1856.
25 GP (BL Add. MSS 44164), Sir James Graham, Bt, to Gladstone, 3 December 1856.
26 Glynne-Gladstone Papers (box 9/1), Gladstone to R. Gladstone, 1 May 1855.
27 GP (BL Add. MSS 44164), Gladstone to Graham, 1 December 1856.
28 GP (BL Add. MSS 44388), Gladstone to E. G. Salisbury, MP, 10 July 1857.
29 Hansard (third series), CXLIV, col. 167 (3 February 1857).
30 In support of his brother-in-law's candidacy for Flintshire, *The Times*, 6 April 1857.
31 GP (BL Add. MSS 44388), Gladstone to E. G. Salisbury, MP, 10 July 1857.
32 Ibid. (BL Add. MSS 44345), Bishop Wilberforce to Gladstone, 8 March 1858.
33 Ibid., Wilberforce to Gladstone, 26 June 1857.
34 Newcastle Papers, NeC 11743, Nottingham University Library, the Duke of Newcastle to Gladstone, 24 June 1857.
35 GP (BL Add. MSS 44263), Gladstone to the Duke of Newcastle, 22 June 1857.
36 Hansard (third series), CXLVII, col. 853 (31 July 1857).
37 B. Porter, *The Refugee Question in Mid-Victorian Politics* (Cambridge, 1979), ch. 6.
38 Glynne-Gladstone Papers (box 28/6), Gladstone to C. Gladstone, 18, 19 February 1858.
39 Hansard (third series), CXLVIII, cols. 1806–20 (19 February 1858); quotations from 1819–20. For the Rumanian question see ch. 11, pp. 283–5.
40 A. Tilney Bassett (ed.), *Gladstone to his Wife* (London, 1936), p. 121, Gladstone to C. Gladstone, 22 February 1858.
41 Glynne-Gladstone Papers (box 9/2), Gladstone to R. Gladstone, 18 March 1858.
42 Papers of the first Earl Canning (box 4), Leeds City Archives, Gladstone to Canning, 25 February 1858.
43 *Annual Summaries reprinted from The Times* (London, 1893), 1858, p. 64.
44 Glynne-Gladstone Papers (box 18/2), Capt J. Gladstone to Gladstone, 22 February 1858.
45 Ibid. (box 15/5), R. Gladstone to Gladstone, 22 February 1858.
46 Ibid. (box 9/2), Gladstone to R. Gladstone, 13 April 1858.

47 Aberdeen Papers (BL Add. MSS 43071), Gladstone to Aberdeen, 30 October 1858.

48 Lewis's diary records the Palmerstonian conciliation of Russell; for its beginnings, Harpton Court Collection (3572), 4 to 6, 10 March 1858.

49 K. Robbins, *John Bright* (London, 1979), pp. 130–47.

50 Although in 1859 Palmerston was prepared to let the Derby ministry introduce a reform bill, he meant 'then to deal with it according to its merits', as he did. Clarendon Papers (MS Clar. Dep. c. 524), Bodleian Library, Oxford, Palmerston to Clarendon, 19 December 1858.

51 Aberdeen Papers (Add. MSS 43071), Gladstone to Aberdeen 20 September 1858.

52 GP (BL Add. MSS 44551), Gladstone to Newcastle, 31 September 1858.

53 Lytton Papers (D/EK/028/2), Hertfordshire Record Office, Sir E. Bulwer-Lytton, Bt, to Gladstone, 1 February 1859.

54 *The Economist*, 30 April 1859, 'The State of the City during the Week'.

55 Malmesbury Papers (9M 73), Hampshire Record Office, MS political diary of the third Earl of Malmesbury, 12 April 1859.

56 *The Economist*, 30 April 1859, 'The State of the City during the Week' and 'The Banker's Gazette' section in the same issue.

57 *The Times*, 29 April 1859, 'Money Market and City Intelligence'.

58 Ibid., 2 May 1859.

59 Ibid., 3, 4 May 1859.

60 Ibid., 30 April 1859.

61 D. E. D. Beales, *England and Italy, 1859–60* (Edinburgh, 1961), pp. 62–75.

62 GP (BL Add. MSS 44211), Gladstone to Sidney Herbert, 18 May 1859.

63 GP (BL Add. MSS 44209), Gladstone to Sir W. Heathcote, Bt, 16 June 1859.

64 Glynne-Gladstone Papers (box 9/2), Gladstone to R. Gladstone, 30 November 1857.

65 *The Times*, 2 May 1859.

66 Glynne-Gladstone Papers (box 28/5), Gladstone to C. Gladstone, 23 July 1856.

67 GP (BL Add. MSS 44345), Gladstone to Bishop Wilberforce, 17 June 1859.

68 H. C. G. Matthew, (ed.), *The Gladstone Diaries*, vols. V and VI (Oxford, 1978) p. xxvii, n. 6.

69 Harpton Court Collection (3573), Lewis's diary, 13 June 1859.

70 Matthew, *Gladstone Diaries*, V, p. 432, 19 October 1859.

71 At Holyhead, *The Times*, 21 October 1859.

72 A summary of this momentous interview is printed from Palmerston's diary in Matthew, *Gladstone Diaries*, VI, p. 495, n. 1.

73 Harpton Court Collection (3578), Lewis's diary, 12 July 1860.

74 *The Times* 15 April 1863, editorial on Lewis's death, and obituary; for Disraeli's high estimate of him, see L. Strachey and R. Fulford, *The Greville Memoirs*, 8 vols. (London, 1938), VII, p. 321, 17 December 1857.

75 Clarendon Papers (MS Clar. Dep. c. 531), Sir G. C. Lewis to Lord Clarendon, 19 July [1860].

76 Glynne-Gladstone Papers (box 28/6), Gladstone to C. Gladstone, 24 January 1861.

77 Hansard (third series), CLXII, col. 586 (15 April 1861).

78 Expenditure in 1865 stood at £67.1 millions, nearly 12 millions above the 1853 figure, to which Gladstone looked back. Debt and interest fell from £808.8 to £790.7 millions, and £28.7 to £26.4 millions, respectively, between 1859 and 1865, B. R. Mitchell and P. Deane, *Abstract of British Historical Statistics* (Cambridge, 1962), pp. 397, 403. There is an authoritative reconsideration of Gladstonian finance in H. C. G. Matthew, 'Disraeli, Gladstone, and the Politics of Mid-Victorian Budgets', *Historical Journal* (1979).

79 P. Guedalla (ed.), *The Palmerston Papers: Gladstone and Palmerston, 1851–1865* (London, 1928), pp. 327–8, Palmerston to Gladstone, 27 November 1865.

80 'It is not easy for us to explain why we revert to the exploded system of a treaty about tariffs without saying that it was the choice of the French Government', Cowley Papers (PRO, FO 519/292), Palmerston to Lord Cowley, ambassador at Paris, 30 January 1860; Guedalla, *The Palmerston Papers*, pp. 166–7, Palmerston to Gladstone, 14 April 1861.

81 Guedalla, *The Palmerston Papers*, pp. 169–70, Palmerston to Gladstone, 16 May 1861.

82 Hansard (third series), CLXIII, col. 331 (30 May 1861).

83 As in the Holyhead speech, *v. supra*; and, an earlier example, in Hansard (third series), CXLIV, col. 995 ff. (20 February 1857), on Lewis's budget of that year.

84 Hansard (third series), CLXVI, cols. 1643–55 (13 May 1862); quotations from 1653, 1655.

85 Ibid., CLXX, cols. 616–23, 245 (23, 16 April 1863); quotations from 622, 245.

86 Ibid. CLXI, cols. 619–24 (19 February 1861); quotation from 624.

87 9 June 1860, B.P. (D/20).

88 Connell, *Regina v. Palmerston*, p. 291, Palmerston to the Queen, 2 July 1860.

89 Guedalla, *The Palmerston Papers*, pp. 236–9, Gladstone to Palmerston, 28 September 1862.

90 Benson and Esher, *The Letters of Queen Victoria*, first series, 3 vols. (London, 1908), III, pp. 416–17, Palmerston to the Queen, 2 December 1860.

91 Glynne-Gladstone Papers (box 29/1), Gladstone to C. Gladstone, 15 November 1862.

92 Ashwell and Wilberforce, *Life of the Rt. Rev. Samuel Wilberforce*, III, pp. 80–4, Gladstone to Wilberforce, 21 March 1863.

93 Glynne-Gladstone Papers (box 29/1), Gladstone to C. Gladstone, 15 November 1864.

94 Hansard (third series), CLXX, col. 434 (20 April 1863); CLXVI, col. 967 (11 April 1862).

95 GP (BL Add. MSS 44752), Gladstone's 'Memorandum on the Roman Question', 27 March 1863. The circumstances of its composition and its predictable treatment by the Italian government are related in C. Lacaita, *An Italian Englishman: Sir James Lacaita, 1813–1895* (London, 1933), pp. 187–92.

96 A concern illustrated by entries on this subject in Lord Stanley's published diary, Vincent, *Disraeli, Derby and the Conservative Party*, 20 March, 25 August, 6 October 1861, pp. 167–8, 175–7.

97 *The Times*, 13 January 1862.

98 Ibid., 27 November 1861.

99 Ibid., 9 October 1862.

100 Ibid., 11 August 1862.

101 Ibid., 1 April 1863.

102 Quotations in this sentence are from speeches by Gladstone at York and Hawarden, ibid., 11 October 1862, 15 September 1865.

103 In London, at the annual dinner of the thirteenth and fourteenth companies of the Queen's Westminster Volunteers, ibid., 11 November 1864.

104 At Bolton, ibid., 13 October 1864.

105 Gladstone at the North London Industrial Exhibition, ibid., 8 November 1864; Palmerston to the local Ragged School Society, *Leeds Mercury*, 27 October 1860.

106 R. Harrison, *Before the Socialists: Studies in Labour and Politics 1861–1881* (London, 1965), pp. 25–33.

107 At Sheffield, *The Times*, 11 August 1862.

108 To an agricultural dinner in Flintshire, ibid., 25 September 1862.

109 At Romsey, ibid., 5 January 1865.

110 At the Mansion House, ibid., 28 July 1864.

111 At Liverpool and the Trinity House, London, ibid., 13 October, 4 July 1864; the two speeches should be read together. The prime minister's performance at the Trinity House, in the shadow of a motion of no confidence in his Danish policy, impressed Gladstone: 'Lord Palmerston was really marvellous', Matthew, *Gladstone Diaries*, VI, p. 286, 2 July 1864.

112 *The Times*, 9 October 1860.

113 Ibid., editorial comment.

114 Bright Papers (BL Add. MSS 44384), Bright to Cobden, [October/November] 1860.

115 *The Times*, 11 November 1864.

116 At Tiverton, ibid., 24 August 1864.

117 BP (GC/RU/878), Russell to Palmerston, 8 September 1864.

118 RP (PRO 30/22/22), Palmerston to Russell, 19 September 1863.

119 Cowley Papers (PRO FO 519/292), Palmerston to Cowley, 16 October 1859.

120 Hammond Papers (PRO FO 391/7), Palmerston's minute of 28 September 1865.

121 Palmerston to Hansard (third series), CXLIII, col. 609 (10 July 1856); O. Anderson, 'The Wensleydale Peerage Case and the Position of the House of Lords in the Mid-nineteenth century', *English Historical Review* (1967).

122 F. Awdry, *A Country Gentleman of the Nineteenth Century* (London, 1906), pp. 109–10, Sir W. Heathcote, Bt to Sir J. Coleridge, 18 January 1856.

123 Hansard (third series), CXLIII, col. 603 (10 July 1856).

124 Harpton Court Collection (3571), Lewis's diary, 2, 8, 9, 16, 19, 23 February, 12 March 1856; quotation from 8 February.

125 Wilberforce Papers (d. 37), Gladstone to Wilberforce, 12 July 1856.

126 F. M. L. Thompson, *English Landed Society in the Nineteenth Century* (London, 1963), pp. 292–3. The elevation of H. A. Bruce to the peerage as Lord Aberdare in 1873 was a marginal case, ibid., p. 63.

127 Hansard (third series), CXLVII, cols. 1858–9 (18 August 1857).

128 Ibid., cols. 1861–2. The bill had to be withdrawn.

129 GP (BL Add. MSS 44534), Gladstone to H. A. Bruce, Parliamentary under-secretary of state at the Home Office, 13 February 1864.

130 RP (PRO 30/22/23), Palmerston to Russell, 19 March 1865.

131 Guedalla, *The Palmerston Papers*, pp. 321–2, Palmerston to Gladstone, 31 January 1865.

132 Palmerston repeatedly indicated the attendant risks to him, as on 29 April, 25 May 1862, ibid., pp. 205–9.

133 One such was the reference to political pressures on him in his speech of 24 April 1862 to the Manchester Chamber of Commerce, *The Times*, 25 April. This public hint elicited the prime ministerial admonition of 29 April cited in the previous footnote.

134 Guedalla, *The Palmerston Papers*, pp. 282–3, Gladstone to Palmerston, 13 May 1864.

135 W. E. Williams, *The Rise of Gladstone to the Leadership of the Liberal Party, 1859 to 1868* (Cambridge, 1934), chs. 1–6.

136 Bright Papers (BL Add. MSS 43384), Bright to Cobden, 16 November 1859.

137 Cobden Papers (BL Add. MSS 43651), Cobden to Bright, 19 February 1861.

138 Vincent, *Disraeli, Derby and the Conservative Party*, pp. 219–20, entry in Lord Stanley's journal for 23 June 1864.

139 In the encounter of 6 June 1860 with Gladstone, Palmerston declared the suppression of slavery to be one of 'two great objects before him in life'. Gladstone to Argyll, 6 June 1860, Matthew, *Gladstone Diaries*, VI, p. 494.

140 '...the Italians deserve freedom – the black millions are forgotten', wrote Bright when Gladstone proclaimed his Confederate sympathies. Bright Papers (BL Add. MSS 43384), to Cobden, 8 October 1862. Gladstone's fears of unrest in Lancashire feature prominently in his letter of 25 September 1862 to Palmerston, Guedalla, *The Palmerston Papers*, pp. 233–6.

141 Harpton Court Collection (3575), Lewis's diary, 11, 12 November 1862.

142 RP (PRO 30/22/14D), Palmerston to Russell, 2 November 1862.

143 Glynne-Gladstone Papers (box 29/1), Gladstone to C. Gladstone, 13 November 1862.

144 GP (BL Add. MSS 44532), Gladstone to Argyll, 26 August 1861.

145 Printed in Matthew, *Gladstone Diaries*, VI, p. 139.

146 Exemplified in his reverent comment after visiting the monks of Platutera on Corfu. 'I have not in the Latin countries seen any monastery like this.' 2 December 1858, Matthew, *Gladstone Diaries*, V, p. 344.

147 *Quarterly Review*, April 1859, 'Foreign Affairs – War in Italy', p. 528.

148 See his article on 'Sardinia and Rome', ibid., June 1855, pp. 42–3.

149 Malmesbury Papers (9 M73/1/5), Malmesbury to Cowley, 7 December 1858. This letter became known to Liberal politicians in England following an audience granted by Napoleon III to Lord Granville, Harpton Court Collection (3573), Lewis's diary, 28 January 1859.

150 Sir G. Douglas and Sir G. P. Ramsay, *The Panmure Papers* (London, 1908), II, pp. 436, 446–7, Palmerston to Lord Panmure, secretary of state for war, 28 September, 11 October 1857.

151 Hansard (third series), CL, cols. 1616–17 (7 June 1858); speech at Chester in aid of foreign missions, *The Times*, 14 October 1857.

152 GP (BL Add. MSS 44394), Gladstone to Massari, 30 August 1860.

153 The Confederation's triumph over Denmark did not shake his view that 'Germany in the aggregate should be strong...'. Palmerston to Russell, 30 September 1865, Palmerston Letter Books (BL Add. MSS 44583).

154 As in 'the Declining Efficiency of Parliament', *Quarterly Review*, September 1856.

155 At Tiverton, *The Times*, 28 May 1857.

156 Malmesbury Papers (9 M73/1/5), Malmesbury to Cowley, 13 November 1858.

157 GP (BL Add. MSS 44745), Gladstone's memorandum of 28 February 1855.

158 Lewis went so far as to say at one point, 'I consider the Liberal party at present to be extinct as a *party*', to Henry Reeve, 7 September 1858, in the Rev. Sir Gilbert Lewis, Bt (ed.), *The Letters of Sir George Cornewall Lewis, Bt* (London, 1870), p. 344.

159 *The Times*, 2 June 1865.

160 Hansard (third series), CLXVIII, cols. 1116–26 (1 August 1862); quotation from 1125.

161 *The Times*, 19 July 1865.

162 Ibid., 24 July 1865.

163 RP (PRO 30/22/14B), Palmerston to Russell, 18 October 1861.

164 GP (BL Add. MSS 44753), 13 November 1864.

165 GP (BL Add. MSS 44754), 18 September 1863.

3 THE POLITICS OF WAR AND PEACE

1 J. B. Conacher, *Britain and the Crimea, 1855–56: Problems of War and Peace* (London, 1987); a detailed narrative of war and diplomacy with some Parliamentary background; O. Anderson, *A Liberal State at War: English Politics and Economics during the Crimean War* (London, 1967); J. R. Vincent, 'The Parliamentary Dimension of the Crimean War', *Transactions of the Royal Historical Society* (1981), and Taylor, *The Struggle for Mastery in Europe, 1848–1918*, are essential.

2 Palmerston Letter Books (BL Add. MSS 48579), Palmerston to Clarendon, 25 September 1855.

3 Connell, *Regina v. Palmerston*, p. 159, entry in the Queen's journal for 3 February 1855, Clarendon Papers (MS Clar. Dep. c 31), Palmerston to Clarendon, 5 February 1855.

4 Spencer Walpole Papers, Walpole's memorandum of 1 February on Lord Derby's audience of the Queen on 31 January 1855.

5 G. P. Gooch (ed.), *The Later Correspondence of Lord John Russell, 1840–1878*, 2 vols. (London, 1925), II, pp. 160–1, memorandum by Lord Palmerston, 19 March 1854. Vincent, *Disraeli, Derby and the Conservative Party*, p. 136, Stanley's 'Memorandum on Public Affairs, November 1855'; GP (BL Add. MSS 44210), Sidney Herbert to Gladstone, 18 November 1855.

6 Harpton Court Collection (3569), Lewis's diary 13, 20 November 1855.

7 Ibid., 11 November 1855.

8 *The Times*, 5 October 1855.

9 Ibid., 5 May 1856.

10 Sir V. Wellesley and R. Sencourt, *Conversations with Napoleon III* (London, 1934), p. 69, Lord Cowley, ambassador at Paris, to Clarendon, 21 January 1855.

11 Comte de Hübner, *Neuf Ans de Souvenirs d'un Ambassadeur d'Autriche à Paris sous la Second Empire*, 2 vols. (Paris, 1904), I, p. 385, Hübner to Count Buol-Schauenstein, Austrian foreign minister, 25 January 1856.

12 *The Times*, 15 September, 6 October 1855.

13 Villiers Papers, British Library of Political and Economic Science (M.759), Clarendon to C. P. Villiers [April 1859].

14 Prince Jerome Napoleon, 'Les Préliminaires de la Paix, 11 juillet 1859, Journal de ma Mission à Vérone auprès de l'Empereur de l'Autriche', *Revue des Deux Mondes* (1909), vol. 52, pp. 481–503, esp. p. 496.

15 Guedalla, *The Palmerston Papers*, pp. 104–6, Palmerston to Gladstone, 6 February 1855.

16 Harpton Court Collection (3569), Lewis's diary, 6 July 1855, recalling Russell's statement to the cabinet.

17 Ibid., 11 September 1855: 'Lord Palmerston's sanguine expectation [of taking Sebastopol]...I confess I did not share.'

18 Lord Edmond Fitzmaurice, *The Life of Granville George Leveson Gower, Second Earl Granville, K.G.*, 2 vols. (London, 1905), 1, pp. 105–8, Granville to Argyll, 3 May 1855.

19 Harpton Court Collection (3569), Lewis's diary, 20, 23, 26 July 1855.

20 Ibid., 1 August, 11 September 1855.

21 Morley, *Cobden*, II, p. 175, Cobden to Bright, 18 September 1855.

22 BP (GC/LE/35), Lewis to Palmerston, 18 September 1855.

23 Ripon Papers (BL Add. MSS 43534), H. A. Bruce, MP to Lord Goderich, MP, 1 September 1855.

24 Benson and Esher, *Letters of Queen Victoria*, III, pp. 58–60, memorandum by Prince Albert, 9 December 1854.

25 R. A. J. Walling (ed.), *The Diaries of John Bright* (London, 1930), pp. 185–6, 20 February 1855.

26 GP (BL Add. MSS 44745), Gladstone's memorandum of 18 February 1855.

27 Walling, *Diaries of John Bright*, pp. 185–7, 191; 20–22, 24, 25 February 1855.

28 The diaries of Sir Hamilton Seymour (BL Add. MSS 60306), 19 January 1855; Morley, *Cobden*, II, p. 171, Cobden to Bright, 11 February 1855.

29 E. I. Barrington, *The Servant of All: Pages from the Family, Social and Political Life of my Father, James Wilson*, 2 vols. (London, 1927), I, p. 249.

30 Morley, *Cobden*, II, p. 166, Cobden to Bright, 5 January 1855.

31 *Economist*, 5 May 1855; and see O. Anderson, 'The Administrative Reform Association, 1855–7', in P. Hollis (ed.), *Pressure from Without in Early Victorian England* (London, 1974).

32 *The Times*, 14 June 1855.

33 Hansard (third series), CXXXVI, cols. 1592 (19 February), 2161–5 (1 March 1855).

34 Douglas and Ramsay, *The Panmure Papers*, II, p. 199, Lord Panmure to the Queen, 20 April 1856.

35 Hansard (third series), CXXXVII, col. 1760 (23 February 1855); *The Times*, 10 February 1855.

36 *Economist*, 17 February 1855.

37 Lewis, *Letters*, p. 298, Lewis to Sir E. W. Head, Bt, 17 August 1855.

38 Glynne-Gladstone Papers (box 9/1), Gladstone to Robertson Gladstone,

6 August 1855. While the index of estimated industrial production (Appendix 3 above) drops in 1855, the output of iron, consumption of raw cotton and total exports continued to rise.

39 *The Times*, 1 January 1856.

40 Morley, *Cobden*, II, p. 167, Cobden to Bright, 5 January 1855.

41 Palmerston Letter Books (BL Add. MSS 48580), Palmerston to Clarendon, 11 March 1856.

42 Cobden Papers (BL Add. MSS 43655), Cobden to William Hargreaves, 12 November 1855; ibid. (BL Add. MSS 43650), Cobden to Bright, 26 June 1855.

43 Lady Rose Weighall, *The Correspondence of Priscilla, Countess of Westmorland* (London, 1909), Prince Metternich to Lady Westmorland, 25 February 1855; K. Marx and F. Engels, *Articles on Britain* (Moscow, 1975), pp. 223–5, Marx on 'The Crisis in Britain' in the *New York Daily Tribune*, 24 March 1855.

44 Hübner, *Neuf Ans de Souvenirs d'un Ambassadeur*, 1, p. 308, Hübner to Count Buol-Schauenstein, 1 February 1855.

45 Wellesley and Sencourt, *Conversations with Napoleon III*, pp. 115–19, Cowley to Clarendon, 13 October, Hübner to Buol-Schauenstein, 27 October 1856.

46 Wodehouse Papers (BL Add. MSS 46692), Clarendon to Lord Wodehouse, 22 July 1856.

47 *The Times*, 7 November 1856.

48 Third Earl of Malmesbury, *Memoirs of an Ex-Minister: An Autobiography*, new edn (London, 1885), p. 384, entry in Malmesbury's journal for 12 November 1856; H. Acton, *The Last Bourbons of Naples (1825–1861)* (London, 1961), ch. 16.

49 *Leeds Mercury*, 29 May 1858.

50 Wellesley and Sencourt, *Conversations with Napoleon III*, pp. 115–16, Cowley to Clarendon, 13 October 1856.

51 BP (GC/CL/945), Clarendon to Palmerston, 10 October 1856; Clarendon Papers (MS Clar. Dep. c 50), Palmerston to Clarendon, 10 October 1856.

52 K. Bourne, *Britain and the Balance of Power in North America, 1815–1908* (London, 1967), ch. 3.

53 Douglas and Ramsay, *The Panmure Papers*, I, pp. 402–3, Palmerston to Panmure, 24 September 1855.

54 Clarendon Papers (MS Clar. Dep. c 49), Palmerston's minute of 3 June 1856; Ashley, *The Life and Correspondence of Viscount Palmerston*, II, pp. 125–6, Palmerston to Clarendon, 1 March 1857.

55 Hickleton Papers, Leeds University microfilm (A4/57, pt. iii), Clarendon to Sir Charles Wood, Bt, 22 June 1856.

56 F. R. Flournoy, *British Policy towards Morocco in the Age of Palmerston, 1830–1865* (Baltimore, 1935), pp. 165–81.

57 W. C. Costin, *Great Britain and China, 1835–1860* (Oxford, 1968), chs. 4 and 5.

58 Clarendon Papers (MS Clar. Dep. c 50), Lewis's memorandum on 'Despatches respecting China and Japan', 3 January 1856 [*recte* 1857], enclosed with Lewis to Edmund Hammond, permanent under-secretary at the Foreign Office, 4 January 1857.

59 Ibid. (MS Clar. Dep. c 69, c 533), Palmerston to Clarendon, 7 January, Clarendon to Lewis, 11 January 1857.

60 Ibid. (MS Clar. Dep. c 50), Lewis to Clarendon, 31, 9 January 1857.

61 Harpton Court Collection (3571), Lewis's diary, 26 February 1857.

62 Clarendon Papers (MS Clar. Dep. c 69), Palmerston to Clarendon, 3 March 1857; Hansard (third series), CXLIV, cols. 1810–34, quotations from cols. 1810, 1813, 1833.

63 Connell, *Regina v. Palmerston*, p. 213, entry in the Queen's journal for 4 March 1857.

64 *The Times*, 7 March 1857, 'Money Market and City Intelligence'.

65 Ibid., 10 March 1857.

66 Ibid., 9, 7 March 1857; the quotation is from J. A. Turner, chairman of the Manchester Commercial Association.

67 Hansard (third series), CXLIV, col. 1792 (3 March 1857).

68 Malmesbury, *Memoirs*, p. 374, Herbert to Malmesbury, 8 December 1855.

69 Clarendon Papers (MS Clar. Dep. c 69), Palmerston to Clarendon, 20 July 1857.

70 GB (BL Add. MSS 44530), Gladstone to G. W. Hope, 15 February 1855. Conacher, *Britain and the Crimea, 1855–56*, p. 2, gives figures that classify virtually all MPs as Tories, Liberals, Peelites, or adherents of the Independent Irish Party. For a selection of the literature on party, see the first footnote to each of the three chapters on the subject, 4, 5 and 6 below.

71 In deploring the weakness of party, Gladstone's *Quarterly Review* article of September 1856 on 'The Declining Efficiency of Parliament' reflected his isolation and reluctance to end it except on his own terms.

72 Malmesbury, *Memoirs*, p. 387, entry in Malmesbury's journal for 3 February 1857; the number of political rebels may have been higher, Matthew, *Gladstone Diaries*, V, p. 22, Gladstone's memorandum of 10 February 1855.

73 Malmesbury, *Memoirs*, pp. 399–400, 349–51, entries in Malmesbury's journal for 9, 13 February 1855, 29 January 1857.

74 Benson and Esher, *The Letters of Queen Victoria*, III, pp. 83–5, memorandum by Prince Albert, 1 February 1855.

75 Malmesbury, *Memoirs*, pp. 349–50, entry in Malmesbury's journal for 9 February 1855.

76 Ibid., pp. 356–8, 370–2, Malmesbury to Derby, 14 April, to Stanley, 21 October 1855; Vincent, *Disraeli, Derby and the Conservative Party*, p. 135, Stanley's 'Memorandum on Public Affairs, November 1855'.

77 Malmesbury, *Memoirs*, p. 379, entry in Malmesbury's journal for 26 April 1856.

78 Clarendon Papers (MS Clar. Dep. c 69), Palmerston to Clarendon, 24 February 1857.

79 Bright Papers (BL Add. MSS 43388), Milner Gibson to Bright, 14 November 1855.

80 Bourne, *Palmerston-Sulivan Letters, 1804–1863*, p. 311, Palmerston to Laurence Sulivan, 17 May 1856.

81 Hansard (third series), CXXXVII, col. 1633 (7 June 1855); Walling, *Diaries of John Bright*, pp. 197–8, 7 June 1855.

82 Malmesbury, *Memoirs*, pp. 370–2, Malmesbury to Stanley, 21 October 1855.

83 Hansard (third series), CXXXVII, col. 1186 (27 March 1855).

84 Walling, *Diaries of John Bright*, pp. 199–201, 30 June, 26 July 1855.

85 *The Times*, 1 March, 2 June 1855.

86 Ibid., 25 May 1855.
87 Glynne-Gladstone Papers (box 9/1), Gladstone to Robertson Gladstone, 28 February 1855.
88 Matthew, *Gladstone Diaries*, V, p. 123, Gladstone's memorandum of 17 April 1856.
89 Glynne-Gladstone Papers (box 9/1), Gladstone to Robertson Gladstone, 12 November; GP (44164), Gladstone to Sir James Graham, 4 December 1856.
90 Ripon Papers (BL Add. MSS 43534), H. A. Bruce, MP to Lord Goderich, MP, 1 September 1855.
91 Bright Papers (BL Add. MSS 43386), Villiers to Bright, 10 November [1855].
92 Ibid., Villiers to Bright, [13 August 1855], 3 August 1856.
93 *The Times*, 31 January; Cobden Papers (BL Add. MSS 43662), Milner Gibson to Cobden, 14 January 1857.

4 PARTY: WHIGS AND LIBERALS

1 Gladstone Papers (BL Add. MSS 44547), Gladstone to the Rev Malcolm MacColl, 30 January 1884.
   Vincent, *The Formation of the Liberal Party 1857–1863* (London, 1966), D. Southgate, *The Passing of the Whigs, 1832–1886* (London, 1962), Hawkins, *Parliament, Party, and the Art of Politics in Britain* and R. Shannon, *Gladstone, I: 1809–1865* (London, 1982) are important for this chapter. D. F. Krein, *The Last Palmerston Government* (Ames, Iowa, 1978) is helpful.
2 May, *The Constitutional History of England*, I, p. 166.
3 Ibid., 2, pp. 223, 225, 1, pp. 165–6.
4 Morley, *Cobden*, II, p. 220, Cobden to W. S. Lindsay, MP, 23 March 1858.
5 Cobden Papers (BL Add. MSS 43650), Cobden to Bright, 20 February, 31 March, [14 April] 1858.
6 May, *Constitutional History of England*, II, p. 220.
7 Lewis, *Letters*, pp. 344–5, Lewis to Reeve, 7 September 1858.
8 Glynne-Gladstone Papers (box 9/2), Gladstone to Robertson Gladstone, 2 July 1859.
9 May, *Constitutional History of England*, I, p. 165, II, p. 220.
10 Douglas and Ramsay, *The Panmure Papers*, I, p. 51, Palmerston to Panmure, 7 February 1855.
11 Vincent, *The Formation of the Liberal Party*, p. 25; Southgate, *The Passing of the Whigs*, p. xv; H. J. Hanham, *Elections and Party Management: Politics in the Time of Disraeli and Gladstone* (London, 1959) and D. Fraser, *Power and Authority in the Victorian City* (London, 1979) depict the notables' control of local politics.
12 Guedalla, *The Palmerston Papers*, pp. 281–3, Palmerston to Gladstone, 12 May 1864; Gladstone to Palmerston, 13 May 1864.
13 BP (GC/TE 356), Palmerston to Sir William Temple, 15 February 1855.
14 Ibid.
15 GP (BL Add. MSS 44745), Gladstone's memorandum of 28 February 1855.
16 Ibid.
17 BP (GC/TE 356), Palmerston to Temple, 15 February 1855; BP (GC/GR 831), Granville to Palmerston 24 February 1855; Lewis, *Letters*, p. 293, Lewis to Sir E. W. Head, Bt, 18 March 1855.

18 Cobden Papers (BL Add. MSS 43665), Cobden to Col. J. W. Fitzmayer, 10 March 1855.

19 Clarendon Papers (MS Clar. Dep. c 31), Palmerston to Clarendon, 5 February 1855.

20 BP (GC/TE 357, 358), Palmerston to Temple, 9 March, 12 June 1855.

21 Douglas and Ramsay, *The Panmure Papers*, I, p. 233, Panmure to Lord Raglan, 11 June 1855.

22 Bourne, *Palmerston–Sulivan Letters, 1804–1863*, p. 319, Palmerston to Laurence Sulivan, 14 April 1863.

23 Lewis has no biography. A selection from his correspondence edited by his brother, the Rev. Sir Gilbert Lewis, Bt, illustrates the man's temper and political beliefs.

24 BP (GC/LE/35), Lewis to Palmerston, 18 September 1855.

25 Ibid. (GC/TE 364), Palmerston to Temple, 24 December 1855.

26 Vincent, *Disraeli, Derby and the Conservative Party*, p. 139, Stanley's 'Memorandum on Public Affairs', November 1855.

27 Harpton Court Collection (3570), Lewis's diary, 28 April 1856.

28 Palmerston's diary (BP, D/16), 3 February 1855.

29 Palmerston Letter Books (BL Add. MSS 48579), Palmerston to Cheetham, 28 August 1855; Harpton Court Collection (3570), Lewis's diary, 21 January 1856.

30 Hansard (third series), CXLIII, col. 609 (10 July 1856).

31 Mill, *Considerations on Representative Government*, ch. 13.

32 BP (SHA/PD/7), Shaftesbury Papers, diary, 11, 20 February 1856.

33 Hansard (third series), CXLIII, col. 609 (10 July 1856), Palmerston.

34 Harpton Court Collection (3570), Lewis's diary, 8 February 1856.

35 BP (GC/GR/1844), Granville to Palmerston, 8 February 1856.

36 Malmesbury, *Memoirs*, p. 376, Derby to Malmesbury, 19 July 1856.

37 Hansard (third series), CXLIII, cols. 1461, 1469 (25 July 1856).

38 Matthew, *Gladstone Diaries*, V, pp. 150–1, 25 July 1856.

39 Hansard (third series), CXLIII, col. 1465 (25 July 1856).

40 Hansard (third series), CXLIII, cols. 1473–4 (25 July 1856).

41 BP (GC/TE 365), Palmerston to Temple, 15 July 1856.

42 *The Times*, 27 October 1856.

43 Ibid., 12 November 1856.

44 Ibid., 10 November 1856.

45 Ibid., 18 November 1856.

46 Benson and Esher, *Letters of Queen Victoria*, III, p. 226, Palmerston to the Queen, 13 January 1857; Douglas and Ramsay, *The Panmure Papers*, I, p. 347, Palmerston to Panmure, 5 February 1857.

47 Harpton Court Collection (3571), Lewis's diary, 23 February 1857.

48 Matthew, *Gladstone Diaries*, V p. 203, 6 March 1857.

49 Hansard (third series), CXLIV, col. 2064 (9 March 1857).

50 Connell, *Regina v. Palmerston*, p. 214, Palmerston to the Queen, 6 March 1857. The results of the election are summarized in Appendix 2 above.

51 *The Times*, 17 March 1857.

52 Ibid., 19 March 1857.

53 Ibid., 21 March 1857.

54 Ibid., 30 March 1857.

55 *Leeds Intelligencer*, 14 March 1857.

56 Clarendon Papers (MS Clar. Dep. c 69), Palmerston to Clarendon, 26 April 1857.

57 Ibid., Palmerston to Clarendon, 24 March 1857.

58 Wodehouse Papers (BL Add. MSS 46692), Clarendon to Wodehouse, 19 March 1857.

59 *The Times*, 20, 28 March 1857.

60 RP (PRO 30/22/13C), Hayter to Russell, 25 March 1857.

61 D. MacCarthy and A. Russell. *Lady John Russell. A Memoir* (London, 1926), p. 170, Lord John Russell to Lady Melgund, 1 April 1857; RP (PRO 30/22/13C), Russell to Elliot, 4 April 1857.

62 Ibid., Russell to Elliot, 23 April 1857.

63 Newcastle Papers (NeC12347–381), Newcastle to Abraham Hayward, 10 April 1857.

64 *The Times*, 28 March 1857.

65 Clarendon Papers (MS Clar. Dep. c 69), Palmerston to Clarendon, 26 April 1857.

66 Hickleton Papers (A4/63), Wood to Palmerston, 7 May 1857.

67 Ibid., Palmerston to Wood, 7 May 1857.

68 Harpton Court Collection (3571), Lewis's diary, 7 May 1857.

69 *The Times*, 20 March 1857.

70 Ibid.

71 Ibid., 19 March 1857.

72 Ibid., 25 March 1857.

73 Ibid., 28 March 1857.

74 Ibid., 28, 31 March 1857.

75 Hansard (third series), CLIII, col. 785 (24 March 1859).

76 *The Times*, 25, 28 March 1857.

77 Ibid., 23 March 1857.

78 Lewis, *Letters*, p. 329, Lewis to Head, 5 February 1858.

79 Harpton Court Collection (3572), Lewis's diary, 16 September 1857; the second entry for that date following 22 September.

80 BP (D/17), Palmerston's diary, 28 November 1857; F. B. Smith, *The Making of the Second Reform Bill* (Cambridge, 1966), p. 40.

81 Harpton Court Collection (3572), Lewis's diary, 28 November, 16, 18 December.

82 Ibid., 11 December 1857. Clanricarde's morals had been the subject of unfavourable comment following a case in the Irish courts several years earlier.

83 Ibid., 21 February 1858.

84 Lewis, *Letters*, p. 332, Lewis to Reeve, 5 March 1858.

85 Harpton Court Collection (3572), Lewis's diary, 19 February 1858.

86 Ibid., 27, 14 January 1857.

87 Malmesbury, *Memoirs*, p. 416, entry in Malmesbury's journal for 9 February 1858.

88 Harpton Court Collection (3572), Lewis's diary, 19 February 1858; Vincent,

Disraeli, Derby and the Conservative Party, pp. 153–4, entry in Stanley's journal for 20 February 1858.

89 Harpton Court Collection (3572), Lewis's diary, 26 February 1858; Benson and Esher, *Letters of Queen Victoria*, III, pp. 266–8, memorandum by Prince Albert, 21 February 1858.

90 Harpton Court Collection (3572), Lewis's diary, 4 March 1858.

91 BP (D/18), Palmerston's diary, 20 February 1858.

92 *The Times*, 8 May 1858.

93 Ibid., 25 January 1858.

94 Ibid., 1 March 1858.

95 Lewis, *Letters*, p. 347, Lewis to Reeve, 16 September 1858.

96 P. Gordon (ed.), *The Red Earl: The Papers of the Fifth Earl Spencer, 1835–1910*, 2 vols. (Northampton, 1981–86), I, p. 44, Althorp to the fourth Earl Spencer, 4 September 1857.

97 Harpton Court Collection (3572), Lewis's diary, 7 March 1857.

98 RP (PRO 30/22/13E), Russell to Elliot, 8 January, 3 March 1858.

99 Ibid., Russell to Elliot, 15 March 1858.

100 Ibid., Russell to Elliot, 3 March 1858.

101 Harpton Court Collection (3572), Lewis's diary, 10 May 1858.

102 Matthew, *Gladstone Diaries*, V, p. 298, 19 May 1858.

103 Harpton Court Collection (3572), Lewis's diary, 21 May 1858.

104 Ibid., 14 May 1858; BP (D/18), Palmerston's diary, 14 May 1858.

105 Clarendon Papers (MS Clar. Dep. c 524), Palmerston to Clarendon, n.d. but 1858.

106 BP (D/18), Palmerston's diary, 21 May 1858.

107 Harpton Court Collection (3572), Lewis's diary, 31 July 1858.

108 *The Times*, 18 August 1858.

109 Ibid., 25 August 1858.

110 Ibid., 23 September 1858.

111 Ibid., 27 September 1858.

112 Ibid., 28 September 1858.

113 Ibid., 19 October 1858.

114 Clarendon Papers (MS Clar. Dep. c 524), Palmerston to Clarendon, 31 October, 3 November 1858.

115 Benson and Esher, *Letters of Queen Victoria*, III, pp. 300–1, memorandum by Prince Albert, 4 September 1858.

116 BP (D/18), Palmerston's diary, 16 November 1858.

117 Ibid., 14 September 1858.

118 Barrington, *The Servant of All*, II, pp. 104–5, Lewis to James Wilson, MP, 28 November 1858.

119 G. W. Curtis (ed.), *The Correspondence of John Lothrop Motley*, 2 vols. (London, 1889), I, pp. 254–5, Motley to his wife, 6 June 1858.

120 Ibid., p. 262, Motley to his wife, 13 June 1858.

121 Barrington, *The Servant of All*, II, p. 98, Wilson to Lewis, 21 November 1858.

122 RP (PRO 30/22/13 F), Russell to Elliot, 4, 11 November 1858.

123 Harpton Court Collection (3572), Lewis's diary, 14 May; Tilney Bassett, *Gladstone to his Wife*, pp. 123–4, 9 April 1859.

124 Benson and Esher, *Letters of Queen Victoria*, III, pp. 300–1, memorandum by Prince Albert, 4 September 1858.

125 Ibid.

126 Douglas and Ramsay, *The Panmure Papers*, II, p. 480, Wood to Panmure, 16 June 1859.

127 BP (GC/R/496), Russell to Palmerston, 13 February 1859.

128 RP (PRO 30/22/13G), Palmerston to Russell, 14 February 1859; Hansard third series), CLIII, col. 75 (3 February 1859).

129 Harpton Court Collection (3573), Lewis's diary, 3 February 1859; Barrington, *The Servant of All*, II, p. 131, Lewis to Wilson, 12 January 1859.

130 BP (GC/CL/1184), Clarendon to Palmerston, 22 January 1859.

131 Clarendon Papers (MS Clar. Dep. c 524), Palmerston to Clarendon, 20 January 1859.

132 Ibid.

133 Ibid. (MS Clar. Dep. c 531), Lewis to Clarendon, 7 January 1859.

134 Ibid. (MS Clar. Dep. c 524), Palmerston to Clarendon, 15 April, 20 January 1859.

135 Hickleton Papers (A4/56), Russell to Wood, 28 May 1859.

136 Ibid.; RP (PRO 30/22/13F), Russell to Elliot, 15 December, 19 October 1858; S. Koss, *The Rise and Fall of the Political Press in Britain*, 2 vols. (London, 1981–84), I: *The Nineteenth Century*, p. 115.

137 Clarendon Papers (MS Clar. Dep. c 524), Palmerston to Clarendon, 4 January 1859.

138 RP (PRO 30/22/13F), Russell to Elliot, 15 December 1858.

139 Clarendon Papers (MS Clar. Dep. c 533), Clarendon to Lewis, 16 November, 14 December 1858.

140 J. K. Laughton, *Memoirs of the Life and Correspondence of Henry Reeve*, 2 vols. (London, 1898), I, pp. 401–2, Clarendon to Reeve, 18 December 1858.

141 RP (PRO 30/22/13F), Russell to Elliot, 18 December 1858.

142 Clarendon Papers (MS Clar. Dep. c 524), Palmerston to Clarendon, 19 December 1858; BP (D/19), Palmerston's diary, 7 March 1859.

143 Hansard (third series), CLIII, cols. 873–89 (25 March 1859); A. L. Kennedy, '*My Dear Duchess*': *Social and Political Letters to the Duchess of Manchester, 1858–1869* (London, 1956), pp. 167–8, Granville to the Duchess of Manchester, 28 March 1859; Malmesbury Papers (9M73), MS diary, 19 March 1859.

144 BP (D/19), Palmerston's diary, 4 and 6 April 1859; Hansard (third series), CLIII, cols. 1415–18 (6 April 1859).

145 RP (PRO 30/22/13G), Russell to Elliot, 12 April 1859.

146 Lord Stanmore, *Sidney Herbert, Lord Herbert of Lea. A Memoir*, 2 vols. (London, 1906), II, pp. 190–2, Palmerston to Herbert, 24 May 1859.

147 RP (PRO 30/22/13G), Palmerston to Russell, 18 May 1859.

148 *The Times*, 16 April 1859.

149 Ibid.

150 Ibid., 25 April 1859.

151 Lamb Papers (BL Add. MSS 45554), Lady Palmerston to Palmerston, 29 April 1859.

152 *The Times*, 30 April 1859.

153 Ibid., 2 May 1859.

154 Ibid., 3 May 1859.

155 Ibid., 30 April 1859.

156 Clarendon Papers (MS Clar. Dep. c 524), Palmerston to Clarendon, 5 May 1859. For a summary of the election's outcome, see Appendix 2 above.

157 BP (GC/HA/314), Hayter to Palmerston, 22 May 1859.

158 RP (PRO 30/22/139), Russell to Elliot, 13 May 1859.

159 Graham Papers, Cambridge University Library microfilm (MS 37), Graham to Russell, 17 May 1859.

160 BP (GC/WO/131), Wood to Palmerston, 24 May 1859.

161 Graham Papers (MS 47), Russell to Graham, 26 May; RP (PRO 30/22/13G) Russell to Elliot, 13 May; Harpton Court Collection (3573), Lewis's diary, 2 June 1859.

162 Ibid.

163 Graham Papers (MS 47), Graham to Russell, 18 May; Harpton Court Collection (33573), Lewis's diary, 30 May, 2 June 1859.

164 BP (D/19), Palmerston's diary, 6 June 1859.

165 Harpton Court Collection (33573), Lewis's diary, 6 June 1859; *Guardian*, 8 June, quoting from the *Morning Star* – the paper of Cobden and his friends – as giving the best account of this private meeting.

166 Ibid.

167 *The Times*, 7 June 1859.

168 Hansard (third series), CLIV, cols. 117–18 (7 June 1859).

169 Ibid., col. 134.

170 BP (GC/HA/314), Hayter to Palmerston, 22 May; BP (SHA/PD/7), Shaftesbury Papers, diary, 3 June 1859.

171 Benson and Esher, *Letters of Queen Victoria*, III, pp. 336–9, Derby to the Queen, 2 June 1859.

172 Connell, *Regina v. Palmerston*, pp. 255–6, entry in the Queen's journal for 11 June 1859.

173 Harpton Court Collection (3573), Lewis's diary, 11 June; BP (D/19), Palmerston's diary, 12 June 1859.

174 Harpton Court Collection (3573), Lewis's diary, 11 June 1859; BP (RC/FF/36), Palmerston to the Queen, 11 June 1859.

175 A. I. Dasent, *John Thadeus Delane, Editor of The Times: His Life and Correspondence*, 2 vols. (London, 1908), I, p. 313, Granville to Delane, 12 June 1859.

176 With the Board of Trade vacant pending Cobden's return from America: Palmerston's diary, BP (D/19), 13 June 1859; a postscript written two weeks later.

177 Douglas and Ramsay, *The Panmure Papers*, II, p. 478, Panmure to Palmerston, 15 June 1859. Argyll was a survivor from the old cabinet who was not regarded, and did not regard himself, as a Whig.

178 Palmerston Letter Books (BL Add. MSS 48582), Palmerston to Bruce, 26 November 1860.

179 BP (SHA/PD/7), Shaftesbury Papers, diary, 21 June 1859.

180 Morley, *Cobden*, II, pp. 228–9, Cobden to his wife, 30 June 1859.

181 Cobden Papers (BL Add. MSS 43653), Cobden to Ashworth, 10 July 1859.

182 Morley, *Cobden*, II, pp. 228–34, Cobden to Sale, 4 July 1859.

183 *Memoirs of Ernest II, Duke of Saxe-Coburg-Gotha* (trans. P. Andreae), 4 vols. (London, 1890), III, pp. 307–8, Albert to Ernest II, 18 June 1859.

184 Benson and Esher, *Letters of Queen Victoria*, III, pp. 446–7, Palmerston to the Queen, 26 July 1861; Layard Papers (BL Add. MSS 38987), Palmerston's undated minute from 1861–65, the period of Layard's under-secretaryship in his second government.

185 *The Times*, 18 August 1859.

186 Morley, *Cobden*, II, p. 230, Cobden to Sale, 4 July 1859.

187 BP (GC/LE/228), Palmerston to Lewis, 31 January 1861.

188 Clarendon Papers (MS Clar. Dep. c 524), Palmerston to Clarendon, 4 November, 7 September 1859.

189 Cowley Papers (PRO FO 519/292), Palmerston to Cowley, 30 January 1860.

190 Clarendon Papers (MS Clar. Dep. c 31), Lewis to Clarendon, 13 March 1860.

191 Bright Papers (BL Add. MSS 43384), Bright to Cobden, 5 February 1860.

192 Malmesbury, *Memoirs*, p. 512, Clarendon to Malmesbury, 8 February 1860.

193 Hansard (third series), CLVII, col. 136 (8 March 1860).

194 Cobden Papers (43662), Milner Gibson to Cobden, 1 January 1860.

195 Palmerston Letter Books (BL Add. MSS 48081), Palmerston to Russell, 4 November 1859.

196 Somerset Papers, Buckingham RO, Gladstone to the Duke of Somerset, 8 September 26 December 1859.

197 Guedalla, *The Palmerston Papers*, pp. 113–14, Gladstone to Palmerston, 25 November 1859.

198 GP (BL Add. MSS 44591), Gladstone's memorandum on 'Fortifications and Fortification Loan' of 26 May 1860.

199 Ibid.

200 Guedalla, *The Palmerston Papers*, pp. 115–18, Palmerston to Gladstone, 15 December 1859.

201 *The Times*, 9 September 1859.

202 Bright Papers (BL Add. MSS 43384), Bright to Cobden, 15 July 1860; Cobden Papers (BL Add. MSS 43651), Cobden to Bright, 22 June 1860.

203 Graham Papers (MS 47), Graham to Gladstone, 2 June 1860.

204 GP (BL Add. MSS 44211), Gladstone to Herbert, 10 April 1860.

205 *The Times*, 3 March 1860.

206 Hansard (third series), CLVII, cols. 485–90 (13 March), Palmerston, 1252–8 (26 March) Russell.

207 BP (D/20), Palmerston's diary, 9 June 1860.

208 *The Times*, 19 August 1859.

209 BP (D/20), Palmerston's diary, 4 and 9 December 1859; BP (GC/VI/14), Villiers to Palmerston, 17 January 1860.

210 Ibid. (GC/VI/13), Villiers to Palmerston, 10 December 1859.

211 Ibid. (GC/RU/1132), Palmerston to Russell, 29 December 1859.

212 BP (D/20), Palmerston's diary, 3 May 1860.

213 Hansard (third series), CLVIII, cols. 146, 161–3 (26 April 1860); Harpton Court Collection (3574), Lewis's diary, 26 April 1860.

214 RP (PRO 30/22/25), Villiers to Russell, 10 June 1860.

215 Ibid. (PRO 30/22/14A), Palmerston to Russell, 21 May 1860; Clarendon Papers (MS Clar. Dep. c 531), Lewis to Clarendon, 18 June 1860.

216 Harpton Court Collection (3574), Lewis's diary, 31 January 1860; Bright Papers (BL Add. MSS 43384), Bright to Cobden, 3 July 1860.

217 Harpton Court Collection (3574), Lewis's diary, 22 May 1860.

218 Benson and Esher, *Letters of Queen Victoria*, III, pp. 401–2, Palmerston to the Queen, 22 May 1860.

219 Harpton Court Collection (3574), Lewis's diary, 25 June 1860.

220 Connell, *Regina v. Palmerston*, p. 291, Palmerston to the Queen, 2 July 1860; Guedalla, *The Palmerston Papers*, pp. 139–40, Gladstone to Palmerston, 4 July 1860; Hansard (third series), CLIX, cols. 1430–41 (5 July 1860).

221 Harpton Court Collection (3574), Lewis's diary, 8 May 1860.

222 Malmesbury, *Memoirs*, p. 521, entry in Malmesbury's journal for 13 May 1860.

223 BP (GC/GR/1874), Granville to Palmerston, 17 May 1860; Granville Papers (PRO 30/29/19), Palmerston to Granville, 21 May 1860.

224 Harpton Court Collection (3574), Lewis's diary, 21, 25 May 1860; Kennedy, '*My Dear Duchess*', pp.104–5, Clarendon to the Duchess of Manchester, 27 May 1860.

225 Malmesbury, *Memoirs*, p. 522, entries in Malmesbury's journal for 1 and 2 June 1860.

226 BP (D/20), Palmerston's diary, 5 [recte 6] June; Clarendon Papers (MS Clar. Dep. c 531), Lewis to Clarendon 18 June 1860.

227 Connell, *Regina v. Palmerston*, p. 292, Palmerston to the Queen, 22, 24 July 1860.

228 Phillimore Papers (Christ Church, Oxford), diary, 12 July 1860.

229 BP (D/20), Palmerston's diary, 6 August; Guedalla, *The Palmerston Papers*, pp. 145–7, Palmerston to Gladstone, 23, 24 July, Gladstone to Palmerston, 24 July 1860.

230 Guedalla, *The Palmerston Papers*, p. 150, Palmerston to Gladstone, 16 August 1860.

231 BP (GC/RU/631), Russell to Palmerston, 30 October 1860.

232 RP (PRO 30/22/21), Palmerston to Russell, 29 October 1860.

233 Cowley Papers (PRO FO 519/292), Palmerston to the Duc de Persigny, 18 September 1860; RP (PRO 30/22/21), Palmerston to Russell, 16 November 1860.

234 Harpton Court Collection (3574), Lewis's diary, 17 November 1860.

235 RP (PRO 30/22/21), Palmerston to Russell, 16 November 1860.

236 GP (BL Add. MSS 44636), Gladstone's note of the decision on 'Reform Bills' in the cabinet, 9 February 1861.

237 Matthew, *Gladstone Diaries*, VI, p. 24, 13 April 1861.

238 Harpton Court Collection (3575), Lewis's diary, 11, 12 April; BP (D/21), Palmerston's diary, 11, 12 April; Matthew, *Gladstone Diaries*, VI, pp. 23–4, undated notes, on the cabinets of 11 and 12 April; Clarendon Papers (MS Clar. Dep. c 531), Lewis to Clarendon, 12 April 1861.

239 Clarendon Papers (MS Clar. Dep. c 531), Lewis to Clarendon, 13 April; Guedalla, *The Palmerston Papers*, pp. 166–7, Palmerston to Gladstone, 14 April; Matthew, *Gladstone Diaries*, VI, p. 25, Gladstone's note of his calculations, 13 April 1861.

240 GP (BL Add. MSS 44184), Wood to Gladstone 12 April 1861.

241 Guedalla, *The Palmerston Papers*, pp. 166–7, Palmerston to Gladstone, Gladstone to Palmerston, 14 April 1861.
242 Hansard (third series), CLXII, cols. 1106–7 (25 April 1861).
243 Ibid., col. 1423.
244 GP (BL Add. MSS 44531), Gladstone to Gregory Burnett, his agent, 21 May 1861, on the issues in the impending Flintshire by-election.
245 Hansard (third series), CLXII, cols. 1106–7 (25 April 1861).
246 GP (BL Add. MSS 44209), Gladstone to Heathcote, 15 May 1861.
247 Vincent, *Disraeli, Derby and the Conservative Party*, pp. 170–1, entries in Stanley's journal for 23 and 30 May 1861.
248 Guedalla, *The Palmerston Papers*, p. 169–70. Palmerston to Gladstone, 16 May 1861.
249 Ibid., pp. 174–7, Palmerston to Gladstone, 19 July 1861.
250 GP (BL Add. MSS 44099), Argyll to Gladstone, 23 August; ibid. (BL Add. MSS 44532), Gladstone to Argyll, 26 August 1861.
251 Ibid., Gladstone to W. S. Lindsay, MP, 26 November 1861.
252 Ibid., Gladstone to Phillimore, 4 September 1861.
253 *The Times*, 16 October 1861.
254 BP (SHA/PD/7), Shaftesbury Papers, diary, 15 June 1861.

5 PEELITES AND RADICALS

1 For the Peelites, see Conacher, *The Aberdeen Coalition* supplemented by *Britain and the Crimea*; W. D. Jones and A. B. Erickson, *The Peelites, 1846–1857* (Columbus, Ohio, 1972) and Lord Stanmore, *Sidney Herbert, Lord Herbert of Lea*, II, ch. 3 'The Extinction of Peelism (1857–58)'. The extensive literature on radicalism includes: S. Maccoby, *English Radicalism, 1853–1886* (London, 1928); Vincent, *The Formation of the Liberal Party*; Morley, *Cobden*; W. Hinde, *Richard Cobden: A Victorian Outsider* (New Haven, Conn., 1987); H. Ausubel, *John Bright, Victorian Reformer* (New York, 1966). Robbins, *John Bright*; and D. Read, *Cobden and Bright: A Victorian Partnership* (London, 1967).
2 Granville Papers (PRO 30/29/19), Newcastle to Granville, 18 April 1855.
3 Ibid., Palmerston to Granville, 2 December 1857.
4 BP (GC/RU/579), Russell to Palmerston, 16 February 1860.
5 GP (BL Add. MSS 44098), Argyll to Gladstone, 20 February 1855.
6 Walling, *Diaries of John Bright*, p. 193, 3 April 1855.
7 BP (GC/AR/7), Argyll to Palmerston, 30 May 1855.
8 Douglas and Ramsay, *The Panmure Papers*, I, p. 51, Palmerston to Panmure, 7 February 1855.
9 Clarendon Papers (MS Clar. Dep. c 69), Palmerston to Clarendon, 24 February 1857.
10 GP (BL Add. MSS 44210), Herbert to Gladstone, 16 November, 19 December 1856.
11 Ibid. (BL Add. MSS 44530), Gladstone to G. W. Hope, 15 February 1855.
12 Aberdeen Papers (BL Add. MSS 43071), Gladstone to Aberdeen, 13 October 1856. The words in quotation marks applied to the Liberal Disraeli's well-known remark in 1845 that 'a Conservative Government was an organized hypocrisy'.

13 GP (BL Add. MSS 44164), Gladstone to Graham, 29 November 1856.

14 Matthew, *Gladstone Diaries*, V, p. 203, Gladstone's memorandum of his interview with Derby on 6 March; Malmesbury, *Memoirs*, pp. 392–3, entry in Malmesbury journal for 6, 7, 8 March 1857.

15 *The Times*, 6 April 1857.

16 Glynne-Gladstone Papers (box 9/2), Gladstone to Robertson Gladstone, 28 March 1857.

17 Malmesbury, *Memoirs*, p. 393, entry in Malmesbury's journal for 16 March 1857.

18 Aberdeen Papers (BL Add. MSS 43071), Aberdeen to Palmerston, 3 April 1857.

19 GP (BL Add. MSS 44545), Gladstone to John Morley, 24 October 1881.

20 *The Times*, 28 March 1857.

21 Aberdeen Papers (BL Add. MSS 43071), Gladstone to Aberdeen, 4 April 1857.

22 Ibid., Aberdeen to Gladstone, 8 April 1857.

23 GP (BL Add. MSS 44210), Herbert to Gladstone, 4 January 1857.

24 Ibid., Gladstone to Herbert, 22 March 1857.

25 Eighth Duke of Argyll, *India under Dalhousie and Canning*, (London, 1865), p. 142. Reprinted from *The Edinburgh Review*, January and April 1863.

26 J. G. A. Baird (ed.), *Private Letters of the Marquess of Dalhousie* (Shannon, Ireland, 1972), Dalhousie to Sir George Couper, Bt, 17 March 1855.

27 GP (BL Add. MSS 44211), Herbert to Gladstone, 10 February 1858.

28 Glynne-Gladstone Papers (box 4/2), Gladstone to Robertson Gladstone, 29 January 1858.

29 GP (BL Add. MSS 44164), Graham to Gladstone, 31 August 1857.

30 Ibid. (BL Add. MSS 44211), Herbert to Gladstone, 10 February 1858.

31 Graham Papers (MS 46), Gladstone to Graham, 23 January 1858.

32 *Quarterly Review*, April 1858, 'France and the late Ministry', pp. 560, 569.

33 Matthew, *Gladstone Diaries*, V, p. 279, 20 February 1858.

34 GP (BL Add. MSS 44164), Graham to Gladstone, 25 May 1858.

35 Ibid., Gladstone to Graham, 26 May 1858.

36 Glynne-Gladstone Papers (box 9/2), Gladstone to Robertson Gladstone, 15 June 1858.

37 *Quarterly Review*, October 1858, 'The Past and Present Administrations', p. 522.

38 Lewis, *Letters*, p. 261, Lewis to Hayward, 28 October 1858; Harpton Court Collection (3572), Lewis's diary, 22 to 27 October 1858.

39 Aberdeen Papers (BL Add. MSS 43071), Gladstone to Aberdeen, 30 October 1858.

40 Graham Papers (MS 47), Graham to Russell, 9, 17, 18 May 1859.

41 Morley, *Gladstone*, (London, 1905), I, pp. 623–4, quoting Phillimore's diary, 18 May 1859.

42 GP (BL Add. MSS 44164), Gladstone to Graham, 29 November; Matthew, *Gladstone Diaries*, V, pp. 112–14, Gladstone to Aberdeen, 13 March; Aberdeen Papers (BL Add. MSS 43071), Gladstone to Aberdeen, 27 September 1856.

43 Glynne-Gladstone Papers (9/2), Gladstone to Robertson Gladstone, 2 July 1859. Palmerston's acknowledgement of Graham's services, dated 29 June, is in the Graham Papers (MS 47).

44 BP (GC/HE/48), Palmerston's endorsement of 24 May on a copy of Herbert to Russell, 21 May 1859.

45 Phillimore Papers, diary, 26 May 1859.

46 Graham Papers (MS 47), Graham to Russell, 9 May 1859.

47 Hansard (third series), CLXXIII, col. 84 (4 February 1864).

48 *The Times*, 20 March 1857.

49 Graham Papers (MS 47), Graham to Russell, 17 May 1859.

50 Walling, *Diaries of John Bright*, pp. 237–40, 3 and 5 June 1859.

51 *Guardian*, 8 June 1859.

52 Walling, *Diaries of John Bright*, pp. 240–1, 243, 12, 15 June 1859; Benson and Esher, *Letters of Queen Victoria*, III, pp. 349–50, Palmerston to the Queen, the Queen to Palmerston, 2 July 1859.

53 Morley, *Cobden*, II, p. 232, Cobden to Sale, 4 July 1859.

54 BP (GC/SH/37), Shaftesbury to Palmerston, 23 June 1859.

55 Morley, *Cobden*, II, pp. 219–20, Cobden to Lindsay, 23 March 1858.

56 Ibid., pp. 396–7, Cobden to Henry Ashworth, 7 February 1862.

57 Cobden Papers (BL Add. MSS 43655), Cobden to Hargreaves, 6 June 1857.

58 Ibid. (BL Add. MSS 43650), Cobden to Bright, 6 March 1857; Bright Papers (BL Add. MSS 43384), Bright to Cobden, 25 October 1860.

59 Ibid., Bright to Cobden, 2 November 1856.

60 Morley, *Cobden*, II, p. 220, Cobden to Lindsay, 23 March 1858; Cobden Papers (BL Add. MSS 43655), Cobden to Hargreaves, 6 June 1857.

61 Ibid. (BL Add. MSS 43650), Cobden to Bright, 31 March 1858.

62 Bright Papers (BL Add. MSS 43384), Bright to Cobden, 9 April, 2 September 1858.

63 Cobden Papers (BL Add. MSS 43650), Cobden to Bright, 17 October 1858.

64 J. E. T. Rogers, (ed.), *Speeches on Questions of Public Policy by the Rt. Hon. John Bright* (London, 1878), p. 472, Birmingham, 29 October 1858.

65 Bright Papers (BL Add. MSS 43384), Bright to Cobden, 26 September 1858.

66 Rogers, *Speeches by...Bright*, pp. 471–3, Birmingham, 29 October 1858.

67 *The Times*, 18, 29 January 1859; Rogers, *Speeches by...Bright*, p. 289, Bright at Birmingham, 27 October 1858.

68 Barrington, *The Servant of All*, II, pp. 103–7, Wilson to Lewis, 17 December 1858.

69 Rogers, *Speeches by...Bright*, p. 470, Birmingham, 29 October 1858.

70 Barrington, *The Servant of All*, II, pp. 105–6, Wilson to Lewis, 19 December 1858.

71 Bright Papers (BL Add. MSS 43384), Bright to Cobden, 14 November 1858.

72 Barrington, *The Servant of All*, II, p. 95, Lewis to Wilson, 16 November 1858.

73 Rogers, *Speeches by...Bright*, pp. 313–15, Glasgow, 21 December 1858.

74 Cobden Papers (BL Add. MSS 43650), Cobden to Bright, 26 December 1858.

75 RP (PRO 30/22/13G), Russell to Elliot, 5 January 1859.

76 Ibid., Lewis to Russell, 12, 21 January, Russell to Elliot, 19 January 1859.

77 Hickleton Papers (A4/63), Palmerston to Wood, 26 December 1858.

78 Ibid., Wood to Palmerston, 30 December 1858.

79 BP (D/19), Palmerston's diary, 7 March; Walling, *Diaries of John Bright*, p. 236, 4 March 1859.

80 BP (D/19), Palmerston's diary, 7 March 1859; Palmerston preferred £8 rental

in view of a possible change in the law of rating which would have enlarged the scope of £6 rateable value.

81 Walling, *Diaries of John Bright*, pp. 236–7, 22 March 1859.

82 Hickleton Papers (A4/63), Wood to Palmerston, 16 April and BP (GC/WO/129), 1 May 1859.

83 Ibid. (GC/WO/130), Wood to Palmerston, 6 May 1859.

84 *The Times*, 13, 16 April 1859.

85 Ibid., 25, 29 April 1859.

86 Ibid., 9 December 1858, 30 April 1859.

87 Graham Papers (MS 47), Russell to Graham, 7 May 1859.

88 *The Times*, 27, 28 January 1859.

89 Ibid., 28 June 1859.

90 Cobden Papers (BL Add. MSS 43655), Cobden to Hargreaves, 14 June 1860.

91 *The Times*, 24, 28 November 1860.

92 Connell, *Regina v. Palmerston*, p. 305, Palmerston to the Queen, 23 July 1861.

93 *The Times*, 29 April 1863.

94 BP (GC/WO/169), Wood to Palmerston, 21 April 1863.

95 Malmesbury, *Memoirs*, p. 593, 18 March; Hansard (third series), CLXXIV, cols. 268–70 (17 March), Palmerston; BP (GC/SO/119), the Duke of Somerset, first lord of the Admiralty, to Palmerston, 26 March; Somerset Papers, Palmerston to Somerset, 8 April; BP (GC/WO/176), Wood to Palmerston, 4 April 1864.

96 Bright Papers (BL Add. MSS 43386), Villiers to Bright [23], 25 November, [25 December] 1859.

97 Ibid., (BL Add. MSS 43388), Milner Gibson to Bright, 30 January 1861.

98 *The Times*, 27 June 1859.

99 Bright Papers (BL Add. MSS 43384), Bright to Cobden, 13 August 1860, 6 February 1861; Vincent, *Disraeli, Derby and the Conservative Party*, p. 167, entry in Stanley's journal for 15 March 1861.

100 Bright Papers (BL Add. MSS 43388), Bright to Milner Gibson, 7 December, Milner Gibson to Bright, 18 December 1861.

101 Ibid., Milner Gibson to Bright, 14 November 1862, 16 September 1863.

102 Ibid., Milner Gibson to Bright, 12 January 1865.

103 *The Times*, 25 January 1865.

104 Bright Papers (BL Add. MSS 43386), Villiers to Bright, 4 January 1860.

105 Rogers, *Speeches by...Bright*, p. 311, Glasgow, 21 December 1858; Hansard (third series), CLIII, col. 791 (24 March 1859).

106 Rogers, *Speeches by...Bright*, pp. 313–14, Glasgow, 21 December 1858; BP (D/21), Palmerston's diary, 25 January 1861; Connell, *Regina v. Palmerston*, pp. 299–300, Palmerston to the Queen, 27 January 1861; Morley, *Cobden*, II, pp. 227–8, Russell to Cobden, 25 June 1859; Vincent, *Disraeli Derby and the Conservative Party*, p. 167, entry in Stanley's journal for 15 March 1861.

107 Bright Papers (BL Add. MSS 43386), Villiers to Bright, 3, 14 December 1861.

108 Ibid., Villiers to Bright, 15, 25 January 1862, 20 November 1863.

109 Morley, *Cobden*, II, p. 365, Cobden to Hargreaves, 1 March 1861.

110 Cobden Papers (BL Add. MSS 43651), Cobden to Bright, 16 June, 30 January, 30 June 1860.

111 Ibid. (BL Add. MSS 43655), Cobden to Hargreaves, 31 January 1861.

112 Ibid. (BL Add. MSS 43651), Cobden to Bright, 25 August 1860.

113 Ibid., Cobden to Bright, 27 December 1861, 30 June 1860.

114 Ibid., Cobden to Bright, 19 October 1861.

115 Ibid. (BL Add. MSS 43652), Cobden to Bright, 7 October 1862, 25 August 1860.

116 Bright Papers (BL Add. MSS 43384), Bright to Cobden, 6 February 1861, 13 April 1860, 31 August, 6 September 1861.

117 Ibid., Bright to Cobden, 6 August, 6 September, 8 October 1862.

118 *The Times*, 9 January 1860.

119 Ibid., 21 January 1860.

120 Ibid.

121 Ibid., 14 April 1860.

122 Ibid.

123 Cobden Papers (BL Add. MSS 43655), Cobden to Hargreaves, 30 April 1860.

124 *The Times*, 31 May 1860.

125 Bright Papers (BL Add. MSS 43384), Bright to Cobden, 17 June, 3 July 1860.

126 Ibid., Bright to Cobden, 17 July 1860.

127 *The Times*, 30 January 1861.

128 Ibid., 7 October 1861.

129 Ibid., 14 March 1862.

130 Cobden Papers (BL Add. MSS 43651), Cobden to Bright, 31 October, 21 November 1861, 7 August 1862.

131 Ibid., Cobden to Bright, 7 January 1864. For Crossley, see ch. 7, p. 181.

6 TORYISM

1 The Conservatives and their leaders during these years have been studied in R. M. Stewart, *The Foundations of the Conservative Party, 1830–1867* (London, 1978); R. Blake, *The Conservative Party from Peel to Churchill* (London, 1970), chs. 3–4, and *Disraeli* (London, 1966); W. D. Jones, *Lord Derby and Victorian Conservatism* (Oxford, 1956), chs. 8–10; P. Ghosh, 'Disraelian Conservatism: a Financial Approach', *English Historical Review* (1984); B. Coleman, *Conservatism and the Conservative Party in Nineteenth-Century Britain* (London, 1988). W. F. Monypenny and G. E. Buckle, *The Life of Benjamin Disraeli, Earl of Beaconsfield*, new edn, 2 vols. (London, 1929) remains indispensable.

2 Malmesbury, *Memoirs*, pp. 399–400, entry in Malmesbury's journal for 29 June 1857.

3 Ibid., p. 511, Malmesbury to Derby, 6 February 1860; *Codino*, literally a pigtail, was a popular Italian term for a reactionary.

4 Canning Papers, Ellenborough to Canning, 21 August 1855.

5 Malmesbury, *Memoirs*, pp. 397–8, Derby to Malmesbury, 6 May 1857.

6 Vincent, *Disraeli, Derby and the Conservative Party*, p. 166, entry in Stanley's journal for 11 February 1861; BP (GC/TE/364), Palmerston to Temple, 24 December 1855. A. L. Lowell, *The Government of England*, 2 vols. (New York, 1908), II, ch. 35, 'The Strength of Party Ties', especially p. 89; and see H. Berrington, 'Partisanship and Dissidence in the Nineteenth-Century House of Commons', *Parliamentary Affairs* (1968), esp. p. 349.

7　Malmesbury, *Memoirs*, p. 541, entry in Malmesbury's journal for 2 June 1861.

8　Ibid., pp. 385–6, Derby to Malmesbury, 15 December 1856.

9　Ibid., p. 396, entries in Malmesbury's journal for 1 and 2 May 1857.

10　Vincent, *Disraeli, Derby and the Conservative Party*, pp. 155–8, 179, entries in Stanley's journal for 21 February 1858, 30 November 1861.

11　Ibid., p. 171, 30 May 1861; Malmesbury, *Memoirs*, pp. 556–7, 3 June 1862.

12　Ashwell and Wilberforce, *Life of Samuel Wilberforce*, III, p. 314, entry in Bishop Wilberforce's diary for 19 January 1856.

13　Stewart, *The Foundations of the Conservative Party, 1830–1867*, pp. 343–4.

14　*The Times*, 12 October 1863.

15　Lewis, *Letters*, p. 332, Lewis to Reeve, 5 March 1858.

16　Hughenden Papers (B/XX/S/654), Stanley to Disraeli, 26 October 1858.

17　Ibid. (B/XX/S/675), Stanley to Derby, 8 February 1859.

18　Malmesbury, *Memoirs*, p. 464, entries in Malmesbury's journal for 8 and 9 February; Hughenden Papers (B/XX/S/675, 676), Stanley to Derby, 8 February, Stanley to Disraeli, 9/10 February 1859.

19　Ibid. (B/XX/S/676), Stanley to Disraeli, 9/10 February 1859.

20　Ibid. (B/XX/S/193), Derby to Disraeli, 30 December 1858; Hansard (third series), CLIII, col. 1245 (31 March 1859).

21　Sotheron Estcourt Papers, Gloucestershire RO (D 1571/F409), diary, 31 March 1859.

22　Hughenden Papers (B/XX.W/44), Walpole to Disraeli, 25 January 1859.

23　Malmesbury Papers (9M73), MS diary, 17 May 1859.

24　Hughenden Papers (B/XX/S/676), Stanley to Disraeli, 9/10 February 1859.

25　Ibid. (B/XX/S/205), Derby to Disraeli, 2 January 1859.

26　Harpton Court Collection (3573), Lewis's diary, 1 March 1859.

27　Lytton Papers (D/EK/028/1), Lytton to Gladstone, 11 December 1858.

28　Hughenden Papers (B/XX/S/701), Stanley to Disraeli, 6 April 1860.

29　Ibid. (B/XX/S/325), Derby to Disraeli, 15 October 1864.

30　Ibid. (B/XX/S/702), Stanley to Disraeli 13 October 1860.

31　*The Times*, 31 October 1859.

32　Vincent, *Disraeli, Derby and the Conservative Party*, pp. 203, 206, entries in Stanley's journal for 10 December 1863, 27 January 1864: 'I do not think these speculations are likely soon to be put into practice' commented Stanley on the latter occasion.

33　Hughenden Papers (B/XX/S/262), Derby to Disraeli, 19 January 1860.

34　Malmesbury, *Memoirs*, p. 532, Derby to Malmesbury, 4 December 1860.

35　*The Times*, 2 July 1863.

36　Ibid.

37　Hughenden Papers (B/XX/S/331), Derby to Disraeli, 30 January 1865.

38　*The Times*, 31 October 1859.

39　Hansard (third series), CL, cols. 161, Ebury, 173–6, Derby (6 May 1858).

40　Harpton Court Collection (3573), Lewis's diary, 21 February 1859.

41　Spencer Walpole Papers, memorandum on church rates by Lord John Manners, 8 April 1858.

42　Ibid., memorandum on church rates by Lord Stanley, 8 March 1858.

43　Hughenden Papers (B/XX/S/277), Derby to Disraeli, 12 December 1860; Malmesbury, *Memoirs*, pp. 533–5, Derby to Malmesbury, 26 December 1860.

44 Sotheron Estcourt Papers (D1571/F367), Wilson Patten to Sotheron Estcourt, 7 February 1863.

45 Spencer Walpole Papers, memorandum on church rates by Lord Stanley, 8 April 1858.

46 Hansard (third series), CXLV, cols. 323–4 (15 May 1857).

47 Carnarvon Papers (BL Add. MSS 60892), Carnarvon's résumé of the session, 12 August 1858; M. C. N. Salbstein, *The Emancipation of the Jews in Britain: the Question of the Admission of the Jews to Parliament, 1828–1860* (London and Toronto, 1982), ch. 12.

48 Ibid. (BL Add. MSS 60765), Derby to Carnarvon, 9 June 1858, a circular to Conservative peers

49 Ibid. (BL Add. MSS 60892), Carnarvon's résumé of the session, 12 August 1858; Hansard (third series), CLI, col. 1252 (12 July 1858).

50 Wilberforce Papers (c. 12), Warren to Wilberforce, 12 August 1858.

51 Hansard (third series), CLI, col. 1886 (21 July 1858).

52 GP (BL Add. MSS 44211), Herbert to Gladstone, 17 May 1859.

53 *The Times*, 13 September 1858.

54 Carnarvon Papers (BL Add. MSS 60892), Carnarvon's résumé of the session, 12 August 1858.

55 Mayo Papers, National Library of Ireland (11031), the thirteenth Earl of Eglinton and Winton, Viceroy of Ireland, to Lord Naas, chief secretary, 4 February 1859; Hughenden Papers (B/XX/S/671), Stanley to Disraeli, 10 January 1859.

56 Mayo Papers (11031), Eglinton and Winton to Naas, 8 March 1859.

57 K. T. Hoppen, 'Tories, Catholics and the General Election of 1859', *Historical Journal* (1970), pp. 50–3; Hughenden Papers (B/XX/S/692), Stanley to Disraeli, 5 September 1859.

58 Malmesbury Papers (9M 73/1/5), Malmesbury to Cowley, 7 December 1858; Malmesbury, *Memoirs*, p. 453, Malmesbury to Cowley, 7 January 1859.

59 Hoppen, 'Tories, Catholics, and the General Election of 1859', pp. 54–6; Mayo Papers (11031), Eglinton and Winton to Naas, 10 July 1858.

60 *The Times*, 21 May 1859, Wiseman to T. F. Strange, 13, 23 April 1859; E. D. Steele, 'Cardinal Cullen and Irish Nationality', *Irish Historical Studies* (1975), pp. 253–5.

61 Hughenden Papers (B/XX/S/692), Stanley to Disraeli, 5 September 1859.

62 Ibid. (B/XX/S/322), Derby to Disraeli, 10 March 1865.

63 Malmesbury, *Memoirs*, pp. 593–4, entries in Malmesbury's journal for 13, 15 April 1864.

64 Hansard (third series), CLXXX, cols. 5789–90 (26 June 1865); Hughenden Papers (B/XX/S/335), Derby to Disraeli, 4 August 1865.

65 Ibid.; Matthew, *Gladstone Diaries*, V, pp. 384–5, 16, 19 September 1865.

66 L. Wolf, *Life of the Marquess of Ripon, K. G.*, 2 vols. (London, 1921), I, pp. 128–9, Goderich to Thomas Hughes, 4 February 1857.

67 Wodehouse Papers (BL Add. MSS 46692), Clarendon to Wodehouse, 19 March 1857; Malmesbury, *Memoirs*, p. 404, entry in Malmesbury's journal for 31 August 1857.

68 Hansard (third series), CXLV, col. 28 (7 May 1857).

69 Ibid., CXLVII, col. 1434 (11 August 1857).

70 Malmesbury Papers (9M73), MS diary, 28 February 1, 3, 6 March 1858; ibid. (9M73/1/5), Malmesbury to Cowley, 6 March 1858.

71 Ibid., Malmesbury to Cowley, 2 March 1858; partly printed in Malmesbury, *Memoirs*, p. 420, 2 March 1858.

72 Malmesbury Papers (9M73/1/5), Malmesbury to Cowley, 22 January 1859; for the *Charles et Georges* affair, see ch. 13, pp. 363–4.

73 Ibid., Malmesbury to Derby, 27 October 1858; and (9M73), Malmesbury's MS diary, 13 March 1858.

74 Malmesbury Papers (9M73/1/5), Malmesbury to Lord Augustus Loftus, minister at Vienna, 10 November 1858.

75 Malmesbury, *Memoirs*, p. 446.

76 Hansard (third series), CXLIX, col. 1939 (29 April 1858).

77 Malmesbury, *Memoirs* , pp. 433, 438, entries in Malmesbury's journal for 29 April, 11, 12 June 1858; Hansard (third series), CL, col. 282 (7 May 1858), Lord John Russell.

78 Malmesbury Papers (9M73/1/5), Malmesbury to Cowley, 7 December 1858; Clarendon Papers (MS Clar. Dep. c 524), Palmerston to Clarendon, 20 January 1859; Harpton Court Collection (3573), Lewis's diary, 28 January 1859; BP (GC/CL/1184), Clarendon to Palmerston, 22 January 1859.

79 Hansard (third series), CLIII, cols. 1831–3 (8 April 1859).

80 Malmesbury, *Memoirs*, p. 459, entry in Malmesbury's journal for 12 January 1859; ibid., Malmesbury to Cowley, 15 January 1859.

81 Malmesbury Papers (9M73/1/5), Malmesbury to Cowley, 7 December 1858; Hughenden Papers (B/XX/S/208), Derby to Disraeli, 8 January 1859.

82 Malmesbury Papers (9M73/1/5), Malmesbury to Cowley, 13 January 1859.

83 *The Times*, 2, 3 May 1859.

84 Malmesbury Papers (9M73/1/6), Malmesbury to the Queen, 3 May 1859.

85 Malmesbury, *Memoirs*, pp. 491–2; the *Press*, mentioned here, was a weekly and Disraeli's organ.

86 Hansard (third series), CLXI, col. 24 (5 February 1861), from *Macbeth*, Act 3, scene 1:

Ay, in the catalogue ye go for men;
As hounds, and greyhounds, mongrels, spaniels, curs,
Shoughs, water-rugs, and demi-wolves are clept
All by the name of dogs;

Layard Papers (BL Add. MSS 38987), Derby to Layard, 20 February 1861.

87 Hansard (third series), CLXI, cols. 795–7 (19 April 1861).

88 Ibid., CLXX, col. 1486 (8 May 1863); CLXI, col. 1195 (1 March 1861).

89 Ibid., CLXXII, col. 1352 (24 July 1863).

90 Rogers, *Speeches by...Bright*, p. 328, the wording in Hansard differs slightly, CLIII, col. 712 (24 March 1859).

91 Hansard (third series), CLXIX, cols. 942–3 (27 February 1863), Disraeli; CLXXII, col. 1353 (24 July 1863), Malmesbury.

92 Malmesbury, *Memoirs*, pp. 592–3, entries in Malmesbury's journal for 9 and 12 March 1864.

93 Count Vitzthum von Eckstädt, *St Petersburg and London in the years 1852–1864*, trans. H. Reeve, 2 vols. (London, 1887), II, p. 267, Vitzthum to Beust,

3 January 1864; Malmesbury, *Memoirs*, p. 592–3, entry in Malmesbury's journal for 12 March 1864.

94 Ibid., pp. 598–9, entry in Malmesbury's journal for 3 July 1864.

95 *Guardian*, 13 July 1864; Vincent, *Disraeli, Derby and the Conservative Party*, pp. 221–2, entry in Stanley's journal for 17 July 1864; Hansard (third series), CLXXIV, col. 777 (11 April 1864).

96 Vincent, *Disraeli, Derby and the Conservative Party*, pp. 221–2, entry in Stanley's journal for 17 July 1864.

97 Lytton Papers (D/EK/C5), Disraeli to Lytton, 19 September 1864.

98 Malmesbury, *Memoirs*, pp. 539–40, entry in Malmesbury's journal for 16 April 1861.

99 Ibid.

100 Hughenden Papers (B/XX/S/261), Derby to Disraeli, 15 January 1860.

101 Vitzthum von Eckstädt, *St Petersburg and London*, II, p. 25, Vitzthum to Beust, 28 January 1860.

102 Hughenden Papers (B/XX/S/311, 315), Derby to Disraeli, 29 January, 5 November 1863.

103 Malmesbury, *Memoirs*, p. 566, Derby to Malmesbury, 31 October 1862.

104 BP (GC/CL/1207), Clarendon to Palmerston, 16 October 1862, reporting his conversation with Derby at Knowsley.

105 Malmesbury, *Memoirs*, pp. 556, 562, entry in Malmesbury's journal for 23 May 1862, and the account of his French visit in October that year.

106 Vincent, *Disraeli, Derby and the Conservative Party*, p. 199, entries in Stanley's journal for 2 and 9 July 1863.

107 Rogers, *Speeches by…Bright*, p. 91, Rochdale, 4 December 1861.

108 Hughenden Papers (B/XX/S/708), Stanley to Disraeli, 15 July 1862.

109 Harpton Court Collection (3572), Lewis's diary, 12, 13 May 1858; Hansard (third series), CL, cols. 590, 594 (14 May 1858).

110 Ibid., cols. 601–2, 607–8.

111 Ibid., cols. 645–7, 661, Derby, 605–6, Ellenborough.

112 BP (GC/WO/113), Wood to Palmerston, 6 September 1857.

113 Hughenden Papers (B/XX/S/150), Derby to Disraeli, 15 November 1857.

114 Hansard (third series), CXLVII, cols. 440–81 (27 July 1857); quotation from col. 442.

115 Tilney Bassett, *Gladstone to his Wife*, p. 116, Gladstone to Catherine Gladstone, 28 July 1857.

116 Hughenden Papers (B/XX/Hs/59), Malmesbury to Disraeli, 15 October 1857.

117 Benson and Esher, *Letters of Queen Victoria*, III, p. 286, the Queen to Derby, 14 May 1858.

118 Hansard (third series), CL, col. 624 (14 May 1858).

119 Dasent, *John Thadeus Delane*, I, pp. 298–9, Stanley to Delane, 17 August, 14 October 1858.

120 Benson and Esher, *Letters of Queen Victoria*, III, p. 298, the Queen to Derby, 15 April 1858; Malmesbury Papers (9M73/1/5), Malmesbury to Stanley, 15 August 1858.

121 *The Times*, 1 December 1858.

122 Rogers, *Speeches by…Bright*, p. 472, Birmingham, 29 October 1858;

Vincent, *Disraeli, Derby and the Conservative Party*, p. 373, nn. 50–1; Hughenden Papers (B/XX.S/651), Stanley to Disraeli, 4 October 1858.

123 Lytton Papers (D/EK/028/1), Bulwer Lytton to Stanley, 19 October 1858.

124 W. C. Costin, *Great Britain and China*, new edn (Oxford, 1968), p. 288.

125 Hansard (third series), CLVII, cols. 1597–1601 (30 March 1860).

126 Ibid., cols. 1601–6; quotations from cols. 1604–5.

127 Ibid., col. 1599.

128 Ibid., CLXXI, col. 1132 (19 June 1863).

129 Ibid., CXLIX, cols. 1151–8 (6 March 1863); *Quarterly Review*, April 1864, 'Foreign Policy of England', pp. 485–92.

130 Hansard (third series), CLXXI, col. 1120 (19 June 1863).

131 Ibid., CLII, col. 70 (3 February 1859).

132 *Leeds Intelligencer*, 11 July 1865.

133 Hughenden Papers (B/XX/P/33), Pakington to Disraeli, 8 October 1857.

134 Ibid. (B/XX/P/44), Disraeli to Pakington, 21 December 1858.

135 Ibid. (B/XX/P/45), Pakington to Disraeli, 21 December 1858.

136 Harpton Court Collection (3572), Lewis's diary, 26 March 1858.

137 Hansard (third series), CXLIX, col. 844 (26 March 1858).

138 Ibid., cols. 1069–70 (26 April 1858).

139 Lytton Papers (D/EK/024/318), Disraeli to Lytton, 7 April 1858.

140 Hughenden Papers (B/XX/M/101A), memorandum on Tory prospects by Lord John Manners, 10 March 1857.

141 Hughenden Papers (B/XX/S/640), Stanley to Disraeli, 12 April 1858.

142 Malmesbury, *Memoirs*, pp. 456, 465, entries in Malmesbury's journal for 3 December 1858, 9 February 1859; Lytton Papers (D/EK/028/1), Bulwer Lytton to Gladstone, 11 December 1858.

143 Sotheron Estcourt Papers, diary, 1, 15 March 1858; Malmesbury's MS diary, 17 March 1858.

144 BP (GC/CL/1195), Clarendon to Palmerston, 5 June 1859.

145 Malmesbury, *Memoirs*, p. 512, Malmesbury to Derby, 6 February 1860.

146 Ibid., p. 511, entry in Malmesbury's journal for 24 January 1860.

147 Connell, *Regina v. Palmerston*, pp. 298–9, Prince Albert to Palmerston, 24 January 1861.

148 Hughenden Papers (B/XX/P/64), Pakington to Disraeli, 8 June 1861.

149 Vincent, *Disraeli, Derby and the Conservative Party*, p. 172, entry in Stanley's journal for 3 June 1861; Hughenden Papers (B/XX/P/64), Pakington to Disraeli, 8 June 1861.

150 Vincent, *Disraeli, Derby and the Conservative Party*, pp. 155–8, entry in Stanley's journal for 21 February 1858; Malmesbury, *Memoirs*, pp. 385–6, Derby to Malmesbury, 15 December 1856.

151 Malmesbury, *Memoirs*, p. 556, entry in Malmesbury's journal for 2 June 1862.

152 Hughenden Papers (B/XX/S/300), Derby to Disraeli, 7 June 1862, a reminder of how he had viewed the Tory move; Vincent, *Disraeli, Derby and the Conservative Party*, p. 185, entry in Stanley's journal for 24 May 1862.

153 Iddesleigh Papers (BL Add. MSS 50015), Northcote to Disraeli, 19 April 1862.

154 Ibid.

155 Ibid., Northcote to Disraeli, 19, 25 April 1862.

156 Vincent, *Disraeli, Derby and the Conservative Party*, p. 186, entry in Stanley's

journal for 3 June; Malmesbury, *Memoirs*, pp. 556–7, entry in Malmesbury's journal for 3 June 1862.

157 A. E. Gathorne Hardy, *Gathorne Hardy, First Earl of Cranbrook, A Memoir*, 2 vols. (London, 1910), I, pp. 156–7, entry in Hardy's diary for 5 June 1862.

158 J. E. Denison, First Viscount Ossington, *Notes from my Journal when Speaker of the House of Commons*, ed. L. E. Denison (London, 1900), pp. 117–23, entry in Denison's diary for 3 June 1862.

159 Matthew, *Gladstone Diaries*, VI, p. 126, 3 June 1862.

160 Vincent, *Disraeli, Derby and the Conservative Party*, pp. 186–7, entry in Stanley's journal for 3 June 1862.

161 BP (D/22), Palmerston's diary, 3 June 1862.

162 Hughenden Papers (B/XX/S/308), Derby to Disraeli, 7 June 1862.

163 Harpton Court Collection (3575), Lewis's diary, 3 June 1862.

164 Hughenden Papers (B/XX/S/311), Derby to Disraeli, 29 January 1863.

165 Vincent, *Disraeli, Derby and the Conservative Party*, p. 227, entry in Stanley's journal for 11 February 1865.

166 *The Times*, 29 June 1863.

167 Ibid., 2 July 1863.

168 Ibid., 1 October 1863.

169 Ibid., 16 October 1861.

170 Ibid., 2 July 1863, 2 May 1861.

171 Hughenden Papers (B/XX/S/336), Derby to Disraeli, 12 August 1865.

172 Vincent, *Disraeli, Derby and the Conservative Party*, p. 221, entry in Stanley's journal for 15 July 1864.

173 *The Times*, 20 July 1865.

174 Ibid.

175 Iddesleigh Papers (BL Add. MSS 50015), Northcote to Disraeli, 3, 16, 17 February, 6 July 1864.

7 RELIGION AND POLITICS

1 *Nonconformist*, 20 July 1865; based on returns in the closing stages of the election.

2 The diary of R. J. Phillimore, transcript of extracts in the Phillimore Papers, Christ Church, Oxford (Box 2), 9 March 1860.

3 Palmerston Letter Books (BL Add. MSS 48579), Palmerston to Lord Carlisle, viceroy of Ireland, 25 April 1855.

4 G. I. T. Machin, *Politics and the Churches in Great Britain 1832 to 1868* (Oxford, 1977); W. O. Chadwick, *The Victorian Church*, parts 1 and 2 (London, 1966–70); G. Finlayson, *The Seventh Earl of Shaftesbury* (London, 1981) and A. D. Gilbert, *Religion and Society in Industrial England. Church, Chapel and Social Change, 1740–1914* (London, 1976) are standard for this subject and period. W. H. Mackintosh, *Disestablishment and Liberation: The Movement for the Separation of the Anglican Church from State Control* (London, 1972) is a valuable guide to the details of enacted and attempted legislation.

5 BP (SHA/PD/7), Shaftesbury Papers, diary 31 May 1856.

6 Ibid. (GC/ST/23/2), A. P. Stanley to Lord Stanley of Alderley, president of the Board of Trade, 24 September 1856.

7 R. T. Davidson and W. Benham, *Life of Archibald Campbell Tait, Archbishop of Canterbury*, 2 vols. (London, 1891), I, pp. 495–7, Tait's memorandum of 12 September 1863.

8 BP (SHA/PD/7) Shaftesbury Papers, diary, 18 June 1855.

9 *Guardian*, 30 March 1864 on the circulation of religious and secular weeklies published in the capital.

10 Phillimore Papers, diary, 9 March 1860.

11 BP (GC/WO/94 and 106), Wood to Lord Palmerston, 19 November 1856, 13 March 1857.

12 Benson and Esher, *Letters of Queen Victoria*, III, p. 217, the Queen to Palmerston, 24 November 1856.

13 Palmerston Letter Books (BL Add. MSS 48580), Palmerston to Wood, 20 November 1856.

14 Wilberforce Papers, (d. 38), Hook to Wilberforce, 15 September 1858.

15 *Record*, 14 January 1859.

16 Phillimore Papers, diary, 9 March 1860.

17 Palmerston Letter Books (BL Add. MSS 48580), Palmerston to Wood, 20 November 1856.

18 Glynne-Gladstone Papers (Box 28/5), Gladstone to his wife, 23 July 1856.

19 BP (SHA/PD/7), Shaftesbury Papers, diary, 4 August 1856.

20 Hansard (third series), CXLIV, cols. 2332–3 (16 March 1857).

21 Ibid., col. 2337.

22 E. Hodder, *The Life and Work of the Seventh Earl of Shaftesbury, K. G.*, 3 vols. (London, 1886), III, pp. 30–2, quoting Shaftesbury's diary for 17 May 1856.

23 *Record*, 26 May 1856.

24 Connell, *Regina v. Palmerston*, p. 202, Palmerston to the Queen, 10 May 1856.

25 B. Harrison, 'The Sunday Trading Riots of 1855', *Historical Journal* (1965), pp. 219–45'; BP (SHA/PD/7), Shaftesbury Papers, diary, 27 June 1855.

26 R. J. Moore, *Sir Charles Wood's Indian Policy, 1853–1866* (Manchester, 1966), p. 119.

27 *Guardian*, 9 March 1859.

28 *Record*, 16 April 1858.

29 Ibid., 11 May 1860.

30 Ibid., 2 March 1864.

31 Ibid., 9 March 1856.

32 Ibid., 4 May 1860.

33 Ibid., 9 May 1862.

34 Ibid., 12 May 1862.

35 Rogers, *Speeches by…Bright*, p. 284, Birmingham, 27 October 1858; BP (GC/SH/35) Shaftesbury to Palmerston, 30 June 1859.

36 Walling, *Diaries of John Bright*, pp. 240–2, 12 to 14 June 1859.

37 *Record*, 9 May 1856.

38 *The Times*, 21 November 1857; *Nonconformist*, 9 June 1859.

39 Cobden Papers (BL Add. MSS 43664), Baines to Cobden, 19 January 1856.

40 Ibid. (BL Add. MSS 43650), Cobden to Bright, 11 August 1856.

41 *Leeds Mercury*, 27 February 1858.

42 Ibid., 2 March 1858.

43 Ibid., 20 October 1860.

44 Hansard (third series), CLIX, col. 1714 (11 July 1860).

45 BP (CAB/132), Palmerston's minute of 5 July 1860.

46 Hansard (third series), CLIX, col. 1715 (11 July 1860).

47 RP (PRO 30/22/13F), Russell to Dean Elliot, 4 October 1858.

48 GP (BL Add. MSS 44636), Gladstone's minute of 9 July 1860.

49 Bright Papers (BL Add. MSS 43384), Bright to Cobden, 17 June 1860.

50 Hansard (third series), CLIX, col. 1702 (11 July 1860).

51 Baines Papers, Leeds City Archives (bundle 45/15), Baines to Alexander Ritchie, 12 May 1865; *Leeds Mercury*, 1 July 1865.

52 Walling, *Diaries of John Bright*, p. 283, 15 February 1865.

53 *Guardian*, 24 September 1862.

54 Hansard (third series), CLXIV, cols. 732–4 (11 July 1861); Lowe cited with 'much pleasure' the advocacy of his compromise by Connop Thirlwall, Bishop of St David's and one of the broadest of Broad Churchmen.

55 Hansard (third series), CXL, col. 2011 (6 March 1856).

56 *The Times*, 13 May 1862.

57 *Guardian*, 19 September 1860.

58 *Record*, 7 July 1862.

59 BP (GC/SH/48), Shaftesbury to Palmerston, 30 July 1862.

60 *Record*, 9 January 1863; Hansard (third series), CLXX, cols. 140–1 (15 April 1863).

61 BP (GC/SH/35), Shaftesbury to Palmerston, 20 June 1859.

62 BP (GC/WO/169), Wood to Palmerston, 21 April 1863.

63 Hansard (third series), CLXX, col. 928 (29 April 1863).

64 *The Times*, 19 October 1861.

65 *Nonconformist*, 23 November 1864.

66 E. D. Steele, 'The Leeds Patriciate and the Cultivation of Learning, 1819–1905: A Study of the Leeds Philosophical and Literary Society', *Proceedings of the Leeds Philosophical and Literary Society* (1978), pp. 183–9.

67 *The Times*, 5 October 1858.

68 Ibid., 30 September 1857.

69 Ibid., 25 January 1865.

70 *Leeds Mercury*, 13 December 1860.

71 S. Gilley, 'The Garibaldi Riots of 1862' *Historical Journal* (1975), pp. 692–732; L. Thouvenel (ed.), *Le Secret de l'Empereur: correspondance confidentielle et inédite échangée entre M. Thouvenel, le Duc de Gramont et le Général Comte de Flahaut 1860–63*, 2 vols. (Paris 1889), I, pp. 431–3, Palmerston to Flahaut, 26 September 1862 with postscript dated 6 October; English version in BP (PM/J/I), private letter book.

72 Thouvenel, *Le Secret de l'Empereur*, 1, pp. 434–5, Flahaut to Palmerston, 9 October 1862.

73 RP (PRO 30/22/15D), Palmerston to Russell, 19, 20 February 1865; (PRO 30/22/23) to Russell, 7 May 1865, objecting to Manning as the new archbishop.

74 BP (GC/RU/899 and 900), Russell to Palmerston, – May and 15 May 1865.

75 E. D. Steele, 'The Irish Presence in the North of England, 1850–1914', *Northern History* (1976), pp. 229–30. PP 1861, IX, Select Committee on Poor

Relief (England), answer 8887; evidence of Fr John Morris, citing a statement submitted on behalf of the Catholic clergy of Bradford.

76 P. MacSuibhne, *Paul Cullen and his Contemporaries with their Letters from 1820–1920*, 5 vols. (Naas, Co Kildare, 1961–77), II, pp. 197–200, Cullen to Mgr Barnabo of the Congregation De Propaganda Fide, 28 July 1855, III, pp. 246–7 to Cardinal Barnabo, 19 November 1856.

77 Ibid., II, p. 155, Cullen to Barnabo, 21 February 1854.

78 J. H. Newman, *Apologia Pro Vita Sua*, Everyman's Library edn (London, 1949), p. 239.

79 Malmesbury, *Memoirs*, p. 537, Disraeli to Malmesbury, 22 February 1861.

80 Hughenden Papers (B/XX/S/332), Derby to Disraeli, 10 March 1865.

81 Phillimore Papers (Box 1), Northcote to Phillimore, 10 April 1863.

82 *The Times*, 31 March 1864.

83 Hughenden Papers (B/XX/W/361), Wilberforce to Disraeli, 15 December 1862.

84 Wilberforce Papers (c. 13), Disraeli to Wilberforce, 30 November 1862.

85 Vincent, *Disraeli, Derby and the Conservative Party*, pp. 203–4, entry in Stanley's journal for 18 December 1863.

86 Carnarvon Papers (BL Add. MSS 60758), Cecil to the fourth Earl of Carnarvon, 18 November 1861.

87 *Record*, 4 May 1860.

88 *The Times*, 31 October 1862.

89 Vincent, *Disraeli, Derby and the Conservative Party*, p. 208, entry in Stanley's journal for 19 February 1864.

90 Newcastle Papers (NeC10890), Newcastle to Palmerston, 22 August 1861.

91 BP (GC/HE/69), Herbert to Palmerston, 19 June 1860.

92 Vincent, *Disraeli, Derby and the Conservative Party*, p. 174, entry in Stanley's journal for 14 July 1861; Guedalla, *The Palmerston Papers*, p. 137, Palmerston to Herbert, 20 June 1860.

93 Palmerston Letter Books (BL Add. MSS 48582), Palmerston to the Hon. George Denman, MP, 8 April 1861.

94 Ibid. (BL Add. MSS 48583), Palmerston to Sir Augustus Clifford, 11 October 1865.

95 BP (SHA/PC/68), Palmerston to Shaftesbury, 29 April 1864.

96 Palmerston Letter Books (BL Add. MSS 48583), Palmerston to Sir George Grey Bt, Home Secretary, 24 May 1865.

97 GP (BL Add. MSS 44534), Gladstone to Pusey, 15 March 1864; Wilberforce Papers (d. 37), Gladstone to Wilberforce, 21 March 1863.

98 Ibid. (BL Add. MSS 44532), Gladstone to Mayow, 10 June 1862.

99 Ibid. (BL Add. MSS 44535), Gladstone to Hall, 18 June 1865.

100 Ibid. (BL Add. MSS 544534), Gladstone to the Rev. R. W. Barnes, 13 January 1865.

101 BP (SHA/PC/70), Shaftesbury Papers, Palmerston to Shaftesbury, 21 June 1865.

102 Guedalla, *The Palmerston Papers*, p. 338, Gladstone to Palmerston, 17 June 1865.

103 Ibid., Palmerston to Gladstone, 23 June 1865; BP (GC/SH/70), Shaftesbury to Palmerston, 21 June 1865.

104 Guedalla, *The Palmerston Papers*, pp. 326–7, Palmerston to Gladstone, 27 March
     1865; Hansard (third series), CLXXVIII, cols. 420–34 (28 March 1865).
105 GP (44535), Gladstone to Mr Justice O'Hagan, 2 May 1865.

8 THE FACTOR OF CONFIDENCE

 1 Matthew, *Gladstone Diaries*, V, pp. 104–6, Gladstone's 'memorandum of
    finance', 16 February 1856; with notes by Graham added in December of that
    year, p. 105, n. 4.
 2 Mill, *Considerations on Representative Government*, p. 209.
 3 *Banker's Magazine*, July 1862, pp. 409–10.
 4 The economy at this time is well covered in J. H. Clapham, *Economic History of
    Modern Britain*, vol. II (Cambridge, 1932); J. R. T. Hughes *Fluctuations in Trade,
    Industry, and Finance: a Study of British Economic Development, 1850–1860* (Oxford,
    1960); S. G. Checkland, *The Rise of Industrial Society in England, 1815–1885*,
    paperback edn (London, 1971), and A. H. Imlah, *Economic Elements in the Pax
    Britannica: Studies in British Foreign Trade in the Nineteenth Century* (Cambridge,
    Mass, 1958). Unless otherwise stated, statistics in this chapter are taken from
    Mitchell and Deane, *Abstract of British Historical Statistics*; selected tables are
    printed in Appendix 3, above.
 5 N. St John Stevas (ed.), *The Collected Works of Walter Bagehot*, 14 vols. (London,
    1968–86), IX, p. 433 (*The Economist*, 24 September 1864).
 6 Harpton Court Collection (3572), Lewis's diary, 12 November 1857.
 7 Barrington, *The Servant of All*, II, pp. 111–12, Wilson to Lewis, 25 December
    1857.
 8 Lewis, *Letters*, p. 328, Lewis to Head, 5 February 1858.
 9 D. P. O'Brien (ed.), *The Correspondence of Lord Overstone*, 3 vols. (Cambridge,
    1971), II, pp. 813–16, Lewis to Overstone, 20 November 1857.
10 Ibid.; Sir J. Clapham, *The Bank of England: a History*, 2 vols. (Cambridge,
    1944), II, ch. 5 describes the crisis from the Bank's angle.
11 BP (GC/LE/105), unsigned memorandum in Lewis's hand, 12 November
    1857.
12 O'Brien, *The Correspondence of Lord Overstone*, II, pp. 813–16, 819–20, Lewis to
    Overstone, 20, 22 November 1857.
13 *The Times*, 1 January 1858.
14 Dasent, *John Thadeus Delane*, I, p. 271.
15 *The Times*, 1 January 1858.
16 Ibid., 2 September 1858.
17 Fitzmaurice, *The Life of Granville*, I, p. 267, Granville to Canning,
    24 November 1857.
18 Barrington, *The Servant of All*, II, pp. 111–12, Wilson to Lewis, 25 December
    1857.
19 Harpton Court Collection (3572), Lewis's diary, 12 October 1857.
20 *The Times*, 15 March 1861.
21 *The Economist*, 23 February 1861.
22 *The Times*, 14 October 1864.
23 Matthew, *Gladstone Diaries*, V, pp. xxxiii–iv; S. A. Wallace and F. E. Gillespie,

The Journal of Benjamin Moran, 2 vols. (Chicago, 1948–49), I, pp. 179–80, 18 November 1857.

24 Figures from A. H. Imlah, *Economic Elements in the Pax Britannica*, esp. pp. 155–8; L. Davis and R. A. Huttenback, 'The Export of British Finance, 1865–1914', *Journal of Imperial and Commonwealth History* (1985), pp. 50–9. For criticism of the statistics here and in the authors' *Mammon and the Pursuit of Empire: the Political Economy of British Imperialism, 1860–1912* (Cambridge, 1986), see D. C. M. Platt, *English Historical Review* (1988), pp. 695–9 and A. G. Hopkins, *Journal of Imperial and Commonwealth History* (1988), pp. 234–7.

25 O'Brien, *The Correspondence of Lord Overstone*, II, pp. 853–4, Cardwell to Overstone, 21 April 1858.

26 E. V. Morgan and W. A. Thomas, *The Stock Exchange: its History and Functions* (London, 1962), pp. 280–1; *The Times*, 22 February 1858.

27 Ibid., 2 January 1860.

28 Ibid., 4 August 1864.

29 Ibid., 11 August 1862.

30 Ibid., 10 November 1860.

31 Hansard (third series), CLV, cols. 211–12 (21 July 1859).

32 Lewis, *Letters*, p. 298, Lewis to Head, 17 August 1855.

33 *The Times*, 28 March 1857.

34 Ibid., 10 August 1864.

35 Guedalla, *The Palmerston Papers*, pp. 305, 312–13, Gladstone to Palmerston, 22 October, Palmerston to Gladstone, 7 November 1864.

36 GP (BL Add. MSS 44591), Gladstone's memorandum of 20 April 1860.

37 GP (BL Add. MSS 44530), Gladstone to Robertson Gladstone, 18 August 1859.

38 Ibid. (BL Add. MSS 44531), Gladstone to Sir James Lacaita, 1 December 1860.

39 *The Times*, 11 November 1864.

40 Guedalla, *The Palmerston Papers*, p. 160, Palmerston to Gladstone, 25 February 1861.

41 *The Times*, 25 April 1862.

42 GP (BL Add. MSS 44591), Gladstone's memorandum of 20 April 1860.

43 Ibid. (BL Add. MSS 44304), Somerset's memorandum with his letter to Gladstone of 17 May 1860.

44 BP (GC/SO/6), Somerset to Palmerston, 28 September 1859; Somerset Papers, Palmerston to Somerset, 30 September 1859.

45 Ibid., Gladstone to Somerset, 13 December 1864.

46 Hansard (third series), CLXIX, col. 1075 (5 March 1863).

47 H. Cawley (ed.), *The American Diaries of Richard Cobden* (Princeton, 1952), pp. 187–8, 10 May 1859.

48 Morley, *Cobden*, II, p. 251, entry in Cobden's journal for 2 November 1859.

49 Cobden Papers (BL Add. MSS 43651), Cobden to Bright, 23 January 1860.

50 Ibid., Cobden to Bright, 10 February 1860.

51 Hansard (third series), CLXIX, cols. 690–99 (23 February 1863).

52 Ibid., CLXVIII, col. 69 (8 July 1862).

53 Ibid., CLV, col. 203 (21 July 1859).

54 J. Brooke and M. Sorensen, *The Prime Ministers' Papers: W. E. Gladstone*, I: *Autobiographica* (London, 1971), p. 75, 'Protectionism, 1840–1860'.

55 Hansard (third series), CLXV, cols. 289–90 (14 February 1862).

56 PP 1864, VII, Report and Evidence from the Select Committee on Trade with Foreign Nations, p. 348, A. 936, evidence of Henry Ashworth, president of the Manchester Chamber of Commerce.

57 Ibid., p. 504, A. 3068.

58 GP (BL Add. MSS 44531), Gladstone to Lacaita, 1 December 1860.

59 Morley, *Cobden*, II, pp. 260–1, Cobden to Bright, 29 December 1859.

60 St John Stevas (ed.), *The Collected Works of Walter Bagehot*, IX, p. 473, (*Economist*, 19 November 1864).

61 *The Times*, 25 January 1865.

62 Guedalla, *The Palmerston Papers*, p. 111, Gladstone to Palmerston, 12 September 1859.

63 Malmesbury, *Memoirs*, p. 533, entry in Malmesbury's journal for 10 December 1860: 'The English and French in China hate each other'.

64 *The Times*, 27 July, 18 August 1857.

65 Barrington, *The Servant of All*, II, p. 56, Lewis to Wilson, 11 September 1857; BP (GC/LE/102, 104), Lewis to Palmerston, 28 October, 8 November 1857.

66 Douglas and Ramsay, *The Panmure Papers*, II, p. 392, Panmure to Clarendon [June 1857].

67 *Leeds Mercury*, 9 February 1861.

68 *The Times*, 24 September 1864.

69 St John Stevas (ed.), *The Collected Works of Walter Bagehot*, IX, p. 423 (*The Economist*, 3 September 1864).

70 A. Howe, *The Cotton Masters, 1830–1860* (Oxford, 1984), p. 24.

71 Hansard (third series), CLIII, col. 790 (24 March 1859).

72 Rogers, *Speeches by…Bright*, p. 453, Birmingham, 26 January 1864.

73 Ibid., p. 311, Glasgow, 21 December 1858.

74 Morley, *Cobden*, II, p. 486, Cobden to T. B. Potter, 22 March 1865.

75 Clarendon Papers (MS Clar. Dep. box 82), Clarendon to Bedford, 17 July 1858.

76 Checkland, *Rise of Industrial Society*, ch. 7; E. J. Hobsbawm, 'The Labour Aristocracy in Nineteenth Century Britain' in his *Labouring Men: Studies in the History of Labour* (London, 1964), pp. 272–315; A. Briggs *Victorian People* (London, 1954), chs. 5 and 7; Harrison, *Before the Socialists*, ch. 1; N. Kirk, *The Growth of Working Class Reformism in Mid-Victorian England* (London, 1985), ch. 1; M. C. Curthoys, 'Trade Union Legislation 1871–6: Government Responses to the Development of Organized Labour' (Oxford D Phil thesis, 1988), ch. 1.

77 Morley, *Cobden*, II, p. 486, Cobden to T. B. Potter, 22 March 1865.

78 J. O. Foster, *Class Struggle and the Industrial Revolution: Early Industrial Capitalism in Three English Towns* (London, 1974), pp. 7, 236.

79 *The Times*, 1 April 1863.

80 Ibid.

81 Ibid., 2 April 1863.

82 St John Stevas, *The Collected Works of Walter Bagehot*, III, p. 281 (*The Economist*, 13 August 1864).

83 Guedalla, *The Palmerston Papers*, p. 280, Palmerston to Gladstone, 11 May 1864; H. Collins and C. Abramsky, *Karl Marx and the British Labour Movement: Years of the First International* (London, 1965), ch. 5.

84 Morley, *Cobden*, II, pp. 416–7, Cobden to Hargreaves, 5 April 1863.

85 Ch. 2 above, pp. 33–4, 39; Vincent, *Disraeli, Derby and the Conservative Party*, p. 221, entry in Stanley's journal for 15 July 1864.

86 GP (BL Add. MSS 44534), Gladstone to Hon. Arthur Kinnaird MP, 5 December 1864.

87 Hansard (third series), CLXXIX, cols. 696–700 (22 May 1865).

88 GP (BL Add. MSS 44591), Gladstone's memorandum of 20 April 1860.

89 Lewis, *Letters*, pp. 304–5, Lewis to Henry Reeve, 2 December 1855.

90 Ibid., pp. 373–4, Lewis to Reeve, 4 December 1859; Lewis contributed the last five pages to W. R. Greg's article on 'British Taxation' in the *Edinburgh Review* for January 1860.

91 Matthew, *Gladstone Diaries*, VI, p. 11, 16 and 19 February 1861; J. S. Mill, *Principles of Political Economy with some of their Applications to Social Philosophy*, vols. II and III in *The Collected Works of John Stuart Mill* (Toronto, 1965), III, p. 817.

92 Hansard (third series), CLXVI, col. 1653 (13 May 1862).

93 Guedalla, *The Palmerston Papers*, p. 324, Gladstone to Palmerston, 2 February 1865.

94 PP 1861, VII, Report and Evidence from the Select Committee on Income and Property Tax, p. 252, A. 3597.

95 Hansard (third series), CLXXIV, cols. 587–8 (7 April 1864).

96 Ibid., CXLIX, col. 2128 (3 May 1858).

97 Ibid., CXXXVII, col. 1561 (20 April 1855), Lewis.

98 Guedalla, *The Palmerston Papers*, p. 323, Gladstone to Palmerston, 2 February 1865.

99 Hansard (third series), CLXVII, col. 1488 (12 August 1857).

100 BP (PM/J/1), Palmerston to C. P. Villiers, 23 November 1862.

101 Vincent, *Disraeli, Derby and the Conservative Party*, p. 191, entry in Stanley's journal for 4 September 1862; for the scale of disruption by war in America and previous overproduction, see D. A. Farnie, *The English Cotton Industry and the World Market, 1815–1896* (Oxford, 1979), ch. 4.

102 BP (PM/J/1), Palmerston to Sir George Grey, Bt., 13 November 1862.

103 BP (GC/VI/18), Villiers to Palmerston, 23 November 1862, quoting a letter from Cobden.

104 W. O. Henderson, *The Lancashire Cotton Famine, 1861–65*, second edn (Manchester, 1969), pp. 57–67, 87–8.

105 Ibid., pp. 101–3; BP (GC/VI/21), Villiers to Palmerston [February 1864].

106 Henderson, *The Lancashire Cotton Famine*, pp. 68–81; Vincent, *Disraeli, Derby and the Conservative Party*, p. 189, entry in Stanley's journal for 20 July 1862.

107 BP (GC/LE/217), Palmerston to Lewis, 6 May 1860.

108 Harpton Court Collection (3574), Lewis's diary, 9 May 1860.

109 Palmerston Letter Books (BL Add. MSS 48581), Palmerston to Milner Gibson, 13 July 1860; W. L. Burn, *The Age of Equipoise: a Study of the Mid-Victorian Generation* (London, 1964), ch. 4; O. MacDonagh, *Early Victorian Government, 1830–1870* (London, 1977); R. J. Lambert, *Sir John Simon, 1816–1904 and English Social Administration* (London, 1963).

110 Lewis, *Letters*, p. 351, Lewis to Abraham Hayward, 28 October 1858.
111 *Leeds Mercury*, 27 October 1860.
112 RP (PRO 30/22/27), Palmerston's memorandum of January 1862; D. W. Sylvester, *Robert Lowe and Education* (Cambridge, 1974), pp. 47–8.
113 *The Times*, 7 November 1856.
114 Matthew, *Gladstone Diaries*, V, p. 451, Gladstone's memorandum of 2 January 1860.
115 *The Times*, 25 November 1863.
116 Cobden Papers (BL Add. MSS 43654), Cobden to Henry Ashworth, 27 August 1864.
117 Ibid. (BL Add. MSS 43652), Cobden to Bright, 7 January 1864.
118 Morgan and Thomas, *The Stock Exchange*, pp. 280–1; *The Times*, 2 September 1858, 17 September 1862.
119 O'Brien, *The Correspondence of Lord Overstone*, II, pp. 642–4, Overstone to Granville, 21 March 1856.
120 Hansard (third series), CXXXIX, cols. 1389–90 (26 July 1855).
121 Ibid., CXLIII, cols. 343–4 (4 July 1856).
122 O'Brien, *The Correspondence of Lord Overstone*, II, pp. 642–4, Overstone to Granville, 21 March 1856.
123 Hansard (third series), CXXXIX, cols. 1389–90 (26 July 1855); CXLIII, cols. 343–4 (4 July 1856).
124 Cobden Papers (BL Add. MSS 43654), Cobden to Henry Ashworth, 27 August 1864.

9 THE POLITICAL NATION AND THE PEOPLE

1 Harpton Court Collection (3575), Lewis's diary, 5 February 1863.
2 *The Times*, 2 October, 10 December 1863.
3 *Economist*, 25 March 1865.
4 Morley, *Cobden*, II, pp. 417–18. Cobden to Hargreaves, 5 April 1863.
5 Smith, *The Making of the Second Reform Bill*, ch. 3.
6 *The Times*, 11 December 1863.
7 Harrison, *Before the Socialists*, ch. 2.
8 Kirk, *The Growth of Working Class Reformism in Mid-Victorian England*, chs. 4–6; Briggs, *Victorian People*, ch. 7.
9 *The Times*, 15 October 1864.
10 *Economist*, 22 July 1865; *Churchman*, 27 April 1865.
11 Trelawny diary (MS Eng. hist. d 413–4), 7 August 1862, 15 May 1863.
12 Ashwell and Wilberforce, *Life of the Rt. Rev. Samuel Wilberforce*, III, p. 91, Wilberforce to the Hon. Arthur Gordon, June 1863.
13 Trelawny diary (MS Eng. hist. d 414), 27 March 1863; Ashwell and Wilberforce, *Life of the Rt. Rev. Samuel Wilberforce*, III, p. 91, Wilberforce to Gordon, June 1863.
14 Harpton Court Collection (3575), Lewis's diary, 8 January 1862.
15 *The Times*, 25 April 1862; Cobden Papers (BL Add MSS 43654), Cobden to Ashworth, 16 April, Ashworth to Cobden, 24 April 1862.
16 Guedalla, *The Palmerston Papers*, pp. 205–17, Palmerston to Gladstone, 24 April, 7, 8 May. Gladstone to Palmerston 30 April, 2, 8 May 1862.

17 Brand Papers, Palmerston to Brand, 15 January 1861.

18 Guedalla, *The Palmerston Papers*, pp. 210–14, Gladstone to Palmerston, 2 May 1862.

19 Ibid., pp. 223–5, Gladstone to Palmerston, 27 May 1862.

20 Ibid., pp. 217–18, Gladstone to Palmerston, 9 May 1862; Brand Papers, Brand to Stansfeld, 17 May 1862.

21 Harpton Court Collection (3575), Lewis's diary, 3 June 1862.

22 Hansard (third series), CLXVII, col. 381 (3 June 1862).

23 Trelawny diary (MS Eng. hist. d 413), 3 June 1862.

24 Harpton Court Collection (3575), Lewis's diary, 3 June 1862; Hansard (third series), CLXVII, cols. 322–33 (3 June 1862).

25 Morley, *Cobden*, II, pp. 399–400, Cobden to Hargreaves, 7 August 1862.

26 Figures from Mitchell and Deane, *Abstract of British Historical Statistics*, p. 397.

27 Brand Papers, Gladstone to Brand, 16 October 1863.

28 Guedalla, *The Palmerston Papers*, pp. 292–304, Gladstone to Palmerston, 6 October, Palmerston to Gladstone, 19 October 1864.

29 Ibid., p. 305, Gladstone to Palmerston, 22 October 1864.

30 Tilney Bassett, *Gladstone to His Wife*, p. 164, Gladstone to Catherine Gladstone, 9 November 1864.

31 *The Times*, 9 November 1863.

32 Brand Papers, Palmerston to Brand, 12 December 1863; Hansard (third series), CL, cols. 1875–81 (10 June 1858); BP (GC/BR/20), Brand's memorandum on 'County Franchise Bill', 9 August 1864, with his letter of the same day to Palmerston.

33 BP (CAB/148), Palmerston's note of the voting in cabinet and Brand's memorandum, both 9 February 1864.

34 Harpton Court Collection (3575), Lewis's diary, 9 February 1861.

35 BP (CAB/148), Palmerston's note of the voting.

36 Ibid. (GC/GR/2568), Grey to Palmerston, 2 May 1865.

37 Hansard (third series), CLXXIV, cols. 953–4 (13 April 1864).

38 BP (GC/BR/25), Brand to Palmerston, 5 May 1865.

39 Hansard (third series), CLXXVIII, col. 1638 (8 May 1865).

40 BP (GC/GR/2569), Grey to Palmerston, 2 and 3 May 1865.

41 Guedalla, *The Palmerston Papers*, pp. 279–80, Palmerston to Gladstone, 11 May 1864.

42 Mill, *Considerations on Representative Government*, pp. 280–7.

43 Hansard (third series), CLXXVIII, col. 1644 (8 May 1865).

44 Morley, *Cobden*, II, pp. 416–19, Cobden to Hargreaves, 5 April 1863; Bright Papers (BL Add. MSS 62079), Bright to Hargreaves, 13 May 1863.

45 BP (GC/BR/28), Palmerston to Brand, 14 August 1863.

46 Trelawny diary (MS Eng. hist. d 415), 11 May 1864.

47 Hansard (third series), CLXXV, col. 324 (11 May 1864).

48 Ibid., CLXXIV, cols. 952–4 (13 April 1864).

49 Trelawny diary (MS Eng. hist. d 415), 11 May 1864.

50 Vincent, *Disraeli, Derby and the Conservative Party*, pp. 215–16, entry in Stanley's journal for 11 May 1864.

51 Guedalla, *The Palmerston Papers*, pp. 282–3, 286–7, Gladstone to Palmerston, 13 May, Palmerston to Gladstone, 23 May 1864.

52 BP (GC/BR/27), Brand to Palmerston, 8 May, 29 July, Palmerston to Brand, 3 August 1865.

53 Cobden Papers (BL Add. MSS 43652), Cobden to Bright, 30 March 1864.

54 Ibid. (BL Add. MSS 43655), Cobden to Hargreaves, 11 February 1865.

55 Strachey and Fulford, *The Greville Memoirs*, VII, p. 374, 22 June 1858.

56 Clarendon Papers (MS Clar. Dep. c 531), Lewis to Clarendon, 20 January 1863.

57 Lewis, *A Dialogue on the Best Form of Government*, pp. 17, 20–1.

58 Somerset Papers, Palmerston to Somerset, 10 May 1862; BP (SHA/PC/68), Shaftesbury Papers, Palmerston to Shaftesbury, 29 April 1864.

59 Somerset Papers, Palmerston to Somerset, 10 May 1862.

60 Clarendon Papers (MS Clar. Dep. c 531), Lewis to Clarendon, 26 March 1863.

61 Guedalla, *The Palmerston Papers*, pp. 256–9, Gladstone to Palmerston, 23, 24, 25 March, Palmerston to Gladstone, 23, 26 March 1863.

62 Ibid., pp. 250–3, Gladstone to Palmerston, 7 January, 10 February, Palmerston to Gladstone, 7, 11 February 1863.

63 RP (PRO 30/22/14E), Palmerston to Russell, 19 January 1863; Clarendon Papers (MS Clar. Dep. c 531), Lewis to Clarendon, 26 March 1863.

64 GP (BL Add. MSS 44534), Gladstone to Argyll, 13 September, to Russell, 26 September 1864.

65 Dasent, *John Thadeus Delane*, II, pp. 129–33; BP (GC/BR/21), Palmerston to Russell, 11 June 1864; the thought was one that Brand 'did not like to put on paper'.

66 Ibid. (GC/GR/1415), Granville to Palmerston, 18 February 1865.

67 Fitzmaurice, *The Life of Granville*, I, p. 139, Granville to Canning, 8 January 1856. Instead of Greg and Marshall, Granville, backed by Lord Lansdowne, the Whig elder statesman, put forward the name of Edward Strutt, created Baron Belper that year; a large landowner who represented 'the bygone generation of manufacturers', BP (GC/GR/1842), Lansdowne to Granville, 13 January, in Granville to Palmerston, 14 January 1856. Strutt's peerage nevertheless gratified the cotton trade, Howe, *The Cotton Masters*, pp. 267–8.

68 BP (GC/GR/1915), Granville to Palmerston, 18 February 1865; N. Mitford, *The Stanleys of Alderley* (London, 1939), p. 239.

69 Vincent, *Disraeli, Derby and the Conservative Party*, pp. 176–7, entry in Stanley's journal for 6 October 1861.

70 *The Times*, 31 October 1863.

71 Vincent, *Disraeli, Derby and the Conservative Party*, pp. 167–8, 175–6, 207, 223, entries in Stanley's journal for 20 March, 25 August 1861, 16 February, 31 July 1864.

72 Mill, *Principles of Political Economy*, II, pp. 226–32; and the comment in E. D. Steele, 'J. S. Mill and the Irish Question: the Principles of Political Economy, 1848–65', *Historical Journal* (1970), pp. 222–3.

73 *The Times*, 4 February 1864.

74 Vincent, *Disraeli, Derby and the Conservative Party*, p. 205, entry in Stanley's journal for 1 January 1864; Kennedy, '*My Dear Duchess*', p. 112, Clarendon to the Duchess of Manchester, 7 August 1860.

75 Thompson, *English Landed Society*, p. 210.

76 H. Perkin, *The Origins of Modern English Society, 1780–1880* (London, 1969),

pp. 414–17; W. D. Rubinstein, *Men of Property: the Very Wealthy in Britain since the Industrial Revolution* (London, 1981).

77 Perkin, *The Origins of Modern English Society*, pp. 414–17; and for the acceptance of their social obligations by businessmen, Howe, *The Cotton Masters*, ch. 8.

78 Thompson, *English Landed Society*, p. 62.

79 Vincent, *Disraeli, Derby and the Conservative Party*, pp. 175–6, 152, entries in Stanley's journal for 25 August 1861, 22 June 1857.

80 Lewis, *A Dialogue on the Best Form of Government*, pp. 70, 72, 77–8, 82, 103.

81 Mill, *Considerations on Representative Government*, pp. 245–6.

82 Rogers, *Speeches by…Bright*, p. 453, Birmingham, 26 January 1864.

83 J. R. Vincent, *Pollbooks: How Victorians Voted* (Cambridge, 1967), p. 23.

84 Bright Papers (BL Add. MSS 43384), Bright to Cobden, 6 September 1861; Morley, *Cobden*, II, Cobden to Henry Ashworth, 7 February 1862.

85 Rogers, *Speeches by…Bright*, p. 311, Glasgow, 21 December 1858.

86 *The Times*, 11 August 1862, 1 April 1863; Hansard (third series), CLIII, col. 789 (24 March 1859).

87 *The Times*, 17 December 1863.

88 Harrison, *Before the Socialists*, ch. 1.

89 G. Boyce et al., *Newspaper History from the Seventeenth Century to the Present Day* (London, 1978), ch. 13.

90 *The Times*, 15 October 1864.

91 *Beehive*, 17, 10 June 1865.

92 Ibid., 28, 7 January 1865.

93 Karl Marx, F. Engels, *Collected Works* (London, 1975), vol. 41, p. 430, Marx to Engels, 17 November 1862.

94 Buckle, *Letters of Queen Victoria* (second series), I, pp. 171–3, Palmerston to the Queen, 18 April 1864.

95 Morley, *Cobden*, II, pp. 447–8, Cobden to Chevalier, 3 May 1864.

96 RP (PRO 30/22/23), Palmerston to Russell, 23 March 1864; Ripon Papers (BL Add. MSS 43512), Palmerston to de Grey, 21 March 1864.

97 RP (PRO 30/22/15B), Palmerston to Russell, 6 April 1864.

98 *The Times*, 9 April 1864.

99 Buckle, *Letters of Queen Victoria* (second series), I, pp. 175–6, Granville to the Queen, 21 April 1864; Malmesbury, *Memoirs*, pp. 593–4, entries in Malmesbury's journal for 13 and 15 April 1864.

100 Guedalla, *The Palmerston Papers*, p. 297, Gladstone to Palmerston, 27 March 1864.

101 *Guardian*, 20 April 1864.

102 Ibid., 27 April 1864.

103 Lady Burghclere (ed.), *A Great Lady's Friendships: Letters of Mary, Marchioness of Salisbury, Countess of Derby, 1862–1876* (London, 1933), p. 59, Lord Cowley, ambassador in Paris, to Lady Salisbury, 4 August 1864.

104 RP (PRO 30/22/15B), Palmerston to Russell, 6 April; BP (D/24), Palmerston's diary, 12 April 1864; *Guardian*, 27 April 1864.

105 Matthew, *Gladstone Diaries*, VI, p. 269, 17 April; Buckle, *Letters of Queen Victoria* (second series), I, pp. 172–3, Palmerston to the Queen, 18 April; Malmesbury, *Memoirs*, pp. 594–5, entry in Malmesbury's journal for 20 April 1864.

106 F. E. Gillespie, *Labour and Politics in England, 1850–1867*, (Durham, North Carolina, 1927), pp. 218–19; *Beehive*, 7 January 1865.

107 Vincent, *Disraeli, Derby and the Conservative Party*, p. 213, entry in Stanley's journal for 16 April 1864.

108 *Beehive*, 7 January 1865.

109 H. Cunningham, *The Volunteer Force: a Social and Political History, 1859–1902* (London, 1975), ch. 3.

110 Howe, *The Cotton Masters*, p. 259.

111 Cunningham, *The Volunteer Force*, p. 30.

112 Cobden Papers (BL Add. MSS 43384), Bright to Cobden, 6 September 1861.

113 *The Times*, 12 November 1863; Cunningham, *The Volunteer Force*, ch. 2.

114 *The Times*, 23 October 1862.

115 *Saturday Review*, 8 April 1865.

116 *Daily Telegraph*, 3 April 1865.

117 *Saturday Review*, 8 April 1865.

118 Guedalla, *The Palmerston Papers*, pp. 287, 325–6, Gladstone to Palmerston, 23 May 1864, Palmerston to Gladstone, 12 March 1865.

119 Mill, *Considerations on Representative Government*, pp. 280–7, 277.

120 Mill, *Principles of Political Economy*, III, bk. iv, ch. vii, 'On the Probable Futurity of the Labouring Classes'.

121 Mill, *Considerations on Representative Government*, p. 265.

122 Mill, *Principles of Political Economy*, II, bk. ii, ch. ii, sec. 4, chs. vi and vii; III, bk iv, ch. vii, secs. 4–7.

123 For the uninhibited expression of Mill's impatience with 'the ridiculous appeals to humanity and Christianity in favour of ruffians' like the Chinese, see: F. E. Mineka and D. N. Lindley (eds.), *The Later Letters of John Stuart Mill*, 4 vols. (Toronto, 1972), forming vols. XIV–XVII of J. M. Robson et al., *The Collected Works of J. S. Mill* (Toronto, 1963); XV, p. 528, Mill to Edwin Chadwick, 13 March 1857.

124 Wallace and Gillespie, *The Journal of Benjamin Moran*, I, p. 176, 6 November 1857.

125 Mineka and Lindley, *The Later Letters of John Stuart Mill*, XV, pp. 607–8, 552–3, Mill to Lewis, 20 March 1859, to Giuseppe Mazzini, 15 April 1858.

126 *The Times*, 25 July, 1862.

127 Hansard (third series), CXXXVI, col. 2165 (1 March 1855).

128 *Daily News*, 25 October 1862.

129 Ibid., 2 June 1865; for the results, see Appendix 2 above.

130 BP (D/24), Palmerston's diary, 8 July 1864.

131 *Economist*, 25 March 1865.

132 The Times, 2 April 1863, Palmerston at Glasgow.

133 Ibid., 18 September 1862.

134 Ibid., 23 October 1862.

135 *Quarterly Review*, July 1865, 'The Election', pp. 284–6; Hughenden Papers (B/XX/S/335), Derby to Disraeli, 4 August 1865.

136 Vincent, *Disraeli, Derby and the Conservative Party*, p. 233–4, entry in Stanley's journal for 27 July 1865.

137 *Daily Telegraph*, 7, 13 July 1865.

138 Mineka and Lindley, *The Later Letters of John Stuart Mill*, XVI, pp. 1031–5,

Mill to James Beal, 17 April 1865; *Quarterly Review*, July 1864, 'The House of Commons', p. 276.

139　*The Times*, 24 November 1864.

140　*Nonconformist*, 25 October 1865.

141　*The Times*, 2 June 1865.

142　Malmesbury, *Memoirs*, p. 606, entry in Malmesbury's journal for 30 April 1865.

143　*Churchman*, 27 April 1865.

144　G. I. T. Machin, *Politics and the Churches in Great Britain 1832–1868* (Oxford, 1977), pp. 333–4; Chadwick, *The Victorian Church*, Part 2, pp. 83–4.

145　*Quarterly Review*, July 1865, 'The Church in her Relations to Political Parties', p. 212; *Churchman*, 27 April 1865.

146　*Economist*, 25 March, 1 July 1865.

147　*Guardian*, 24 May, 19 July 1865.

148　*Quarterly Review*, July 1865, 'The Church in her Relations to Political Parties', pp. 204–6; J. P. Parry, *Democracy and Religion: Gladstone and the Liberal Party, 1867–1875* (Cambridge, 1986), pp. 80–102, has reassessed this underrated element in the Church.

149　*Churchman*, 22 June, 18 May, 15 June 1865.

150　GP (BL Add. MSS 44535), Gladstone to Sir Thomas Fremantle, 25 July 1865.

151　Ibid.

152　*Guardian*, 7 June 1865.

153　*The Times*, 24 July 1865.

154　Ibid., 21, 2 June 1865.

155　Ibid., 12 June, 24 July 1865.

156　Ibid., 2 June; GP (BL Add. MSS 44534), Gladstone to Abraham Hayward, 19 May 1864.

157　*The Times*, 13 July, *Daily Telegraph*, 12 April 1865.

158　*Economist*, 8 July 1865.

159　Laughton, *Memoirs of…Henry Reeve*, II, p. 114, Clarendon to Reeve, 11 June 1865; Morley, *Cobden*, II, p. 232, Cobden to Sale, 4 July 1859.

160　*Daily Telegraph*, 6, 7 July 1865.

161　*Saturday Review*, 29 July 1865.

162　*Quarterly Review*, July 1865, 'The Election', p. 295.

163　GP (BL Add. MSS 44535), Gladstone to Sir Thomas Gladstone, Bt, 19 July 1865; R. M. Stewart, 'The Conservative Reaction: Lord Robert Cecil and Party Politics' in Lord Blake and H. P. Cecil, *Salisbury: the Man and his Policies* (London, 1987).

164　W. E. Gladstone, 'Notes and Queries on the Irish Demand', *The Nineteenth Century*, February 1887, p. 81.

165　M. J. Cowling, *1867: Disraeli, Gladstone and Revolution: the Passing of the Second Reform Bill* (Cambridge, 1967).

166　W. E. Gladstone, 'England's Mission', *The Nineteenth Century*, September 1878, p. 569.

167　Steele, 'Gladstone and Ireland', *Irish Historical Studies* (1970).

168　*Daily Telegraph*, 19 October, *Daily News*, 20 October 1865.

169　*The Times*, 19 October 1865.

170　Rolo, *George Canning*, p. 187.

171 S. G. Checkland, *The Gladstones: A Family Biography, 1764–1851* (Cambridge, 1971), ch. 23.

10 THE REVISION OF BRITAIN'S GREAT POWER DIPLOMACY

1 Hickleton Papers (A4/137), Delane to Wood, 18 October 1863. For the context of this chapter and the following one, Taylor, *The Struggle for Mastery in Europe* and Bourne, *The Foreign Policy of Victorian England* should be supplemented by the studies of particular problems cited below.

2 A. Saitta (ed.), *La Questione Italiana dalle Annessioni al Regno d'Italia nei Rapporte fra la Francia e l'Europa* III Serie: 1848–1860, 4 vols. (Rome, 1968), Fonti per la Storia d'Italia per l'Età Moderna e Contemporanea, 89–92: II, pp. 12–18, 31–33, Persigny to Napoleon III, 21 November 1859, 15 December 1859.

3 Clarendon Papers (MS Clar. Dep. c 82), Palmerston to Clarendon, 1 January 1858.

4 Ibid., 18 May 1858.

5 Malmesbury, *Memoirs*, p. 482, Malmesbury to Lord Cowley, 2 May 1859.

6 Malmesbury Papers (9M73/1/5), Malmesbury to Sir Henry Bulwer, 23 August 1858.

7 K. Jagow, *Letters of the Prince Consort, 1831–1861* (London, 1938), pp. 361–3, Albert to the Crown Princess of Prussia, 24 April 1861.

8 Hansard (third series), CLV, col. 578 (28 July 1859).

9 Grant Papers (Southwark Diocesan Archives), George Bowyer, MP to Bishop Thomas Grant, 25 August 1859.

10 RP (PRO 30/22/13F), Russell to Dean Elliot, 11 November 1858.

11 RP (PRO 30/22/14F), Palmerston to Russell, 11 May 1863.

12 BP (CAB/89), Palmerston's memorandum of 21 January 1858.

13 Count E. Corti (trans L. M. Sieveking and I. F. D. Morrow), *The Downfall of Three Dynasties* (London, 1934), pp. 365–8, Alexander of Hesse to Tsar Alexander II, 18 May 1863.

14 Ibid., pp. 369–70, 132, Tsar Alexander II to Alexander of Hesse, 24 June 1863, 18 May 1859.

15 Ibid., p. 371, Francis Joseph to Alexander of Hesse, 14 July 1863.

16 Vitzthum von Eckstädt, *St Petersburg and London, 1852–1864*, I, p. 381, Vitzthum to Beust, 10 August 1859.

17 Lewis, *A Dialogue on the Best Form of Government*, p. 25.

18 Ibid., p. 82

19 Vitzthum von Eckstädt, *St Petersburg and London, 1852–1864*, II, pp. 266–8, Vitzthum to Beust, 7 December 1863.

20 Corti, *The Downfall of Three Dynasties*, p. 147, Tsarina Marie to Alexander of Hesse, 18 July 1863.

21 Clarendon Papers (MS Clar, Dep, c 82), Palmerston to Clarendon, 18 May 1858.

22 Ibid. (MS Clar. Dep. c 524), Palmerston to Clarendon, 20 January 1859.

23 Ibid. (MS Clar. Dep. c 82), Palmerston to Clarendon, 18 May 1858.

24 Ibid. (MS Clar. Dep. c 524), Palmerston to Clarendon, 3 January 1860.

25 Ibid., Palmerston to Clarendon, 4 November 1859.

26 Ibid.

27 Ibid., Palmerston to Clarendon, 3 January 1860; T. Pinney (ed.), *The Letters of Thomas Babington Macaulay*, 6 vols. (Cambridge, 1974–81), VI, pp. 94–6, Macaulay to H. S. Randall, 23 May 1857.

28 Clarendon Papers (MS Clar. Dep. c 524), Palmerston to Clarendon, 27 November 1858.

29 Ibid., Palmerston to Clarendon, 15 May 1859.

30 Cowley Papers (PRO, FO 519/292), Palmerston to Cowley, 2 October 1860, the first letter of that date.

31 Clarendon Papers (MS Clar. Dep. c 524), Palmerston to Clarendon, 7 September 1859.

32 Ibid. (MS Clar. Dep. c 533), Clarendon to Lewis, 12 March 1856.

33 Harpton Court Collection (3570), Lewis's diary, 15 March, 5 April 1856 and (3571), 14 June 1857.

34 Clarendon Papers (MS Clar. Dep. c 531), Lewis to Clarendon, 21 May [1860].

35 Wellesley and Sencourt, *Conversations with Napoleon III*, p. 185, Palmerston to Cowley, 30 June 1860; Cowley Papers (PRO FO 519/292) Palmerston to Cowley, 30 January 1860.

36 Clarendon Papers (MS Clar. Dep. c 524), Palmerston to Clarendon, 9 February 1860, returning Malmesbury to Clarendon, 'Thursday' [January/February 1860].

37 Malmesbury, *Memoirs*, p. 512, Clarendon to Malmesbury, 8 February 1860.

38 Guedalla, *The Palmerston Papers*, p. 127, Palmerston to Gladstone, 14 February 1860.

39 Taylor, *The Struggle for Mastery in Europe, 1848–1918*, p. 81 n. 1.

40 Ibid., p. xxxv; Wellesley and Sencourt, *Conversations with Napoleon III*, p. 190, Cowley to Russell, 20 November 1860.

41 Harpton Court Collection (3575), Lewis's diary, 14 July 1862.

42 BP (CAB/89), Palmerston's memorandum of 21 January 1858.

43 Ibid. (CAB/97 and 94), undated memoranda by Cranworth and Argyll.

44 Porter, *The Refugee Question in Mid-Victorian Politics*, pp. 175–6.

45 Malmesbury, *Memoirs*, p. 424, entry in Malmesbury's journal for 13 March 1858.

46 R. Lucas, *Lord Glenesk and the 'Morning Post'* (London, 1910), pp. 142–6, Palmerston to Borthwick, 19 August 1858.

47 Wellesley and Sencourt, *Conversations with Napoleon III*, pp. 148–9, Cowley to Malmesbury, 30 August 1858.

48 Harpton Court Collection (3571), Lewis's diary, 3 February 1859; Hansard (third series), CLII, cols. 74–6 (3 February 1859).

49 Wellesley and Sencourt, *Conversations with Napoleon III*, pp. 212–13, Cowley to Russell, 7 December 1862.

50 RP (PRO 30/22/21), Palmerston to Russell, 11 November 1860.

51 Malmesbury, *Memoirs*, p. 492, Malmesbury to Cowley, 14 June 1859.

52 Somerset Papers, Palmerston to Somerset, 27 August 1865.

53 Morley, *Cobden*, II, p. 305.

54 Benson and Esher, *Letters of Queen Victoria*, III, p. 462, the Queen to Palmerston, 25 October 1861. P. M. Kennedy, *The Rise of the Anglo-German Antagonism, 1860–1914* (London, 1980) is authoritative; see also W. E. Mosse, *The European*

Powers and the German Question 1848–71, with special reference to England and Russia (Cambridge, 1958) and L. D. Steefel, *The Schleswig-Holstein Question* (Cambridge, Mass., 1932).

55 Tilney Bassett, *Gladstone to his Wife*, pp. 131–2, Gladstone to Catherine Gladstone, 15 December 1860.

56 Benson and Esher, *Letters of Queen Victoria*, III, p. 359, the Queen to Russell, 18 July 1859.

57 Jagow, *Letters of the Prince Consort*, pp. 361–3, Albert to the Crown Princess of Prussia, 24 April 1861.

58 Vincent, *Disraeli, Derby and the Conservative Party*, pp. 178–81, entry in Stanley's journal for 16 December 1861.

59 Aberdeen Papers (BL Add. MSS 43071), Gladstone to Aberdeen, 7 July 1855.

60 Harpton Court Collection (3571), Lewis's diary, 28 February 1857.

61 Connell, *Regina v. Palmerston*, pp. 245–9, minute of cabinet, 11 March 1857.

62 Benson and Esher, *Letters of Queen Victoria*, III, pp. 196–7, Derby to the Queen, 23 June 1856.

63 Connell, *Regina v. Palmerston*, p. 247, minute of cabinet, 15 March 1857.

64 Aberdeen Papers (BL Add. MSS 43071), Gladstone to Aberdeen, 26 June 1856.

65 Jagow, *Letters of the Prince Consort*, p. 275, Albert to Marie, Duchess of Saxe Coburg-Gotha, June 1857.

66 *The Times*, 18 February 1858.

67 Vitzthum von Eckstädt, *St. Petersburg and London, 1852–1864*, I, p. 359, Albert to Vitzthum, 24 June 1859.

68 Jagow, *Letters of the Prince Consort*, pp. 340–1, Albert to Princess Victoria of Prussia, 13 September 1859.

69 RP (PRO 30/22/20), Palmerston to Russell, 23 August, 6 December 1859.

70 BP (GC/RU/1130), Palmerston to Russell, 28 April 1859.

71 Malmesbury Papers (9M73/1/6), Malmesbury to the Queen, 3 May 1859; Malmesbury, *Memoirs*, p. 482, Malmesbury to Cowley, 2 May 1859.

72 Malmesbury Papers (9M73), MS diary, 2, 20, 28 May 1859.

73 Malmesbury, *Memoirs*, p. 488, entry in Malmesbury's journal for 29 May 1859.

74 Benson and Esher, *Letters of Queen Victoria*, III, pp. 335–9, the Queen to Derby, 1 June, Derby to the Queen, 2 June 1859.

75 O. Ernst, *Franz Joseph as revealed by his Letters*, trans A. Blake (London, 1927), pp. 11–14, nd [March] 1859.

76 RP (PRO 30/22/20), Palmerston to Russell, 8 September 1859.

77 Connell, *Regina v. Palmerston*, p. 277, memorandum by the Prince Consort, 31 December 1859.

78 RP (PRO 30/22/20), Palmerston to Russell, 6 December 1859.

79 Vitzthum von Eckstädt, *St. Petersburg and London, 1852–1864*, II, pp. 35–7, Vitzthum to Beust, 14 February 1860.

80 RP (PRO 30/22/21), Palmerston to Russell, 25 December 1860.

81 *Die Auswärtige Politik Preussens 1858–1871: Diplomatische Aktenstücke*, 9 vols. (Oldenburg, 1932–45), Subsequently cited as *APP*, II, part. 2, pp. 190–1, m. 3, Count Bernstorff, Prussian minister in London, to King William I, 18 February 1861.

82 RP (PRO 30/22/14B), Palmerston to Russell, 27 October 1861.

83 Vitzthum von Eckstädt, *St. Petersburg and London 1852–1864*, II pp. 14–16, Vitzthum to Beust, 14 January 1860.

84 RP (PRO 30/22/22 and 15C), Palmerston to Russell, 16 November 1863, 13 June 1864.

85 R. Fulford (ed.), *Dearest Mama: Letters between Queen Victoria and the Crown Princess of Prussia, 1861–1864* (London, 1968), p. 297, the Queen to the Crown Princess, 3 February 1864.

86 Guedalla, *The Palmerston Papers*, p. 290, Palmerston to Gladstone, 3 July 1864.

87 Layard Papers (BL Add. MSS 38951), Edmund Hammond to A. H. Layard, 27 October 1862.

88 *APP*, II, part. 2, pp. 190–1, n. 3, Bernstorff to William I, 18 February 1861.

89 RP (PRO 30/22/14F), Palmerston to Russell, 7 September 1863.

90 Ibid. (PRO 30/22/21), Palmerston to Russell, 5 April 1860.

91 Taylor, *The Struggle for Mastery in Europe*, pp. 12–15, 46, 142–55.

92 RP (PRO 30/22/21), Palmerston to Russell, 23 March 1860; ibid. (PRO 30/22/14G), memorandum by Palmerston, 3 December 1863.

93 Hansard (third series), CLXXII, col. 1252 (23 July 1863).

94 Ernst, *Franz Joseph as revealed by his Letters*, pp. 144–6, Francis Joseph to Crown Prince Albert of Saxony, 16 February 1864.

95 GP (BL Add. MSS 44534), Gladstone to the Duke of Somerset, 15 January 1864; to Lord Brougham, 2 February 1864.

96 *APP*, IV, pp. 603–4, Baron Adelsward, Swedish minister in Paris, to Count Manderstrom, minister of foreign affairs, 24 February 1864.

97 RP (PRO 30/22/15A), Palmerston to Russell, 18 January 1864.

98 *APP*, IV, pp. 560–3, Bernstorff to William I, 17 February 1864.

99 GP (BL Add MSS 44534), Gladstone to Lord Brougham, 2 February 1864.

100 Vitzthum von Eckstädt, *St. Petersburg and London, 1852–1864*, II, pp. 305–13, Derby to Vitzthum, 10 January, Vitzthum to Derby, 13 January 1864.

101 RP (PRO 30/22/) Palmerston to Russell, 3 January, 13 February 1864.

102 BP (D/24), Palmerston's diary, 3 February 1864.

103 Connell, *Regina v. Palmerston*, p. 353, entry in the Queen's journal for 21 June 1864.

104 Dasent, *John Thadeus Delane*, II, pp. 105–6, Palmerston to Delane, 9 May 1864.

105 *APP*, V, pp. 239–41, Sir Andrew Buchanan to Russell, 18 June 1864.

106 Matthew, *Gladstone Diaries*, VI, pp. 284–5, Gladstone's memorandum of the proceedings in cabinet, 24 and 25 June 1864.

107 Brooke and Sorensen, *The Prime Ministers' Papers: W. E. Gladstone, I: Autobiographica*, pp. 89–91, '1864, The Danish Question'.

108 GP (BL Add. MSS 44534), Gladstone to Robertson Gladstone, 1 February 1864.

109 Palmerston Letter Books (BL Add. MSS 48583), Palmerston to Russell, 13 September 1865.

110 *APP*, V, pp. 732–3, Bernstorff to William I, 8 March 1865.

111 *Les Origines Diplomatiques de la Guerre de 1870–1: Receuil de Documents publiée par le Ministère des Affaires Étrangères*, 29 vols. (Paris, 1910–32), subsequently cited as *Origines*: V, pp. 349–51, Prince de la Tour d'Auvergne, ambassador in London, to Edouard Drouyn de Lhuys, foreign minister of France, 24 January 1865.

112 *APP*, VI, pp. 328–3, Baron von Oubril, Russian minister in Berlin, to Prince Gortchakov, foreign minister of Russia, 1, 13 September 1865.

113 *Origines*, V, pp. 181–3, de la Tour d'Auvergne to Drouyn de Lhuys, 13 December 1864.

114 RP (PRO 30/22/23), minute by Palmerston, 24 January 1864.

115 *Leaves from the Diary of Henry Greville* (ed. Alice, Countess of Strafford), fourth series (London, 1905), p. 182, entry for 26 February 1864.

116 GP (BL Add. MSS 44534), Gladstone to Fould, 6 April 1864.

117 RP (PRO 30/22/14D), Palmerston to Russell, 16 September 1862.

118 Buckle, *Letters of Queen Victoria* (second series), I, p. 271, the Queen to Leopold I, 3 August 1865.

119 T. Martin, *The Life of H. R. H the Prince Consort*, 5 vols. (London, 1875–80), V, pp. 349–50, Albert to an unnamed correspondent, 9 May 1861.

120 Ibid., IV, p. 92, Albert to Stockmar, August 1857.

121 Dasent, *John Thadeus Delane*, II, pp. 107–110, Torrington to Delane, 7, 10 May 1864.

122 First Earl Russell, *Selections from the Speeches of Earl Russell, 1817 to 1841, and from Despatches, 1859–1865*, 2 vols. (London, 1870), II, pp. 328–32, Russell to Sir James Hudson, minister at Turin, 27 October 1860. Beales, *England and Italy, 1859–60* is standard, as are D. Mack Smith, *Cavour and Garibaldi, 1860: a Study in Political Conflict* (Cambridge, 1954) and the same author's *Victor Emanuel, Cavour and the Risorgimento* (London, 1971); see also C. T. McIntire, *England against the Papacy 1858–1861: Tories, Liberals and the Overthrow of Papal Temporal Power during the Italian Risorgimento* (Cambridge, 1983).

123 *Origines*, II, pp. 123–5, Comte de Massignac, chargé d'affaires at St Petersburg, to Drouyn de Lhuys, 14 March 1864.

124 Wellesley and Sencourt, *Conversations with Napoleon III*, pp. 190–1, Prince Richard Metternich to Count Rechberg-Rothenlöwen, foreign minister of Austria, 9 December 1860.

125 Ibid., Cowley to Russell, pp. 192–4, 11 January 1861.

126 Ibid., pp. 215–16, Cowley to Russell, 26 February 1863.

127 Russell, *Selections from Speeches ... and Despatches*, II, pp. 339–41, Gortchakov to Prince Gagarine, Russian chargé d'affaires at Turin, 28 September 1860; *APP*, II, part 1, pp. 739–41, Bernstorff to the Prince Regent of Prussia, 1 December 1860.

128 *I Documenti Diplomatichi Italiani* (Prima Serie 1861–1870), (Rome, 1952), vol. I, pp. 141–4, Marchese d'Azeglio to Baron Ricasoli, premier and foreign minister of Italy, 19–20 December 1861.

129 Jagow, *Letters of the Prince Consort*, pp. 361–3, Albert to the Crown Princess of Prussia, 24 April 1861.

130 RP (PRO 30/22/21), Palmerston to Russell, 17 September 1861.

131 L. Fagan, *The Life of Sir Anthony Panizzi, K.C.B* 2 vols. (London, 1880), II, pp. 193–7, Cavour to Panizzi, 24 October 1859. For Cullen and MacHale, archbishops of Dublin and Tuam, see E. D. Steele, 'Cardinal Cullen and Irish Nationality' *Irish Historical Studies* (1975), pp. 239–60 and ch. 12 below.

132 Lewis, *Letters*, p. 389, Lewis to Mrs Austin, 26 December 1860.

133 GP (BL Add. MSS 44530), Gladstone to the Duke of Somerset, 31 December 1859.

134 D. Mack Smith, *Cavour and Garibaldi, 1860*, pp. 137–8.

135 Saitta, *La Questione Italiana*, II, p. 245, Russell to Persigny, 13 June 1860.

136 Thouvenel, *Le Secret de l'Empereur*, I, pp. 187–91, E. A. Thouvenel, foreign minister of France to the Duc de Gramont, ambassador to the Holy See, 9 September 1860.

137 RP (PRO 30/22/21 and 15B), Palmerston to Russell, 26 October 1860; 6 April 1864.

138 Malmesbury Papers (9M73), MS diary, 14 April 1860.

139 Hansard (third series), CLVII, cols. 485, Palmerston, and 1252–8, Russell (13 and 26 March 1860).

140 BP (CAB/103), Palmerston's memorandum of 5 January 1860.

141 Ibid. (CAB/106), Gladstone's memorandum of 7 January 1860.

142 BP (GC/WO/141), Wood to Palmerston, 7 January 1860; ibid. (GC/AR/20), Argyll to Palmerston, 5 January 1860.

143 Halifax Papers (BL Add. MSS 49531), Palmerston to Wood, 7 January 1860; Clarendon papers (MS Clar. Dep. c 531), Lewis to Clarendon, 9 and 10 January 1860.

144 Morley, *Cobden*, II, pp. 281–4, entry in Cobden's journal for 30 March 1860.

145 Cobden Papers (BL Add. MSS 43651), Cobden to Bright, 28 May 1860.

146 Morley, *Cobden*, II, pp. 302–3, entry in Cobden's journal for 14 June 1860.

147 Saitta, *La Questione Italiana*, II, pp. 82–5, Persigny to Thouvenel, 16 February 1860.

148 Hansard (third series), CLVII, cols. 1258–8 (26 March 1860); Malmesbury, *Memoirs*, p. 518, entry in Malmesbury's journal for 26 March 1860.

149 Benson and Esher, *Letters of Queen Victoria*, III, pp. 390–4, Cowley to Russell, 7 March 1860 (despatch).

150 Cowley Papers (PRO, FO 519/292), Palmerston to Persigny, 17 April 1860.

151 Benson and Esher, *Letters of Queen Victoria*, III, p. 393, Cowley to Russell, 7 March 1860 (despatch).

152 Cowley Papers (PRO, FO 519/292), Palmerston to Persigny, 17 April 1860.

153 Connell, *Regina v. Palmerston*, pp. 268, 275, the Queen to Palmerston, 6 September, 6 December 1859.

154 Wellesley and Sencourt, *Conversations with Napoleon III*, pp. 196–8, Prince Richard Metternich, ambassador in Paris, to Count Rechberg-Rothenlöwen, foreign minister of Austria, 30 June; Cowley to Russell, 2 July 1861; Kennedy, *My Dear Duchess*, pp. 170–2, Clarendon to the Duchess of Manchester, 28 August 1861.

155 RP (PRO 30/22/14D), Palmerston to Russell, 17 September 1862.

156 Ibid., Palmerston to Russell, 15 October 1862.

157 Thouvenel, *Le Secret de l'Empereur*, I, pp. 440–2, II, pp. 423–5, Thouvenel to the Comte de Flahaut, ambassador in London, 21 February 1861, 4 October 1862.

158 RP (PRO 30/22/14D), Palmerston to Russell, 6 October 1862.

159 Cowley Papers (PRO, FO 519/292), Palmerston to Cowley, 2 March 1862.

160 Wellesley and Sencourt, *Conversations with Napoleon III*, p. 211, Cowley to Russell, 3 October 1862.

161 Mack Smith, *Victor Emanuel, Cavour and the Risorgimento*, pp. 230–1; A. C. Jemolo, *Church and State in Italy, 1850–1950* (Oxford, 1960), pp. 24–5.

162 Wellesley and Sencourt, *Conversations with Napoleon III*, pp. 206, 211–12, Cowley to Russell, 11 February, 3 October 1862.

163 RP (PRO 30/22/14E), Palmerston to Russell, 11 January 1863; Hansard (third series), CLXIX, cols. 45–7 (5 February 1863).

164 Mack Smith, *Victor Emanuel, Cavour and the Risorgimento*, pp. 300–2, 337–8.

165 Hammond Papers (PRO, FO 391/7), minute by Palmerston, 3 March 1861.

166 Mack Smith, *Victor Emanuel, Cavour and the Risorgimento*, pp. 288–92.

167 Wellesley and Sencourt, *Conversations with Napoleon III*, pp. 228–9, Cowley to Russell, 18 December 1864.

168 RP (PRO 30/22/14D), Palmerston to Russell, 23 September 1862.

169 I. Scott, *The Roman Question and the Powers, 1848–1865* (The Hague, 1969), pp. 206, 229–30, 299–301.

170 Clarendon Papers (MS Clar. Dep. c 531), Lewis to Clarendon, 29 November [1859].

171 Morley, *Cobden*, II, pp. 272–7, entry in Cobden's journal for 30 January 1860.

172 Harpton Court Collection (3574), Lewis's diary, 30 November, 15 December 1860; Clarendon Papers (MS Clar. Dep. c 531), Lewis to Clarendon, 30 November 1860.

173 Ibid. (MS Clar. Dep. c 524), Palmerston to Clarendon, 2 December 1859.

174 Morley, *Cobden*, II, pp. 272–7, entry in Cobden's journal for 30 January 1860.

175 RP (PRO 30/22/21), Palmerston to Russell, 14 January 1861; Wellesley and Sencourt, *Conversations with Napoleon III*, pp. 192–4, Cowley to Russell, 11 January 1861.

176 RP (PRO 30/22/14D), Palmerston to Russell, 18 October 1861.

177 Wellesley and Sencourt, *Conversations with Napoleon III*, pp. 201–5, Cowley's memorandum of 10 January 1862.

178 PP 1860, LXVIII, pp. 127–8, Correspondence respecting the Affairs of Italy, Loftus to Russell, 15 September 1859.

11 THE EXTENSION OF REALISM IN FOREIGN AFFAIRS

1 Quarterly Review, April 1864, 'Foreign Policy of England', p. 483, ibid., July 1864, 'The House of Commons', p. 276.

2 *Leeds Mercury*, 27 October 1860.

3 Wellesley and Sencourt, *Conversations with Napoleon III*, p. 149, Cowley to Malmesbury, 30 August 1858, reporting an interview between Palmerston and the Emperor; BP (MM/TU/50), Palmerston's memorandum of 8 October 1860. For the context, R. H. Davison, *Reform in the Ottoman Empire, 1856–1876* (Princeton, 1963) and D. C. Blaisdell, *European Financial Control in the Ottoman Empire* (New York, 1929) are standard.

4 Layard Papers (BL Add. MSS 389887), Bulwer to Layard, undated but from late 1860 or early 1861.

5 Ibid., Bulwer to Layard, undated but from late 1860.

6 GP (BL Add. MSS 44534), Gladstone's 'Memorandum on Turkish Budget', 11 December 1864.

7 Ibid., Gladstone's memorandum on Turkish finance, 27 February 1864.

8 GP (BL Add. MSS 44534), Gladstone's 'Memorandum on Turkish Budget', 11 December 1864.

9 Blaisdell, *European Financial Control in the Ottoman Empire*, pp. 34–5.

10 Hansard (third series), CLXXI, cols. 125–40, Cobden; 140–7, Gladstone (29 May 1863).

11 Matthew, *Gladstone Diaries*, V, p. 204, 29 May 1863; GP (BL Add. MSS 44533), Gladstone to Bulwer, 4 July 1863.

12 Vincent, *Disraeli, Derby and the Conservative Party*, p. 194, entry in Stanley's journal for 11 January 1863.

13 Aali Pasha Papers (BL Add. MSS 46695), Bulwer to Aali Pasha, 23 January 1865.

14 Carlisle, *Correspondence of Abraham Hayward*, II, pp. 93, 95 Bulwer to Hayward, April 29 [? 1863], [? January 1863]

15 Malmesbury Papers (9M73/1/5), Malmesbury to Cowley, 22 January 1859.

16 S. Lane-Poole, *The Life of the Rt. Hon. Stratford Canning, Viscount Stratford de Redcliffe*, 2 vols. (London, 1888), II, pp. 439–40, Stratford de Redcliffe to Clarendon, 3 June 1855.

17 PP 1861, LXVII, pp. 612–15, Papers relating to Administrative and Financial Reforms in Turkey, 1858–61, memorandum by Viscount Stratford de Redcliffe, 22 October 1858.

18 Ibid., pp. 616–18, 667–72, Bulwer to Russell, 26 July 1859, 16 November 1860.

19 Ibid., p. 638 Russell to Bulwer, 12 May 1860.

20 Wellesley and Sencourt, *Conversations with Napoleon III*, p. 149, Cowley to Malmesbury, 30 August 1858.

21 BP (BL Add. MSS 48582), Palmerston to Bulwer, 26 June 1861.

22 Layard Papers (BL Add. MSS 38987), minute by Russell, 17 September 1861.

23 RP (PRO 30/22/21), Palmerston to Russell, 12 October 1861.

24 Ibid. (PRO 30/22/14D), Palmerston to Russell, 6 November 1862.

25 Vincent, *Disraeli, Derby and the Conservative Party*, pp. 224–5, entry in Stanley's journal for 23 October 1864.

26 RP (PRO 30/22/14E), Palmerston to Russell, 6 January 1863; ibid. (PRO 30/22/14D), Palmerston to Russell, 16 November 1862.

27 Ibid. (PRO 30/22/14E), Palmerston to Russell, 6 January, 7 February 16 March 1863.

28 E. Prevelakis, *British Policy towards the Change of Dynasty in Greece 1862–1863* (Athens, 1955); Wellesley and Sencourt, *Conversations with Napoleon III*, p. 212, Cowley to Russell, 7 December 1862; RP (PRO 30/22/14D), Palmerston to Russell, 16, 17 November 1862; ibid. (PRO 30/22/14E), minute by Palmerston, 8 February 1863; Harpton Court Collection (3575), Lewis's diary, 22 November, 2 December 1862.

29 *The Times*, 12 December 1862, 5, 6, 7, 10, 11, 25 February, 17, 18, 27 March 1863.

30 BP (GC/RU/1142), Palmerston to Russell, 6 November 1862; RP (PRO 30/22/14D), Palmerston to Russell, 4, 7 December 1862; Harpton Court Collection (3575), Lewis's diary, 8 December 1862, 7 March 1863; R. Clogg, *A Short History of Modern Greece* (Cambridge, 1978), p. 90.

31 Wellesley and Sencourt, *Conversations with Napoleon III*, p. 228, Cowley to Russell, 18 December 1864.

32 Ibid., pp. 213–14, Metternich to Rechberg, 8 January 1863.

33 RP (PRO 30/22/14D), Palmerston to Russell, 25 November 1862, first letter of that date.

34 Ibid., minute by Palmerston, 22 October 1862.

35 PP 1863, LXXIII, Correspondence relating to the Bombardment of Belgrade in June 1862, pp. 37–9, Russell to Bulwer, 3 July 1862.

36 Carlisle, *Correspondence of Abraham Hayward*, II, pp. 95–7, Bulwer to Hayward, 12 July 1863.

37 See n. 3 above.

38 PP 1863, LXXIII, Correspondence relating to the Bombardment of Belgrade in June 1862, Russell to J. S. Lumley, chargé d'affaires at St Petersburg, 25 August 1862.

39 Carlisle, *Correspondence of Abraham Hayward*, II, pp. 95–7, Bulwer to Hayward, 12 July 1863.

40 Layard Papers (BL Add. MSS 38991), minute by Palmerston, 14 January 1865.

41 T. W. Riker, *The Making of Roumania: A Study of an International Problem, 1850–1866* (London, 1931), is a detailed account.

42 Wellesley and Sencourt, *Conversations with Napoleon III*, p. 127, Cowley to Clarendon, 4 August 1857.

43 Ibid., pp. 126–7, Cowley to Clarendon, 2 and 4 August 1857.

44 Wodehouse Papers (BL Add. MSS 46693), Clarendon to Wodehouse, 11 August 1857.

45 Ibid., Clarendon to Sir Hamilton Seymour, 11 August 1857.

46 Malmesbury Papers (9M73/1858/3), Palmerston to Malmesbury, 15 June 1858.

47 Wellesley and Sencourt, *Conversations with Napoleon III*, pp. 121, 169–71, Hübner to Rechberg, 7 December 1856, Metternich to Rechberg, 5 September 1859.

48 Wodehouse Papers (BL Add. MSS 46693), Wodehouse to Clarendon, 14 August 1857.

49 Hansard (third series), CL, cols. 59–63 (4 May 1858).

50 Malmesbury, *Memoirs*, pp. 403–4, entry in Malmesbury's journal for 14 August 1857.

51 Wodehouse Papers (BL Add. MSS 46693), Clarendon to Wodehouse, 11 August 1857, to Seymour, 11 August 1857; Malmesbury Papers (9M73/1858/3), Palmerston to Malmesbury, 15 June 1858.

52 Wodehouse Papers (BL Add. MSS 46693), Wodehouse to Clarendon, 14 August 1857.

53 Palmerston Letter Books (BL Add. MSS 48582), Palmerston to Bulwer, 26 June 1861.

54 Cowley Papers (PRO, FO 519/292), Palmerston to Cowley, 31 July 1860.

55 Sir. A. Lyall, *The Life of the Marquis of Dufferin and Ava*, 2 vols. (London, 1905), I, pp. 106–9, 118.

56 Ibid., pp. 117–19.

57 Wellesley and Sencourt, *Conversations with Napoleon III*, p. 194, Cowley to Russell, 11 January 1861.

58 Thouvenel, *Le Secret de l'Empereur*, I, pp. 390–2, 442–6, Thouvenel to Flahaut, 4 February, to Gramont, 24 February 1861.

59 Wodehouse Papers (BL Add. MSS 46693), Wodehouse to Clarendon, 31 July 1857.

60 Thouvenel, *Le Secret de l'Empereur*, I, pp. 390–2, 442–6, Thouvenel to Flahaut, 4 February, to Gramont, 24 February 1861.

61 RP (PRO 30/22/21), Palmerston to Russell, 31 January 1861.

62 Ibid.

63 Wellesley and Sencourt, *Conversations with Napoleon III*, p. 230, Cowley to Russell, 13 April 1865.

64 Lyall, *The Life of the Marquis of Dufferin and Ava*, I, p. 119.

65 GP (BL Add. MSS 44304), memorandum by Somerset accompanying his letter to Gladstone of 17 May 1860.

66 Layard Papers (BL Add. MSS 38991), Palmerston to Layard, 8 January 1865; ibid. (BL Add. MSS 38990), minute by Palmerston, 24 December 1864.

67 Ibid.

68 BP (D/22), Palmerston's diary, 19 June 1862.

69 Dasent, *John Thadeus Delane*, I, pp. 326–8, Palmerston to Delane, 16 December 1859.

70 RP (PRO 30/22/21), Palmerston's memorandum of 23 November 1861.

71 BP (D/22), Palmerston's diary, 19 June 1862.

72 Salisbury Papers (HHM/3M/C4), Salisbury to the Earl of Lytton, viceroy of India, 20 July 1877.

73 Aali Pasha Papers (BL Add. MSS 46695), Bulwer to Aali Pasha [1864].

74 PP 1865, LVII, pp. 885–8, Correspondence respecting Protestant Missionaries and Converts in Turkey, Bulwer to Russell, 7 September 1864.

75 Malmesbury, *Memoirs*, pp. 373–5, Herbert to Malmesbury, 8 December 1855.

76 GP (BL Add. MSS 44533), Gladstone to MacColl, 8 September 1863.

77 RP (PRO 30/22/14E), Palmerston to Russell, 7 April 23 February 1863.

78 RP (PRO 30/22/14F), Palmerston to Russell, 15 May 1863.

79 Kriegel, *The Holland House Diaries*, p. 40, entry in Holland's diary for 26 August 1831.

80 Hansard (third series), CLXVI, col. 17 (25 March 1862), Earl Russell; W. E. Mosse, 'England and the Polish Insurrection of 1863', *E.H.R.* (1967) pp. 28–35.

81 RP (PRO 30/22/14E), Palmerston to Russell, 10 February 1863; ibid (PRO 30/22/22), to Russell, 20 June 1863.

82 Hansard (third series), CLXVI, cols. 568, 570 (4 April 1862).

83 Ibid., CLXIX, col. 935 (27 February 1863).

84 RP (PRO 30/22/22), Palmerston to Russell, 27 February 1863, the second letter of that date.

85 Morley, *Cobden*, II, p. 404, Cobden to Michel Chevalier, 22 June 1863.

86 Matthew, *Gladstone Diaries*, VI, p. 215, 20 July 1863; Hansard (third series) CLXXII, cols. 1098, 1103–5 (20 July 1863).

87 Palmerston Letter Books (BL Add. MSS 48583), Palmerston to Russell 13 September 1865.

88 Layard Papers (BL Add. MSS 38991), minute by Palmerston, 1 May 1865.

89 Somerset Papers, Palmerston to Somerset, 25 September 1859, 23 June 1861.

90 Benson and Esher, *Letters of Queen Victoria*, III, pp. 447–50, Palmerston to the Queen, 14 August 1861.

91 Somerset Papers, Palmerston to Somerset, 3 May 1862.

92 BP (PM/J/1), Palmerston to Russell, 11 September 1864.

93 Benson and Esher, *Letters of Queen Victoria*, III, pp. 203–5, Granville to the Queen, 30 August 1856.

94 *The Times*, 17 October 1861.

95 F. Venturi (trans. F. Haskell), *The Roots of Revolution: A History of the Populist and Socialist Movement in Nineteenth-Century Russia* (New York, 1966), pp. 2–3, 220–31.

96 Russell, *Selections from Speeches...and Despatches*, II, pp. 331–2, Russell to Sir James Hudson, minister at Turin, 27 October 1860.

97 Malmesbury, *Memoirs*, p. 529, entry in Malmesbury's journal for 10 November 1860.

98 *APP*, VI, pp. 382–3, Baron von Oubril, Russian minister in Berlin to Gortchakov, 1/13 September 1865; W. E. Mosse, *The Rise and Fall of the Crimean System, 1865–1871* (London, 1963), pp. 129–30.

99 Hammond Papers (PRO, FO 391/7), minute by Palmerston, 17 September 1863.

100 Bourne, *The Foreign Policy of Victorian England*, pp. 334–6, Palmerston to Clarendon, 31 December 1857. For this period in Anglo-American relations see E. D. Adams, *Great Britain and the American Civil War*, 2 vols. (London, 1925), H. C. Allen, *Great Britain and the United States: A History of Anglo-American Relations 1783–1952* (London, 1954) chs. 12–13, Bourne, *Britain and the Balance of Power in North America*, chs. 6–8, and N. B. Ferris, *The Trent Affair: a Diplomatic Crisis* (Knoxville, Tennessee, 1977).

101 Lewis, *Letters*, pp. 313–17, Lewis to Head, 6 July 1856.

102 Ibid., pp. 310–12, Lewis to Head, 13 April 1856; GP (BL Add. MSS 44595), memorandum by Lewis, 7 November 1862.

103 Hansard (third series), CXLIX, col. 954 (12 April 1858); CLXIV, col. 1658 (26 July 1861).

104 RP (PRO 30/22/21), Palmerston to Russell, 24 September 1861.

105 Newcastle Papers (NeC 10889), Newcastle to Russell, 11 February 1860.

106 RP (PRO 30/22/25), Argyll to Russell, 19 and 21 December 1859.

107 Ibid., Argyll to Russell, 21 December 1859.

108 Lewis, *Letters*, pp. 310–12, Lewis to Head, 13 April 1856.

109 Clarendon Papers (MS Clar. Dep. c 69), Palmerston to Clarendon, 22 December 1857.

110 Wellesley and Sencourt, *Conversations with Napoleon III*, p. 124, Cowley to Clarendon, 19 June 1857.

111 BP (GC/CL/1180), Clarendon to Palmerston, 6 January 1859.

112 Malmesbury, *Memoirs*, pp. 448–9, Malmesbury to Cowley, 28 September 1858.

113 RP (PRO 30/22/22), Palmerston to Russell, 19 January 1862.

114 Hammond Papers (FO 391/7), minute by Palmerston, 20 October, with Russell's comment, 21 October 1861.

115 Ibid.

116 RP (PRO 30/22/21), Palmerston to Russell, 26 September 1861.

117 Hammond Papers (PRO, FO 391/7), minute by Palmerston, 21 October [1861]; RP (PRO 30/22/21), Palmerston to Russell, 26 September 1861; Cowley Papers (PRO, FO 519/292), Palmerston to Cowley, 13 August 1863.

118 Somerset Papers, Palmerston to Somerset, 25 September 1861.

119 RP (PRO 30/22/22), Palmerston to Russell, 19 January 1862; ibid. (PRO 30/22/21), Palmerston to Russell, 24 September 1861.

120 Layard Papers (BL Add. MSS 38987), minute by Palmerston, 20 October 1861.

121 RP (PRO 30/22/21), Palmerston to Russell, 18 July 1861.

122 Harpton Court Collection (3575), Lewis's diary, 30 November, 4 December 1861.

123 RP (PRO 30/22/21), Palmerston to Russell, 6 December 1861, the second letter of that date.

124 Lewis, *Letters*, pp. 405–6, Lewis to Twistleton, 30 November, with postscript dated 3 December 1861.

125 Morley, *Cobden*, II, pp. 390–3, Cobden to Sumner, 29 November, 6, 12, 19 December 1861.

126 Harpton Court Collection (3575), Lewis's diary, 11 January 1862.

127 Ibid.

128 Bourne, *Palmerston-Sulivan Letters, 1804–1863*, p. 319, Palmerston to Laurence Sulivan, 26 January 1862.

129 BP (D/22), Palmerston's diary, 8 January 1862.

130 Thouvenel, *Le Secret de l'Empereur*, II, pp. 215–17, Thouvenel to Flahaut, 26 December 1861.

131 Harpton Court Collection (3575), Lewis's Diary, 11 January 1862.

132 Matthew, *Gladstone Diaries*, V, p. 76, 28 November 1861; Benson and Esher *Letters of Queen Victoria*, III, pp. 469–70, the Queen to Russell, 1 December 1861, with the Queen's annotation: 'This draft was the last the beloved Prince ever wrote…'

133 Dasent, *John Thadeus Delane*, II, pp. 34–5, W. H. Russell to Delane, 13 September 1861.

134 Bright Papers (BL Add. MSS 43386), C. P. Villers to Bright, 14 December 1861; *The Times*, 10 January 1862.

135 Bourne, *Palmerston-Sulivan Letters, 1804–1863*, p. 319, Palmerston to Laurence Sulivan, 26 January 1862; Connell, *Regina v. Palmerston*, p. 322, Palmerston to the Queen, 12 January 1862.

136 RP (PRO 30/22/21), Palmerston's memorandum of 11 December 1860.

137 Guedalla, *The Palmerston Papers*, pp. 233–6, Gladstone to Palmerston, 25 September 1862.

138 Thouvenel, *Le Secret de l'Empereur*, II, pp. 247–9, Thouvenel to Flahaut, 13 March 1862.

139 Wellesley and Sencourt, *Conversations with Napoleon III*, p. 198, Cowley to Russell, 2 July 1861.

140 GP (BL Add. MSS 44532), Gladstone to J. E. Denison, the Speaker, 16 August 1861; ibid. (BL Add. MSS 44325), Harriet, Duchess of Sutherland to Gladstone, nd [1861].

141 Ibid. (BL Add. MSS 44532), Gladstone to Argyll, 26 August 1861; ibid. (BL Add. MSS 44531), Gladstone to Argyll, 15 July 1861.

142 RP (PRO 30/22/14D), Palmerston to Russell, 20 October 1862, Matthew, *Gladstone Diaries*, V, p. 495, Gladstone to Argyll, 6 June 1860.

143 Guedalla, *The Palmerston Papers*, pp. 239–47, Gladstone's memorandum of

24 October 1862 on the war in America; GP (BL Add. MSS 44533), Gladstone to Argyll, 19 September 1862.

144 RP (PRO 30/22/14D), Russell to Lewis, 26 October, Palmerston to Russell, 14 September 1862; ibid. (PRO 30/22/22), Palmerston to Russell, 24 April 1862.

145 *The Times*, 9 October 1862; the quotations are from GP (44533), Gladstone to the Hon. Arthur Gordon, 22 September 1862.

146 RP (PRO 30/22/22), Palmerston to Russell, 12 October 1862; Morley, *Gladstone*, I, p. 709, Gladstone to his wife, 29 July 1862.

147 Morley, *Gladstone*, I, p. 714, n. 2, entries for 8 and 9 October in the diary of C. F. Adams.

148 RP (PRO 30/22/14D), Palmerston to Russell, 20, 21 October, 2 November 1862; BP (GC/CL/1207), Clarendon to Palmerston, 16 October 1862; Clarendon Papers (MS Clar. Dep. c 524), Palmerston to Clarendon, 20 October 1862.

149 Harpton Court Collection (3575), Lewis's diary, 11, 12 November 1862; Morley, *Gladstone*, I, p. 719, Gladstone to his wife, 12, 13 November 1862.

150 Harpton Court Collection (3575), Lewis's diary, 23 October 1862; GP (BL Add. MSS 44595), memorandum by Lewis, 17 October 1862.

151 Harpton Court Collection (3575), Lewis's diary, 25 to 28 November 1862.

152 Morley, *Gladstone*, I, p. 719, Gladstone to his wife, 13 November 1862.

153 Eg, RP (PRO 30/22/15C), Palmerston to Russell, 4 August 1864.

154 Ibid. (PRO 30/22/14F), Palmerston to Russell, 7, 9 September 1863.

155 GP (BL Add. MSS 44534), Gladstone to Sumner, 1 February 1864.

156 Lewis, *Letters*, pp. 406–7, Lewis to Twistleton, 5 December 1861; Clarendon Papers (MS Clar. Dep. c 531). Lewis to Clarendon, 11 November 1862.

157 Wellesley and Sencourt, *Conversations with Napoleon III*, p. 212, Cowley to Russell, 3 October 1862; Clarendon Papers (MS Clar. Dep. c 531), Lewis to Clarendon, 13 November 1862; RP (PRO 30/22/15C), Palmerston to Russell, 4 August 1864.

158 Curtis, *Correspondence of J. L. Motley*, II, pp. 81–2, Motley to his mother, 18 August 1862.

159 GP (BL Add. MSS 44533), Gladstone to Argyll, 19 September 1862.

160 *Papers relating to Foreign Affairs accompanying the Annual Message of the President of the United States to Congress (1861–62)*, part 1, p. 568, Motley, US minister to Austria, to William H. Seward, secretary of state, October 1862; subsequently cited as *Foreign Relations of the US*

161 *Edinburgh Review*, April 1861, 'The Election of the President Lincoln and its Consequences', quotations from pp. 586–7.

162 Cobden Papers (BL Add. MSS 43655), Cobden to Hargreaves, 22 June 1861, 5, 21 January 1862.

163 Ibid., Cobden to Hargreaves, 19 July, 18 December 1862.

164 Bright Papers (BL Add. MSS 62079), Bright to Hargreaves, 10 November 1862.

165 Ibid. (BL Add. MSS 43388), Milner Gibson to Bright, 14 November 1862.

166 Morley, *Cobden*, II, p. 232, Cobden to Sale, 4 July 1859.

167 Cobden Papers (BL Add. MSS 43652), Cobden to Bright, 29 December, 7 October 1862.

168 *Foreign Relations of the US 1862–63*, part 1, pp. 349–50, C. F. Adams, minister to Great Britain, to Seward, 3 July 1863.

169 Hansard (third series), CLXXI, cols. 1771–80, Roebuck; cols. 1826–38, Bright; cols. 1800–12, Gladstone (30 June 1863).

170 *Foreign Relations of the US 1862–63*, part 1, pp. 249–50, Adams to Seward, 3 July 1863.

171 Hansard (third series), CLXXI, col. 1831 (30 June 1863).

172 Bright Papers (BL Add. MSS 62079), Bright to Hargreaves, 30 January 1863, 10 November 1862, 16 August 1863.

173 *Foreign Relations of the US 1862–63*, part 1, pp. 636–7, William L. Doyle, minister to France, to Seward, 30 July 1863.

174 R. Wemyss Reid, *Memoirs and Letters of the Rt. Hon. Sir Robert Morier from 1826 to 1876*, 2 vols. (London, 1911), I, pp. 401–8, Morier to Lady Salisbury, 15 March 1864.

175 Lord Augustus Loftus, *The Diplomatic Reminiscences of Lord Augustus Loftus, 1837–1862*, 2 vols. (London, 1892). II, pp. 373–9.

176 Cobden Papers (BL Add. MSS 43654), Cobden to Ashworth, 10 July 1860; partly printed and misdated in Morley, *Cobden*, II, pp. 381–3, where the recipient is wrongly given as William Hargreaves.

177 Morley, *Cobden*, II, pp. 302–3, entry in Cobden's journal for 14 June 1860; Cobden Papers (BL Add. MSS 43651), Cobden to Bright, 28 May 1860.

178 E.g. Guedalla, *The Palmerston Papers*, pp. 207–8, Palmerston to Gladstone, 29 April 1862.

179 Clarendon Papers (MS Clar. Dep. c 533), Clarendon to Lewis, 24 October 1859; ibid. (MS Clar. Dep. c 531), Lewis to Clarendon, 21 May [1860].

180 BP (GC/RU/599), Russell to Palmerston, 18 May 1860; Kennedy, '*My Dear Duchess*,' p. 101, Clarendon to the Duchess of Manchester, 21 April 1860.

181 The Marquis of Lorne, *Viscount Palmerston* (London, 1906), pp. 197–202, Palmerston's draft minute of cabinet to the Queen, May 1860.

182 BP (CAB/117), memorandum by Lewis, 17 June 1860.

183 BP (CAB/119), memorandum by Wood, 19 June 1860.

184 Ibid. (CAB/120), undated memorandum by Granville.

185 Hansard (third series), CLVII, cols. 1252–8 (26 March 1860).

186 Saitta, *La Questione Italiana*, II, pp. 153–5, Persigny to Thouvenel, 21 March 1860.

187 *The Times*, 1 August 1860.

188 Kennedy, '*My Dear Duchess*', pp. 109–10, Clarendon to the Duchess of Manchester, 2 August 1860.

189 Cowley Papers (PRO FO 519/292), Palmerston to Persigny, 18 September 1860 (copy).

190 Benson and Esher, *Letters of Queen Victoria*, III, pp. 408–9, the Queen to Russell, 21 September 1860.

191 Cowley Papers (PRO FO 519/292), Palmerston to Cowley, 13 and 2 October 1860, the first letter of that date.

192 Hansard (third series), CLVII, col. 1258 (26 March 1860).

193 Cowley Papers (PRO, FO 519/292), Palmerston to Cowley, 2 October 1860, the first letter of the date.

194 Wellesley and Sencourt *Conversations with Napoleon III*, pp. 185–6, Cowley to Russell, 13 July 1860.

195 Clarendon Papers (MS Clar. Dep. c 524), Palmerston to Clarendon, 10 October 1860.

196 BP (GC/LE/221), Palmerston to Lewis, 22 November 1860; printed with Lewis's reply in Ashley, *Life of Viscount Palmerston*, II, pp. 33–4.

197 Somerset Papers, Palmerston to Somerset, 29 December 1860.

198 Clarendon Papers (MS Clar, Dep. c 50), Palmerston to Clarendon, 14 December 1856.

199 RP (PRO 30/22/21), Palmerston to Russell, 8 February 1861.

200 Wellesley and Sencourt, *Conversations with Napoleon III*, p. 192, Cowley to Russell, 11 January 1861.

201 RP (PRO 30/22/14B), minutes by Palmerston, 14 March, Wood, 24 March and Gladstone, 1 March 1861.

202 Wellesley and Sencourt, *Conversations with Napoleon III*, pp. 194–6, Cowley to Russell, 1 March, 1 April 1861.

203 GP (BL Add. MSS 44531), Gladstone to Brougham, 15 March 1861.

204 Kennedy, '*My Dear Duchess*', pp. 142–3, Clarendon to the Duchess of Manchester, 27 March 1861.

205 BP (RC/F/1073), the Queen to Palmerston, 25 October 1861.

206 Benson and Esher, *Letters of Queen Victoria*, III, pp. 462–4, Delane to Palmerston. 28 October, Palmerston to the Queen, 30 October 1861.

207 RP(PRO 30/22/21), Palmerston to Russell, 10 February 1860.

208 Connell, *Regina v. Palmerston*, pp. 266–7, Palmerston to the Queen, 13 August 1859.

209 RP (PRO 30/22/14B), Palmerston to Russell, 27 October 1861.

210 R. Ringhoffer (ed.) (trans C. E. Barrett-Lennard and M. W. Hoper), *The Bernstorff Papers: the Life of Count Albrecht Bernstorff*, 2 vols. (London 1908), II, p. 811, Prince Albert to Bernstorff, 15 September 1861.

211 Clarendon Papers (MS Clar. Dep. c 531), Lewis to Clarendon, 28 November 1859.

212 Morley, *Cobden*, II, p. 255

213 E. B. Eastwick, *Journal of a Diplomat's Three Years' Residence in Persia*, 2 vols. (London, 1864), I, pp. 18–19.

214 Kennedy, '*My Dear Duchess*', p. 100, Clarendon to the Duchess of Manchester, 21 April 1860.

215 Guedalla, *The Palmerston Papers*, p. 185, Palmerston to Gladstone, 21 July 1861.

216 Somerset Papers, Palmerston to Somerset, 27 March 1861.

217 Wellesley and Sencourt, *Conversations with Napoleon III*, p. 205, Cowley's memorandum of 10 January 1862.

218 Guedalla, *The Palmerston Papers*, pp. 113–14, Gladstone to Palmerston, 23 November 1859.

219 Somerset Papers, Gladstone to Somerset, 13 December 1864.

220 Malmesbury, *Memoirs*, p. 533, entry in Malmesbury's journal for 10 December 1860.

221 BP (RC/H/124), Albert to Palmerston, 16 November 1861.

222 Wellesley and Sencourt, *Conversations with Napoleon III*, pp. 201, 204–5, Cowley's memorandum of 10 January 1862.

223 Cambridge Papers (Leeds University microfilm, Vic. Add. MSS E/1: reel 16), Colonel Claremont to the Duke of Cambridge, 19 February 1864.

224 T. Zeldin, *France, 1848–1945* (Oxford, 1973), p. 555.

225 Wellesley and Sencourt, *Conversations with Napoleon III*, pp. 226, Cowley to Russell, 24 February 1864, report by Prince Heinrich VII von Reuss on his interview with the Emperor, 9 June 1863.

226 Ibid., pp. 216–17, 223–4, Cowley to Russell, 1 March, 10 April, 13 November 1863; Taylor, *The Struggle for Mastery in Europe*, p. 136.

227 RP (PRO 30/22/22), Palmerston to Russell, 8 November 1863.

228 Ibid. (PRO 30/22/14G), Palmerston to Russell, 12 November 1863; for Russell's speech at Blairgowrie, see *The Times*, 28 September 1864.

229 BP (PM/J/1), Palmerston to Russell, 2 December 1863.

230 Ibid., Palmerston to Leopold II, 15 November, to Russell, 18 November 1863.

231 PP, 1864, LXVI, pp. 8–11, Correspondence respecting the Congress proposed to be held at Paris, Russell to Cowley, 25 November 1863; Wellesley and Sencourt, *Conversations with Napoleon III*, pp. 224–5, Cowley to Russell, 11 December 1863.

232 Malmesbury, *Memoirs*, p. 583, entry in Malmesbury's journal for 12 November 1863; ibid., pp. 585–6, Derby to Malmesbury, 10 January 1864.

233 Buckle, *Letters of Queen Victoria* (second series) I, pp. 113–14, the Queen to Leopold II, 12 November 1863.

234 Wellesley and Sencourt, *Conversations with Napoleon III*, pp. 226–7, Cowley to Russell, 13 June 1864.

235 Matthew, *Gladstone Diaries*, VI, pp. 284–5, Gladstone's memorandum of the decision in cabinet, 25 June 1864.

236 Vitzthum von Eckstädt, *St Petersburg and London, 1852–1864*, II, pp. 258, 280–3, 305–7, Vitzthum to Beust, 27 August, quoting *The Times*, and 31 December 1863; Derby to Vitzthum, 10 January 1864.

237 Lady Burghclere, *A Great Lady's Friendships*, pp. 57–8 Cowley to Lady Salisbury, 3 February 1864.

238 Wellesley and Sencourt, *Conversations with Napoleon III*, pp. 233–7, von der Goltz to William I of Prussia, 29 August 1865.

239 RP (PRO 30/22/14G), memoranda by Palmerston, 14 March, Sir Charles Wood, 24 March, and Gladstone, 26 March 1861; E. d'Hauterive (trans. H. Wilson) *The Second Empire and its Downfall: the Correspondence of the Emperor Napoleon III and his cousin Prince Napoleon* (London, 1927), pp. 261–8, the prince's memorandum on the affairs of Poland, 20 February 1863.

240 BP (GC/HA/264), Hammond to Palmerston, 3 October 1863.

241 Cowley Papers (PRO, FO 519/292), Palmerston to Cowley, 3 September 1865; Vincent, *Disraeli, Derby and the Conservative Party*, pp. 235–6, where the entry in Stanley's journal for 18 September describes Cowley's reaction to this letter.

242 *Origines*, V, pp. 349–51, VI, pp. 437–9, La Tour d'Auvergne to Drouyn de Lhuys, 24 January, Baron Baude, chargé d'Affaires at London, to Drouyn de Lhuys, 23 August 1865; Palmerston Letter Books (BL Add. MSS 48583), Palmerston to Russell, 13 September 1865.

12 IRELAND

1 There are important studies by J. H. Whyte, Emmet Larkin and K. T. Hoppen on this comparatively neglected period in Irish history: Whyte's *The Independent Irish Party, 1850–9* (Oxford, 1958), and his *Political Problems, 1850–60*, published together with P. J. Corish, *Political Problems, 1860–78* as vol. V parts 2 and 3 (Dublin, 1967) of *A History of Irish Catholicism*; Hoppen's 'National Politics and Local Realities in Mid-Nineteenth Century Ireland' in A. Cosgrove and D. McCartney, *Studies in Irish History presented to R. Dudley Edwards* (Dublin, 1979), followed by *Elections, Politics and Society in Ireland 1832–85* (Oxford, 1984); and E. Larkin's *The Making of the Roman Catholic Church in Ireland, 1850–1860* (Chapel Hill, 1980) and *The Consolidation of the Roman Catholic Church in Ireland, 1860–1870* (Dublin, 1987).

2 Clarendon Papers (MS Clar. Dep. c 69), Palmerston to Clarendon, 7 October 1857.

3 Hansard (third series), CXLVIII, col. 1331 (12 February 1858).

4 BP (GC/BR/12), memorandum by Palmerston, 2 August 1861 with Brand to Palmerston, 31 July 1861.

5 Palmerston Letter Books (BL Add. MSS 48581), Palmerston to Cardwell, chief secretary for Ireland, 1 December 1859.

6 Douglas and Ramsay, *The Panmure Papers*, II, pp. 446–7, Palmerston to Panmure, 11 October 1857.

7 Ibid., p. 447, Carlisle to Palmerston, 8 October 1857; BP (GC/CA/509, 518), Carlisle to Palmerston, 15 July 1860, 24 August 1863.

8 Mill, *Considerations on Representative Government*, pp. 364–5.

9 Palmerston Letter Books (BL Add. MSS 48583), Palmerston to Wodehouse, 18 March 1865.

10 BP (GC/PE/29), Peel to Palmerston, 5 December 1863.

11 PP 1864, Land and Marine Forces (Religious Denominations), pp. 586–7; H. J. Hanham, 'Religion and Nationality in the Mid-Victorian Army' in M. R. D. Foot (ed.), *War and Society. Historical Essays in Honour of J. R. Western, 1928–1971* (London, 1973).

12 Ibid., p. 162.

13 Ibid., pp. 164–7; Palmerston Letter Books (BL Add MSS 48582), Palmerston to Herbert, secretary of state for war, 4 June 1861; Bourne, *Britain and the Balance of Power in North America*, p. 217, n. 2.

14 Brand Papers, Palmerston to Brand, 4 and 8 September 1864; RP (PRO 30/22/15C), Palmerston to Grey, 22 April, to Russell, 28 April 1864. Abolition of the viceroyalty had come up before within his governments and in Parliament: R. B. McDowell, *The Irish Administration, 1801–1914* (London, 1964), pp. 67–8; BP (GC/LE/202), Palmerston to Lewis, 18 March 1858.

15 Mack Smith, *Victor Emanuel, Cavour and the Risorgimento*, p. 89, Palmerston to Clarendon, 29 June 1856.

16 Palmerston Letter Books (BL Add. MSS 48581), Palmerston to Cardwell, 15 September 1859.

17 BP (GC/BR/10 and 12), Brand to Palmerston, 1 June, 31 July 1861.

18 E. D. Steele, *Irish Land and British Politics: Tenant-Right and Nationality, 1865–1870* (Cambridge, 1974), pp. 68–9.

19 Hansard (third series), CLXXVII, col. 823 (27 February 1865).

20 PP 1845, XIX, Report and Evidence from the Royal Commission on the State of the Law and Practice in respect to the Occupation of Land in Ireland, p. 95, Qs 75, 77, As 75–77.

21 Hansard (third series), CXXXVIII, cols. 167–71 (4 May 1855).

22 Ibid., CLXIV, cols. 240–51 (2 July 1861).

23 BP (GC/PE/29), Peel to Palmerston, 5 December 1863.

24 E. D. Steele, 'Cardinal Cullen and Irish Nationality' *Irish Historical Studies* (1975); P. J. Corish, 'Cardinal Cullen and the National Association of Ireland' *Reportorium Novum* (1961–2): both reprinted in A. O'Day, *Reactions to Irish Nationalism 1865–1914* (London, 1987).

25 Buckle, *Letters of Queen Victoria* (second series), I, pp. 255–7, Palmerston to the Queen, 24 February 1865.

26 Palmerston Letter Books (BL Add MSS 48583), Palmerston to Grey, 30 September, 2 October 1865.

27 BP (GC/LE/212), Palmerston to Lewis, 26 December 1859.

28 Ibid.

29 BP (PM/J/1), Palmerston to Russell, 2 December 1863.

30 Ibid., Palmerston to Chichester Fortescue, MP, under-secretary of state for the Colonies, 15 September 1864.

31 Hansard (third series), CXLIV, col. 917ff. (19 February 1857).

32 C. S. Dessain et al. (eds.), *The Letters and Diaries of John Henry Newman*, 31 vols. (London and Oxford, 1961–78), XVII, pp. 385–6, Newman to J. E. Wallis, 23 September 1856.

33 J. H. Newman, *The Idea of a University*, ed. I. T. Ker (Oxford, 1976), pp. 388–90.

34 Palmerston Letter Books (BL Add. MSS 48583), Palmerston to Wodehouse, 28 July 1865.

35 Rev. F. X. Martin (ed.), *The Easter Rising, 1916, and University College, Dublin* (Dublin, 1966).

36 Vincent, *Disraeli, Derby and the Conservative Party*, pp. 167, 172–3, 177–8, entries in Stanley's journal for 18 February, 17 June, 17 November 1861.

37 Ibid., p. 167, entry in Stanley's journal for 18 February 1861.

38 Steele, *Irish Land and British Politics*, p. 16; *The Times*, 7 October 1859, Derby's second speech at Liverpool, 29 October.

39 Vincent, *Disraeli, Derby and the Conservative Party*, pp. 172–3, entry in Stanley's journal for 17 June 1861.

40 Ibid.

41 BP (GC/GR/1888), Granville to Palmerston, 31 August 1861.

42 Ibid.; Palmerston Letter Books (BL Add. MSS 48582), Palmerston to Carlisle, 28 July 1861.

43 Ibid., Palmerston to Carlisle, 28 July, 28 December 1861.

44 Ibid., Palmerston to Carlisle, 28 July 1861, 7 January 1862; BP (GC/BR/12), Brand to Palmerston, 31 July, memorandum by Palmerston, 2 August 1861.

45 Vincent, *Disraeli, Derby and the Conservative Party*, pp. 177–8, entry in Stanley's journal for 17 November 1861.

46 Palmerston Letter Books (BL Add. MSS 48582), Palmerston to Carlisle, 7 January 1862.

47 Ibid.

48 BP (GC/GR/1888), Granville to Palmerston, 31 August 1861.

49 *Dod's Parliamentary Companion* (1864); *The Tablet*, 14, 21 May, 18 June 1859, 16 July 1864.

50 Dublin Diocesan Archives, Cullen to The O'Donoghue, 17 September 1859.

51 *Cork Examiner*, 3 December 1860.

52 BP (GC/LE/135), Lewis to Palmerston, 6 December 1860.

53 MacSuibhne, *Paul Cullen and his Contemporaries with their Letters*, V, pp. 115–16, Cullen to O'Reilly, 22 June 1863.

54 Palmerston Letter Books (BL Add. MSS 48582), Palmerston to Peel, 9 December 1861.

55 Dublin Diocesan Archives, Maguire to Cullen, n.d. but probably 1859; The O'Donoghue to Cullen, 26 September [1859].

56 Ibid., Cullen to Bishop J. J. Lynch of Toronto, 13 May 1864.

57 Palmerston Letter Books (BL Add. MSS 48582), Palmerston to Carlisle, 28 July 1861.

58 Dublin Diocesan Archives, Acton to Cullen, 18, 23 November 1857.

59 D. Mathew, *Lord Acton and his Times* (London, 1968), pp. 106–9; J. J. Auchmuty, 'Acton's Election as an Irish Member of Parliament', *English Historical Review* (1946), pp. 394–405.

60 PP 1867, VIII, Report and Evidence from the Select Committee on the Tipperary Election Petition, pp. 191–8, evidence of the Most Rev. Patrick Leahy.

61 BP (GC/BR/12), Brand to Palmerston, 31 July 1861.

62 *Dod's Parliamentary Companion* (1864); *The Tablet*, 16 July 1864.

63 Dublin Diocesan Archives, Cullen to William Monsell, MP, 15 July 1864.

64 Matthew, *Gladstone Diaries*, VI, p. 345, 31 March 1865.

65 Lord Aberdare, *Letters of the Rt. Hon. Henry Austin Bruce, G.C.B., Lord Aberdare of Duffryn* (Oxford, 1902), I, pp. 22–8, Bruce to Granville, 7 October 1865.

66 Ibid., p. 221, Bruce to Rachel Bruce, 8 August, 1865.

67 Ibid., pp. 226–8, Bruce to Granville, 7 October 1865.

68 BP (PM/J/1), Palmerston to Fortescue, 12, 15 September 1864.

69 Steele, *Irish Land and British Politics*, especially chs. 4 and 9.

70 A. Ramm (ed.). *The Political Correspondence of Mr Gladstone and Lord Granville, 1863–1876*, 2 vols., Camden third series LXXXI–II (London, 1952), I, p. 96, Granville to Gladstone, 31 March 1870.

71 BP (GC/LE/212), Palmerston to Lewis, 26 December 1859.

72 J. J. Figgis and R. V. Laurence (eds.), *Selections from the Correspondence of the First Lord Acton* (London, 1917), pp. 97–8, Gladstone to Acton, 8 January 1870.

73 BP (PM/J/1), Palmerston to Fortescue, 15 September 1864.

74 E. D. Steele, 'Gladstone, Irish Violence and Conciliation' in Cosgrove and McCartney, *Studies in Irish History Presented to R. Dudley Edwards* (Dublin, 1979).

13 EMPIRE

1 Statistics from Mitchell and Deane, *Abstract of British Historical Statistics*, pp. 315–22, and L. Davis and R. A. Huttenback, 'The Export of British Finance' *Journal of Imperial and Commonwealth History* (1985), pp. 50–1.

2 Cambridge Papers (Leeds University Library microfilm, Vic Add MSS E/1: reel 10), Palmerston to the Duke of Cambridge, C-in-C at the Horse Guards, 4 November 1860; H. Knollys (ed.), *Incidents of the China War of 1860 compiled from the private journals of Sir Hope Grant, G.C.B.* (London, 1875), p. 144ff., Herbert to Grant, 9 April 1860.

3 These contributions to the literature of empire are especially useful: J. W. Cell, *British Colonial administration in the Mid-Nineteenth Century: The Policy-making Process* (New Haven, 1970); R. Robinson and J. Gallagher, *Africa and the Victorians: The Official Mind of Imperialism* (London, 1961), and 'The Imperialism of Free Trade', *Economic History Review* (1953), pp. 1–15; D. C. M. Platt, *Finance, Trade and Politics in British Foreign Policy, 1815–1914* (Oxford, 1968) and 'The Imperialism of Free Trade: Some Reservations', *Economic History Review* (1968); Sir F. T. Piggott, *Extraterritoriality: the Law relating to Consular Jurisdiction and Residence in Oriental Countries*, second edn (Hong Kong, 1907).

4 J. S. Mill, *On Liberty*, Everyman's Library edn (London, 1954), p. 73.

5 BP (GC/LE/201), Palmerston to Lewis, 24 January 1859.

6 Hansard (third series), CXLVIII, cols. 169–70 (4 December 1857).

7 Rogers, *Speeches by…Bright*, p. 105, Birmingham, 18 December 1862.

8 Hickleton Papers (A4/63/146), Palmerston to Wood, 19 April 1864.

9 *The Times*, 13 February 1862.

10 Rogers, *Speeches by…Bright*, pp. 108–9, Birmingham, 18 December 1862.

11 Mill, *Considerations on Representative Government*, pp. 376, 380.

12 *The Times*, 14 July 1858.

13 Ibid., 14 June 1858.

14 On the Mutiny the following are indispensable: S. N. Sen, *Eighteen Fifty Seven* (Calcutta, 1967); M. Maclagan, *'Clemency' Canning* (London, 1962); R. C. Majumdar, *The Sepoy Mutiny and the Revolt of 1857*, second edn (Calcutta, 1963); S. B. Chaudhuri, *Theories of the Indian Mutiny* (Calcutta, 1965); and E. Stokes, *The Peasant and the Raj: Studies in Agrarian Society and Peasant Rebellion in Colonial India* (Cambridge, 1978), chs. 6–8. For India over the rest of this period there are, *inter alia*, R. J. Moore, *Sir Charles Wood's Indian Policy*; S. Gopal, *British Policy in India, 1858–1905* (Cambridge, 1965) and T. R. Metcalf, *The Aftermath of Revolt: India, 1857–1870* (Princeton, 1964).

15 Douglas and Ramsay, *The Panmure Papers*, II, p. 399, Palmerston to Panmure, 30 June 1857.

16 Ibid., pp. 446, 449, Palmerston to Panmure, 8 and 30 October 1857.

17 Cambridge Papers (Vic. Add. MSS E/1: reel 6), Campbell to the Duke of Cambridge, 9, 24 July 1858.

18 R. Bosworth Smith, *Life of Lord Lawrence*, 2 vols. (London, 1883), II, pp. 299–305, Lawrence to Lord Dalhousie and to Lord Stanley, president of

the Board of Control, both 16 June 1858; Cambridge Papers (Vic. Add. MSS E/1: reel 6), Campbell to Cambridge, 24 July 1858.

19 Hansard (third series), CL, cols. 1613–33 (7 June 1859); quotations from cols. 1617, 1621.

20 Hansard (third series), CL, cols. 949–50 (20 May 1858); CLV, col. 822 (1 August 1859); Rogers, *Speeches by...Bright*, p. 105, Birmingham, 18 December 1862.

21 Canning Papers (letters from HM ministers), Palmerston to Canning, 9 October 1857.

22 Vernon Smith Papers (MSS Eur. B 324/2), Canning to Vernon Smith, 23 November 1857.

23 Canning Papers (letters from HM ministers), Palmerston to Canning, 9 October 1857.

24 BP (GC/WO/113), Wood to Palmerston, 6 September 1857; J. Martineau, *The Life and Correspondence of Sir Bartle Frere, Bart.*, 2 vols. (London, 1895), I, pp. 446–7, Wood to Frere, the governor of Bombay, 17 April 1863.

25 Sir W. T. Denison, *Varieties of Viceregal Life*, 2 vols. (London, 1870), II, p. 128, Denison to Canning, 7 March 1861.

26 BP (GC/WO/113), Wood to Palmerston, 6 September 1857.

27 W. T. Denison, *Varieties of Viceregal Life*, II, p. 61, n.1, Canning's note on Denison's 'Memorandum on the Reorganization of the Indian Native Army' [1861].

28 Moore, *Sir Charles Wood's Indian Policy*, p. 104, Dalhousie to Wood, 13 July 1864.

29 Ibid., p. 180, Wood to Dalhousie, 24 April 1854.

30 Hansard (third series), CL col. 1621 (7 June 1858); Clarendon Papers (MS Clar. Dep. c 49), minute by Palmerston, 2 June 1856.

31 Canning Papers (large despatch box), Canning's memorandum of the discussion, 13 November 1855.

32 BP (GC/WO/113), Wood to Palmerston, 6 September 1857.

33 Vernon Smith Papers (MSS Eur. B 324/2), Canning to Vernon Smith, 20 February 1858.

34 Ibid., and Gopal, *British Policy in India*, pp. 8–10.

35 Fitzmaurice, *The Life of Granville*, I, p. 384, Canning to Granville, 4 July 1860.

36 Martineau, *The Life and Correspondence of Sir Bartle Frere*, I, p. 449, Wood to Frere, 1 August 1862.

37 Denison, *Varieties of Viceregal Life*, II, p. 128, Denison to Sir George Clerk, governor of Bombay, 15 October 1861.

38 Hansard (third series), CLXIII, cols. 631–45 (6 June 1861); quotations from cols. 641, 643.

39 C. H. Philips (ed.), *The Evolution of India and Pakistan, 1858–1947: Select Documents* (London, 1967), pp. 40–1, Wood to Sir Bartle Frere, member of the viceroy's council, 18 August 1861.

40 Denison, *Varieties of Viceregal Life*, II, p. 128, Denison to Clerk, 15 October 1861.

41 J. D. Lunt (ed.), *From Sepoy to Subadar: Being the Life and Adventures of Subadar Sita Ram* (London, 1970), p. xxi, citing Sir Thomas Munro, governor of Madras 1820–27.

42 Gopal, *British Policy in India*, p. 1.

43 Denison, *Varieties of Viceregal Life*, II, p. 61, n. 1, Denison's 'Memorandum on the Reorganization of the Indian Native Army' [1861], and Lord Canning's note.

44 Ibid.

45 Fitzmaurice, *The Life of Granville*, I, pp. 377–9, Canning to Granville, 29 May 1860; E. D. Steele, 'Ireland and the Empire in the 1860s: Imperial Precedents for Gladstone's first Irish Land Act' *Historical Journal* (1968), pp. 66–8, 72; George Campbell, 'The Tenure of Land in India' in *Systems of Land Tenure in Various Countries. A Series of Essays published with the sanction of the Cobden Club* (London, 1870), pp. 216–18.

46 Steele, 'Ireland and the Empire in the 1860s', pp. 66–8.

47 Moore, *Sir Charles Wood's Indian Policy*, ch. 5.

48 Gopal, *British Policy in India*, pp. 22–32; Moore, *Sir Charles Wood's Indian Policy*, pp. 77–85; BP (GC/LE/228), Palmerston to Lewis, 31 January 1861.

49 Hansard (third series), CLXIV, col. 1517 (25 July 1861).

50 Moore, *Sir Charles Wood's Indian Policy*, pp. 32–5; Gopal, *British Policy in India*, pp. 27–9; T. Walrond (ed.), *Letters and Journals of James, 8th Earl of Elgin* (London, 1872), pp. 446–7, Elgin to Maine, 25 February 1863; Bosworth Smith, *Life of Lord Lawrence*, II, pp. 551–2.

51 G. Feaver, *From Status to Contract: a Biography of Sir Henry Maine* (London, 1959).

52 Wood Papers (MSS Eur. F 78/114/2), Maine to Wood, 2 April 1864.

53 Lawrence Papers (MSS Eur. F 90/26), Wood to Lawrence 10 April 1865; Wood Papers (MSS Eur. F 78/L.B. 18), Wood to Maine, 9 September 1864.

54 Ibid.

55 Lawrence Papers (MSS Eur. F 90/26), Wood to Lawrence, 27 March 1865.

56 Wood Papers (MSS Eur. F 78/L.B. 14), Wood to Sir C. Trevelyan, finance member of the viceroy's council, 10 November 1863; ibid. (MSS Eur. F 78/114/4), Maine to Wood, 12 January 1865.

57 Ibid., Maine to Wood, 13 August 1865.

58 J. M. Winter, *Robert Lowe* (Toronto, 1976). There is a daily record of leader writers for this period in the archives of *The Times*.

59 *The Times*, 9 August 1865.

60 Lawrence Papers (MSS Eur. F 90/25), Wood to Lawrence, 10 September 1864.

61 Hansard (third series), CLXIII, col. 641 (6 June 1861); Mill, *Considerations on Representative Government*, p. 386.

62 *The Times*, 12 February 1863.

63 Ibid., 14 February 1863.

64 Printing House Square Papers. Delane Correspondence (vol. 14), Wood to Delane, 'Saturday morning'.

65 Wood Papers (MSS Eur. F 78/L.B. 11), Wood to Trevelyan, 22 December 1862.

66 A. W. Silver, *Manchester Men and Indian Cotton, 1847–1872* (Manchester, 1966), pp. 111–20, quotation from p. 117.

67 Campbell, 'Tenure of Land in India', p. 227.

68 Moore, *Sir Charles Wood's Indian Policy*, pp. 190–4; Printing House Square Papers, Delane Correspondence (vol. 12), Wood to Delane, 4 February 1863.

69 *Manchester Guardian*, 22 November 1862.

70 Printing House Square Papers, Delane Correspondence (vol. 14), Wood to Delane, 'Saturday morning'.

71 Wood Papers (MSS Eur. F 78/LB 11), Wood to Trevelyan, 22 December 1862.

72 Moore, *Sir Charles Wood's Indian Policy*, 138–50.

73 *Leeds Mercury*, 16 August 1860.

74 Gopal, *British Policy in India*, pp. 11–12, 48–56; A. Redford, *Manchester Merchants and Foreign Trade*, 2 vols. (Manchester, 1934–56), II, pp. 23–6; R. C. Dutt, *The Economic History of India in the Victorian Age* (London, 1906), pp. 401–2.

75 *The Times*, 6 February 1862.

76 Ibid., 13 February 1862.

77 Denison, *Varieties of Viceregal Life*, 2, II. 393, Denison to Sir Roderick Murchison, 30 May 1865.

78 *The Times*, 14 January 1863.

79 Ibid., 27 January 1863.

80 Ibid.

81 Hansard (third series), CLI, cols. 344–5 (24 June 1858).

82 Ibid., CLXIII, cols. 641, 634–5 (6 June 1861).

83 Philips, *The Evolution of India and Pakistan*, pp. 40–1, Wood to Frere, 18 August 1861.

84 *The Times*, 30 September 1857.

85 Mill, *On Liberty*, p. 92 n.

86 *The Times*, 8 October 1857.

87 Harpton Court Collection (3571–2), Lewis's diary, 1 August, 4 September 1857.

88 *The Times*, 30 September 1857.

89 Ibid., 27 November 1857.

90 Ibid., 21 and 2 November 1857.

91 *Record*, 11 January 1858.

92 *Guardian*, 25 May 1858.

93 Moore, *Sir Charles Wood's Indian Policy*, p. 119.

94 *Economist*, 19 December 1857.

95 Harpton Court Collection (3572), Lewis's diary, 16 September 1857.

96 Bosworth Smith, *Life of Lord Lawrence*, II, p. 112.

97 Philips, *The Evolution of India and Pakistan*, pp. 41–2, Wood to Elgin, 19 May 1862.

98 Cambridge Papers (Vic. Add. MSS E/1: reel 17), Lt-Gen. Sir Hugh Rose, commander-in-chief in India, to Cambridge, 30 June 1864, Wood to Cambridge, 8 March 1864.

99 P. Mason, *A Matter of Honour: An Account of the Indian Army, its Officers and Men* (London, 1974), ch. 13.

100 Denison, *Varieties of Viceregal Life*, II, p. 65, n. 3, Canning's note and Denison's rejoinder on the latter's 'Memorandum on the Reorganization of the Indian Native Army' [1861].

101 Ibid., p. 70, n. 1.
102 Canning Papers (large despatch box), Ellenborough to Canning, 19 August and 8 July 1855, with part of Edwards's letter.
103 Hansard (third series), CLI, cols. 342–4 (24 June 1858).
104 Harpton Court Collection (3572), Lewis's diary, 16 September 1857.
105 G. O. Trevelyan, *The Life and Letters of Lord Macaulay*, 2 vols. (London, 1961), II, pp. 359–60, entry in Macaulay's journal for 19 September 1857.
106 Bosworth Smith, *Life of Lord Lawrence*, II, pp. 254–65.
107 Vincent, *Disraeli, Derby and the Conservative Party*, pp. 194–5, entry in Lord Stanley's journal for 11 January 1863.
108 Mill, *Considerations on Representative Government*, pp. 384–8.
109 *Edinburgh Review*, April 1863, 'India under Lord Canning', p. 472.
110 Hansard (third series), CLXIII, col. 634 (6 June 1861), Wood.
111 *Manchester Guardian*, 22 November 1862.
112 *Edinburgh Review*, April 1863, 'India under Lord Canning', pp. 485–6.
113 *British Colonial Administration in the Mid-Nineteenth Century*, chs. 3–6; Mitchell and Deane, *Abstract of British Historical Statistics*, pp. 315–27. D. G. Creighton, *The Road to Confederation: the Emergence of Canada, 1863–1867* (Toronto, 1964), and G. Serle, *The Golden Age: A History of the Colony of Victoria, 1851–1861* (Melbourne, 1963) are notable studies of individual colonies.
114 GP (BL Add MSS 44118), Gladstone to Cardwell, 23 May 1865.
115 J. K. Chapman, *The Career of Arthur Hamilton Gordon, First Lord Stanmore, 1829–1912* (Toronto, 1964), p. 18, Gordon to Sir Roundell Palmer, 8 November 1863; GP (BL Add MSS 44534), Gladstone to Bishop G. A. Selwyn of New Zealand, 20 April 1864.
116 Palmerston Letter Books (BL Add MSS 485582), Palmerston to the Duke of Newcastle, 7 November 1861.
117 Hansard (third series), CXLVII, cols. 1136–7 (6 August 1857).
118 GP (BL Add MSS 44534), Gladstone to Cardwell, 25 October 1864.
119 Guedalla, *The Palmerston Papers*, pp. 325–6, Palmerston to Gladstone, 12 March 1865.
120 Hansard (third series), CLXXVII, cols. 1613–33 (13 March 1865).
121 Cambridge Papers (Vic. Add. MSS E/1: reel 13), Lewis to Cambridge, 9 June, 21 April 1862.
122 Cell, *British Colonial Administration in the Mid-Nineteenth Century*, p. 208; BP (GC/SO/84), Somerset's memorandum of April 1862 with minute by Palmerston, 14 May.
123 Hansard (third series), CLXXVIII, col. 820 (6 April 1865).
124 *Edinburgh Review*, January 1862, 'Military Defence of the Colonies', p 125.
125 Lytton Papers (D/EK/028/1), Sir E. Bulwer Lytton, secretary of state for the colonies, to Sir H. Barkly, governor of Victoria, 22 November 1858.
126 BP (RC/F/737), the Queen to Palmerston, 2 July 1856.
127 Lytton Papers (D/EK/C25/96), Derby to Lytton, 21 August 1858.
128 Ibid. (D/EK/028/1), Lytton to Gladstone, 11 December 1858.
129 Newcastle Papers (NeC 10885), Newcastle to Sir H. Barkly, 26 April 1861.
130 Lytton Papers (D/EK/028/1), Lytton to Gladstone, 11 December 1858.
131 Morley, *Cobden*, II, pp. 470–1, Cobden to Colonel Cole, 20 March 1865.
132 Newcastle Papers (NeC 10889), Newcastle to Palmerston, 30 September 1860.

133 D. G. G. Kerr, *Sir Edmund Head: A Scholarly Governor* (Toronto, 1954), pp. 219–20, Head to Newcastle, 9 September 1861.

134 Newcastle Papers (NeC 10889), Newcastle to Palmerston, 30 September 1860.

135 Rogers, *Speeches by…Bright*, p. 300, Manchester, 10 December 1858.

136 Kerr, *Sir Edmund Head*, pp. 169–71, memorandum by Head for the Colonial Secretary [1857].

137 Lytton Papers (D/EK/028/2), Lytton to Sir George Bowen, governor of Queensland, 29 April 1859.

138 S. Lane-Poole (ed.), *Thirty Years of Colonial Government: A Selection from the Despatches and Letters of Sir George Ferguson Bowen*, 2 vols. (London, 1889), I, pp. 156–7, 194–9, Bowen to Chichester Fortescue, Parliamentary under-secretary for the Colonies, 6 June 1860, to Cobden, 18 March 1862.

139 Denison, *Varieties of Viceregal Life*, I, pp. 370, 467, Denison to Henry Lawrence, 23 September 1856, to Lady Hornby, 31 October 1859.

140 GP (BL Add. MSS 44535), Gladstone to Lord Lyttelton, 27 July 1865.

141 Roundell Palmer, *First Earl of Selborne, Memorials, Part 1, Family and Personal, 1766–1865*, 2 vols. (London, 1896), II, p. 467, Selwyn to Sir Roundell Palmer, 30 September 1863.

142 GP (BL Add. MSS 44535), Gladstone to Lord Lyttelton, 27 July 1865.

143 B. J. Dalton, *War and Politics in New Zealand, 1855–1870* (Sydney, 1969), ch. 8.

144 Trelawny diary (MSS Eng. hist. d 415), 18 July 1864.

145 Newcastle Papers (NeC 10887), Newcastle to Sir George Grey, governor of New Zealand, 26 February 1863.

146 BP (PM/J/1), Palmerston to Newcastle, 30 June 1863.

147 Steele, 'Ireland and the Empire in the 1860s', pp. 64–5, 81–3.

148 BP (GC/CA/414), Palmerston to Cardwell, 21 May 1865.

149 Hansard (third series), CLXXVIII, cols. 164–170 (23 March 1865).

150 Quoted in the *Autobiography of Sir Henry Taylor 1800–1875*, 2 vols. (London, 1885), II, pp. 241–2.

151 Hansard (third series), CLXVIII, col. 867 (25 July 1862).

152 Clarendon Papers (MS Clar. Dep. c 69), minute by Palmerston, 12 January 1857.

153 Platt, *Finance, Trade and Politics*, pp. 11, 35–7.

154 Clarendon Papers (MS Clar. Dep. c 49), Palmerston to Clarendon, 26 August 1856.

155 Ibid. (MS Clar. Dep. c 524), Palmerston to Clarendon, 4 January 1859.

156 *The Times*, 'Money Market and City Intelligence', 4, 5 July, 4, 25, 26 September 1861; Platt, *Finance, Trade and Politics*, pp. 334–6.

157 Layard Papers (BL Add. MSS 38987), minute by Russell [November 1861].

158 Ibid., minute by Layard, 27 November 1861.

159 RP (PRO 30/22/21), Palmerston to Russell, 7 October 1861.

160 Platt, *Finance, Trade and Politics*, pp. 335–6; Hansard (third series), CLXVIII, cols. 363–71 (15 July 1862).

161 Layard Papers (BL Add. MSS 38990), minute by Palmerston, 5 June 1864.

162 Ibid. (BL Add. MSS 38987), minute by Russell, 7 September 1861.

163 Ibid. (BL Add. MSS 38989), minute by Palmerston, 6 February 1863.

164 Hansard (third series), CLXXI, col. 1120 (19 June 1863), Malmesbury; CLXIX, col. 1194, Cobden, cols. 1176–87, Layard; the Foreign Office circular

is printed in Platt, *Finance, Trade and Politics,* pp. 398–9; L. A. Bethell, *The Abolition of the Brazilian Slave Trade: Britain, Brazil and the Slave Trade Question, 1807–1869* (Cambridge, 1970), ch. 13 shows how friction over the continued existence of slavery in Brazil affected relations with Britain.

165　RP (PRO 30/22/22), Palmerston to Russell, 4 May 1863.

166　BP (PM/J/1), Palmerston to Russell, 5 October 1864.

167　W. C. Costin, *Great Britain and China,* chs. 6–8; quotation from p. 269, W. B. Reed, United States minister in China to Cass, secretary of state, 29 July 1858, citing Elgin.

168　Sir G. E. P. Hertslet, *Hertslet's China Treaties,* 2 vols. (London, 1908), I, pp. 22–3, 51; H. Knollys *Incidents of the China War of 1860,* p. 144ff., Herbert to Grant, 9 April 1860.

169　J. S. Gregory, *Great Britain and the Taipings,* (London, 1969), pp. 148–9.

170　Lewis, *Letters,* pp. 349–50, Lewis to Head, 22 September 1858; W. G. Beasley, *Great Britain and the Opening of Japan, 1834–1858* (London, 1951), and G. Fox, *Britain and Japan, 1858–1883* (Oxford, 1969) are standard.

171　Sir W. L. Clowes, *The Royal Navy. A History from the Earliest Times to the Death of Queen Victoria,* 7 vols. (London, 1897–1903), VII, pp. 190–208.

172　Somerset Papers, Palmerston to Somerset, 20 November 1864.

173　Guedalla, *The Palmerston Papers,* p. 111, Gladstone to Palmerston, 12 September 1859.

174　GP (BL Add. MSS 44531), Gladstone to Harriet, Duchess of Sutherland, 12 December 1860.

175　Ibid. (BL Add. MSS 44533), Gladstone's memorandum on Japan, 9 December 1862.

176　Hansard (third series), CLXXIII, col. 394 (9 February 1864).

177　Matthew, *Gladstone Diaries,* VI, p. 254, 9 February 1864.

178　GP (BL Add. MSS 44395), Elgin to Gladstone, 2 March 1861.

179　Hansard (third series), CLXXV, col. 973 (31 May 1864).

180　Flournoy, *British Policy towards Morocco in the Age of Palmerston,* ch. 8.

181　Harpton Court Collection (3574), Lewis's diary, 21, 30 November 1860.

182　RP (PRO 30/22/21), Palmerston to Russell, 31 December 1860; Tilney Bassett, *Gladstone to His Wife,* pp. 132–3, Gladstone to Catherine Gladstone, 19 January 1861.

183　Layard Papers (BL Add. MSS 38987), memorandum by Gladstone on the Moroccan loan, 26 September 1861.

184　Clarendon Papers (MS Clar. Dep. c 531), Lewis to Clarendon, 1 December 1860.

185　Layard Papers (BL Add. MSS 38987), memorandum by Palmerston, 25 September 1861.

186　Ibid., minutes by Layard, 19, 20 September 1861.

187　Ibid., memorandum by Palmerston 25 September 1861.

188　Ibid., memorandum by Gladstone, 26 September 1861.

189　Ibid., Lewis to Layard, 25 September 1861.

190　Ibid., memorandum by Palmerston, 25 September 1861.

191　Harpton Court Collection (3575), Lewis's diary, 16 October 1861.

192　*Bankers' Magazine,* February 1862, pp. 71–2 *The Times,* 14 January 1862.

193　Cell, *British Colonial Administration in the Mid-Nineteenth Century,* pp. 254–74;

C. Lloyd, *The Navy and the Slave Trade: the Suppression of the African Slave Trade in the Nineteenth Century*, second edn (London, 1963), remains the best general account.

194 Clarendon Papers (MS Clar. Dep. c 69), Palmerston to Clarendon, 22 November, 3 December 1857.

195 BP (D/18), Palmerston's diary, 14 September 1858.

196 PP 1859 (Sess. 2), XXVII, pp. 119, 201. Correspondence respecting the *Charles et Georges*.

197 Malmesbury Papers (9M73/1/5), Malmesbury to Cowley, 30 October 1858.

198 Cell, *British Colonial Administration in the Mid-Nineteenth Century*, pp. 254–65.

199 G. E. Marindin (ed.), *Letters of Frederic, Lord Blachford* (London, 1896), pp. 172–3, Sir Frederic Rogers, Bt, to his mother, January 1858.

200 *The Times*, 9 November 1858; Clarendon Papers (MS Clar. Dep. c 524), Palmerston to Clarendon, 19 December 1858.

201 Malmesbury Papers (9M73/1/5), Malmesbury to Wilberforce, 11 November; to Stanley, 26 December 1858. The Bishop was the son of William Wilberforce, of anti-slavery fame.

202 Cell, *British Colonial Administration in the Mid-Nineteenth Century*, pp. 269–74; PP 1861, LXV, p. 260, Napoleon III to E. A. Thouvenel, minister of foreign affairs, 1 July 1861; printed with the Anglo-French Convention relative to Emigration of Labourers from India to the French Colonies.

203 Palmerston Letter Books (BL Add. MSS 48581), Palmerston to Archbishop Longley of Canterbury, 15 July 1860.

204 R. Coupland, *The Exploitation of East Africa, 1856–1890: the Slave Trade and the Scramble for Africa*, second edn (London, 1968), chs. 1 and 2.

205 Layard Papers (BL Add. MSS 38987), minutes by Layard, 14, 21 September 1861, undated minutes by Russell in reply.

206 Robinson and Gallagher, *Africa and the Victorians*, pp. 44–5, quoting Capt C. P. Rigby, Consul at Zanzibar.

207 Hansard (third series), CLXXIII, col. 395 (9 February 1864).

208 Benson and Esher, *Letters of Queen Victoria*, III, p. 391, Cowley to Russell, 7 March 1863 [*recte* 1860].

209 Cell, *British Colonial Administration in the Mid-Nineteenth Century*, pp. 274–85, argues that regional Anglo-French rivalry may have been a factor in the decision to annex Lagos.

Epilogue

1 G. W. E. Russell (ed.), *Malcolm MacColl, Memoirs and Correspondence* (London, 1914), p. 110.

2 Bourne, *Palmerston-Sulivan Letters*, pp. 3, 5, Palmerston to Laurence Sulivan, 31 December 1852.

3 Granville Papers (PRO 30/29/19), Palmerston to Granville, 2 December 1857.

4 Rogers, *Speeches by...Bright*, p. 300, Manchester, 10 December 1858.

5 Morley, *Gladstone*, I, pp. 785–6, Gladstone to Anthony Panizzi, 18 October 1865.

Bibliography

Manuscript sources

Aberdeen Papers (British Library)
Aali Pasha Papers (British Library)
Baines Papers (West Yorkshire Archives Service, Leeds)
Brand Papers (House of Lords Record Office)
Bright Papers (British Library)
Broadlands Papers (third Viscount Palmerston and seventh Earl of Shaftesbury: Southampton University Library)
Cambridge Papers (Leeds University Library: microfilm)
Canning Papers (West Yorkshire Archives Service, Leeds)
Carnarvon Papers (British Library)
Clarendon Papers (Bodleian Library, Oxford)
Cobden Papers (British Library)
Cowley Papers (Public Record Office)
Cullen Papers (Dublin Diocesan Archives)
Delane Correspondence (*The Times*, Printing House Square Papers)
Sotheron Estcourt Papers (Gloucestershire Record Office; transcripts provided by Dr Mark Curthoys)
Gladstone Papers (British Library)
Glynne-Gladstone Papers (Clwyd Record Office, Hawarden)
Graham Papers (Cambridge University Library: microfilm)
Grant Papers (Southwark Roman Catholic Diocesan Archives)
Granville Papers (Public Record Office)
Halifax Papers (British Library)
Hammond Papers (Public Record Office)
Harpton Court Collection (National Library of Wales)
Hickleton Papers (Leeds University Library: microfilm)
Hughenden Papers (Cambridge University Library: microfilm)
Iddesleigh Papers (British Library)
Kitson Papers (West Yorkshire Archives Service, Leeds)
Lamb Papers (British Library)

Layard Papers (British Library)
Lawrence Papers (India Office Library)
Lytton Papers (Hertfordshire Record Office)
Malmesbury Papers (Hampshire Record Office)
Mayo Papers (National Library of Ireland)
Newcastle Papers (Nottingham University Library)
Palmerston Letter Books (British Library)
Phillimore Papers (Christ Church, Oxford)
Ripon Papers (British Library)
Russell Papers (Public Record Office)
Salisbury Papers (Hatfield House)
Sir Hamilton Seymour Diaries (British Library)
Vernon Smith Papers (India Office Library)
Somerset Papers (Buckinghamshire Record Office)
Trelawny Diaries (Bodleian Library, Oxford)
Villiers Papers (London School of Economics)
Spencer Walpole Papers (in private hands; transcripts provided by Dr Mark Curthoys)
Wilberforce Papers (Bodleian Library, Oxford)
Wodehouse Papers (British Library)
Wood Papers (India Office Library)

Newspapers and periodicals

Banker's Magazine
Beehive
Churchman
Daily News
Daily Telegraph
Economist
Edinburgh Review
Guardian
Leeds Mercury
Leeds Intelligencer
Manchester Guardian
Nonconformist
Quarterly Review
Record
Saturday Review
Tablet
The Times

Official publications

PP 1845, XIX, Report and Evidence from the Royal Commission on the State of the Law and Practice in respect to the Occupation of Land in Ireland
PP 1859 (Sess. 2), XXVII, Correspondence respecting the *Charles et Georges*

PP 1860, LXVIII, Correspondence respecting the Affairs of Italy

PP 1861, VII, Report and Evidence from the Select Committee on Income and Property Tax

PP 1861, LXV, Anglo-French Convention relative to Emigration of Labourers from India to the French Colonies

PP 1861, LXVII, Papers relating to Administrative and Financial Reforms in Turkey, 1858–61

PP 1863, LXXIII, Correspondence relating to the Bombardment of Belgrade in June 1862

PP 1864, VII, Report and Evidence of the Select Committee on Trade with Foreign Nations

PP 1864, XXXV, Land and Marine Forces (Religious Denominations)

PP 1864, XLVI, Correspondence respecting the Congress proposed to be held at Paris

PP 1865, LVII, Correspondence respecting Protestant Missionaries and Converts in Turkey

PP 1867, VIII, Report and Evidence from the Select Committee on the Tipperary Election Petititon

Les Origines Diplomatiques de la Guerre de 1870–1: Recueil de Documents publiée par le Ministère des Affaires Étrangères, 29 vols. (Paris, 1910–32)

I Documenti Diplomatichi Italiani (Prima Serie 1861–1870), (Rome, 1952–)

La Questione Italiana dalle Annessioni al Regno d' Italia nei Rapporti fra la Francia e l' Europa III serie: 1848–1860, ed. A. Saitta, 4 vols. (Rome, 1968); Fonti per la Storia d'Italia per l'Età Moderna e Contemporanea, 89–92.

Die Auswärtige Politik Preussens, 1858–1871: Diplomatische Aktenstücke, 9 vols. (Oldenburg, 1932–45).

Papers relating to Foreign Affairs accompanying the Annual Message of the President of the United States to Congress, 1861–62, 1862–63.

Other sources cited in the text and notes

Lord Aberdare, *Letters of the Rt. Hon. Henry Austin Bruce, G.C.B., Lord Aberdare of Duffryn*, 2 vols. (Oxford, 1902)

Acton, H., *The Last Bourbons of Naples (1825–1861)* (London, 1961)

Adams, E. D., *Great Britain and the American Civil War*, 2 vols. (London, 1925)

Allen, H. C., *Great Britain and the United States: A History of Anglo-American Relations (1783–1952)* (London, 1954)

Anderson, O., *A Liberal State at War: English Politics and Economics during the Crimean War* (London, 1967)

Anderson, O. 'The Administrative Reform Association, 1855–7' in P. Hollis (ed.), *Pressure from Without in Early Victorian England* (London, 1974)

Anderson, O. 'The Wensleydale Peerage Case and the Position of the House of Lords in the Mid-Nineteenth Century', *English Historical Review* (1967)

Argyll, eighth Duke of, *India under Dalhousie and Canning* (London, 1865); reprinted from *The Edinburgh Review*, (January and April 1863)

Ashley, Hon. E., *Life of Henry John Temple, Viscount Palmerston, 1846–65, with Selections from his Speeches and Correspondence*, 2 vols. (London, 1876)

Ashwell, A. R. and Wilberforce, R. G., *Life of the Right Reverend Samuel Wilberforce. D.D*, 3 vols. (London, 1880–83)

Auchmuty, J. J., 'Acton's Election as an Irish Member of Parliament', *English Historical Review* (1946)

Ausubel, H., *John Bright, Victorian Reformer* (New York, 1966)

Awdry, F., *A Country Gentleman of the Nineteenth Century* (London, 1906)

Baird, J. G. A., *Private Letters of the Marquess of Dalhousie* (Shannon, Ireland, 1972)

Barrington, E. I., *The Servant of All: Pages from the Family, Social and Political Life of my Father, James Wilson*, 2 vols. (London, 1927)

Bassett, A. Tilney (ed.), *Gladstone to his Wife* (London, 1936)

Bateman, J., *The Great Landowners of Great Britain and Ireland*, fourth edn (London, 1883; reprinted by Leicester University Press, 1971)

Beales, D. E. D., *England and Italy, 1859–60* (Edinburgh, 1961)

Beasley, W. G., *Great Britain and the Opening of Japan, 1834–1858* (London, 1951)

Bell, H. C. F., *Lord Palmerston*, 2 vols. (London, 1936)

Benson, A. C., and Esher, Viscount (eds.), *The Letters of Queen Victoria*, first series, 3 vols. (London, 1908)

Berrington, H., 'Partisanship and Dissidence in the Nineteenth-Century House of Commons', *Parliamentary Affairs* (1968)

Bethell, L. A., *The Abolition of the Brazilian Slave Trade: Britain, Brazil and the Slave Trade Question, 1807–1869* (Cambridge, 1970)

Blaisdell, D. C., *European Financial Control in the Ottoman Empire* (New York, 1929)

Blake, R., *The Conservative Party from Peel to Churchill* (London, 1970)

Blake, R., *Disraeli* (London, 1966)

Bosworth Smith, R., *Life of Lord Lawrence*, 2 vols. (London, 1883)

Bourne, K., *Britain And the Balance of Power in North America, 1815–1908* (London, 1967)

Bourne, K., *The Foreign Policy of Victorian England, 1830–1902* (Oxford, 1970)

Bourne, K., 'The Foreign Office under Palmerston' in R. Bullen (ed.) *The Foreign Office, 1782–1982* (Frederick, Maryland, 1982)

Bourne, K. (ed.), *The Letters of the Third Viscount Palmerston to Laurence and Elizabeth Sulivan, 1804–1863*, Camden fourth series (London, 1979)

Bourne, K., *Palmerston: The Early Years, 1784–1841* (London, 1982)

Boyce, G. et al., *Newspaper History from the Seventeenth Century to the Present Day* (London, 1978)

Briggs, A., *Victorian People* (London, 1954)

Brooke, J. and Sorensen, M. (eds.), *The Prime Ministers' Papers: W. E. Gladstone, I: Autobiographica* (London, 1971)

Buckle, G. E. (ed.), *The Letters of Queen Victoria*, second series, 2 vols. (London, 1926)

Bullen, R., and Strong, F., *Palmerston: Private Correspondence with Sir George Villiers (Afterwards Fourth Earl of Clarendon) as Minister to Spain, 1833–1837*, Prime Ministers' Papers Series (London, 1985)

Bulwer, Sir H. L., (Lord Dalling and Bulwer) *The Life of Henry John Temple, Viscount Palmerston, with Selections from his Diaries and Correspondence*, 3 vols. (London, 1870–74); vol. 3 edited by the Hon. Evelyn Ashley

Burghclere, Lady (ed.), *A Great Lady's Friendships: Letters of Mary, Marchioness of Salisbury, Countess of Derby, 1862–1876* (London, 1933)

Burn, W. L., *The Age of Equipoise: A Study of the Mid-Victorian Generation* (London, 1964)

Bylsma, J. R., 'Party Structure in the 1852–1857 House of Commons', *Journal of Interdisciplinary History* (1977)

Campbell, G., 'The Tenure of Land in India' in *Systems of Land Tenure in Various Countries, a Series of Essays published with the sanction of the Cobden Club* (London, 1870)

Carlisle, H.E. (ed.), *A Selection from the Correspondence of Abraham Hayward, Q.C. from 1834 to 1884, with an Account of his Early Life*, 2 vols. (London, 1886)

Cawley, E. H. (ed.), *The American Diaries of Richard Cobden* (Princeton, 1952)

Cecil, Lord Robert, 'The Church in her Relations to Political Parties', *Quarterly Review*, (July 1865)

Cecil, Lord Robert, 'The Elections', *Quarterly Review*, (July 1865)

Cecil, Lord Robert, 'Foreign policy in England', *Quarterly Review*, (April 1864)

Cecil, Lord Robert, 'The House of Commons', *Quarterly Review*, (July 1864)

Cell, J. W., *British Colonial Administration in the Mid-Nineteenth Century: The Policy-making Process* (New Haven, 1970)

Chadwick, W. O., *The Victorian Church*, Parts 1 and 2 (London, 1966–70)

Chamberlain, M. E., *Lord Palmerston* (Cardiff, 1987)

Chapman, J. K., *The Career of Arthur Hamilton Gordon, First Lord Stanmore, 1829–1912* (Toronto, 1964)

Chaudhuri, S. B., *Theories of the Indian Mutiny* (Calcutta, 1965)

Checkland, S. G., *The Gladstones: A Family Biography, 1764–1851* (Cambridge, 1971)

Checkland, S. G., *The Rise of Industrial Society in England, 1815–1885*, paperback edn (London, 1971)

Clapham, J. H., *The Bank of England: A History*, 2 vols. (Cambridge, 1944)

Clapham, J. H., *Economic History of Modern Britain*, vol. 2 (Cambridge, 1932)

Clogg, R., *A Short History of Modern Greece* (Cambridge, 1978)

Clowes, Sir W. L., *The Royal Navy. A History from the Earliest Times to the Death of Queen Victoria*, 7 vols. (London, 1897–1903)

Coleman, B., *Conservatism and the Conservative Party in Nineteenth-Century Britain* (London, 1988)

Collins, H. and Abramsky, C., *Karl Marx and the British Labour Movement: Years of the First International* (London, 1965)

Conacher, J. B., *The Aberdeen Coalition, 1852–1855: A Study in Mid-Nineteenth Century Party Politics* (London, 1965)

Conacher, J. B., *Britain and the Crimea 1855–56: Problems of War and Peace* (London, 1987)

Connell, B. (ed.), *Regina v. Palmerston: The Correspondence between Queen Victoria and her Foreign and Prime Minister 1837–1865* (London, 1962)

Corish, P. R. J., 'Cardinal Cullen and the National Association of Ireland', *Reportorium Novum* (1961–62)

Corish, P. J., *Political Problems, 1860–78* (Dublin, 1967)

Corti, Count E., *The Downfall of Three Dynasties*, trans. L. M. Sieveking and I. F. D. Morrow (London, 1934)

Costin, W. C., *Great Britain and China*, new edn (Oxford, 1968)

Coupland, R., *The Exploitation of East Africa, 1856–1890: The Slave Trade and the Scramble for Africa*, second edn (London, 1968)

Cowling, M. J., *1867: Disraeli, Gladstone and Revolution: The Passing of the Second Reform Bill* (Cambridge, 1967)

Craig, F. W. S. (ed.), *British Electoral Facts, 1832–1987* (Aldershot, 1989)

Creighton, D. G., *The Road to Confederation: The Emergence of Canada, 1863–1867* (Toronto, 1964)

Cromwell, V., 'Mapping the Political World of 1861: A Multidimensional Analysis of House of Commons Division Lists', *Legislative Studies Quarterly* (1982)

Cunningham, H., *The Volunteer Force: a Social and Political History, 1859–1901* (London, 1975)

Curthoys, M. C., 'Trade Union Legislation, 1871–76: Government Responses to the Development of Organised Labour' (Oxford D Phil thesis, 1988)

Curtis, G. W. (ed.), *The Correspondence of John Lothrop Motley*, 2 vols. (London, 1889)

Dalton, B. J., *War and Politics in New Zealand, 1855–1870* (Sydney, 1969)

Dasent, A. I., *John Thadeus Delane, Editor of The Times: His Life and Correspondence*, 2 vols. (London, 1908)

Davidson, R. T. and Benham, W., *Life of Archibald Campbell Tait, Archbishop of Canterbury*, 2 vols. (London, 1891)

Davis, L and Huttenback, R. A., 'The Export of British Finance 1865–1914', *Journal of Imperial and Commonwealth History* (1985)

Davis, L. and Huttenback, R. A., *Mammon and the Pursuit of Empire: the Political Economy of British Imperialism 1860–1912* (Cambridge, 1986)

Davison, R. H., *Reform in the Ottoman Empire 1856–1876* (Princeton, 1963)

Denison, J. E., First Viscount Ossington, *Notes from my Journal when Speaker of the House of Commons*, ed. L. E. Denison (London, 1900)

Denison, Sir W. T., *Varieties of Viceregal Life*, 2 vols. (London, 1870)

Dessain, C. S. et al. (eds.)., *The Letters and Diaries of John Henry Newman*, 31 vols. (London and Oxford, 1961–78)

Dod's Parliamentary Companion, (London, 1855–1865)

Douglas, Sir G. and Ramsay, Sir G. D., *The Panmure Papers*, 2 vols. (London, 1908)

D'Hauterive, E., *The Second Empire and its Downfall: the Correspondence of the Emperor Napoleon III and his Cousin Prince Napoleon*, trans. H. Wilson (London, 1927)

Dutt, R. C., *The Economic History of India in the Victorian Age* (London, 1906)

Eastwick, E. B., *Journal of a Diplomat's Three Years' Residence in Persia,* 2 vols. (London, 1864)

Ernest II of Coburg, *Memoirs of Ernest II, Duke of Saxe-Coburg-Gotha*, trans. P. Andreae 4 vols. (London, 1890)

Ernst O., (ed.), *Franz Joseph as revealed by his Letters*, trans. A. Blake (London, 1927)

Fagan, L., *The Life of Sir Anthony Panizzi, K. C. B.*, 2 vols. (London, 1880)

Farnie, D. A., *The English Cotton Industry and the World Market, 1815–1896* (Oxford, 1979)

Feaver, G., *From Status to Contract: a Biography of Sir Henry Maine* (London, 1969)

Ferris, N. B., *The Trent Affair: a Diplomatic Crisis* (Knoxville, Tennessee. 1977)

Figgis J. J. and Lawrence, R. V. (eds.), *Selections from the Correspondence of the first Lord Acton* (London. 1917)

Finlayson, G., *The Seventh Earl of Shaftesbury* (London, 1981)

Fitzmaurice, Lord Edmond, *The Life of Granville George Leveson Gower, Second Earl Granville, K. G.*, 2 vols. (London, 1905)

Flournoy, F. R., *British Policy towards Morocco in the Age of Palmerston 1830–1865* (Baltimore, 1935)

Foot M. R. D. and Matthew, H. C. G. (eds.), *The Gladstone Diaries,* vols. III and IV (Oxford, 1974)

Foster, J. O., *Class Struggle and the Industrial Revolution: Early Industrial Capitalism in Three English Towns* (London, 1974)

Fox, G., *Britain and Japan, 1858–1883* (Oxford, 1969)

Fraser, D., *Power and Authority in the Victorian City* (Oxford, 1979)

Fulford, R. (ed.), *Dearest Mama: Letters between Queen Victoria and the Crown Princess of Prussia, 1861–1864* (London, 1968)

Gash, N., *Aristocracy and People: Britain 1815–1865* (London, 1979)

Ghosh, P., 'Disraelian Conservatism: a financial approach', *English Historical Review* (1984)

Gilbert, A. D., *Religion and Society in Industrial England. Church, Chapel and Social Change, 1740–1914* (London, 1976)

Gillespie, F. E., *Labour and Politics in England, 1850–1867* (Durham, North Carolina, 1927)

Gilley, S., 'The Garibaldi Riots of 1862', *Historical Journal* (1975)

Gladstone, W. E., 'The Declining Efficiency of Parliament', *Quarterly Review* (September 1856)

Gladstone, W. E., 'England's Mission', *The Nineteenth Century,* (September 1878)

Gladstone, W. E., 'Foreign Affairs – War in Italy', *Quarterly Review* (April 1854)

Gladstone, W. E., 'France and the Late Ministry', *Quarterly Review* (April 1858)

Gladstone, W. E., 'Notes and Queries on the Irish Demand', *The Nineteenth Century* (February 1887)

Gladstone, W. E., 'The Past and Present Administrations', *Quarterly Review* (October 1858)

Gladstone, W. E., 'Sardinia and Rome', *Quarterly Review* (June 1855)

Gooch, G. P. (ed.), *The Later Correspondence of Lord John Russell, 1840–1878*, 2 vols. (London, 1925)

Gopal, S., *British Policy in India, 1858–1905* (Cambridge, 1965)

Gordon, P. (ed.), *The Red Earl: The Papers of the Fifth Earl Spencer 1835–1910*, 2 vols. (Northampton, 1981–86)

Gregory, J. S., *Great Britain and the Taipings* (London, 1969)

Guedalla, P. (ed.), *The Palmerston Papers: Gladstone and Palmerston, 1851–1865* (London, 1928)

Gurowich, R. M., 'The Continuation of War by Other Means: Party and Politics, 1855–1865', *Historical Journal* (1984)

Hanham, H.J., *Elections and Party Management: Politics in the Time of Disraeli and Gladstone* (London, 1959)

Hanham, H. J., 'Religion and Nationality in the Mid-Victorian Army' in M. R. D. Foot (ed.), *War and Society, Historical Essays in Honour of J. R. Western, 1928–1971* (London, 1973)

Hardy, A. E. Gathorne, *Gathorne Hardy, First Earl of Cranbrook. A Memoir.* 2 vols. (London, 1910)

Harrison, B., 'The Sunday Trading Riots of 1855', *Historical Journal* (1965)

Harrison, R., *Before the Socialists: Studies in Labour and Politics, 1861–1881* (London, 1965)

Hawkins, A., *Parliament, Party, and the Art of Politics in Britain, 1855–1859* (London, 1987)

Henderson, W. O., *The Lancashire Cotton Famine 1861–65*, second edn (Manchester, 1969)

Hertslet, Sir G. E. P., *Hertslet's China Treaties*, third edn, 2 vols. (London, 1908)

Hewett, O. W. (ed.), '...*And Mr Fortescue'. A Selection from the Diaries from 1851 to 1862 of Chichester Fortescue, Lord Carlingford* (London, 1958)

Hinde, W., *Richard Cobden: a Victorian Outsider* (New Haven, Connecticut, 1987)

Hobsbawm, E. J., 'The Labour Aristocracy in Nineteenth Century Britain', in *Labouring Men: Studies in the History of Labour* (London, 1964)

Hodder, E., *The Life and Work of the Seventh Earl of Shaftesbury, K. G.*, 3 vols. (London, 1886)

Hoppen, K. T., *Elections, Politics and Society in Ireland, 1832–85* (Oxford, 1984)

Hoppen, K. T., 'National Politics and Local Realities in Mid-Nineteenth Century Ireland', in A. Cosgrove and D. McCartney, *Studies in Irish History presented to R. Dudley Edwards* (Dublin, 1979)

Hoppen, K. T., 'Tories, Catholics, and the General Election of 1859', *Historical Journal* (1970)

Howe, A., *The Cotton Masters, 1830–1860* (Oxford, 1984)

Hübner, Comte de, *Neuf Ans de Sôuvenirs d'un Ambassadeur d'Autriche à Paris sous le Second Empire*, 2 vols. (Paris, 1904)

Hughes, J. R. T., *Fluctuations in Trade, Industry, and Finance: a Study of British Economic Development, 1850–1860* (Oxford, 1960)

Imlah, A. H., *Economic Elements in the Pax Britannica: Studies in British Foreign Trade in the Nineteenth Century* (Cambridge, Massachusetts, 1958)

Jagow, K., *Letters of the Prince Consort, 1831–1861* (London, 1938)

Jemolo, A. C., *Church and State in Italy, 1850–1950* (Oxford, 1960)

Jerome Napoleon, Prince, 'Les Préliminaires de la Paix, 11 juillet 1859: Journal de ma Mission à Vérone auprès de l'Empereur d'Autriche', *Revue des Deux Mondes* (1909)

Jones, W. D., *Lord Derby and Victorian Conservatism* (Oxford, 1956)

Jones, W. D and Erickson, A. B., *The Peelites, 1846–1857* (Columbus, Ohio, 1972)

Kennedy, A. L. (ed.), '*My Dear Duchess': Social and Political Letters to the Duchess of Manchester, 1858–1869* (London, 1956)

Kennedy, P. M., *The Rise of the Anglo-German Antagonism, 1860–1914* (London, 1980)

Kerr, D. G. G., *Sir Edmund Head: a Scholarly Governor* (Toronto, 1954)

Kirk, N., *The Growth of Working Class Reformism in Mid-Victorian England* (London, 1985)

Koss, S., *The Rise and Fall of the Political Press in Britain*, 1: *The Nineteenth Century* (London, 1981)

Knollys, H. (ed.), *Incidents of the China War of 1860 compiled from the private journals of Sir Hope Grant, G.C.B.* (London, 1875)

Krein, D. F., *The Last Palmerston Government* (Ames, Iowa, 1978)

Kriegel, A. D. (ed.), *The Holland House Diaries: the Diary of Henry Richard Vassall Fox, third Lord Holland, with extracts from the Diary of Dr John Allen* (London, 1977)

Lacaita, L., *An Italian Englishman: Sir James Lacaita, 1813–1895* (London, 1933)

Lambert, R. J., *Sir John Simon, 1816–1904 and English Social Administration* (London, 1963)

Lane-Poole, S., *The Life of the Rt. Hon. Stratford Canning, Viscount Stratford de Redcliffe* 2 vols. (London, 1888).

Lane-Poole, S. (ed.), *Thirty Years of Colonial Government: A Selection from the Despatches and Letters of Sir George Ferguson Bowen*, 2 vols. (London, 1889)

Larkin, E., *The Consolidation of the Roman Catholic Church in Ireland, 1860–1870* (Dublin, 1987)

Larkin, E., *The Making of the Roman Catholic Church in Ireland, 1850–1860* (Chapel Hill, 1980)

Laughton, J. K., *Memoirs of the Life and Correspondence of Henry Reeve*, 2 vols. (London, 1898)

Lecky, W. E. H., *Democracy and Liberty*, 2 vols. (London, 1908)

Lewis, Sir George Cornewall, Bt, *A Dialogue on the Best Form of Government* (London, 1863)

Lewis, Sir George Cornewall, Bt, 'The Election of President Lincoln and its Consequences', *Edinburgh Review* (April 1861)

Lewis, Sir George Cornewall, Bt, 'Military Defence of the Colonies', *Edinburgh Review* (January 1862)

Lewis, The Rev. Sir Gilbert, Bt (ed.), *The Letters of Sir George Cornewall Lewis, Bt* (London, 1870)

Lloyd, C., *The Navy and the Slave Trade: the Suppression of the African Slave Trade in the Nineteenth Century*, second edn. (London 1963)

Loftus, Lord Augustus, *The Diplomatic Reminiscences of Lord Augustus Loftus, 1837–1862*, 2 vols. (London, 1892)

Lorne, The Marquis of, *Viscount Palmerston* (London, 1906)

Lowell, A. L., *The Government of England*, 2 vols. (New York, 1908)

Lucas, R., *Lord Glenesk and the 'Morning Post'* (London, 1910)

Lunt, J. D. (ed.), *From Sepoy to Subadar: Being the Life and Adventures of Subadar Sita Ram* (London, 1970)

Lyall, Sir A., *The Life of the Marquis of the Dufferin and Ava*, 2 vols. (London, 1905)

MacCarthy, D. and Russell, A., *Lady John Russell: A Memoir* (London, 1926)

Maccoby, S., *English Radicalism, 1853–1886* (London, 1928)

MacDonagh, O., *Early Victorian Government, 1830–1870* (London, 1977)

McDowell, R. B., *The Irish Administration, 1801–1914* (London, 1966)

Machin, G. I. T., *Politics and the Churches in Great Britain, 1832–1868* (Oxford, 1977)

McIntire, C. T., *England against the Papacy, 1858–1861: Tories, Liberals and the Overthrow of Papal Temporal Power during the Italian Risorgimento* (Cambridge, 1983)

Mack Smith, D., *Cavour and Garibaldi, 1860: A Study in Political Conflict* (Cambridge, 1954)

Mack Smith, D., *Victor Emanuel, Cavour and the Risorgimento* (London, 1971)

Mackintosh, W. H., *Disestablishment and Liberation: The Movement for the Separation of The Anglican Church from State Control* (London 1972)

MacLagan, M., *'Clemency' Canning* (London, 1962)

MacSuibhne, P., *Paul Cullen and his Contemporaries with their Letters from 1820–1902*, 5 vols. (Naas, Co Kildare, 1961–77)

Majumdar, R. C., *The Sepoy Mutiny and the Revolt of 1857*, second edn (Calcutta, 1963)

Malmesbury, Third Earl of, *Memoirs of an Ex-Minister: An Autobiography*, new edn (London, 1885)

Marindin, G. E. (ed.), *Letters of Frederic, Lord Blachford* (London, 1896)

Martin, Rev F. X. (ed.), *The Easter Rising, 1916, and University College, Dublin* (Dublin, 1966)

Martin, K., *The Triumph of Lord Palmerston: A Study of Public Opinion in England before the Crimean War*, new edn (London, 1963)

Martin, T., T*he Life of H.R.H. the Prince Consort*, 5 vols. (London, 1875–80)

Martineau, J., *The Life and Correspondence of Sir Bartle Frere, Bart.*, 2 vols. (London, 1895)

Marx, K. and Engels, F., *Articles on Britain* (Moscow, 1895)

Marx, K. and Engels, F., *Collected Works*, vol. 41 (London, 1975)

Mason, P., *A Matter of Honour: An Account of the Indian Army, its Officers and Men* (London, 1974)

Mathew, D., *Lord Acton and his Times* (London, 1968)

Matthew, H. C. G., 'Disraeli, Gladstone, and the Politics of Mid-Victorian Budgets', *Historical Journal* (1979)

Matthew, H. C. G. (ed.), *The Gladstone Diaries*, vols. V and VI (Oxford, 1978)

May, Sir T. E., *The Constitutional History of England since the Accession of George the Third*, third edn, 3 vols. (London, 1871)

Metcalf, T. R., *The Aftermath of Revolt: India, 1857–1870* (Princeton, 1964)

Mill, J. S., *On Liberty* and *Considerations on Representative Government*, Everyman's Library edn (London, 1954)

Mill, J. S., *Principles of Political Economy with some of their Applications to Social Philosophy*, 2 vols. (Toronto, 1965), vols. II and III in *The Collected Works of John Stuart Mill*

Mineka, F. E. and Lindley, D. N. (eds.), *The Later Letters of John Stuart Mill*, 4 vols. (Toronto, 1972), vols. XIV to XVII of *The Collected Works of John Stuart Mill* (Toronto, 1963)

Mitchell, B. R. and Deane, P., *Abstract of British Historical Statistics* (Cambridge, 1962)

Mitford, N., *The Stanleys of Alderley* (London, 1939)

Monypenny, W. F. and Buckle, G. E., *The Life of Benjamin Disraeli, Earl of Beaconsfield*, new edn, 2 vols. (London, 1929)

Moore, R. J., *Sir Charles Wood's Indian Policy, 1853–1866* (Manchester 1966)

Morgan, E. V. and Thomas, W. A., *The Stock Exchange: its History and Functions* (London, 1962)

Morley, J., *The Life of Richard Cobden*, 2 vols. (London, 1896)

Morley, J., *The Life of William Ewart Gladstone*, 2 vols. (London, 1905)

Mosse, W. E., 'England and the Polish Insurrection of 1863', *English Historical Review* (1967)

Mosse, W. E., *The European Powers and the German Question, 1848–1871, with special reference to England and Russia* (Cambridge, 1958)

Mosse, W. E., *The Rise and Fall of the Crimean System, 1856–1871* (London, 1963)

Newman, J. H., *Apologia Pro Vita Sua*, Everyman's Library edn (London, 1949)

Newman, J. H. *The Idea of a University*, ed., I. T. Ker (Oxford, 1976)

O'Brien, D. P. (ed)., *The Correspondence of Lord Overstone*, 3 vols. (Cambridge, 1971)

Palmer, R., First Earl of Selborne, *Memorials Part I, Family and Personal, 1766–1865*, 2 vols. (London, 1896)

Parry, J. P., *Democracy and Religion: Gladstone and the Liberal Party, 1867–1875* (Cambridge, 1986)

Perkin, H., *The Origins of Modern English Society, 1780–1880* (London, 1969)

Philips, C. H. (ed.), *The Evolution of India and Pakistan, 1858–1947: Select Documents* (London, 1967)

Piggott, Sir F. T., *Extraterritoriality: the Law relating to Consular Jurisdiction and Residence in Oriental Countries*, second edn (Hong Kong, 1907)

Pinney, T. (ed.)., *The Letters of Thomas Babington Macaulay*, 6 vols. (Cambridge, 1974–81)

Platt, D. C. M., *Finance, Trade and Politics in British Foreign Policy, 1815–1914* (Oxford, 1968)

Platt, D. C. M., 'The Imperialism of Free Trade: Some Reservations', *Economic History Review* (1968).

Porter, B., *The Refugee Question in Mid-Victorian Politics* (Cambridge, 1979)

Prest, J. M., *Lord John Russell* (London, 1972)

Prevelakis, E., *British Policy towards the Change of Dynasty in Greece, 1862–1863* (Athens, 1955)

Ramm, A. (ed.), *The Political Correspondence of Mr Gladstone and Lord Granville, 1863–1876*, 2 vols. Camden third series. LXXXI–II (London, 1952)

Read, D., *Cobden and Bright: a Victorian Partnership* (London, 1967)

Redford, A., *Manchester Merchants and Foreign Trade*, 2 vols. (Manchester, 1934–56)

Reid, R. Wemyss, *Memoirs and Letters of the Rt. Hon. Sir Robert Morier from 1826 to 1876*, 2 vols. (London, 1911)

Ringhoffer, R. (ed.), *The Bernstorff Papers: the Life of Count Albrecht Bernstorff*, trans. C. E. Barrett-Lennard and M. W. Hoper, 2 vols. (London, 1908)

Riker, T. W., *The Making of Roumania: A Study of an International Problem, 1850–1866* (London, 1931)

Ridley, J., *Lord Palmerston* (London, 1970)

Robbins, K., *John Bright* (London, 1979)

Robinson, R. and Gallagher, J., *Africa and the Victorians: The Official Mind of Imperialism* (London, 1961)

Robinson, R. and Gallagher, J., 'The Imperialism of Free Trade', *Economic History Review* (1953)

Rogers, J. E. T. (ed.), *Speeches on Questions of Public Policy by the Rt. Hon. John Bright* (London, 1878)

Rolo, P. J. V., *George Canning: Three Biographical Studies* (London, 1965)

Rubinstein, W. D., *Men of Property: The Very Wealthy in Britain Since the Industrial Revolution* (London, 1981)

Russell, First Earl, *Selections from the Speeches of Earl Russell, 1817 to 1841, and from Despatches, 1859–1865*. 2 vols. (London, 1870)

Russell, G. W. E. (ed.), *Malcolm MacColl, Memoirs and Correspondence* (London, 1914)

Salbstein, M. C. N., *The Emancipation of the Jews in Britain: the Question of the Admission of the Jews to Parliament, 1828–1860* (London and Toronto, 1982)

Scott, I. *The Roman Question and the Powers, 1848–1865* (The Hague, 1969)

Sen, S., *Eighteen Fifty Seven* (Calcutta, 1967)

Serle, G., *The Golden Age: A History of the Colony of Victoria, 1851–1861* (Melbourne, 1963)

Shannon, R., *Gladstone, I.: 1809–1865* (London, 1982)

Silver, A. W., *Manchester Men and Indian Cotton, 1847–1872* (Manchester, 1966)

Smith, F. B., *The Making of the Second Reform Bill* (Cambridge, 1966)

Southgate, D., '*The Most English Minister...*' *The Policies and Politics of Palmerston* (London, 1966)

Southgate, D., *The Passing of the Whigs* (London, 1962)

Stanmore, Lord, *Sidney Herbert, Lord Herbert of Lea. A Memoir*, 2 vols. (London, 1906)

Steefel, L. D., *The Schleswig-Holstein Question* (Cambridge, Massachusetts, 1932)

Steele, E. D. 'Cardinal Cullen and Irish Nationality', *Irish Historical Studies* (1975)

Steele, E. D. 'Gladstone and Ireland', *Irish Historical Studies* (1970)

Steele, E. D. 'Gladstone, Irish Violence and Conciliation' in A. Cosgrove and D. McCartney, *Studies in Irish History Presented to R. Dudley Edwards* (Dublin, 1979)

Steele, E. D., 'Ireland and the Empire in the 1860s: Imperial Precedents for Gladstone's First Irish Land Act', *Historical Journal* (1968)

Steele, E. D., *Irish Land and British Politics: Tenant-Right and Nationality 1865–1870* (Cambridge, 1974)

Steele, E. D., 'The Irish Presence in the North of England 1850–1914', *Northern History* (1976)

Steele, E. D., 'The Leeds Patriciate and the Cultivation of Learning, 1819–1905: A Study of the Leeds Philosophical and Literary Society', *Proceedings of the Leeds Philosophical and Literary Society* (1978)

Steele, E. D., 'Liberalism' in M. A. Riff (ed.), *Dictionary of Modern Political Ideologies* (Manchester, 1987)

Steele, E. D., 'J. S. Mill and the Irish Question: The Principles of Political Economy, 1848–65', *Historical Journal* (1970)

St John Stevas, J. (ed.), *The Collected Works of Walter Bagehot*, 14 vols. (London, 1968–86)

Stewart, R. M., 'The Conservative Reaction: Lord Robert Cecil and Party Politics' in Lord Blake and H. P. Cecil (eds.), *Salisbury: The Man and His Policies* (London, 1987)

Stewart, R. M., *The Foundations of the Conservative Party, 1830–1867* (London, 1978)

Stokes, E., *The Peasant and the Raj: Studies in Agrarian Society and Peasant Rebellion in Colonial India* (Cambridge, 1978)

Strachey, L. and Fulford, R., *The Greville Memoirs*, 8 vols. (London, 1938)

Strafford, Alice, Countess of, *Leaves from the Diary of Henry Greville* (London, 1905)

Sylvester, D. W., *Robert Lowe and Education* (Cambridge, 1974)

Trevelyan, G. O., *The Life and Letters of Lord Macaulay*, 2 vols. (London, 1961)

Taylor, A. J. P., *Essays in English History*, Penguin edn (London, 1976)

Taylor, A. J. P., *The Italian Problem in European Diplomacy, 1847–1849* (Manchester, 1934)

Taylor, A. J. P., *The Struggle for Mastery in Europe, 1848–1918* (Oxford, 1957)

Taylor, Sir H., *Autobiography of Sir Henry Taylor*, 2 vols. (London, 1885)

Thompson, F. M. L., *English Landed Society in the Nineteenth Century* (London, 1963)

Thouvenel, L. (ed.), *Le Secret de l'Empereur: correspondance confidentielle et inédite échangée entre M. Thouvenel, le Duc de Gramont et le Général Comte de Flahaut*, 1860–63, 2 vols. (Paris, 1889)

The Times: Annual Summaries reprinted from The Times (London, 1893)

The Times: The History of The Times, 5 vols. (London, 1925–52)

Venturi, F., *The Roots of Revolution: A History of the Populist and Socialist Movement in Nineteenth-Century Russia*, trans. F. Haskell (New York, 1966)

Vincent, J. R., *The Formation of the Liberal Party, 1857–1868* (London, 1966)

Vincent, J. R., *Pollbooks: How Victorians Voted* (Cambridge, 1967)

Vincent, J. R., 'The Parliamentary Dimension of the Crimean War', *Transactions of the Royal Historical Society* (1981)

Vincent, J. R., (ed.)., *Disraeli, Derby and the Conservative Party: Journals and Memoirs of Edward Henry, Lord Stanley, 1849–69* (Hassocks, Sussex, 1978)

Vitzthum von Eckstädt, Count, *St Petersburg and London in the Years 1852–1864*, trans. H. Reeve, 2 vols. (London, 1887)

Wallace, S. A. and Gillespie, F. E., *The Journal of Benjamin Moran*, 2 vols. (Chicago, 1948–49)

Walling, R. A. J. (ed), *The Diaries of John Bright* (London, 1930)

Walpole, S., *The History of Twenty-five Years*, 4 vols. (London, 1904–08)

Walpole, S., *The Life of Lord John Russell*, 2 vols. (London, 1889)

Walrond, T. (ed), *Letters and Journals of James, 8th Earl of Elgin* (London, 1872)

Webster, Sir C., *The Foreign Policy of Palmerston, 1830–41: Britain, the Liberal Movement, and the Eastern Question*, 2 vols. (London, 1951)

Weighall, Lady Rose, *The Correspondence of Priscilla, Countess of Westmorland* (London, 1909)

Wellesley, Sir V. and Sencourt, R., *Conversations with Napoleon III* (London, 1934)

Whyte, J. H., *The Independent Irish Party, 1850–59* (Oxford, 1958)

Whyte, J. H., *Political Problems, 1850–60* (Dublin, 1967)

Williams, W. E., *The Rise of Gladstone to the Leadership of the Liberal Party, 1859 to 1868* (Cambridge, 1934)

Wilson, K. M. (ed.), *British Foreign Secretaries and Foreign Policy: From Crimean War to World War* (London, 1987)

Winter, J. M., *Robert Lowe* (Toronto, 1976)

Wolf, L., *Life of the Marquess of Ripon, K. G.*, 2 vols. (London, 1921)

Zeldin, T., *France, 1848–1945* (Oxford, 1973)

Index